NATIONAL LEAGUE GREEN BOOK—1992
THE NATIONAL LEAGUE OF PROFESSIONAL BASEBALL CLUBS
350 Park Avenue, New York, New York 10022
TABLE OF CONTENTS

ATLANTA BRAVES
Atlanta National League Baseball Club, Inc.

P.O. Box 4064
Atlanta, GA 30302
(404) 522-7630
FAX: (404) 614-1391

Chairman of the Board	William C. Bartholomay
Directors	Henry L. Aaron, Stanley H. Kasten, Rubye M. Lucas, Terence F. McGuirk, John Schuerholz, M.B. Seretean, Allison Thornwell, Jr., R.E. Turner, III
President	Stanley H. Kasten
Senior Vice President & Assistant to the President	Henry L. Aaron
Executive Vice President & General Manager	John Schuerholz
Senior Vice President/Administration & Finance	Charles Sanders
Vice President, Director of Marketing & Broadcasting	Wayne Long
Assistant Vice President & Special Assistant to General Manager	Paul Snyder
Assistant General Manager	Dean Taylor
Director of Scouting & Player Development	Chuck LaMar
Assistant Director of Player Development	Rod Gilbreath
Assistant Director of Scouting	Scott Proefrock
Director of Team Travel & Equipment Manager	Bill Acree
Director of Public Relations	Jim Schultz
Director of Community Relations	Danny Goodwin
Director of Promotions	Miles McRea
Director of Ticket Sales	Jack Tyson
Director of Merchandising	Robert A. Hope
Director of Ticket Operations	Ed Newman
Assistant Director of Ticket Operations	Sam Williams
Director of Advertising	Peter Diffin
Assistant Controller	Chip Moore
Director of Stadium Operations & Security	Terri Brennan
Media Relations Manager	Glen Serra
Publications Manager	Mike Ringering

Games At: Atlanta-Fulton County Stadium
521 Capitol Avenue, SW
Atlanta, GA 30312

Capacity: 52,013   Surface: Natural Grass
Playing Field Distances:

Left Field Fence	330 feet
Center Field Fence	402 feet
Right Field Fence	330 feet
Plate to Grandstand	60 feet
Power Alleys (Left and Right)	385 feet

Height of Walls:

All	10 feet

CHICAGO CUBS
Chicago National League Ball Club, Inc.

1060 West Addison St.
Chicago, IL 60613
(312) 404-2827
FAX: (312) 404-4129

BOARD OF DIRECTORS
Stanton R. Cook, (Chairman), Thomas G. Ayers,
Charles T. Brumback, Donald C. Grenesko, Andrew J. McKenna

BASEBALL OPERATIONS

Executive Vice President, Baseball Operations	Larry Himes
Senior Vice President/Special Player Consultant	Jim Frey
Assistant General Manager	Syd Thrift
Vice President, Scouting and Player Development	Dick Balderson
Vice President, Baseball Administration	Ned Colletti
Director, Minor League Operations	Bill Harford
Special Player Consultants	Hugh Alexander, Eddie Lyons
Traveling Secretary	Peter Durso

BUSINESS OPERATIONS

Executive Vice President, Business Operations	Mark McGuire
Vice President, Finance and Information Systems	Keith Bode
Vice President, Marketing and Broadcasting	John McDonough
Director, Stadium Operations	Tom Cooper
Director, Human Resources	Wendy Lewis
Director, Ticket Operations	Frank Maloney
Director, Media Relations	Sharon Pannozzo
Corporate Counsel	Geoff Anderson
Corporate Secretary	Stanley Gradowski

Games At: Wrigley Field

Capacity: 38,710   Surface: Natural Grass
Playing Field Distances:

Left Field Fence	355 feet
Center Field Fence	400 feet
Right Field Fence	353 feet
Plate to Grandstand	60½ feet
Power Alleys (Left and Right)	368 feet

Height of Walls:

Left and Right Field	11½ feet

CINCINNATI REDS
The Cincinnati Reds

100 Riverfront Stadium
Cincinnati, OH 45202
(513) 421-4510
FAX: (513) 421-7342

President & Chief Executive Officer	Marge Schott
Vice President & General Manager	Bob Quinn

BUSINESS ADMINISTRATION

Controller	Ernie Brubaker
Director Stadium Operations	Tim O'Connell
Director Ticket Department	John O'Brien
Director Season Ticket Sales	Pat McCaffrey
Director Group Sales	Susan Toomey
Director Marketing	Chip Baker
Director Publicity	Jon Braude
Assistant Publicity Director	Joe Kelley
Director Speakers Bureau	Gordy Coleman
Assistant Ticket Director	Ken Ayer
Field Superintendent	Tony Swain
Manager Gift Shop	Roberta Moore
Chief Administrative Assistant	Joyce Pfarr
Administrative Assistant/Business	Ginny Kamp

BASEBALL ADMINISTRATION

Director Player Development	James G. Bowden IV
Director Scouting	Julian Mock
Special Player Consultant	Sheldon Bender
Traveling Secretary	Joel Pieper
Administrative Assistant/Scouting	Wilma Mann
Administrative Assistant/Player Development	Lois Schneider

Games At: Riverfront Stadium

Capacity: 52,952   Surface: Artificial
Playing Field Distances:

Left Field Fence	330 feet
Center Field Fence	404 feet
Right Field Fence	330 feet
Plate to Grandstand	51 feet
Power Alleys (Left and Right)	375 feet

Height of Walls:

Outfield Fence	8 feet

HOUSTON ASTROS
The Houston Sports Association

P.O. Box 288
Houston, TX 77001-0288
(713) 799-9500
FAX: (713) 799-9562

Chairman of the Board ....Dr. John J. McMullen

BASEBALL ADMINISTRATION

General Manager.. Bill Wood
Assistant General Manager .... Bob Watson
Director of Minor League Operations .... Fred Nelson
Director of Scouting .... Dan O'Brien
Director of Public Relations ....Rob Matwick
Traveling Secretary ....Barry Waters
Asst. to Dir. of Minor Leagues and Scouting.................. Lew Temple
Asst. Scouting Dir./Dir. Inter. Dev. ....David Rawnsley
Assistant Director of Public Relations .... Chuck Pool
Staff Publicist...Tyler Barnes
Assistant to General Manager .... Tim Hellmuth
Admin. Asst. Major League Operations .... Beverly Rains

MARKETING ADMINISTRATION

Vice President Marketing...................................... Ted Haracz
Director, Broadcasting .... Jamie Hildreth
Director, Advertising Sales/Promotions ....Norm Miller
Director, Communications .... Pam Gardner
Director, Sales..David Matlin
Director, Group Sales...Debra Fulmer
Director, Community Services .... Gayle Mongan
Marketing Operations Manager ....Matt Kastel
Ticket Director .... Mark Lavaway
Scoreboard Operations .... Paul Darst

Games At: The Astrodome
    8400 Kirby Dr.
    Houston, TX 77054-1599

    Capacity: 54,816   Surface: Artificial

Playing Field Distances:
    Left Field Fence .... 330 feet
    Center Field Fence.. 400 feet
    Right Field Fence .... 330 feet
    Plate to Grandstand .... 66 feet
Power Alleys (Left and Right) .... 380 feet
Height of Walls:
    All .... 10 feet

LOS ANGELES DODGERS
Los Angeles Dodgers, Inc.

1000 Elysian Park Avenue
Los Angeles, CA 90012
(213) 224-1500
FAX: (213) 224-1459

President .... Peter O'Malley
Executive Vice President, Player Personnel ....Fred Claire
Vice President, Communications ....Tommy Hawkins
Vice President, Finance ....Bob Graziano
Vice President, Marketing ....Barry Stockhamer
Vice President, Stadium Operations .... Bob Smith
Vice President, Ticket Operations .... Walter Nash
Vice President, Treasurer .... Roland Seidler
Assistant to the President .... Ike Ikuhara
Asst. Sec. & General Counsel .... Santiago Fernandez
Director, Accounting & Finance............................Bill Foltz
Director, Advertising & Special Events..........................Paul Kalil
Director, Broadcasting & Publications .... Brent Shyer
Director, Community Relations ....Don Newcombe
Community Relations .... Roy Campanella
Director, Human Resources & Administration...................Irene Tanji
Director, Data Processing .... Mike Mularky
Director, Minor League Operations ....Charlie Blaney
Director, Scouting .... Terry Reynolds
Director, Publicity ....Jay Lucas
Assistant Director, Publicity............................... Chuck Harris
Traveling Secretary ....Bill DeLury
Director, Stadium Operations ....Jim Italiano
Director, Ticket Department .... Debra Duncan

Games At: Dodger Stadium

    Capacity: 56,000   Surface: Natural Grass
Playing Field Distances:
    Left Field Fence .... 330 feet
    Center Field Fence.. 395 feet
    Right Field Fence .... 330 feet
    Plate to Grandstand .... 75 feet
Power Alleys (Left and Right) .... 385 feet
Height of Walls:
    Outfield Fence .... 8 feet

MONTREAL EXPOS
Montreal Baseball Club, Inc.

P.O. Box 500, Station M
Montreal, Quebec
H1V 3P2 Canada
(514) 253-3434
FAX: (514) 253-8282

President and General Partner.......................Claude R. Brochu
Chairman of the Board ....Jacques Menard
Vice Chairmen of the Board ....Jacques Berube,
                        Claude Blanchet, Jocelyn Proteau

BASEBALL MANAGEMENT

Vice-President & General Manager .... Dan Duquette
Vice-President, Baseball Operations..........................Bill Stoneman
Director, Scouting ....Kevin Malone
Director, Minor League Field Operations .... Kevin Kennedy
Director, Minor League Operations ....Kent Qualls
Director, Team Travel ....Erik Ostling
Director, Latin America Operations ....Fred Ferreira
Executive Advisor, Baseball Operations .... Eddie Haas
Special Consultant, Baseball Operations ....Jim Fanning
General Manager, West Palm Beach Operations .... Rob Rabenecker
Administrative Assistant, Scouting ....Gregg Leonard
Administrator, Baseball Operations......................Roberta Mazur

BUSINESS MANAGEMENT

Vice-President, Marketing.....................................Michel Lagace
Vice-President, Communications ....Richard Morency
Vice-President, Business Operations ....Gerry Trudeau
Controller .... Raymond St. Pierre
Director, Marketing & Communications ....Carole Boivin
Director, Ticket Office .... Luigi Carolo
Director, Food Concessions ....Claude Delorme
Director, Media Services ....Monique Giroux
Director, Media Relations ....Richard Griffin
Director, Advertising ....Johanne Heroux
Director, Stadium Operations ....Monique Lacas
Director, Retailing ....Susan LeBlanc
Director, Ticket Sales.................................Ronald Martineau
Director, Corporate Affairs .... Pierre O. Touchette

Games At: Olympic Stadium
    4549 Pierre De Coubertin Ave.
    Montreal, Quebec H1V 3P2

    Capacity: 43,739   Surface: Artificial
Playing Field Distances:
    Left Field Fence .... 325 feet
    Center Field Fence.. 404 feet
    Right Field Fence .... 325 feet
    Plate to Grandstand .... 53 feet
Power Alleys (Left and Right) .... 375 feet
Height of Walls:
    All .... 12 feet

NEW YORK METS
Sterling Doubleday Enterprises, L.P.

126th St. & Roosevelt Ave.
Flushing, NY 11368
(718) 507-6387
FAX: (718) 565-4382

Chairman of the Board .... Nelson Doubleday
Directors .... Nelson Doubleday, Fred Wilpon,
J. Frank Cashen, Saul Katz, Marvin Tepper
Special Advisor to the Board of Directors .... Richard Cummins
President/Chief Executive Officer .... Fred Wilpon
Chief Operating Officer & Senior Executive
Vice President .... J. Frank Cashen
Executive Vice President & General Manager .... Alan Harazin
Assistant V.P., Baseball Operations .... Gerald Hunsicker
Vice President, Treasurer .... Harold O'Shaughnessy
Vice President, Operations .... Robert Mandt
Traveling Secretary .... Bob O'Hara
Director of Ticket Operations .... William Ianniciello
Controller .... Rick Iandoli
Director, Public Relations .... Jay Horwitz
Vice President, Marketing .... Jim Ross
Director, Promotions .... Jim Plummer
Vice President, Broadcasting .... Mike Ryan
Stadium Manager .... John McCarthy
Assistant Public Relations Director .... Craig Sanders

Games At: Shea Stadium

Capacity: 55,601	Surface: Natural Grass	
Playing Field Distances:		
Left Field Fence	....	338 feet
Center Field Fence	....	410 feet
Right Field Fence	....	338 feet
Plate to Grandstand	....	80 feet
Power Alleys (Left and Right)	....	371 feet
Height of Walls:		
All	....	8 feet

PHILADELPHIA PHILLIES
The Phillies

P.O. Box 7575
Philadelphia, PA 19101
(215) 463-6000
FAX:
(215) 389-3050 (PR/Admin./Fin.)
(215) 755-9324 (BB Ops)
(215) 463-8765 (Com Rel/TravSec/
Stad Ops/Merch)
(215) 463-6025 (Mktg/Prom/Tix)

Phillies (cont.)

President, CEO and General Partner .... Bill Giles
Partners .... Clair S. Betz, Estate of John Drew Betz,
Tri-Play Associates (Alexander K. Buck, J. Mahlon Buck, Jr.,
William C. Buck), Fitz Eugene Dixon, Jr., Mrs. Rochelle Levy

ADMINISTRATION

President, CEO and General Partner .... Bill Giles
Exec. Vice President and COO .... David Montgomery
Executive Secretary .... Nancy Deren
Secretary & General Counsel .... William Y. Webb
Dir., Planning/Development & Super Boxes .... Tom Hudson
Financial Consultant .... Robert D. Hedberg

BASEBALL ADMINISTRATION

Senior Vice President, General Manager .... Lee Thomas
Player Personnel Administrator .... Ed Wade
Director, Player Development .... Del Unser
Director, Scouting .... Jay Hankins
Assistant to the President .... Paul Owens
Business Manager, Minor Leagues .... Bill Gargano
Secretary, Baseball Administration .... Susan Ingersoll
Computer Analysis .... Jay McLaughlin
Secretary, Minor Leagues .... Maryann Skedzielewski
Traveling Secretary .... Eddie Ferenz
Video Operations .... Dan Stephenson

ACCOUNTING/FINANCE

Senior Vice President, Finance & Planning .... Jerry Clothier
Payroll Administrator .... Karen Wright
Secretary, Finance .... JoAnn Marano
Accountant .... Scott Schneider
Bookkeeper .... Reeny Dunn
Payroll/Purchasing .... Pat McKee
Controller .... Lou Perez

PUBLIC RELATIONS/COMMUNITY RELATIONS

Vice President, Public Relations .... Larry Shenk
Broadcaster; Director Speakers' Bureau .... Chris Wheeler
Director, Community Relations .... Regina Castellani
Administrator, Public Relations .... Tina Urban
Assistant Director, Community Relations .... Karen Howard
Manager, Media Relations .... Gene Dias
Manager, Publicity .... Leigh McDonald
Speakers' Bureau Representative .... Maje McDonnell
Community Relations Representative .... Kelly Nanni

MARKETING/PROMOTIONS

Vice President, Marketing .... Dennis Mannion
Director, Promotions .... Frank Sullivan
Broadcaster and Corporate Marketing Rep. .... Garry Maddox
Manager, Advertising and Broadcasting .. Jo-Anne Levy-Lamoreaux
Assistant Director, Promotions .... Chris Legault
Phanatic, Promotions Representative .... David Raymond
Assistant to the VP of Marketing .... Debbie Nocito
Marketing Coordinator .... Kurt Funk
Manager, Corporate Marketing .... Dave Buck
Fan Development Representative .... Rob Holiday
Phanavision and Scoreboard Operations .... Anthony Fanticola
Manager, Merchandising .... Dan Ingersoll
Corporate Marketing Representative .... Agnes Gillin
Receptionist, Assistant to Marketing .... Karen Nocella
Merchandising Representative .... Mike Connor
Promotions Representative .... Tom Burgoyne

Phillies (cont.)

SALES/TICKETS

Vice President, Ticket Operations .... Richard Deats
Director, Sales .... Rory McNeil
Director, Ticket Department .... Dan Goroff
Manager, Group Sales .... Kathy Killian
Manager, Sales Operations .... John Weber
Super Box Coordinator .... Lynn Samuels
Corporate Sales Representative .... Tom Mashek
Sales Office Representatives .... Joanne Hudson,
Jim Getgey, Laura Horn
Ticket Office Representatives .... Lori Loughlin, Cathy Krise,
Jack Hardiman, Andrea Hobbs, Sharon Snyder, Corning Pearson

COMPUTER OPERATIONS

Director, Information Systems .... Brian Lamoreaux
Computer Operations Manager .... Christopher Pohl
Manager, Software & Analysis .... Donna Underwood
System & Software Support .... George Wagner
Analysis & Support .... Phil Feather

STADIUM OPERATIONS

Director, Stadium Operations .... Mike DiMuzio
Director, Office Operations .... Pat Cassidy
Super Box Administrator .... Carmen DiNovi
Field Superintendent .... Ralph Frangipani
Assistant Field & Maintenance Supervisor .... Jody Boon
Secretary, Stadium Operations .... Bernie Mansi
Switchboard Receptionist .... Kelly Addario
Maintenance .... Jack Kelleher, Tony McClean, James Rodriquez
Office Security .... Foster Mears, Ted DiMuzio, Ed Berry

Games At: Veterans Stadium

Broad & Pattison Sts.
Philadelphia, PA 19148

Capacity: 62,382	Surface: Artificial	
Playing Field Distances:		
Left Field Fence	....	330 feet
Center Field Fence	....	408 feet
Right Field Fence	....	330 feet
Plate to Grandstand	....	60 feet
Power Alleys (Left and Right)	....	371 feet
Height of Walls:		
All	....	12 feet

PITTSBURGH PIRATES
Pittsburgh Associates

P.O. Box 7000
Pittsburgh, PA 15212
(412) 323-5000
FAX: (412) 323-9133 (P.R.)
(412) 323-5024

Board of Directors ....Joe L. Brown, Frank V. Cahouet,
Richard M. Cyert, Douglas D. Danforth, Eugene Litman,
John Marous, Sophie Masloff, John H. McConnell,
Thomas H. O'Brien, Paul H. O'Neill, David M. Roderick,
Vincent A. Sarni, Harvey M. Walken

STAFF DIRECTORY

Chairman of the Board ....Douglas D. Danforth
President and CEO ....Mark Sauer
Senior VP and GM for Baseball Operations ....Ted Simmons
Senior VP for Business Operations ....Douglas Bureman
Vice President, Finance & Administration ....Kenneth C. Curcio
Vice President, Marketing & Operations ....Steven N. Greenberg
Vice President, Public Relations ....Richard J. Cerrone
Assistant to the President.. Ken Wilson
Assistant General Manager .... Cam Bonifay
Assistant Vice President, Finance ....Patti Mistick
Executive Director of Broadcasting
   and Advertising Sales ....Mark Driscoll
Director of Minor League Operations ....Chet Montgomery
Director of Scouting ....Jack Zdurience k
Traveling Secretary .... Greg Johnson
Senior Director of Sales & Marketing ....Bob Derda
Senior Director of Sales & Marketing ....Mark Norelli
Manager of Ticket Operations.............................Gary Remlinger
Director of Bradenton Baseball Operations ....Jeff Podobnik
Director of Community Relations .... Patty Paytas
Director of Community Services & Sales ....Al Gordon
Director of Corporate Sales .... Nellie Briles
Director of Diamond Club .... Chris Cronin
Director of Finance...Jim Plake
Director of In-Game Entertainment .... Mike Gordon
Director of Media Relations.................................... Jim Trdinich
Director of Merchandising ....Joe Billetdeaux
Director of Promotions...Kathy Guy
Director of Publications & Special Projects .... Jim Lachimia
Director of Stadium Operations............................ Dennis DaPra
Director of Telemarketing ....Phillip Trozzi
Senior Account Executive..................................Mark Ferraco
Account Executive...Karin Kmetz
Account Executive...Harold Balk
Broadcast Administration Coordinator......................Declan Bolger
Comm. & Mgmt. Info. Sys. Coordinator ....Sanjay Chakrabarty
Customer Service Coordinator .... Kathy Murphy
Guest Relations & Food Service Coordinator .... Elliott Falcione
Mini-Clubhouse Store & Warehouse Manager ....Judy Gardner
Ticket Processing Coordinator .... Dave Wysocki
Pirate Clubhouse Catalog Manager ....Mark DeLuca
Assistant, Baseball Operations..........................John Sirignano
Assistant Director of Public Relations ....Sally O'Leary
Assistant Manager of Ticket Operations .... Jon Mercurio
Assistant, Minor Leagues & Scouting........................Tom Treece

Games At: Three Rivers Stadium
   600 Stadium Circle
   Pittsburgh, PA 15212

   Capacity: 58,729   Surface: Artificial
Playing Field Distances:
   Left Field Fence .... 335 feet
   Center Field Fence .... 400 feet
   Right Field Fence .... 335 feet
   Plate to Grandstand .... 60 feet
Power Alleys (Left and Right) .... 375 feet
Height of Walls:
   All .... 10 feet

ST. LOUIS CARDINALS
St. Louis National Baseball Club, Inc.

250 Stadium Plaza
St. Louis, MO 63102
(314) 421-3060
FAX: (314) 425-0640

Chairman of the Board .... August A. Busch, III
Vice Chairman ....Fred L. Kuhlmann
President & Chief Executive Officer .... Stuart F. Meyer
Vice President, Business Operations .... Mark Gorris
Controller ....Brad Wood
Vice President, General Manager .... Dal Maxvill
Administrative Assistant to
   President & Chief Executive Officer ....Elaine Milo
Administrative Assistant to
   Vice President, General Manager ....Judy Carpenter Barada
Administrative Assistant to Vice President,
   Business Operations .... Renee Garrett
Vice President, Marketing ....Marty Hendin
Administrative Assistant to
   Vice President, Marketing .... Mary Ellen Edmiston
Director of Promotions ....Nancy Trammell
Director of Player Development .... Mike Jorgensen
Director of Scouting ....Fred McAlister
Assistant Director of Scouting ....Marty Maier
Assistant to Player Development & Scouting ....Scott Smulczenski
Director of Public Relations .... Jeff Wehling
Public Relations Manager .... Brian Bartow
Director of Broadcasting & Market Development .... Dan Farrell
Promotions Supervisor ....Joe Strohm
Director of Community Relations .... Joe Cunningham
Director of Sales ....Sue Ann McClaren
Director, Target Marketing ....Ted Savage
Director, Ticket Systems........................... Josephine Arnold
Director, Human Resources .... Marian Rhodes
Director, Ticket Services.. Kevin Wade
Director, Tickets and Office Administration .... Colin Allsop
Manager, Office Services ....Patti McCormick
Traveling Secretary ....C.J. Cherre

Games At: Busch Stadium

   Capacity: 56,627   Surface: Artificial
Playing Field Distances:
   Left Field Fence .... 330 feet
   Center Field Fence .... 402 feet
   Right Field Fence .... 330 feet
   Plate to Grandstand .... 64 feet
Power Alleys (Left and Right) .... 375 feet
Height of Walls:
   All .... 8 feet

SAN DIEGO PADRES
San Diego Padres Baseball Partnership

P.O. Box 2000
San Diego, CA 92112-2000
(619) 283-7294
FAX: (619) 282-8886 (Media Rel.)
   (619) 282-2228 (BB Op.)

Chairman/Managing Partner ....Tom Werner
Vice Chairmen ....Art Engel, Russell Goldsmith, Art Rivkin
Partners ....Malin Burnham, Bruce Corwin, John Earhart,
   Jack Goodall, Keith Matson, Michael Monk, Leon Parma,
   Bob Payne, Peter Peckham, Ernest Rady, Scott Wolfe
President .... Dick Freeman
Executive Vice President/Baseball
   Operations & General Manager .... Joe McIlvaine
Vice President/Business Operations .... Bill Adams
Vice President/Public Relations .... Andy Strasberg
Vice President/Finance ....Bob Wells
Assistant Vice President/Baseball
   Operations & Assistant General Manager ....John Barr
Director/Ticket Sales ....Jack Autrey
Director/Stadium Operations .... Doug Duennes
Director/Media Relations .... Jim Ferguson
Director/Administrative Services .... Lucy Freeman
Director/Community Relations & Publications .... Jim Geschke
Director/Ticket Operations.................................. Dave Gilmore
Director/Scoreboard Operations .... Mark Guglielmo
Director/Marketing .... Don Johnson
Director/Minor Leagues .... Ed Lynch
Traveling Secretary .... John (Doc) Mattei
Director/Promotions .... Tom Ryba
Director/Scouting .... Reggie Waller
Director/Broadcasting .... TBA
Assistant Director/Media Relations .... Roger Riley
Manager/Accounting ....Bob Croasdale
Administrator/Minor Leagues .... Priscilla Oppenheimer

Games At: San Diego/Jack Murphy Stadium
   9449 Friars Road
   San Diego, CA 92108

   Capacity: 59,700   Surface: Natural Grass
Playing Field Distances:
   Left Field Fence .... 327 feet
   Center Field Fence .... 405 feet
   Right Field Fence .... 327 feet
   Plate to Grandstand .... 75 feet
Power Alleys (Left and Right) .... 370 feet
Height of Walls:
   All .... 8½ feet

SAN FRANCISCO GIANTS
San Francisco Giants Baseball Club

Candlestick Park
San Francisco, CA 94124
(415) 468-3700
FAX: (415) 467-0485

Board of Directors .... Robert A. Lurie, H. Michael Kurzman,
Connie Lurie, Corey Busch, Eugene L. Valla, James L. Hunt, Esq.,
Albert L. Rosen, Peter A. McGowan
Chairman .... Bob Lurie
President and General Manager .... Al Rosen
Executive Vice President .... Corey Busch
Senior Vice President .... Pat Gallagher
Staff Counsel .... Michael Shapiro, Esq.
Govt. Affairs/Broadcast Coordinator .... Bob Hartzell

BASEBALL ADMINISTRATION

Vice President & Assistant General Manager .... Ralph Nelson
Vice President, Baseball Operations .... Bob Kennedy
Vice President, Scouting .... Bob Fontaine
Director of Scouting .... Dave Nahabedian
Director of Minor League Operations .... Tony Siegle
Director of Player Development .... Jack Hiatt
Director of Travel .... Dirk Smith

BUSINESS ADMINISTRATION

Vice President, Public Relations .... Duffy Jennings
Vice President, Stadium Operations .... Jorge Costa
Vice President, Tickets .... Arthur Schulze
Director of Media Relations .... Matt Fischer
Director of Marketing .... Mario Alioto
Director of Ticket Operations .... Judy Jones
Director of Ticket Sales .... Pennie Lundberg
Director of Community Services .... David Craig
Director of Communications .... Robin Carr Locke
Director of Retail Operations .... Robert Tolifson
Controller .... Jeannie Hurley
Director of Publications .... Mark Ray
Promotions Manager .... Valerie McGuire

Games At: Candlestick Park

Capacity: 62,000   Surface: Natural Grass
Playing Field Distances:
    Left Field Fence .... 335 feet
    Center Field Fence .... 400 feet
    Right Field Fence .... 335 feet
    Plate to Grandstand .... 66 feet
Power Alleys (Left and Right) .... 365 feet
Height of Walls:
    All .... 9 feet

COLORADO ROCKIES
Colorado Rockies Baseball Club

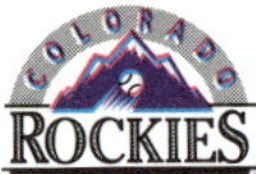

Suite 2100
1700 Broadway
Denver, CO 80290
(303) 292-0200
FAX: (303) 830-8977

Chairman and Chief Executive Officer .... John Antonucci
President and Chief Operating Officer .... Steve Ehrhart
Senior Vice President/General Manager .... Bob Gebhard
Executive Vice President/General Counsel .... Paul Jacobs
Executive Vice President/Baseball Operations .... John McHale, Jr.
Senior Vice President/Business Operations .... Bernie Mullin
Senior Vice President/Public Affairs .... Dean Peeler
Director, Public Relations .... Mike Swanson
Director, Community Services .... Roger Kinney
Manager, Community Relations .... Jackie Sarmiento
Vice President/Finance .... Michael Kent
Director of Scouting .... Pat Daugherty
Director of Corporate Marketing .... Dave Glazier
Director of Merchandising .... Mark Ehrhart
Director of Ticket Operations .... Chuck Javernick
Assistant General Manager .... Randy Smith
Special Assistant to the General Manager .... Larry Bearnarth
Assistant Director of Scouting .... Paul Egins
Assistant to President .... Jennifer Moore
Special Events Coordinator .... Alan Bossart
Administrator/Baseball Operations .... Mary Cheney
Administrative Assistant/Baseball Operations .... Chris Rice
Assistant to Senior Vice President/
    Business Operations .... Liz Stecklein
Administrative Assistant/Public Affairs .... Barb Maniscalco
Executive Administrator .... Wendy Jobe
Administrative Assistant ....Lisa Quarton
Secretary/Scouting Department .... Penny Biever
Sales Assistant ....Jan Giovino
Store Manager, Rockies Dugout Store .... Steve Tomlinson

Games At: Mile High Stadium (1993-94)

Capacity: 76,100   Surface: Natural Grass
Playing Field Distances:
    Left Field Fence .... 335 feet
    Center Field Fence .... 423 feet
    Right Field Fence .... 370 feet
    Plate to Grandstand .... 60 feet
Power Alleys (Left) .... 375 feet
    (Right) .... 390 feet

FARM CLUBS

Bend, Northwest (Rookie) .... PDC
Mesa, Arizona (Rookie) (sharing with Cubs) .... PDC
Visalia, California (Rookie) (supplying players) .... PDC

FLORIDA MARLINS
Florida Marlins Baseball Club

100 N.E. Third Avenue
Ft. Lauderdale, FL 33301
(305) 779-7070
FAX: (305) 779-7130

Chairman .... Wayne Huizenga
President .... Carl Barger
Executive Vice President & General Manager .... Dave Dombrowski
Vice President of Business Operations .... Richard Andersen
Vice President/Expansion Coordinator .... Don Smiley
Vice President of Finance .... Jonathan D. Mariner
Vice President of Communications .... Dean Jordan
Director of Scouting and Special Assistant
    to the General Manager .... Gary Hughes
Director of Player Development .... John Boles
Director of Minor League Administration .... Dan Lunetta
Assistant General Manager .... Frank Wren
Senior Advisor, Player Personnel .... Carrol "Whitey" Lockman
Special Assistant to the General Manager ......Octavio "Cookie" Rojas
Director of Latin American Operations and
    Special Consultant to the General Manager ....Angel Vazquez
Coordinator of Team Development and Scout.................. Jim Hendry
Traveling Secretary ....John Panagakis
Home Run Club .... William Beck
Staff Assistant .... Patrick McNamara
Staff Assistant .... Royal "Tripp" McKenney

Games At: Joe Robbie Stadium

Capacity: 46,500   Surface: Natural Grass
Playing Field Distances:
    Left Field Fence .... 335 feet
    Center Field Fence .... 410 feet
    Right Field Fence .... 345 feet
    Plate to Grandstand .... 60 feet
Power Alleys (Left and Right) .... 380 feet

FARM CLUBS

Erie, NY-Penn (Rookie) .... PDC
Kissimmee, Gulf Coast (Rookie) 0

NATIONAL LEAGUE UNIFORM INFORMATION

ATLANTA BRAVES

Caps—Navy blue with scarlet bill and button, white script letter "A". Uniforms: Home Jersey—Solid white body and sleeve, button down placket neck, scarlet braid with navy trim extends around collar and down front and around sleeves ½" up from edge. Emblem—On front, scarlet "BRAVES" with navy outline, slanted upward, left to right, with Tomahawk emblem, scarlet with navy border, gold chain stitch laces bordered in navy, navy detail in head, slanted under lettering. Back—8" number, scarlet on navy, white name plate with 3" name arched in navy. Home Pants—Solid white with scarlet braid with navy trim on outseam, navy belts, solid white tunnel belt loops trimmed with scarlet braid with navy trim. Socks: Navy blue. Road Uniforms: Jersey—Solid gray body and sleeve, front emblem is scarlet "ATLANTA," otherwise same specifications as home jersey. Pants—Solid gray, otherwise same specifications as home pants.

CHICAGO CUBS

Caps—Royal blue with red "C" 1¾" high; white border; red button on top. Home uniform—White with royal blue pinstriped body and sleeves; saddle shoulder; button down front with placket neck; sleeve rib—royal blue 1"; curved bottom; front emblem, positioned at left side of chest—"CUBS" logo 7" diameter; left sleeve emblem—blue cub inside red circle 4¼" diameter. Back—royal blue number 8" high. Pants—White with royal blue pinstripe; tunnel belt loops to hold blue belt. Road uniform—Gray body and sleeves; saddle shoulder; button down front placket neck; curved bottom; front emblem—2¼" blue with white trim "CHICAGO" straight across jersey front with 2nd "C" of "CHICAGO" on placket; front numbers—4" red numbers trimmed with blue (inside) and white with 1st number ¾" below "A" of "CHICAGO"; left sleeve emblem—official team logo 4½" diameter. Back—3½" blue with white trim arched player's name above 8" blue with white trim player's number. Pants—Gray with ⅜" blue and ⅜" white side seam stripes; tunnel belt loops to hold blue belt.

CINCINNATI REDS

Caps—Scarlet with wishbone "C" in white. Home uniforms—White knit pullover shirt. Wishbone "C" in white outlined in scarlet. "REDS" in white block letters on red background inside the "C". Red-white-red trim on sleeves and neckline. Scarlet numbers on right shirt front and on back. Names on back same color as numbers. White knit pants with built-in elastic waistband. Red-white-red trim down side of pants. Road uniforms—Gray with "CINCINNATI" in scarlet block letters across front of shirt. Rest of uniform same as home. Secondary road shirt—Scarlet with "CINCINNATI" in white block letters across the front. Number in white, front and back. Name in white on back.

HOUSTON ASTROS

Caps—Solid navy; white "H" logo 2½" high with LOGO orange star. Home shirt—Solid white button down front with ⅞" navy neck piping and rounded bottom. Set-in sleeves with sleeve stripe insert on top shoulder and down sleeve; striping measures ⅝" navy, ⅝" red, ⅝" UNIFORM orange, ⅝" yellow, ⅝" UNIFORM orange, ⅝" red, ⅝" navy. 1" navy insert underneath arm and down length of jersey. Navy "Astros" lettering trimmed in white (uppercase 3⅝", lowercase 2⅝") centered on chest. Navy star trimmed in white 5⅝" high, located ¼" below Astros "o". Home trousers—White, with navy 1" striping down entire side of pant leg; to be worn with blue belt. Road shirt—Solid cream button down front with ⅞" navy neck piping and rounded bottom. Set-in sleeves with sleeve stripe insert on top shoulder and down sleeve; striping measures ⅝" navy, ⅝" red, ⅝" UNIFORM orange, ⅝" yellow, ⅝" UNIFORM orange, ⅝" red, ⅝" navy. 1" navy insert underneath arm and down length of jersey. Navy "Astros" lettering trimmed in white (uppercase 3⅝", lowercase 2⅝") centered on chest. Navy star trimmed in white 5⅝" high, located ¼" below Astros "o". Road trousers—Cream, with navy 1" striping down entire side of pant leg; to be worn with blue belt.

LOS ANGELES DODGERS

Caps—Royal blue with white button and white full block monogram "LA" (superimposed). Uniforms—White knit with no trim. "DODGERS" in royal blue script and underlined across shirt front. Royal blue belt. Royal blue numbers and players' names on back and red numbers on lower left shirt front. Royal blue sleeves on sweatshirts. Patch on left sleeve of jersey commemorating the 30th Anniversary of Dodger Stadium. Socks—Royal blue. Road uniforms—Blue-gray knit with white trim around number, "DODGERS" and name. White-blue-white trim on sleeve. Rest same as home uniforms.

MONTREAL EXPOS

Caps—Solid Montreal Expos Blue (PMS 287) with blue button and visor. Montreal's Official team logo 2" high outlined in white. Helmet same as cap. Home uniform—White with Montreal Expos blue pinstriped body and sleeves—no trim. Set in sleeves, button down front with placket neck. "Expos" script in Montreal Expos blue outlined in red and underlined across shirt front. Montreal Expos secondary logo patch on sleeve 4¼" in diameter. Blue belt. Number on left front, name and number on back all in block letters/numbers in Montreal Expos blue with red outline. Montreal Expos blue sweatshirt and white sox with blue stirrups. Road uniforms—Gray with ¾" blue, ¼" white, ¾" red stripe down side and on outer sleeve. Numbers on lower right front, back and names in block letters are red on blue on white. "Montreal" script in red on blue on white and underlined across shirt front with a blue fleur de lys above the "E". Sleeve patch is same as on home.

NATIONAL LEAGUE UNIFORM INFORMATION

NEW YORK METS

Caps—Royal blue with orange monogram "NY" (superimposed). Home uniform: White with blue pin stripe body and sleeve; orange and blue stripes across shoulders and down both sides; set-in sleeves with stripe from collar to sleeve end; curved bottom; Button-down front; Shoulder stripes—centered on shoulder, orange ½", blue 1", orange ½"; Side stripes—starting under armpit, ½" orange, 1" blue, ½" orange. Front emblem—"METS" lettering blue outlined with orange and white angled upward with top of "e" 4½" from middle of V-neck. Player's number 4" high centered directly under "s". Pants—White with blue pin stripes and orange and blue stripes down sides—orange ½", blue 1", orange ½". Road uniform—Solid gray body and set in sleeves, Button-down front with orange, blue, orange striping outlined with white border on shoulder and sleeve top. Lettering across front blue, New York block letters outlined in orange and white arched across chest with no number on front. Back—Blue number with orange and white trim. Pants—Grey with orange, blue, orange striping with white border. Names on all home and road game jerseys.

PHILADELPHIA PHILLIES

NEW UNIFORM TO BE UNVEILED OPENING DAY

During the off-season, the Phillies changed their logo and uniforms. The new logo appears on Page 4. The change includes a switch from the burgundy color the Phillies have been using since 1970, the last time they made a uniform change. The new color is red (PMS 200). The Phillies began using the new logo over the winter but the uniforms are being kept secret until opening day. Major League Baseball Properties Design Service and Dick Perez, the Phillies artist and the official artist of the Baseball Hall of Fame, assisted the Phillies in designing the new logo and uniform. The Phillies home uniforms have featured a red pinstripe since 1950. Their road uniform has been grey, then blue and back to gray again.

PITTSBURGH PIRATES

Caps—Black with block letter "P" in gold. Uniform—Home—Solid white body and sleeves; Saddle shoulder; Curved bottom; Button-down front with a placket neck; Sleeve stripes—½" black (outside), ½" gold, ½" black. Front emblem—4" black "PIRATES" lettering outlined in gold vertically arched across front; black 5" player's number outlined in gold positioned under lettering on left side. Sleeve emblem—Official Team Logo—same 3/colors as logo, 4"x4"; Back—black 3½" player's name arched in block lettering, outlined in gold above 9" black with gold outlining player's number. Pants: Solid white; Side stripes—½" black, ½" gold, ½" black; tunnel belt loops. Road—Solid gray body and sleeves; Saddle shoulder; Curved bottom; Button-down front with a placket neck; Sleeve stripes—½" black (outside), ½" gold, ½" black. Front emblem—black "Pittsburgh" with gold outlining (uppercase 5", lowercase 2¼"), angled upward from right to left across front; black 5" player's number outlined in gold positioned under lettering on left side. Sleeve emblem—Official team logo—same 3/colors as logo, 4"x4"; Back—black 3½" player's name outlined in gold above 9" black with gold outlining player's number. Pants: Solid gray. Same specs as home trousers.

ST. LOUIS CARDINALS

Caps (Home)—Red with white "StL" logo trimmed in blue. Shirt (Home)—White, traditional style, button-down front with centered "Birds-On-Bat" logo, quarter sleeves. Pants (Home)—White, belted (red), three-quarter length. Caps (Road)—Blue with red "StL" logo trimmed in white, red button on top. Shirt (Road)—Light gray, traditional style, button-down front with centered "Birds-On-Bat" logo, quarter sleeves. Pants (Road)—Light gray, belted (blue), three-quarter length. Players' numbers and names will be red on both home and road uniforms.

SAN DIEGO PADRES

Caps—Solid navy blue with white "S" and orange "D" interlocking. Shirt (home)—White with navy blue pin-striped body and sleeves; set-in sleeves; button down placket neck (2" interfacing). Navy blue PADRES lettering outlined in white with orange dropshadow, angled with "P" top 1¾" below "S" top. Shirt (road)—gray body and sleeves; saddle shoulder; button down placket neck (2" interfacing). Navy blue 3¾" block style "SAN DIEGO" outlined in white (inside) with orange dropshadow, arched across front. Pants (home)—white with navy blue pinstripes, belt loops on waistband. Pants (road)—Gray with belt loops to hold Navy blue belt.

SAN FRANCISCO GIANTS

Caps—Black with orange button and orange monogram "SF" (superimposed). Home uniform shirt—White, button-down style, with orange and black stripes on sleeves and "GIANTS" across chest in arched black block letters outlined in orange; number and name on back. Home uniform pants—White, with black leg stripes flanked by thin orange stripes. Road uniform shirt—Gray, button-down style, with orange and black stripes in sleeves and black trim around neckline and down both sides of front buttons; monogram "SF" (superimposed) over left breast; number and name on back. Road uniform pants—Gray, with black leg stripes flanked by thin orange stripes.

FARM CLUB AFFILIATIONS

ATLANTA

Richmond, International (AAA) .... O
Greenville, Southern (AA) .... O
Durham, Carolina (A) .... PDC
Macon, South Atlantic (A) .... O
PULASKI, APPALACHIAN (Rookie) .... PDC
Bradenton, Gulf Coast (Rookie) .... O
Idaho Falls, Pioneer (Rookie) .... PDC

CHICAGO

Iowa, American Association (AAA) .... PDC
Charlotte, Southern (AA) .... PDC
Winston-Salem, Carolina (A) .... PDC
Peoria, Midwest (A) .... PDC
Geneva, NY-Penn (Rookie) .... PDC
Huntington, W.VA, Appalachian (Rookie) .... O
Mesa, Arizona (Rookie) .... PDC

CINCINNATI

Nashville, American Association (AAA) .... PDC
Chattanooga, Southern (AA) .... PDC
Cedar Rapids, Midwest (A) .... PDC
Charleston, W.Va, South Atlantic (A) .... PDC
Billings, Pioneer (Rookie) .... PDC
Princeton, W.VA, Appalachian (Rookie) .... PDC

HOUSTON

TUCSON, PACIFIC COAST (AAA) .... PDC
Jackson, Texas (AA) .... PDC
Asheville, South Atlantic (A) .... PDC
Burlington, Midwest (A) .... PDC
Osceola, FL, Florida State (A) .... O
Auburn, NY-Penn (Rookie) .... PDC
Kissimmee, Gulf Coast (Rookie) .... O

LOS ANGELES

Albuquerque, Pacific Coast (AAA) .... PDC
San Antonio, Texas (AA) .... PDC
Bakersfield, California (A) .... PDC
Vero Beach, Florida State (A) .... O
Salem, OR, Northwest (A) .... PDC
Great Falls, Pioneer (Rookie) .... PDC
Port St. Lucie, Gulf Coast (Rookie) .... O
Santo Domingo, Dominican Summer League (Rookie) .... O

MONTREAL

Indianapolis, American Association (AAA) .... PDC
Harrisburg, Eastern (AA) .... PDC
WEST PALM BEACH, FLORIDA STATE (A) .... O
Rockford, Midwest (A) .... PDC
Albany, South Atlantic (A) .... PDC
JAMESTOWN, NY-PENN (A) .... O
GULF COAST, GULF COAST (Rookie) .... O

NEW YORK

Tidewater, VA, International (AAA) .... PDC
Binghamton, Eastern (AA) .... O
St. Lucie, Florida State (A) .... O
COLUMBIA, SC, SOUTH ATLANTIC (A) .... PDC
Pittsfield, NY-Penn (A) .... PDC
Kingsport, Appalachian (Rookie) .... O
Sarasota, Gulf Coast (Rookie) .... O

PHILADELPHIA

Scranton/Wilkes-Barre, International (AAA) .... PDC
Reading, Eastern (AA) .... PDC
Clearwater, Florida State (A) .... O
Spartanburg, South Atlantic (A) .... PDC
Batavia, NY-Penn (A) .... PDC
Martinsville, Appalachian (Rookie) .... O

PITTSBURGH

Buffalo, American Association (AAA) .... PDC
Carolina, Southern (AA) .... PDC
Salem, VA, Carolina (A) .... PDC
Augusta, South Atlantic (A) .... PDC
Welland, NY-Penn (A) .... PDC
Bradenton, Gulf Coast (Rookie) .... O

ST. LOUIS

Louisville, American Association (AAA) .... PDC
Arkansas, Texas (AA) .... PDC
St. Petersburg, Florida State (A) .... PDC
Savannah, South Atlantic (A) .... PDC
Springfield, IL, Midwest (A) .... O
Johnson City, Appalachian (Rookie) .... PDC
Hamilton, Ont, NY-Penn (Rookie) .... PDC
Peoria, AZ, Arizona (Rookie) .... PDC

SAN DIEGO

Las Vegas, Pacific Coast (AAA) .... PDC
Wichita, KS, Texas (AA) .... PDC
HIGH DESERT, CALIFORNIA (A) .... PDC
Waterloo, Midwest (A) .... PDC
Charleston, South Atlantic (A) .... PDC
Scottsdale, Arizona (Rookie) .... PDC
Spokane, Northwest (Rookie) .... PDC

SAN FRANCISCO

Phoenix, Pacific Coast (AAA) .... PDC
SHREVEPORT, TEXAS (AA) .... PDC
San Jose, California (A) .... PDC
CLINTON, MIDWEST (A) .... PDC
Everett, WA, Northwest (Rookie) .... PDC
Scottsdale, Arizona (Rookie) .... PDC
San Pedro de Macoris, Dominican Summer (Rookie) .... PDC

ALL CAPS—WON LEAGUE CHAMPIONSHIP   PDC—Player Development Contract   O—Owned

NATIONAL LEAGUE RETIRED UNIFORM NUMBERS

ATLANTA

21 Warren Spahn
35 Phil Niekro
41 Eddie Mathews
44 Henry Aaron

CHICAGO

14 Ernie Banks
26 Billy Williams

CINCINNATI

1 Fred Hutchinson
5 Johnny Bench

HOUSTON

32 Jim Umbricht
40 Don Wilson

LOS ANGELES

1 Pee Wee Reese
4 Duke Snider
19 Jim Gilliam
24 Walt Alston
32 Sandy Koufax
39 Roy Campanella
42 Jackie Robinson
53 Don Drysdale

MONTREAL

None

NEW YORK

14 Gil Hodges
37 Casey Stengel
41 Tom Seaver

PHILADELPHIA

1 Richie Ashburn
20 Mike Schmidt
32 Steve Carlton
36 Robin Roberts

PITTSBURGH

1 Billy Meyer
4 Ralph Kiner
8 Willie Stargell
9 Bill Mazeroski
20 Pie Traynor
21 Roberto Clemente
33 Honus Wagner
40 Danny Murtaugh

ST. LOUIS

6 Stan Musial
14 Ken Boyer
17 Dizzy Dean
20 Lou Brock
45 Bob Gibson

SAN DIEGO

6 Steve Garvey

SAN FRANCISCO

Christy Mathewson
John McGraw
3 Bill Terry
4 Mel Ott
11 Carl Hubbell
24 Willie Mays
27 Juan Marichal
44 Willie McCovey

FIRST GAME PLAYED

(National League teams)

Team	First Game
Boston	April 22, 1876—Boston 6, Philadelphia Athletics 5 (road)
Philadelphia Athletics	April 22, 1876—Boston 6, Philadelphia 5 (home)
New York Mutuals	April 25, 1876—Boston 7, New York 6 (home)
Chicago	April 25, 1876—Chicago 4, Louisville 0 (road)
Cincinnati	April 25, 1876—Cincinnati 2, St. Louis 1 (home)
St. Louis	April 25, 1876—Cincinnati 2, St. Louis 1 (road)
Philadelphia	May 1, 1883—Providence 4, Philadelphia 3 (home)
New York (original club)	May 1, 1883—New York 7, Boston 5 (home)
Pittsburgh	April 30, 1887—Pittsburgh 6, Chicago 2 (home)
Brooklyn	April 19, 1890—Boston 15, Brooklyn 9 (road)
Milwaukee	April 13, 1953—Milwaukee 2, Cincinnati 0 (road)
Los Angeles	April 15, 1958—San Francisco 8, Los Angeles 0 (road)
San Francisco	April 15, 1958—San Francisco 8, Los Angeles 0 (home)
Houston	April 10, 1962—Houston 11, Chicago 2 (home)
New York (present club)	April 11, 1962—St. Louis 11, New York 4 (road)
Atlanta	April 12, 1966—Pittsburgh 3, Atlanta 2 (home)
San Diego	April 8, 1969—San Diego 2, Houston 1 (home)
Montreal	April 8, 1969—Montreal 11, New York 10 (road)

NATIONAL LEAGUE STADIUMS

ATLANTA BRAVES

ATLANTA FULTON COUNTY STADIUM
First game played—April 12, 1966

GROUND RULES

DUGOUTS—Dugouts are bounded by guard rails and any ball hitting guard rail is IN PLAY. Ball hitting netting on home plate side of either dugout is IN PLAY. Ball hitting facing on or over either dugout is IN PLAY. Ball hitting front ledge of lip in front of dugout is IN PLAY.

BACKSTOP—Ball lodging in padding or on top of camera booth is dead—ONE BASE on pitch and TWO BASES on throw by a fielder. Ball thrown into stands under fence going from dugout to dugout—ONE BASE on pitch and TWO BASES on throw by a fielder.

CANVAS—Catch may be made off of canvas. Ball lodged behind or under canvas is dead—ONE BASE on pitch and TWO BASES on throw by a fielder. Batted ball lodging behind or under canvas—TWO BASES.

FOUL POLES—Ball hitting any part of screen area supported by poles down left or right field line—HOME RUN. Ball going over outfield fence into open space directly below screen area—HOME RUN.

HOUSTON ASTROS

ASTRODOME
First game played—April 12, 1965

GROUND RULES

DUGOUTS—The ball remains in play unless it enters the dugout. ONE BASE on throw by pitcher; TWO BASES on throw by a fielder.

BEHIND HOME PLATE—Any thrown ball hitting above, on or below canvas padding behind home plate remains IN PLAY if it rebounds onto field. If ball lodges and remains in canvas padding—ONE BASE on pitch; TWO BASES on throw by a fielder.

HITTING ROOF OR SPEAKERS—Ball hitting roof or speakers in fair territory is playable if caught by fielder—batter is out. Ball hitting roof or speakers in fair territory shall be judged fair or foul in relation to where it hits the ground or is touched by a fielder. Any ball that hits speakers or roof in foul territory is a foul ball and the ball is dead.

OUTFIELD AREA—Fairly batted ball in left, center and right field hitting ABOVE yellow or orange line—HOME RUN. Any ball bouncing above line is considered to have left the playing field and should be ruled a TWO BASE hit.

CHICAGO CUBS

WRIGLEY FIELD
First game played—April 20, 1916

GROUND RULES

WHEN BALL:

Hits railing or screen above bleacher wall, and bounces back on playing field—IN PLAY.

Sticks in screen in front of bleachers—TWO BASES.

Sticks in vines on bleacher walls—TWO BASES. If ball comes out—IN PLAY.

Hits left field or right field foul markers above painted mark—HOME RUN.

Hits foul markers below painted mark, and bounces back on playing field—IN PLAY.

Goes in or under grates in left or right field and remains there—TWO BASES.

Goes in or under grates, on either side of home plate, and remains there—ONE BASE on pitched ball. TWO BASES on thrown ball.

LOS ANGELES DODGERS

DODGER STADIUM
First game played—April 10, 1962

GROUND RULES

LEFT- AND RIGHT-FIELD FOUL POLES—Ball IN PLAY when it hits below railing (white section of foul pole). HOME RUN on ball hitting foul pole above railing (yellow section).

DUGOUTS—All Television and Photography booths, as well as Dugouts, considered bench. Ball striking any forward facing of Dugouts—IN PLAY.

BACKSTOP SCREEN—Screen Roof of Fans' Dugout Boxes considered same as sloping area of a Backstop. Ball striking guide wire supporting Backstop—OUT OF PLAY.

CINCINNATI REDS

RIVERFRONT STADIUM
First game played—June 30, 1970

GROUND RULES

FOUL SCREEN—Any ball hitting foul screen in left or right field—HOME RUN.

THE OUTFIELD—Any ball bouncing over fence—TWO BASE HIT. Any ball hit down right or left field line and bouncing into box seats in stands—TWO BASES.

CANVAS (TARP)—Ball remaining behind or underneath canvas—ONE BASE on pitch and TWO BASES on throw by fielder. TWO BASES on batted ball, otherwise in play. Fielder may make catch standing on canvas.

DUGOUTS—Everything in play unless the ball goes into the dugout.

MONTREAL EXPOS

OLYMPIC STADIUM
First game played—April 15, 1977

GROUND RULES

Ball hitting roof on outfield side of yellow line is a HOME RUN.

Everything in play—

EXCEPT: Ball going beyond or on lines in front of dugout and camera pits—BOOK RULE. Popup or fly ball hit into any one of four designated camera areas is out of play.

If ball hits overhanging speakers in fair territory, it is a HOME RUN.

If ball hits overhanging speakers in foul territory, it is a DEAD BALL.

Ball caught in padding of outfield fence is GROUND RULE DOUBLE.

NATIONAL LEAGUE STADIUMS

NEW YORK METS

SHEA STADIUM
First game played—April 17, 1964

PHILADELPHIA PHILLIES

VETERANS STADIUM
First game played—April 10, 1971

PITTSBURGH PIRATES

THREE RIVERS STADIUM
First game played—July 16, 1970

GROUND RULES

Ball rolling under any part of field boxes and staying out of sight—ONE BASE on throw by pitcher from rubber—TWO BASES on throw by infielder. Ball hitting side of facing of dugout considered IN DUGOUT.

Ball going into dugout—ONE BASE on throw by pitcher from rubber—TWO BASES from field.

Fair ball bouncing over fence—TWO BASES.

Fair ball bouncing over temporary fence in foul territory in left and right field—TWO BASES.

GROUND RULES

DUGOUTS—Ball has to actually enter dugout area or hit the yellow bars or yellow line to be considered out of play. Ball entering open area above end of dugout inside yellow line is considered OUT OF PLAY.

FOUL POLES—Are outside playing area and balls hitting them are to be considered HOME RUN.

FENCES—Glass areas have openings at top. If ball sticks in opening it is a GROUND RULE DOUBLE. Ball sticking underneath padding in outfield fence is IN PLAY. In left and right field the stands protrude to a point near the foul lines. If ball lands in fair territory and bounces over the points and lands in the playing area, it is considered to be in the stands and ruled a GROUND RULE DOUBLE. Ball off screen behind home plate is IN PLAY. Ball hitting pipe to right of right field foul pole is IN PLAY.

GROUND RULES

Ball hitting any part of foul-line screen above top of outfield fence—HOME RUN.

For purpose of Ground Rules photographers' benches which about outfield ends of home and visiting clubs' benches are considered to be part of player's bench.

Fair hit ball striking screen in front of right or left field bullpen is IN PLAY.

Fair hit ball sticking in screen in front of right or left field bullpen—TWO BASES.

Fair hit ball going through or under screen in front of right or left field bullpen—TWO BASES.

ST. LOUIS CARDINALS

BUSCH STADIUM
First game played—May 12, 1966

SAN DIEGO PADRES

SAN DIEGO/JACK MURPHY STADIUM
First game played—April 8, 1969

SAN FRANCISCO GIANTS

CANDLESTICK PARK
First game played—April 12, 1960

GROUND RULES

OUTFIELD AREA—Fair ball hitting above yellow line on outfield wall—HOME RUN. Ball hitting on or below yellow line is IN PLAY. Fair ball bounding into field boxes, bleachers, over fence in outfield, or enclosed area in left or right field corners or going through or under fences—TWO BASES.

DUGOUTS—Ball rolling onto top step of dugouts (which are at ground level) is IN PLAY. Photographer's area on outfield end of each dugout shall be regarded as part of the dugout. Ball thrown by pitcher from the rubber to catch base-runner off first or third base that goes into stand or dugout—ONE BASE. A pitched, thrown or batted ball that hits anyone on the playing field, except as otherwise provided for in the Official Playing Rules is IN PLAY. Any batted ball hitting automatic tarpaulin container would be FOUL BALL. Ball going through wire behind plate or lodging in it—ONE BASE on throw by a pitcher—TWO BASES on throw by fielder.

GROUND RULES

Photographers' areas adjacent to first base and third base dugouts are considered part of dugouts. Ball out of play, same as both dugouts (Field Level).

Bullpens are IN PLAY.

Everything else is standard ground rules.

GROUND RULES

1. Ball hitting either foul pole (or screen attached) *above* black ring painted on foul pole—HOME RUN. Hitting black ring or below on foul pole or hitting top of fence and bounding onto playing field—IN PLAY. If bounding into stands or over fence—TWO BASES.

2. Thrown ball going behind backstop screen—ONE BASE, if thrown by pitcher from rubber. Other overthrows—TWO BASES.

3. Ball going over fence under screen attached to foul poles—HOME RUN.

4. Ball hitting face of dugouts or face of bat racks—IN PLAY. Must go *into* dugouts to be out of play.

5. Ball IN PLAY in bullpens.

6. Ball hitting any portion of right field stands above the top of the outfield fence and bounding onto playing field—HOME RUN.

Atlanta Braves

MANAGER
BOBBY COX (6)

Coaches:
JIM BEAUCHAMP (37)
PAT CORRALES (39)
CLARENCE JONES (28)
LEO MAZZONE (54)
JIMY WILLIAMS (22)

Team Physician—DR. DAVID T. WATSON
Trainer—DAVE PURSLEY
Assistant Trainer—JEFF PORTER

Director of Public Relations—JIM SCHULTZ
Traveling Secretary—BILL ACREE

No. PITCHERS (18)	B	T	Ht.	Wt.	Born	Birthplace	Residence	1991 Club	W-L	ERA	G	GS	CG	SV	IP	H	R	ER	BB	SO	M.L. Service
33 AVERY, STEVE	L	L	6-4	190	4-14-70	Trenton, MI	Taylor, MI	Atlanta	18-8	3.38	35	35	3	0	210.1	189	89	79	65	137	1.113
48 BERENGUER, JUAN	R	R	5-11	220	11-30-54	Aguadulce, Pan.	Longwood, FL	Atlanta	0-3	2.24	49	0	0	17	64.1	43	18	16	20	53	10.151
36 BIELECKI, MIKE	R	R	6-3	195	7-31-59	Baltimore, MD	Crownsville, MD	Chicago NL	13-11	4.50	39	25	0	0	172.0	169	91	86	54	72	
								Atlanta	0-0	0.00	2	0	0	0	1.2	2	0	0	2	3	
								(Composite)	13-11	4.46	41	25	0	0	173.2	171	91	86	56	75	5.068
67 BURLINGAME, DENNIS★	R	R	6-4	200	6-17-69	Woodbury, NJ	Mullica Hill, NJ	Durham	11-7	3.01	26	26	3	0	161.1	143	60	54	80	95	0.000
40 FREEMAN, MARVIN	R	R	6-7	222	4-10-63	Chicago, IL	Chicago, IL	Atlanta	1-0	3.00	34	0	0	1	48.0	37	19	16	13	34	3.015
47 GLAVINE, TOM	L	L	6-1	190	3-25-66	Concord, MA	Atlanta, GA	Atlanta	20-11	2.55	34	34	9	0	246.2	201	83	70	69	192	4.052
56 GOMEZ, PAT★	L	L	5-11	185	3-17-68	Roseville, CA	Citrus Heights, CA	Richmond	2-9	4.39	16	14	0	0	82.0	99	55	40	41	41	
								Greenville	5-2	7.00	13	13	0	0	79.2	58	20	62	31	71	0.000
32 LEIBRANDT, CHARLIE	R	L	6-3	200	10-4-56	Chicago, IL	Leawood, KS	Atlanta	15-13	3.49	36	36	1	0	229.2	212	105	89	56	128	10.010
50 MERCKER, KENT	L	L	6-2	195	2-1-68	Dublin, OH	Dublin, OH	Atlanta	5-3	2.58	50	4	0	6	73.1	56	23	21	35	62	1.148
63 MURRAY, MATT★	L	R	6-6	200	9-26-70	Boston, MA	Swampscott, MA	Durham	1-0	1.29	2	2	0	0	7.0	5	1	1	0	7	0.000
62 NIED, DAVID★	R	R	6-2	175	12-22-68	Dallas, TX	Duncanville, TX	Greenville	7-3	2.41	15	15	1	0	89.2	79	26	24	20	101	
								Durham	8-3	1.56	13	12	2	0	80.2	46	19	14	23	77	0.000
26 PENA, ALEJANDRO	R	R	6-1	203	6-25-59	Camb., Puerto Plata, D.R.	Montebello, CA	New York NL	6-1	2.71	44	0	0	4	63.0	63	20	19	19	49	
								Atlanta	2-0	1.40	15	0	0	11	19.1	11	3	3	3	13	
								(Composite)	8-1	2.40	59	0	0	15	82.1	74	23	22	22	62	9.162
42 REYNOSO, ARMANDO★	R	R	6-0	186	5-1-66	San Luis Potosi, Mexico	Jalisco, Mex.	Richmond	10-6	2.61	22	19	3	0	131.0	117	44	38	39	97	
								Atlanta	2-1	6.17	6	5	0	0	23.1	26	18	16	10	10	0.059
51 RIVERA, BEN★	R	R	6-6	210	1-11-69	San Pedro de Macoris, D.R.	San Pedro de Macoris, D.R.	Greenville	11-8	3.57	26	26	3	0	158.2	155	76	63	75	116	0.000
25 SMITH, PETE	R	R	6-2	200	2-27-66	Weymouth, MA	Burlington, MA	Macon	0-0	0.00	3	3	0	0	9.2	15	11	0	2	14	
								Richmond	3-3	7.24	10	10	1	0	51.0	66	44	41	24	41	
								Atlanta	1-3	5.06	14	10	0	0	48.0	48	33	27	22	29	4.000
29 SMOLTZ, JOHN	R	R	6-3	185	5-15-67	Warren, MI	Atlanta, GA	Atlanta	14-13	3.80	36	36	5	0	229.2	206	101	97	77	148	3.072
30 STANTON, MIKE	L	L	6-1	190	6-2-67	Houston, TX	Houston, TX	Atlanta	5-5	2.88	74	0	0	7	78.0	62	27	25	21	54	2.039
43 WOHLERS, MARK★	R	R	6-4	207	1-23-70	Holyoke, MA	Holyoke, MA	Richmond	1-0	1.03	23	0	0	11	26.1	23	4	3	12	22	
								Atlanta	3-1	3.20	17	0	0	2	19.2	17	7	7	13	13	0.052

No. CATCHERS (5)	B	T	Ht.	Wt.	Born	Birthplace	Residence	1991 Club	AVG.	G	AB	R	H	2B	3B	HR	RBI	BB	SO	SB	M.L. Service
11 BERRYHILL, DAMON	S	R	6-0	205	12-3-63	South Laguna, CA	Laguna Niguel, CA	Chicago NL	.189	62	159	13	30	7	0	5	14	11	41	1	
								Atlanta	.000	1	1	0	0	0	0	0	0	0	1	0	
								(Composite)	.188	63	160	13	30	7	0	5	14	11	42	1	3.159
19 CABRERA, FRANCISCO	R	R	6-4	193	10-10-66	Santo Domingo, D.R.	Santo Domingo, D.R.	Richmond	.261	32	119	22	31	7	1	7	24	10	21	0	
								Atlanta	.242	44	95	7	23	6	0	4	23	6	20	1	1.139
8 HEATH, MIKE	R	R	5-11	180	2-5-55	Tampa, FL	Brandon, FL	Atlanta	.209	49	139	4	29	3	1	1	12	7	26	0	13.039
64 LOPEZ, JAVIER★	R	R	6-3	185	11-5-70	Ponce, PR	Ponce, PR	Durham	.245	113	384	43	94	14	2	11	51	25	87	10	0.000
10 OLSON, GREG	R	R	6-0	200	9-6-60	Marshall, MN	Edina, MN	Atlanta	.241	133	411	46	99	25	0	6	44	44	48	1	2.013

No. INFIELDERS (10)	B	T	Ht.	Wt.	Born	Birthplace	Residence	1991 Club	AVG.	G	AB	R	H	2B	3B	HR	RBI	BB	SO	SB	M.L. Service
2 BELLIARD, RAFAEL	R	R	5-6	160	10-24-61	Pueblo Nuevo Mao, D.R.	Santa Cruz, CA	Atlanta	.249	149	353	36	88	9	2	0	27	22	63	3	7.080
4 BLAUSER, JEFF	R	R	6-0	170	11-8-65	Los Gatos, CA	Atlanta, GA	Atlanta	.259	129	352	49	91	14	3	11	54	54	59	5	3.100
12 BREAM, SID	L	L	6-4	220	8-3-60	Carlisle, PA	Wexford, PA	Atlanta	.253	91	265	32	67	12	0	11	45	25	31	0	7.002
65 CARABALLO, RAMON*	S	R	5-7	150	5-23-69	Rio San Juan, D.R.	Santo Domingo, D.R.	Durham	.250	120	444	73	111	13	8	6	52	38	91	53	0.000
45 CASTILLA, VINNY*	R	R	6-1	175	7-4-67	Oaxaca, Mex.	Oaxaca, Mex.	Richmond	.225	67	240	25	54	7	4	7	36	14	31	1	
								Greenville	.270	66	259	34	70	17	3	7	44	9	35	0	
								Atlanta	.200	12	5	1	1	0	0	0	0	0	2	0	0.036
14 HUNTER, BRIAN	R	L	6-0	195	3-4-68	Tor, CA	Long Beach, CA	Richmond	.260	48	181	28	47	7	0	10	30	11	24	3	
								Atlanta	.251	97	271	32	68	16	1	12	50	17	48	0	0.129
20 LEMKE, MARK	S	R	5-9	167	8-13-65	Utica, NY	Whitesboro, NY	Atlanta	.234	136	269	36	63	11	2	2	23	29	27	1	2.036
18 LYONS, STEVE	L	R	6-3	192	6-3-60	Tacoma, WA	Scottsdale, AZ	Boston	.241	87	212	15	51	10	1	4	17	11	35	10	6.131
9 PENDLETON, TERRY	S	R	5-9	195	7-16-60	Los Angeles, CA	Oxnard, CA	Atlanta	.319	153	586	94	187	34	8	22	86	43	70	10	7.075
15 TREADWAY, JEFF	L	R	5-11	170	1-22-63	Columbus, GA	Griffin, GA	Atlanta	.320	106	306	41	98	17	2	3	32	23	19	2	4.034

No. OUTFIELDERS (8)	B	T	Ht.	Wt.	Born	Birthplace	Residence	1991 Club	AVG.	G	AB	R	H	2B	3B	HR	RBI	BB	SO	SB	M.L. Service
5 GANT, RON	R	R	6-0	172	3-2-65	Victoria, TX	Smyrna, GA	Atlanta	.251	154	561	101	141	35	3	32	105	71	104	34	3.133
16 GREGG, TOMMY	L	L	6-1	190	7-29-63	Boone, NC	Smyrna, GA	Atlanta	.187	72	107	13	20	8	1	1	4	12	24	2	3.089
23 JUSTICE, DAVID	L	L	6-3	200	4-14-66	Cincinnati, OH	Atlanta, GA	Atlanta	.275	109	396	67	109	25	1	21	87	65	81	8	2.000
17 MITCHELL, KEITH*	R	R	5-10	180	8-6-69	San Diego, CA	San Diego, CA	Greenville	.327	60	214	46	70	15	3	10	47	29	29	12	
								Richmond	.326	25	95	16	31	6	1	2	17	9	13	0	
								Atlanta	.318	48	66	11	21	0	0	2	5	8	12	3	0.081
66 NIEVES, MELVIN*	S	R	6-2	186	12-28-71	San Juan, PR	Bayamon, PR	Durham	.264	64	201	31	53	11	0	9	25	40	53	3	0.000
1 NIXON, OTIS@	S	R	6-2	180	1-9-59	Evergreen, NC	Atlanta, GA	Atlanta	.297	124	401	81	119	10	1	0	26	47	40	72	6.085
24 SANDERS, DEION	L	L	6-1	195	8-9-67	Ft. Myers, FL	Alpharetta, GA	Richmond	.262	29	130	20	34	6	3	5	16	10	28	12	
								Atlanta	.191	54	110	16	21	1	2	4	13	12	23	11	1.052
27 SMITH, LONNIE	R	R	5-9	190	12-22-55	Chicago, IL	Atlanta, GA	Atlanta	.275	122	353	58	97	19	1	7	44	50	64	9	12.082

*Rookie
@On Disqualified List

FULL NAMES AND PHONETICS

Avery, Steven Thomas
Belliard, Rafael Leonidas (BELL-ee-ard)
Berenguer, Juan Bautista, Jr. (BAIR-un-gair)
Berryhill, Damon Scott
Bielecki, Michael Joseph (BIL-leck-ee)
Blauser, Jeffrey Michael (BLAU-zer)
Bream, Sidney Eugene
Burlingame, Dennis Arthur
Cabrera, Francisco Paulino (ca-BRER-ah)
Caraballo, Ramon (car-ah-BYE-yoh)
Castilla, Vinicio (Cass-TEE-uh)
Freeman, Marvin
Gant, Ronald Edwin
Glavine, Thomas Michael (GLA-vin)

Gomez, Patrick Alexander
Gregg, William Thomas
Heath, Michael Thomas
Hunter, Brian Ronald
Justice, David Christopher
Leibrandt, Charles Louis, Jr. (LEE-brant)
Lemke, Mark Alan (LEM-kee)
Lopez, Javier Torres
Lyons, Stephen John
Mercker, Kent Franklin
Mitchell, Keith Alexander
Murray, Matthew Michael
Nied, David Glen (as in need)
Nieves, Melvin Ramos (nee-EV-es)

Nixon, Otis Junior
Olson, Gregory William
Pena, Alejandro (Vasquez) (PAYN-yuh)
Pendleton, Terry Lee
Reynoso, Martin Armando (Gutierrez) (ray-NOH-so)
Rivera, Bienvenido Santana (ree-VAIR-uh)
Sanders, Deion Luwynn
Smith, Lonnie
Smith, Peter John
Smoltz, John Andrew
Stanton, William Michael
Treadway, Hugh Jeffrey
Wohlers, Mark Edward (wowl-ers)

MANAGER AND COACHES

Robert J. Cox
James E. Beauchamp (BEACH-im)
Patrick Corrales
Clarence Woodrow Jones
Leo O. Mazzone
James F. Williams

Chicago Cubs

MANAGER
JIM LEFEBVRE (5)

Coaches:
BILLY CONNORS (4)
CHUCK COTTIER (15)
SAMMY ELLIS (46)
JOSE MARTINEZ (3)
TOM TREBELHORN (41)

Team Physicians—JOHN MARQUARDT, M.D.,
MICHAEL SCHAFER, M.D.
Trainer—JOHN FIERRO
Assistant Trainer—DAVE CILLADI
Media Relations Director—SHARON PANNOZZO
Traveling Secretary—PETER DURSO

No. PITCHERS (16)	B	T	Ht.	Wt.	Born	Birthplace	Residence	1991 Club	W-L	ERA	G	GS	CG	SV	IP	H	R	ER	BB	SO	M.L. Service
45 ASSENMACHER, PAUL	L	L	6-3	200	12-10-60	Detroit, MI	Stone Mountain, GA	Chicago NL	7-8	3.24	75	0	0	15	102.2	85	41	37	31	117	5.158
47 BOSKIE, SHAWN	R	R	6-3	205	3-28-67	Hawthorne, NV	Reno, NV	Iowa	2-2	3.57	7	6	2	0	45.1	43	19	18	11	29	
								Chicago NL	4-9	5.23	28	20	0	0	129.0	150	78	75	52	62	1.110
52 BULLINGER, JIM*	R	R	6-2	185	8-21-65	New Orleans, LA	Sarasota, FL	Iowa	3-4	5.40	8	8	0	0	46.2	47	32	28	23	30	
								Charlotte	9-9	3.53	20	20	8	0	142.2	132	62	56	61	128	0.000
49 CASTILLO, FRANK	R	R	6-1	180	4-1-69	El Paso, TX	El Paso, TX	Iowa	3-1	2.52	4	4	1	0	25.0	20	7	7	7	20	
								Chicago NL	6-7	4.35	18	18	4	0	111.2	107	56	54	33	73	0.102
33 DICKSON, LANCE*	R	L	6-1	185	10-19-69	Fullerton, CA	La Mesa, CA	Iowa	4-4	3.11	18	18	1	0	101.1	85	39	35	57	101	0.057
22 HARKEY, MIKE	R	R	6-5	220	10-25-66	San Diego, CA	Chino Hills, CA	Chicago NL	0-2	5.30	4	4	0	0	18.2	21	11	11	6	15	2.031
44 HARTSOCK, JEFF*	R	R	6-0	190	11-19-66	Fairfield, OH	Greensboro, NC	Albuquerque	12-6	3.80	29	26	0	0	154.0	153	80	65	78	123	0.000
32 JACKSON, DANNY	R	L	6-0	205	1-5-62	San Antonio, TX	Overland Park, KS	Iowa	0-0	1.80	1	1	0	0	5.0	2	1	1	2	4	
								Chicago NL	1-5	6.75	17	14	0	0	70.2	89	59	53	48	31	7.131
50 LANCASTER, LES	R	R	6-2	200	4-21-62	Dallas, TX	Irving, TX	Chicago NL	9-7	3.52	64	11	1	3	156.0	150	68	61	49	102	4.057
31 MADDUX, GREG	R	R	6-0	175	4-14-66	San Angelo, TX	Las Vegas, NV	Chicago NL	15-11	3.35	37	37	7	0	263.0	232	113	98	66	198	5.021
35 McELROY, CHUCK	L	L	6-0	180	10-1-67	Galveston, TX	Beaumont, TX	Chicago NL	6-2	1.95	71	0	0	3	101.1	73	33	22	57	92	1.088
36 MORGAN, MIKE	R	R	6-2	210	10-8-59	Tulare, CA	Ogden, UT	Los Angeles	14-10	2.78	34	33	5	1	236.1	197	85	73	61	140	9.111
30 SCANLAN, BOB	R	R	6-8	215	8-9-66	Los Angeles, CA	Beverly Hills, CA	Iowa	2-0	2.95	4	3	0	0	18.1	14	8	6	10	15	
								Chicago NL	7-8	3.89	40	13	0	1	111.0	114	60	48	40	44	0.160
51 SLOCUMB, HEATHCLIFF	R	R	6-3	210	6-7-66	Jamaica, NY	Richmond Hills, NY	Iowa	1-0	4.05	12	0	0	1	13.1	10	8	6	6	9	
								Chicago NL	2-1	3.45	52	0	0	1	62.2	53	29	24	30	34	0.155
42 SMITH, DAVE	R	R	6-1	195	1-21-55	San Francisco, CA	Olivenhain, CA	Chicago NL	0-6	6.00	35	0	0	17	33.0	39	22	22	19	16	12.000
43 WENDELL, TURK*	S	R	6-2	175	5-19-67	Pittsfield, MA	Dalton, MA	Greenville	11-3	2.56	25	20	1	0	147.2	130	47	42	51	122	
								Richmond	0-2	3.43	3	3	1	0	21.0	20	9	8	16	18	0.000

No. CATCHERS (4)	B	T	Ht.	Wt.	Born	Birthplace	Residence	1991 Club	AVG.	G	AB	R	H	2B	3B	HR	RBI	BB	SO	SB	M.L. Service
7 GIRARDI, JOE	R	R	5-11	195	10-14-64	Peoria, IL	Highland Park, IL	Iowa	.222	12	36	3	8	1	0	0	4	4	8	2	
								Chicago NL	.191	21	47	3	9	2	0	0	6	6	6	0	2.140
53 PEDRE, GEORGE*	R	R	6-0	205	10-12-66	Culver City, CA	Buena Park, CA	Omaha	.216	31	116	12	25	4	0	1	4	4	18	2	
								Memphis	.253	100	363	43	92	28	1	9	59	24	72	1	
								Kansas City	.263	10	19	2	5	1	1	0	3	3	5	0	0.032
19 VILLANUEVA, HECTOR	R	R	6-1	220	10-2-64	San Juan, PR	Rio Piedras, PR	Iowa	.360	6	25	2	9	3	0	2	9	1	6	0	
								Chicago NL	.276	71	192	23	53	10	1	13	32	21	30	0	1.125
2 WILKINS, RICK	L	R	6-2	210	6-4-67	Jacksonville, FL	Jacksonville, FL	Iowa	.271	38	107	12	29	3	1	5	14	11	17	1	
								Chicago NL	.222	86	203	21	45	9	0	6	22	19	56	3	0.124

No. INFIELDERS (11)	B	T	Ht.	Wt.	Born	Birthplace	Residence	1991 Club	AVG.	G	AB	R	H	2B	3B	HR	RBI	BB	SO	SB	M.L. Service
21 ARIAS, ALEX*	R	R	6-3	185	11-20-67	New York, NY	New York, NY	Charlotte	.275	134	488	69	134	26	0	4	47	47	42	23	0.000
37 CASTELLANO, PEDRO*	R	R	6-1	175	3-11-70	Lara, Ven.	Lara, Ven.	Charlotte	.421	7	19	2	8	0	0	0	2	1	6	0	
								Winston-Salem	.303	129	459	59	139	25	3	10	87	72	97	11	0.000
12 DUNSTON, SHAWON	R	R	6-1	175	3-21-63	Brooklyn, NY	Fremont, CA	Chicago NL	.260	142	492	59	128	22	7	12	50	23	64	21	6.093
17 GRACE, MARK	L	L	6-2	190	6-28-64	Winston-Salem, NC	Pacific Palisades, CA	Chicago NL	.273	160	619	87	169	28	5	8	58	70	53	3	3.154
9 PAULINO, ELVIN*	L	R	6-1	190	11-6-67	Moca, D.R.	Moca, D.R.	Charlotte	.257	132	460	67	118	27	1	24	81	55	110	8	0.000
10 SALAZAR, LUIS	R	R	5-10	190	5-19-56	Barcelona, Ven.	Caracas, Ven.	Chicago NL	.258	103	333	34	86	14	1	14	38	15	45	0	11.052
6 SANCHEZ, REY*	R	R	5-9	165	10-5-67	Rio Piedras, PR	Rio Piedras, PR	Iowa	.290	126	417	60	121	16	5	2	46	37	27	13	
								Chicago NL	.261	13	23	1	6	0	0	0	2	4	3	0	0.031
23 SANDBERG, RYNE	R	R	6-2	185	9-18-59	Spokane, WA	Phoenix, AZ	Chicago NL	.291	158	585	104	170	32	2	26	100	87	89	22	10.034
25 SCOTT, GARY*	R	R	6-0	175	8-22-68	New Rochelle, NY	Pelham, NY	Iowa	.208	63	231	21	48	10	2	3	34	20	45	0	
								Chicago NL	.165	31	79	8	13	3	0	1	5	13	14	0	0.041
1 STRANGE, DOUG	S	R	6-2	170	4-13-64	Greenville, SC	Scottsdale, AZ	Iowa	.293	131	509	76	149	35	5	8	56	49	75	10	
								Chicago NL	.444	3	9	0	4	1	0	0	1	0	1	1	0.112
16 VIZCAINO, JOSE	S	R	6-1	180	3-26-68	San Cristobal, DR	El Cajon, CA	Chicago NL	.262	93	145	7	38	5	0	0	10	5	18	2	1.115

No. OUTFIELDERS (9)	B	T	Ht.	Wt.	Born	Birthplace	Residence	1991 Club	AVG.	G	AB	R	H	2B	3B	HR	RBI	BB	SO	SB	M.L. Service
11 BELL, GEORGE	R	R	6-1	202	10-21-59	S.P. de Macoris, D.R.	S.P. de Macoris, D.R.	Chicago NL	.285	149	558	63	159	27	0	25	86	32	62	2	9.084
29 DASCENZO, DOUG	S	L	5-8	160	6-30-64	Cleveland, OH	LaBelle, PA	Chicago NL	.255	118	239	40	61	11	0	1	18	24	26	14	2.093
8 DAWSON, ANDRE	R	R	6-3	197	7-10-54	Miami, FL	Miami, FL	Chicago NL	.272	149	563	69	153	21	4	31	104	22	80	4	15.025
28 LANDRUM, CED	L	R	5-8	170	9-3-63	Butler, AL	Sweet Water, AL	Iowa	.336	38	131	14	44	8	2	1	11	5	21	13	
								Chicago NL	.233	56	86	28	20	2	1	0	6	10	18	27	0.133
27 MAY, DERRICK*	L	R	6-4	205	7-14-68	Rochester, NY	Newark, DE	Iowa	.297	82	310	47	92	18	4	3	49	19	38	7	
								Chicago NL	.227	15	22	4	5	2	0	1	3	2	1	0	0.060
34 ROBERSON, KEVIN*	S	R	6-4	210	1-29-68	Decatur, IL	Decatur, IL	Charlotte	.256	136	507	77	130	24	2	19	67	39	129	17	0.000
18 SMITH, DWIGHT	L	R	5-11	175	11-8-63	Tallahassee, FL	Atlanta, GA	Chicago NL	.228	90	167	16	38	7	2	3	21	11	32	2	2.154
24 WALKER, CHICO	S	R	5-9	185	11-26-58	Jackson, MS	Chicago, IL	Chicago NL	.257	124	374	51	96	10	1	6	34	33	57	13	2.165
20 WALTON, JEROME	R	R	6-1	175	7-8-65	Newnan, GA	Fairburn, GA	Chicago NL	.219	123	270	42	59	13	1	5	17	19	55	7	3.000

*Rookie
#Rehabilitation Assignment

FULL NAMES AND PHONETICS

Arias, Alejandro (air-REE-ahs)
Assenmacher, Paul Andre (AHSS-em-mahk-ur)
Bell, George Antonio
Boskie, Shawn Keahola (BAH-skee)
Bullinger, James Eric (BULL-in-jer)
Castellano, Pedro (kas-ta-YAH-no)
Castillo, Frank Anthony (cas-TEE-yoh)
Dascenzo, Douglas Craig (duh-SEN-zoh)
Dawson, Andre Nolan
Dickson, Lance Michael
Dunston, Shawn Donnell (DUNN-stun)
Girardi, Joseph Elliott (jeh-RAR-dee)

Grace, Mark Eugene
Harkey, Michael Anthony
Hartsock, Jeffrey Roger
Jackson, Danny Lynn
Lancaster, Lester Wayne
Landrum, Cedric Bernard
Maddux, Gregory Alan (MADD-ucks)
May, Derrick Brant
McElroy, Charles Dwayne (MAC-il-roy)
Morgan, Michael Thomas
Paulino, Elvin (pah-LEE-no)
Pedre, Jorge Enrique (PAY-dray)

Roberson, Kevin Lynn (ROH-bur-sun)
Salazar, Luis Ernesto
Sanchez, Rey (Guadalupe)
Sandberg, Ryne Dee
Scanlan, Robert Guy
Scott, Gary Thomas
Slocumb, Heathcliff
Smith, David Stanley Jr.
Smith, John Dwight
Strange, Joseph Douglas
Villanueva, Hector
Vizcaino, Jose Luis (Pimental) (vis-KAH-ee-no)

Walker, Cleotha
Walton, Jerome O'Terrell
Wendell, Steven John (WEN-d'l)
Wilkins, Richard David

MANAGER AND COACHES

James Kenneth Lefebvre (lu-FEE-ver)
William Joseph Connors III
Charles Keith Cottier (kah-TEE-air)
Samuel Joseph Ellis
Jose Martinez (Azcuiz)
Thomas Lynn Trebelhorn

Cincinnati Reds

MANAGER
LOU PINIELLA (41)

Coaches:
JOHN McLAREN (8)
JACKIE MOORE (4)
TONY PEREZ (24)
SAM PERLOZZO (2)
LARRY ROTHSCHILD (3)

Medical Consultant—RICHARD JOLSON
Trainer—LARRY STARR
Assistant Trainer—DOUG SPREEN

Publicity Director—JON BRAUDE
Traveling Secretary—JOEL PIEPER

No.	PITCHERS (21)	B	T	Ht.	Wt.	Born	Birthplace	Residence	1991 Club	W-L	ERA	G	GS	CG	SV	IP	H	R	ER	BB	SO	M.L. Service
62	AYALA, BOBBY★	R	R	6-2	190	7-8-69	Ventura, CA	Oxnard, CA	Chattanooga	3-1	4.67	39	8	1	4	90.2	79	52	47	58	92	0.000
50	BANKHEAD, SCOTT	R	R	5-10	185	7-31-63	Raleigh, NC	Asheboro, NC	#San Bernardino	0-1	5.06	2	2	0	0	5.1	4	4	3	2	4	
									#Bellingham	1-0	0.00	1	0	0	0	4.0	1	0	0	1	8	
									#Calgary	0-0	1.04	5	0	0	1	8.2	7	1	1	1	10	
									Seattle	3-6	4.90	17	9	0	0	60.2	73	35	33	21	28	5.138
31	BELCHER, TIM	R	R	6-3	220	10-19-61	Sparta, OH	Mt. Gilead, OH	Los Angeles	10-9	2.62	33	33	2	0	209.1	189	76	61	75	156	4.032
32	BROWNING, TOM	L	L	6-1	195	4-28-60	Casper, WY	Edgewood, KY	Cincinnati	14-14	4.18	36	36	1	0	230.1	241	124	107	56	115	7.011
37	CHARLTON, NORM	S	L	6-3	205	1-6-63	Ft. Polk, LA	Jamaica Beach, TX	Cincinnati	3-5	2.91	39	11	0	1	108.1	92	37	35	34	77	3.128
49	DIBBLE, ROB	L	R	6-4	230	1-24-64	Bridgeport, CT	Cincinnati, OH	Cincinnati	3-5	3.17	67	0	0	31	82.1	67	32	29	25	124	3.097
54	FOSTER, STEVE★	R	R	6-0	180	8-16-66	Dallas, TX	Waxahachie, TX	Chattanooga	0-2	1.15	17	0	0	10	15.2	10	4	2	4	18	
									Nashville	2-3	2.14	41	0	0	12	54.2	46	17	13	29	52	
									Cincinnati	0-0	1.93	11	0	0	0	14.0	7	5	3	4	11	0.046
61	GARCIA, VICTOR★	R	R	6-2	195	9-15-69	Bonao, D.R.	Bonao, D.R.	Chattanooga	5-3	1.98	40	0	0	5	50.0	41	12	11	20	51	
									Nashville	2-0	2.63	15	0	0	0	24.0	15	7	7	14	12	0.000
45	HAMMOND, CHRIS	L	L	6-1	190	1-21-66	Atlanta, GA	Birmingham, AL	Cincinnati	7-7	4.06	20	18	0	0	99.2	92	51	45	48	50	1.040
48	HENRY, DWAYNE	R	R	6-3	230	2-16-62	Elkton, MD	Glen Allen, VA	Houston	3-2	3.19	52	0	0	2	67.2	51	25	24	39	51	3.107
39	HILL, MILTON★	R	R	6-0	180	8-22-65	Atlanta, GA	Stone Mountain, GA	Nashville	3-3	2.94	37	0	0	3	67.1	59	26	22	15	62	
									Cincinnati	1-1	3.78	22	0	0	0	33.1	36	14	14	8	20	0.068
53	HOFFMAN, TREVOR★	R	R	6-1	200	10-13-67	Bellflower, CA	Anaheim, CA	Cedar Rapids	1-1	1.87	27	0	0	12	33.2	22	8	7	13	52	
									Chattanooga	1-0	1.93	14	0	0	8	14.0	10	4	3	7	23	0.000
43	LAYANA, TIM	R	R	6-2	190	3-2-64	Inglewood, CA	Florence, KY	Nashville	3-1	3.23	26	2	0	1	47.1	41	17	17	28	43	
									Cincinnati	0-2	6.97	22	0	0	0	20.2	23	18	16	11	14	1.084
33	MINUTELLI, GINO★	L	L	6-0	190	5-23-64	Wilmington, DE	Nashville, TN	#Char. (W.Va.)	1-0	0.00	2	2	0	0	8.0	2	0	0	4	8	
									Nashville	4-7	1.90	13	13	1	0	80.1	57	25	17	35	64	
									Cincinnati	0-2	6.04	16	3	0	0	25.1	30	17	17	18	21	0.100
60	POWELL, ROSS★	L	L	6-0	180	1-24-68	Grand Rapids, MI	Sand Lake, MI	Nashville	8-8	4.37	24	24	1	0	129.2	125	74	63	63	82	0.000
55	PUGH, TIM★	R	R	6-6	225	1-26-67	Lake Tahoe, CA	Bartlesville, OK	Chattanooga	3-1	1.64	5	5	0	0	38.1	20	7	7	11	24	
									Nashville	7-11	3.81	23	23	3	0	148.2	130	68	63	56	89	0.000
27	RIJO, JOSE	R	R	6-2	210	5-13-65	San Cristobal, D.R.	Delray Beach, FL	Cincinnati	15-6	2.51	30	30	3	0	204.1	165	69	57	55	172	6.118
28	RUSKIN, SCOTT	R	L	6-2	195	6-8-63	Jacksonville, FL	Jacksonville, FL	Montreal	4-4	4.24	64	0	0	6	63.2	57	31	30	30	46	2.000
36	SANFORD, MO★	R	R	6-6	225	12-24-66	Americus, GA	Starkville, MS	Chattanooga	7-4	2.74	16	16	1	0	95.1	69	37	29	55	124	
									Nashville	3-0	1.60	5	5	2	0	33.2	19	7	6	22	38	
									Cincinnati	1-2	3.86	5	5	0	0	28.0	19	14	12	15	31	0.064
63	SATRE, JASON★	R	R	6-1	180	8-24-70	Tampa, FL	Abilene, TX	Cedar Rapids	8-6	2.58	21	20	4	1	132.2	101	48	38	67	130	
									Chattanooga	1-7	5.11	8	8	0	0	44.0	37	26	25	26	44	0.000
29	SWINDELL, GREG	R	L	6-3	225	1-2-65	Fort Worth, TX	Sugar Land, TX	Cleveland	9-16	3.48	33	33	7	0	238.0	241	112	92	31	169	5.046

No.	CATCHERS (4)	B	T	Ht.	Wt.	Born	Birthplace	Residence	1991 Club	AVG.	G	AB	R	H	2B	3B	HR	RBI	BB	SO	SB	M.L. Service
25	GEREN, BOB	R	R	6-3	225	9-22-61	San Diego, CA	San Diego, CA	New York AL	.219	64	128	7	28	3	0	2	12	9	31	0	3.035
9	OLIVER, JOE	R	R	6-3	210	7-24-65	Memphis, TN	Orlando, FL	Cincinnati	.216	94	269	21	58	11	0	11	41	18	53	0	2.079
34	REED, JEFF	L	R	6-2	190	11-12-62	Joliet, IL	Elizabethton, TN	Cincinnati	.267	91	270	20	72	15	2	3	31	23	38	0	6.074
42	SUTKO, GLENN	R	R	6-3	225	5-9-68	Atlanta, GA	Alpharetta, GA	Chattanooga	.286	23	63	12	18	3	0	3	11	9	20	0	
									Nashville	.209	45	134	9	28	2	1	3	15	22	67	1	
									Cincinnati	.100	10	10	0	1	0	0	0	1	2	6	0	0.079

No.	INFIELDERS (7)	B	T	Ht.	Wt.	Born	Birthplace	Residence	1991 Club	AVG.	G	AB	R	H	2B	3B	HR	RBI	BB	SO	SB	M.L. Service
12	BENAVIDES, FREDDIE*	R	R	6-2	185	4-7-66	Laredo, TX	Laredo, TX	Nashville	.242	94	331	24	80	8	0	0	21	16	55	7	
									Cincinnati	.286	24	63	11	18	1	0	0	3	1	15	1	0.076
58	BRANSON, JEFF*	L	R	6-0	180	1-26-67	Waynesboro, MS	Millry, AL	Chattanooga	.263	88	304	35	80	13	3	2	28	31	51	3	
									Nashville	.241	43	145	10	35	4	1	0	11	8	31	5	0.000
19	DORAN, BILL	S	R	6-0	180	5-28-58	Cincinnati, OH	Cincinnati, OH	Cincinnati	.280	111	361	51	101	12	2	6	35	46	39	5	9.031
51	LANE, BRIAN*	R	R	6-3	215	6-15-69	Waco, TX	Waco, TX	Cincinnati					DID NOT PLAY								1.000
11	LARKIN, BARRY	R	R	6-0	190	4-28-64	Cincinnati, OH	Cincinnati, OH	Cincinnati	.302	123	464	88	140	27	4	20	69	55	64	24	5.054
23	MORRIS, HAL	L	L	6-4	215	4-9-65	Fort Rucker, AL	Richwood, KY	Cincinnati	.318	136	478	72	152	33	1	14	59	46	61	10	2.089
17	SABO, CHRIS	R	R	6-0	185	1-19-62	Detroit, MI	Cincinnati, OH	Cincinnati	.301	153	582	91	175	35	3	26	88	44	79	19	4.000

No.	OUTFIELDERS (8)	B	T	Ht.	Wt.	Born	Birthplace	Residence	1991 Club	AVG.	G	AB	R	H	2B	3B	HR	RBI	BB	SO	SB	M.L. Service
15	BRAGGS, GLENN	R	R	6-4	220	10-17-62	San Bernardino, CA	San Bernardino, CA	Cincinnati	.260	85	250	36	65	10	0	11	39	23	46	11	5.080
46	BRUMFIELD, JACOB*	R	R	6-0	170	5-27-65	Bogalusa, LA	Atlanta, GA	Omaha	.267	111	397	62	106	14	7	3	43	33	64	36	0.000
22	HATCHER, BILLY	R	R	5-10	190	10-4-60	Williams, AZ	Houston, TX	Cincinnati	.262	138	442	45	116	25	3	4	41	26	55	11	6.110
68	HERNANDEZ, CESAR*	R	R	6-0	160	9-28-66	Yamasa, D.R.	Santo Domingo, D.R.	Harrisburg	.254	128	418	58	106	15	2	13	52	25	106	34	0.000
30	MARTINEZ, DAVE	L	L	5-10	175	9-26-64	New York, NY	Bartlett, IL	Montreal	.295	124	396	47	117	18	5	7	42	20	54	16	5.085
21	O'NEILL, PAUL	L	L	6-4	215	2-25-63	Columbus, OH	Cincinnati, OH	Cincinnati	.256	152	532	71	136	36	0	28	91	73	107	12	5.047
10	ROBERTS, BIP	S	R	5-7	165	10-27-63	Berkeley, CA	San Diego, CA	San Diego	.281	117	424	66	119	13	3	3	32	37	71	26	4.014
16	SANDERS, REGGIE*	R	R	6-1	180	12-1-67	Florence, SC	Florence, SC	Chattanooga	.315	86	302	50	95	15	8	8	49	41	67	15	
									Cincinnati	.200	9	40	6	8	0	0	1	3	0	9	1	0.046

*Rookie
#Rehabilitation Assignment

FULL NAMES AND PHONETICS

Ayala, Robert Joseph (Eye-YA-luh)
Bankhead, Michael Scott
Belcher, Timothy Wayne
Benavides, Alfredo, III (Ben-uh-VEE-diss)
Braggs, Glenn Erick
Branson, Jeffery Glenn
Browning, Thomas Leo
Brumfield, Jacob Donnell
Charlton, Norman Wood, III
Dibble, Robert Keith
Doran, William Donald (DOOR-in)
Foster, Stephen Eugene, Jr.

Garcia, Victoriano
Geren, Robert Peter, III (GAIR-in)
Hammond, Christopher Andrew
Hatcher, William Augustus
Henry, Dwayne Allen
Hernandez, Cesar Dario
Hill, Milton Giles
Hoffman, Trevor William
Lane, Brian Conley
Larkin, Barry Louis
Layana, Timothy Joseph (Lay-YONNA)
Martinez, David

Minutelli, Gino Michael (Min-you-TELL-ee)
Morris, William Harold, III
Oliver, Joseph Melton
O'Neill, Paul Andrew
Powell, Ross John
Pugh, Timothy Dean
Reed, Jeffrey Scott
Rijo, Jose Antonio (REE-ho)
Roberts, Leon Joseph, III
Ruskin, Scott Drew
Sabo, Christopher Andrew (SAY-bo)
Sanders, Reginald Laverne

Sanford, Meredith LeRoy, Jr.
Satre, Jason Robert (Sat-TREE)
Sutko, Glenn Edward (SUTT-ko)
Swindell, Forest Gregory (Swin-DELL)

MANAGER AND COACHES

Louis Victor Piniella (Pin-ELL-uh)
John Lowell McLaren
Jackie Spencer Moore
Atanasio Rigal Perez
Samuel Benedict Perlozzo (Per-LAHZ-oh)
Larry L. Rothschild

Houston Astros

MANAGER
ART HOWE (18)

Coaches:
BOB CLUCK (55)
MATT GALANTE (48)
RUDY JARAMILLO (42)
ED OTT (14)
TOM SPENCER (52)

Team Physician—DR. BILL BRYAN
Trainer—DAVE LABOSSIERE
Trainer Emeritus—JIM 'DOC' EWELL

Public Relations—ROB MATWICK
Traveling Secretary—BARRY WATERS

No.	PITCHERS (20)	B	T	Ht.	Wt.	Born	Birthplace	Residence	1991 Club	W-L	ERA	G	GS	CG	SV	IP	H	R	ER	BB	SO	M.L. Service
41	BLAIR, WILLIE	R	R	6-1	185	12-18-65	Paintsville, KY	Lexington, KY	Colorado Spr.	9-6	4.99	26	15	0	4	113.2	130	74	63	30	57	
									Cleveland	2-3	6.75	11	5	0	0	36.0	58	27	27	10	13	1.047
46	BOWEN, RYAN	R	R	6-0	185	2-10-68	Hanford, CA	Hanford, CA	Tucson	5-5	4.38	18	18	2	0	98.2	114	56	48	56	78	
									Houston	6-4	5.15	14	13	0	0	71.2	73	43	41	36	49	0.080
35	CAPEL, MIKE	R	R	6-1	175	10-13-61	Marshall, TX	Houston, TX	Tucson	4-2	2.40	30	0	0	3	56.1	49	16	15	17	44	
									Houston	1-3	3.03	25	0	0	3	32.2	33	14	11	15	23	1.009
39	GARDNER, CHRIS*	R	R	6-0	175	3-30-69	Long Beach, CA	Paso Robles, CA	Jackson	13-5	3.15	22	22	1	0	131.1	116	57	46	75	72	
									Houston	1-2	4.01	5	4	0	0	24.2	19	12	11	14	12	0.031
60	GRIFFITHS, BRIAN*	R	R	6-2	190	5-29-68	Portland, OR	Milwaukie, OR	Osceola	4-3	1.92	18	8	0	0	61.0	43	18	13	17	44	0.000
27	HARNISCH, PETE	R	R	6-0	207	9-23-66	Commack, NY	Belmar, NJ	Houston	12-9	2.70	33	33	4	0	216.2	169	71	65	83	172	2.135
50	HENRY, BUTCH*	L	L	6-1	195	10-7-68	El Paso, TX	El Paso, TX	Tucson	10-11	4.80	27	27	2	0	153.2	192	92	82	42	97	0.000
31	HERNANDEZ, XAVIER	L	R	6-2	185	8-16-65	Port Arthur, TX	Missouri City, TX	Tucson	2-1	2.75	16	3	0	4	36.0	35	16	11	9	34	
									Houston	2-7	4.71	32	6	0	3	63.0	66	34	33	32	55	2.015
37	JONES, JIMMY	R	R	6-2	190	4-20-64	Dallas, TX	Highland Village, TX	Houston	6-8	4.39	26	22	1	0	135.1	143	73	66	51	88	4.019
59	JONES, TODD*	L	R	6-3	200	4-24-68	Marietta, GA	Pell City, AL	Osceola	4-4	4.35	14	14	0	0	72.1	69	38	35	35	52	
									Jackson	4-3	4.88	10	10	0	0	55.1	51	37	30	39	37	0.000
44	JUDEN, JEFF*	R	R	6-7	245	1-19-71	Salem, MA	Salem, MA	Jackson	6-3	3.10	16	16	0	0	95.2	84	43	33	44	75	
									Tucson	3-2	3.18	10	10	0	0	56.2	56	28	20	25	51	
									Houston	0-2	6.00	4	3	0	0	18.0	19	14	12	7	11	0.023
57	KILE, DARRYL	R	R	6-5	185	12-2-68	Garden Grove, CA	Corona, CA	Houston	7-11	3.69	37	22	0	0	153.2	144	81	63	84	100	1.000
56	MALLICOAT, ROB*	L	L	6-3	180	11-16-64	St. Helen's, OR	Hillsboro, OR	Jackson	4-1	3.77	18	0	0	1	31.0	20	15	13	11	34	
									Tucson	4-4	5.48	19	6	0	1	47.2	43	32	29	38	32	
									Houston	0-2	3.86	24	0	0	1	23.1	22	10	10	13	18	0.084
29	OSUNA, AL	L	L	6-3	200	8-10-65	Inglewood, CA	Houston, TX	Houston	7-6	3.42	71	0	0	12	81.2	59	39	31	46	68	1.033
51	PORTUGAL, MARK	R	R	6-0	190	10-30-62	Los Angeles, CA	Missouri City, TX	Houston	10-12	4.49	32	27	1	1	168.1	163	91	84	59	120	4.165
38	REYNOLDS, SHANE*	R	R	6-3	210	3-26-68	Bastrop, LA	Bastrop, LA	Jackson	8-9	4.47	27	27	2	0	151.0	165	93	75	62	116	0.000
19	SCHILLING, CURT	R	R	6-4	215	11-14-66	Anchorage, AK	Sugar Land, TX	Tucson	0-1	3.42	13	0	0	3	23.2	16	9	9	12	21	
									Houston	3-5	3.81	56	0	0	8	75.2	79	35	32	39	71	1.134
45	SIMON, RICHIE*	R	R	6-2	200	11-29-65	Brooklyn, NY	Brooklyn, NY	Jackson	4-2	2.18	56	0	0	20	70.1	55	23	17	30	54	0.000
63	TURNER, MATT*	R	R	6-5	215	2-18-67	Lexington, KY	Lexington, KY	Richmond	1-3	4.75	23	0	0	5	36.0	33	21	19	20	33	
									Tucson	1-1	4.15	13	0	0	1	26.0	27	12	12	14	25	0.000
53	WILLIAMS, BRIAN*	R	R	6-2	195	2-15-69	Lancaster, SC	Columbia, SC	Osceola	6-4	2.91	15	15	0	0	89.2	72	41	29	40	67	
									Jackson	2-1	4.20	3	3	0	0	15.0	17	8	7	7	15	
									Tucson	0-1	4.93	7	7	0	0	38.1	39	25	21	22	29	
									Houston	0-1	3.75	2	2	0	0	12.0	11	5	5	4	4	0.023

CATCHERS (5)

No.		B	T	Ht.	Wt.	Born	Birthplace	Residence	1991 Club	AVG.	G	AB	R	H	2B	3B	HR	RBI	BB	SO	SB	M.L. Service
7	BIGGIO, CRAIG	R	R	5-11	180	12-14-65	Smithtown, NY	Houston, TX	Houston	.295	149	546	79	161	23	4	4	46	53	71	19	3.099
10	EUSEBIO, TONY★	R	R	6-2	180	4-27-67	San Jose de Los Llamos, D.R.	San Pedro de Macoris, D.R.	Jackson	.261	66	222	27	58	8	3	2	31	25	54	3	
									Tucson	.400	5	20	5	8	1	0	0	2	3	3	1	
									Houston	.105	10	19	4	2	1	0	0	0	6	8	0	0.064
9	SERVAIS, SCOTT★	R	R	6-2	195	6-4-67	LaCrosse, WI	Coon Valley, WI	Tucson	.324	60	219	34	71	12	0	2	27	13	19	0	
									Houston	.162	16	37	0	6	3	0	0	6	4	8	0	0.088
6	TAUBENSEE, ED★	L	R	6-4	205	10-31-68	Beeville, TX	Longwood, FL	Colorado Spr.	.310	91	287	53	89	23	3	13	39	31	61	0	
									Cleveland	.242	26	66	5	16	2	1	0	8	5	16	0	0.062
20	TUCKER, EDDIE★	R	R	6-2	205	11-18-66	Greenville, MS	Greenville, MS	Shreveport	.284	110	352	49	100	29	1	4	49	48	57	3	0.000

INFIELDERS (9)

No.		B	T	Ht.	Wt.	Born	Birthplace	Residence	1991 Club	AVG.	G	AB	R	H	2B	3B	HR	RBI	BB	SO	SB	M.L. Service
5	BAGWELL, JEFF	R	R	6-0	195	5-27-68	Boston, MA	Houston, TX	Houston	.294	156	554	79	163	26	4	15	82	75	116	7	1.000
11	CAMINITI, KEN	S	R	6-0	200	4-21-63	Hanford, CA	Richmond, TX	Houston	.253	152	574	65	145	30	3	13	80	46	85	4	3.137
1	CANDAELE, CASEY	S	R	5-9	165	1-12-61	Lompoc, CA	San Luis Obispo, CA	Houston	.262	151	461	44	121	20	7	4	50	40	49	9	3.132
17	CEDENO, ANDUJAR	R	R	6-1	168	8-21-69	La Romana, D.R.	La Romana, D.R.	Tucson	.303	93	347	49	105	19	6	7	55	19	68	5	
									Houston	.243	67	251	27	61	13	2	9	36	9	74	4	0.104
36	COOPER, GARY★	R	R	6-1	200	8-13-64	Lynwood, CA	Orem, UT	Tucson	.305	120	406	86	124	25	6	14	75	66	107	7	
									Houston	.250	9	16	1	4	1	0	0	2	3	6	0	0.023
43	GUERRERO, JUAN★	R	R	5-11	160	2-1-67	S.P. de Macoris, D.R.	Haina, D.R.	Shreveport	.334	128	479	78	160	40	2	19	94	46	86	14	0.000
64	MILLER, ORLANDO★	R	R	6-1	180	1-13-69	Changlonola, Pan.	Estafeta el Dorado, Pan.	Osceola	.298	74	272	27	81	11	2	0	36	13	30	1	
									Jackson	.186	23	70	5	13	6	0	1	5	5	13	0	0.000
3	MOTA, ANDY★	R	R	5-10	180	3-4-66	Santo Domingo, D.R.	Tucson, AZ	Tucson	.299	123	462	65	138	19	4	2	46	22	76	14	
									Houston	.189	27	90	4	17	2	0	1	6	1	17	2	0.038
15	YELDING, ERIC	R	R	5-11	165	2-22-65	Montrose, AL	Daphne, AL	Tucson	.395	11	43	6	17	3	0	0	3	4	4	4	
									Houston	.243	78	276	19	67	11	1	1	20	13	46	11	2.111

OUTFIELDERS (6)

No.		B	T	Ht.	Wt.	Born	Birthplace	Residence	1991 Club	AVG.	G	AB	R	H	2B	3B	HR	RBI	BB	SO	SB	M.L. Service
21	ANTHONY, ERIC	L	L	6-2	195	11-8-67	San Diego, CA	Houston, TX	Tucson	.336	79	318	57	107	22	2	9	63	25	58	11	
									Houston	.153	39	118	11	18	6	0	1	7	12	41	1	1.067
12	FINLEY, STEVE	L	L	6-2	180	3-12-65	Union City, TN	Houston, TX	Houston	.285	159	596	84	170	28	10	8	54	42	65	34	3.000
26	GONZALEZ, LUIS	L	R	6-2	180	9-3-67	Tampa, FL	Houston, TX	Houston	.254	137	473	51	120	28	9	13	69	40	101	10	1.032
4	RHODES, KARL	L	L	5-11	170	8-21-68	Cincinnati, OH	Cincinnati, OH	Tucson	.260	84	308	45	80	17	1	1	46	38	47	5	
									Houston	.213	44	136	7	29	3	1	1	12	14	26	2	0.116
22	SIMMS, MIKE	R	R	6-4	185	1-12-67	Orange, CA	Houston, TX	Tucson	.246	85	297	53	73	20	2	15	59	36	94	2	
									Houston	.203	49	123	18	25	5	0	3	16	18	38	1	0.118
2	YOUNG, GERALD	S	R	6-2	185	10-22-64	Tela, Hond.	Houston, TX	Tucson	.304	24	79	14	24	2	3	0	17	14	8	3	
									Houston	.218	108	142	26	31	3	1	1	11	24	17	16	3.154

★Rookie
#Rehabilitation Assignment

FULL NAMES AND PHONETICS

Anthony, Eric Todd
Bagwell, Jeffery Robert (BAG-well)
Biggio, Craig Alan (BIDG-ee-oh)
Blair, William Allen
Bowen, Ryan Eugene (BOW-un)
Caminiti, Kenneth Gene (kam-un-NET-ee)
Candaele, Casey Todd (can-dell)
Capel, Michael Lee (K-pull)
Cedeno, Andujar (sa-DAYN-yo)
Cooper, Gary Clifton

Eusebio, Raul Antonio (you-SAY-be-oh)
Finely, Steven Allen (FIN-lee)
Gardner, Chrsitopher John
Gonzalez, Luis Emilio
Griffiths, Brian David
Guerrero, Juan Antonio (guh-RAIR-oh)
Harnisch, Peter Thomas (HAR-nish)
Henry, Floyd Bluford
Hernandez, Francis Xavier
Jones, James Condia

Jones, Todd Barton
Juden, Jeffrey Daniel (JU-den)
Kile, Darryl Andrew
Mallicoat, Robin Dale (MAL-a-coat)
Miller, Orlando Salmon
Mota, Andres Alberto
Osuna, Alfonso, Jr., (oh-SUE-na)
Portugal, Mark Steven
Reynolds, Richard Shane
Rhodes, Karl Derrick

Schilling, Curt Montague (SHILL-ing)
Servais, Scott Daniel (same as "service")
Simms, Michael Howard
Simon, Richard
Taubensee, Edward Kenneth (TAW-ben-see)
Tucker, Eddie Jack
Turner, William Matthew
Williams, Brian, O.
Yelding, Eric Girard (YELL-ding)
Young, Gerald Anthony

MANAGER AND COACHES

Arthur Henry Howe, Jr. (HOW)
Robert Cluck
Matthew J. Galante (guh-LAHN-tee)
Rudolfo Jaramillo (hahd-ah-MEE-oh)
Edward Nathan Ott
Thomas Spencer

Los Angeles Dodgers

MANAGER
TOM LASORDA (2)

Coaches:
JOE AMALFITANO (8)
MARK CRESSE (58)
JOE FERGUSON (13)
BEN HINES (37)
RON PERRANOSKI (16)

Team Physicians—FRANK W. JOBE, M.D.,
MICHAEL F. MELLMAN, M.D.,
HERNDON P. HARDING, JR., M.D.
Trainer—BILL BUHLER
Assistant Trainer—CHARLIE STRASSER
Director of Publicity—JAY LUCAS
Traveling Secretary—BILL DeLURY

No. PITCHERS (17)	B	T	Ht.	Wt.	Born	Birthplace	Residence	1991 Club	W-L	ERA	G	GS	CG	SV	IP	H	R	ER	BB	SO	M.L. Service
56 ASTACIO, PEDRO*	R	R	6-2	174	11-28-69	Hato Mayor, D.R.	Hato Mayor, D.R.	Vero Beach	5-3	1.67	9	9	3	0	59.1	44	19	11	8	45	
								San Antonio	4-11	4.78	19	19	2	0	113.0	142	67	60	39	62	0.000
54 CANDELARIA, JOHN	S	L	6-6	225	11-6-53	Brooklyn, NY	Laguna Hills, CA	Los Angeles	1-1	3.74	59	0	0	2	33.2	31	16	14	11	38	16.117
49 CANDIOTTI, TOM	R	R	6-2	200	8-31-57	Walnut Creek, CA	Danville, CA	Cleveland	7-6	2.24	15	15	3	0	108.1	88	35	27	28	86	
								Toronto	6-7	2.98	19	19	3	0	129.2	114	47	43	45	81	
								(Composite)	13-13	2.65	34	34	6	0	238.0	202	82	70	73	167	6.138
52 CREWS, TIM	R	R	6-0	195	4-3-61	Tampa, FL	Ocoee, FL	Los Angeles	2-3	3.43	60	0	0	6	76.0	75	30	29	19	53	4.041
35 GOTT, JIM	R	R	6-4	220	8-3-59	Hollywood, CA	S. Pasadena, CA	Los Angeles	4-3	2.96	55	0	0	2	76.0	63	28	25	32	73	10.000
46 GROSS, KEVIN	R	R	6-5	215	6-8-61	Downey, CA	Claremont, CA	Los Angeles	10-11	3.58	46	10	0	3	115.2	123	55	46	50	95	8.100
57 GROSS, KIP	R	R	6-2	190	8-24-64	Scottsbluff, NE	Gering, NE	Nashville	5-3	2.08	14	6	1	0	47.2	39	13	11	16	28	
								Cincinnati	6-4	3.47	29	9	1	0	85.2	93	43	33	40	40	0.165
55 HERSHISER, OREL	R	R	6-3	192	9-16-58	Buffalo, NY	Pasadena, CA	#Bakersfield	2-0	0.82	2	2	0	0	11.0	5	2	1	1	6	
								#San Antonio	0-1	2.57	1	1	0	0	7.0	11	3	2	1	5	
								#Albuquerque	0-0	0.00	1	1	0	0	5.0	5	0	0	0	5	
								Los Angeles	7-2	3.46	21	21	0	0	112.0	112	43	43	32	73	8.032
50 HOWELL, JAY	R	R	6-3	212	11-26-55	Miami, FL	Cumming, GA	Los Angeles	6-5	3.18	44	0	0	16	51.0	39	19	18	11	40	9.145
59 JAMES, MIKE*	R	R	6-3	180	8-15-67	Ft. Walton, FL	Mary Ester, FL	San Antonio	9-5	4.53	15	15	2	0	89.1	88	54	45	51	74	
								Albuquerque	1-3	6.60	13	8	0	0	45.0	51	36	33	30	39	0.000
45 MARTINEZ, PEDRO*	R	R	5-11	150	7-25-71	Manoguyabo, D.R.	Santo Domingo, D.R.	Bakersfield	8-0	2.05	10	10	0	0	61.1	41	17	14	19	83	
								San Antonio	7-5	1.76	12	12	4	0	76.2	57	21	15	31	74	
								Albuquerque	3-3	3.66	6	6	0	0	39.1	28	17	16	16	35	0.000
48 MARTINEZ, RAMON	R	R	6-4	173	4-22-68	Santo Domingo, D.R.	Santo Domingo, D.R.	Los Angeles	17-13	3.27	33	33	6	0	220.1	190	89	80	69	150	2.133
51 McANDREW, JAMIE*	R	R	6-2	190	9-2-67	Williamsport, PA	Paducah, KY	Albuquerque	12-10	5.04	28	26	0	1	155.1	167	105	87	76	91	0.000
31 McDOWELL, ROGER	R	R	6-1	182	12-21-60	Cincinnati, OH	Jackson, MS	Philadelphia	3-6	3.20	38	0	0	3	59.0	61	28	21	32	28	
								Los Angeles	6-3	2.55	33	0	0	7	42.1	39	12	12	16	22	
								(Composite)	9-9	2.93	71	0	0	10	101.1	100	40	33	48	50	7.000
17 OJEDA, BOB	L	L	6-1	195	12-17-57	Los Angeles, CA	Upland, CA	Los Angeles	12-9	3.18	31	31	2	0	189.1	181	78	67	70	120	10.088
40 SEANEZ, RUDY	R	R	5-10	185	10-20-68	Brawley, CA	Brawley, CA	Colorado Spr.	0-0	7.27	16	0	0	0	17.1	17	14	14	22	19	
								Canton-Akron	4-2	2.58	25	0	0	7	38.1	17	12	11	30	73	
								Cleveland	0-0	16.20	5	0	0	0	5.0	10	12	9	7	7	1.016
38 WILSON, STEVE	L	L	6-4	195	12-13-64	Victoria, B.C., Canada	Tempe, AZ	Iowa	3-8	3.87	25	16	1	0	114.0	102	55	49	45	83	
								Chicago NL	0-0	4.38	8	0	0	0	12.1	13	7	6	5	9	
								Los Angeles	0-0	0.00	11	0	0	2	8.1	1	0	0	4	5	
								(Composite)	0-0	2.61	19	0	0	2	20.2	14	7	6	9	14	2.095

No. CATCHERS (4)	B	T	Ht.	Wt.	Born	Birthplace	Residence	1991 Club	AVG.	G	AB	R	H	2B	3B	HR	RBI	BB	SO	SB	M.L. Service
61 BAAR, BRYAN*	R	R	6-3	205	4-10-68	Zeeland, MI	Jennison, MI	San Antonio	.224	101	348	33	78	19	0	10	51	21	92	3	0.000
41 HERNANDEZ, CARLOS	R	R	5-11	185	5-24-67	San Felix, Bolivar, Ven.	Santa Monica, Caracas, Ven.	Albuquerque	.345	95	345	60	119	24	2	8	44	24	36	5	
								Los Angeles	.214	15	14	1	3	1	0	0	1	0	5	1	0.099
60 PIAZZA, MIKE*	R	R	6-3	200	9-4-68	Norristown, PA	Valley Forge, PA	Bakersfield	.277	117	448	71	124	27	2	29	80	47	83	0	0.000
14 SCIOSCIA, MIKE	L	R	6-2	220	11-27-58	Upper Darby, PA	Claremont, CA	Los Angeles	.264	119	345	39	91	16	2	8	40	47	32	4	11.116

No.	INFIELDERS (10)	B	T	Ht.	Wt.	Born	Birthplace	Residence	1991 Club	AVG.	G	AB	R	H	2B	3B	HR	RBI	BB	SO	SB	M.L. Service
36	BENZINGER, TODD	S	R	6-1	190	2-11-63	Dayton, KY	Cincinnati, OH	Cincinnati	.187	51	123	7	23	3	2	1	11	10	20	2	
									Kansas City	.294	78	293	29	86	15	3	2	40	17	46	2	4.108
3	HAMILTON, JEFF	R	R	6-3	207	3-19-64	Flint, MI	Fenton, MI	Albuquerque	.000	2	7	0	0	0	0	0	0	0	2	0	
									Los Angeles	.223	41	94	4	21	4	0	1	14	4	21	0	5.034
15	HANSEN, DAVE	L	R	6-0	180	11-24-68	Long Beach, CA	Long Beach, CA	Albuquerque	.303	68	254	42	77	11	1	5	40	49	33	4	
									Los Angeles	.268	53	56	3	15	4	0	1	5	2	12	1	0.125
29	HARRIS, LENNY	L	R	5-10	205	10-28-64	Miami, FL	Miami, FL	Los Angeles	.287	145	429	59	123	16	1	3	38	37	32	12	3.031
23	KARROS, ERIC*	R	R	6-4	205	11-4-67	Hackensack, NJ	San Diego, CA	Albuquerque	.316	132	488	88	154	33	8	22	101	58	80	3	
									Los Angeles	.071	14	14	0	1	1	0	0	1	1	6	0	0.036
30	OFFERMAN, JOSE	S	R	6-0	160	11-8-68	San Pedro de Macoris, D.R.	San Pedro de Macoris, D.R.	Albuquerque	.298	79	289	58	86	8	4	0	29	47	58	32	
									Los Angeles	.195	52	113	10	22	2	0	0	3	25	32	3	0.129
10	SAMUEL, JUAN	R	R	5-11	183	12-9-60	San Pedro de Macoris, D.R.	Santo Domingo, D.R.	Los Angeles	.271	153	594	74	161	22	6	12	58	49	133	23	8.041
27	SHARPERSON, MIKE	R	R	6-3	190	10-4-61	Orangeburg, SC	Stone Mountain, GA	Los Angeles	.278	105	216	24	60	11	2	2	20	25	24	1	3.074
21	SMITH, GREG*	S	R	5-11	170	4-5-67	Baltimore, MD	Sykesville, MD	Albuquerque	.217	48	161	25	35	3	2	0	17	10	30	11	
									Los Angeles	.000	5	3	1	0	0	0	0	0	0	2	0	0.098
62	YOUNG, ERIC*	R	R	5-9	180	11-26-66	Jacksonville, FL	Jacksonville, FL	San Antonio	.280	127	461	82	129	17	4	3	35	67	36	71	
									Albuquerque	.400	1	5	0	2	0	0	0	0	0	0	0	0.000

No.	OUTFIELDERS (9)	B	T	Ht.	Wt.	Born	Birthplace	Residence	1991 Club	AVG.	G	AB	R	H	2B	3B	HR	RBI	BB	SO	SB	M.L. Service
63	ASHLEY, BILLY*	R	R	6-7	220	7-11-70	Taylor, MI	Belleville, MI	Vero Beach	.252	61	206	18	52	11	2	7	42	7	69	9	0.000
22	BUTLER, BRETT	L	L	5-10	160	6-15-57	Los Angeles, CA	Atlanta, GA	Los Angeles	.296	161	615	112	182	13	5	2	38	108	79	38	10.009
28	DANIELS, KAL	L	R	5-11	205	8-20-63	Vienna, GA	Warner Robins, GA	Los Angeles	.249	137	461	54	115	15	1	17	73	63	116	6	5.135
33	DAVIS, ERIC	R	R	6-3	185	5-29-62	Los Angeles, CA	Cincinnati, OH	Cincinnati	.235	89	285	39	67	10	0	11	33	48	92	14	7.033
47	GOODWIN, TOM*	L	R	6-1	165	7-27-68	Fresno, CA	Fresno, CA	Albuquerque	.273	132	509	84	139	19	4	1	45	59	83	48	
									Los Angeles	.143	16	7	3	1	0	0	0	0	0	0	1	0.036
5	JAVIER, STAN	S	R	6-0	185	1-9-64	San Francisco de Macoris, D.R	Santo Domingo, D.R.	Los Angeles	.205	121	176	21	36	5	3	1	11	16	36	7	5.116
43	MONDESI, RAUL*	R	R	5-11	150	3-12-71	San Cristobal, D.R.	San Cristobal, D.R.	Bakersfield	.283	28	106	23	30	7	2	3	13	5	21	9	
									San Antonio	.272	53	213	32	58	10	5	5	26	8	47	7	
									Albuquerque	.333	2	9	3	3	0	1	0	0	0	1	1	0.000
26	RODRIGUEZ, HENRY*	L	L	6-1	180	11-8-67	Santo Domingo, D.R.	New York, NY	Albuquerque	.271	121	446	61	121	22	5	10	67	25	62	4	0.000
44	STRAWBERRY, DARRYL	L	L	6-6	200	3-12-62	Los Angeles, CA	Los Angeles, CA	Los Angeles	.265	139	505	86	134	22	4	28	99	75	125	10	8.150

*Rookie
#Rehabilitation Assignment

FULL NAMES AND PHONETICS

Ashley, Billy Manual
Astacio, Pedro Julio (a-STA-see-oh)
Baar, Bryan David (Bar)
Benzinger, Todd Eric (BEN-zing-er)
Butler, Brett Morgan
Candelaria, John (Kan-del-AHR-e-a)
Candiotti, Thomas Cesar (Kan-dee-AH-tee)
Crews, Stanley Timothy
Daniels, Kalvoski
Davis, Eric Keith
Goodwin, Thomas Jones
Gott, James William
Gross, Kevin Frank

Gross, Kip Lee
Hamilton, Jeffrey Robert
Hansen, David Andrew
Harris, Leonard Anthony
Hernandez, Carlos Alberto
Hershiser, Orel Leonard (hersh-HYZ-ur)
Howell, Jay Canfield
James, Michael Elmo
Javier, Stanley Julian (HAV-ee-air)
Karros, Eric Peter (CARE-ose)
Martinez, Pedro Jaime (mar-TEE-nezz)
Martinez, Ramon Jaime (mar-TEE-nezz)
McAndrew, Jamie B.

McDowell, Roger Alan
Mondesi, Raul (MON-de-see)
Offerman, Jose Antonio
Ojeda, Robert Michael (oh-HEED-uh)
Piazza, Michael Joseph (PEE-ah-za)
Rodriguez, Henry Anderson
Samuel, Juan Milton (SAHM-well)
Scioscia, Michael Lorri (SOH-shuh)
Seanez, Rudy C. (SEE-ahn-yez)
Sharperson, Michael Tyrone
Smith, Gregory Alan
Strawberry, Darryl Eugene
Wilson, Stephen Douglas

Young, Eric Orlando

MANAGER AND COACHES

Thomas Charles Lasorda
John Joseph Amalfitano (uh-mahl-fuh-TAWN-oh)
Mark Emery Cresse (CRESS-ee)
Joseph Vance Ferguson
Benjamin T. Hines
Ronald Peter Perranoski (pair-uh-NOSS-kee)

Montreal Expos

MANAGER
TOM RUNNELLS (10)

Coaches:
FELIPE ALOU (17)
TOMMY HARPER (21)
JOE KERRIGAN (45)
JERRY MANUEL (6)
JAY WARD (35)

Team Physician—DR. ROBERT BRODRICK
Team Orthopedist—DR. LARRY COUGHLIN
Trainers—RON McCLAIN, MIKE KOZAK

Director, Media Relations—RICHARD GRIFFIN
Director, Media Services—MONIQUE GIROUX
Director, Team Travel—ERIK OSTLING

No. PITCHERS (19)	B	T	Ht.	Wt.	Born	Birthplace	Residence	1991 Club	W-L	ERA	G	GS	CG	SV	IP	H	R	ER	BB	SO	M.L. Service
47 BARNES, BRIAN	L	L	5-9	170	3-25-67	Roanoke Rapids, NC	Roanoke Rapids, NC	#Indianapolis	2-0	1.64	2	2	0	0	11.0	6	2	2	8	10	
								#W. Palm Beach	0-0	0.00	2	2	0	0	7.0	3	0	0	4	6	
								Montreal	5-8	4.22	28	27	1	0	160.0	135	82	75	84	117	1.020
46 BOTTENFIELD, KENT★	S	R	6-3	225	11-14-68	Portland, OR	Lake Clarke Shor., FL	Indianapolis	8-15	4.06	29	27	5	0	166.1	155	97	75	61	108	0.000
49 FARMER, HOWARD★	R	R	6-3	192	1-18-66	Gary, IN	Gary, IN	Indianapolis	6-4	3.86	20	19	0	0	105.0	93	55	45	37	67	0.093
39 FASSERO, JEFF	L	L	6-1	195	1-5-63	Springfield, IL	Indianapolis, IN	Indianapolis	3-0	1.47	18	0	0	4	18.1	11	3	3	7	12	
								Montreal	2-5	2.44	51	0	0	8	55.1	39	17	15	17	42	0.135
41 FREY, STEVE	R	L	5-9	170	7-29-63	Southampton, PA	Newtown, PA	Indianapolis	3-1	1.51	30	0	0	3	35.2	25	6	6	15	45	
								Montreal	0-1	4.99	31	0	0	1	39.2	43	31	22	23	21	2.034
28 GARDNER, MARK	R	R	6-1	200	3-1-62	Los Angeles, CA	Fresno, CA	#Indianapolis	2-0	3.48	6	6	0	0	31.0	26	13	12	16	38	
								Montreal	9-11	3.85	27	27	0	0	168.1	139	78	72	75	107	2.044
42 HANEY, CHRIS	L	L	6-3	185	11-16-68	Baltimore, MD	Barboursville, VA	Harrisburg	5-3	2.16	12	12	3	0	83.1	65	21	20	31	68	
								Indianapolis	1-1	4.35	2	2	0	0	10.1	14	10	5	6	8	
								Montreal	3-7	4.04	16	16	0	0	84.2	94	49	38	43	51	0.091
44 HILL, KEN	R	R	6-2	175	12-14-65	Lynn, MA	Lynn, MA	#Louisville	0-0	0.00	1	0	0	0	1.0	0	2	0	0	2	
								St. Louis	11-10	3.57	30	30	0	0	181.1	147	76	72	67	121	2.161
56 HURST, JONATHAN★	R	R	6-3	175	10-20-66	New York, NY	Spartanburg, SC	Miami	8-2	2.90	15	15	0	0	99.1	89	41	32	31	91	
								Tulsa	2-1	2.16	5	2	1	1	25.0	18	6	6	6	17	
								Harrisburg	5-0	0.86	6	6	1	0	42.0	26	4	4	12	34	0.000
52 KARCHNER, MATT★	R	R	6-4	215	6-28-67	Berwick, PA	Berwick, PA	Baseball City	6-3	1.97	38	0	0	5	73.0	49	28	16	25	65	0.000
32 MARTINEZ, DENNIS	R	R	6-1	180	5-14-55	Granada, Nicaragua	Miami, FL	Montreal	14-11	2.39	31	31	9	0	222.0	187	70	59	62	123	15.026
43 NABHOLZ, CHRIS	L	L	6-5	212	1-5-67	Harrisburg, PA	Pottsville, PA	#Indianapolis	2-2	1.86	4	4	0	0	19.1	13	5	4	5	16	
								Montreal	8-7	3.63	24	24	1	0	153.2	134	66	62	57	99	1.058
48 PIATT, DOUG★	L	R	6-1	190	9-26-65	Beaver, PA	Beaver, PA	Indianapolis	6-4	3.45	44	0	0	13	47.0	40	24	18	27	61	
								Montreal	0-0	2.60	21	0	0	0	34.2	29	11	10	17	29	0.069
50 RISLEY, BILL★	R	R	6-2	210	5-29-67	Chicago, IL	Farmington, NM	Chattanooga	5-7	3.16	19	19	3	0	108.1	81	48	38	60	77	
								Nashville	3-5	4.91	8	8	1	0	44.0	45	27	24	26	32	0.000
51 ROJAS, MEL	R	R	5-11	185	12-10-66	Haina, D.R.	Santo Domingo, D.R.	Indianapolis	4-2	4.10	14	10	0	1	52.2	50	29	24	14	55	
								Montreal	3-3	3.75	37	0	0	6	48.0	42	21	20	13	37	1.008
55 SAMPEN, BILL	R	R	6-2	195	1-18-63	Lincoln, IL	Havana, IL	Indianapolis	4-0	2.04	7	7	1	0	39.2	33	13	9	19	41	
								Montreal	9-5	4.00	43	8	0	0	92.1	96	49	41	46	52	1.141
40 WAINHOUSE, DAVID★	L	R	6-2	185	11-7-67	Toronto, Ont.	Mercer Island, WA	Harrisburg	2-2	2.60	33	0	0	11	52.0	49	17	15	17	46	
								Indianapolis	2-0	4.08	14	0	0	1	28.2	28	14	13	15	13	
								Montreal	0-1	6.75	2	0	0	0	2.2	2	2	2	4	1	0.008
57 WETTELAND, JOHN	R	R	6-2	195	8-21-66	San Mateo, CA	Cedar Crest, NM	Albuquerque	4-3	2.79	41	4	0	20	61.1	48	22	19	26	55	
								Los Angeles	1-0	0.00	6	0	0	0	9.0	5	2	0	3	9	1.087
60 YOUNG, PETE★	R	R	6-0	225	3-19-68	Meadville, MS	Summit, MS	Harrisburg	7-5	2.60	54	0	0	13	90.0	82	28	26	24	74	0.000

No.	CATCHERS (7)	B	T	Ht.	Wt.	Born	Birthplace	Residence	1991 Club	AVG.	G	AB	R	H	2B	3B	HR	RBI	BB	SO	SB	M.L. Service
8	CARTER, GARY	R	R	6-2	214	4-8-54	Culver City, CA	Palm Bch. Gard., FL	Los Angeles	.246	101	248	22	61	14	0	6	26	22	26	2	17.017
15	COLBRUNN, GREG*	R	R	6-0	190	7-26-69	Fontana, CA	Fontana, CA	Indianapolis				DID NOT PLAY									
24	FLETCHER, DARRIN	L	R	6-1	199	10-3-66	Elmhurst, IL	Fithin, IL	Scranton	.284	90	306	39	87	13	1	8	50	23	29	1	
									Philadelphia	.228	46	136	5	31	8	0	1	12	5	15	0	0.140
54	KREMERS, JIMMY	L	R	6-3	210	10-8-65	Little Rock, AR	Fithin, IL	Indianapolis	.241	98	290	34	70	14	0	11	42	40	97	2	0.086
53	LAKER, TIM*	R	R	6-3	195	11-27-69	Encino, CA	Simi Valley, CA	Harrisburg	.286	11	35	4	10	1	0	1	5	2	5	0	
									W. Palm Beach	.231	100	333	36	77	15	2	5	33	22	52	10	0.000
58	NATAL, ROBERT	R	R	5-11	190	11-13-65	Long Beach, CA	Chula Vista, CA	Indianapolis	.317	16	41	2	13	4	0	0	9	6	9	1	
									Harrisburg	.256	100	336	47	86	16	3	13	53	49	90	1	0.000
20	REYES, GILBERTO	R	R	6-2	212	12-10-63	Santo Domingo, D.R.	Santo Domingo, D.R.	Montreal	.217	83	207	11	45	9	0	0	13	19	51	2	2.051

No.	INFIELDERS (7)	B	T	Ht.	Wt.	Born	Birthplace	Residence	1991 Club	AVG.	G	AB	R	H	2B	3B	HR	RBI	BB	SO	SB	M.L. Service
25	BARBERIE, BRET	S	R	5-11	180	8-16-67	Long Beach, CA	Cerritos, CA	Indianapolis	.312	71	218	45	68	10	4	10	48	59	47	10	
									Montreal	.353	57	136	16	48	12	2	2	18	20	22	0	0.114
26	CANALE, GEORGE*	L	R	6-1	190	8-11-65	Memphis, TN	Roanoke, VA	Denver	.234	88	274	36	64	10	2	10	47	51	49	6	
									Milwaukee	.176	21	34	6	6	2	0	3	10	8	6	0	0.118
12	CORDERO, WILFREDO*	R	R	6-2	185	10-3-71	Mayaguez, PR	Mayaguez, PR	Indianapolis	.261	98	360	48	94	16	4	11	52	26	89	8	0.000
4	DeSHIELDS, DELINO	L	R	6-1	170	1-15-69	Seaford, DE	Seaford, DE	Montreal	.238	151	563	83	134	15	4	10	51	95	151	56	2.000
16	FOLEY, TOM	L	R	6-1	175	9-9-59	Columbus, GA	Miami, FL	Montreal	.208	86	168	12	35	11	1	0	15	14	30	2	9.000
11	OWEN, SPIKE	S	R	5-10	170	4-19-61	Cleburne, TX	Austin, TX	Montreal	.255	139	424	39	108	22	8	3	26	42	61	2	8.100
29	WALLACH, TIM	R	R	6-3	202	9-14-57	Huntington Park, CA	Yorba Linda, CA	Montreal	.225	151	577	60	130	22	1	13	73	50	100	2	11.031

No.	OUTFIELDERS (7)	B	T	Ht.	Wt.	Born	Birthplace	Residence	1991 Club	AVG.	G	AB	R	H	2B	3B	HR	RBI	BB	SO	SB	M.L. Service
18	ALOU, MOISES*	R	R	6-3	190	7-3-66	Atlanta, GA	Santo Domingo, D.R.	Montreal				DID NOT PLAY									1.037
22	CALDERON, IVAN	R	R	6-1	221	3-19-62	Fajardo, PR	Loiza, PR	Montreal	.300	134	470	69	141	22	3	19	75	53	64	31	6.159
9	GRISSOM, MARQUIS	R	R	5-11	190	4-17-67	Atlanta, GA	Riverdale, GA	Montreal	.267	148	558	73	149	23	9	6	39	34	89	76	2.042
5	REED, DARREN*	R	R	6-1	205	10-16-65	Ventura, CA	Ventura, CA	Montreal				DID NOT PLAY									1.066
59	STAIRS, MATT*	R	R	5-9	175	2-27-69	Fredericton, N.B.	Stanley, N.B.	Harrisburg	.333	129	505	87	168	30	10	13	78	66	47	23	0.000
23	VANDERWAL, JOHN*	L	L	6-2	190	4-29-66	Grand Rapids, MI	Jenison, MI	Indianapolis	.293	133	478	84	140	36	8	15	71	79	118	8	
									Montreal	.213	21	61	4	13	4	1	1	8	1	18	0	0.031
33	WALKER, LARRY	L	R	6-3	215	12-1-66	Maple Ridge, B.C.	Montreal, Que.	Montreal	.290	137	487	59	141	30	2	16	64	42	102	14	3.045

*Rookie   #Rehabilitation Assignment

FULL NAMES AND PHONETICS

Alou, Moises Rojas (ah-LOO) (MOI-shuh)
Barberie, Bret Edward (bar-ber-ee)
Barnes, Brian Keith
Bottenfield, Kent Dennis
Calderon, Ivan Perez (CALL-der-OWN)
Canale, George Anthony (cah-NAL-ee)
Carter, Gary Edmund
Colbrunn, Gregory Joseph
Cordero, Wilfredo Nieva (COR-DAIR-OH)
DeShields, Delino Lamont (duh-LYNE-oh)
Farmer, Howard Earl
Fassero, Jeffrey Joseph (fuh-SAIR-oh)

Fletcher, Darrin Glen
Foley, Thomas Michael
Frey, Steven Francis (fry)
Gardner, Mark Allen
Grissom, Marquis Deon (mar-KEESE)
Haney, Christopher Deane
Hill, Kenneth Wade
Hurst, Jonathan
Karchner, Matthew Dean
Kremers, James Edward
Laker, Timothy John
Martinez, Jose Dennis (mar-TEE-nezz)

Nabholz, Christopher William (NAB-holts)
Natal, Robert Marcel
Owen, Spike Dee
Piatt, Douglas William (PIE-utt)
Reed, Darren Douglas
Reyes, Gilberto Rolando (RAY-us)
Risley, William Charles (RIZZ-lee)
Rojas, Melquiades (ROH-hoss)
Sampen, William Albert
Stairs, Matthew Wade
Vanderwal, John Henry
Wainhouse, David Paul

Walker, Larry Kenneth
Wallach, Timothy Charles
Wetteland, John Karl
Young, Bryan O.

MANAGER AND COACHES

Thomas William Runnells
Felipe Rojas Alou (feh-lee-pay) (ah-LOO)
Thomas Harper
Joseph Thomas Kerrigan
Jerry Manuel
John Francis Ward

New York Mets

MANAGER
JEFF TORBORG (10)

Coaches:
MIKE CUBBAGE (4)
BARRY FOOTE (26)
DAVE LaROCHE (28)
TOM McCRAW (27)
MEL STOTTLEMYRE (30)

Team Physician—DR. DAVID ALTCHEK
Trainer—STEVE GARLAND
Assistant Trainer—SAM McCRARY

Director, Public Relations—JAY HORWITZ
Traveling Secretary—BOB O'HARA

No.	PITCHERS (19)	B	T	Ht.	Wt.	Born	Birthplace	Residence	1991 Club	W-L	ERA	G	GS	CG	SV	IP	H	R	ER	BB	SO	M.L. Service
46	BROSS, TERRY*	R	R	6-9	230	3-30-66	El Paso, TX	Bridgewater, CT	Tidewater	2-0	4.36	27	0	0	2	33.0	31	21	16	32	23	
									Williamsport	2-0	2.49	20	0	0	5	25.1	13	12	7	11	28	
									New York NL	0-0	1.80	8	0	0	0	10.0	7	2	2	3	5	0.036
44	BURKE, TIM	R	R	6-3	205	2-19-59	Omaha, NE	Palm Bch. Gardens, FL	Montreal	3-4	4.11	37	0	0	5	46.0	41	24	21	14	25	
									New York NL	3-3	2.75	35	0	0	1	55.2	55	22	17	12	34	
									(Composite)	6-7	3.36	72	0	0	6	101.2	96	46	38	26	59	7.000
17	CONE, DAVID	L	R	6-1	190	1-2-63	Kansas City, MO	Kansas City, MO	New York NL	14-14	3.29	34	34	5	0	232.2	204	95	85	73	241	5.058
50	FERNANDEZ, SID	L	L	6-1	215	10-12-62	Honolulu, HI	Hawaii Kai, HI	#St. Lucie	0-0	0.00	1	1	0	0	3.0	1	0	0	1	4	
									#Williamsport	0-0	0.00	1	1	0	0	6.0	3	0	0	1	5	
									#Tidewater	1-0	1.15	3	3	0	0	15.2	9	2	2	6	22	
									New York NL	1-3	2.86	8	8	0	0	44.0	36	18	14	9	31	7.089
31	FRANCO, JOHN	L	L	5-10	185	9-17-60	Brooklyn, NY	Staten Island, NY	New York NL	5-9	2.93	52	0	0	30	55.1	61	27	18	18	45	7.160
45	GIBSON, PAUL	R	L	6-0	185	1-4-60	Center Moriches, NY	Center Moriches, NY	Detroit	5-7	4.59	68	0	0	8	96.0	112	51	49	48	52	4.000
16	GOODEN, DWIGHT	R	R	6-3	210	11-16-64	Tampa, FL	St. Petersburg, FL	New York NL	13-7	3.60	27	27	3	0	190.0	185	80	76	56	150	8.000
13	HILLMAN, ERIC*	L	L	6-10	225	4-27-66	Gary, IN	Citrus Heights, CA	Tidewater	5-12	4.01	27	27	2	0	161.2	184	89	72	58	91	0.000
40	INNIS, JEFF	R	R	6-1	168	7-5-62	Decatur, IL	Jupiter, FL	New York NL	0-2	2.66	69	0	0	0	84.2	66	30	25	23	47	3.009
38	JOHNSTONE, JOHN*	R	R	6-3	195	11-25-68	Liverpool, NY	Liverpool, NY	Williamsport	7-9	3.97	27	27	2	0	165.1	159	94	73	79	99	0.000
39	ROSENBERG, STEVE	L	L	6-0	190	10-31-64	Brooklyn, NY	Coral Springs, FL	Las Vegas	2-4	7.54	36	8	0	0	68.0	95	62	57	26	61	
									San Diego	1-1	6.94	10	0	0	0	11.2	11	9	9	5	6	2.011
18	SABERHAGEN, BRET	R	R	6-1	200	4-11-64	Chicago Heights, IL	Thousand Oaks, CA	Kansas City	13-8	3.07	28	28	7	0	196.1	165	76	67	45	136	8.000
48	SCHOUREK, PETE	L	L	6-5	205	5-10-69	Austin, TX	Falls Church, VA	Tidewater	1-1	2.52	4	4	0	0	25.0	18	7	7	10	17	
									New York NL	5-4	4.27	35	8	1	2	86.1	82	49	41	43	67	0.156
43	SIMONS, DOUG	L	L	6-0	160	9-15-66	Bakersfield, CA	Orlando, FL	New York NL	2-3	5.19	42	1	0	1	60.2	55	40	35	19	38	1.000
34	VALERA, JULIO*	R	R	6-2	215	10-13-68	San Sebastian, PR	San Sebastian, PR	Tidewater	10-10	3.83	26	26	3	0	176.1	152	79	75	70	117	
									New York NL	0-0	0.00	2	0	0	0	2.0	1	0	0	4	3	0.041
66	VASQUEZ, JULIAN*	R	R	6-3	165	5-24-68	Puerto Plata, D.R.	Puerto Plata, D.R.	St. Lucie	3-2	0.28	56	0	0	25	64.0	35	6	2	39	56	0.000
63	VITKO, JOE*	R	R	6-8	210	2-1-70	Somerville, NY	Ebensburg, PA	St. Lucie	11-8	2.24	22	22	5	0	140.1	102	40	35	39	105	0.000
47	WHITEHURST, WALLY	R	R	6-3	195	4-11-64	Shreveport, LA	Houma, LA	New York NL	7-12	4.19	36	20	0	1	133.1	142	67	62	25	87	2.067
19	YOUNG, ANTHONY*	R	R	6-2	200	1-19-66	Houston, TX	Houston, TX	Tidewater	7-9	3.73	25	25	3	0	164.0	172	74	68	67	93	
									New York NL	2-5	3.10	10	8	0	0	49.1	48	20	17	12	20	0.041

No. CATCHERS (4)	B	T	Ht.	Wt.	Born	Birthplace	Residence	1991 Club	AVG.	G	AB	R	H	2B	3B	HR	RBI	BB	SO	SB	M.L. Service
64 FORDYCE, BROOK*	R	R	6-1	185	5-7-70	New London, CT	Old Lyme, CT	St. Lucie	.239	115	406	42	97	19	3	7	55	37	50	4	0.000
9 HUNDLEY, TODD*	S	R	5-11	185	5-27-69	Martinsville, VA	Palatine, IL	Tidewater	.273	125	454	62	124	24	4	14	66	51	95	1	
								New York NL	.133	21	60	5	8	0	1	1	7	6	14	0	0.098
22 O'BRIEN, CHARLIE	R	R	6-2	200	5-1-61	Tulsa, OK	Tulsa, OK	New York NL	.185	69	168	16	31	6	0	2	14	17	25	0	4.053
2 SASSER, MACKEY	L	R	6-1	210	8-3-62	Fort Gaines, GA	Lynn Haven, FL	New York NL	.272	96	228	18	62	14	2	5	35	9	19	0	4.045

No. INFIELDERS (10)	B	T	Ht.	Wt.	Born	Birthplace	Residence	1991 Club	AVG.	G	AB	R	H	2B	3B	HR	RBI	BB	SO	SB	M.L. Service
11 BAEZ, KEVIN*	R	R	6-0	170	1-10-67	Brooklyn, NY	Brooklyn, NY	Tidewater	.171	65	210	18	36	8	0	0	13	12	32	0	0.360
23 DONNELS, CHRIS	L	R	6-0	185	4-21-66	Los Angeles, CA	Torrance, CA	Tidewater	.303	84	287	45	87	19	2	8	56	62	56	1	
								New York NL	.225	37	89	7	20	2	0	0	5	14	19	1	0.069
15 ELSTER, KEVIN	R	R	6-2	200	8-3-64	San Pedro, CA	Huntington Bch., CA	New York NL	.241	115	348	33	84	16	2	6	36	40	53	2	4.061
21 HANSEN, TERREL*	R	R	6-3	210	9-25-66	Bremerton, WA	Bremerton, WA	Tidewater	.272	107	368	54	100	20	2	12	62	40	82	0	0.000
29 MAGADAN, DAVE	L	R	6-3	205	9-30-62	Tampa, FL	Tampa, FL	New York NL	.258	124	418	58	108	23	0	4	51	83	50	1	5.029
33 MURRAY, EDDIE	S	R	6-2	222	2-24-56	Los Angeles, CA	Canyon Country, CA	Los Angeles	.260	153	576	69	150	23	1	19	96	55	74	10	15.000
65 NAVARRO, TITO*	S	R	5-10	155	9-12-70	Rio Piedras, PR	Hato Rey, PR	Williamsport	.288	128	482	69	139	9	4	2	42	73	63	42	0.000
3 NOBOA, JUNIOR	R	R	5-10	170	11-10-64	Azua, D.R.	Santo Domingo, D.R.	Montreal	.242	67	95	5	23	3	0	1	2	1	8	2	3.083
32 PECOTA, BILL	R	R	6-2	190	2-16-60	Redwood City, CA	Overland Park, KS	Kansas City	.286	125	398	53	114	23	2	6	45	41	45	16	4.076
12 RANDOLPH, WILLIE	R	R	5-11	171	7-6-54	Holly Hill, SC	Franklin Lakes, NJ	Milwaukee	.327	124	431	60	141	14	3	0	54	75	38	4	16.064

No. OUTFIELDERS (6)	B	T	Ht.	Wt.	Born	Birthplace	Residence	1991 Club	AVG.	G	AB	R	H	2B	3B	HR	RBI	BB	SO	SB	M.L. Service
25 BONILLA, BOBBY	S	R	6-3	240	2-23-63	New York, NY	Bradenton, FL	Pittsburgh	.302	157	577	102	174	44	6	18	100	90	67	2	6.103
6 BOSTON, DARYL	L	L	6-3	210	1-4-63	Cincinnati, OH	Cincinnati, OH	New York NL	.275	137	255	40	70	16	4	4	21	30	42	15	6.047
1 COLEMAN, VINCE	S	R	6-1	185	9-22-61	Jacksonville, FL	St. Louis, MO	New York NL	.255	72	278	45	71	7	5	1	17	39	47	37	7.000
8 GALLAGHER, DAVE	R	R	6-0	184	9-20-60	Trenton, NJ	Trenton, NJ	California	.293	90	270	32	79	17	0	1	30	24	43	2	3.163
62 HOWELL, PAT*	S	R	5-11	155	8-31-68	Mobile, AL	Prichard, AL	Williamsport	.281	70	274	43	77	5	1	1	26	21	50	27	0.000
								St. Lucie	.220	62	240	36	54	8	2	0	10	14	47	37	
20 JOHNSON, HOWARD	S	R	5-10	195	11-29-60	Clearwater, FL	Woodbury, NY	New York NL	.259	156	564	108	146	34	4	38	117	78	120	30	8.129

*Rookie
#Rehabilitation Assignment

FULL NAMES AND PHONETICS

Baez, Kevin (BY-az)
Bonilla, Roberto Martin Antonio (boh-NEE-yuh)
Boston, Daryl Lamont
Bross, Terrence Paul (brahs)
Burke, Timothy Phillip
Castillo, Antonio Jose (Cass-TEE-oh)
Coleman, Vincent Maurice
Cone, David Brian
Donnels, Chris Barton (DONN-uls)
Elster, Kevin Daniel
Fernandez, Charles Sid
Fordyce, Brook Alexander (Four-dice)

Franco, John Anthony
Gallagher, David Thomas
Gibson, Paul Marshall
Gooden, Dwight Eugene
Hansen, Terrell Ernest
Hillman, John Eric
Howell, Patrick O'Neal
Hundley, Todd Randolph
Innis, Jeffrey David (ENN-is)
Johnson, Howard Michael
Johnstone, John William
Magadan, David Joseph (MAG-uh-dun)

Murray, Eddie Clarence
Navarro (Rodriguez), Norberto
Noboa, Milciades Arturo (nah-BOE-ah)
O'Brien, Charles Hugh
Pecota, William Joseph (Puh-COAT-uh)
Rosenberg, Steven
Saberhagen, Bret William (SAY-ber-hay-gun)
Sasser, Mackey Daniel
Schourek, Peter Alan (SHUR-ek)
Simons, Douglas Eugene
Valera, Julio (vuh-LAIR-uh)
Vasquez, Julian

Vitko, Joseph John III (VIT-co)
Whitehurst, Walter Richard
Young, Anthony Wayne

MANAGER AND COACHES

Jeffrey Allen Torborg
Michael Lee Cubbage
Barry Clifton Foote
David Eugene LaRoche
Tom McCraw
Melvin Leon Stottlemyre (STOTT-ul-myr)

Philadelphia Phillies

MANAGER
JIM FREGOSI (11)

Coaches:
LARRY BOWA (2)
DENIS MENKE (14)
JOHNNY PODRES (46)
MEL ROBERTS (26)
JOHN VUKOVICH (18)

Team Physician—DR. PHILLIP MARONE
Trainer—JEFF COOPER
Assistant Trainer—MARK ANDERSEN

Vice President, Public Relations—LARRY SHENK
Traveling Secretary—EDDIE FERENZ

No. PITCHERS (17)	B	T	Ht.	Wt.	Born	Birthplace	Residence	1991 Club	W-L	ERA	G	GS	CG	SV	IP	H	R	ER	BB	SO	M.L. Service
47 ABBOTT, KYLE*	L	L	6-4	200	2-18-68	Newburyport, MA	Mission Viejo, CA	Edmonton	14-10	3.99	27	27	4	0	180.1	173	84	80	46	120	
								California	1-2	4.58	5	3	0	0	19.2	22	11	10	13	12	0.031
40 ASHBY, ANDY*	R	R	6-5	180	7-11-67	Kansas City, MO	Kansas City, MO	Scranton	11-11	3.46	26	26	6	0	161.1	144	78	62	60	113	
								Philadelphia	1-5	6.00	8	8	0	0	42.0	41	28	28	19	26	0.041
53 AYRAULT, BOB*	R	R	6-4	230	4-27-66	S. Lake Tahoe, CA	Carson City, NV	Scranton	8-5	4.83	68	0	0	3	98.2	91	58	53	47	103	0.000
55 BORLAND, TOBY*	R	R	6-6	180	5-29-69	Quitman, LA	Quitman, LA	Reading	8-3	2.70	59	0	0	24	76.2	68	31	23	56	72	0.000
51 BRANTLEY, CLIFF*	R	R	6-1	190	4-12-68	Staten Island, NY	Staten Island, NY	Reading	4-3	1.94	11	11	2	0	69.2	50	17	15	25	51	
								Scranton	2-4	3.80	8	8	0	0	47.1	44	26	20	25	28	
								Philadelphia	2-2	3.41	6	5	0	0	31.2	26	12	12	19	25	0.034
41 CHAPIN, DARRIN*	R	R	6-0	170	2-1-66	Warren, OH	Cortland, OH	Columbus (O.)	10-3	1.95	55	0	0	12	78.1	54	23	17	40	69	
								New York AL	0-1	5.06	3	0	0	0	5.1	3	3	3	6	5	0.020
21 COMBS, PAT	L	L	6-4	207	10-29-66	Newport, RI	Sugarland, TX	#Scranton	2-2	6.67	6	6	1	0	27.0	39	23	20	16	14	
								Philadelphia	2-6	4.90	14	13	1	0	64.1	64	41	35	43	41	2.028
54 DeJESUS, JOSE	R	R	6-5	213	1-6-65	Brooklyn, NY	Cidra, PR	Philadelphia	10-9	3.42	31	29	3	1	181.2	147	74	69	128	118	1.164
49 GREENE, TOMMY	R	R	6-5	227	4-6-67	Lumberton, NC	Richmond, VA	Philadelphia	13-7	3.38	36	27	3	0	207.2	177	85	78	66	154	1.108
48 GRIMSLEY, JASON	R	R	6-3	182	8-7-67	Cleveland, TX	Cleveland, TX	Scranton	2-3	4.35	9	9	0	0	51.2	48	28	25	37	43	
								Philadelphia	1-7	4.87	12	12	0	0	61.0	54	34	33	41	42	1.063
42 HARTLEY, MIKE	R	R	6-1	197	8-31-61	Hawthorne, CA	El Cajon, CA	Los Angeles	2-0	4.42	40	0	0	1	57.0	53	29	28	37	44	
								Philadelphia	2-1	3.76	18	0	0	1	26.1	21	11	11	10	19	
								(Composite)	4-1	4.21	58	0	0	2	83.1	74	40	39	47	63	2.022
43 HOWELL, KEN	R	R	6-3	237	11-28-60	Detroit, MI	Farmington, MI	#Scranton	2-0	5.11	6	6	0	0	24.2	30	15	14	16	20	7.022
50 JONES, BARRY	R	R	6-4	225	2-15-63	Centerville, IN	Anna Maria, FL	Montreal	4-9	3.35	77	0	0	13	88.2	76	35	33	33	46	5.038
45 MULHOLLAND, TERRY	R	L	6-3	206	3-9-63	Uniontown, PA	Phoenix, AZ	Philadelphia	16-13	3.61	34	34	8	0	232.0	231	100	93	49	142	3.155
39 RITCHIE, WALLY	L	L	6-2	180	7-12-65	Glendale, CA	Provo, UT	Scranton	1-0	2.42	7	2	0	2	26.0	17	8	7	7	25	
								Philadelphia	1-2	2.50	39	0	0	0	50.1	44	17	14	17	26	2.047
24 SEARCY, STEVE	L	L	6-1	195	6-5-64	Knoxville, TN	Knoxville, TN	Detroit	1-2	8.41	16	5	0	0	40.2	52	40	38	30	32	
								Philadelphia	2-1	4.15	18	0	0	0	30.1	29	16	14	14	21	2.028
28 WILLIAMS, MITCH	L	L	6-4	205	11-17-64	Santa Ana, CA	Arlington, TX	Philadelphia	12-5	2.34	69	0	0	30	88.1	56	24	23	62	84	6.000

No. CATCHERS (3)	B	T	Ht.	Wt.	Born	Birthplace	Residence	1991 Club	AVG.	G	AB	R	H	2B	3B	HR	RBI	BB	SO	SB	M.L. Service
10 DAULTON, DARREN	L	R	6-2	200	1-3-62	Arkansas City, KS	Safety Harbor, FL	#Reading	.250	1	4	0	1	0	0	0	0	1	0	0	
								#Scranton	.222	2	9	1	2	0	0	1	1	0	0	0	
								Philadelphia	.196	89	285	36	56	12	0	12	42	41	66	5	7.008
35 LINDSEY, DOUG*	R	R	6-2	200	9-22-67	Austin, TX	Austin, TX	Reading	.259	94	313	26	81	13	0	1	34	21	49	1	
								Philadelphia	.000	1	3	0	0	0	0	0	0	0	3	0	0.017
23 PRATT, TODD*	R	R	6-3	195	2-9-67	Bellevue, NE	Chula Vista, CA	Pawtucket	.292	68	219	27	64	16	0	11	41	23	42	0	0.000

No.	INFIELDERS (9)	B	T	Ht.	Wt.	Born	Birthplace	Residence	1991 Club	AVG.	G	AB	R	H	2B	3B	HR	RBI	BB	SO	SB	M.L. Service
6	BACKMAN, WALLY	S	R	5-9	168	9-22-59	Hillsboro, OR	Kona, HI	Philadelphia	.243	94	185	20	45	12	0	0	15	30	30	3	9.153
5	BATISTE, KIM*	R	R	6-0	175	3-15-68	New Orleans, LA	Prairieville, LA	Scranton	.292	122	462	54	135	25	6	1	41	11	72	18	
									Philadelphia	.222	10	27	2	6	0	0	0	1	1	8	0	0.032
7	DUNCAN, MARIANO	R	R	6-0	185	3-13-63	S.P. de Macoris, D.R.	Los Angeles, CA	Cincinnati	.258	100	333	46	86	7	4	12	40	12	57	5	6.000
15	HOLLINS, DAVE	S	R	6-1	207	5-25-66	Buffalo, NY	West Seneca, NY	Scranton	.266	72	229	37	61	11	6	8	35	43	42	4	
									Philadelphia	.298	56	151	18	45	10	2	6	21	17	26	1	1.104
17	JORDAN, RICKY	R	R	6-3	209	5-26-65	Richmond, CA	Gold River, CA	Philadelphia	.272	101	301	38	82	21	3	9	49	14	49	0	3.068
29	KRUK, JOHN	L	L	5-10	200	2-9-61	Charleston, WV	Burlington, WV	Philadelphia	.294	152	538	84	158	27	6	21	92	67	100	7	6.000
19	LINDEMAN, JIM	R	R	6-1	200	1-10-62	Evanston, IL	Chicago, IL	Scranton	.275	11	40	7	11	1	1	2	7	5	6	0	
									Philadelphia	.337	65	95	13	32	5	0	0	12	13	14	0	4.009
12	MORANDINI, MICKEY	L	R	5-11	167	4-22-66	Kittanning, PA	Marlton, NJ	Scranton	.261	12	46	7	12	4	0	1	9	5	6	2	
									Philadelphia	.249	98	325	38	81	11	4	1	20	29	45	13	1.034
9	SVEUM, DALE	S	R	6-3	185	11-23-63	Richmond, CA	Glendale, AZ	Milwaukee	.241	90	266	33	64	19	1	4	43	32	78	2	5.095

No.	OUTFIELDERS (9)	B	T	Ht.	Wt.	Born	Birthplace	Residence	1991 Club	AVG.	G	AB	R	H	2B	3B	HR	RBI	BB	SO	SB	M.L. Service
33	AMARO, RUBEN*	S	R	5-10	170	2-12-65	Philadelphia, PA	Philadelphia, PA	Edmonton	.326	121	472	95	154	42	6	3	42	63	48	36	
									California	.217	10	23	0	5	1	0	0	2	3	3	0	0.028
16	CASTILLO, BRAULIO*	R	R	6-0	180	5-13-68	Elias Pina, D.R.	Santo Domingo, D.R.	San Antonio	.300	87	297	40	89	19	3	8	48	32	73	22	
									Scranton	.350	16	60	14	21	9	1	0	15	6	7	2	
									Philadelphia	.173	28	52	3	9	3	0	0	2	1	15	1	0.052
44	CHAMBERLAIN, WES	R	R	6-2	210	4-13-66	Chicago, IL	Chicago, IL	Scranton	.257	39	144	12	37	7	2	2	20	8	13	7	
									Philadelphia	.240	101	383	51	92	16	3	13	50	31	73	9	0.164
57	DOSTAL, BRUCE*	L	L	6-0	195	3-10-65	Montville, NJ	West Orange, NJ	Reading	.313	96	364	68	114	11	5	5	34	58	55	38	0.000
4	DYKSTRA, LEN	L	L	5-10	186	2-10-63	Santa Ana, CA	Philadelphia, PA	Philadelphia	.297	63	246	48	73	13	5	3	12	37	20	24	6.116
27	LONGMIRE, TONY*	L	R	6-1	195	6-12-68	Vallejo, CA	Vallejo, CA	Reading	.288	85	323	43	93	23	1	9	56	32	45	10	
									Scranton	.261	36	111	11	29	3	2	0	9	8	20	4	0.000
3	MURPHY, DALE	R	R	6-4	221	3-12-56	Portland, OR	Roswell, GA	Philadelphia	.252	153	544	66	137	33	1	18	81	48	93	1	14.046
58	PEGUERO, JULIO*	S	R	6-0	180	9-7-68	San Isidor, D.R.	El Bonito, D.R.	Scranton	.273	133	506	71	138	20	9	2	39	40	71	21	0.000
56	WILLIAMS, CARY*	R	R	6-3	190	7-29-69	San Antonio, TX	San Antonio, TX	Reading	.278	116	421	55	117	21	3	6	62	27	69	12	0.000

*Rookie
#Rehabilitation Assignment

FULL NAMES AND PHONETICS

Abbott, Lawrence Kyle
Amaro, Ruben
Ashby, Andrew Jason
Ayrault, Robert C. (AY-ralt)
Backman, Walter Wayne
Batiste, Kimothy Emil (bah-TEEST)
Borland, Toby Shawn
Brantley, Clifford
Castillo, Braulio (cass-TEE-yoh)
Chamberlain, Wesley Polk
Chapin, Darrin John (CHAY-pin)
Combs, Patrick Dennis
Daulton, Darren Arthur (DALL-tun)

DeJesus, Jose Luis (day-HAY-zeus)
Dostal, Bruce Wayne
Duncan, Mariano
Dykstra, Lenny Kyle (DYK-struh)
Greene, Ira Thomas
Grimsley, Jason Allen
Hartley, Michael Edward
Hollins, David Michael
Howell, Kenneth, Jr.
Jones, Barry Louis
Jordan, Paul Scott
Kruk, John Martin (as in truck)
Lindeman, James William

Lindsey, Michael Douglas
Longmire, Anthony Eugene
Morandini, Michael Robert (MOR-an-deeni)
Mulholland, Terence John
Murphy, Dale Bryan
Peguero, Julio Cesar (peh-GAIR-oh)
Pratt, Todd Alan
Ritchie, Wallace Reid
Searcy, William Stephen
Sveum, Dale Curtis (swaim)
Williams, Cary Wayne
Williams, Mitchell Steven

MANAGER AND COACHES

James Louis Fregosi
Larry Robert Bowa
Denis John Menke
John Joseph Podres
Melvin Henry Roberts
Michael James Ryan

Pittsburgh Pirates

MANAGER
JIM LEYLAND (10)

Coaches:
TERRY COLLINS (44)
RICH DONNELLY (45)
MILT MAY (39)
RAY MILLER (31)
TOMMY SANDT (37)

Team Physician—DR. JOSEPH COROSO
Team Orthopedist—DR. JACK FAILLA
Trainers—KENT BIGGERSTAFF, DAVE TUMBAS

Vice-President, Public Relations—RICK CERRONE
Director of Media Relations—JIM TRDINICH
Traveling Secretary—GREG JOHNSON

No. PITCHERS (18)	B	T	Ht.	Wt.	Born	Birthplace	Residence	1991 Club	W-L	ERA	G	GS	CG	SV	IP	H	R	ER	BB	SO	M.L. Service
60 AUSANIO, JOE★	R	R	6-1	205	12-9-65	Kingston, NY	Kingston, NY	Carolina	0-0	0.00	3	0	0	2	3.0	0	0	0	0	2	
								Buffalo	2-2	3.86	22	0	0	3	30.1	33	17	13	19	26	0.000
53 BATISTA, MIGUEL★	R	R	6-0	160	2-19-71	Santo Domingo, D.R.	S.P. de Macoris, D.R.	Rockford	11-5	4.04	23	23	2	0	133.2	126	74	60	57	90	0.000
50 BELINDA, STAN	R	R	6-3	187	8-6-66	Huntingdon, PA	Port Matilda, PA	Pittsburgh	7-5	3.45	60	0	0	16	78.1	50	30	30	35	71	1.162
61 COLE, VICTOR★	R	R	5-10	160	1-23-68	Leningrad, USSR	Monterey, CA	Omaha	1-1	4.15	6	0	0	0	13.0	9	6	6	9	12	
								Buffalo	1-2	3.75	19	1	0	0	24.0	23	11	10	20	24	
								Carolina	0-2	1.91	20	0	0	12	28.1	13	8	6	19	32	0.000
15 DRABEK, DOUG	R	R	6-1	185	7-25-62	Victoria, TX	The Woodlands, TX	Pittsburgh	15-14	3.07	35	35	5	0	234.2	245	92	80	62	142	5.132
26 HEATON, NEAL	L	L	6-1	205	3-3-60	Jamaica, NY	E. Patchoque, NY	Pittsburgh	3-3	4.33	42	1	0	0	68.2	72	37	33	21	34	9.032
43 LANDRUM, BILL	R	R	6-2	205	8-17-58	Columbia, SC	Columbia, SC	Pittsburgh	4-4	3.18	61	0	0	17	76.1	76	32	27	19	45	4.010
48 MASON, ROGER	R	R	6-6	220	9-18-58	Bellaire, MI	Bellaire, MI	Buffalo	9-5	3.08	34	15	2	0	122.2	115	47	42	44	80	
								Pittsburgh	3-2	3.03	24	0	0	3	29.2	21	11	10	6	21	2.036
64 MILLER, PAUL★	R	R	6-5	220	4-27-65	Burlington, WI	Richmond, IL	Carolina	7-2	2.42	14	14	1	0	89.1	69	29	24	35	69	
								Buffalo	5-2	1.48	10	10	2	0	67.0	41	17	11	29	30	
								Pittsburgh	0-0	5.40	1	1	0	0	5.0	4	3	3	3	2	0.002
58 PALACIOS, VICENTE	R	R	6-3	175	7-19-63	Mataloma, Mex.	Veracruz, Mex.	Buffalo	0-0	1.42	3	0	0	2	6.1	7	1	1	2	8	
								Pittsburgh	6-3	3.75	36	7	1	3	81.2	69	34	34	38	64	1.105
38 PATTERSON, BOB	R	L	6-2	192	5-16-59	Jacksonville, FL	Hickory, NC	Pittsburgh	4-3	4.11	54	1	0	2	65.2	67	32	30	15	57	3.019
34 REED, RICK	R	R	6-0	205	8-16-64	Huntington, WV	Huntington, WV	Buffalo	14-4	2.15	25	25	5	0	167.2	151	45	40	26	102	
								Pittsburgh	0-0	10.38	1	1	0	0	4.1	8	6	5	1	2	1.025
30 RODRIGUEZ, ROSARIO	R	L	6-0	205	7-8-69	Los Mochis, Mex.	Los Mochis, Mex.	Buffalo	4-3	3.00	48	0	0	8	51.0	38	22	17	31	43	
								Pittsburgh	1-1	4.11	18	0	0	0	15.1	14	7	7	8	10	0.129
35 ROESLER, MIKE★	R	R	6-5	200	9-12-63	Ft. Wayne, IN	Ft. Wayne, IN	Carolina	2-4	4.91	20	0	0	6	25.2	20	15	14	15	31	
								Buffalo	5-4	3.56	33	0	0	8	48.0	46	19	19	21	34	0.085
57 SMILEY, JOHN	L	L	6-4	200	3-17-65	Phoenixville, PA	Wexford, PA	Pittsburgh	20-8	3.08	33	32	2	0	207.2	194	78	71	44	129	5.035
41 SMITH, ZANE	L	L	6-1	200	12-28-60	Madison, WI	Stone Mountain, GA	Pittsburgh	16-10	3.20	35	35	6	0	228.0	234	95	81	29	120	7.027
29 TOMLIN, RANDY	L	L	5-11	170	6-14-66	Bainbridge, MA	Mars, PA	Pittsburgh	8-7	2.98	31	27	4	0	175.0	170	75	58	54	104	1.059
17 WALK, BOB	R	R	6-3	217	11-26-56	Van Nuys, CA	Frazier Park, CA	#Carolina	0-1	1.80	1	1	0	0	5.0	5	1	1	2	3	
								Pittsburgh	9-2	3.60	25	20	0	0	115.0	104	53	46	35	67	9.085

No. CATCHERS (4)	B	T	Ht.	Wt.	Born	Birthplace	Residence	1991 Club	AVG.	G	AB	R	H	2B	3B	HR	RBI	BB	SO	SB	M.L. Service
12 LaVALLIERE, MIKE	L	R	5-10	210	8-18-60	Charlotte, NC	Bradenton, FL	Pittsburgh	.289	108	336	25	97	11	2	3	41	33	27	2	6.047
14 PRINCE, TOM	R	R	5-11	185	8-13-64	Kankakee, IL	Bradenton, FL	Buffalo	.208	80	221	29	46	8	3	6	32	37	31	3	
								Pittsburgh	.265	26	34	4	9	3	0	1	2	7	3	0	1.108
77 ROMERO, MANDY★	S	R	5-11	196	10-19-67	Miami, FL	Miami, FL	Carolina	.217	98	323	28	70	12	0	3	31	45	53	1	0.000
11 SLAUGHT, DON	R	R	6-1	190	9-11-58	Long Beach, CA	Arlington, TX	Pittsburgh	.295	77	220	19	65	17	1	1	29	21	32	1	9.090

No. INFIELDERS (10)	B	T	Ht.	Wt.	Born	Birthplace	Residence	1991 Club	AVG.	G	AB	R	H	2B	3B	HR	RBI	BB	SO	SB	M.L. Service
3 BELL, JAY	R	R	6-1	185	12-11-65	Eglin AFB, FL	Valrico, FL	Pittsburgh	.270	157	608	96	164	32	8	16	67	52	99	10	3.110
22 BUECHELE, STEVE	R	R	6-2	200	9-26-61	Lancaster, CA	Arlington, TX	Texas	.267	121	416	58	111	17	2	18	66	39	69	0	
								Pittsburgh	.246	31	114	16	28	5	1	4	19	10	28	0	6.080
51 GARCIA, CARLOS*	R	R	6-1	185	10-15-67	Tachira, Ven.	Bolivar, Ven.	Buffalo	.266	127	463	62	123	21	6	7	60	33	78	30	
								Pittsburgh	.250	12	24	2	6	0	2	0	1	1	8	0	0.069
7 KING, JEFF	R	R	6-1	185	12-26-64	Marion, IN	Wexford, PA	#Buffalo	.222	9	18	3	4	1	1	0	2	6	3	1	
								Pittsburgh	.239	33	109	16	26	1	1	4	18	14	15	3	2.124
13 LIND, JOSE	R	R	5-11	170	5-1-64	Toabaja, PR	Dorado, PR	Pittsburgh	.265	150	502	53	133	16	6	3	54	30	56	7	4.039
6 MERCED, ORLANDO	S	R	5-11	170	11-2-66	San Juan, PR	San Juan, PR	Buffalo	.167	3	12	1	2	0	0	0	0	1	4	1	
								Pittsburgh	.275	120	411	83	113	17	2	10	50	64	81	8	1.065
2 REDUS, GARY	R	R	6-1	185	11-1-56	Tanner, AL	Decatur, AL	Pittsburgh	.246	98	252	45	62	12	2	7	24	28	39	17	9.027
27 RICHARDSON, JEFF	R	R	6-2	180	8-26-65	Grand Island, NE	Carrollton, TX	Buffalo	.258	62	186	21	48	16	2	1	24	18	29	5	
								Pittsburgh	.250	6	4	0	1	0	0	0	0	0	3	0	0.097
46 SHELTON, BEN*	R	L	6-3	210	9-21-69	Chicago, IL	Oak Park, IL	Salem	.261	65	203	37	53	10	2	14	56	45	65	4	
								Carolina	.231	55	169	19	39	8	3	1	19	29	57	2	0.000
52 WEHNER, JOHN*	R	R	6-3	204	6-29-67	Pittsburgh, PA	Pittsburgh, PA	Carolina	.265	61	234	30	62	5	1	3	21	24	32	17	
								Buffalo	.304	31	112	18	34	9	2	1	15	14	12	6	
								Pittsburgh	.340	37	106	15	36	7	0	0	7	7	17	3	0.083

No. OUTFIELDERS (8)	B	T	Ht.	Wt.	Born	Birthplace	Residence	1991 Club	AVG.	G	AB	R	H	2B	3B	HR	RBI	BB	SO	SB	M.L. Service
24 BONDS, BARRY	L	L	6-1	185	7-24-64	Riverside, CA	Rancho, CA	Pittsburgh	.292	153	510	95	149	28	5	25	116	107	73	43	5.129
47 BULLETT, SCOTT*	L	L	6-2	200	12-25-68	Martinsburg, WV	Martinsburg, WV	Augusta	.284	95	384	61	109	21	6	1	36	27	79	48	
								Salem	.333	39	156	22	52	7	5	2	15	8	29	15	
								Pittsburgh	.000	11	4	2	0	0	0	0	0	0	3	1	0.036
28 MARTIN, ALBERT*	L	L	6-2	220	11-24-67	West Covina, CA	West Covina, CA	Greenville	.243	86	301	38	73	13	3	7	38	32	84	19	
								Richmond	.278	44	151	20	42	11	1	5	18	7	33	11	0.000
23 McCLENDON, LLOYD	R	R	5-11	210	1-11-59	Gary, IN	Boulder, CO	Pittsburgh	.288	85	163	24	47	7	0	7	24	18	23	2	4.106
36 McDANIEL, TERRY	S	R	5-9	205	12-6-66	Kansas City, MO	Kansas City, MO	Tidewater	.248	118	399	63	99	23	6	9	42	50	117	18	
								New York NL	.207	23	29	3	6	1	0	0	2	1	11	2	0.038
16 RATLIFF, DARYL*	R	R	6-1	180	10-15-69	Santa Cruz, CA	Santa Cruz, CA	Salem	.293	88	352	60	103	8	4	2	23	27	43	35	
								Carolina	.215	24	93	10	20	3	0	0	9	6	16	8	0.000
18 VAN SLYKE, ANDY	L	R	6-2	195	12-21-60	Utica, NY	Chesterfield, MO	Pittsburgh	.265	138	491	87	130	24	7	17	83	71	85	10	8.108
42 VARSHO, GARY	L	R	5-11	190	6-20-61	Marshfield, WI	Marshfield, WI	Pittsburgh	.273	99	187	23	51	11	2	4	23	19	34	9	3.002

*Rookie   #Rehabilitation Assignment

FULL NAMES AND PHONETICS

Ausanio, Joseph John (ah-SAIN-ee-oh)
Batista, Miguel Jerez Decartes (bah-TEES-tah)
Belinda, Stanley Peter (bah-LYN-dah)
Bell, Jay Stuart
Bonds, Barry Lamar
Buechele, Steven Bernard (boo-SHELL)
Bullett, Scott Douglas
Cole, Victor Alexander
Drabek, Douglas Dean (DRAY-bek)
Garcia, Carlos Jesus
Heaton, Neal
King, Jeffrey Wayne

Landrum, Thomas William
LaValliere, Michael Eugene (luh-VAL-yur)
Lind, Jose (Salgado) (LEEND)
Martin, Albert Lee
Mason, Roger Leroy
McClendon, Lloyd Glenn
McDaniel, Terrance Keith
Merced, Orlando L. (mer-SED)
Miller, Paul Robert
Palacios, Vicente Hernandez (pa-lah-SEE-os)
Patterson, Robert Chandler
Prince, Thomas Albert

Ratliff, Daryl Reynard
Redus, Gary Eugene (REED-us)
Reed, Richard Allen
Richardson, Jeffrey Scott
Rodriguez, Rosario (ro-DREE-gezz)
Roesler, Michael Joseph (RESS-ler)
Romero, Armando
Shelton, Benjamin Davis
Slaught, Donald Martin (slought)
Smiley, John Patrick
Smith, Zane William
Tomlin, Randy Leon

Van Slyke, Andrew James
Varsho, Gary Andrew
Walk, Robert Vernon
Wehner, John Paul (WAIN-uhr)

MANAGER AND COACHES

James Richard Leyland (LEE-land)
Terry Lee Collins
Richard Francis Donnelly
Milton S. May
Raymond Roger Miller
Thomas James Sandt

St. Louis Cardinals

MANAGER
JOE TORRE (9)

Coaches:
DON BAYLOR (24)
JOE COLEMAN (40)
DAVE COLLINS (15)
BUCKY DENT (30)
GAYLEN PITTS (4)

Team Physician—DR. STAN LONDON
Trainer—GENE GIESELMANN
Assistant Trainer—BRAD HENDERSON

Director of Public Relations—JEFF WEHLING
Manager of Public Relations—BRIAN BARTOW
Traveling Secretary—C.J. CHERRE

No. PITCHERS (17)	B	T	Ht.	Wt.	Born	Birthplace	Residence	1991 Club	W-L	ERA	G	GS	CG	SV	IP	H	R	ER	BB	SO	M.L. Service
49 AGOSTO, JUAN	L	L	6-2	190	2-23-58	Rio Piedras, PR	Sarasota, FL	St. Louis	5-3	4.81	72	0	0	2	86.0	92	52	46	39	34	7.164
44 CARPENTER, CRIS	R	R	6-1	185	4-5-65	St. Augustine, FL	Gainesville, GA	St. Louis	10-4	4.23	59	0	0	0	66.0	53	31	31	20	47	2.004
55 CLARK, MARK★	R	R	6-5	225	5-12-68	Bath, IL	Bath, IL	Arkansas	5-5	4.00	15	15	4	0	92.1	99	50	41	30	76	
								Louisville	3-2	2.98	7	6	1	0	45.1	43	17	15	15	29	
								St. Louis	1-1	4.03	7	2	0	0	22.1	17	10	10	11	13	0.032
65 COMPRES, FIDEL★	R	R	6-0	165	5-10-65	Bacuiabaso Lauego, D.R.	LaVega, D.R.	Arkansas	4-2	3.94	27	0	0	9	32.0	37	17	14	12	18	
								Louisville	0-2	3.07	10	0	0	0	14.2	22	5	5	8	7	0.000
52 CORMIER, RHEAL	L	L	5-10	185	4-23-67	Moncton, B.C.	Shediac, B.C.	Louisville	7-9	4.23	21	21	3	0	127.2	140	64	60	31	74	
								St. Louis	4-5	4.12	11	10	2	0	67.2	74	35	31	8	38	0.054
48 DeLEON, JOSE	R	R	6-3	226	12-20-60	R.V., LaVega, D.R.	Perth Amboy, NJ	St. Louis	5-9	2.71	28	28	1	0	162.2	144	57	49	61	118	7.161
35 DiPINO, FRANK	L	L	6-0	194	10-22-56	Syracuse, NY	Manilus, NY	Louisville	0-0	36.00	2	0	0	0	1.0	2	4	4	3	0	9.067
66 ERICKS, JOHN★	R	R	6-7	220	9-16-67	Oaklawn, IL	Tinley Park, IL	Arkansas	5-14	4.77	25	25	1	0	139.2	138	94	74	84	103	0.000
32 MAGRANE, JOE	R	L	6-6	230	7-2-64	Des Moines, IA	St. Louis, MO	St. Louis					DID NOT PLAY								4.164
22 McCLURE, BOB	R	L	5-11	188	4-29-53	Oakland, CA	Los Altos, CA	California	0-0	9.31	13	0	0	0	9.2	13	11	10	5	5	
								St. Louis	1-1	3.13	32	0	0	0	23.0	24	8	8	8	15	15.107
53 MILCHIN, MIKE★	L	L	6-3	190	2-28-68	Knoxville, TN	Richmond, VA	Arkansas	3-2	3.06	6	6	1	0	35.1	27	13	12	8	38	
								Louisville	5-9	5.07	18	18	2	0	94.0	132	64	53	40	47	0.000
26 OLIVARES, OMAR	R	R	6-1	193	7-6-67	Mayaguez, PR	San German, PR	Louisville	1-2	3.47	6	6	0	0	36.1	39	15	14	16	27	
								St. Louis	11-7	3.71	28	24	0	1	167.1	148	72	69	61	91	1.030
36 SMITH, BRYN	R	R	6-2	205	8-11-55	Marietta, GA	Santa Maria, CA	St. Louis	12-9	3.85	31	31	3	0	198.2	188	95	85	45	94	10.012
47 SMITH, LEE	R	R	6-6	269	12-4-57	Jamestown, LA	Castor, LA	St. Louis	6-3	2.34	67	0	0	47	73.0	70	19	19	13	67	11.035
37 TERRY, SCOTT	R	R	5-11	195	11-21-59	Hobbs, NM	St. Louis, MO	St. Louis	4-4	2.80	65	0	0	1	80.1	76	31	25	32	52	5.003
39 TEWKSBURY, BOB	R	R	6-4	208	11-30-60	Concord, NH	Concord, NH	St. Louis	11-12	3.25	30	30	3	0	191.0	206	86	69	38	75	3.120
38 WORRELL, TODD	R	R	6-5	222	9-28-59	Arcadia, CA	St. Louis, MO	#Louisville	0-0	18.00	3	0	0	0	3.0	4	6	6	3	4	6.041

No. CATCHERS (3)	B	T	Ht.	Wt.	Born	Birthplace	Residence	1991 Club	AVG.	G	AB	R	H	2B	3B	HR	RBI	BB	SO	SB	M.L. Service
64 FERNANDEZ, JOSE★	L	R	6-3	210	8-24-67	New York, NY	Jupiter, FL	Arkansas	.228	94	285	46	65	14	1	12	28	62	86	0	0.000
29 GEDMAN, RICH	L	R	6-0	211	9-26-59	Worcester, MA	Framingham, MA	St. Louis	.106	46	94	7	10	1	0	3	8	4	15	0	11.004
19 PAGNOZZI, TOM	R	R	6-1	190	7-30-62	Tucson, AZ	St. Louis, MO	St. Louis	.264	140	459	38	121	24	5	2	57	36	63	9	4.087

No. INFIELDERS (12)	B	T	Ht.	Wt.	Born	Birthplace	Residence	1991 Club	AVG.	G	AB	R	H	2B	3B	HR	RBI	BB	SO	SB	M.L. Service
18 ALICEA, LUIS	S	R	5-9	177	7-29-65	Santurce, PR	Guaynabo, PR	Louisville	.393	31	112	26	44	6	3	4	16	14	8	5	
								St. Louis	.191	56	68	5	13	3	0	0	0	8	19	0	1.069
33 BREWER, ROD*	L	L	6-3	218	2-24-66	Eustis, FL	Zellwood, FL	Louisville	.225	104	382	39	86	21	1	8	52	35	57	4	
								St. Louis	.077	19	13	0	1	0	0	0	1	0	5	0	0.066
67 CARMONA, GREG*	S	R	6-0	150	5-9-68	Bani, D.R.	Peravia, D.R.	Arkansas	.182	13	33	1	6	0	0	0	1	5	9	0	0.000
								Louisville	.175	56	143	16	25	2	1	2	10	13	25	7	
41 GALARRAGA, ANDRES	R	R	6-3	235	6-18-61	Caracas, Ven.	Caracas, Ven.	Montreal	.219	107	375	34	82	13	2	9	33	23	86	5	6.046
8 JONES, TIM	L	R	5-10	175	12-1-62	Sumter, SC	Sumter, SC	Louisville	.255	86	306	34	78	9	1	5	29	36	59	19	
								St. Louis	.167	16	24	1	4	2	0	0	2	2	6	0	2.147
11 OQUENDO, JOSE	S	R	5-10	171	7-4-63	Rio Piedras, PR	St. Louis, MO	St. Louis	.240	127	366	37	88	11	4	1	26	67	48	1	7.120
7 PENA, GERONIMO	S	R	6-1	195	3-29-67	Dist. Nacional, D.R.	Los Alcarrizos, D.R.	St. Louis	.243	104	185	38	45	8	3	5	17	18	45	15	1.094
21 PERRY, GERALD	L	R	6-0	201	10-30-60	Savannah, GA	Smyrna, GA	St. Louis	.240	109	242	29	58	8	4	6	36	22	34	15	7.102
5 ROYER, STAN*	R	R	6-3	221	8-31-67	Olney, IL	Springfield, IL	Louisville	.254	138	523	48	133	30	6	14	74	43	126	1	
								St. Louis	.286	9	21	1	6	1	0	0	1	1	2	0	0.028
1 SMITH, OZZIE	S	R	5-10	168	12-26-54	Mobile, AL	St. Louis, MO	St. Louis	.285	150	550	96	157	30	3	3	50	83	36	35	14.000
12 WILSON, CRAIG	R	R	5-11	208	11-28-64	Anne Arundel, MD	Annapolis, MD	St. Louis	.171	60	82	5	14	2	0	0	13	6	10	0	1.149
27 ZEILE, TODD	R	R	6-1	190	9-9-65	Van Nuys, CA	Valencia, CA	St. Louis	.280	155	565	76	158	36	3	11	81	62	94	17	2.046

No. OUTFIELDERS (8)	B	T	Ht.	Wt.	Born	Birthplace	Residence	1991 Club	AVG.	G	AB	R	H	2B	3B	HR	RBI	BB	SO	SB	M.L. Service
23 GILKEY, BERNARD	R	R	6-0	190	9-24-66	St. Louis, MO	St. Louis, MO	Louisville	.146	11	41	5	6	2	0	0	2	6	10	1	
								St. Louis	.216	81	268	28	58	7	2	5	20	39	33	14	1.030
28 GUERRERO, PEDRO	R	R	6-0	197	6-29-56	San Pedro de Macoris, D.R.	Rio Rancho, NM	Louisville	.455	3	11	2	5	0	0	1	2	0	0	0	
								St. Louis	.272	115	427	41	116	12	1	8	70	37	46	4	12.077
10 HUDLER, REX	R	R	6-0	195	9-2-60	Tempe, AZ	Grover, MO	St. Louis	.227	101	207	21	47	10	2	1	15	10	29	12	4.131
50 JORDAN, BRIAN*	R	R	6-1	205	3-29-67	Baltimore, MD	Baltimore, MD	Louisville	.264	61	212	35	56	11	4	4	24	17	41	10	0.000
34 JOSE, FELIX	S	R	6-1	221	5-8-65	Santo Domingo, D.R.	Oakland, CA	St. Louis	.305	154	568	69	173	40	6	8	77	50	113	20	2.101
16 LANKFORD, RAY	L	L	5-11	190	6-5-67	Modesto, CA	Stockton, CA	St. Louis	.251	151	566	83	142	23	15	9	69	41	114	44	1.044
51 MACLIN, LONNIE*	L	L	5-11	185	2-17-67	Clayton, MO	St. Louis, MO	Louisville	.287	84	327	35	91	12	2	4	37	16	50	19	0.000
25 THOMPSON, MILT	L	R	5-11	200	1-5-59	Washington, DC	Ballwin, MO	St. Louis	.307	115	326	55	100	16	5	6	34	32	53	16	6.086

*Rookie
#Rehabilitation Assignment

FULL NAMES AND PHONETICS

Agosto, Juan Robert (a-GUST-oh)
Alicea, Luis Rene (ah-la-SAY-ya)
Brewer, Rodney Lee
Carmona, Gregorio
Carpenter, Cris Howell
Clark, Mark Willard
Compres, Fidel A.
Cormier, Rheal Paul (RAY-al, KOR-mee-ay)
DeLeon, Jose (Chestaro) (day-LEE-own)
DiPino, Frank Michael (duh-PEE-noh)
Ericks, John Edward
Fernandez, Jose Ignacio

Galarraga, Andres Jose (gala-RAH-guh)
Gedman, Richard Leo, Jr.
Gilkey, Otis Bernard
Guerrero, Pedro (guh-RAIR-oh)
Hudler, Rex Allen
Jones, William Timothy
Jose, Domingo Felix
Jordan, Brian O'Neal
Lankford, Raymond Lewis
Maclin, Lonnie Lee
Magrane, Joseph David
McClure, Robert Craig

Milchin, Michael Wayne
Olivares, Omar (Palqu) (ah-liv-AIR-es)
Oquendo, Jose Manuel (oh-KEN-doh)
Pagnozzi, Thomas Alan (pag-NOHZ-ee)
Pena, Geronimo (PAYN-yuh)
Perry, Gerald June
Royer, Stanley Dean
Smith, Bryn Nelson
Smith, Lee Arthur, Sr.
Smith, Osborne Earl
Terry, Scott Ray
Tewksbury, Robert Alan

Thompson, Milton Bernard
Wilson, Craig
Worrell, Todd Roland (wor-RELL)
Zeile, Todd Edward (ZEAL)

MANAGER AND COACHES

Joseph Paul Torre
Don Edward Baylor
Joseph Howard Coleman
David S. Collins
Russell Dent
Gaylen R. Pitts

San Diego Padres

MANAGER
GREG RIDDOCH (3)

Coaches:
BRUCE KIMM (34)
ROB PICCIOLO (5)
MERV RETTENMUND (16)
MIKE ROARKE (36)
JIM SNYDER (17)

Team Physician—SCRIPPS CLINIC MEDICAL STAFF
Trainer—BOB DAY
Assistant Trainer—TODD HUTCHESON

Director of Media Relations—JIM FERGUSON
Traveling Secretary—JOHN 'DOC' MATTEI

No. PITCHERS (17)	B	T	Ht.	Wt.	Born	Birthplace	Residence	1991 Club	W-L	ERA	G	GS	CG	SV	IP	H	R	ER	BB	SO	M.L. Service
27 ANDERSEN, LARRY	R	R	6-3	205	5-6-53	Portland, OR	San Diego, CA	San Diego	3-4	2.30	38	0	0	13	47.0	39	13	12	13	40	11.059
40 BENES, ANDY	R	R	6-6	240	8-20-67	Evansville, IN	Poway, CA	San Diego	15-11	3.03	33	33	4	0	223.0	194	76	75	59	167	2.054
56 BONES, RICKY	R	R	6-0	190	4-7-69	Salinas, PR	Guayama, PR	Las Vegas	8-6	4.22	23	23	1	0	136.1	155	90	64	43	95	
								San Diego	4-6	4.83	11	11	0	0	54.0	57	33	29	18	31	0.059
49 BROCAIL, DOUG*	L	R	6-5	220	5-16-67	Clearfield, PA	Lamar, CO	Wichita	10-7	3.87	34	16	3	6	146.1	147	77	63	43	108	0.000
46 HARRIS, GREG	R	R	6-2	195	12-1-63	Greensboro, NC	Del Mar, CA	#Las Vegas	1-2	7.40	4	4	0	0	20.2	24	20	17	8	16	
								San Diego	9-5	2.23	20	20	3	0	133.0	116	42	33	27	95	3.015
50 HERNANDEZ, JEREMY*	R	R	6-6	205	7-6-66	Burbank, CA	Walnut Creek, CA	Las Vegas	4-8	4.74	56	0	0	13	68.1	76	36	36	25	67	
								San Diego	0-0	0.00	9	0	0	2	14.1	8	1	0	5	9	0.036
47 HURST, BRUCE	L	L	6-3	220	3-24-58	St. George, UT	Rancho Santa Fe, CA	San Diego	15-8	3.29	31	31	4	0	221.2	201	89	81	59	141	10.123
11 LEFFERTS, CRAIG	L	L	6-1	210	9-29-57	Munich, W. Ger.	Poway, CA	San Diego	1-6	3.91	54	0	0	23	69.0	74	35	30	14	48	9.000
37 LINSKEY, MIKE*	L	L	6-5	220	6-18-66	Baltimore, MD	Baltimore, MD	Hagerstown	6-5	4.46	16	16	1	0	107.0	128	62	53	37	71	
								Rochester	1-5	7.24	10	9	0	0	41.0	67	34	33	17	25	0.000
51 MADDUX, MIKE	L	R	6-2	190	8-27-61	Dayton, OH	Las Vegas, NV	San Diego	7-2	2.46	64	1	0	5	98.2	78	30	27	27	57	3.092
48 MELENDEZ, JOSE	R	R	6-2	175	9-2-65	Naguabo, PR	Naguabo, PR	Las Vegas	7-0	3.99	9	8	1	0	58.2	54	27	26	11	45	
								San Diego	8-5	3.27	31	9	0	3	93.2	77	35	34	24	60	0.159
28 MYERS, RANDY	L	L	6-1	215	9-19-62	Vancouver, WA	Vancouver, WA	Cincinnati	6-13	3.55	58	12	1	6	132.0	116	61	52	80	108	5.088
32 PETERSON, ADAM	R	R	6-3	190	12-11-65	Long Beach, CA	Vancouver, WA	Las Vegas	2-2	4.50	8	8	0	0	42.0	41	25	21	20	37	
								San Diego	3-4	4.45	13	11	0	0	54.2	50	33	27	28	37	1.093
42 RODRIGUEZ, RICH	R	L	6-0	200	3-1-63	Downey, CA	Knoxville, TN	San Diego	3-1	3.26	64	1	0	0	80.0	66	31	29	44	40	1.097
44 SEMINARA, FRANK*	R	R	6-2	205	5-16-67	Brooklyn, NY	Brooklyn, NY	Wichita	15-10	3.38	27	27	6	0	176.0	173	86	66	68	107	0.000
35 VALDEZ, RAFAEL*	R	R	5-11	185	12-17-68	Nizao Bani, D.R.	Nizao Bani, D.R.	Las Vegas	0-2	5.94	5	5	0	0	16.2	22	13	11	16	9	0.029
31 WHITSON, ED	R	R	6-3	200	5-19-55	Johnson City, TN	Dublin, OH	San Diego	4-6	5.03	13	12	2	0	78.2	93	47	44	17	40	13.159

No. CATCHERS (3)	B	T	Ht.	Wt.	Born	Birthplace	Residence	1991 Club	AVG.	G	AB	R	H	2B	3B	HR	RBI	BB	SO	SB	M.L. Service
7 BILARDELLO, DANN	R	R	6-0	190	5-26-59	Santa Cruz, CA	W. Palm Beach, FL	Las Vegas	.314	44	140	17	44	13	1	4	29	9	19	2	
								San Diego	.269	15	26	4	7	2	1	0	5	3	4	0	4.090
25 LAMPKIN, TOM	L	R	5-11	185	3-4-64	Cincinnati, OH	San Diego, CA	Las Vegas	.317	45	164	25	52	11	1	2	29	10	20	2	
								San Diego	.190	38	58	4	11	3	1	0	3	3	9	0	1.057
09 SANTIAGO, BENITO	R	R	6-1	185	3-9-65	Ponce, PR	Chula Vista, CA	San Diego	.267	152	580	60	155	22	3	17	87	23	114	8	5.022

No. INFIELDERS (13)	B	T	Ht.	Wt.	Born	Birthplace	Residence	1991 Club	AVG.	G	AB	R	H	2B	3B	HR	RBI	BB	SO	SB	M.L. Service
23 FARIES, PAUL	R	R	5-10	170	2-20-65	Berkeley, CA	Moraga, CA	#High Desert	.310	10	42	6	13	2	2	0	5	2	3	1	
								Las Vegas	.307	20	75	16	23	2	1	1	12	12	5	7	
								San Diego	.177	57	130	13	23	3	1	0	7	14	21	3	1.019
1 FERNANDEZ, TONY	S	R	6-2	175	6-30-62	S.P. de Macoris, D.R.	Santo Domingo, D.R.	San Diego	.272	145	558	81	152	27	5	4	38	55	74	23	7.164
41 GARDNER, JEFF*	L	R	5-11	165	2-4-64	Newport Beach, CA	Newport Beach, CA	Tidewater	.292	136	504	73	147	23	4	1	56	84	48	6	0.000
								New York NL	.162	13	37	3	6	0	0	0	1	4	6	0	0.031
53 HOLBERT, RAY*	R	R	6-0	170	9-25-70	Torrance, CA	Moreno Valley, CA	High Desert	.264	122	386	76	102	14	2	4	51	56	83	19	0.000
14 LOPEZ, LUIS*	S	R	5-11	155	9-4-70	Cidra, PR	Cidra, PR	Wichita	.268	125	452	43	121	17	1	1	41	18	70	6	0.000
29 McGRIFF, FRED	L	L	6-3	210	10-31-63	Tampa, FL	Tampa, FL	San Diego	.278	153	528	84	147	19	1	31	106	105	135	4	5.009
10 REDINGTON, TOM*	R	R	6-1	200	2-13-69	Fullerton, CA	Anaheim, CA	Wichita	.284	116	394	54	112	23	0	5	57	67	66	2	0.000
18 SHIPLEY, CRAIG	R	R	6-1	185	1-7-63	Sydney, Australia	Jupiter, FL	Las Vegas	.300	65	230	27	69	9	5	5	34	10	32	2	
								San Diego	.275	37	91	6	25	3	0	1	6	2	14	0	1.040
26 STATON, DAVE*	R	R	6-5	220	4-12-68	Seattle, WA	Auburn, CA	Las Vegas	.267	107	375	61	100	19	1	22	74	44	89	1	0.000
20 TEUFEL, TIM	R	R	6-0	175	7-7-58	Greenwich, CT	Greenwich, CT	New York NL	.118	20	34	2	4	0	0	1	2	2	8	1	
								San Diego	.228	97	307	39	70	16	0	11	42	49	69	8	
								(Composite)	.217	117	341	41	74	16	0	12	44	51	77	9	8.030
8 VALENTIN, JOSE*	S	R	5-10	175	10-12-69	Manati, PR	Manati, PR	Wichita	.251	129	447	73	112	22	5	17	68	55	115	8	0.000
15 VELASQUEZ, GUILLERMO*	L	R	6-3	220	4-23-68	Mexicali, Mex.	Calexico, CA	Wichita	.295	130	501	72	148	26	3	21	100	48	75	4	0.000
39 WORTHINGTON, CRAIG	R	R	6-0	200	4-17-65	Los Angeles, CA	San Diego, CA	Rochester	.298	19	57	10	17	4	0	2	9	6	8	0	
								Baltimore	.225	31	102	11	23	3	0	4	12	12	14	0	2.114

No. OUTFIELDERS (7)	B	T	Ht.	Wt.	Born	Birthplace	Residence	1991 Club	AVG.	G	AB	R	H	2B	3B	HR	RBI	BB	SO	SB	M.L. Service
22 AZOCAR, OSCAR	L	L	6-1	195	2-21-65	Soro, Ven.	Valencia, Ven.	Las Vegas	.296	107	361	51	107	23	3	7	50	21	26	4	
								San Diego	.246	38	57	5	14	2	0	0	9	1	9	2	0.139
24 CLARK, JERALD	R	R	6-4	205	8-10-63	Crockett, TX	San Diego, CA	San Diego	.228	118	369	26	84	16	0	10	47	31	90	2	2.021
19 GWYNN, TONY	L	L	5-11	215	5-9-60	Los Angeles, CA	Poway, CA	San Diego	.317	134	530	69	168	27	11	4	62	34	19	8	9.077
33 HOWARD, THOMAS	S	R	6-2	205	12-11-64	Middletown, OH	Middletown, OH	Las Vegas	.309	25	94	22	29	3	1	2	16	10	16	11	
								San Diego	.249	106	281	30	70	12	3	4	22	24	57	10	1.014
4 JACKSON, DARRIN	R	R	6-0	185	8-22-63	Los Angeles, CA	Mesa, AZ	San Diego	.262	122	359	51	94	12	1	21	49	27	66	5	3.105
57 TAYLOR, WILL*	R	R	6-2	170	8-19-68	Alexandria, LA	Alexandria, LA	Las Vegas	.259	125	468	82	121	11	5	4	33	56	101	62	0.000
2 VATCHER, JIM	R	R	5-9	175	5-27-66	Santa Monica, CA	Pacific Palisades, CA	Las Vegas	.266	117	395	67	105	28	6	17	67	53	76	4	
								San Diego	.200	17	20	3	4	0	0	0	2	4	6	1	0.156

*Rookie   #Rehabilitation Assignment

FULL NAMES AND PHONETICS

Andersen, Larry Eugene
Azocar, Oscar Gregorio (ah-ZOH-car)
Benes, Andrew Charles (BEN-es)
Bilardello, Dann James (bill-ar-DELL-oh)
Bones, Ricardo (BONE-us)
Brocail, Douglas Keith (Broh-KALE)
Clark, Jerald Dwayne
Faries, Paul Tyrell (FAIR-ees)
Fernandez, Octavio Antonio
Gardner, Jeffrey Scott
Gwynn, Anthony Keith (GWIN)
Harris, Gregory Wade

Hernandez, Jeremy Stuart
Holbert, Ray Arthur
Howard, Thomas Sylvester
Hurst, Bruce Vee
Jackson, Darrin Jay
Lampkin, Thomas Michael
Lefferts, Craig Lindsay
Linskey, Michael Shawn (LINN-skey)
Lopez, Luis Manuel
Maddux, Michael Ausley
McGriff, Frederick Stanley
Melendez, Jose Luis (muh-LEN-dez)

Myers, Randall Kirk
Peterson, Adam Charles
Redington, Thomas Richard
Rodriguez, Richard Anthony
Santiago, Benito (Rivera) (sahn-tee-AH-go)
Seminara, Frank Peter (sem-ah-NAIR-ah)
Shipley, Craig Barry
Staton, David Alan (STAY-ton)
Taylor, William Christopher
Teufel, Timothy Shawn (TUFF-ul)
Valdez, Rafael Emilio (Val-DEZZ)
Valentin, Jose Antonio (VAL-un-teen)

Vatcher, James Ernest
Velasquez, Guillermo (Ve-LAS-quez)
Whitson, Eddie Lee
Worthington, Craig Richard

MANAGER AND COACHES

Gregory Lee Riddoch (RID-ock)
Bruce Edward Kimm
Robert Michael Picciolo (PEACH-ah-low)
Mervin Weldon Rettenmund (RETT-un-mund)
Michael Roarke
James Robert Snyder

San Francisco Giants

MANAGER
ROGER CRAIG (38)

Coaches:
CARLOS ALFONSO (16)
DUSTY BAKER (12)
BOB BRENLY (14)
WENDELL KIM (20)
BOB LILLIS (5)

Team Physician—DR. GORDON CAMPBELL
Trainer—MARK LETENDRE
Assistant Trainer—GREG LYNN

Director of Media Relations—MATT FISCHER
Director of Travel—DIRK SMITH

No. PITCHERS (21)	B	T	Ht.	Wt.	Born	Birthplace	Residence	1991 Club	W-L	ERA	G	GS	CG	SV	IP	H	R	ER	BB	SO	M.L. Service
64 ARD, JOHNNY*	R	R	6-5	220	6-1-67	Las Vegas, NV	Sarasota, FL	Phoenix	3-5	5.78	10	10	1	0	62.1	76	42	40	33	30	0.000
								Shreveport	9-3	2.74	13	13	4	0	88.2	77	31	27	36	58	
47 BECK, ROD	R	R	6-1	215	8-3-68	Burbank, CA	Van Nuys, CA	Phoenix	4-3	2.02	23	5	3	6	71.1	56	18	16	13	35	
								San Francisco	1-1	3.78	31	0	0	1	52.1	53	22	22	13	38	0.104
40 BLACK, BUDDY	L	L	6-2	185	6-30-57	San Mateo, CA	San Diego, CA	San Francisco	12-16	3.99	34	34	3	0	214.1	201	104	95	71	104	9.167
49 BRANTLEY, JEFF	R	R	5-11	190	9-5-63	Florence, AL	Clinton, MS	San Francisco	5-2	2.45	67	0	0	15	95.1	78	27	26	52	81	3.061
34 BURBA, DAVE*	R	R	6-4	220	7-7-66	Dayton, OH	Springfield, OH	Calgary	6-4	3.53	23	9	0	4	71.1	82	35	28	27	42	
								Seattle	2-2	3.68	22	2	0	1	36.2	34	16	15	14	16	0.117
33 BURKETT, JOHN	R	R	6-2	210	11-28-64	New Brighton, PA	Jackson, TN	San Francisco	12-11	4.18	36	34	3	0	206.2	223	103	96	60	131	2.030
37 DOWNS, KELLY	R	R	6-4	205	10-25-60	Ogden, UT	Centerville, UT	San Francisco	10-4	4.19	45	11	0	0	111.2	99	59	52	53	62	5.070
50 GARRELTS, SCOTT	R	R	6-4	210	10-30-61	Urbana, IL	Shreveport, LA	San Francisco	1-1	6.41	8	3	0	0	19.2	25	14	14	9	8	7.142
53 GUNDERSON, ERIC*	L	L	6-0	175	3-29-66	Portland, OR	Vancouver, WA	Phoenix	7-6	6.14	40	14	0	3	107.0	153	85	73	44	53	
								San Francisco	0-0	5.40	2	0	0	1	3.1	6	4	2	1	2	0.051
60 HANCOCK, CHRIS*	L	L	6-3	175	9-12-69	Lynwood, CA	Fontana, CA	San Jose	4-3	2.03	9	9	0	0	53.1	42	16	12	33	59	0.000
36 HEREDIA, GIL*	R	R	6-1	190	10-26-65	Nogales, AZ	Tucson, AZ	Phoenix	9-11	2.82	33	15	5	1	140.1	155	60	44	28	75	
								San Francisco	0-2	3.82	7	4	0	0	33.0	27	14	14	7	13	0.043
41 HICKERSON, BRYAN	L	L	6-2	195	10-13-63	Bemidji, MN	Bemidji, MN	Shreveport	3-4	3.00	23	0	0	2	39.0	36	15	13	14	41	
								Phoenix	1-1	3.80	12	0	0	2	21.1	29	10	9	5	21	
								San Francisco	2-2	3.60	17	6	0	0	50.0	53	20	20	17	43	0.074
42 JACKSON, MIKE	R	R	6-0	200	12-22-64	Houston, TX	Houston, TX	Seattle	7-7	3.25	72	0	0	14	88.2	64	35	32	34	74	5.059
21 MASTERS, DAVE*	R	R	6-9	225	8-13-64	San Diego, CA	Honolulu, HI	Indianapolis	4-6	6.04	27	9	1	1	70.0	82	56	47	63	64	0.000
								Phoenix	1-2	6.46	8	4	0	0	30.2	34	24	22	17	28	
54 MYERS, JIM*	R	R	6-1	185	4-28-69	Oklahoma City, OK	Crowder, OK	Shreveport	6-4	2.48	62	0	0	24	76.1	71	22	21	30	51	0.000
45 OLIVERAS, FRANCISCO	R	R	5-10	180	1-31-63	Santurce, PR	Caguas, PR	Phoenix	2-0	2.45	3	3	1	0	18.1	18	5	5	7	12	
								San Francisco	6-6	3.86	55	1	0	3	79.1	69	36	34	22	48	2.025
52 QUIRICO, RAFAEL*	L	L	6-3	170	9-7-69	Santo Domingo, D.R.	Santo Domingo, D.R.	Greensboro	12-8	2.26	26	26	1	0	155.1	103	59	39	80	162	0.000
19 RIGHETTI, DAVE	L	L	6-4	212	11-28-58	San Jose, CA	San Jose, CA	San Francisco	2-7	3.39	61	0	0	24	71.2	64	29	27	28	51	10.151
58 ROGERS, KEVIN*	S	L	6-1	190	8-20-68	Cleveland, MS	Parchman, MS	Shreveport	4-6	3.36	22	22	2	0	118.0	124	63	44	54	108	0.000
26 SWIFT, BILL	R	R	6-0	180	10-27-61	S. Portland, ME	Redmond, WA	Seattle	1-2	1.99	71	0	0	17	90.1	74	22	20	26	48	5.093
32 WILSON, TREVOR	L	L	6-0	195	6-7-66	Torrance, CA	Scottsdale, AZ	San Francisco	13-11	3.56	44	29	2	0	202.0	173	87	80	77	139	2.059

No. CATCHERS (2)	B	T	Ht.	Wt.	Born	Birthplace	Residence	1991 Club	AVG.	G	AB	R	H	2B	3B	HR	RBI	BB	SO	SB	M.L. Service
35 DECKER, STEVE	R	R	6-3	205	10-25-65	Rock Island, IL	Salem, OR	Phoenix	.252	31	111	20	28	5	1	6	14	13	29	0	
								San Francisco	.206	79	233	11	48	7	1	5	24	16	44	0	0.164
8 MANWARING, KIRT	R	R	5-11	190	7-15-65	Elmira, NY	Scottsdale, AZ	Phoenix	.222	24	81	8	18	0	0	4	14	8	15	0	
								#San Jose	.000	1	3	1	0	0	0	0	0	1	1	0	
								San Francisco	.225	67	178	16	40	9	0	0	19	9	22	1	2.140

No. INFIELDERS (9)	B	T	Ht.	Wt.	Born	Birthplace	Residence	1991 Club	AVG.	G	AB	R	H	2B	3B	HR	RBI	BB	SO	SB	M.L. Service
18 BENJAMIN, MIKE	R	R	6-2	175	11-22-65	Euclid, OH	Mesa, AZ	Phoenix	.204	64	226	34	46	13	2	6	31	20	67	3	
								San Francisco	.123	54	106	12	13	3	0	2	8	7	26	3	1.023
22 CLARK, WILL	L	L	6-1	190	3-13-64	New Orleans, LA	New Orleans, LA	San Francisco	.301	148	565	84	170	32	7	29	116	51	91	4	6.000
10 CLAYTON, ROYCE*	R	R	6-0	175	1-2-70	Burbank, CA	N. Inglewood, CA	Shreveport	.280	126	485	84	136	22	8	5	68	61	104	36	
								San Francisco	.115	9	26	0	3	1	0	0	2	1	6	0	0.017
15 LITTON, GREG	R	R	6-0	190	7-13-64	New Orleans, LA	Pensacola, FL	Phoenix	.407	8	27	9	11	1	0	4	9	8	5	0	
								San Francisco	.181	59	127	13	23	7	1	1	15	11	25	0	2.153
57 PATTERSON, JOHN*	S	R	5-9	160	2-11-67	Key West, FL	Phoenix, AZ	Shreveport	.295	117	464	81	137	31	13	4	56	30	63	40	0.000
56 SANTANA, ANDRES*	S	R	5-11	150	3-19-68	S.P. de Macoris, D.R.	S.P. de Macoris, D.R.	Phoenix	.316	113	456	84	144	7	5	1	35	36	46	45	0.018
6 THOMPSON, ROBBY	R	R	5-11	170	5-10-62	W. Palm Beach, FL	Tequesta, FL	San Francisco	.262	144	492	74	129	24	5	19	48	63	95	14	6.000
23 URIBE, JOSE	S	R	5-10	170	1-21-60	San Cristobal, D.R.	Santo Domingo, D.R.	#San Jose	.111	3	9	0	1	0	1	0	1	1	2	0	
								#Phoenix	.341	11	41	7	14	1	1	0	4	1	2	0	
								San Francisco	.221	90	231	23	51	8	4	1	12	20	33	3	7.020
9 WILLIAMS, MATT	R	R	6-2	210	11-28-65	Bishop, CA	Scottsdale, AZ	San Francisco	.268	157	589	72	158	24	5	34	98	33	128	5	3.113

No. OUTFIELDERS (8)	B	T	Ht.	Wt.	Born	Birthplace	Residence	1991 Club	AVG.	G	AB	R	H	2B	3B	HR	RBI	BB	SO	SB	M.L. Service
17 BASS, KEVIN	S	R	6-0	190	5-12-59	Redwood City, CA	Sugar Land, TX	#San Jose	.105	5	19	1	2	2	0	0	1	2	3	2	
								#Phoenix	.317	10	41	8	13	3	1	2	7	2	4	1	
								San Francisco	.233	124	361	43	84	10	4	10	40	36	56	7	9.073
25 FELDER, MIKE	S	R	5-8	160	11-18-62	Vallejo, CA	Richmond, CA	San Francisco	.264	132	348	51	92	10	6	0	18	30	31	21	5.097
63 HOSEY, STEVE*	R	R	6-3	215	4-2-69	Oakland, CA	Inglewood, CA	Shreveport	.293	126	409	79	120	21	5	17	74	56	88	24	0.000
30 JAMES, CHRIS	R	R	6-1	190	10-4-62	Rusk, TX	Alto, TX	Cleveland	.238	115	437	31	104	16	2	5	41	18	61	3	5.125
1 LEONARD, MARK	L	R	6-0	195	8-14-64	Mountain View, CA	Cupertino, CA	Phoenix	.253	41	146	27	37	7	0	8	25	21	29	1	
								San Francisco	.240	64	129	14	31	7	1	2	14	12	25	0	1.041
2 LEWIS, DARREN	R	R	6-0	175	8-28-67	Berkeley, CA	Union City, CA	Phoenix	.340	81	315	63	107	12	10	2	52	41	36	32	
								San Francisco	.248	72	222	41	55	5	3	1	15	36	30	13	0.130
51 McGEE, WILLIE	S	R	6-1	195	11-2-58	San Francisco, CA	Hercules, CA	#Phoenix	.500	4	10	4	5	1	0	0	1	3	1	2	
								San Francisco	.312	131	497	67	155	30	3	4	43	34	74	17	9.148
39 WOOD, TED*	L	L	6-2	178	1-4-67	Mansfield, OH	New Orleans, LA	Phoenix	.311	137	512	90	159	38	6	11	109	86	96	12	
								San Francisco	.120	10	25	0	3	0	0	0	1	2	11	0	0.034

*Rookie
#Rehabilitation Assignment

FULL NAMES AND PHONETICS

Ard, Broni Johnny
Bass, Kevin Charles
Beck, Rodney Roy
Benjamin, Michael Paul
Black, Harry Ralston, Jr.
Brantley, Jeffrey Hoke
Burba, David Allen
Burkett, John David (bur-KETT)
Clark, William Nuschler, Jr.
Clayton, Royce Spender
Decker, Steven Michael
Downs, Kelly Robert

Felder, Michael Otis
Garrelts, Scott William (guh-RELTS)
Gunderson, Eric A.
Hancock, Christopher Martin
Heredia, Gilbert (err-A-Dee-uh)
Hickerson, Bryan David
Hosey, Steven Bernard
Jackson, Michael Ray
Leonard, Mark David
Lewis, Darren Joel
Litton, Jon Gregory
Manwaring, Kirt Dean (MAN-wair-ing)

Masters, David William
McClellan, Paul William
McGee, Willie Dean
Myers, James Xavier
Oliveras, Francisco Javier (all-e-VER-us)
Patterson, John Allen
Quirico, Rafael Octavio (kier-E-ko)
Righetti, David Allen (ri-GET-tee)
Rogers, Charles Kevin
Santana, Andres Confesor
Swift, William Charles
Thompson, Robert Randall

Uribe, Jose A. (oo-REE-bay)
Williams, Matthew Derrick
Wilson, Trevor Kirk
Wood, Edward Robert, Jr.

MANAGER AND COACHES

Roger Lee Craig
Carlos Alfonso
Johnnie B. Baker
Robert Earl Brenly
Wendell Kim
Robert Perry Lillis

NATIONAL LEAGUE MANAGERS 1992

ATLANTA—BOBBY COX

Born May 21, 1941, Tulsa, OK . . . Resides: Marietta, GA . . . 6'0" . . . 185 . . . Married Pam Boswell . . . Three children, Keisha, Kami and Skyla.

In 1991, Bobby Cox became the first manager to take a team with the worst record in the Major Leagues one year (65-97 in '90) to first place the following season. He guided the Braves to the best record in Atlanta history (94-68), a National League pennant and a dramatic seven-game World Series. Cox's accomplishments brought him several post-season honors, including being named Major League Manager of the Year by the Associated Press and National League Manager of the Year by the BBWAA and The Sporting News. Cox became the first manager to earn the A.P. accolade in both leagues, having also won it while with Toronto in 1985.

Cox, 50, is in the third season of his second stint with the Braves. He also managed the Braves from 1978-81, compiling a 266-323 record. Cox began a four-year tenure as the Blue Jays' manager in 1982, lifting an habitual seventh-place team to within one game of attaining a 1985 World Series berth.

In 1982, Cox led the Blue Jays to a 78-84 mark, the best record in their six-year existence. Toronto improved to 89-73 each of the next two seasons and then won the American League East crown by going 99-62 in 1985.

Cox returned to the Braves as General Manager in October 1985 and oversaw a farm system which produced many of the team's current standouts. He added the field managing responsibilities June 22, 1990, then was able to devote fulltime to those duties when the Braves named John Schuerholz GM in October 1990.

Cox signed with the Dodgers in 1959. He won the Pioneer League batting title with Great Falls in 1963, hitting .337 with 19 home runs and 85 RBIs. He led his league in fielding percentage on three occasions (1961 as a second baseman, 1963 and 1965 as a third baseman).

He spent seven years in the Dodgers' farm system before being acquired by Atlanta late in 1966. After playing in 1967 for AAA Richmond, Cox was traded to the New York Yankees in 1968. He went on to make the Topps Rookie All-Star team that season.

Bad knees forced Cox to retire at the age of 30. He was appointed manager of the Yankees' Class A Fort Lauderdale club in 1971. His teams never finished lower than fourth in his six seasons in the Yankees' system. He won the Eastern League pennant and championship with West Haven in 1972 and placed second twice and third twice in four years at Syracuse, winning the International League's Governor's Cup in 1976.

After serving as the Yankees' first base coach in 1977, Cox moved south to manage the Braves.

CHICAGO—JIM LEFEBVRE

Born January 7, 1942, Inglewood, CA . . . Resides: Scottsdale, AZ . . . 5'11" . . . 190 . . . Married Ruth Endersby . . . Four children, Ryan, Briana, Bryce and Brittany.

Jim Lefebvre was named the 43rd manager in Cubs history November 22, 1991. He spent the previous three years as the manager of the Seattle Mariners, leading the franchise to its first winning season in 1991 with an 83-79 record.

Lefebvre was the winningest manager in Seattle's history, posting a 233-253 mark. His .479 winning percentage also was best in club annals.

He began his managerial career in 1978 with Los Angeles' Lethbridge affiliate in the short-season Pioneer League (Rookie) and was promoted to the Dodgers' coaching staff in September and remained with the club for the 1979 season. He joined the San Francisco Giants in 1980, spending seven seasons with that organization and serving as manager at Phoenix of the Pacific Coast League (AAA) in 1985-1986. He was the league's Manager of the Year during both campaigns and earned Baseball America's Minor League Manager of the Year award in 1985. Lefebvre returned to the majors in 1987, serving as Oakland's third base coach and hitting instructor for two seasons before being hired as Seattle's manager.

A former second baseman, Jim played eight seasons with the Dodgers, batting .251 in 922 major league games. He was the Baseball Writers' Association of America's Rookie of the Year in 1965, hitting .250 with 12 home runs and 69 RBI. He was a National League All-Star in 1966, finishing the campaign with a .274 batting average, 24 homers and 74 RBI.

Following the conclusion of his M.L. career, he played four seasons (1973-1976) with the Lotte Orions of the Japanese Pacific League. He served as a coach for the team in 1977.

This past winter, he helped conduct a series of clinics in Holland, Italy and Czechoslovakia.

CINCINNATI—LOU PINIELLA

Born August 28, 1943, Tampa, FL . . . Resides: Allendale, NJ . . . 6'2" . . . 200 . . . Married Anita Garcia . . . Three children, Lou Jr., Kristi, and Derek.

Lou Piniella is in his third season in the National League as manager of the Reds after spending the first 22 years of his major league baseball career (1968-89) in the American League, first as a player and then as a coach, manager and front office executive. Lou Piniella made the transition to the National League in 1990 with sensational results. He guided the Reds to their first Western Division title since 1979; their first N.L. pennant since 1976; and then a stunning World Series sweep over Oakland. His Reds set a team record by winning their first 9 games and then stayed in first place through the entire season to become the first N.L. team to go wire-to-wire in a 162-game season.

Lou began his managerial career in 1986, when he led the Yankees to a second place finish in the A.L. East with a 90-72 record. His '87 New York club won 89 games. Piniella then moved to the front office as Yankees' General Manager in October, 1987. He resigned that post in May, 1988, to assume other responsibilities with the team, then returned to the dugout as manager on June 23, replacing Billy Martin. He was a special adviser to Yankees' owner George Steinbrenner in 1989 as well as a Yankee TV broadcaster. Lou moved to the N.L. as manager of the Reds on November 3, 1989. His overall managerial record is 389-352 (.525).

Piniella had a long, distinguished career as a player, including 18 major league seasons in a 23-year pro career. He produced a .291 big league career average; batted .319 in 22 World Series games; and hit .305 in 18 Championship Series games. Lou was named A.L. Rookie of the Year in 1969 at Kansas City, where he played for five seasons before he was traded to New York. He retired as a player in June, 1984, then was a Yankee coach from that time until being named manager.

HOUSTON—ART HOWE

Born December 15, 1946, Pittsburgh, PA . . . Resides: Houston, TX . . . 6' 1" . . . 200 . . . Married Elizabeth (Betty) Louise Falconio . . . Three children, Stephanie, Gretchen and Matthew.

After spending more than seven seasons in an Astros uniform as a player, Art Howe returned to the Houston organization on November 7, 1988, when he was named the 10th manager in franchise history.

Despite being a rookie major league skipper in 1989, Howe guided the Astros to an 86-76 mark. The club finished in third place in the National League West, only six games behind the pennant-winning Giants. In 1990, he guided a club in its first year of a rebuilding process to a 75-87 mark and fourth place tie with the San Diego Padres. Howe was an All-Star coach in 1991 and guided the youngest club in baseball to a 65-97 record.

Howe returned to the Astros after working as a coach for the Texas Rangers for four seasons. During his tenure with the Rangers, he worked as a third base coach, first base coach and hitting instructor. His previous managing experience included four winters in the Puerto Rican Winter League at Bayamon in 1979, 1980 and 1982, and at Ponce in 1985. He was named Manager of the year in 1980.

A .260 lifetime hitter, Howe played in 891 major league games. His playing career spanned more than 10 seasons and included stops in Pittsburgh, Houston and St. Louis. His best single-season was 1981 when he led the Astros with a .296 average. In May 1981, he established what is still the Houston all-time best hitting streak at 23 games.

Howe was a member of Houston's 1980 West Division championship team. He had a homer, two singles and four RBI in the Astros' division-clinching 7-1 win over Los Angeles in a one-game playoff at Dodger Stadium.

The 1992 season is Howe's 22nd in professional baseball. Born in Pittsburgh, he starred in football and baseball at Shaler High in Glenshaw, PA, graduating in 1964. He played four years of baseball and one year of football at the University of Wyoming. He was a quarterback for the Cowboys' football team before a back injury ended his grid career.

LOS ANGELES—TOM LASORDA

Born September 22, 1927, Norristown, PA . . . Resides: Fullerton, CA . . . 5'9" . . . 185 . . . Married Jo . . . One child, Laura.

The "dean" of Major League managers, Tom Lasorda enters his 16th season as manager of the Los Angeles Dodgers. Only two men in Dodger history have skippered the Dodgers longer or won more games than Lasorda—Walter Alston (23 years and 2,042 wins) and Wilbert Robinson (18 years and 1,375 wins).

Lasorda, who took over as Dodger manager upon Alston's retirement on Sept. 29, 1976, has a 1276-1100 record and has been with one club longer than any other active manager in the majors.

In Lasorda's 16 seasons, he has guided the Dodgers to a World Championship in 1981 and '88, National League pennants in 1977, '78, '81 and '88 and Western Division titles in 1977, '78, '81, '83, '85 and '88. His 1980 club tied for the division title with Houston, only to lose in a one-game playoff.

The 1992 season marks Lasorda's 43rd year in the Dodger organization. His Dodger career began in 1949 after he signed his first professional contract with the Philadelphia Phillies in 1945. He played 11 years in the Dodger organization, mostly in Montreal. He was with the Brooklyn club parts of the 1954 and '55 seasons. He also played for Kansas City in 1956. Lasorda ended his playing career in 1960 and became a scout for the Dodgers for five years. He was the manager in the Dodgers minor league system for seven years, his teams winning five pennants. Lasorda was selected The Sporting News' Minor League Manager of the Year in 1970. He served as third-base coach for the Dodgers from 1973-76.

Lasorda has earned Manager of the Year awards from the BBWAA (1983 and '88), AP (1977, '81 and '83) and UPI (1977, '83 and '88). He finished tied for third in the 1990 BBWAA Manager of the Year voting last season.

By guiding the Dodgers to a pennant in 1977, Lasorda became only the 19th manager in history to win a league title in his first year of managing in the majors. He also became only the second manager in N.L. history to win league titles in his first two full years of managing in the majors, 1977 and '78.

MONTREAL—TOM RUNNELLS

Born April 17, 1955, Greeley, CO . . . Resides: Greeley, CO . . . 6' . . . 175 . . . Married Kathy . . . Two children, April and Tom, Jr.

Tom Runnells, at 36, became the youngest manager in the majors when he was named on June 3, 1991, succeeding Buck Rodgers after the Expos began the season with a 20-29 record. He is the second Expos' manager to have previously coached third base for the club. Dick Williams coached third in 1970 and took over as manager in 1977.

Under Runnells, the Expos posted a 51-61 record, for a 71-90 final mark. Greeley, Colorado, a town of 20,000, boasts two major league managers, Greg Riddoch of the Padres and Runnells, living six blocks apart.

Runnells was named the American Association's All-Star Manager in 1989 and was winner of the Casey Stengel Award as the league's Manager of the Year. Managed the Indianapolis Indians to an 87-59 record and the regular season championship in the American Association. In 1988 at AA Chattanooga, in the Reds' organization, he led his team to the first-half title and the post-season championship. In 1987, his first managerial assignment was at Vermont of the Eastern League.

Was appointed Expos' third base coach and infield instructor on November 15, 1989, for the 1990 season, until being named manager.

NEW YORK—JEFF TORBORG

Born November 26, 1941, Westfield NJ . . . Resides: Mountainside, NJ . . . 6' . . . 210 . . . Married Sue Barber . . . Three sons, Doug, Greg, Dale.

Jeff Torborg signed a four-year contract on October 11, 1991 to become the 14th manager in New York Mets history.

For the last three seasons, the 50-year-old Mountainside, NJ resident, managed the Chicago White Sox. In 1990, he was a unanimous choice as the American League Manager of the Year as he guided the Sox to a 94-68 record (after a 69-92 mark in 1989) and second place in the West. Last season Chicago was 87-75 and again finished in second place.

Torborg, who earned his BS Degree in Education from Rutgers University and holds a Master's Degree in Athletic Administration from Montclair State, began his managerial career on June 19, 1977 when he succeeded Frank Robinson at Cleveland. He stayed with the Indians until July 23, 1979.

The Westfield, NJ native played 10 years in the major leagues as a catcher, seven with the Dodgers and three with the Angels. He was a member of LA's 1965 World Championship team and the 1966 NL pennant-winning club. He also caught three no-hitters in his career, Sandy Koufax in 1965, Billy Singer in 1970 and Nolan Ryan with the Angels in 1973. Jeff was behind the plate when Don Drysdale threw his fifth consecutive shutout in 1968.

Jeff also was a coach with the Indians from 1975-1977 and the Yankees from 1979-1988.

While at Rutgers, Torborg batted .537 as a senior to lead the NCAA in hitting. He is a member of the New Jersey Governor's Council on Physical Fitness and Sports. Incidentally, his Master's Thesis at Montclair State was written on "The Effects of Platooning in Baseball."

PHILADELPHIA—JIM FREGOSI

Born April 4, 1942, San Francisco, CA . . . Resides: Tarpon Springs, FL . . . 6'2" . . . 210 . . . Married Joni Dunn . . . Four children, Jim Jr., Jennifer, Nicole and Robert.

Became the 44th manager in Phillies history, April 23, 1991, replacing Nick Leyva after 13 games. Had a 74-75 record with the Phils, leading them to a third place finish, best since 1986.

Fregosi came to the Phillies organization as a Special Assignment Scout for Lee Thomas, May 29, 1989 and was named Minor League Pitching Instructor/Special Assignment for the 1990 season.

Prior to the Phillies, Fregosi managed the California Angels from 1978-1981 leading them to their first AL pennant in 1979. He then managed the Louisville Redbirds from 1983-1986, winning the Eastern Division championship in 1983 and 1985. League's Manager of the Year in 1983 and shared the honor in 1985. Replaced Tony LaRussa as the Chicago White Sox manager, June 22, 1986, where he remained through the 1988 season.

Retired after an 18-year major league career, June 1, 1978 to manage the California Angels. Was an American League All-Star six times in his career and a Gold Glove recipient in 1967. Played mainly at shortstop for the Angels (1961-71), New York Mets (1972-73), Texas Rangers (1973-77) and Pittsburgh Pirates (1977-78). Upon retiring, Fregosi held the Angels all-time records in games, at-bats, runs, hits, doubles, triples, extra-base hits and total bases.

PITTSBURGH—JIM LEYLAND

Born December 15, 1944, Toledo, OH . . . Resides: Pittsburgh, PA . . . 6'0" . . . 180 . . . Married Katie O'Connor . . . One son, Patrick.

In terms of seniority in the National League, only Los Angeles' Tom Lasorda and San Francisco's Roger Craig have been with their teams longer than Jim Leyland.

Since his first season with the Pirates in 1986, Leyland has guided Pittsburgh to a 496-474 record and back-to-back division titles in 1990 and 1991. With the club's 44th victory this season, Leyland will become the fourth winningest manager in Pirate history.

Following the 1990 season, Jim Leyland earned 17 of the 24 first-place votes by the Baseball Writers' Association of America for National League Manager of the Year after leading the Pirates to a 95-67 mark and their first Eastern Division title in 11 years. He also was named N.L. Manager of the Year by United Press International and The Sporting News.

Leyland became skipper of the Pirates on November 20, 1985, following more than 22 years of professional experience, including 11 as a manager in the Detroit Tigers' farm system. Just prior to joining the Bucs, Jim spent four seasons as the Chicago White Sox's third-base coach and outfield instructor.

In 1971, at the age of 26, Leyland received his first managerial assignment, taking over the Tigers' Bristol club in the Appalachian Rookie League. The former catcher capped off his 11-year minor league managerial career with three seasons at the Triple-A Evansville club. His teams advanced to the playoffs in five of his last six seasons, winning three league titles. For these accomplishments, he was named Manager-of-the-Year in the Class-A Florida State League in 1977 and 1978 and also for the Triple-A American Association in 1979.

ST. LOUIS—JOE TORRE

Born July 18, 1940, Brooklyn, NY . . . Resides: St. Louis, MO . . . 6'1" . . . 195 . . . Married Alice . . . Three children, Michael, Lauren and Tina.

Joe Torre finished his first full season as the Cardinals' manager in 1991 by guiding the team to a surprising second-place finish. Although picked by many to finish last, Torre's club finished with an 84-78 record. Since he returned to the organization where he spent six outstanding seasons as a player, Torre has posted a managerial record of 108-112. The Brooklyn native has been involved in professional baseball as a player, manager and broadcaster since 1960.

Torre broke into the major leagues with the Milwaukee Braves in 1960. In 1964, and again in 1966, Torre became the first major-league catcher since 1955 to bat over .300, hit at least 20 home runs and drive in 100 or more runs.

The Braves moved to Atlanta in 1966, and Torre smacked the first regular-season home run in Atlanta's Fulton County Stadium history on April 12, 1966. His 36 home runs in 1966 remains the Braves' record for catchers.

The Cardinals acquired Torre for Orlando Cepeda on March 17, 1969. Torre played both first and third base for St. Louis and won the N.L. Most Valuable Player award in 1971 and the N.L. batting title with a .363 average. He also led the National League with 230 hits and 137 RBIs during the '71 campaign.

On October 13, 1974, the Cardinals traded Torre to the New York Mets for Ray Sadecki and Tommy Moore. Torre was named the player-manager of the Mets on May 31, 1977, becoming the first N.L. player-manager since the Cardinals' Solly Hemus in 1959. His playing career ended only 18 days later, when Torre became a full-time manager. He retired with a .297 batting average, 2,342 hits and 1,185 RBIs.

Torre earned many honors as a player, including nine All-Star Game invitations.

Torre spent five years as the Mets' manager and accumulated a 286-420 record. In 1982, he was named the Atlanta Braves' manager, and guided them to their first divisional title in 13 seasons. Torre was named the Associated Press Manager of the Year in 1982.

Torre left the Braves after three seasons with a 257-229 record. He spent the next six years as a television broadcaster for the California Angels.

On August 1, 1990, Torre was named manager of the Cardinals, following Whitey Herzog's resignation.

SAN DIEGO—GREG RIDDOCH

Born July 17, 1945 in Greeley, CO . . . Resides: Greeley, CO . . . 5'11" . . . 175 . . . Married Linda . . . Two sons, Rory and Raliegh.

Greg Riddoch guided the Padres to an 84-78 record, the third best mark in club history, in his first full season as manager. The Padres had a 44-35 record after the All-Star break to earn a third place finish in the Western Division. His overall record with the Padres is 122-122.

Riddoch took over as manager of the Padres on July 11, 1990, during the All-Star break. The team lost 11 of its first 12 games, then posted a 37-33 record for the last 70 games. Overall, the team was 38-44 after Riddoch took over.

Greg had been a coach for the Padres since 1987, serving at first base and in the dugout at various times. Prior to joining the major league team, he was in the San Diego organization in 1986 as Director of Minor League Instruction.

Riddoch's previous managing experience included eight seasons in the Cincinnati Reds farm system at Eugene and Seattle of the Northwest League and Billings of the Pioneer League with an overall record of 295-289 (.505). His 1975 Eugene team won the league title and his 1980 team tied for first place.

Greg spent a total of 19 years in the Cincinnati organization as a minor league infielder, minor league manager, scout and Director of Minor League Clubs.

He played baseball and basketball at Northern Colorado University, where he earned a B.A. degree in Business Administration. He has a Master's Degree in Education Administration from Colorado State University.

SAN FRANCISCO GIANTS—ROGER CRAIG

Born February 17, 1930 in Durham, NC . . . Resides: Warner Springs, CA . . . 6'4" . . . 195 . . . Married Carolyn . . . Four children, Sherry, Roger Jr., Teresa and Vikki.

Roger Craig is now the San Francisco Giants all-time record holder for games managed with 990. Craig's .519 winning percentage is the best by a SF Giants skipper. Five of his six years at the helm have produced winning campaigns.

In 1989 Craig became the first manager ever to win two championships within four years of a 100-loss campaign. In 1987, just two years after a 100-loss season in 1985, Roger guided the Giants to the National League West title and their first LCS appearance since 1971. In 1989 Roger took San Francisco one step further, leading the team to its first World Series berth since 1962, despite manipulating a team record 21 starting pitchers.

Roger has coached, managed or scouted for the past 23 seasons, since his retirement as a player in 1967. He managed the San Diego Padres in 1978 and 1979 and was the pitching coach for the Detroit Tigers from 1980 through their World Championship 1984 campaign. Craig also served as pitching coach for the Astros (1974-75) and Padres (1976-77). He instructed the Dodgers' minor league hurlers in 1973 and managed Albuquerque in 1968.

Craig broke into the Majors in 1955 with the Brooklyn Dodgers, and ended with a 74-98 mark and a 3.82 ERA in 12 big league seasons. He has played or coached for five World Championship teams: Brooklyn 1955-56, Los Angeles 1959, St. Louis 1964 and Detroit 1984.

NATIONAL LEAGUE MANAGERS, 1876 TO 1992

BRAVES

1876-1881	Harry Wright
1882-1888	John F. Morrill
1889	Jim Hart
1890-1901	Frank Selee
1902-1904	Al Buckenberger
1905-1907	Fred Tenney
1908	Joe Kelley
1909	Frank Bowerman & Harry Smith
1910	Fred Lake
1911	Fred Tenney
1912	John Kling
1913-1920	George Stallings
1921-1923	Fred Mitchell
1924-1927	Dave Bancroft
1928	Jack Slattery & Rogers Hornsby
1929	Emil Fuchs & Rabbit Maranville
1930-1937	Bill McKechnie
1938-1943	Casey Stengel
1944	Bob Coleman
1945	Coleman & Del Bissonette
1946-1950	Billy Southworth
1951	Southworth & Tommy Holmes
1952	Holmes & Charlie Grimm
1953-1955	Charlie Grimm
1956	Grimm & Fred Haney
1957-1959	Fred Haney
1960	Charlie Dressen
1961	Dressen & Birdie Tebbetts
1962	Birdie Tebbetts
1963-1965	Bobby Bragan
1966	Bragan & Billy Hitchcock
1967	Hitchcock & Ken Silvestri
1968-1971	Luman Harris
1972	Harris & Eddie Mathews
1973	Eddie Mathews
1974	Mathews & Clyde King
1975	King & Connie Ryan
1976-1977	Dave Bristol
1978-1981	Bobby Cox
1982-1984	Joe Torre
1985	Eddie Haas & Bobby Wine
1986-1987	Chuck Tanner
1988	Tanner & Russ Nixon
1989	Russ Nixon
1990	Nixon & Bobby Cox
1991-1992	Bobby Cox

CUBS

1876-1877	Al Spalding
1878	Bob Ferguson
1879-1897	Cap Anson
1898-1899	Tom Burns
1900-1901	Tom Loftus
1902-1904	Frank Selee
1905	Selee & Frank Chance
1906-1912	Frank Chance
1913	John Evers
1914	Hank O'Day
1915	Roger Bresnahan
1916	Joe Tinker
1917-1920	Fred Mitchell
1921	John Evers & Bill Killefer
1922-1924	Bill Killefer
1925	Killefer, Rabbit Maranville & George Gibson
1926-1929	Joe McCarthy
1930	McCarthy & Rogers Hornsby
1931	Rogers Hornsby
1932	Hornsby & Charlie Grimm
1933-1937	Charlie Grimm
1938	Grimm & Gabby Hartnett
1939-1940	Gabby Hartnett
1941-1943	Jimmy Wilson
1944	Wilson & Charlie Grimm
1945-1948	Charlie Grimm
1949	Grimm & Frank Frisch
1950	Frank Frisch
1951	Frisch & Phil Cavarretta
1952-53	Phil Cavarretta
1954-1956	Stan Hack
1957-1959	Bob Scheffing
1960	Charlie Grimm & Lou Boudreau
1961-1965	None
1966-1971	Leo Durocher
1972	Durocher & Whitey Lockman
1973	Whitey Lockman
1974	Lockman & Jim Marshall
1975-1976	Jim Marshall
1977-1979	Herman Franks
1980	Preston Gomez & Joe Amalfitano
1981	Joe Amalfitano
1982	Lee Elia
1983	Elia & Charlie Fox
1984-1985	Jim Frey
1986	Frey & Gene Michael
1987	Michael & Frank Lucchesi
1988-1990	Don Zimmer
1991	Zimmer & Jim Essian
1992	Jim Lefebvre

REDS

1876	Charles Gould
1877	Gould & Lipman Pike
1878	Calvin McVey
1879	McVey & James "Deacon" White
1880	John Clapp
1881-1889	Not in league
1890-1891	Tom Loftus
1892-1894	Charles Comiskey
1895-1899	Buck Ewing
1900	Robert Allen
1901	John McPhee
1902	McPhee, Frank Bancroft & Joe Kelley
1903-1905	Joe Kelley
1906-1907	Ned Hanlon
1908	John Ganzel
1909-1911	Clark Griffith
1912	Hank O'Day
1913	Joe Tinker
1914-1915	Buck Herzog
1916	Herzog & Christy Mathewson
1917	Christy Mathewson
1918	Mathewson & Heinie Groh
1919-1923	Pat Moran
1924-1929	Jack Hendricks
1930-1932	Dan Howley
1933	Donie Bush
1934	Bob O'Farrell & Chuck Dressen
1935-1936	Chuck Dressen
1937	Dressen & Bobby Wallace
1938-1946	Bill McKechnie
1947	Johnny Neun
1948	Neun & Bucky Walters
1949	Bucky Walters
1950-1951	Luke Sewell
1952	Sewell & Rogers Hornsby
1953	Rogers Hornsby
1954-1957	Birdie Tebbetts
1958	Tebbetts & Jimmy Dykes
1959	Mayo Smith & Fred Hutchinson
1960-1964	Fred Hutchinson
1965	Dick Sisler
1966	Don Heffner & Dave Bristol
1967-1969	Dave Bristol
1970-1978	George "Sparky" Anderson
1979-1981	John McNamara
1982	McNamara & Russ Nixon
1983	Russ Nixon
1984	Vern Rapp & Pete Rose
1985-1988	Pete Rose
1989	Rose & Tommy Helms
1990-1992	Lou Piniella

ASTROS

1962-1963	Harry Craft
1964	Craft & Lum Harris
1965	Lum Harris
1966-1967	Grady Hatton
1968	Hatton & Harry Walker
1969-1971	Harry Walker
1972	Walker & Leo Durocher
1973	Leo Durocher
1974	Preston Gomez
1975	Gomez & Bill Virdon
1976-1981	Bill Virdon
1982	Virdon & Bob Lillis
1983-1985	Bob Lillis
1986-1988	Hal Lanier
1989-1992	Art Howe

DODGERS

1890	William McGunnigle
1891-1892	John Montgomery Ward
1893-1896	Dave Foutz
1897	William Barnie
1898	Barnie, Mike Griffin & C.H. Ebbets
1899-1905	Ned Hanlon
1906-1908	Patsy Donovan
1909	Harry Lumley
1910-1913	Bill Dahlen
1914-1931	Wilbert Robinson
1932-1933	Max Carey
1934-1936	Casey Stengel
1937-1938	Burleigh Grimes
1939-1946	Leo Durocher
1947	Burt Shotton
1948	Leo Durocher & Burt Shotton
1949-1950	Burt Shotton
1951-1953	Chuck Dressen
1954-1976	Walter Alston
1977-1992	Tom Lasorda

EXPOS

1969-1975	Gene Mauch
1976	Karl Kuehl & Charlie Fox
1977-1980	Dick Williams
1981	Williams & Jim Fanning
1982	Jim Fanning
1983	Bill Virdon
1984	Virdon & Jim Fanning
1985-1990	Buck Rodgers
1991	Rodgers & Tom Runnells
1992	Tom Runnells

METS

1962-1964	Casey Stengel
1965	Stengel & Wes Westrum
1966	Wes Westrum
1967	Westrum & Salty Parker
1968-1971	Gil Hodges
1972-1974	Yogi Berra
1975	Berra & Roy McMillan
1976	Joe Frazier
1977	Frazier & Joe Torre
1978-1981	Joe Torre
1982	George Bamberger
1983	Bamberger & Frank Howard
1984-1989	Dave Johnson
1990	Johnson & Bud Harrelson
1991	Harrelson & Mike Cubbage
1992	Jeff Torborg

PHILLIES

1876	A.L.H. Wright
1877-1882	Not in league
1883	Horace Phillips
1884-1893	Harry Wright
1894-1895	Arthur Irwin
1896	Billy Nash
1897	George Stallings
1898	Stallings & Bill Shettsline
1899-1902	Bill Shettsline
1903	Chief Zimmer
1904-1906	Hugh Duffy
1907-1909	Billy Murray
1910-1914	Charlie Dooin
1915-1918	Pat Moran
1919	Jack Coombs & Gavvy Cravath
1920	Gavvy Cravath
1921	Wild Bill Donovan & Irvin Wilhelm
1922	Irvin Wilhelm
1923-1926	Art Fletcher
1927	Stuffy McInnis
1928-1933	Burt Shotton
1934-1937	Jimmy Wilson
1938	Wilson & Hans Lobert
1939-1941	Doc Prothro
1942	Hans Lobert
1943	Bucky Harris & Fred Fitzsimmons
1944	Fred Fitzsimmons
1945	Fitzsimmons & Ben Chapman
1946-1947	Ben Chapman
1948	Chapman & Eddie Sawyer
1949-1951	Eddie Sawyer
1952	Sawyer & Steve O'Neill
1953	Steve O'Neill
1954	O'Neill & Terry Moore
1955-1957	Mayo Smith
1958	Smith & Eddie Sawyer
1959	Eddie Sawyer
1960	Sawyer & Gene Mauch
1961-1967	Gene Mauch
1968	Mauch & Bob Skinner
1969	Skinner & George Myatt
1970-1971	Frank Lucchesi
1972	Lucchesi & Paul Owens
1973-1978	Danny Ozark
1979	Ozark & Dallas Green
1980-1981	Dallas Green
1982	Pat Corrales
1983	Corrales & Paul Owens
1984	Paul Owens
1985-1986	John Felske
1987	John Felske & Lee Elia
1988	Elia & John Vukovich
1989-1990	Nick Leyva
1991	Leyva & Jim Fregosi
1992	Jim Fregosi

PIRATES

1887-1888	Horace B. Phillips
1889	Phillips, Fred Dunlap & Ned Hanlon
1890	Guy Hecker
1891	Ned Hanlon & Bill McGunnigle
1892	Tommy Burns & Al Buckenberger
1893	Al Buckenberger
1894	Buckenberger & Connie Mack
1895-1896	Connie Mack
1897	Patsy Donovan
1898	W.H. Watkins
1899	Watkins & Patsy Donovan
1900-1915	Fred Clarke
1916	Jimmy Callahan
1917	Callahan, Hans Wagner & Hugo Bezdek
1918-1919	Hugo Bezdek
1920-1921	George Gibson
1922	Gibson & Bill McKechnie
1923-1926	Bill McKechnie
1927-1928	Donie Bush
1929	Bush & Jewel Ens
1930-1931	Jewel Ens
1932-1933	George Gibson
1934	Gibson & Pie Traynor
1935-1939	Pie Traynor
1940-1946	Frank Frisch
1947	Billy Herman
1948-1952	Bill Meyer
1953-1955	Fred Haney
1956	Bobby Bragan
1957	Bragan & Danny Murtaugh
1958-1964	Danny Murtaugh
1965-1966	Harry Walker
1967	Walker & Danny Murtaugh
1968-1969	Larry Shepard
1970-1971	Danny Murtaugh
1972	Bill Virdon
1973	Virdon & Danny Murtaugh
1974-1976	Danny Murtaugh
1977-1985	Chuck Tanner
1986-1992	Jim Leyland

CARDINALS

1876	S.M. Graffen
1877	J.R. Lucas & George McManus
1878-1884	Not in league
1885	Fred Dunlap, Benjamin Fine & H.V. Lucas
1886	Gus Schmelz
1887-1891	Not in league
1892	Chris Von Der Ahe
1893	W.H. Watkins
1894	George Miller & H.B. Martin
1895	Al Buckenberger, Joe Quinn, Lewis Phelan & Chris Von Der Ahe
1896	Harry Diddledock, Arlie Latham, Roger Connor & Tom Dowd
1897	Dowd, Hugh Nicol, Billy Hallman & Chris Von Der Ahe
1898	Tim Hurst
1899	Oliver Tebeau
1900	Tebeau & Louis Heilbroner
1901-1903	Patsy Donovan
1904	Charles "Kid" Nichols
1905	Nichols, Jimmy Burke & Matthew Robison
1906-1908	John J. McCloskey
1909-1912	Roger Bresnahan
1913-1917	Miller Huggins
1918	Jack Hendricks
1919-1924	Branch Rickey
1925	Rickey & Rogers Hornsby
1926	Rogers Hornsby
1927	Bob O'Farrell
1928	Bill McKechnie
1929	McKechnie & Billy Southworth
1930-1932	Gabby Street
1933	Street & Frank Frisch
1934-1937	Frank Frisch
1938	Frisch & Mike Gonzalez
1939	Ray Blades
1940	Blades, Gonzalez & Billy Southworth
1941-1945	Billy Southworth
1946-1950	Eddie Dyer
1951	Marty Marion
1952-1954	Eddie Stanky
1955	Stanky & Harry Walker
1956-1957	Fred Hutchinson
1958	Hutchinson & Stan Hack
1959-1960	Solly Hemus
1961	Hemus & Johnny Keane
1962-1964	Johnny Keane
1965-1976	Red Schoendienst
1977	Vern Rapp
1978	Rapp & Ken Boyer
1979	Ken Boyer
1980	Boyer & Whitey Herzog
1981-1989	Whitey Herzog
1990	Herzog & Joe Torre
1991-1992	Joe Torre

PADRES

1969-1971	Preston Gomez
1972	Gomez & Don Zimmer
1973	Don Zimmer
1974-1976	John McNamara
1977	McNamara & Alvin Dark
1978-1979	Roger Craig
1980	Jerry Coleman
1981	Frank Howard
1982-1985	Dick Williams
1986	Steve Boros
1987	Larry Bowa
1988	Bowa & Jack McKeon
1989	Jack McKeon
1990	McKeon & Greg Riddoch
1991-1992	Greg Riddoch

GIANTS

1876	W.H. Cammeyer
1877-1882	Not in league
1883	John Clapp
1884	James L. Price
1885-1891	Jim Mutrie
1892	Pat Powers
1893-1894	John Montgomery Ward
1895	George Davis, Jack Doyle & Harvey Watkins
1896	Arthur Irwin & Bill Joyce
1897	Bill Joyce
1898	Joyce & Cap Anson
1899	John B. Day & Fred Hoey
1900	Buck Ewing & George Davis
1901	George Davis
1902	Horace Fogel, George Smith & John McGraw
1903-1931	John J. McGraw
1932	McGraw & Bill Terry
1933-1941	Bill Terry
1942-1947	Mel Ott
1948	Ott & Leo Durocher
1949-1955	Leo Durocher
1956-1959	Bill Rigney
1960	Rigney & Tom Sheehan
1961-1964	Alvin Dark
1965-1968	Herman Franks
1969	Clyde King
1970	King & Charlie Fox
1971-1973	Charlie Fox
1974	Fox & Wes Westrum
1975	Wes Westrum
1976	Bill Rigney
1977-1978	Joe Altobelli
1979	Altobelli & Dave Bristol
1980	Dave Bristol
1981-1983	Frank Robinson
1984	Robinson & Danny Ozark
1985	Jim Davenport & Roger Craig
1986-1992	Roger Craig

MEET THE ROOKIES 1992

THE FOLLOWING ARE SHORT BIOS OF SOME OF THE NEW YOUNG PLAYERS WE MIGHT SEE IN NATIONAL LEAGUE GAMES DURING 1992.

for Atlanta—

KEITH MITCHELL, outfielder, hit .318, including .452 (14-for-31) in 48 games for Atlanta after being called up July 18, 1991. He started 0-for-5 as a pinch-hitter, then went on a 19-for-46 (.413) tear. He batted .390 (16-for-41) in his nine starts. He started the season at AA Greenville, where he hit .327 with 10 HRs and 47 RBIs in 60 games before being promoted to AAA Richmond (.330, 2 HRs, 17 RBIs in 25 games). Keith is a second cousin of Seattle's Kevin Mitchell.

MARK WOHLERS, righthanded pitcher, was named USA Today's Minor League Player of the Year after posting 32 saves in 33 opportunities in 1991 (21-for-21 at AA Greenville, 11-for-12 at AAA Richmond). He had his contract purchased by Atlanta August 16 and earned his first Major League save the next night at San Diego. He did not allow an earned run in his first six appearances (7.1 innings). He pitched two perfect innings in the Braves' combined no-hitter vs. Padres September 11, relieving Kent Mercker and serving as setup man for Alejandro Pena. Wohlers went 2-for-3 in save chances for Atlanta (3-1, 3.20, 13 Ks, 19.2 IP, 17 Gs).

for Chicago—

LANCE DICKSON, 22, spent his first full professional season at Iowa of the American Association (AAA) in 1991, going 4-4 with a 3.11 ERA in 18 starts. The left-hander ranked seventh in the league in strikeouts with 101 in 101.1 innings and averaged 9.0 strikeouts per 9.0 innings, the highest ratio in the league. Since being selected 23rd overall in the 1991 June free agent amateur draft, he has made 29 minor league starts and has 212 strikeouts in 177.2 innings (10.7 per 9.0 innings).

TURK WENDELL, 24, was acquired from the Atlanta organization last September after combining for an 11-5 mark with a 2.67 ERA in 28 games (23 starts) at Greenville of the Southern League (AA) and Richmond of the International League (AAA). A right-hander, Wendell was 11-3 with a 2.56 ERA at Greenville, striking out 122 batters and allowing only four homers in 147.2 innings. He led Southern League pitchers in winning percentage (.786), ranked sixth in ERA and tied for sixth in victories. He pitched in Puerto Rico this off-season and was 7-1 with a 0.94 ERA in nine starts.

for Cincinnati—

REGGIE SANDERS, a 24-year-old outfielder, spent most of the 1991 season at Double-A Chattanooga, before earning a late-season callup to the Reds. In his first year at Double-A, he hit .315 with 8 homers, 49 RBI and 15 steals in 86 games. Sanders was named to the Southern League's post-season All-Star team, to Baseball America's All-Star team for all Double-A leagues and was selected the second-best major league prospect in the Southern League. Baseball America named Reggie the Southern League's Best Batting Prospect, Best Defensive Outfielder and Most Exciting Player. He was promoted to the Reds on Aug. 22, but played in only 9 games for Cincinnati, suffering a shoulder separation in his second game and re-aggravating the injury in late September.

DAN WILSON, a 23-year-old catcher, was the Reds' No. 1 draft choice (7th pick in the nation) in June, 1990, out of the University of Minnesota, where he earned first team All-America honors. In 1991, his first full year of pro ball, Wilson hit .315 in 52 games for Class A Charleston (WV), then was promoted to Double-A Chattanooga in June and batted .257 in 81 games. Although he did not spend even half the season at Charleston, South Atlantic League managers named him the league's best defensive catcher. At Charleston, he threw out 44% of runners trying to steal and he gunned down 38% of would-be base stealers after his move to Double-A.

for Houston—

JEFF JUDEN, 21, was Houston's top pick in the June 1989 draft (12th selection overall). The hard-throwing right-hander pitched at three levels in 1991, landing in Houston in only his third season as a pro. Opened the year at Double A Jackson and went 6-3 with a 3.10 ERA in 16 starts. Was promoted to Triple A Tucson and had a 3-2 mark with a 3.18 ERA in 10 outings. He won Game Three of the PCL Championship Series with the Toros facing elimination. Juden worked eight innings and allowed one run as Tucson rallied to win the series, 3-2. Was 0-2 with a 6.00 ERA in four September appearances for the Astros.

SCOTT SERVAIS, 24, is a catcher who will have an opportunity to win Houston's every-day job with Craig Biggio's move to second base. He opened 1991 at Triple A Tucson, but joined the Astros in mid-July. Hit .324 in 60 games for the Toros. Was on the DL

from August 4-September 7 after fracturing a bone in his right hand when he was struck by a foul tip. Went hitless in his first 22 major league at-bats, then finished the season going 6-for-19 (.315). Batted .295 for Magallanes in Venezuela this past winter.

for Los Angeles—

ERIC KARROS, 24, played in 14 games for the Dodgers in 1991 and was 1-for-14 with an RBI . . . his one hit was a pinch-hit, game-tying double in the 12th inning of L.A.'s 6-5, 12-inning win. Was selected as the Dodgers' Minor League (Position) Player of the Year. He batted .316 with 22 home runs and 101 RBI at Albuquerque (AAA) in 1991. He also slugged 33 doubles and had a .551 slugging percentage.

PEDRO MARTINEZ, 20, was a combined 18-8 with a 2.29 ERA at three different levels in the Dodgers minor league system in 1991. Martinez, the younger brother of Ramon Martinez, was 8-0 with a 2.05 ERA at Bakersfield (A), 7-5 with a 1.76 ERA at San Antonio (AA) and 3-3 with a 3.66 ERA for Albuquerque (AAA). For his success in 1991, Martinez was named THE SPORTING NEWS Minor League Player of the Year and the Dodgers' Pitcher of the Year.

CARLOS HERNANDEZ, 24, appeared in 15 games with the Dodgers in 1991 and batted .214 with one RBI. Had an outstanding season for Albuquerque, batting .345 with eight home runs and 44 RBI. He fell one at bat short of qualifying for the league leaders in batting, but his .345 average was second best in the PCL. He was selected to the PCL All-Star team.

for Montreal—

MATT STAIRS, 23, was the 1991 AA-Eastern League's MVP and batting champion. The lefthanded hitter batted .333 for Harrisburg with 30 doubles, 10 triples, 13 home runs and 78 RBIs in his first year at the AA level. He also collected 23 stolen bases. He was selected on the AA All-Star squad at the end of the season. Stairs played second, third and the outfield. Stairs is from Stanley, New Brunswick and was a member of the Canadian Olympic Team at the 1988 games in Seoul, Korea. He was signed by the Expos as a free agent.

JOHN VANDER WAL, 25, is a lefthanded hitting outfielder who was named on the 1991 American Association All-Star team. He finished among the top 10 in the league in nine offensive categories. He was second in runs (84), doubles (36), extra-base hits (59) and slugging average (.496); third in total bases (237); fourth in walks (79) and on-base percentage (.393); eighth in runs batted in (71) and ninth in average (.392). He was promoted to the Expos' roster last September.

for New York—

ANTHONY YOUNG, 26, appeared in 10 games for the Mets last September, picking up his first two major league wins while also winning seven games at AAA-Tidewater and ranking 10th in the International League with a 3.73 ERA at the time of his callup. The righthanded pitcher was Pitcher of the Year in the Texas League in 1990 after leading the circuit in wins (15), and ERA (1.65). Started eight games for the Mets in 1991, including an outing vs. St. Louis on September 22 in which he tossed six shutout innings before allowing a home run to Felix Jose.

TODD HUNDLEY, 22, will be given the chance to be the Mets starting catcher after brief appearances in the majors in both 1990 and 91. The switch-hitter batted .273 in 125 games at AAA-Tidewater in 1991 with 14 homers and 66 RBI. He was also named the fourth-best prospect in the International League in a vote of managers conducted by Baseball America.

for Philadelphia—

ANDY ASHBY, a 24-year-old righthanded pitcher made his major league debut June 6, last year, starting at Cincinnati. He became the 11th major league pitcher, first Phillie, to strike out the side on nine pitches, June 15. He tied for the International League lead in complete games (6) and shutouts (3) and finished 5th in strikeouts (113) last season with Scranton. Was the Paul Owens Award winner for Best Pitcher in the Phillies minor leagues in 1990.

KIM BATISTE, a 24-year-old shortstop earned a September call-up last season, making his major league debut September 9 at Houston, where he also got his first hit (single). Was the Paul Owens Award winner for Best Player in the Phillies minor league system last season. He set career-highs last year at triple A in batting (.292), doubles (25) and hits (135). He was the Phillies 3rd pick in the June 1987 draft.

for Pittsburgh—

CARLOS GARCIA, shortstop, saw action in 12 games for the Pirates last year after his recall in September. He batted .250 (6-for-24) with two triples and one RBI in limited action. In 127 games with Buffalo (AAA), the 24-year-old Venezuelan batted .266 with

seven home runs, 60 RBI and 30 stolen bases. In addition, Garcia led American Association shortstops with 211 putouts.

PAUL MILLER, righthanded pitcher, pitched only one game at the major-league level last year (5.0 IP/3 ER), but put together a fine season in the minors. Miller, the Pirates' 53rd selection in the 1987 draft, was 12-4 with a 2.01 ERA in 25 starts with Carolina (AA) and Buffalo. In the last two seasons, the 26-year-old righty has gone 22-11 with a 2.22 ERA in 42 minor league starts.

for St. Louis—

MARK CLARK, pitcher, got off to a slow start last season after suffering off-the-field ankle injury prior to spring training. Started the year in May at Arkansas (AA), where he was 5-5 in 15 starts. Was promoted to Louisville (AAA) in late July, and posted a 3-2 mark with a 2.98 ERA in 7 games. Right-hander earned a September recall to St. Louis, where he impressed Cardinals' coaching staff in two late-season starts. Will be trying to crack Cards' pitching staff this season as a starter or middle reliever. The 23-year-old Clark was Cardinals 9th round selection in June, 1988, free-agent draft.

STAN ROYER, third baseman, enjoyed a productive season in his first full season at Triple-A Louisville. Had 14 home runs and 74 RBI to go along with a .254 batting average. Was recalled by the Cardinals in September and batted .286 (6-for-21) in 9 games after his promotion. The 24-year-old will need to have impressive spring in order to make opening day roster, for Cards management would prefer he see plenty of playing time at AAA rather than be used as bench player in St. Louis. Royer, who was drafted by Oakland in 1988, was involved in four-player trade to St. Louis in August, 1990, for outfielder Willie McGee.

for San Diego—

JEFF GARDNER had his third consecutive solid season at the Triple-A level with Tidewater, earning a late-season promotion to the Mets. Gardner batted .292 with 56 RBIs and 84 walks. He ranked among league leaders in batting average, walks, hits, at-bats and runs scored. He played in the Triple-A All-Star game and was named to the International League post-season All-Star team. He once drew 142 walks in 123 games, setting a South Atlantic League (A) record with Columbia in 1985. The infielder has been primarily a second baseman. He came to the Padres in an off-season trade with the Mets for pitcher Steve Rosenberg.

JEREMY HERNANDEZ is a hard-thrower who fanned 67 batters in 68.1 innings at Las Vegas (AAA) last summer while making the conversion from a starting pitcher to a bullpen closer. The tall (6-6) right-hander had 13 saves and a 4-8 record to go with a 4.53 ERA in 56 appearances, allowing just one home run. In a late-season trial with the Padres, Hernandez gave up just one unearned run in 14.1 innings over 9 appearances, fanning 9. It was his second full season in the Padres organization after a 1989 trade from St. Louis.

FRANK SEMINARA led the Class AA Texas League with 15 wins, setting a Wichita club record, in his first season in the Padres organization after being drafted from the Yankees organization in December, 1990. Seminara also led the TL with 6 complete games and 176 innings. The right-hander from Columbia University posted a 16-8 record and a 1.90 in 1990 and was named Pitcher of the Year in the Carolina League (A) for Prince William.

for San Francisco—

DAVE BURBA—Acquired from Seattle during the Winter Meetings in the Kevin Mitchell trade, this hard-throwing righthanded pitcher has a chance to help the Giants either as a starter or a reliever. With a 3.34 ERA in 113 minor league games and a 2-2 mark in 28 games for the Mariners over the past two seasons, this Ohio State grad is thought to be ready for full-time Major League service.

ROYCE CLAYTON—This slick-fielding shortstop helped Shreveport to its second consecutive Texas League title in 1991, while being tabbed as the top prospect in all of minor league baseball by The Sporting News and the No. 2 prospect in the Texas League by Baseball America. After posting a .280 average with 68 RBIs and 36 stolen bases in 126 games for Shreveport last season, this 22-year-old will battle for the Giants starting shortstop job in spring training.

TED WOOD—Has a chance to help the Giants off the bench in 1992 after a record-setting season at triple-A Phoenix in 1991. Led all triple-A players last season with 109 RBIs, setting a new record for a Phoenix franchise that had been in existence over 30 years. Also led the Pacific Coast League last year with 137 games played, 86 walks and 10 sacrifice flies. Has a .281 average with 73 doubles, 18 triples, 28 home runs and 224 RBIs in 382 minor league games since helping the 1988 Olympic Team to a gold medal by batting .474 in that competition.

COLLEGE PLAYING EXPERIENCE

ATLANTA
Damon Berryhill—Orange Coast College
Mike Bielecki—Valencia JC, Loyola College (MD)
Jeff Blauser—Sacramento City College
Sid Bream—Liberty Baptist (VA)
Marvin Freeman—Jackson State
Tommy Gregg—Wake Forest University
Brian Hunter—Cerritos Junior College
David Justice—Thomas More College
Charlie Leibrandt—Miami (OH) University
Greg Olson—University of Minnesota
Terry Pendleton—Fresno St., Oxnard JC
Deion Sanders—Florida State
Mike Stanton—Alvin (TX) Community College
Jeff Treadway—University of Georgia, Middle Georgia

CHICAGO
Paul Assenmacher—Aquinas College
Shawn Boskie—Modesto Junior College
Jim Bullinger—University of New Orleans
Doug Dascenzo—Florida College, Oklahoma State
Andre Dawson—Florida A&M University
Lance Dickson—University of Arizona
Joe Girardi—Northwestern University
Mark Grace—Saddleback College (CA), San Diego St.
Mike Harkey—Cal-State Fullerton
Jeff Hartsock—North Carolina State
Danny Jackson—U. of Oklahoma, Trinidad St. JC
Les Lancaster—U. of Arkansas, Dallas Baptist College
Ced Landrum—University of North Alabama
George Pedre—West Los Angeles College, Los Angeles
   Harbor JC
Kevin Roberson—Parkland Junior College
Gary Scott—Villanova University
Dave Smith—San Diego State University
Dwight Smith—Spartanburg Methodist College
Doug Strange—North Carolina State
Hector Villanueva—Univ. of Alabama-Birmingham
Jerome Walton—Enterprise State Junior College (AL)
Turk Wendell—Quinnipiac College
Rick Wilkins—Furman University, Florida JC

CINCINNATI
Scott Bankhead—University of North Carolina
Tim Belcher—Mt. Vernon Nazarene College
Freddie Benavides—Texas Christian University
Glenn Braggs—University of Hawaii
Jeff Branson—Livingston University
Tom Browning—LeMoyne College, Tenn. Wesleyan
Norm Charlton—Rice University
Rob Dibble—Florida Southern
Bill Doran—Miami University (OH)
Steve Foster—Blinn College, University of Texas-Arlington
Bob Geren—Mesa Community College, Point Loma College
Chris Hammond—Alabama-Birmingham, Gulf Coast CC
Billy Hatcher—Yavapai Community College
Cesar Hernandez—Autonoma University (Dom. Rep.)
Milton Hill—DeKalb Community College, Georgia College
Trevor Hoffman—Cypress College, University of Arizona
Barry Larkin—University of Michigan
Tim Layana—Loyola Marymount
Dave Martinez—Valencia Community College
Gino Minutelli—Southwestern Junior College
Hal Morris—University of Michigan
Ross Powell—University of Michigan
Tim Pugh—Oklahoma State University
Bip Roberts—University of Nevada-Las Vegas,
   Chabot College
Scott Ruskin—University of Florida
Chris Sabo—University of Michigan
Reggie Sanders—Spartanburg Methodist College
Mo Sanford—University of Alabama
Glenn Sutko—Spartanburg Methodist College, DeKalb CC
Greg Swindell—University of Texas

HOUSTON
Jeff Bagwell—Hartford
Craig Biggio—Seton Hall

Willie Blair—Morehead State
Ken Caminiti—San Jose State
Casey Candaele—Arizona
Mike Capel—Texas
Gary Cooper—Brigham Young
Steve Finley—Southern Illinois
Chris Gardner—Cuesta JC
Luis Gonzalez—South Alabama
Brian Griffiths—Mt. Hood JC
Pete Harnisch—Fordham
Xavier Hernandez—Southwestern Louisiana
Todd Jones—Jacksonville State
Darryl Kile—Chaffey JC
Rob Mallicoat—Taft
Andy Mota—Cal State-Fullerton
Al Osuna—Stanford
Mark Portugal—Grand Canyon College
Shane Reynolds—Texas
Scott Servais—Creighton
Curt Schilling—Yavapai JC
Eddie Tucker—Delta State
Matt Turner—Middle Georgia
Brian Williams—South Carolina
Eric Yelding—Chipola JC

LOS ANGELES
Bryan Baar—Western Michigan University
Brett Butler—Southeastern Oklahoma State U.
Tom Candiotti—St. Mary's (Calif.)
Tim Crews—Valencia Community College
Kal Daniels—Middle Georgia JC
Jim Gott—Brigham Young University
Kevin Gross—California Lutheran
Kip Gross—Murray State JC, University of Nebraska
Orel Hershiser—Bowling Green University
Jay Howell—Colorado
Mike James—L.B. Wallace JC
Eric Karros—UCLA
Jamie McAndrew—University of Florida
Roger McDowell—Bowling Green State
Jose Offerman—Colegio Biblico Cristiano
Bob Ojeda—College of the Sequoias JC
Mike Piazza—Miami Dade North JC
Mike Sharperson—South Dekalb Junior College
Steve Wilson—University of Portland
Eric Young—Rutgers University

MONTREAL
Moises Alou—Canada College (CA)
Bret Barberie—Southern California
Brian Barnes—Clemson University
George Canale—Virginia Tech University
Howard Farmer—Jackson State College
Jeff Fassero—University of Mississippi
Darrin Fletcher—University of Illinois
Tom Foley—Dade South Community College
Steve Frey—Bucks Community College
Mark Gardner—Fresno State University
Marquis Grissom—Florida A&M
Chris Haney—University of North Carolina
Ken Hill—No. Adams State College
Jon Hurst—Spartanburg Methodist University
Matt Karchner—Bloomsburg State University
Jimmy Kremers—University of Arkansas
Tim Laker—Oxnard Community College
Chris Nabholz—Towson State College
Bob Natal—Univ. of California at San Diego
Spike Owen—University of Texas
Doug Piatt—Western Kentucky University
Darren Reed—Ventura Junior College
Bill Sampen—McMurray College
John VanderWal—Western Michigan
Dave Wainhouse—Washington State
Tim Wallach—Cal State-Fullerton
Pete Young—Mississippi State

NEW YORK
Kevin Baez—Dominican (NY) College
Terry Bross—St. John's University
Tim Burke—University of Nebraska
Vince Coleman—Florida A&M
Chris Donnels—Loyola Marymount (CA)
Kevin Elster—Golden West Junior College
John Franco—St. John's University
Dave Gallagher—Mercer (NJ) Junior College
Terrel Hansen—Washington State University
Eric Hillman—Eastern Illinois University
Jeff Innis—University of Illinois
Howard Johnson—St. Petersburg Junior College
Dave Magadan—University of Alabama
Charlie O'Brien—Wichita State University
Bill Pecota—DeAnza Junior College (CA)
Steve Rosenberg—University of Florida
Mackey Sasser—George Wallace (GA) CC
Doug Simons—Pepperdine University
Joe Vitko—St. Francis (PA) College
Wally Whitehurst—University of New Orleans
Anthony Young—University of Houston

PHILADELPHIA
Kyle Abbott—UC San Diego
Ruben Amaro—Stanford University
Andy Ashby—Crowder Junior College
Bob Ayrault—Moorpark Junior College & University
   of Nevada-Las Vegas
Wes Chamberlain—Jackson State University
Pat Combs—Baylor University
Darren Daulton—Cowley County Community College
Bruce Dostal—William Patterson College
Mike Hartley—Grossmont College
Dave Hollins—University of South Carolina
Ken Howell—Tuskegee Institute
Barry Jones—Indiana University
John Kruk—Allegheny Community College
Jim Lindeman—Bradley University
Doug Lindsey—Seminole Junior College
Mickey Morandini—Indiana University
Terry Mulholland—Marietta College
Dale Murphy—Brigham Young University
Wally Ritchie—Glendale Junior College &
   Brigham Young University
Steve Searcy—University of Tennessee
Cary Williams—John C. Calhoun Junior College

PITTSBURGH
Joe Ausanio—Jacksonville University
Stan Belinda—Allegany (MD) Community College
Barry Bonds—Arizona State University
Steve Buechele—Stanford University
Victor Cole—Santa Clara University
Doug Drabek—University of Houston
Neal Heaton—University of Miami
Jeff King—University of Arkansas
Bill Landrum—Spartanburg Meth. & U. of So. Carolina
Mike LaValliere—University of Lowell
Roger Mason—Saginaw Valley State College
Lloyd McClendon—Valparaiso University
Blas Minor—Arizona State University
Bob Patterson—East Carolina
Tom Prince—Kankakee (IL) Community College
Gary Redus—Calhoun JC (AL), Athens (AL) State College
Rick Reed—Marshall University (WV)
Jeff Richardson—Louisiana Tech
Mike Roesler—Ball State University
Don Slaught—Western Carolina University
Zane Smith—Indiana State University
Randy Tomlin—Liberty Baptist (VA)
Gary Varsho—University of Wisconsin-Oshkosh
Bob Walk—College of the Canyons JC
John Wehner—Indiana University

ST. LOUIS
Luis Alicea—Florida State University
Rod Brewer—University of Florida

Cris Carpenter—University of Georgia
Mark Clark—Lincoln Land CC
Frank DiPino—St. Leo College
John Ericks—University of Illinois
Rheal Cormier—Rhode Island Community College
Jose Fernandez—University of Florida
Tim Jones—The Citadel
Brian Jordan—Richmond University
Ray Lankford—Modesto Junior College
Lonnie Maclin—St. Louis Community College
Joe Magrane—University of Arizona
Bob McClure—Matteo Junior College
Mike Milchin—Clemson University
Omar Olivares—Miami Dade Junior College
Tom Pagnozzi—University of Arkansas
Stan Royer—Eastern Illinois University
Bryn Smith—Allen Hancock Junior College
Ozzie Smith—California State Poly, San Luis Obispo
Scott Terry—Southwestern University
Bob Tewksbury—Rutgers University, St. Leo (FL)
Milt Thompson—Howard University
Craig Wilson—Anne Arundel Community College (MD)
Todd Worrell—Biola University
Todd Zeile—UCLA

SAN DIEGO
Larry Andersen—Bellevue Community College
Andy Benes—University of Evansville
Dann Bilardello—Cabrillo College (CA)
Doug Brocail—Lamar Community College
Jerald Clark—Lamar University
Paul Faries—Pepperdine University
Jeff Gardner—Orange Coast Community College (CA)
Tony Gwynn—San Diego State University
Jeremy Hernandez—Cal State Northridge
Greg Harris—Elon College
Thomas Howard—Ball State University
Bruce Hurst—Dixie Junior College
Tom Lampkin—Portland University
Craig Lefferts—University of Arizona
Mike Linskey—James Madison University
Randy Myers—Clark Community College
Frank Seminara—Columbia University
Craig Shipley—University of Alabama
Dave Staton—Orange Coast CC (CA); Cal State Fullerton
Tim Teufel—Clemson University
Jim Vatcher—West Los Angeles JC; Cal State Northridge
Ed Whitson—University of Tennessee

SAN FRANCISCO
Mike Benjamin—Arizona State University
Bud Black—Lower Columbia (WA) JC, San Diego State
Jeff Brantley—Mississippi State University
Dave Burba—Ohio State University
Will Clark—Mississippi State University
Steve Decker—Lewis-Clark State (ID)
Mike Felder—Contra Costa College (CA)
Eric Gunderson—Portland State University
Gil Heredia—University of Arizona
Bryan Hickerson—University of Minnesota
Steve Hosey—Fresno State University
Mike Jackson—Hill Junior College
Mark Leonard—Univ. of California, Santa Barbara
Darren Lewis—Univ. of California, Berkeley
Greg Litton—Pensacola Junior College
Kirt Manwaring—Coastal Carolina College
Dave Masters—Univ. of California, Berkeley
Paul McClellan—College of San Mateo (CA)
Willie McGee—Diablo Valley JC (CA)
John Patterson—Grand Canyon College (AZ)
Dave Righetti—San Jose City College
Kevin Rogers—Mississippi Delta CC
Bill Swift—University of Maine
Robby Thompson—Palm Beach JC, Univ. of Florida
Matt Williams—University of Nevada, Las Vegas
Trevor Wilson—Oregon State University
Ted Wood—University of New Orleans

BASIC AGREEMENT ARTICLE XX
MAJOR LEAGUE FREE AGENTS
(Unsigned At Press Time)

PITCHERS (17)	B	T	Ht.	Wt.	Born	1991 Club	W-L	ERA	SV	M.L. Service
ACKER, JIM	R	R	6-2	215	9/24/58	Toronto	3-5	5.20	1	9.000
BEDROSIAN, STEVE	R	R	6-3	205	12/ 6/57	Minnesota	5-3	4.42	6	10.053
BLYLEVEN, BERT	R	R	6-3	220	4/ 6/51	California	Did not play			21.117
BOYD, DENNIS	R	R	6-1	160	10/ 6/59	Texas	2-7	6.68	0	8.116
CERUTTI, JOHN	L	L	6-2	200	4/28/60	Detroit	3-6	4.57	2	6.007
CRAWFORD, STEVE	R	R	6-6	240	4/29/58	Kansas City	3-2	5.98	1	8.101
GLEATON, JERRY	L	L	6-3	210	9/14/57	Detroit	3-2	4.06	2	6.028
HAMMAKER, ATLEE	S	L	6-2	204	1/24/58	San Diego	0-1	5.79	0	10.056
KRUEGER, BILL	L	L	6-5	205	4/24/58	Seattle	11-8	3.60	0	7.012
LAMP, DENNIS	R	R	6-3	215	9/23/52	Boston	6-3	4.70	0	14.017
LEACH, TERRY	R	R	6-0	190	3/13/54	Minnesota	1-2	3.61	0	6.101
ONTIVEROS, STEVE	R	R	6-0	197	3/ 5/61	Philadelphia	Did not play			6.118
PETRY, DAN	R	R	6-4	215	11/13/58	Detroit/Boston	2-3	4.79	1	
						Atlanta	0-0	5.55	0	12.075
POWER, TED	R	R	6-4	220	1/31/55	Cincinnati	5-3	3.62	3	9.079
*RASMUSSEN, D.	L	L	6-7	233	4/18/59	San Diego	6-13	3.74	0	7.124
SISK, DOUG	R	R	6-2	210	9/26/57	Atlanta	2-1	5.02	0	7.035
YOUNG, CURTIS	R	L	6-1	175	4/16/60	Oakland	4-2	5.00	0	7.110

CATCHERS (6)	B	T	Ht.	Wt.	Born	1991 Club	AVG.	HR	RBI	M.L. Service
FITZGERALD, MIKE	R	R	5-11	190	7/13/60	Montreal	.202	4	28	7.151
HASSEY, RON	L	R	6-2	195	2/27/53	Montreal	.227	1	14	13.017
KENNEDY, TERRY	L	R	6-4	220	6/ 4/56	San Francisco	.234	3	13	12.110
LAKE, STEVE	R	R	6-1	202	3/14/57	Philadelphia	.228	1	11	8.114
RUSSELL, JOHN	R	R	6-0	200	1/ 5/61	Texas	.111	0	1	6.043
SALAS, MARK	L	R	6-0	205	3/ 8/61	Detroit	.088	1	7	6.089

INFIELDERS (11)	B	T	Ht.	Wt.	Born	1991 Club	AVG.	HR	RBI	M.L. Service
ANDERSON, DAVE	R	R	6-2	184	8/ 1/60	San Francisco	.248	2	13	8.150
FLETCHER, SCOTT	R	R	5-11	150	1/20/64	Chicago (AL)	.206	1	28	9.082
GRIFFIN, ALFREDO	S	R	5-11	166	3/ 6/57	Los Angeles	.243	0	27	13.081
HILL, DONNIE	S	R	5-10	160	11/12/60	California	.239	1	20	7.032
HOWELL, JACK	L	R	6-0	185	8/18/61	California	.210	2	7	
						San Diego	.206	6	16	6.008
*JACOBY, BROOK	R	R	5-11	195	11/23/59	Cleve./Oak.	.224	4	44	8.055
NEWMAN, AL	S	R	5-9	198	6/30/60	Minnesota	.191	0	19	6.069
RILES, ERNEST	L	R	6-1	180	10/ 2/60	Oakland	.214	5	32	6.131
STILLWELL, KURT	S	R	5-11	185	6/ 4/65	Kansas City	.265	6	51	6.000
TEMPLETON, GARRY	S	R	6-0	209	3/24/56	SD/NY (NL)	.221	3	26	15.057
WILKERSON, CURTIS	R	R	5-9	173	4/26/61	Pittsburgh	.188	2	18	8.026

OUTFIELDERS (7)	B	T	Ht.	Wt.	Born	1991 Club	AVG.	HR	RBI	M.L. Service
*INCAVIGLIA, PETE	R	R	6-1	230	4/ 2/64	Detroit	.214	11	38	6.000
JONES, TRACY	R	R	6-3	220	3/31/61	Seattle	.251	3	24	6.000
MARTINEZ, C.	R	R	6-2	225	7/28/60	Pit./Cin.	.234	6	19	
						Kansas City	.207	4	17	8.042
MOSEBY, LLOYD	L	R	6-3	200	11/ 5/59	Detroit	.262	6	35	11.135
PARKER, DAVE	L	R	6-5	250	6/ 9/51	Cal./Toronto	.239	11	59	18.082
VENABLE, MAX	L	R	5-10	185	6/ 6/57	California	.246	3	21	7.152
WILSON, MOOKIE	S	R	5-10	175	2/ 9/56	Toronto	.241	2	28	11.034

*Signed minor league contract.

SERVICE MILESTONES

3 YEAR MEN

ATLANTA
Damon Berryhill
Jeff Blauser
Marvin Freeman
Ron Gant
Tom Glavine
Tommy Gregg
Pete Smith
John Smoltz
Jeff Treadway
CHICAGO
Mark Grace
Les Lancaster
Jerome Walton
CINCINNATI
Tim Belcher
Norm Charlton
Rob Dibble

Bob Geren
Dwayne Henry
Bip Roberts
Chris Sabo
HOUSTON
Craig Biggio
Ken Caminiti
Casey Candaele
Steve Finley
Jimmy Jones
Mark Portugal
Gerald Young
LOS ANGELES
Todd Benzinger
Tim Crews
Lenny Harris
Mike Sharperson

MONTREAL
Larry Walker
NEW YORK
Kevin Elster
Dave Gallagher
Paul Gibson
Jeff Innis
Junior Noboa
Charlie O'Brien
Bill Pecota
Mackey Sasser
PHILADELPHIA
Ricky Jordan
Jim Lindeman
Terry Mulholland
PITTSBURGH
Jay Bell
Bill Landrum

Jose Lind
Lloyd McClendon
Bob Patterson
Gary Varsho
ST. LOUIS
Rex Hudler
Joe Magrane
Tom Pagnozzi
Bob Tewksbury
SAN DIEGO
Dann Bilardello
Greg Harris
Darrin Jackson
Mike Maddux
SAN FRANCISCO
Jeff Brantley
Matt Williams

5 YEAR MEN

ATLANTA
Mike Bielecki
CHICAGO
Paul Assenmacher
Greg Maddux
CINCINNATI
Scott Bankhead
Glenn Braggs
Barry Larkin
Dave Martinez

Paul O'Neill
Greg Swindell
LOS ANGELES
Kal Daniels
Jeff Hamilton
Stan Javier
NEW YORK
David Cone
Dave Magadan

PHILADELPHIA
Barry Jones
Dale Sveum
PITTSBURGH
Barry Bonds
Doug Drabek
John Smiley
ST. LOUIS
Scott Terry

SAN DIEGO
Fred McGriff
Randy Myers
Benito Santiago
SAN FRANCISCO
Kelly Downs
Mike Felder
Mike Jackson
Chris James
Bill Swift

6 YEAR MEN

ATLANTA
Rafael Belliard
Sid Bream
Steve Lyons
Alejandro Pena
Terry Pendleton
CHICAGO
George Bell
Shawon Dunston
Danny Jackson
Mike Morgan
CINCINNATI
Tom Browning
Bill Doran
Billy Hatcher
Jeff Reed
Jose Rijo
LOS ANGELES
Tom Candiotti
Eric Davis

Kevin Gross
Orel Hershiser
Jay Howell
Roger McDowell
Juan Samuel
Darryl Strawberry
MONTREAL
Ivan Calderon
Tom Foley
Spike Owen
NEW YORK
Bobby Bonilla
Daryl Boston
Tim Burke
Vince Coleman
Sid Fernandez
John Franco
Dwight Gooden
Howard Johnson
Bret Saberhagen

PHILADELPHIA
Wally Backman
Darren Daulton
Mariano Duncan
Lenny Dykstra
Ken Howell
John Kruk
Mitch Williams
PITTSBURGH
Steve Buechele
Neal Heaton
Mike LaValliere
Gary Redus
Don Slaught
Zane Smith
Andy Van Slyke
Bob Walk
ST. LOUIS
Juan Agosto
Jose DeLeon

Frank DiPino
Andres Galarraga
Jose Oquendo
Gerald Perry
Milt Thompson
Todd Worrell
SAN DIEGO
Tony Fernandez
Tony Gwynn
Craig Lefferts
Tim Teufel
SAN FRANCISCO
Kevin Bass
Bud Black
Will Clark
Scott Garrelts
Willie McGee
Robby Thompson
Jose Uribe

10 YEAR MEN

ATLANTA
Juan Berenguer
Mike Heath
Charlie Leibrandt
Lonnie Smith
CHICAGO
Andre Dawson**
Luis Salazar
Ryne Sandberg**
Dave Smith

LOS ANGELES
Brett Butler
John Candelaria
Jim Gott
Bob Ojeda
Mike Scioscia**
MONTREAL
Gary Carter
Dennis Martinez**
Tim Wallach**

NEW YORK
Eddie Murray
Willie Randolph
PHILADELPHIA
Dale Murphy
ST. LOUIS
Rich Gedman
Pedro Guerrero
Bob McClure
Bryn Smith

Lee Smith
Ozzie Smith**
SAN DIEGO
Larry Andersen
Bruce Hurst
Ed Whitson**
SAN FRANCISCO
Dave Righetti

**Spent last 5 years with club

1991-1992 DEALS MADE BY NATIONAL LEAGUE CLUBS

3/17/91 — Pirates sign free agent (RHR) **Jay Tibbs**.

3/25/91 — Dodgers sign free agent (LHS) **John Candelaria**.

3/26/91 — Dodgers sign free agent (C) **Gary Carter**.

3/26/91 — Padres are awarded the contract of (RHR) **Jose Melendez** from Seattle on waiver claim.

3/29/91 — Cubs trade the contract of (OF) **Gary Varsho** to the Pirates in exchange for the contract of (OF) **Steven Carter**.

3/31/91 — Padres trade the contracts of (2B) **Joey Cora** and (1B) **Kevin Garner** and minor leaguer Warren Newson to Chicago (AL) in exchange for the contracts of (RHS) **Adam Peterson** and (LHS) **Steven Rosenberg**.

4/1/91 — Braves trade the contract of (C) **Jim Kremers** to the Expos in exchange for the contract of (OF) **Otis Nixon.**

4/2/91 — Expos trade the contract of (OF) **Terrell Hansen** to the Mets in exchange for the contract of (OF) **Darren Reed**.

4/5/91 — Pirates sign free agent (OF) **Mike Aldrete**.

4/6/91 — Giants sign free agent (OF) **Mike Felder**.

4/7/91 — Pirates trade the contract of (SS) **Kevin Burdick** to Cleveland for a player to be named later.

4/7/91 — Cubs acquire the contracts of (RHS) **Bob Scanlan** and (LHR) **Chuck McElroy** from the Phillies in exchange for the contract of (LHR) **Mitch Williams**.

4/7/91 — Reds sign free agent (LHR) **Don Carman**.

4/8/91 — Phillies sign free agent (LHS) **Dave LaPoint**.

5/4/91 — Pirates trade the contract of (OF) **Carmelo Martinez** to Kansas City in exchange for the contract of (RHR) **Victor Cole**.

5/9/91 — Mets are awarded the contract of (RHR) **Mark Dewey** from the Giants on waiver claim.

5/16/91 — Pirates trade the contract of (RHS) **Michael York** to Cleveland in exchange for the contract of (OF) **Mitch Webster**.

5/31/91 — Mets trade the contract of (2B) **Tim Teufel** to the Padres in exchange for the contract of (SS) **Garry Templeton**.

6/4/91 — Expos are awarded the contract of (OF) **Ken Williams** from Toronto on waiver claim.

6/14/91 — Reds trade the contract of (1B) **Reggie Jefferson** to Cleveland in exchange for the contract of minor leaguer Tim Costo.

6/14/91 — Braves are awarded the contract of (RHR) **Rick Mahler** from Seattle on waiver claim.

6/24/91 — Cardinals sign free agent (LHR) **Bob McClure**.

6/25/91 — Braves acquire the contract of (RHR) **Dan Petry** from Detroit in exchange for the contract of minor leaguer Victor Rosario.

6/26/91 — Cardinals are awarded the contract of (RHR) **Willie Fraser** from Toronto on waiver claim.

6/26/91 — Cubs acquire the contract of minor leaguer Steve Adkins from New York (AL) to be sent to Iowa in exchange for the contract of **David Rosario**.

7/3/91 — Dodgers trade the contract of (OF) **Jose Gonzalez** to the Pirates in exchange for the contract of (OF) **Mitch Webster**.

7/8/91 — Expos are awarded the contract of (RHS) **Chris Johnson** from Milwaukee on waiver claim.

7/12/91 — Reds trade the contract of (1B) **Todd Benzinger** to Kansas City in exchange for the contract of (OF) **Carmelo Martinez** and cash.

7/15/91 — Expos trade the contract of (RHR) **Tim Burke** to the Mets in exchange for the contract of (RHS) **Ron Darling**.

7/15/91 — Phillies sign free agent (LHS) **Steve Searcy**.

7/21/91 — Expos trade the contract of (RHS) **Dennis Boyd** to Texas in exchange for the minor league contracts of Jonathan Hirst, Joseph Eischen and a player to be named later or cash.

7/30/91 — Padres trade the contract of (OF) **Shawn Abner** to California in exchange for the contract of (3B) **Jack Howell, Jr.**.

7/31/91 — Braves trade the contract of (RHR) **Matt Turner** to the Astros in exchange for the contract of (RHR) **Jim Clancy**.

7/31/91 — Dodgers trade the contract of (RHR) **Mike Hartley** and minor leaguer Braulio Castillo to the Phillies in exchange for the contract of (RHR) **Roger McDowell**.

7/31/91 — Expos trade the contract of (RHS) **Ron Darling** to Oakland in exchange for the minor league contracts of Matthew Grott and Russ Cormier.

8/6/91 — Giants award the contract of (2B) **Tony Perezchica** to Cleveland on waiver claim.

8/15/91 — Pirates award the contract of (OF) **Jose Gonzalez** to Cleveland on waiver claim.

8/16/91 — Braves trade the contract of (RHR) **Dan Petry** to Boston in exchange for a player to be named later.

8/16/91 — Giants sign free agent (2B) **Tom Herr**.

8/24/91 — Expos trade minor leaguer Richie Lewis to Baltimore in exchange for the contract of (LHS) **Chris Myers**.

8/29/91 — Braves trade the contracts of (LHR) **Antonio Castillo** and a player to be named later to the Mets in exchange for the contract of (RHR) **Alejandro Pena**.

8/30/91 — Pirates trade the minor league contracts of Kurt Miller and a player to be named later to Texas in exchange for the contract of (3B) **Steve Buechele**.

9/6/91 — Pirates send the contract of (RHS) **Hector Fajardo** to Texas as the player to be named later to complete the trade of 8/30/91.

9/25/91 — Astros are awarded the contract of (C) **Eddie Tucker** from the Giants on waiver claim.

9/29/91 — Braves trade the contracts of (LHR) **Yorkis Perez** and minor leaguer Steven J. Wendell to the Cubs in exchange for the contracts of (RHR) **Mike Bielecki** and (C) **Damon Berryhill**.

10/8/91 — Expos award the contract of (2B) **Junior Noboa** to the Mets on a waiver claim.

10/15/91 — Expos award the contract of (1B) **George Canale** to Milwaukee in exchange for the contract of minor leaguer Alex Diaz.

11/15/91 — Dodgers award the contract of (C) **Gary Carter** to the Expos on a waiver claim.

11/15/91 — Reds trade the contract of (RHS) **Jack Armstrong** and **Scott Scudder** to Cleveland in exchange for the contract of (LHS) **Greg Swindell**.

11/19/91 — Mets award the contract of (OF) **Terry McDaniel** to the Pirates on a waiver claim.

11/20/91 — Padres award the contract of (LHS) **Derek Lilliquist** to Cleveland on a waiver claim.

11/20/91 — Padres are awarded the contract of (LHS) **Mike Linskey** from Baltimore on a waiver claim.

11/25/91 — Expos trade the contract of (1B) **Andres Galarraga** to the Cardinals in exchange for the contract of (RHS) **Ken Hill**.

11/26/91 — Astros award the contract of (RHR) **Dwayne Henry** to the Reds on a waiver claim.

11/27/91 — Reds trade the contracts of (OF) **Eric Davis** and (RHR) **Kip Gross** to the Dodgers in exchange for the contracts of (RHS) **Tim Belcher** and (RHR) **John Wetteland**.

11/27/91 — Mets sign free agent (1B) **Eddie Murray**.

12/2/91 — Cubs are awarded the contract of (C) **George Pedre** from Kansas City on a waiver claim.

12/2/91 — Reds are awarded the contract of (OF) **Cesar Hernandez** from the Expos on a waiver claim.

12/2/91 — Reds are awarded the contract of (C) **Bob Geren** from New York (AL) on a waiver claim.

12/2/91 — Mets sign free agent (OF) **Bobby Bonilla**.

12/3/91 — Dodgers re-sign free agent (RHS) **Orel Hershiser**.

12/3/91 — Dodgers sign free agent (RHS) **Tom Candiotti**.

12/8/91 — Phillies trade the contract of (OF) **Von Hayes** to California in exchange for the contracts of (LHS) **Kyle Abbott** and (OF) **Ruben Amaro, Jr.**.

12/9/91 — Cubs sign free agent (RHS) **Mike Morgan**.

12/9/91 — Reds trade the contract of (LHR) **Randy Myers** to the Padres in exchange for the contract of (SS) **Bip Roberts**.

12/9/91 — Expos trade the contract of (RHR) **Barry Jones** to the Phillies in exchange for the contract of (C) **Darrin Fletcher** and cash.

12/10/91 — Mets trade the contract of (OF) **Hubie Brooks** to California in exchange for the contract of (OF) **Dave Gallagher**.

12/10/91 — Astros trade the contracts of (OF) **Ken Lofton** and (SS) **David Rohde** to Cleveland in exchange for the contracts of (C) **Ed Taubensee** and **Willie Blair**.

12/10/91 — Phillies sign free agent (2B) **Mariano Duncan**.

12/11/91 — Reds trade the contracts of (RHR) **John Wetteland** and (RHS) **Bill Risley** to the Expos in exchange for the contracts of (OF) **Dave Martinez**, (LHR) **Scott Ruskin** and minor leaguer Willie Greene.

12/11/91 — Dodgers acquire the contract of (RHS) **Rudy Seanez** from Cleveland in exchange for the contracts of (LHR) **Dennis Cook** and (RHR) **Mike Christopher**.

12/11/91 — Dodgers acquire the contract of (1B) **Todd Benzinger** from Kansas City in exchange for the contract of (OF) **Chris Gwynn**.

12/11/91 — Phillies acquire the contract of (SS) **Dale Sveum** from Milwaukee in exchange for the contract of (LHS) **Bruce Ruffin** and cash.

12/11/91 — Giants trade the contracts of (OF) **Kevin Mitchell** and (LHS) **Mike Remlinger** to Seattle in exchange for the contracts of (RHR) **Bill Swift**, (RHR) **Mike Jackson** and (RHS) **Dave Burba**.

12/11/91 — Mets trade the contracts of (OF) **Kevin McReynolds**, (OF) **Keith Miller** and (2B) **Gregg Jefferies** to Kansas City in exchange for the contracts of (RHS) **Bret Saberhagen** and (3B) **Bill Pecota**.

12/12/91 — Mets trade the contract of (2B) **Jeff Gardner** to the Padres in exchange for the contract of (LHS) **Steve Rosenberg**.

12/12/91 — Pirates re-sign free agent (3B) **Steve Buechele**.

12/13/91 — Braves re-sign free agent (OF) **Otis Nixon**.

12/20/91 — Mets sign free agent (2B) **Willie Randolph**.

12/20/91 — Pirates sign free agent (RHS) **Bob Walk**.

12/21/91 — Cardinals sign free agent (RHR) **Scott Terry**.

1/8/92 — Phillies acquire the contract of (RHS) **Darrin Chapin** from New York (AL) in exchange for a player to be named later.

1/8/92 — Braves sign free agent (OF) **Steve Lyons**.

1/8/92 — Padres re-sign free agent (2B) **Tim Teufel**.

1/16/92 — Giants sign free agent (OF) **Chris James**.

1/22/92 — Mets acquire the contracts of (LHR) **Paul Gibson** and minor leaguer **Randy Marshall** from Detroit for the contracts of (OF) **Mark Carreon** and (LHR) **Antonio Castillo**.

1/23/92 — Reds sign free agent (RHS) **Scott Bankhead**.

2/17/92 — Padres acquire contracts of (3B) **Craig Worthington** and minor league pitcher Tom Martin from Baltimore in exchange for the contracts of (RHR) **Jim Lewis** and minor league outfielder Steve Martin.

1991 PINCH-HITTING LEADERS

Batting Average	:	.406	Walker, Chi.
Runs	:	8	Redus, Pitt.
Hits	:	14	Noboa, Mon.
Total Bases	:	22	Carreon, N.Y.
Doubles	:	4	Backman, Phi. & Gregg, Atl.
Triples	:	1	17 players tied.
Home Runs	:	3	Carreon, N.Y.
Runs Batted In	:	13	Gwynn, L.A. & Perry, St.L.
Bases on Balls	:	8	Backman, Phi., Kingery, S.F. & Ready, Phi.
Slugging Percentage	:	.629	Carreon, N.Y.
On-Base Percentage	:	.500	Walker, Chi.

1991 ROAD-HITTING LEADERS

Batting Average	:	.345	McGee, S.F.
Runs	:	53	Butler, L.A.
Hits	:	95	McGee, S.F.
Total Bases	:	146	Johnson, N.Y.
Doubles	:	24	Jose, St.L.
Triples	:	7	Gwynn, S.D. & Owen, Mon.
Home Runs	:	18	Mitchell, S.F.
Runs Batted In	:	69	Clark, S.F.
Bases on Balls	:	58	Bonds, Pitt.
Slugging Percentage	:	.582	Bonds, Pitt.
On-Base Percentage	:	.436	Bonds, Pitt.

1992 NATIONAL LEAGUE UMPIRES

DIRECTOR OF UMPIRE SUPERVISION—Ed Vargo

34 GREGORY BONIN

Born June 15, 1955 in Lafayette, LA . . . Resides in Lafayette . . . 5'10'' . . . 160 lbs . . . Married Judith Norton October 10, 1986 . . . Played Colt League and American Legion Baseball . . . Graduate of University of South West Louisiana . . . Worked first National League game on April 25, 1984 . . . Became regular member of N.L. staff in April, 1986 . . . Previously umpired in Florida State League, Texas League, International League, Colombia Winter League, and Dominican Republic Winter League . . . Works in family business during off-season . . . Hobbies include fishing, golf and hunting.

2 GERALD JOSEPH (JERRY) CRAWFORD

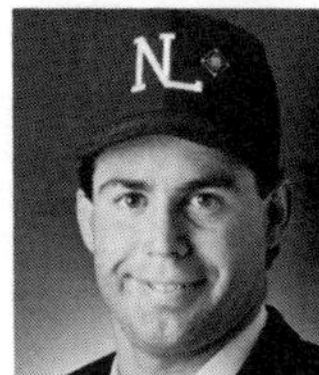

Born August 13, 1947 in Philadelphia, PA . . . Resides in Havertown, PA . . . 6' . . . 194 lbs . . . Married Carol Alessi February 24, 1968 . . . Two children, Christopher and Alyson . . . Played American Legion and Connie Mack baseball . . . Worked first National League game in 1975 . . . Became regular member of N.L. staff May 15, 1976 . . . Previously umpired in Florida State League, Carolina League, Eastern League and International League . . . Hobbies include HO trains and music.

35 GARY RICHARD DARLING

Born October 9, 1957 in San Francisco, CA . . . Resides in Phoenix, AZ . . . 6'3'' . . . 208 lbs . . . Married Cheryl Hellmann December 19, 1987 . . . Two children, Cameron and Courtney . . . Graduated from Cosumnes River Junior College . . . Played high school, college and American Legion base-ball . . . Worked first National League game on June 6, 1986 . . . Became regular member of N.L. staff in April 1988 . . . Previously umpired in North-west League, California League, Arizona Instructional League, Columbian Winter League, Puerto Rico Winter League and Pacific Coast League . . . Hobbies include golf and basketball.

31 ROBERT ALLAN (BOB) DAVIDSON

Born August 3, 1952 in Chicago, IL . . . Resides in Altoona, IA . . . 6'2'' . . . 224 lbs . . . Married Denise Nesheim September 27, 1980 . . . Two children, Amber Adelle and Andrea Lynn . . . Attended University of Minnesota, where he played baseball . . . Also played high school baseball . . . Worked first National League game May 31, 1982 . . . Became regular member of N.L. staff for 1983 season . . . Previously umpired in Midwest League, Florida State League, Florida Instructional League, Southern League, Do-minican Republic Winter League and the American Association . . . During off-season Bob is a high school basketball official.

12 GERALD (GERRY) DAVIS

Born February 22, 1953 in St. Louis, MO . . . Resides in Appleton, WI . . . 6'2'' . . . 236 lbs . . . Married Lynn Mentzel October 9, 1980 . . . One child, Jeremy Joseph . . . Played semi-pro baseball as a pitcher, first baseman in St. Louis . . . Worked first National League game June 9, 1982 . . . Became regular member of staff for 1985 season . . . Previously umpired in Midwest League, Eastern League, American Association, Florida Instructional League, and Puerto Rico Winter League . . . During the off-season Gerry coaches the University of Wisconsin-Fox Valley Junior College basketball team . . . His hobby is golf.

32 DANA ANDREW DeMUTH

Born May 30, 1956 in Fremont, OH . . . Resides in Gilbert, AZ . . . 6' . . . 216 lbs . . . Married Marjorie Whitaker December 2, 1978 . . . One child, Dane . . . Worked first National League game June 3, 1983 . . . Became a regular member of the N.L. staff in April, 1985 . . . Previously umpired in California League, Texas League, and Pacific Coast League . . . Also worked in Colombia and Dominican Republic Winter Leagues.

UMPIRE SUPERVISORS—Al Barlick, Nick Colosi

6 BRUCE NEAL FROEMMING*

Born September 28, 1939 in Milwaukee, WI . . . Resides in Vero Beach, FL . . 5'8'' . . 252 lbs . . . Married Rose Marie Loch May 2, 1959 . . . Two children, Kevin and Steven . . . Played high school and semi-pro baseball . . . Worked first National League game in April, 1971, when he became regular member of the staff . . . Previously umpired in Nebraska State League, Midwest League, Northern League, Northwest League, Texas League and Pacific Coast League . . . Began umpiring professionally when he was 18 years old, which made him the youngest professional umpire . . . Has been on Board of Directors of Major League Umpires' Association since 1972 . . . Partner in umpire school in Cocoa, FL . . . His hobby is golf.

7 ERIC EUGENE GREGG

Born May 18, 1951 in Philadelphia, PA . . . Resides in Philadelphia . . . 6'3'' . . . 325 lbs . . . Married Ramona Camilo December 31, 1974 . . . Four children, Eric, Kevin, Ashley and Jamie . . . Played high school baseball . . . Worked first National League game September 26, 1975 . . . Became regu-lar member of N.L. staff in 1978 . . . Previously umpired in New York-Penn League, Florida State League, Eastern League, Dominican Republic League and Pacific Coast League.

20 THOMAS FRANCIS (TOM) HALLION

Born September 5, 1956 in Saugerties, NY . . . Resides in Louisville, KY . . . 5'10'' . . . 168 lbs . . . Married Elizabeth Carnright September 11, 1983 . . . Two children, Corey Nicholas and Kyle Matthew . . . Lettered in football, basketball and baseball in high school . . . Attended University of Buffalo . . . Worked first National League game on June 10, 1985 . . . Became regular member of N.L. staff in April, 1986 . . . Previously umpired in New York-Penn League, Carolina League, Eastern League and American As-sociation . . . Hobbies include golf, tennis and antiques.

8 DOUG HARVEY*

Born March 13, 1930 in Southgate, CA . . . Resides in San Diego, CA . . . 6'2'' . . . 196 lbs . . . Married Joy Ann Glascock September 24, 1960 . . . Three children, Douglas, Scott and Todd . . . Attended San Diego State, where he played basketball, football and baseball . . . Became regular member of National League staff April 10, 1962, when he worked his first N.L. game . . . Previously umpired in California State League and Pacific Coast League . . . Also worked as a professional basketball referee for 6 years . . . Doug's hobbies include golf and fishing.

4 MARK HIRSCHBECK

Born September 22, 1960 in Bridgeport, CT . . . Resides in Stratford, CT . . . 5'9'' . . . 189 lbs . . . Married Mary Frances Mallon November 20, 1982 . . . Two children, Jaclyn and Nikki . . . Played football in high school . . . Also participated in Little League and Pony League . . . Worked first Na-tional League game on June 19, 1987 . . . Became regular member of N.L. staff in April, 1988 . . . Previously umpired in Gulf Coast League, Florida State League, Midwest League, Eastern League, Dominican Republic League, Florida Instructional League and American Association . . . In the off-season Mark referees high school basketball . . . Hobbies include hunting, fishing and golf.

29 WILLIAM JOHN (BILL) HOHN

Born June 29, 1955 in Butler, PA . . . Resides in Collegeville, PA . . . 6' . . . 175 lbs . . . Married Grace Grippo December 26, 1983 . . . One child, Meredith . . . Played high school and amateur baseball . . . Worked first National League game on May 29, 1987 . . . Became regular member of N.L. staff in April, 1989 . . . Previously umpired in Gulf Coast League, Florida Instructional League, Florida State League, Southern League, Puerto Rico Winter League and Pacific Coast League . . . In the off-season Bill works for a security company . . . Hobbies include hunting, archery and aerobics.

24 JERRY BLAKE LAYNE

Born September 28, 1958 in Pikeville, KY . . . Resides in Winter Haven, FL . . . 6'4'' . . . 249 lbs . . . Married Jacqueline Heck September 19, 1982 . . . Two children, Brittany and Monica . . . Became regular member of N. L. staff in April, 1989 . . . Previously umpired in Appalachian League, Florida State League, Florida Instructional League, Southern League and Pacific Coast League . . . Hobbies include golf.

30 RANDALL GILBERT (RANDY) MARSH

Born April 8, 1949 in Covington, KY . . . Resides in Edgewood, KY . . . 6' . . . 210 lbs . . . Married Roxanne McFarland October 7, 1978 . . . One child, Lauren . . . Attended University of Kentucky . . . Played high school baseball . . . Worked first National League game in May, 1981 . . . Became regular member of N.L. staff for 1982 season . . . Previously umpired in Appalachian League, Florida State League, Eastern League, Florida Instructional League, Dominican Republic League and Pacific Coast League . . . Was Umpire-in-Chief of Pacific Coast League . . . Hobbies include photography and golf.

10 JOHN PATRICK McSHERRY*

Born September 11, 1944 in New York, NY . . . Resides in Dobbs Ferry, NY . . . 6'2½'' . . . 328 lbs . . . Single . . . Attended St. John's University . . . Umpired sandlot and high school baseball . . . Worked first National League game June 1, 1971, when he became regular member of staff . . . Previously umpired in Carolina League, International League and Florida Instructional League.

11 EDWARD MICHAEL (ED) MONTAGUE

Born November 3, 1948 in San Francisco, CA . . . Resides in San Mateo, CA . . . 5'10'' . . . 184 lbs . . . Married Marcia Simons October 14, 1978 . . . Three children, Edward Michael, Brooke and Brett . . . Attended San Francisco City College, where he played baseball . . . Worked first National League games last two days of 1974 season . . . Became regular member of N.L. staff in April, 1976 . . . Previously umpired in California League, Arizona Instructional League, Pacific Coast League and Puerto Rico Winter League . . . During off-season Ed volunteers his time at VA hospitals around the country for Disabled American Veterans . . . Hobbies include magic, guitar, running and golf.

14 FRANK VICTOR PULLI

Born March 22, 1935 in Easton, PA . . . Resides in Palm Harbor, FL . . . 5'11'' . . . 194 lbs . . . Married Kim Hale December 29, 1984 . . . Six children, Vicky, Michelle, Frank, Jr., Michael, Candice and Nikki . . . Played high school baseball and basketball . . . Worked first National League game in April, 1972, when he became regular member of staff . . . Previously umpired in Midwest League, Eastern League and International League.

15 JAMES EDWARD (JIM) QUICK

Born September 6, 1943 in Sacramento, CA . . . Resides in Incline Village, NV . . . 6' . . . 229 lbs . . . Married Sandra Smith July 6, 1985 . . . Three children, Kresten, Kimberly and Kara . . . Has AA degree from Yuba Junior College, where he played football and baseball . . . Worked first National League game in August, 1974 . . . Became regular member of N.L. staff in 1976 . . . Previously umpired in Northwest League, California League, Texas League and Pacific Coast League . . . During off-season Jim helps his wife in their group tour business . . . Hobbies include golf, skiing and hunting.

23 EDWARD RAPUANO, JR.

Born September 30, 1957 in New Haven, CT . . . Resides in North Haven, CT . . . 5'10'' . . . 185 lbs . . . Married Valerie Funaro October 12, 1984 . . . Two children, Eddie III and Rosalie Ann . . . Graduate of Technical Careers Institute . . . Played high school baseball . . . Worked first National League game May 11, 1990 . . . Became regular member of N.L. staff April 8, 1991 . . . Previously umpired in NY-Penn League, Florida State League, Southern League and Triple Alliance . . . Hobbies include youth hockey and golf.

18 CHARLES HAROLD RELIFORD

Born September 19, 1956 in Ashland, KY . . . Resides in Ashland . . . 5'9'' . . . 180 lbs . . . Single . . . Attended University of Kentucky and Ohio University . . . Worked first National League game May 29, 1989 . . . Became regular member of N.L. staff April 8, 1991 . . . Previously umpired in Appalachian League, Florida State League, Southern League, American Association and Triple Alliance . . . In the off-season Charlie is a high school basketball referee.

16 LAURENCE HENRY (DUTCH) RENNERT, JR

Born June 12, 1934 in Oshkosh, WI . . . Resides in Vero Beach, FL . . . 5'8'' . . . 180 lbs . . . Married Shirley Malchow June 16, 1964 . . . Four children, Jeff, Greg, Kevin and Melissa . . . Played high school football, basketball and baseball . . . Also played semi-pro football and baseball . . . Worked first National League game September 6, 1973 . . . Became regular member of N.L. staff in April, 1974 . . . Previously umpired in Alabama-Florida League, Pioneer League, Three-I League, Southern Association, Texas League and Pacific Coast League . . . Hobbies include woodcutting and golf.

27 THOMAS STEVEN (STEVE) RIPPLEY

Born May 2, 1954 in St. Petersburg, FL . . . Resides in Seminole, FL . . . 6' . . . 206 lbs . . . Married Gaye Broshears February 16, 1991 . . . One child, Tiffany Marie . . . Lettered in football, basketball and baseball in high school . . . Worked first National League game on May 30, 1983 . . . Became regular member of N.L. staff for 1984 season . . . Previously umpired in Gulf Coast League, Florida State League, Eastern League, Southern League, American Association, Dominican Republic Winter League, and Puerto Rico Winter League . . . During the off-season Steve is an instructor at an umpire school . . . Steve's hobbies include golf, racquetball and running.

17 PAUL EDWARD RUNGE*

Born October 20, 1940 in St. Catharines, Ontario, Canada . . . Resides in El Cajon, CA . . . 6'1'' . . . 206 lbs . . . Married Anastasia Mouzas October 17, 1965 . . . Two children, Brian and Renee . . . Graduate of Arizona State University . . . Played minor league ball for Houston and California . . . Worked first National League game in September, 1973 . . . Became regular member of N.L. umpire staff in April, 1974 . . . Previously umpired in California League, Eastern League and Pacific Coast League . . . During off-season Paul is a real estate broker in El Cajon . . . Hobbies include golf, bowling, racquetball, fishing, swimming and camping.

19 TERRY ANTHONY TATA*

Born April 24, 1940 in Waterbury, CT . . . Resides in Cheshire, CT . . . 5'10'' . . . 200 lbs . . . Married Janice Membrino October 5, 1973 . . . One child, Lisa . . . Was very active in amateur sports, baseball, basketball and football on sandlot level . . . Worked first National League game April 5, 1973, when he became regular member of staff . . . Previously umpired in Midwest League, Northern League, Texas League and International League . . . Hobbies include reading, aerobics, wood splitting and he is a fine wine collector.

21 HARRY HUNTER WENDELSTEDT, JR*

Born July 27, 1938 in Baltimore, MD . . . Resides in Ormond Beach, FL . . . 6'2" . . . 278 lbs . . . Married Cheryl Maher November 2, 1970 . . . Two children, Harry, III and Amy . . . Attended Essex Community College and University of Maryland where he played basketball and baseball . . . Also played high school and American Legion baseball and professional soccer . . . Became regular member of N.L. umpire staff in April, 1966 . . . Previously umpired in Georgia-Florida League, Northwest League, Texas League and International League . . . During off-season Harry is owner-operator of umpire school in Florida . . . Served four terms as President of Major League Umpire Association . . . Hobbies include fishing.

22 JOSEPH HENRY (JOE) WEST

Born October 31, 1952 in Asheville, NC . . . Resides in Ft. Lauderdale, FL and Kilby Island, NC . . . 6'1" . . . 278 lbs . . . Married Jean Jo Mason December 25, 1988 . . . Quarterbacked Elon College to three conference championships, 1971-1973 and set three passing records there . . . Elected to Elon Sports Hall of Fame in '86 . . . Worked first National League game in September, 1976 . . . Became regular member of N.L. staff in April, 1978 . . . Previously umpired in Western Carolinas League, Carolina League, Southern League, American Association and Puerto Rico Winter League . . . Singer and songwriter.

25 CHARLES HERMAN (CHARLIE) WILLIAMS

Born December 20, 1943, in Denver, CO . . . Resides in Chicago, IL . . . 5'9" . . . 211 lbs . . . Married Diana Gilkes June 20, 1979 . . . Two children, Charles and Gaberial . . . Attended Long Beach City College and Cal State, Los Angeles . . . Worked first National League game April 26, 1978 . . . Became regular member of N.L. staff for 1982 season . . . Previously umpired in California League, Texas League and Pacific Coast League . . . During the off-season Charlie is a salesman . . . His hobbies include golf, bowling and reading.

33 MICHAEL JOHN (MIKE) WINTERS

Born November 19, 1958, in Oceanside, CA . . . Resides in San Diego, CA . . . 6' . . . 193 lbs . . . Married Cindy Livingston January 7, 1989 . . . Two children, Sean and Erin . . . Received associate degree from San Diego Mesa College . . . Also attended San Diego State . . . Worked first National League game July 9, 1988 . . . Became regular member of NL staff April 9, 1990 . . . Previously umpired in Northwest League, California League, Arizona Instructional League, Texas League, Dominican Republic Winter League and Pacific Coast League . . . Hobbies include golf and racquetball.

*Crew Chief

In addition to the regular staff umpires working spring training games for the National League, the following minor league umpires will also be seen at spring training games: **Ron Barnes** (PCL), **Wally Bell** (IL), **Kerwin Danley** (PCL), **Brian Gorman** (AA), **Angel Hernandez** (AA), **Jeffrey Kellogg** (IL), **Larry Poncino** (PCL), **Phil Cuzzi** (IL), **Scott Potter** (AA), **Larry Vanover** (AA), **Dan Wickham** (PCL), **Jerry Meals** (IL), **Rich Rieker** (AA), **Mark Barron** (AA), and **Bob Long** (IL).

UMPIRES' UNIFORMS

National League umpires wear grey slacks, navy blazers, light blue short-sleeved cotton shirts or light grey turtlenecks and black leather belts. They are also issued navy blue windbreakers and navy blue V-neck sweaters. National League logos are on the left breast pocket of the blazer and the left breast of the windbreaker and sweater. Umpires' numbers are worn on the right sleeve of the blazers, shirts, sweaters and windbreakers. Caps are navy blue with white embroidered "NL" on the front.

UMPIRES' SERVICE

	Years Service Thru 1991	All-Star Games	Championship Series	World Series
Doug Harvey	30	1963, '64, '71, '77, '82	1970, '72, '76, '80, '83, '86, '89, '91	1968, '74, '81, '84, '88
Harry Wendelstedt	26	1968, '76, '83	1970, '72, '77, '81 '82, '84, '88, '90	1973, '80, '86, '91
Bruce Froemming	21	1975, '86	1973, '77, '80, '82, '85, '89, '91	1976, '84, '88
John McSherry	21	1975, '82, '91	1974, '78, '83, '85, '88, '90	1977, '87
Frank Pulli	20	1977, '88	1975, '79, '84, '86, '91	1978, '83, '90
Terry Tata	19	1978, '88	1976, '80, '83, '85, '89	1979, '87, '91
Dutch Rennert	18	1979, '84	1977, '81, '82, '86, '88, '90	1980, '83, '89
Paul Runge	18	1978, '86	1977, '81, '82, '85, '88, '90	1979, '84, '89
Jim Quick	16	1981, '83, '91	1979, '87, '89	1985, '90
Ed Montague	16	1982. '90	1979, '84, '87	1986, '91
Jerry Crawford	15	1989	1980, '83, '85, 90	1988
Eric Gregg	14½	1986	1981, '87, '91	1989
Joe West	14	1987	1981, '86, '88	—
Charlie Williams	11	1985	1989	—
Randy Marsh	10	1985, '88	1989	1990
Bob Davidson	10	1987	1988, '91	—
Steve Rippley	8½	1990	—	—
Gerry Davis	8	1989	1990	—
Dana DeMuth	8	1990	1991	—
Greg Bonin	6	1991	—	—
Tom Hallion	6	—	—	—
Gary Darling	5	—	—	—
Mark Hirschbeck	4	—	—	—
Bill Hohn	3	—	—	—
Jerry Layne	3	—	—	—
Mike Winters	2	—	—	—
Charlie Reliford	2	—	—	—
Ed Rapuano	1½	—	—	—

ED VARGO—Begins his sixth year as Director of Umpire Supervision. Umpired in the NL from 1960-1983. Became an umpire consultant in 1984. Ed worked 4 All Star Games, 4 League Championships and 4 World Series.

AL BARLICK—Began his NL career towards the end of the 1940 season. Retired as an active umpire in 1971. Has been an umpire consultant since 1972. Al worked 7 All Star Games and 7 World Series. He was inducted into the Baseball Hall of Fame in 1989.

NICK COLOSI—Began his career in the NL at the end of the 1968 season. Retired as an active umpire following the 1982 season. This marks his third year as a consultant. Nick worked 2 All-Star Games, 3 League Championships and 2 World Series.

ALL-STAR GAME SCORES

1933	AL	4	NL	2
1934	AL	9	NL	7
1935	AL	4	NL	1
1936	NL	4	AL	3
1937	AL	8	NL	3
1938	NL	4	AL	1
1939	AL	3	NL	1
1940	NL	4	AL	0
1941	AL	7	NL	5
1942	AL	3	NL	1
1943	AL	5	NL	3
1944	NL	7	AL	1
1946	AL	12	NL	0
1947	AL	2	NL	1
1948	AL	5	NL	2
1949	AL	11	NL	7
1950	NL	4	AL	3
1951	NL	8	AL	3
1952	NL	3	AL	2
1953	NL	5	AL	1
1954	AL	11	NL	9
1955	NL	6	AL	5
1956	NL	7	AL	3
1957	AL	6	NL	5
1958	AL	4	NL	3
1959	NL	5	AL	4
1959	AL	5	NL	3
1960	NL	5	AL	3
1960	NL	6	AL	0
1961	NL	5	AL	4
1961	NL	1	AL	1
1962	NL	3	AL	1
1962	AL	9	NL	4
1963	NL	5	AL	3
1964	NL	7	AL	4
1965	NL	6	AL	5
1966	NL	2	AL	1
1967	NL	2	AL	1
1968	NL	1	AL	0
1969	NL	9	AL	3
1970	NL	5	AL	4
1971	AL	6	NL	4
1972	NL	4	AL	3
1973	NL	7	AL	1
1974	NL	7	AL	2
1975	NL	6	AL	3
1976	NL	7	AL	1
1977	NL	7	AL	5
1978	NL	7	AL	3
1979	NL	7	AL	6
1980	NL	4	AL	2
1981	NL	5	AL	4
1982	NL	4	AL	1
1983	AL	13	NL	3
1984	NL	3	AL	1
1985	NL	6	AL	1
1986	AL	3	NL	2
1987	NL	2	AL	0
1988	AL	2	NL	1
1989	AL	5	NL	3
1990	AL	2	NL	0
1991	AL	4	NL	2

TOTALS
NL—37
AL—24
Tie: 1 (1961)

NATIONAL LEAGUE TOP VOTE-GETTERS

CATCHERS

B. Santiago	San Diego	1,751,399
C. Biggio	Houston	910,659
M. Scioscia	Los Angeles	850,396
T. Pagnozzi	St. Louis	355,768
J. Oliver	Cincinnati	287,124
M. LaValliere	Pittsburgh	277,694
M. Heath	Atlanta	269,604
T. Kennedy	San Francisco	255,529

FIRST BASEMEN

W. Clark	San Francisco	1,534,203
F. McGriff	San Diego	1,474,502
M. Grace	Chicago	541,465
E. Murray	Los Angeles	514,745
P. Guerrero	St. Louis	343,412
H. Morris	Cincinnati	324,120
J. Bagwell	Houston	269,869
S. Bream	Atlanta	260,492

SECOND BASEMEN

R. Sandberg	Chicago	2,526,747
D. DeShields	Montreal	637,022
J. Samuel	Los Angeles	522,468
B. Roberts	San Diego	329,215
B. Doran	Houston	307,436
J. Lind	Pittsburgh	276,106
R. Thompson	San Francisco	264,365
J. Oquendo	St. Louis	247,493

THIRD BASEMEN

C. Sabo	Cincinnati	1,325,774
M. Williams	San Francisco	782,392
T. Wallach	Montreal	715,502
T. Pendleton	Atlanta	637,886
T. Zeile	St. Louis	533,770
K. Caminiti	Houston	443,089
G. Jefferies	New York	357,056
G. Scott	Chicago	265,737

SHORTSTOPS

O. Smith	St. Louis	1,280,495
I. Fernandez	San Diego	1,083,010
B. Larkin	Cincinnati	875,591
S. Dunston	Chicago	623,955
H. Johnson	New York	402,323
J. Bell	Pittsburgh	347,939
A. Griffin	Los Angeles	253,876
S. Owen	Montreal	224,865

OUTFIELDERS

D. Strawberry	Los Angeles	1,393,009
T. Gwynn	San Diego	1,381,602
A. Dawson	Chicago	1,108,585
B. Bonilla	Pittsburgh	1,085,233
K. Mitchell	San Francisco	1,001,357
D. Justice	Atlanta	986,238
G. Bell	Chicago	871,299
B. Bonds	Pittsburgh	870,457
E. Davis	Cincinnati	741,008
A. Van Slyke	Pittsburgh	643,285
W. McGee	San Francisco	593,507
F. Jose	St. Louis	566,966
B. Butler	Los Angeles	522,598
I. Calderon	Montreal	401,186
V. Coleman	New York	382,140
L. Dykstra	Philadelphia	367,013

ALL-STAR MVP's

Year	Player & Club	League
1970	Carl Yastrzemski, Boston	A.L.
1971	Frank Robinson, Baltimore	A.L.
1972	Joe Morgan, Cincinnati	N.L.
1973	Bobby Bonds, San Francisco	N.L.
1974	Steve Garvey, Los Angeles	N.L.
1975	Bill Madlock, Chicago	N.L.
	Jon Matlack, New York	N.L.
1976	George Foster, Cincinnati	N.L.
1977	Don Sutton, Los Angeles	N.L.
1978	Steve Garvey, Los Angeles	N.L.
1979	Dave Parker, Pittsburgh	N.L.
1980	Ken Griffey, Cincinnati	N.L.
1981	Gary Carter, Montreal	N.L.
1982	Dave Concepcion, Cincinnati	N.L.
1983	Fred Lynn, California	A.L.
1984	Gary Carter, Montreal	N.L.
1985	LaMarr Hoyt, San Diego	N.L.
1986	Roger Clemens, Boston	A.L.
1987	Tim Raines, Montreal	N.L.
1988	Terry Steinbach, Oakland	A.L.
1989	Bo Jackson, Kansas City	A.L.
1990	Julio Franco, Texas	A.L.
1991	Cal Ripken Jr., Baltimore	A.L.

1992 marks the second time the All-Star Game will be played at San Diego Jack Murphy Stadium. The last time was 1978, on Tuesday, July 11th. The National League team won that game 7-3. The National League squad will be trying to break out of a 4-game losing streak in this season's contest. The date of the game is Tuesday, July 14th.

ALL-STAR GAME BOX SCORE

NATIONAL (2)

	AB	R	H	BI
Gwynn, cf	4	1	2	0
Butler, pr-cf	1	0	0	0
Sandberg, 2b	3	0	1	0
Samuel, 2b	1	0	1	0
Clark, 1b	2	0	1	0
Murray, 1b	1	0	0	0
Bonilla, dh	4	0	2	1
Dawson, rf	2	1	1	1
Jose, rf	2	0	1	0
Calderon, lf	2	0	0	0
O'Neill, lf	2	0	0	0
Sabo, 3b	2	0	0	0
Johnson, 3b	2	0	0	0
Santiago, c	3	0	0	0
Biggio, c	1	0	0	0
O. Smith, ss	1	0	0	0
Larkin, ss	1	0	0	0
Bell, ph	1	0	0	0
Glavine, p	0	0	0	0
De. Martinez, p	0	0	0	0
Viola, p	0	0	0	0
Harnisch, p	0	0	0	0
Smiley, p	0	0	0	0
Dibble, p	0	0	0	0
Morgan, p	0	0	0	0
TOTALS	35	2	10	2

AMERICAN (4)

	AB	R	H	BI
R. Henderson, lf	2	1	1	0
Carter, lf	1	1	1	0
Boggs, 3b	2	1	1	0
Molitor, 3b	0	0	0	0
C. Ripken, ss	3	1	2	3
Guillen, ss	0	0	0	0
Fielder, 1b	3	0	0	0
Palmeiro, 1b	0	0	0	0
Tartabull, dh	2	0	0	0
Baines, dh	1	0	0	1
D. Henderson, rf	2	0	0	0
Sierra, rf	2	0	0	0
Griffey Jr., cf	3	0	2	0
Puckett, cf	1	0	0	0
S. Alomar, c	2	0	0	0
Fisk, c	2	0	1	0
R. Alomar, 2b	4	0	0	0
Morris, p	0	0	0	0
Key, p	0	0	0	0
Clemens, p	0	0	0	0
McDowell, p	0	0	0	0
Reardon, p	0	0	0	0
Aguilera, p	0	0	0	0
Eckersley, p	0	0	0	0
TOTALS	30	4	8	4

E—Biggio. DP—American 2. LOB—National 8, American 8. 2B—Sandberg. HR—Dawson, C. Ripken. S—Guillen. SF—Baines. SB—Calderon. BB—National 2 (O. Smith, Clark); American 1 (Palmeiro). SO—National 6 (Santiago, Bonilla, Murray, O'Neill, Johnson, Bell); American 6 (Fielder, Tartabull, D. Henderson, Sierra 2, Fisk). GDP—Dawson, Gwynn. T—3:04. A—52,383. Umpires: HP—Joe Brinkman (AL); 1B—John McSherry (NL); 2B—Ken Kaiser (AL); 3B—Jim Quick (NL); LF—Larry Young (AL); RF—Greg Bonin (NL). Official scorers—Kit Stier, Red Foley and Joe Sawchuk.

NATIONAL

	IP	H	R	ER	BB	SO
Glavine	2	1	0	0	1	3
De. Martinez (L)	2	4	3	3	0	0
Viola	1	0	0	0	1	0
Harnisch	1	2	0	0	0	1
Smiley	0	1	1	1	0	0
Dibble	1	0	0	0	1	1
Morgan	1	0	0	0	0	1

AMERICAN

	IP	H	R	ER	BB	SO
Morris	2	4	1	1	0	1
Key (W)	1	1	0	0	0	1
Clemens	1	1	1	1	0	0
McDowell	2	1	0	0	2	0
Reardon	⅔	1	0	0	0	0
Aguilera	1⅓	2	0	0	0	3
Eckersley (S)	1	0	0	0	0	1

```
National ..................... 1 0 0   1 0 0   0 0 0—2
American ..................... 0 0 3   0 0 0   1 0 X—4
```

NATIONAL LEAGUE ALL-STARS BY CLUB

Atlanta (1)
Tom Glavine

Chicago (3)
George Bell
Andre Dawson
Ryne Sandberg

Cincinnati (5)
Tom Browning
Rob Dibble
Barry Larkin
Paul O'Neill
Chris Sabo

Houston (2)
Craig Biggio
Pete Harnisch

Los Angeles (5)
Brett Butler
Ramon Martinez
Eddie Murray
Juan Samuel
Darryl Strawberry*

Montreal (2)
Ivan Calderon
Dennis Martinez

New York (2)
Howard Johnson
Frank Viola

Philadelphia (1)
John Kruk

Pittsburgh (2)
Bobby Bonilla
John Smiley

St. Louis (3)
Felix Jose
Lee Smith
Ozzie Smith

San Diego (2)
Tony Gwynn
Benito Santiago

San Francisco (1)
Will Clark

*Elected starter, unable to play.

LCS MVP

Joe Sebo, Atlanta Braves

STEVE AVERY
ATLANTA BRAVES

Steve Avery of the Atlanta Braves won the National League Championship Series honors with his 2-0 record, 0.00 ERA and 17 strikeouts in the seven-game series. Avery pitched 8 shutout innings in game 2 at Pittsburgh, allowing the Braves to win the 1-0 contest. In game 6, back at Pittsburgh, he pitched another 8 scoreless innings in another 1-0 pitchers' duel. Alejandro Pena pitched the ninth inning in each of Avery's games and recorded two saves. In game 2 Avery was matched against Zane Smith, who pitched 7 innings, allowing the one Braves' run and in game 7 he pitched against Doug Drabek, who also pitched 8 scoreless innings, but allowed the winning run in the ninth inning. The 21-year-old left-hander was untouchable during the League Championship Series.

MVP AWARD WINNERS

1977—Dusty Baker, Los Angeles Dodgers
1978—Steve Garvey, Los Angeles Dodgers
1979—Willie Stargell, Pittsburgh Pirates
1980—Manny Trillo, Philadelphia Phillies
1981—Burt Hooton, Los Angeles Dodgers
1982—Darrell Porter, St. Louis Cardinals
1983—Gary Matthews, Philadelphia Phillies
1984—Steve Garvey, San Diego Padres
1985—Ozzie Smith, St. Louis Cardinals
1986—Mike Scott, Houston Astros
1987—Jeffrey Leonard, San Francisco Giants
1988—Orel Hershiser, Los Angeles Dodgers
1989—Will Clark, San Francisco Giants
1990—Rob Dibble and Randy Myers, Cincinnati Reds
1991—Steve Avery, Atlanta Braves

LEAGUE CHAMPIONSHIP SERIES

ATLANTA BRAVES

PLAYER	AVG	G	AB	R	H	2B	3B	HR	RBI
Belliard, R	.211	7	19	0	4	0	0	0	1
Blauser, J	.000	2	2	0	0	0	0	0	0
Bream, S	.300	4	10	1	3	0	0	1	3
Cabrera, F	.000	0	0	0	0	0	0	0	0
Gant, R	.259	7	27	4	7	1	0	1	3
Gregg, T	.250	4	4	0	1	0	0	0	0
Hunter, B	.333	5	18	2	6	2	0	1	4
Justice, D	.200	7	25	4	5	1	0	1	2
Lemke, M	.200	7	20	1	4	1	0	0	1
RIGHT	.364	--	11	--	4	1	0	0	1
LEFT	.000	--	9	--	0	0	0	0	0
Mitchell, K	.000	5	4	0	0	0	0	0	0
Olson, G	.333	7	24	3	8	1	0	1	4
Pendleton, T	.167	7	30	1	5	1	1	0	1
RIGHT	.294	--	17	--	5	1	1	0	1
LEFT	.000	--	13	--	0	0	0	0	0
Smith, L	.250	7	24	3	6	3	0	0	0
Treadway, J	.333	1	3	0	1	0	0	0	0
Willard, J	.000	2	2	0	0	0	0	0	0
Avery, S	.143	2	7	0	1	0	0	0	0
Glavine, T	.250	2	4	0	1	0	0	0	0
Leibrandt, C	.000	1	1	0	0	0	0	0	0
Smoltz, J	.200	2	5	0	1	0	0	0	0
BRAVES	.231	7	229	19	53	10	1	5	19
PIRATES	.224	7	228	12	51	10	0	3	11

PITCHER		W	L	ERA	IP	H	R	ER	BB	SO
Avery, S	L	2	0	0.00	16.1	9	0	0	4	17
Clancy, J	R	0	0	0.00	0.1	0	0	0	0	0
Glavine, T	L	0	2	3.21	14.0	12	5	5	6	11
Leibrandt, C	L	0	0	1.35	6.2	8	2	1	3	6
Mercker, K	L	0	1	13.50	0.2	0	1	1	2	0
Smoltz, J	R	2	0	1.76	15.1	14	3	3	3	15
St. Claire, R	R	0	0	- - -	0.0	0	0	0	0	0
Stanton, M	L	0	0	2.45	3.2	4	1	1	3	3
Wohlers, M	R	0	0	0.00	1.2	3	0	0	1	1
BRAVES		4	3	1.57	63.0	51	12	11	22	57
PIRATES		3	4	2.57	63.0	53	19	18	22	42

PITTSBURGH PIRATES

PLAYER	AVG	G	AB	R	H	2B	3B	HR	RBI
Bell, J	.414	7	29	2	12	2	0	1	1
Bonds, B	.148	7	27	1	4	1	0	0	0
Espy, C	.000	2	2	0	0	0	0	0	0
RIGHT	.000	--	0	--	0	0	0	0	0
LEFT	.000	--	2	--	0	0	0	0	0
Lind, J	.160	7	25	0	4	0	0	0	3
McClendon, L	.000	3	2	0	0	0	0	0	0
Merced, O	.222	3	9	1	2	0	0	1	1
RIGHT	.000	--	0	--	0	0	0	0	0
LEFT	.222	--	9	--	2	0	0	1	1
Redus, G	.158	5	19	1	3	0	0	0	0
Slaught, D	.235	6	17	0	4	0	0	0	1
Van Slyke, A	.160	7	25	3	4	2	0	1	2
Varsho, G	.500	2	2	0	1	0	0	0	0
Wilkerson, C	.000	4	4	0	0	0	0	0	0
RIGHT	.000	--	1	--	0	0	0	0	0
LEFT	.000	--	3	--	0	0	0	0	0
Drabek, D	.200	2	5	0	1	1	0	0	1
Mason, R	.000	3	1	0	0	0	0	0	0
Smith, Z	.000	2	5	0	0	0	0	0	0
Tomlin, R	.000	1	2	0	0	0	0	0	0
Walk, B	.000	3	2	0	0	0	0	0	0
PIRATES	.224	7	228	12	51	10	0	3	11
BRAVES	.231	7	229	19	53	10	1	5	19

PITCHER		W	L	ERA	IP	H	R	ER	BB	SO
Belinda, S	R	1	0	0.00	5.0	0	0	0	3	4
Drabek, D	R	1	1	0.60	15.0	10	1	1	5	10
Landrum, B	R	0	0	9.00	1.0	2	1	1	2	2
Mason, R	R	0	0	0.00	4.1	3	0	0	1	2
Patterson, B	L	0	0	0.00	2.0	1	0	0	0	3
Rodriguez, R	L	0	0	27.00	1.0	1	3	3	2	1
Smiley, J	L	0	2	23.63	2.2	8	8	7	1	3
Smith, Z	L	1	1	0.61	14.2	15	1	1	3	10
Tomlin, R	L	0	0	3.00	6.0	6	2	2	2	1
Walk, B	R	0	0	1.93	9.1	5	2	2	3	5
PIRATES		3	4	2.57	63.0	53	19	18	22	42
BRAVES		4	3	1.57	63.0	51	12	11	22	57

LINESCORES

GAME 1—Wednesday, October 9 (n)

Atlanta	0 0 0 0 0 0 0 0 1	1 5 1		Time: 2:52
Pittsburgh	1 0 2 0 0 1 0 1 x	5 8 1		Att: 57,347

GLAVINE, Wohlers (7) and Stanton (8)
DRABEK and Walk (S) (7)
HR: Pittsburgh (1)-Van Slyke; Atlanta (1)-Justice

GAME 2—Thursday, October 10 (n)

Atlanta	0 0 0 0 0 1 0 0 0	1 8 0	Time: 2:46
Pittsburgh	0 0 0 0 0 0 0 0 0	0 6 0	Att: 57,533

AVERY and Pena (S) (9)
Z. SMITH, Mason (8) and Belinda (9)

GAME 3—Saturday, October 12

Pittsburgh	1 0 0 1 0 0 1 0 0	3 10 2	Time: 3:22
Atlanta	4 1 1 0 0 0 1 3 x	10 11 0	Att: 50,905

SMILEY, Landrum (3), Patterson (4), Kipper (6) and Rodriguez (8)
SMOLTZ, Stanton (7), Wohlers (8) and Pena (S) (8)
HR: Atlanta (3)-Gant, Olson, Bream; Pittsburgh (2)-Merced, Bell

GAME 4—Sunday, October 13 (n)

Pittsburgh	0 1 0 0 1 0 0 0 1	3 11 1	Time: 3:43
Atlanta	2 0 0 0 0 0 0 0 0	2 7 1	Att: 51,109

Tomlin, Walk (7) and BELINDA (9)
Leibrandt, Clancy (7), Stanton (8), MERCKER (10) and Wohlers (10)

GAME 5—Monday, October 14

Pittsburgh	0 0 0 0 1 0 0 0 0	1 6 2	Time: 2:51
Atlanta	0 0 0 0 0 0 0 0 0	0 9 1	Att: 51,109

Z. SMITH and Mason (S) (8)
GLAVINE and Pena (9)

GAME 6—Wednesday, October 16 (n)

Atlanta	0 0 0 0 0 0 0 0 1	1 7 0	Time: 3:09
Pittsburgh	0 0 0 0 0 0 0 0 0	0 4 0	Att: 54,508

AVERY and Pena (S) (9)
DRABEK

GAME 7—Thursday, October 17 (n)

Atlanta	3 0 0 0 1 0 0 0 0	4 6 1	Time: 3:04
Pittsburgh	0 0 0 0 0 0 0 0 0	0 6 0	Att: 46,932

SMOLTZ
SMILEY, Walk (1), Mason (6) and Belinda (8)
HR: Atlanta (1)-Hunter

NATIONAL LEAGUE CHAMPIONSHIP SERIES RESULTS

1969—New York (E) 3—Atlanta (W) 0
1970—Cincinnati (W) 3—Pittsburgh (E) 0
1971—Pittsburgh (E) 3—San Francisco (W) 1
1972—Cincinnati (W) 3—Pittsburgh (E) 2
1973—New York (E) 3—Cincinnati (W) 2
1974—Los Angeles (W) 3—Pittsburgh (E) 1
1975—Cincinnati (W) 3—Pittsburgh (E) 0
1976—Cincinnati (W) 3—Philadelphia (E) 0
1977—Los Angeles (W) 3—Philadelphia (E) 1
1978—Los Angeles (W) 3—Philadelphia (E) 1
1979—Pittsburgh (E) 3—Cincinnati (W) 0
1980—Philadelphia (E) 3—Houston (W) 2
1981—Los Angeles (W) 3—Montreal (E) 2
1982—St. Louis (E) 3—Atlanta (W) 0
1983—Philadelphia (E) 3—Los Angeles (W) 1
1984—San Diego (W) 3—Chicago (E) 2
1985—St. Louis (E) 4—Los Angeles (W) 2
1986—New York (E) 4—Houston (W) 2
1987—St. Louis (E) 4—San Francisco (W) 3
1988—Los Angeles (W) 4—New York (E) 3
1989—San Francisco (W) 4—Chicago (E) 1
1990—Cincinnati (W) 4—Pittsburgh (E) 2
1991—Atlanta (W) 4—Pittsburgh (E) 3

WORLD SERIES RESULTS

Year—Winner	Loser
1903—Boston A, 5	Pittsburgh N, 3
1904—No Series	
1905—New York N, 4	Philadelphia A, 1
1906—Chicago A, 4	Chicago N, 2
1907—Chicago N, 4	Detroit A, 0; 1 tie
1908—Chicago N, 4	Detroit A, 1
1909—Pittsburgh N, 4	Detroit A, 3
1910—Philadelphia A, 4	Chicago N, 1
1911—Philadelphia A, 4	New York N, 2
1912—Boston A, 4	New York N, 3; 1 tie
1913—Philadelphia A, 4	New York N, 1
1914—Boston N, 4	Philadelphia A, 0
1915—Boston A, 4	Philadelphia N, 1
1916—Boston A, 4	Brooklyn N, 1
1917—Chicago A, 4	New York N, 2
1918—Boston A, 4	Chicago N, 2
1919—Cincinnati N, 5	Chicago A, 3
1920—Cleveland A, 5	Brooklyn N, 2
1921—New York N, 5	New York A, 3
1922—New York N, 4	New York A, 0; 1 tie
1923—New York A, 4	New York N, 2
1924—Washington A, 4	New York N, 3
1925—Pittsburgh N, 4	Washington A, 3
1926—St. Louis N, 4	New York A, 3
1927—New York A, 4	Pittsburgh N, 0
1928—New York A, 4	St. Louis N, 0
1929—Philadelphia A, 4	Chicago N, 1
1930—Philadelphia A, 4	St. Louis N, 2
1931—St. Louis N, 4	Philadelphia A, 3
1932—New York A, 4	Chicago N, 0
1933—New York N, 4	Washington A, 1
1934—St. Louis N, 4	Detroit A, 3
1935—Detroit A, 4	Chicago N, 2
1936—New York A, 4	New York N, 2
1937—New York A, 4	New York N, 1
1938—New York A, 4	Chicago N, 0
1939—New York A, 4	Cincinnati N, 0
1940—Cincinnati N, 4	Detroit A, 3
1941—New York A, 4	Brooklyn N, 1
1942—St. Louis N, 4	New York A, 1
1943—New York A, 4	St. Louis N, 1
1944—St. Louis N, 4	St. Louis A, 2
1945—Detroit A, 4	Chicago N, 3
1946—St. Louis N, 4	Boston A, 3
1947—New York A, 4	Brooklyn N, 3
1948—Cleveland A, 4	Boston N, 2
1949—New York A, 4	Brooklyn N, 1
1950—New York A, 4	Philadelphia N, 0
1951—New York A, 4	New York N, 2
1952—New York A, 4	Brooklyn N, 3
1953—New York A, 4	Brooklyn N, 2
1954—New York N, 4	Cleveland A, 0
1955—Brooklyn N, 4	New York A, 3
1956—New York A, 4	Brooklyn N, 3
1957—Milwaukee N, 4	New York A, 3
1958—New York A, 4	Milwaukee N, 3
1959—Los Angeles N, 4	Chicago A, 2
1960—Pittsburgh N, 4	New York A, 3
1961—New York A, 4	Cincinnati N, 1
1962—New York A, 4	San Francisco N, 3
1963—Los Angeles N, 4	New York A, 0
1964—St. Louis N, 4	New York A, 3
1965—Los Angeles N, 4	Minnesota A, 3
1966—Baltimore A, 4	Los Angeles N, 0
1967—St. Louis N, 4	Boston A, 3
1968—Detroit A, 4	St. Louis N, 3
1969—New York N, 4	Baltimore A, 1
1970—Baltimore A, 4	Cincinnati N, 1
1971—Pittsburgh N, 4	Baltimore A, 3
1972—Oakland A, 4	Cincinnati N, 3
1973—Oakland A, 4	New York N, 3
1974—Oakland A, 4	Los Angeles N, 1
1975—Cincinnati N, 4	Boston A, 3
1976—Cincinnati N, 4	New York A, 0
1977—New York A, 4	Los Angeles N, 2
1978—New York A, 4	Los Angeles N, 2
1979—Pittsburgh N, 4	Baltimore A, 3
1980—Philadelphia N, 4	Kansas City A, 2
1981—Los Angeles N, 4	New York A, 2
1982—St. Louis N, 4	Milwaukee A, 3
1983—Baltimore A, 4	Philadelphia N, 1
1984—Detroit A, 4	San Diego N, 1
1985—Kansas City A, 4	St. Louis N, 3
1986—New York N, 4	Boston A, 3
1987—Minnesota A, 4	St. Louis N, 3
1988—Los Angeles N, 4	Oakland A, 1
1989—Oakland A, 4	San Francisco N, 0
1990—Cincinnati N, 4	Oakland A, 0
1991—Minnesota A, 4	Atlanta N, 3

(A.L. has won 51 series, N.L. has won 37 series.)

WORLD SERIES
MVP

1955	Johnny Podres, Brooklyn Dodgers
1956	Don Larsen, New York Yankees
1957	Lew Burdette, Milwaukee Braves
1958	Bob Turley, New York Yankees
1959	Larry Sherry, Los Angeles Dodgers
1960	Bobby Richardson, New York Yankees
1961	Whitey Ford, New York Yankees
1962	Ralph Terry, New York Yankees
1963	Sandy Koufax, Los Angeles Dodgers
1964	Bob Gibson, St. Louis Cardinals
1965	Sandy Koufax, Los Angeles Dodgers
1966	Frank Robinson, Baltimore Orioles
1967	Bob Gibson, St. Louis Cardinals
1968	Mickey Lolich, Detroit Tigers
1969	Donn Clendenon, New York Mets
1970	Brooks Robinson, Baltimore Orioles
1971	Roberto Clemente, Pittsburgh Pirates
1972	Gene Tenace, Oakland A's
1973	Reggie Jackson, Oakland A's
1974	Rollie Fingers, Oakland A's
1975	Pete Rose, Cincinnati Reds
1976	Johnny Bench, Cincinnati Reds
1977	Reggie Jackson, New York Yankees
1978	Bucky Dent, New York Yankees
1979	Willie Stargell, Pittsburgh Pirates
1980	Mike Schmidt, Philadelphia Phillies
1981	Ron Cey, Los Angeles Dodgers
	Pedro Guerrero, Los Angeles Dodgers
	Steve Yeager, Los Angeles Dodgers
1982	Darrell Porter, St. Louis Cardinals
1983	Rick Dempsey, Baltimore Orioles
1984	Alan Trammell, Detroit Tigers
1985	Bret Saberhagen, Kansas City Royals
1986	Ray Knight, New York Mets
1987	Frank Viola, Minnesota Twins
1988	Orel Hershiser, Los Angeles Dodgers
1989	Dave Stewart, Oakland Athletics
1990	Jose Rijo, Cincinnati Reds
1991	Jack Morris, Minnesota Twins

EXTRA-INNING
WORLD SERIES GAMES

Three of the seven 1991 World Series games went into extra innings, game 3 at Atlanta and games 6 and 7 at Minnesota, with the home team winning each one.

There have been 45 extra-inning games in World Series history. National League clubs have won 23, American League teams have won 19 and three games have ended in a tie. The home team holds a 25-17 advantage in extra-inning games.

The breakdown by innings:

10 innings	26 times
11 innings	8 times
12 innings	10 times
13 innings	None
14 innings	1 time

1991 WORLD SERIES

GAME 1
At MINNESOTA
Saturday, October 19 (night)

Atlanta	0 0 0 0 0 1 0 1 0	2 6 1	Time: 3:00
Minnesota	0 0 1 0 3 1 0 0 x	5 9 1	Att: 55,108

LEIBRANDT, Clancy (5), Wohlers (7) and Stanton (8)
MORRIS, Guthrie (8) and Aguilera (S) (8)
HR: Minnesota (1) - Gagne, Hrbek

GAME 2
At MINNESOTA
Sunday, October 20 (night)

Atlanta	0 1 0 0 1 0 0 0 0	2 8 1	Time: 2:37
Minnesota	2 0 0 0 0 0 0 1 x	3 4 1	Att: 55,145

GLAVINE
TAPANI and Aguilera (S) (9)
HR: Minnesota (2) - Davis, Leius

GAME 3
At ATLANTA
Tuesday, October 22 (night)

Minnesota	1 0 0 0 0 0 1 2 0 0 0 0	4 10 1	Time: 4:04
Atlanta	0 1 0 1 2 0 0 0 0 0 0 1	5 8 2	Att: 50,878

Erickson, West (5), Leach (5), Bedrosian (6), Willis (8), Guthrie (10) and AGUILERA (12)
Avery, Pena (8), Stanton (10), Wohlers (12), Mercker (12) and CLANCY (12)
HR: Atlanta (2) - Justice, Smith; Minnesota (2) - Puckett, Davis

GAME 4
At ATLANTA
Wednesday, October 23 (night)

Minnesota	0 1 0 0 0 0 1 0 0	2 7 0	Time: 2:57
Atlanta	0 0 1 0 0 0 1 0 1	3 8 0	Att: 50,878

Morris, Willis (7), GUTHRIE (8) and Bedrosian (9)
Smoltz, Wohlers (8) and STANTON (8)
HR: Atlanta (2) - Pendleton, Smith; Minnesota (1) - Pagliarulo

GAME 5
At ATLANTA
Thursday, October 24 (night)

Minnesota	0 0 0 0 0 3 0 1 1	5 7 1	Time: 2:59
Atlanta	0 0 0 4 1 0 6 3 x	14 17 1	Att: 50,878

TAPANI, Leach (6), West (7), Bedrosian (7) and Willis (8)
GLAVINE, Mercker (6), Clancy (7) and St. Claire (9)
HR: Atlanta (3) - Justice, Smith, Hunter

GAME 6
At MINNESOTA
Saturday, October 26 (night)

Atlanta	0 0 0 0 2 0 1 0 0 0	3 9 1	Time: 3:36
Minnesota	2 0 0 0 1 0 0 0 0 1	4 9 0	Att: 55,155

Avery, Stanton (7), Pena (9) and LEIBRANDT (11)
Erickson, Guthrie (7), Willis (7) and AGUILERA (10)
HR: Atlanta (1) - Pendleton; Minnesota (1) - Puckett

GAME 7
At MINNESOTA
Sunday, October 27 (night)

Atlanta	0 0 0 0 0 0 0 0 0 0	0 7 0	Time: 3:23
Minnesota	0 0 0 0 0 0 0 0 0 1	1 10 0	Att: 55,118

Smoltz, Stanton (8) and PENA (9)
MORRIS

1991 FINAL STANDINGS

EASTERN DIVISION

	W	L	PCT.	GB		vs. Eastern Division							vs. Western Division				
					Pit.	St.L.	Phi.	Chi.	N.Y.	Mon.	Atl.	L.A.	S.D.	S.F.	Cin.	Hou.
Pittsburgh	98	64	.605	....	....	11	12	11	12	12	3	5	7	7	10	8
St. Louis	84	78	.519	14.0	7	....	12	8	11	11	3	6	3	8	8	7
Philadelphia	78	84	.481	20.0	6	6	....	10	7	14	7	5	9	6	3	5
Chicago	77	83	.481	20.0	7	10	8	....	11	10	6	2	4	6	4	9
New York	77	84	.478	20.5	6	7	11	6	....	14	3	5	7	6	7	5
Montreal	71	90	.441	26.5	6	7	4	7	4	....	7	7	6	7	6	10

WESTERN DIVISION

	W	L	PCT.	GB		vs. Eastern Division							vs. Western Division				
					Pit.	St.L.	Phi.	Chi.	N.Y.	Mon.	Atl.	L.A.	S.D.	S.F.	Cin.	Hou.
Atlanta	94	68	.580	....	9	9	5	6	9	5	....	7	11	9	11	13
Los Angeles	93	69	.574	1.0	7	6	7	10	7	5	11	....	10	8	12	10
San Diego	84	78	.519	10.0	5	9	3	8	5	6	7	8	....	11	10	12
San Francisco	75	87	.463	19.0	5	4	6	6	6	5	9	10	7	....	8	9
Cincinnati	74	88	.457	20.0	2	4	9	8	5	6	7	6	8	10	....	9
Houston	65	97	.401	29.0	4	5	7	3	7	2	5	8	6	9	9	....

STANDINGS OF NATIONAL LEAGUE CLUBS AT HOME AND ROAD FOR 1991

HOME GAMES

	W	L	PCT.	LA		PIT		STL		ATL		PHI		CHI		SF		SD		NY		MON		CIN		HOU		EAST		WEST	
				W	L	W	L	W	L	W	L	W	L	W	L	W	L	W	L	W	L	W	L	W	L	W	L	W	L	W	L
Los Angeles	54	27	.667	--	--	3	3	4	2	5	4	5	1	6	0	5	4	5	4	4	2	5	1	6	3	6	3	27	9	27	18
Pittsburgh	52	32	.619	2	4	--	--	6	3	3	3	7	2	7	2	3	3	3	3	7	2	6	6	5	1	3	3	33	15	19	17
St. Louis	52	32	.619	4	2	4	5	--	--	3	3	7	2	5	4	4	2	1	5	7	2	8	4	4	2	5	1	31	17	21	15
Atlanta	48	33	.593	3	6	6	0	6	0	--	--	3	3	4	2	5	4	4	5	4	2	4	2	3	6	6	3	27	9	21	24
Philadelphia	47	36	.566	4	2	4	5	4	5	4	2	--	--	7	2	4	2	5	1	3	6	8	3	1	5	3	3	26	21	21	15
Chicago	46	37	.554	2	4	5	4	6	3	4	2	6	3	--	--	4	2	2	4	4	5	5	6	3	3	5	1	26	21	20	16
San Francisco	43	38	.531	6	3	2	4	2	4	5	4	4	2	4	2	--	--	4	5	4	2	3	3	5	4	4	5	19	17	24	21
San Diego	42	39	.519	4	5	2	4	4	2	2	7	2	4	4	2	6	3	--	--	3	3	2	4	6	3	7	2	17	19	25	20
New York	40	42	.488	3	3	3	3	4	5	5	4	1	5	5	4	1	7	4	2	--	--	8	3	3	3	2	4	23	23	17	19
Montreal	33	35	.485	6	0	0	6	3	3	5	1	1	6	1	5	4	2	2	4	1	6	--	--	4	2	6	0	6	26	27	9
Cincinnati	39	42	.481	3	6	1	5	2	4	1	8	4	2	5	1	6	3	5	4	2	4	4	2	--	--	6	3	18	18	21	24
Houston	37	44	.457	5	4	1	5	4	2	2	7	4	2	2	4	4	5	4	5	3	3	2	4	6	3	--	--	16	20	21	24

ROAD GAMES

	W	L	PCT.	PIT		ATL		SD		LA		NY		CIN		STL		MON		CHI		SF		PHI		HOU		EAST		WEST	
				W	L	W	L	W	L	W	L	W	L	W	L	W	L	W	L	W	L	W	L	W	L	W	L	W	L	W	L
Pittsburgh	46	32	.590	--	--	0	6	4	2	3	3	5	4	5	1	5	4	6	0	4	5	4	2	7	2	5	1	25	17	21	15
Atlanta	46	35	.568	3	3	--	--	7	2	4	5	5	1	8	1	3	3	1	5	2	4	4	5	2	4	7	2	16	20	30	15
San Diego	42	39	.519	3	3	5	4	--	--	4	5	2	4	4	5	5	1	4	2	4	2	5	4	1	5	5	4	19	17	23	22
Los Angeles	39	42	.481	4	2	6	3	5	4	--	--	3	3	6	3	2	4	0	6	4	2	3	6	2	4	4	5	15	21	24	21
New York	37	42	.468	2	7	2	4	3	3	2	4	--	--	4	2	2	7	6	1	5	4	2	4	6	3	3	3	21	22	16	20
Cincinnati	35	46	.432	1	5	6	3	3	6	3	6	3	3	--	--	2	4	2	4	3	3	4	5	5	1	3	6	16	20	19	26
St. Louis	32	46	.410	3	6	0	6	2	4	2	4	4	5	4	2	--	--	3	3	3	3	4	5	5	1	3	6	18	24	14	22
Montreal	38	55	.409	6	6	2	4	4	2	1	5	3	8	2	4	4	8	--	--	6	5	3	3	3	8	4	2	22	35	16	20
Chicago	31	46	.403	2	7	2	4	2	4	0	6	7	1	1	5	4	5	5	1	--	--	2	4	2	7	4	2	20	21	11	25
San Francisco	32	49	.395	3	3	4	5	3	6	4	5	2	4	3	6	2	4	2	4	2	4	--	--	2	4	5	4	13	23	19	26
Philadelphia	31	48	.392	2	7	3	3	4	2	1	5	4	5	5	1	2	7	6	1	3	6	2	4	--	--	2	4	17	26	14	22
Houston	28	53	.346	3	3	3	6	2	7	3	6	4	2	3	6	1	5	0	6	1	5	5	4	3	3	--	--	12	24	16	29

EASTERN CLUBS vs. EAST

	W	L	PCT.
Pittsburgh	58	32	.644
St. Louis	49	41	.544
Chicago	46	42	.523
New York	44	45	.494
Philadelphia	43	47	.478
Montreal	28	61	.315

EASTERN CLUBS vs. WEST

	W	L	PCT.
Montreal	43	29	.597
Pittsburgh	40	32	.556
Philadelphia	35	37	.486
St. Louis	35	37	.486
New York	33	39	.458
Chicago	31	41	.431

WESTERN CLUBS vs. WEST

	W	L	PCT.
Atlanta	51	39	.567
Los Angeles	51	39	.567
San Diego	48	42	.533
San Francisco	43	47	.478
Cincinnati	40	50	.444
Houston	37	53	.411

WESTERN CLUBS vs. EAST

	W	L	PCT.
Atlanta	43	29	.597
Los Angeles	42	30	.583
San Diego	36	36	.500
Cincinnati	34	38	.472
San Francisco	32	40	.444
Houston	28	44	.389

MONTHLY STANDINGS—1991

THROUGH APRIL 30

EAST	W	L	GB
Pittsburgh	13	7	--
St. Louis	13	8	½
New York	12	8	1
Chicago	10	11	3½
Philadelphia	9	12	4½
Montreal	7	13	6

WEST	W	L	GB
Cincinnati	11	8	--
San Diego	11	10	1
Los Angeles	10	10	1½
Atlanta	8	10	2½
Houston	8	11	3
San Francisco	8	12	3½

THROUGH MAY 31

EAST	W	L	GB
Pittsburgh	30	15	--
New York	26	19	4
St. Louis	24	22	6½
Chicago	24	23	7
Philadelphia	22	25	9
Montreal	20	27	11

WEST	W	L	GB
Los Angeles	27	20	--
Atlanta	25	19	½
Cincinnati	23	23	3½
San Diego	24	25	4
Houston	18	29	9
San Francisco	16	32	11½

THROUGH JUNE 30

EAST	W	L	GB
Pittsburgh	45	27	--
St. Louis	40	34	6
New York	39	34	6½
Chicago	34	41	12½
Montreal	33	42	13½
Philadelphia	32	43	14½

WEST	W	L	GB
Los Angeles	45	29	--
Cincinnati	41	33	4
Atlanta	37	36	7½
San Diego	38	39	8½
San Francisco	33	42	12½
Houston	29	46	16½

THROUGH JULY 31

EAST	W	L	GB
Pittsburgh	60	39	--
New York	55	45	5½
St. Louis	53	47	7½
Chicago	48	52	12½
Montreal	43	57	17½
Philadelphia	42	58	18½

WEST	W	L	GB
Los Angeles	58	42	--
Atlanta	53	46	4½
Cincinnati	49	49	8
San Francisco	48	51	9½
San Diego	48	53	10½
Houston	41	59	17

THROUGH AUGUST 31

EAST	W	L	GB
Pittsburgh	77	51	--
St. Louis	69	59	8
Chicago	65	64	12½
New York	63	66	14½
Philadelphia	62	67	15½
Montreal	52	76	25

WEST	W	L	GB
Atlanta	72	57	--
Los Angeles	71	58	1
Cincinnati	64	65	8
San Diego	63	67	9½
San Francisco	62	67	10
Houston	53	76	19

THROUGH SEPTEMBER 30

EAST	W	L	GB
Pittsburgh	95	62	--
St. Louis	82	75	13
New York	75	81	19½
Philadelphia	75	82	20
Chicago	73	82	21
Montreal	70	86	24½

WEST	W	L	GB
Los Angeles	91	66	--
Atlanta	90	67	1
San Diego	80	77	11
Cincinnati	74	83	17
San Francisco	72	85	19
Houston	63	94	28

1991 SHUTOUT GAMES

Club	Pit	LA	Mon	NY	Cin	Chi	SD	Phi	Hou	Atl	SF	StL	Won	Lost	Pct.
Pittsburgh	—	0	2	1	1	0	1	1	2	0	1	2	11	6	.647
Los Angeles	1	—	2	0	1	1	2	1	1	1	2	2	14	8	.636
Montreal	1	2	—	0	1	1	1	1	1	1	2	3	14	10	.583
New York	1	0	2	—	0	0	1	2	1	0	1	3	11	9	.550
Cincinnati	0	2	0	1	—	0	2	0	2	2	2	0	11	9	.550
Chicago	0	0	0	0	0	—	0	1	1	0	0	2	4	4	.500
San Diego	1	0	0	1	2	1	—	1	2	1	0	2	11	12	.478
Philadelphia	0	0	3	1	0	1	1	—	2	1	2	0	11	12	.478
Houston	0	0	0	2	2	0	2	2	—	2	3	0	13	16	.448
Atlanta	0	2	0	1	1	0	1	0	2	—	0	0	7	9	.438
San Francisco	1	2	0	2	0	0	1	1	2	1	—	0	10	13	.435
St. Louis	1	0	1	0	1	0	0	2	0	0	0	—	5	14	.263
TOTALS	6	8	10	9	9	4	12	12	16	9	13	14	122	122	.500

1991 ONE-RUN MARGINS

Club	SD	StL	Phi	Pit	Chi	LA	Atl	Cin	Mon	SF	NY	Hou	Won	Lost	Pct.
San Diego	—	5	0	1	0	1	4	4	4	3	2	3	27	16	.628
St. Louis	1	—	4	3	5	3	2	4	4	6	4	1	37	22	.627
Philadelphia	2	1	—	3	5	2	5	1	8	3	4	2	36	27	.571
Pittsburgh	3	4	2	—	5	1	0	0	5	2	3	2	27	22	.551
Chicago	1	2	5	3	—	2	1	2	5	4	4	4	33	29	.532
Los Angeles	1	3	4	3	5	—	3	2	2	2	1	3	29	27	.518
Atlanta	3	2	0	1	0	2	—	4	2	2	2	4	22	26	.458
Cincinnati	1	0	1	2	2	2	1	—	2	5	2	3	21	25	.457
Montreal	0	2	1	3	3	4	3	2	—	3	4	3	28	39	.418
San Francisco	1	1	2	1	3	5	4	0	3	—	1	2	23	32	.418
New York	1	1	5	2	1	1	1	3	3	1	—	1	20	29	.408
Houston	2	1	3	0	0	4	2	3	1	1	2	—	19	28	.404
TOTALS	16	22	27	22	29	27	26	25	39	32	29	28	322	322	.500

1991 NIGHT GAME STANDINGS

	HOME		ROAD		SEASON		
	W	L	W	L	W	L	Pct.
Pittsburgh	40	26	33	20	73	46	.613
Atlanta	38	28	35	21	73	49	.598
Los Angeles	42	21	27	27	69	48	.590
St. Louis	40	24	20	32	60	56	.517
San Diego	28	32	30	26	58	58	.500
Philadelphia	38	27	20	31	58	58	.500
New York	28	26	25	29	53	55	.491
Montreal	27	24	27	38	54	62	.466
Cincinnati	27	34	27	33	54	67	.446
Chicago	10	8	24	36	34	44	.436
San Francisco	20	23	21	37	41	60	.406
Houston	29	37	21	37	50	74	.403
TOTALS	367	310	310	367	677	677	

1991 DOUBLEHEADER STANDINGS

	Won	Lost	Split	Total Games W	L	Pct.
Montreal	2	0	2	6	2	.750
Atlanta	1	0	3	5	3	.625
Chicago	1	1	0	2	2	.500
New York	0	0	3	3	3	.500
Cincinnati	0	0	2	2	2	.500
Philadelphia	0	0	1	1	1	.500
St. Louis	0	1	3	3	5	.375
Los Angeles	0	1	2	2	4	.333
Pittsburgh	0	1	2	2	4	.333
Houston	0	0	0	0	0	.000
San Diego	0	0	0	0	0	.000
San Francisco	0	0	0	0	0	.000

1991 EXTRA-INNING GAMES (103)

	Won	Lost	Pct.
St. Louis	10	5	.667
Philadelphia	16	9	.640
Atlanta	8	6	.571
Chicago	12	11	.522
San Diego	8	8	.500
New York	8	8	.500
Pittsburgh	6	6	.500
Montreal	9	10	.474
Los Angeles	9	11	.450
San Francisco	5	8	.385
Cincinnati	5	8	.385
Houston	7	13	.350

1991 STANDINGS ON GRASS (489)

	Won	Lost	Pct.
Los Angeles	75	45	.625
Atlanta	70	50	.583
San Diego	62	58	.517
Chicago	59	56	.513
San Francisco	58	62	.483
Pittsburgh	20	22	.476
New York	54	61	.470
Cincinnati	22	26	.458
Montreal	19	27	.413
Philadelphia	17	25	.405
Houston	18	30	.375
St. Louis	15	27	.357

1991 STANDINGS ON ARTIFICIAL SURFACES (481)

	Won	Lost	Pct.
Pittsburgh	78	42	.650
St. Louis	69	51	.575
Atlanta	24	18	.571
San Diego	22	20	.524
Philadelphia	61	59	.508
New York	23	23	.500
Cincinnati	52	62	.456
Montreal	52	63	.452
Los Angeles	18	24	.429
Houston	47	67	.412
San Francisco	17	25	.405
Chicago	18	27	.400

1991 STANDINGS VS. LEFT-HANDED STARTERS

	Won	Lost	Pct.
Pittsburgh	34	19	.642
Atlanta	28	16	.636
Los Angeles	38	30	.559
Cincinnati	30	25	.545
New York	32	32	.500
St. Louis	35	37	.486
Chicago	31	33	.484
Philadelphia	30	32	.484
San Francisco	23	25	.479
San Diego	27	30	.474
Montreal	21	32	.396
Houston	23	39	.371

1991 STANDINGS VS. RIGHT-HANDED STARTERS

	Won	Lost	Pct.
Pittsburgh	64	45	.587
Los Angeles	55	39	.585
Atlanta	66	52	.559
St. Louis	49	41	.544
San Diego	57	48	.543
Philadelphia	48	52	.480
Chicago	46	50	.479
New York	45	52	.464
Montreal	50	58	.463
San Francisco	52	62	.456
Houston	42	58	.420
Cincinnati	44	63	.411

1991 CLUB HOME RUNS AT EACH PARK

By	Atl	Chi	Cin	Hou	LA	Mtl	NY	Phil	Pitt	StL	SD	SF	1991 Total	1990 Total	Opp. Total
Atlanta	83	4	7	3	5	2	6	4	7	4	7	9	141	162	118
Chicago	8	93	8	4	3	1	9	4	10	6	7	6	159	136	117
Cincinnati	9	9	104	1	8	3	5	5	3	1	7	9	164	125	127
Houston	6	5	8	27	8	1	3	3	3	3	5	7	79	94	129
Los Angeles	6	4	2	11	57	2	8	3	2	2	9	2	108	129	96
Montreal	9	11	7	3	2	35	2	7	7	3	4	5	95	114	111
New York	5	4	9	2	3	5	57	6	9	8	5	4	117	172	108
Philadelphia	4	12	6	0	1	4	8	61	2	3	6	4	111	103	111
Pittsburgh	6	15	9	6	3	5	3	6	61	3	5	4	126	138	117
St. Louis	2	2	6	4	1	2	1	6	4	32	3	5	68	73	114
San Diego	10	7	3	4	5	4	5	2	6	3	65	7	121	123	139
San Francisco	8	2	12	6	7	4	5	7	2	5	14	69	141	152	143
1991 Totals	156	168	181	71	103	68	112	114	116	73	137	131	1430		1430
1990 Totals	155	148	143	82	127	110	138	114	122	90	141	151		1521	

AT ATLANTA (156)

Atlanta (83)—Gant 18, Pendleton 13, Justice 11, Blauser 7, Hunter 7, Olson 6, L. Smith 6, Bream 3, Cabrera 2, Lemke 2, Sanders 2, Bell, Gregg, Heath, Mitchell, Treadway, Willard.
Chicago (8)—Bell 2, Sandberg 2, Dascenzo, Grace, Salazar, Wilkins.
Cincinnati (9)—Oliver 3, Sabo 2, Doran, Duncan, Larkin, Sanders.
Houston (6)—Bagwell 2, Biggio, Caminiti, Cedeno, Simms.
Los Angeles (6)—Daniels, Gwynn, Javier, Murray, Samuel, Strawberry.
Montreal (9)—Wallach 3, Calderon 2, Walker 2, DeShields, Da. Martinez.
New York (5)—Brooks 2, Jefferies 2, Gooden.
Philadelphia (4)—C. Hayes 2, Jordan, Kruk.
Pittsburgh (6)—McClendon 2, Bonds, Bonilla, LaValliere, Redus.
St. Louis (2)—Gilkey, Pena.
San Diego (10)—Jackson 3, Gwynn 2, McGriff 2, Fernandez, Santiago, Teufel.
San Francisco (8)—Bass 3, Benjamin, Clark, Lewis, Thompson, Williams.

AT CHICAGO (168)

Atlanta (4)—Pendleton 2, Gant, Hunter.
Chicago (93)—Dawson 22, Sandberg 15, Villanueva 11, Bell 9, Salazar 8, Dunston 7, Grace 5, Walker 4, Berryhill 3, Walton 3, Dw. Smith 2, Wilkins 2, D. May, Scott.
Cincinnati (9)—Davis 2, O'Neill 2, Sabo 2, Hatcher, Morris, Reed.
Houston (5)—Gonzalez 3, Finley, Rhodes.
Los Angeles (4)—Daniels 2, Harris, Samuel.
Montreal (11)—DeShields 2, Da. Martinez 2, Calderon, Fitzgerald, Galarraga, Noboa, Santovenia, VanderWal, Walker.
New York (4)—Brooks 2, Johnson 2.
Philadelphia (12)—Daulton 3, Kruk 3, Murphy 3, Chamberlain 2, C. Hayes.
Pittsburgh (15)—Merced 3, Van Slyke 3, Bonilla 2, McClendon 2, Varsho 2, Bell, Bonds, Walk.
St. Louis (2)—Gilkey 2.
San Diego (7)—Fernandez 2, Jackson 2, McGriff, Santiago, Teufel.
San Francisco (2)—Mitchell, Williams.

AT CINCINNATI (181)

Atlanta (7)—Cabrera 2, Pendleton 2, Bream, Hunter, Justice.
Chicago (8)—Bell 3, Dunston 2, Boskie, Dawson, Salazar.
Cincinnati (104)—O'Neill 20, Larkin 16, Sabo 15, Duncan 10, Morris 9, Braggs 8, Oliver 7, Davis 5, Doran 3, Hatcher 2, Martinez 2, Quinones 2, Benzinger, Jefferson, Reed, Scudder, Winningham.
Houston (8)—Bagwell 2, Biggio, Gonzalez 2, Candaele, Ramirez.
Los Angeles (2)—Harris, Strawberry.
Montreal (7)—Wallach 3, Calderon 2, Da. Martinez, Walker.
New York (9)—Johnson 3, Brooks, Coleman, Jefferies, McReynolds, Miller, O'Brien.
Philadelphia (6)—Murphy 2, Daulton, C. Hayes, Thon.
Pittsburgh (9)—Bonds 3, Bonilla 3, Bell, Lind, Van Slyke.
St. Louis (6)—Perry 2, Gedman, Oquendo, Pena, Zeile.
San Diego (3)—McGriff 2, Shipley.
San Francisco (12)—Mitchell 3, Williams 3, Bass 2, Clark 2, Thompson, Uribe.

AT HOUSTON (71)

Atlanta (3)—Blauser, Bream, Justice.
Chicago (4)—Bell 3, Berryhill.
Cincinnati (1)—Braggs.
Houston (27)—Caminiti 9, Bagwell 6, Cedeno 4, Gonzalez 4, Candaele, Davidson, Simms, Tolentino.
Los Angeles (11)—Strawberry 6, Murray 2, Scioscia 2, Daniels.
Montreal (3)—DeShields 2, Grissom.
New York (2)—Brooks, Johnson.
Pittsburgh (6)—Bell 4, Bonilla, Van Slyke.
St. Louis (4)—Jose, Lankford, Perry, Thompson.
San Diego (4)—McGriff 2, Coolbaugh, Teufel.
San Francisco (6)—Mitchell 3, Clark, Thompson, Williams.

AT LOS ANGELES (103)

Atlanta (5)—Blauser, Gant, Justice, Sanders, Treadway.
Chicago (3)—Dawson, Dunston, Sandberg.
Cincinnati (8)—O'Neill 2, Braggs, Davis, Jones, Martinez, Quinones, Sabo.
Houston (8)—Finley 3, Bagwell, Cedeno, Gonzalez, Ortiz, Simms.
Los Angeles (57)—Strawberry 14, Daniels 12, Murray 11, Samuel 4, Carter 3, Gwynn 3, Scioscia 3, Butler 2, Hamilton, Harris, Martinez, Sharperson, Webster.
Montreal (2)—DeShields, Galarraga.
New York (3)—McReynolds 2, Johnson.
Philadelphia (1)—Murphy.
Pittsburgh (3)—Redus 2, Bonds.
St. Louis (1)—Lankford.
San Diego (5)—Howell 3, Santiago 2.
San Francisco (7)—Clark 2, McGee 2, Williams 2, Mitchell.

AT MONTREAL (68)

Atlanta (2)—Bream, Gant.
Chicago (1)—Grace.
Cincinnati (3)—Sabo 2, Reed.
Houston (1)—Young.
Los Angeles (2)—Carter, Ojeda.
Montreal (35)—Calderon 7, Walker 5, Wallach 5, DeShields 3, Galarraga 3, Grissom 3, Da. Martinez 3, Barberie 2, Bullock, Fitzgerald, Owen, Santovenia.
New York (5)—Elster 2, Johnson 2, Jefferies.
Philadelphia (4)—Thon 2, Chamberlain, Murphy.
Pittsburgh (5)—Bonds 2, Bell, Bonilla, Van Slyke.
St. Louis (2)—Guerrero 2.
San Diego (4)—McGriff 2, Presley, Santiago.
San Francisco (4)—Mitchell 2, Thompson, Williams.

AT NEW YORK (112)

Atlanta (6)—Hunter 2, Justice 2, Bream, Pendleton.
Chicago (9)—Sandberg 2, Bell, Berryhill, Dawson, Dunston, Salazar, Villanueva, Walker.
Cincinnati (5)—O'Neill 2, Doran, Duncan, Larkin.
Houston (3)—Bagwell, Biggio, Mota.
Los Angeles (8)—Strawberry 3, Murray 2, Carter, Gwynn, Hansen.
Montreal (2)—Walker, Wallach.
New York (57)—Johnson 21, McReynolds 7, Jefferies 5, Brooks 4, Carreon 3, Elster 3, Sasser 3, Boston 2, Magadan 2, Miller 2, Cerone, Hundley, O'Brien, Templeton, Teufel.
Philadelphia (8)—Kruk 2, Campusano, Chamberlain, C. Hayes, Lake, Murphy, Thon.
Pittsburgh (3)—Bonilla, Buechele, McClendon.
St. Louis (1)—Jose.
San Diego (5)—McGriff 2, Santiago 2, Jackson.
San Francisco (5)—Mitchell 2, Williams 2, Clark.

AT PHILADELPHIA (114)

Atlanta (4)—Justice 2, Gant, Pendleton.
Chicago (4)—Sandberg 2, Salazar, Dw. Smith.
Cincinnati (5)—Larkin 2, Braggs, Morris, Sabo.
Houston (3)—Anthony, Caminiti, Finley.
Los Angeles (3)—Samuel 2, Murray.
Montreal (7)—Calderon 2, Walker 2, Fitzgerald, Galarraga.
New York (6)—Boston 2, McReynolds 2, Brooks, Miller.
Philadelphia (61)—Chamberlain 9, Murphy 9, Daulton 8, Kruk 8, C. Hayes 6, Jordan 5, Thon 4, Dykstra 3, Hollins 3, Greene 2, Fletcher, Morandini, Morris, Ready.
Pittsburgh (6)—Bonds 2, King, Merced, Van Slyke, Varsho.
St. Louis (6)—Guerrero 2, Jose, Lankford, Perry, Zeile.
San Diego (2)—Benes, Clark.
San Francisco (7)—Williams 3, Clark 2, Anderson, Mitchell.

AT PITTSBURGH (116)

Atlanta (7)—Gant 2, Bream, Hunter, Justice, Pendleton, Treadway.
Chicago (10)—Wilkins 3, Bell 2, Dawson 2, Salazar, Sandberg, Villanueva.
Cincinnati (3)—Davis 2, Hatcher.
Houston (3)—Bagwell, Davidson, Finley.
Los Angeles (2)—Daniels, Scioscia.
Montreal (7)—Galarraga 2, Calderon, DeShields, Fitzgerald, Hassey, Owen.

AT ST. LOUIS (73)

New York (9)—Johnson 3, Brooks, Carreon, Cerone, Elster, McReynolds, Sasser.
Philadelphia (2)—Kruk, Thon.
Pittsburgh (61)—Bonds 12, Bonilla 9, Van Slyke 9, Bell 7, Merced 5, King 3, Redus 3, Buechele 2, Lind 2, McClendon 2, Wilkerson 2, Espy, Gonzalez, LaValliere, Varsho, Webster.
St. Louis (4)—Zeile 2, Pena, O. Smith.
San Diego (6)—Teufel 2, Ward 2, Gwynn, Jackson.
San Francisco (2)—Clark, Williams.

AT ST. LOUIS (73)

Atlanta (4)—Gant 2, Bream, Sanders.
Chicago (6)—Dawson 3, Bell, Sandberg, Walton.
Cincinnati (1)—Sabo.
Houston (3)—Finley, Gonzalez, Yelding.
Los Angeles (2)—Samuel, Strawberry.
Montreal (3)—Calderon, Grissom, Wallach.
New York (8)—Brooks 2, Johnson 2, McReynolds 2, Magadan, Sasser.
Philadelphia (3)—Kruk 2, C. Hayes.
Pittsburgh (3)—Bell, Bonds, Merced.
St. Louis (32)—Zeile 7, Guerrero 4, Lankford 4, Thompson 4, Jose 3, Gilkey 2, Pagnozzi 2, O. Smith 2, Gedman, Hudler, Pena, Perry.
San Diego (3)—Clark, Santiago, Teufel.
San Francisco (5)—Clark 2, Litton, Thompson, Williams.

AT SAN DIEGO (137)

Atlanta (7)—Gant 2, Pendleton 2, Bream, Justice, L. Smith.
Chicago (7)—Bell 2, Grace, Maddux, Salazar, Sandberg, Walton.
Cincinnati (7)—Browning, Doran, Martinez, Morris, O'Neill, Quinones, Sabo.
Houston (5)—Bagwell, Caminiti, Cedeno, Finley, Gonzalez.
Los Angeles (9)—Samuel 3, Strawberry 2, Carter, Murray, Scioscia, Sharperson.
Montreal (4)—Walker 2, Grissom, Owen.
New York (5)—Brooks, Johnson, Magadan, McReynolds, Templeton.
Philadelphia (6)—Jordan 3, Hollins 2, Kruk.
Pittsburgh (5)—Bonds 2, LaValliere, Redus, Slaught.
St. Louis (3)—Pena, Perry, Thompson.
San Diego (65)—McGriff 18, Jackson 12, Clark 8, Santiago 6, Teufel 5, Howard 4, Howell 3, Roberts 3, Abner, Barrett, Coolbaugh, Fernandez, Gwynn, Templeton.
San Francisco (14)—Mitchell 5, Thompson 3, Leonard 2, Benjamin, Decker, Kennedy, Williams.

AT SAN FRANCISCO (131)

Atlanta (8)—Gant 4, Blauser 2, Bream, Justice, Mitchell.
Chicago (6)—Bell 2, Dawson, Dunston, Sandberg, Walker.
Cincinnati (9)—Martinez 2, Morris 2, Davis, Jones, Oliver, O'Neill, Sabo.
Houston (6)—Candaele 2, Cedeno 2, Bagwell, Caminiti, Gonzalez.
Los Angeles (2)—Murray, Scioscia.
Montreal (5)—Calderon 2, Walker 2, Galarraga.
New York (4)—Johnson 2, Brooks, Herr.
Philadelphia (4)—Kruk 2, Hollins, Murphy.
Pittsburgh (4)—Bell, Buechele, Prince, Van Slyke.
St. Louis (5)—Jose 2, Lankford 2, Gedman.
San Diego (7)—Santiago 3, Jackson 2, McGriff 2.
San Francisco (69)—Clark 17, Williams 17, Thompson 11, Mitchell 9, Bass 5, Decker 4, Kennedy 2, McGee 2, Anderson, Wilson.

LIFETIME GRAND SLAM HOMERS

(Active NL Players for 1992 and those hitting NL grand slams in 1991)
(AL grand slams in parentheses)

Player	Team	No.
Eddie Murray	Mets (14)	15
Gary Carter	Expos	11
George Bell	Cubs (7)	7
Hubie Brooks	Mets	7
Andre Dawson	Cubs	6
Nick Esasky	Braves (1)	6
Howard Johnson	Mets (1)	6
Kevin McReynolds	Mets	6
Eric Davis	Dodgers	5
Dale Murphy	Phillies	5
Darryl Strawberry	Dodgers	5
Tim Wallach	Expos	5
Kevin Bass	Giants	4
Todd Benzinger	Dodgers (2)	4
Kal Daniels	Dodgers	4
Pete Incaviglia	Astros (4)	4
Gary Redus	Pirates (2)	4
Cory Snyder	Giants (4)	4
Matt Williams	Giants	4
Daryl Boston	Mets (2)	3
Will Clark	Giants	3
Mike Fitzgerald	Expos	3
Pedro Guerrero	Cardinals	3
Chris James	Giants	3
John Kruk	Phillies	3
Carmelo Martinez	Reds	3
Fred McGriff	Padres (1)	3
Ernest Riles	Astros (1)	3
Benito Santiago	Padres	3
Tim Teufel	Padres	3
Garry Templeton	Mets	3
Mitch Webster	Dodgers (1)	3
Bobby Bonilla	Mets	2
Sid Bream	Braves	2
Bill Doran	Reds	2
Shawon Dunston	Cubs	2
Tony Fernandez	Padres (2)	2
Andres Galarraga	Cardinals	2
Billy Hatcher	Reds	2
Ricky Jordan	Phillies	2
Terry Kennedy	Giants	2
Terry Pendleton	Braves	2
Rafael Ramirez	Astros	2
Juan Samuel	Dodgers	2
Ryne Sandberg	Cubs	2
Mike Scioscia	Dodgers	2
Lonnie Smith	Braves (2)	2
Robby Thompson	Giants	2
Jay Bell	Pirates	1
Damon Berryhill	Braves	1
Steve Buechele	Pirates (1)	1
Craig Biggio	Astros	1
Jeff Blauser	Braves	1
Barry Bonds	Pirates	1
Brett Butler	Dodgers (1)	1
Ivan Calderon	Expos (1)	1
Ken Caminiti	Astros	1
Rick Cerone	Mets	1
Darren Daulton	Phillies	1
Mariano Duncan	Phillies	1
Len Dykstra	Phillies	1
Steve Finley	Astros (1)	1
Marquis Grissom	Expos	1
Jeff Hamilton	Dodgers	1
Lenny Harris	Dodgers	1
Charlie Hayes	Phillies	1
Tom Herr	Giants	1
Dave Hollins	Phillies	1
Darrin Jackson	Padres	1
Felix Jose	Cardinals (1)	1
David Justice	Braves	1
Jeff King	Pirates	1
Mike LaValliere	Pirates	1
Steve Lyons	Braves (1)	1
Dave Martinez	Reds	1
Lloyd McClendon	Pirates	1
Willie McGee	Giants	1
Orlando Merced	Pirates	1
Joe Oliver	Reds	1
Greg Olson	Braves	1
Paul O'Neill	Reds	1
Tom Pagnozzi	Cardinals	1
Gerald Perry	Cardinals (1)	1
Jeff Reed	Reds	1
Mackey Sasser	Mets	1
Rick Schu	Phillies (1)	1
Don Slaught	Pirates (1)	1
Dwight Smith	Cubs	1
Andy Van Slyke	Pirates	1
Chico Walker	Cubs	1
Curtis Wilkerson	Pirates	1

N.L. ALL-TIME GRAND-SLAM HOMER LEADERS, 1901-1991

Player	No.
Willie McCovey, Giants (16); Padres (2)	18
Hank Aaron, Braves	16
Gil Hodges, Dodgers	14
George Foster, Reds (9); Mets (4)	13
Ernie Banks, Cubs	12
Rogers Hornsby, Cards (7); Giants (1); Cubs (4)	12
Ralph Kiner, Pirates (11); Cubs (1)	12
Johnny Bench, Reds	11
Gary Carter, Expos (7); Mets (4)	11
Dave Kingman, Giants (3); Mets (3); Padres (2); Cubs (3)	11
Willie Stargell, Pirates	11
Joe Adcock, Reds (1); Braves (9)	10
John Milner, Mets (5); Pirates (5)	10
Walker Cooper, Cards (1); Giants (4); Reds (1); Braves (1); Cubs (2)	9
Stan Musial, Cardinals	9
Orlando Cepeda, Giants (4); Braves (4)	8
Carl Furillo, Dodgers	8
George Kelly, Giants (7); Reds (1)	8
Eddie Mathews, Braves	8
Willie Mays, Giants	8
Bill Nicholson, Cubs	8
Ron Northey, Phillies (2); Cardinals (5); Cubs (1)	8
Andy Seminick, Phillies (5); Reds (3)	8
Ted Simmons, Cardinals (7); Braves (1)	8
Bobby Thomson, Giants (4); Braves (4)	8
Billy Williams, Cubs	8
Dick Allen, Phillies (5); Cardinals (2)	7
Ed Bailey, Reds (3); Giants (2); Braves (1); Cubs (1)	7
Wally Berger, Braves (6); Reds (1)	7
Ken Boyer, Cardinals	7
Hubie Brooks, Expos (6); Mets (1)	7
Ron Cey, Dodgers (5); Cubs (2)	7
Jack Clark, Giants (5); Cardinals (1); Padres (1)	7
Roberto Clemente, Pirates	7
Ron Fairly, Dodgers (2); Expos (4); Cardinals (1)	7
Sid Gordon, Giants (3); Braves (4)	7
Keith Hernandez, Cardinals (5); Mets (2)	7
Willie Jones, Phillies (6); Reds (1)	7
Chuck Klein, Phillies (6); Cubs (1)	7
Mike Marshall, Dodgers (6); Mets (1)	7
Mel Ott, Giants	7
Dave Parker, Pirates (2); Reds (5)	7
Mike Schmidt, Phillies	7
Wally Westlake, Pirates	7
Bill White, Cardinals (6); Phillies (1)	7
Fred Williams, Cubs (1); Phillies (6)	7
Bob Aspromonte, Astros	6
Bob Bailey, Pirates (2); Expos (4)	6
Jim Bottomley, Cardinals	6
Roy Campanella, Dodgers	6
Dave Concepcion, Reds	6
Andre Dawson, Expos (2); Cubs (4)	6
Vince DiMaggio, Pirates (2); Phillies (4)	6
Del Ennis, Phillies (5); Cardinals (1)	6
Ernie Lombardi, Reds (3); Giants (3)	6
Lee May, Reds (4); Astros (2)	6
Tim McCarver, Cardinals (5); Phillies (1)	6
Kevin McReynolds, Padres (1); Mets (5)	6
Al Oliver, Pirates (4); Expos (2)	6
Andy Pafko, Cubs (5); Dodgers (1)	6
Vada Pinson, Reds	6
Pee Wee Reese, Dodgers	6
Rusty Staub, Expos (2); Mets (4)	6
Gus Bell, Pirates (2); Reds (3)	5
Dolph Camilli, Phillies (2); Dodgers (3)	5
Cesar Cedeno, Astros (4); Cardinals (1)	5
Nate Colbert, Padres	5
Eric Davis, Reds	5
Jody Davis, Cubs	5
Nick Esasky, Reds	5
Darrell Evans, Braves (3); Giants (2)	5
Elbie Fletcher, Braves (1); Pirates (4)	5
Augie Galan, Cubs (3); Dodgers (1); Reds (1)	5
Steve Garvey, Dodgers (4); Padres (1)	5
Gabby Hartnett, Cubs	5
Jim Hickman, Mets (3); Cubs (2)	5
Howard Johnson, Mets	5
Hank Leiber, Giants (2); Cubs (3)	5
Greg Luzinski, Phillies	5
Johnny Mize, Cardinals (2); Giants (3)	5
Wally Moon, Cardinals (4); Dodgers (1)	5
Dale Murphy, Braves (4); Phillies (1)	5
Tony Perez, Reds	5
Tim Raines, Expos	5
Bill Robinson, Phillies (2); Pirates (3)	5
Frank Robinson, Reds	5
Ron Santo, Cubs	5
Duke Snider, Dodgers	5
Darryl Strawberry, Mets (4); Dodgers (1)	5
Dick Stuart, Pirates (3); Phillies (2)	5
Tim Wallach, Expos	5
Bob Watson, Astros	5
Wes Westrum, Giants	5
Hack Wilson, Cubs (3); Dodgers (2)	5

1991 GRAND SLAMS

Player	No.
Bream, Braves	2
Clark, Giants	2
Dawson, Cubs	2
McGriff, Padres	2
Bell, Pirates	1
Blauser, Braves	1
Boston, Mets	1
Brooks, Mets	1
Caminiti, Astros	1
Daniels, Dodgers	1
Daulton, Phillies	1
Grissom, Expos	1
Harris, Dodgers	1
C. Hayes, Phillies	1
Hollins, Phillies	1
Jackson, Padres	1
Johnson, Mets	1
Jordan, Phillies	1
Kruk, Phillies	1
LaValliere, Pirates	1
McReynolds, Mets	1
Merced, Pirates	1
Murphy, Phillies	1
Oliver, Reds	1
Redus, Pirates	1
Reed, Reds	1
Sandberg, Cubs	1
Strawberry, Dodgers	1
Teufel, Padres	1
Walker, Cubs	1
Wilkerson, Pirates	1

1991 CLUB TOTALS

Club	No.
Philadelphia	6
Pittsburgh	5
Chicago	4
New York	4
San Diego	4
Atlanta	3
Los Angeles	3
Cincinnati	2
San Francisco	2
Houston	1
Montreal	1
St. Louis	0

CAREER FIRSTS

Player	Date	Opp.
LaValliere, Mike	4/20	Chi.
Grissom, Marquis	4/28	St.L.
Bream, Sid	5/17	Pit.
Harris, Lenny	6/10	Chi.
Reed, Jeff	6/25	S.D.
Merced, Orlando	7/4	Chi.
Daulton, Darren	7/15	L.A.
Hollins, Dave	7/19	S.D.
Caminiti, Ken	7/29	St.L.
Jackson, Darrin	8/25	Chi.
Blauser, Jeff	8/26	Mon.
Walker, Chico	8/28	S.F.
Hayes, Charlie	8/28	Hou.
Wilkerson, Curtis	9/19	St.L.
Bell, Jay	9/30	N.Y.
Oliver, Joe	10/2	Atl.

30 OR MORE HOME RUNS—SEASON

Total Homers	Player and Club	Year
56	Hack Wilson, Chicago	1930
54	Ralph Kiner, Pittsburgh	1949
52	Willie Mays, San Francisco	1965
52	George Foster, Cincinnati	1977
51	Ralph Kiner, Pittsburgh	1947
51	Johnny Mize, New York	1947
51	Willie Mays, New York	1955
49	Ted Kluszewski, Cincinnati	1954
49	Willie Mays, San Francisco	1962
49	Andre Dawson, Chicago	1987
48	Willie Stargell, Pittsburgh	1971
48	Dave Kingman, Chicago	1979
48	Mike Schmidt, Philadelphia	1980
47	Ralph Kiner, Pittsburgh	1950
47	Ed Mathews, Milwaukee	1953
47	Ted Kluszewski, Cincinnati	1955
47	Ernie Banks, Chicago	1958
47	Willie Mays, San Francisco	1964
47	Hank Aaron, Atlanta	1971
47	Kevin Mitchell, San Francisco	1989
46	Ed Mathews, Milwaukee	1959
46	Orlando Cepeda, San Francisco	1961
45	Ernie Banks, Chicago	1959
45	Hank Aaron, Milwaukee	1962
45	Willie McCovey, San Francisco	1969
45	Johnny Bench, Cincinnati	1970
45	Mike Schmidt, Philadelphia	1979
44	Ernie Banks, Chicago	1955
44	Hank Aaron, Milwaukee	1957, 1963
	Atlanta	1966, 1969
44	Willie McCovey, San Francisco	1963
44	Willie Stargell, Pittsburgh	1973
44	Dale Murphy, Atlanta	1987
43	Chuck Klein, Philadelphia	1929
43	Johnny Mize, St. Louis	1940
43	Duke Snider, Brooklyn	1956
43	Ernie Banks, Chicago	1957
43	Dave Johnson, Atlanta	1973
42	Rogers Hornsby, St. Louis	1922
42	Mel Ott, New York	1929
42	Ralph Kiner, Pittsburgh	1951
42	Duke Snider, Brooklyn	1953, 1955
42	Gil Hodges, Brooklyn	1954
42	Billy Williams, Chicago	1970
41	Fred Williams, Philadelphia	1923
41	Roy Campanella, Brooklyn	1953
41	Willie Mays, New York	1954
41	Hank Sauer, Chicago	1954
41	Ed Mathews, Milwaukee	1955
41	Ernie Banks, Chicago	1960
41	Darrell Evans, Atlanta	1973
41	Jeff Burroughs, Atlanta	1977
40	Rogers Hornsby, Chicago	1929
40	Chuck Klein, Philadelphia	1930
40	Ralph Kiner, Pittsburgh	1948
40	Johnny Mize, New York	1948
40	Gil Hodges, Brooklyn	1951
40	Ted Kluszewski, Cincinnati	1953
40	Ed Mathews, Milwaukee	1954
40	Duke Snider, Brooklyn	1954, 1957
40	Wally Post, Cincinnati	1955
40	Hank Aaron, Milwaukee	1960
	Atlanta	1973
40	Willie Mays, San Francisco	1961
40	Richie Allen, Philadelphia	1966
40	Tony Perez, Cincinnati	1970
40	Johnny Bench, Cincinnati	1972
40	George Foster, Cincinnati	1978
40	Mike Schmidt, Philadelphia	1983
40	Ryne Sandberg, Chicago	1990
39	Rogers Hornsby, St. Louis	1925
39	Hack Wilson, Chicago	1929
39	Wally Berger, Boston	1930
39	Stan Musial, St. Louis	1948
39	Hank Aaron, Milwaukee	1959
	Atlanta	1967
39	Ed Mathews, Milwaukee	1960
39	Frank Robinson, Cincinnati	1962
39	Willie McCovey, San Francisco	1965, 1970
39	Lee May, Cincinnati	1971
39	Bobby Bonds, San Francisco	1973
39	Greg Luzinski, Philadelphia	1977
39	Darryl Strawberry, New York	1987, 1988
38	Chuck Klein, Philadelphia	1932
38	Mel Ott, New York	1932
38	Joe Adcock, Milwaukee	1956
38	Frank Robinson, Cincinnati	1956
38	Willie Mays, San Francisco	1963
38	Lee May, Cincinnati	1969
38	Hank Aaron, Atlanta	1970
38	Nate Colbert, San Diego	1970, 1972
38	Mike Schmidt, Philadelphia	1975, 1976, 1977
38	Howard Johnson, New York	1991
37	Gabby Hartnett, Chicago	1930
37	Ralph Kiner, Pittsburgh	1952
37	Hank Sauer, Chicago	1952
37	Ed Mathews, Milwaukee	1956
37	Frank Robinson, Cincinnati	1961
37	Ernie Banks, Chicago	1962
37	Willie Mays, San Francisco	1966
37	Jim Wynn, Houston	1967
37	Tony Perez, Cincinnati	1969
37	Billy Williams, Chicago	1972
37	Dave Kingman, New York	1976, 1982
37	Dale Murphy, Atlanta	1985
37	Mike Schmidt, Philadelphia	1986
37	Eric Davis, Cincinnati	1987
37	Darryl Strawberry, New York	1990
36	Mel Ott, New York	1938
36	Willard Marshall, New York	1947
36	Stan Musial, St. Louis	1949
36	Andy Pafko, Chicago	1950
36	Willie Mays, New York	1956
36	Wally Post, Cincinnati	1956
36	Frank Robinson, Cincinnati	1959
36	Willie McCovey, San Francisco	1966, 1968
36	Joe Torre, Atlanta	1966
36	Mike Schmidt, Philadelphia	1974, 1984
36	Dave Kingman, New York	1975
36	Dale Murphy, Atlanta	1982, 1983, 1984
36	Howard Johnson, New York	1987, 1989
35	Babe Herman, Brooklyn	1930
35	Rip Collins, St. Louis	1934
35	Mel Ott, New York	1934
35	Walker Cooper, New York	1947
35	Hank Sauer, Cincinnati	1948
35	Ralph Kiner, Pittsburgh-Chicago	1953
35	Stan Musial, St. Louis	1954
35	Ted Kluszewski, Cincinnati	1956
35	Willie Mays, New York	1957
35	Frank Thomas, Pittsburgh	1958
35	Joe Adcock, Milwaukee	1961
35	Dick Stuart, Pittsburgh	1961
35	Orlando Cepeda, San Francisco	1962
35	Greg Luzinski, Philadelphia	1978
35	Bob Horner, Atlanta	1980
35	Mike Schmidt, Philadelphia	1982, 1987
35	Jack Clark, St. Louis	1987
35	Will Clark, San Francisco	1987
35	Kevin Mitchell, San Francisco	1990
34	Wally Berger, Boston	1934, 1935
34	Dolph Camilli, Brooklyn	1941
34	Willie Mays, San Francisco	1959
34	Hank Aaron, Milwaukee	1961
	Atlanta	1972
34	Frank Thomas, New York	1962
34	Orlando Cepeda, San Francisco	1963
34	Billy Williams, Chicago	1965
34	Richie Allen, St. Louis	1970
34	Orlando Cepeda, Atlanta	1970
34	Lee May, Cincinnati	1970
34	Deron Johnson, Philadelphia	1971
34	Greg Luzinski, Philadelphia	1975
34	Dave Winfield, San Diego	1979
34	Dave Parker, Cincinnati	1985
34	Eric Davis, Cincinnati	1989
34	Glenn Davis, Houston	1989
34	Matt Williams, San Francisco	1991
33	Mel Ott, New York	1936
33	Bill Nicholson, Chicago	1944
33	Roy Campanella, Brooklyn	1951
33	Stan Musial, St. Louis	1955
33	Billy Williams, Chicago	1964
33	Frank Robinson, Cincinnati	1965
33	Ron Santo, Chicago	1965
33	Jim Hart, San Francisco	1966
33	Willie Stargell, Pittsburgh	1966, 1972
33	Richie Allen, Philadelphia	1968
33	Jim Wynn, Houston	1969
33	Bobby Bonds, San Francisco	1971
33	Earl Williams, Atlanta	1971
33	Johnny Bench, Cincinnati	1974
33	Steve Garvey, Los Angeles	1977
33	Bob Horner, Atlanta	1979
33	Dale Murphy, Atlanta	1980
33	Pedro Guerrero, Los Angeles	1985
33	Mike Schmidt, Philadelphia	1985
33	Barry Bonds, Pittsburgh	1990
33	Matt Williams, San Francisco	1990
32	Lefty O'Doul, Philadelphia	1929
32	Hank Sauer, Chicago	1950
32	Gil Hodges, Brooklyn	1950, 1952, 1956
32	Stan Musial, St. Louis	1951
32	Bobby Thomson, New York	1951
32	Roy Campanella, Brooklyn	1955
32	Stan Lopata, Philadelphia	1956
32	Ed Mathews, Milwaukee	1957, 1961
32	Ken Boyer, St. Louis	1960
32	Hank Aaron, Milwaukee	1965
32	John Callison, Philadelphia	1965
32	Deron Johnson, Cincinnati	1965
32	Ed Mathews, Milwaukee	1965
32	Ernie Banks, Chicago	1968
32	Richie Allen, Philadelphia	1969
32	Bobby Bonds, San Francisco	1969
32	Jim Hickman, Chicago	1970
32	Jim Wynn, Los Angeles	1974
32	Rick Monday, Chicago	1976
32	Reggie Smith, Los Angeles	1977
32	Willie Stargell, Pittsburgh	1979
32	Pedro Guerrero, Los Angeles	1982, 1983
32	Bob Horner, Atlanta	1982
32	Andre Dawson, Montreal	1983
32	Gary Carter, New York	1985
32	Bobby Bonilla, Pittsburgh	1990
32	Ron Gant, Atlanta	1990, 1991
31	Jim Bottomley, St. Louis	1928
31	Hack Wilson, Chicago	1928
31	Don Hurst, Philadelphia	1929
31	Chuck Klein, Philadelphia	1931
31	Mel Ott, New York	1935, 1937
31	Joe Medwick, St. Louis	1937
31	Hank Sauer, Cincinnati-Chicago	1949
31	Roy Campanella, Brooklyn	1950
31	Del Ennis, Philadelphia	1950
31	Duke Snider, Brooklyn	1950
31	Gil Hodges, Brooklyn	1953
31	George Crowe, Cincinnati	1957
31	Ed Mathews, Milwaukee	1958
31	Frank Robinson, Cincinnati	1958, 1960
31	Frank Howard, Los Angeles	1962
31	John Callison, Philadelphia	1964
31	Orlando Cepeda, San Francisco	1964
31	Jim Hart, San Francisco	1964
31	Mack Jones, Milwaukee	1965
31	Felipe Alou, Atlanta	1966
31	Willie McCovey, San Francisco	1967
31	Ron Santo, Chicago	1967
31	Willie Stargell, Pittsburgh	1970
31	Johnny Bench, Cincinnati	1977
31	Gary Carter, Montreal	1977
31	Mike Schmidt, Philadelphia	1981
31	Jason Thompson, Pittsburgh	1982
31	Glenn Davis, Houston	1986
31	Dave Parker, Cincinnati	1986
31	Fred McGriff, San Diego	1991
31	Andre Dawson, Chicago	1991
30	Fred Williams, Philadelphia	1927
30	Hack Wilson, Chicago	1927
30	Ival Goodman, Cincinnati	1938
30	Mel Ott, New York	1942
30	Del Ennis, Philadelphia	1948
30	Sid Gordon, New York	1948
30	Andy Pafko, Chicago-Brooklyn	1951
30	Hank Sauer, Chicago	1951
30	Gus Bell, Cincinnati	1953
30	Stan Musial, St. Louis	1953
30	Frank Thomas, Pittsburgh	1953
30	Hank Aaron, Milwaukee	1958
30	Ron Santo, Chicago	1964, 1966
30	Billy Williams, Chicago	1968
30	Rusty Staub, Montreal	1970
30	Willie Montanez, Philadelphia	1971
30	Dusty Baker, Los Angeles	1977
30	Ron Cey, Los Angeles	1977
30	Dave Parker, Pittsburgh	1978
30	George Foster, Cincinnati	1979
30	Larry Parrish, Montreal	1979
30	Darrell Evans, San Francisco	1983
30	Glenn Davis, Houston	1988
30	Ryne Sandberg, Chicago	1989

ALL-TIME NATIONAL LEAGUE LEADERS IN EACH BATTING DEPARTMENT, 1876-1991

★In Hall of Fame, Players in CAPS active in 1991

GAMES

Pete Rose	3,562
★Hank Aaron	3,076
★Stan Musial	3,026
★Willie Mays	2,992
★Honus Wagner	2,785
★Mel Ott	2,730
★Rabbit Maranville	2,670
★Lou Brock	2,616
★Willie McCovey	2,577
★Paul Waner	2,539

AT BATS

Pete Rose	14,053
★Hank Aaron	11,628
★Stan Musial	10,972
★Willie Mays	10,881
★Honus Wagner	10,427
★Lou Brock	10,332
★Rabbit Maranville	10,078
★Mel Ott	9,456
★Roberto Clemente	9,454
★Paul Waner	9,452

RUNS

Pete Rose	2,165
★Hank Aaron	2,107
★Willie Mays	2,062
★Stan Musial	1,949
★Mel Ott	1,859
★Honus Wagner	1,740
★Cap Anson	1,712
★Paul Waner	1,625
★Fred Clarke	1,620
★Lou Brock	1,610

HITS

Pete Rose	4,256
★Stan Musial	3,630
★Hank Aaron	3,600
★Honus Wagner	3,430
★Willie Mays	3,283
★Paul Waner	3,151
★Cap Anson	3,081
★Lou Brock	3,023
★Roberto Clemente	3,000
★Rogers Hornsby	2,895

SINGLES

Pete Rose	3,215
★Honus Wagner	2,426
★Cap Anson	2,331
★Stan Musial	2,253
★Lou Brock	2,247
★Paul Waner	2,246
★Hank Aaron	2,171
★Frank Frisch	2,171
★Roberto Clemente	2,154
Richie Ashburn	2,119

DOUBLES

Pete Rose	746
★Stan Musial	725
★Honus Wagner	651
★Paul Waner	603
★Hank Aaron	600
★Joe Medwick	540
★Rogers Hornsby	532
★Cap Anson	526
★Willie Mays	523
★Mel Ott	488

TRIPLES

★Honus Wagner	252
★Jake Beckley	227
★Fred Clarke	219
★Roger Connor	212
★Paul Waner	190
★Dan Brouthers	183
★Joe Kelley	182
★Rabbit Maranville	177
★Stan Musial	177
★Zack Wheat	171

HOME RUNS

★Hank Aaron	733
★Willie Mays	660
Mike Schmidt	548
★Willie McCovey	521
★Ernie Banks	512
★Mel Ott	511
★Eddie Mathews	503
★Stan Musial	475
★Willie Stargell	475
★Duke Snider	407

TOTAL BASES

★Hank Aaron	6,591
★Stan Musial	6,134
★Willie Mays	6,066
Pete Rose	5,752
★Mel Ott	5,041
★Honus Wagner	4,888
★Ernie Banks	4,706
★Rogers Hornsby	4,660
★Roberto Clemente	4,492
★Paul Waner	4,470

RUNS BATTED IN
(Since 1920)

★Hank Aaron	2,202
★Stan Musial	1,951
★Willie Mays	1,903
★Mel Ott	1,860
★Ernie Banks	1,636
Mike Schmidt	1,595
★Willie McCovey	1,555
★Willie Stargell	1,540
Tony Perez	1,477
★Eddie Mathews	1,426

BATTING PERCENTAGE
(500 or More Games)

★Willie Keeler	.377
★Jesse Burkett	.364
★Rogers Hornsby	.359
Lefty O'Doul	.353
★Billy Hamilton	.351
★Dan Brouthers	.348
★Ed Delahanty	.348
★Elmer Flick	.345
★Bill Terry	.341
★Cap Anson	.339

SLUGGING PERCENTAGE
(500 or More Games)

★Rogers Hornsby	.578
★Johnny Mize	.577
★Hank Aaron	.567
★Stan Musial	.559
★Willie Mays	.557
★Ralph Kiner	.554
★Frank Robinson	.548
★Hack Wilson	.545
★Chuck Klein	.543
★Duke Snider	.540

.400 BATSMEN, SEASON

(Players meeting standards of Section 10.23, Official Rules)

Batter, Club	Avg.	Year	Batter, Club	Avg.	Year
Ross Barnes, Chicago (National League)	.404	1876	Joe Jackson, Cleveland (American League)	.408	1911
Pete Browning, Louisville (Amer. Association)	.418	1887	Willie Keeler, Baltimore (National League)	.432	1897
Jesse Burkett, Cleveland (National League)	.423	1895	Nap Lajoie, Philadelphia (American League)	.422	1901
	.410	1896	Tip O'Neill, St. Louis (American Association)	.442	1887
St. Louis (National League)	.402	1899	George Sisler, St. Louis (American League)	.407	1920
Fred Clarke, Louisville (National League)	.406	1897		.420	1922
Ty Cobb, Detroit (American League)	.420	1911	Harry Stovey, Philadelphia (Amer. Association)	.404	1884
	.410	1912	Bill Terry, New York (National League)	.401	1930
	.401	1922	Sam Thompson, Phil. (National League)	.404	1894
Ed Delahanty, Philadelphia (National League)	.400	1894	Ted Williams, Boston (American League)	.406	1941
	.408	1899			
Hugh Duffy, Boston (National League)	.438	1894			
Fred Dunlap, St. Louis (Union Association)	.420	1884			
Dude Esterbrook, New York (Amer. Assoc.)	.408	1884			
Harry Heilmann, Detroit (American League)	.403	1923			
Rogers Hornsby, St. Louis (National League)	.401	1922			
	.424	1924			
	.403	1925			

Averages for 1887 were recalculated because, for that season only, bases on balls were counted as hits. This resulted in the elimination of the following players:

National League—Adrian Anson, Dennis Brouthers and Samuel Thompson.

American League—Thomas Burns, Dennis Lyons, Joseph Mack, Paul Radford, William Robinson and Harry Stovey.

MOST HOME RUNS, LIFETIME, BY POSITION

1B	439	Willie McCovey (2045 games)
2B	263	Rogers Hornsby (1541 games)
3B	509	Mike Schmidt (2212 games)
SS	277	Ernie Banks (1125 games)
OF	661	Hank Aaron (2756 games)
C	327	Johnny Bench (1744 games)
P	35	Warren Spahn (750 games)

LIFETIME BATTING AVERAGES—NATIONAL LEAGUE PLAYERS

(100 or more games—records compiled in National and American Leagues)

Player	Yrs.	AVG.	G	AB	R	H	TB	2B	3B	HR	RBI	SB
Anderson, Dave	9	.240	822	1942	234	466	607	69	12	16	135	49
Anthony, Eric	3	.179	148	418	44	75	136	16	0	15	43	6
Azocar, Oscar	2	.247	103	271	23	67	92	10	0	5	28	9
Backman, Wally	12	.277	1050	3168	474	876	1081	137	19	10	234	116
8 Bagwell, Jeff	1	.294	156	554	79	163	242	26	4	15	82	7
Bass, Kevin	10	.270	1132	3710	469	1000	1533	180	34	95	468	120
Bell, George	10	.286	1330	5086	704	1453	2462	264	32	227	826	61
Bell, Jay	6	.254	510	1812	262	460	679	89	20	30	184	31
Belliard, Rafael	10	.226	633	1404	151	317	367	25	11	1	99	38
Benzinger, Todd	5	.255	601	2048	233	523	784	99	12	46	286	17
Berryhill, Damon	5	.239	278	884	77	211	311	44	1	18	103	3
Biggio, Craig	4	.272	483	1667	210	454	618	74	9	24	153	71
Bilardello, Dann	7	.207	365	916	77	190	284	38	1	18	90	4
Blauser, Jeff	5	.262	455	1426	176	374	574	71	12	35	161	20
Bonds, Barry	6	.269	870	3111	563	837	1509	184	31	142	453	212
Bonilla, Bobby	6	.283	918	3294	510	931	1554	201	37	116	526	28
Booker, Rod	5	.248	173	274	38	68	84	10	3	0	28	7
Boston, Daryl	8	.250	752	1972	284	493	793	100	19	54	189	85
Braggs, Glenn	6	.260	600	2070	268	538	836	86	13	62	283	55
Bream, Sid	9	.262	800	2398	281	629	1009	147	10	71	352	40
Buechele, Steve	7	.241	911	2813	353	679	1121	120	14	98	357	14
Bullock, Eric	6	.213	123	141	13	30	39	6	0	1	12	9
Butler, Brett	11	.286	1521	5616	962	1606	2107	202	88	41	400	396
Cabrera, Francisco	3	.256	114	258	22	66	115	14	1	11	48	2
Calderon, Ivan	8	.278	794	2903	425	806	1324	176	21	100	398	92
Caminiti, Ken	5	.247	559	1986	203	490	691	90	9	31	233	17
Campusano, Sil	3	.202	154	262	26	53	85	11	3	5	23	1
Candaele, Casey	5	.258	506	1423	156	367	492	63	19	8	106	27
Carter, Gary	18	.264	2201	7686	1001	2030	3400	353	30	319	1196	39
Cerone, Rick	17	.245	1296	4006	383	981	1371	186	15	58	429	5
Chamberlain, Wes	2	.245	119	429	60	105	175	19	3	15	54	13
Clark, Jerald	4	.232	194	526	43	122	195	23	1	16	68	2
4 Clark, Will	6	.302	884	3265	536	985	1673	182	34	146	563	38
Coleman, Vince	7	.264	950	3813	611	1008	1291	113	61	16	234	586
Coles, Darnell	9	.243	706	2253	262	548	856	108	10	60	291	18
Coolbaugh, Scott	3	.217	152	411	40	89	124	15	1	6	35	1
Daniels, Kal	6	.289	644	2126	370	615	1039	114	8	98	335	87
Dascenzo, Doug	4	.232	304	694	96	161	204	24	5	3	60	41
Daulton, Darren	8	.222	561	1629	183	361	586	73	4	48	200	21
Davidson, Mark	6	.225	413	661	88	149	200	27	3	6	57	15
Davis, Eric	8	.268	856	2857	554	767	1453	119	18	177	532	247
Dawson, Andre	16	.282	2167	8348	1199	2354	4086	417	92	377	1335	304
DeShields, Delino	2	.262	280	1062	152	278	383	43	10	14	96	98
Doran, Bill	10	.269	1293	4684	672	1262	1764	200	37	76	444	201
Duncan, Mariano	6	.252	646	2256	297	569	835	83	24	45	203	124
Dunston, Shawon	7	.258	900	3260	399	840	1287	154	37	73	340	131
Dykstra, Len	7	.283	846	2874	480	812	1178	172	28	46	244	190
Elster, Kevin	6	.224	531	1566	166	351	540	75	6	34	174	10
Esasky, Nick	8	.250	810	2703	336	677	1205	120	21	122	427	18
Espy, Cecil	6	.241	394	994	133	240	318	34	13	6	83	95
Felder, Mike	7	.251	587	1481	233	372	480	37	22	9	117	129
Fernandez, Tony	9	.287	1173	4510	591	1294	1777	219	66	44	442	161
Finley, Steve	3	.269	382	1277	165	343	463	49	16	13	116	73
Fitzgerald, Mike	9	.237	753	2127	201	505	742	93	9	42	276	29
Foley, Tom	9	.248	880	2252	208	558	783	111	18	26	219	28
Galarraga, Andres	7	.269	847	3082	394	830	1344	168	14	106	433	54
Gallagher, Dave	5	.275	435	1380	179	380	474	59	7	7	115	15

Player	Yrs.	AVG.	G	AB	R	H	TB	2B	3B	HR	RBI	SB
Gant, Ron	5	.259	548	2042	328	529	954	109	17	94	283	99
Gedman, Rich	12	.253	992	3054	326	772	1229	172	12	87	374	3
Geren, Bob	4	.237	249	620	54	147	221	15	1	19	70	0
Girardi, Joe	3	.258	213	623	54	161	207	36	2	2	58	10
Gonzalez, Luis	2	.251	149	494	52	124	211	30	9	13	69	10
6 Grace, Mark	4	.297	593	2204	298	655	903	111	13	37	276	35
Gregg, Tommy	5	.245	333	674	63	165	242	34	2	13	66	9
Griffin, Alfredo	16	.250	1853	6535	723	1633	2096	235	78	24	514	189
Grissom, Marquis	3	.263	272	920	131	242	333	39	11	10	70	99
3 Guerrero, Pedro	14	.302	1493	5246	720	1586	2545	261	28	214	882	95
1 Gwynn, Tony	10	.328	1335	5181	765	1699	2250	248	72	53	550	246
Hamilton, Jeff	6	.234	416	1205	111	282	421	61	3	24	124	0
Harris, Lenny	4	.282	413	1238	163	349	428	43	6	8	101	45
Hatcher, Billy	8	.265	886	3112	427	824	1139	152	23	39	278	192
Hayes, Charlie	4	.247	388	1336	116	330	482	58	2	30	153	10
Heath, Mike	14	.252	1325	4212	462	1061	1546	173	27	86	469	54
Heep, Danny	13	.257	883	1961	208	503	701	96	6	30	229	12
Herr, Tommy	13	.271	1514	5349	676	1450	1870	254	41	28	574	188
Hollins, Dave	2	.249	128	265	32	66	113	10	2	11	36	1
Howard, Thomas	2	.252	126	325	34	82	114	14	3	4	22	10
Hudler, Rex	7	.251	406	857	118	215	326	43	7	18	65	75
Incaviglia, Pete	6	.244	791	2786	371	679	1244	132	14	135	426	27
Jackson, Darrin	6	.254	362	846	109	215	359	34	4	34	98	13
James, Chris	6	.262	668	2417	258	634	977	112	15	67	301	22
Javier, Stan	7	.245	628	1464	208	359	468	50	16	9	118	65
Jefferson, Stan	6	.216	296	832	125	180	271	25	9	16	67	60
Johnson, Howard	10	.256	1179	3959	624	1014	1845	206	17	197	629	191
Jones, Tim	4	.244	156	279	23	68	88	15	1	1	24	8
Jordan, Ricky	4	.277	406	1421	174	393	597	79	7	37	211	7
Jose, Felix	4	.283	308	1057	128	299	429	59	7	19	135	33
Justice, David	3	.277	252	886	150	245	452	51	3	50	168	21
Kennedy, Terry	14	.264	1491	4979	474	1313	1920	244	12	113	628	6
King, Jeff	3	.229	235	695	93	159	269	31	5	23	90	10
Kingery, Mike	6	.256	466	1079	135	276	396	51	12	15	113	25
Kruk, John	6	.291	786	2441	348	711	1080	112	25	69	376	45
Lake, Steve	9	.238	412	952	75	227	306	33	5	12	93	1
Lankford, Ray	2	.257	190	692	95	178	279	33	16	12	81	52
7 Larkin, Barry	6	.294	695	2589	402	762	1102	118	24	58	290	133
LaValliere, Mike	8	.271	641	1841	144	499	633	84	4	14	214	5
Lemke, Mark	4	.225	268	621	70	140	188	30	3	4	56	1
Lind, Jose	5	.259	644	2348	254	607	772	97	22	8	210	47
Lindeman, Jim	6	.231	261	477	56	110	171	22	0	13	63	4
Litton, Greg	3	.230	223	474	42	109	158	21	5	6	56	1
Lyons, Steve	7	.255	777	2084	255	531	717	99	15	19	192	40
9 Magadan, Dave	6	.294	602	1767	242	519	694	101	10	18	226	4
Manwaring, Kirt	5	.222	206	514	42	114	143	20	3	1	53	3
Martinez, Carmelo	9	.245	1003	2906	350	713	1185	134	7	108	424	10
Martinez, Dave	6	.272	701	2162	282	588	839	79	32	36	197	95
McClendon, Lloyd	5	.248	347	741	94	184	295	31	1	26	103	14
5 McGee, Willie	10	.298	1324	5195	717	1548	2115	237	81	56	603	294
McGriff, Fred	6	.278	731	2472	432	687	1291	118	9	156	411	25
Merced, Orlando	2	.271	145	435	86	118	170	18	2	10	50	8
Morandini, Mickey	2	.248	123	404	47	100	129	15	4	2	23	16
2 Morris, Hal	4	.320	273	825	125	264	390	55	4	21	99	19
Murphy, Dale	16	.267	2136	7856	1191	2095	3709	348	39	396	1252	161
10 Murray, Eddie	15	.292	2288	8573	1279	2502	4181	425	30	398	1469	86
Newman, Al	7	.227	738	1861	239	422	502	63	7	1	144	82

LIFETIME BATTING AVERAGES—NATIONAL LEAGUE PLAYERS

(100 or more games—records compiled in National and American Leagues)

Player	Yrs.	AVG.	G	AB	R	H	TB	2B	3B	HR	RBI	SB
Nixon, Otis	9	.246	749	1540	302	379	446	39	8	4	101	264
Noboa, Junior	6	.243	252	404	37	98	119	12	3	1	24	8
O'Brien, Charlie	6	.203	271	733	72	149	221	36	3	10	79	0
Oliver, Joe	3	.233	264	784	68	183	291	42	0	22	116	1
Olson, Greg	3	.250	236	711	82	178	256	37	1	13	80	2
O'Neill, Paul	7	.262	651	2122	262	557	943	128	6	82	345	55
Oquendo, Jose	8	.261	987	2745	285	717	880	91	18	12	221	33
Owen, Spike	9	.241	1155	3724	447	896	1250	157	49	33	314	65
Pagnozzi, Tom	5	.257	369	1002	86	258	337	51	5	6	107	11
Pecota, Bill	6	.254	445	1084	167	275	401	52	10	18	101	41
Pena, Geronimo	2	.243	122	230	43	56	87	10	3	5	19	16
Pendleton, Terry	8	.267	1080	4019	498	1075	1526	189	32	66	528	109
Perry, Gerald	9	.265	885	2747	333	727	1028	126	11	51	339	137
Ramirez, Rafael	12	.261	1466	5318	545	1388	1824	218	31	52	471	112
Randolph, Willie	17	.277	2112	7732	1210	2138	2727	305	64	52	672	270
Redus, Gary	10	.249	988	3082	535	768	1262	163	44	81	307	307
Reed, Jeff	8	.234	525	1400	101	328	442	63	6	13	117	2
Reyes, Gilberto	7	.202	122	258	13	52	63	11	0	0	14	2
Riles, Ernest	7	.258	786	2300	289	594	843	83	20	42	260	18
Roberts, Bip	5	.291	489	1559	286	454	603	69	16	16	113	107
Sabo, Chris	4	.278	520	1991	300	553	907	134	8	68	232	104
Salazar, Luis	12	.264	1204	3846	418	1017	1483	137	31	89	430	116
Samuel, Juan	9	.259	1234	4922	696	1277	2058	235	81	128	551	341
Sandberg, Ryne	11	.288	1547	6093	976	1753	2774	288	59	205	749	297
Sanders, Deion	3	.183	125	290	47	53	93	5	4	9	29	20
Santiago, Benito	6	.266	683	2486	275	661	1019	103	15	75	333	60
Sasser, Mackey	5	.287	342	830	77	238	339	52	5	13	117	0
Schu, Rick	8	.247	579	1564	189	386	602	67	13	41	134	17
Scioscia, Mike	12	.262	1324	4025	379	1054	1459	192	9	65	422	26
Sharperson, Mike	5	.276	349	789	87	218	278	35	5	5	75	18
Slaught, Don	10	.274	917	2816	294	771	1158	176	23	55	314	14
Smith, Dwight	3	.281	316	800	102	225	336	41	8	18	100	22
Smith, Lonnie	14	.291	1391	4730	830	1375	1987	256	52	84	471	356
Smith, Ozzie	14	.258	2076	7569	1006	1955	2458	327	55	22	650	499
Snyder, Cory	6	.240	728	2597	312	624	1115	117	10	118	357	19
Strawberry, Darryl	9	.263	1248	4408	748	1159	2276	209	34	280	832	201
Sveum, Dale	5	.243	511	1702	210	413	651	80	10	46	236	9
Templeton, Garry	16	.271	2079	7721	893	2096	2847	329	106	70	728	242
Teufel, Tim	9	.257	876	2666	366	684	1087	164	10	73	323	19
Thompson, Milt	8	.280	871	2774	367	777	1059	115	34	33	241	173
Thompson, Robby	6	.257	855	2983	433	768	1196	149	33	71	293	82
Treadway, Jeff	5	.285	494	1638	194	467	645	78	11	26	158	11
Uribe, Jose	8	.241	927	2849	279	686	892	89	33	17	203	71
Van Slyke, Andy	9	.269	1236	4123	617	1109	1845	206	70	130	599	208
Varsho, Gary	4	.251	252	395	49	99	141	22	4	4	35	19
Villanueva, Hector	2	.275	123	306	37	84	162	14	2	20	50	1
Vizcaino, Jose	3	.262	137	206	12	54	62	6	1	0	12	3
Walker, Larry	3	.262	290	953	122	250	413	48	5	35	119	36
Wallach, Tim	12	.263	1617	5992	684	1574	2550	331	30	195	846	48
Walling, Denny	17	.271	1268	2942	371	798	1147	142	30	49	380	44
Walton, Jerome	3	.265	340	1137	169	301	401	52	6	12	84	45
Webster, Mitch	9	.265	906	2845	423	755	1147	127	47	57	278	144
Willard, Jerry	6	.251	293	730	79	183	279	28	1	22	103	1
Williams, Ken	6	.218	451	1154	136	252	391	42	8	27	119	49
Williams, Matt	5	.245	536	1899	235	466	875	84	11	101	310	17
Wilson, Craig	3	.217	121	207	19	45	49	4	0	0	21	0
Yelding, Eric	3	.249	290	877	107	218	258	22	6	2	57	86
Young, Gerald	5	.249	531	1679	235	418	513	54	16	3	105	147
Zeile, Todd	3	.263	327	1142	145	300	459	64	7	27	146	19

HOME RUNS BY PITCHERS

(Pitchers active in 1991 who have hit Major League home runs)

PITCHER	HOME RUNS	LAST HOME RUN DATE	LAST HOME RUN OPPONENT
Don Robinson	13	9/16/90	Hou.
Fernando Valenzuela	8	5/14/90	Mtl.
Dan Schatzeder	5	6/5/86	Phi.
Dwight Gooden	4	6/20/91	Atl.
Jim Gott	4	6/20/87	S.D.
Kevin Gross	4	5/14/90	L.A.
Rick Reuschel	4	5/22/87	Cin.
Eric Show	4	9/27/85	Atl.
Rick Sutcliffe	4	8/31/88	Hou.
Rick Aguilera	3	9/4/87	L.A.
Dennis Eckersley	3	5/26/86	Cin.
Bill Gullickson	3	9/13/90	Cin.
Joe Magrane	3	8/9/89	Pitt.
Bryn Smith	3	10/1/90	Mtl.
Walt Terrell	3	8/23/83	S.D.
Andy Benes	2	4/27/91	Phi.
Ron Darling	2	6/30/89	Cin.
Tommy Greene	2	8/9/91	Mtl.
Jimmy Jones	2	8/22/88	Phi.
Mike LaCoss	2	6/29/86	Cin.
Derek Lilliquist	2	5/1/90	N.Y. NL
Jeff D. Robinson	2	9/9/89	N.Y. NL
Nolan Ryan	2	5/1/87	Atl.
Scott Sanderson	2	5/1/87	S.D.
Calvin Schiraldi	2	7/25/90 (2g)	Cin.
Mike Scott	2	9/23/89	S.F.
Scott Terry	2	6/30/89	S.D.
Bob Welch	2	5/6/86	Chi. NL
Tim Belcher	1	9/11/88	Cin.
Shawn Boskie	1	4/27/91	Cin.
Tom Browning	1	10/4/91	S.D.
John Candelaria	1	7/19/84	S.D.
Dennis Cook	1	5/19/90	L.A.
Danny Darwin	1	9/15/88	Cin.
Mark Davis	1	6/13/88	S.F.
Doug Drabek	1	4/24/90	S.F.
Sid Fernandez	1	9/21/89	St.L.
Scott Garrelts	1	9/5/86	Mtl.
Charlie Hough	1	4/24/77	Atl.
Tim Leary	1	4/20/84	Phi.
Craig Lefferts	1	4/25/86	S.F.
Greg Maddux	1	6/16/91	S.D.
Rick Mahler	1	6/23/82	L.A.
Ramon Martinez	1	9/22/91	Atl.
Bob Ojeda	1	7/11/91	Mtl.
Omar Olivares	1	9/8/90	Chi. NL
Alejandro Pena	1	7/23/83	St.L.
Mark Portugal	1	9/8/89	S.F.
Ted Power	1	7/11/87	Mtl.
Jose Rijo	1	7/19/88	N.Y. NL
Jeff Russell	1	8/23/83	Chi. NL
Scott Scudder	1	6/26/91	S.D.
Lee Smith	1	7/5/82	Atl.
John Smoltz	1	5/3/89	Phi.
Bob Walk	1	4/14/91	Chi. NL
John Wetteland	1	5/27/90	St.L.
Ed Whitson	1	4/25/90	Chi. NL
Mitch Williams	1	9/18/89	N.Y. NL
Trevor Wilson	1	7/25/91	N.Y. NL

CLUBS' ALL-TIME TOP TEN IN BATTING DEPARTMENTS

(Batting percentage column includes only players in 500 or more games.)

BRAVES

GAMES		AT BATS		RUNS		HITS		DOUBLES		TRIPLES	
H. Aaron	3,076	H. Aaron	11,628	H. Aaron	2,107	H. Aaron	3,600	H. Aaron	600	Maranville	103
E. Mathews	2,223	E. Mathews	8,049	E. Mathews	1,452	E. Mathews	2,201	E. Mathews	338	H. Aaron	96
Murphy	1,926	Murphy	7,098	H. Long	1,294	Tenney	2,002	Murphy	306	H. Long	89
Maranville	1,795	H. Long	6,767	Tenney	1,127	H. Long	1,911	T. Holmes	291	Bruton	79
Tenney	1,715	Maranville	6,724	Murphy	1,103	Murphy	1,901	H. Long	277	Tenney	77
H. Long	1,642	Tenney	6,629	Duffy	998	Maranville	1,696	Berger	248	W. Nash	76
R. Lowe	1,403	R. Lowe	5,580	R. Lowe	997	R. Lowe	1,606	Maranville	244	Morrill	75
Crandall	1,394	T. Holmes	4,956	W. Nash	857	Duffy	1,560	Tenney	236	Duffy	72
Logan	1,351	Logan	4,931	Maranville	801	T. Holmes	1,503	Morrill	226	R. Lowe	70
T. Holmes	1,289	Morrill	4,746	Morrill	796	W. Nash	1,345	Logan	207	E. Mathews	70

CUBS

GAMES		AT BATS		RUNS		HITS		DOUBLES		TRIPLES	
Banks	2,528	Banks	9,421	Anson	1,712	Anson	3,081	Anson	530	Ryan	136
Anson	2,253	Anson	9,084	Ryan	1,406	Banks	2,583	Banks	407	Anson	129
B. Williams	2,213	B. Williams	8,479	B. Williams	1,306	B. Williams	2,510	B. Williams	402	Schulte	117
Santo	2,126	Santo	7,768	Banks	1,305	Hack	2,193	Hartnett	391	Dahlen	106
Cavarretta	1,953	Hack	7,278	Hack	1,239	Santo	2,171	Hack	363	Cavarretta	99
Hack	1,938	Ryan	6,803	Santo	1,109	Ryan	2,153	Santo	353	Tinker	93
Hartnett	1,926	Cavarretta	6,592	Sandberg	974	Cavarretta	1,927	Ryan	350	Banks	90
Ryan	1,656	Kessinger	6,355	Cavarretta	968	Hartnett	1,867	W. Herman	346	B. Williams	87
Kessinger	1,648	Hartnett	6,282	Dahlen	899	Sandberg	1,752	Cavarretta	341	Lange	83
Schulte	1,558	Sandberg	6,087	W. Herman	875	W. Herman	1,710	Sandberg	288	Hack	81

REDS

GAMES		AT BATS		RUNS		HITS		DOUBLES		TRIPLES	
Rose	2,722	Rose	10,934	Rose	1,741	Rose	3,358	Rose	601	Roush	153
Concepcion	2,488	Concepcion	8,723	Bench	1,091	Concepcion	2,326	Concepcion	389	Rose	115
Bench	2,158	Bench	7,658	F. Robinson	1,043	Bench	2,048	Bench	381	McPhee	111
Perez	1,948	Perez	6,846	Concepcion	993	Perez	1,934	Pinson	342	Pinson	96
Pinson	1,565	Pinson	6,335	Pinson	978	Pinson	1,881	Perez	339	W.C. Walker	94
F. Robinson	1,502	F. Robinson	5,527	Perez	936	Roush	1,784	F. Robinson	318	M.F. Mitchell	88
Driessen	1,480	Roush	5,384	McPhee	919	F. Robinson	1,673	F. McCormick	285	Beckley	80
Roush	1,399	Kluszewski	4,961	Morgan	816	Kluszewski	1,499	Roush	260	Goodman	79
McMillan	1,348	Corcoran	4,848	Roush	815	F. McCormick	1,439	Kluszewski	244	Daubert	78
Kluszewski	1,339	F. McCormick	4,787	Kluszewski	745	G. Bell	1,343	Driessen	240	Groh	75

ASTROS

GAMES		AT BATS		RUNS		HITS		DOUBLES		TRIPLES	
Cruz	1,870	Cruz	6,629	Cedeno	890	Cruz	1,937	Cedeno	343	Cruz	80
Puhl	1,516	Cedeno	5,732	Cruz	871	Cedeno	1,659	Cruz	335	Morgan	63
Cedeno	1,512	Wynn	5,063	Wynn	829	Watson	1,448	Watson	241	Metzger	62
Wynn	1,426	Watson	4,883	Puhl	676	Puhl	1,357	Wynn	228	Puhl	56
Watson	1,381	Puhl	4,837	Watson	640	Wynn	1,291	Puhl	226	Cedeno	55
Rader	1,178	Doran	4,264	Doran	611	Doran	1,139	Rader	197	Reynolds	55
Reynolds	1,170	Rader	4,232	Morgan	597	Cabell	1,124	Doran	180	Cabell	45
Doran	1,165	Cabell	4,005	Cabell	522	Rader	1,060	Cabell	175	Doran	35
Walling	1,069	Morgan	3,729	Rader	520	Morgan	972	Bass	161	Wynn	32
Cabell	1,067	Metzger	3,678	G. Davis	427	Aspromonte	925	Staub	156	Garner	30
										Rader	30
										Walling	30
										Watson	30

DODGERS

GAMES		AT BATS		RUNS		HITS		DOUBLES		TRIPLES	
Wheat	2,318	Wheat	8,859	Reese	1,338	Wheat	2,804	Wheat	464	Wheat	171
Russell	2,181	Reese	8,058	Wheat	1,255	Reese	2,170	Snider	343	W. Davis	110
Reese	2,166	W. Davis	7,495	Snider	1,199	W. Davis	2,091	Garvey	333	H. Myers	97
Hodges	2,006	Russell	7,318	Gilliam	1,163	Snider	1,995	Reese	330	Daubert	87
Gilliam	1,956	Gilliam	7,119	Hodges	1,088	Garvey	1,968	Furillo	324	Hummel	82
W. Davis	1,952	Hodges	6,881	W. Davis	1,004	Russell	1,926	W. Davis	321	Snider	82
Snider	1,923	Snider	6,640	J. Robinson	947	Furillo	1,910	Gilliam	304	Reese	80
Furillo	1,806	Garvey	6,543	Furillo	895	Gilliam	1,889	Hodges	294	Sheckard	80
Garvey	1,727	Furillo	6,378	Griffin	886	Hodges	1,884	Russell	293	T.P. Daly	74
Wills	1,593	Wills	6,156	Wills	876	Wills	1,732	F. Walker	274	Johnston	73

EXPOS

GAMES		AT BATS		RUNS		HITS		DOUBLES		TRIPLES	
Wallach	1,617	Wallach	5,992	Raines	934	Raines	1,598	Wallach	331	Raines	81
Dawson	1,443	Dawson	5,628	Dawson	828	Dawson	1,575	Dawson	295	Dawson	67
Carter	1,408	Raines	5,305	Wallach	684	Wallach	1,574	Raines	273	Cromartie	30
Raines	1,405	Carter	5,018	Carter	683	Carter	1,365	Carter	256	Wallach	30
Cromartie	1,038	Cromartie	3,796	Cromartie	446	Cromartie	1,063	Cromartie	222	Webster	25
Parrish	967	Parrish	3,411	Parrish	421	Parrish	896	Parrish	208	Parrish	24
Bailey	951	Galarraga	3,082	Bailey	412	Galarraga	830	Galarraga	168	Bailey	23
Speier	895	Bailey	2,991	Galarraga	394	Bailey	791	Brooks	139	Carter	23
Galarraga	847	Speier	2,902	Fairly	303	Speier	710	Valentine	136	Da. Martinez	22
Fairly	718	Foli	2,614	Valentine	297	Brooks	689	Speier	123	Speier	22

CLUBS' ALL-TIME TOP TEN IN BATTING DEPARTMENTS

(Batting percentage column includes only players in 500 or more games.)

BRAVES

HOME RUNS		TOTAL BASES		RUNS BATTED IN		EXTRA BASE HITS		BATTING AVG.		STOLEN BASES (since 1898)	
H. Aaron	733	H. Aaron	6,591	H. Aaron	2,202	H. Aaron	1,429	Hamilton	.338	H. Aaron	240
E. Mathews	493	E. Mathews	4,158	E. Mathews	1,388	E. Mathews	901	Duffy	.336	Tenney	196
Murphy	371	Murphy	3,394	Murphy	1,143	Murphy	714	C.S. Stahl	.328	Maranville	194
Adcock	239	H. Long	2,630	H. Long	961	Berger	499	Garr	.317	Royster	174
Horner	215	Tenney	2,440	Duffy	926	Adcock	458	Carty	.317	Murphy	160
Berger	199	Maranville	2,215	R. Lowe	872	H. Long	454	Richbourg	.311	Sweeney	153
Crandall	170	Berger	2,212	Nash	809	T. Holmes	426	H. Aaron	.310	Bruton	143
J. Torre	142	Adcock	2,162	Adcock	760	Horner	382	J.J. Collins	.310	Garr	137
Evans	131	T. Holmes	2,152	Berger	746	Maranville	370	Berger	.304	Washington	115
Carty	109	R. Lowe	2,113	Horner	652	Crandall	354	T. Holmes	.303	Perry	105

CUBS

HOME RUNS		TOTAL BASES		RUNS BATTED IN		EXTRA BASE HITS		BATTING AVG.		STOLEN BASES (since 1898)	
Banks	512	Banks	4,706	Anson	1,715	Banks	1,009	Anson	.339	Chance	404
B. Williams	392	B. Williams	4,262	Banks	1,636	B. Williams	881	Stephenson	.336	Tinker	304
Santo	337	Anson	4,145	B. Williams	1,354	Santo	756	Lange	.336	Sandberg	297
Hartnett	231	Santo	3,667	Santo	1,290	Anson	751	Everett	.326	Evers	281
Nicholson	205	Hartnett	3,079	Hartnett	1,153	Hartnett	686	Cuyler	.325	Schulte	200
Sandberg	205	Ryan	3,054	Ryan	914	Ryan	579	L. Wilson	.322	Slagle	198
Sauer	198	Hack	2,889	Cavarretta	896	Sandberg	552	Ryan	.316	Hack	165
L. Wilson	190	Sandberg	2,773	Nicholson	833	Cavarretta	532	Gore	.316	Sheckard	163
Dawson	152	Cavarretta	2,742	L. Wilson	768	Nicholson	503	M.J. Kelly	.314	DeJesus	154
Durham	138	Schulte	2,351	Sandberg	749	Hack	501	Demaree	.309	Cuyler	153
										Hofman	153

REDS

HOME RUNS		TOTAL BASES		RUNS BATTED IN		EXTRA BASE HITS		BATTING AVG.		STOLEN BASES (since 1898)	
Bench	389	Rose	4,645	Bench	1,376	Rose	868	Seymour	.333	Morgan	406
F. Robinson	324	Bench	3,644	Perez	1,192	Bench	794	Roush	.331	Concepcion	321
Perez	287	Perez	3,246	Rose	1,036	F. Robinson	692	Beckley	.324	Bescher	320
Kluszewski	251	Concepcion	3,114	F. Robinson	1,009	Perez	682	Holliday	.315	Davis	247
Foster	244	F. Robinson	3,063	Concepcion	950	Pinson	624	Hargrave	.314	Pinson	221
Pinson	186	Pinson	2,973	Kluszewski	886	Concepcion	538	Bressler	.311	Roush	199
Davis	177	Kluszewski	2,542	Foster	861	Kluszewski	518	Lombardi	.311	Corcoran	171
Post	172	Roush	2,488	Pinson	814	Foster	488	C.B. Miller	.308	Lobert	168
G. Bell	160	Foster	2,289	F. McCormick	803	Roush	459	Rose	.307	Mitchell	165
Morgan	152	G. Bell	2,121	Roush	754	G. Bell	423	P. Duncan	.307	F. Robinson	161
Rose	152										

ASTROS

HOME RUNS		TOTAL BASES		RUNS BATTED IN		EXTRA BASE HITS		BATTING AVG.		STOLEN BASES (since 1898)	
Wynn	223	Cruz	2,846	Cruz	942	Cedeno	561	Watson	.297	Cedeno	487
G. Davis	166	Cedeno	2,601	Watson	782	Cruz	553	Cruz	.292	Cruz	288
Cedeno	163	Wynn	2,252	Cedeno	778	Wynn	483	Cedeno	.289	Morgan	219
Watson	139	Watson	2,166	Wynn	719	Watson	410	J. Alou	.282	Puhl	217
Cruz	138	Puhl	1,881	Rader	600	Rader	355	Cabell	.281	Cabell	191
Rader	128	Rader	1,701	G. Davis	518	Puhl	344	Puhl	.281	Doran	191
L. May	81	Doran	1,606	Puhl	432	G. Davis	326	Walling	.277	Wynn	180
Bass	78	Cabell	1,524	Cabell	405	Morgan	288	Bass	.276	Young	147
Morgan	72	Morgan	1,467	Doran	404	Doran	284	Staub	.273	Hatcher	145
Ashby	69	G. Davis	1,463	Bass	396	Bass	268	Thon	.270	Bass	111
Doran	69										

DODGERS

HOME RUNS		TOTAL BASES		RUNS BATTED IN		EXTRA BASE HITS		BATTING AVG.		STOLEN BASES (since 1898)	
Snider	389	Wheat	4,003	Snider	1,271	Snider	814	Keeler	.360	Wills	490
Hodges	361	Snider	3,669	Hodges	1,254	Wheat	766	F. Herman	.339	Lopes	418
Campanella	242	Hodges	3,357	Wheat	1,227	Hodges	703	Fournier	.337	W. Davis	335
Cey	228	W. Davis	3,094	Furillo	1,058	W. Davis	585	Wheat	.317	Sax	290
Garvey	211	Reese	3,038	Garvey	992	Garvey	579	Phelps	.315	Reese	232
Furillo	192	Garvey	3,004	Reese	885	Furillo	572	F.A. Jones	.315	Sheckard	207
Guerrero	171	Furillo	2,922	Campanella	856	Reese	536	Mota	.315	Gilliam	203
W. Davis	154	Gilliam	2,530	W. Davis	849	Cey	469	J. Robinson	.311	Wheat	203
Baker	144	Russell	2,471	Cey	842	J. Robinson	464	F. Walker	.311	J. Robinson	197
Camilli	139	Cey	2,321	J. Robinson	734	Gilliam	440	Guerrero	.309	Daubert	187

EXPOS

HOME RUNS		TOTAL BASES		RUNS BATTED IN		EXTRA BASE HITS		BATTING AVG.		STOLEN BASES (since 1898)	
Dawson	225	Dawson	2,679	Wallach	846	Dawson	587	Raines	.301	Raines	634
Carter	215	Wallach	2,550	Dawson	838	Wallach	556	Staub	.295	Dawson	253
Wallach	195	Raines	2,321	Carter	794	Carter	494	Valentine	.288	Scott	139
Bailey	118	Carter	2,312	Raines	552	Raines	450	Cromartie	.280	Nixon	133
Galarraga	106	Cromartie	1,525	Bailey	466	Parrish	332	Dawson	.280	Grissom	99
Parrish	100	Parrish	1,452	Parrish	444	Cromartie	312	Brooks	.279	DeShields	98
Raines	96	Galarraga	1,344	Galarraga	433	Galarraga	288	Hunt	.277	LeFlore	97
Valentine	95	Bailey	1,307	Brooks	390	Bailey	257	Fairly	.276	Webster	96
Fairly	86	Valentine	1,119	Cromartie	371	Valentine	242	Carter	.272	Lintz	79
Staub	81	Brooks	1,089	Valentine	358	Brooks	232	Galarraga	.269	Da. Martinez	68

CLUBS' ALL-TIME TOP TEN IN BATTING DEPARTMENTS

(Batting percentage column includes only players in 500 or more games.)

METS

GAMES	AT BATS	RUNS	HITS	DOUBLES	TRIPLES
Kranepool 1,853	Kranepool 5,436	Strawberry 662	Kranepool 1,418	Kranepool 225	Wilson 62
Harrelson 1,322	Harrelson 4,390	Wilson 592	C. Jones 1,188	H. Johnson 187	Harrelson 45
Grote 1,235	C. Jones 4,223	C. Jones 563	Wilson 1,112	Strawberry 187	C. Jones 33
C. Jones 1,201	Wilson 4,027	H. Johnson 547	Harrelson 1,029	C. Jones 182	S. Henderson 31
Wilson 1,116	Strawberry 3,903	Kranepool 536	Strawberry 1,025	Wilson 170	Strawberry 30
Strawberry 1,109	Grote 3,881	Harrelson 490	Grote 994	Hernandez 159	Flynn 26
H. Johnson 982	H. Johnson 3,383	Hernandez 455	Hernandez 939	Stearns 152	Kranepool 25
Mazzilli 979	Hernandez 3,164	Mazzilli 404	H. Johnson 863	Mazzilli 148	Mazzilli 22
Staub 942	Mazzilli 3,013	Garrett 389	Mazzilli 796	Grote 143	Garrett 20
Garrett 883	Garrett 2,817	McReynolds 382	McReynolds 745	McReynolds 142	Swoboda 20

PHILLIES

GAMES	AT BATS	RUNS	HITS	DOUBLES	TRIPLES
Schmidt 2,404	Schmidt 8,352	Schmidt 1,506	Schmidt 2,234	Delahanty 432	Delahanty 151
Ashburn 1,794	Ashburn 7,122	Delahanty 1,365	Ashburn 2,217	Schmidt 408	Magee 127
Bowa 1,739	Bowa 6,815	Ashburn 1,114	Delahanty 2,211	Magee 337	S. Thompson 103
Taylor 1,669	Delahanty 6,352	Klein 963	Ennis 1,812	Klein 336	Ashburn 97
Ennis 1,630	Ennis 6,327	S. Thompson 928	Bowa 1,798	Ennis 310	Callison 84
Delahanty 1,544	Taylor 5,799	R. Thomas 916	Klein 1,705	Ashburn 287	Bowa 81
W. Jones 1,520	Hamner 5,772	Magee 898	Magee 1,647	Hamner 271	Cravath 72
Magee 1,518	Magee 5,505	Ennis 891	F. Williams 1,553	Callison 265	Samuel 71
Hamner 1,501	W. Jones 5,419	Hamilton 877	Hamner 1,518	S. Thompson 258	Ennis 65
F. Williams 1,463	Callison 5,306	F. Williams 825	Taylor 1,511	Luzinski 253	Allen 64
					Klein 64
					Lajoie 64
					Titus 64

PIRATES

GAMES	AT BATS	RUNS	HITS	DOUBLES	TRIPLES
Clemente 2,433	Clemente 9,454	Wagner 1,520	Clemente 3,000	Wagner 556	Wagner 231
Wagner 2,432	Wagner 9,046	P. Waner 1,492	Wagner 2,970	P. Waner 556	P. Waner 186
Stargell 2,360	P. Waner 8,429	Clemente 1,416	P. Waner 2,868	Clemente 440	Clemente 166
Carey 2,171	Carey 8,406	Carey 1,414	Carey 2,416	Stargell 423	Traynor 164
Mazeroski 2,163	Stargell 7,927	Stargell 1,195	Traynor 2,416	Carey 375	Clarke 155
P. Waner 2,154	Mazeroski 7,755	Traynor 1,183	L. Waner 2,317	Traynor 371	Carey 148
Traynor 1,941	Traynor 7,559	L. Waner 1,151	Stargell 2,232	Parker 296	Leach 137
L. Waner 1,803	L. Waner 7,256	Clarke 1,017	Mazeroski 2,016	Mazeroski 294	Vaughan 116
Leach 1,548	Leach 5,909	Leach 1,007	Vaughan 1,709	Vaughan 291	Beckley 114
Clarke 1,442	Clarke 5,471	Vaughan 936	Clarke 1,638	Oliver 276	L. Waner 114
				Suhr 276	

CARDINALS

GAMES	AT BATS	RUNS	HITS	DOUBLES	TRIPLES
Musial 3,026	Musial 10,972	Musial 1,949	Musial 3,630	Musial 725	Musial 177
Brock 2,289	Brock 9,125	Brock 1,427	Brock 2,713	Brock 434	Hornsby 143
Slaughter 1,820	Schoendienst 6,841	Hornsby 1,089	Hornsby 2,110	Medwick 377	Slaughter 135
Schoendienst 1,795	Slaughter 6,775	Slaughter 1,071	Slaughter 2,064	Hornsby 367	Brock 121
Flood 1,738	K. Boyer 6,334	Schoendienst 1,025	Schoendienst 1,980	Slaughter 366	Bottomley 119
K. Boyer 1,667	Flood 6,318	K. Boyer 988	K. Boyer 1,855	Schoendienst 352	Konetchy 93
Hornsby 1,580	Hornsby 5,881	Bottomley 921	Flood 1,853	Bottomley 344	Medwick 81
Javier 1,578	Simmons 5,725	Flood 845	Bottomley 1,727	Simmons 332	McGee 76
Simmons 1,564	Javier 5,631	Frisch 831	Simmons 1,704	Frisch 286	J. Martin 75
Marion 1,502	O. Smith 5,333	Medwick 811	Medwick 1,590	Flood 271	Templeton 69

PADRES

GAMES	AT BATS	RUNS	HITS	DOUBLES	TRIPLES
Gwynn 1,335	Gwynn 5,181	Gwynn 765	Gwynn 1,699	Gwynn 248	Gwynn 72
Templeton 1,286	Templeton 4,512	Winfield 599	Templeton 1,135	Templeton 195	Richards 63
Winfield 1,117	Winfield 3,997	Richards 484	Winfield 1,134	Winfield 179	Winfield 39
Flannery 972	Richards 3,414	Colbert 442	Richards 994	Kennedy 158	Templeton 36
Richards 939	Colbert 3,080	Templeton 430	Kennedy 817	Colbert 130	Gaston 29
Colbert 866	Kennedy 2,987	Kennedy 308	Colbert 780	Richards 123	Flannery 25
Kennedy 835	Gaston 2,615	Garvey 291	Gaston 672	Martinez 111	Salazar 24
Martinez 783	Santiago 2,486	Martinez 286	Santiago 661	Garvey 107	Colbert 22
Gaston 766	Flannery 2,473	B. Roberts 286	Flannery 631	Santiago 103	O. Smith 19
Kendall 754	Martinez 2,325	Santiago 275	Garvey 631	Grubb 101	McReynolds 17

GIANTS

GAMES	AT BATS	RUNS	HITS	DOUBLES	TRIPLES
Mays 2,857	Mays 10,477	Mays 2,011	Mays 3,187	Mays 504	Tiernan 159
Ott 2,730	Ott 9,456	Ott 1,859	Ott 2,876	Ott 488	Mays 139
McCovey 2,256	McCovey 7,214	Tiernan 1,312	Terry 2,193	Terry 374	Connor 129
Terry 1,721	Terry 6,428	Terry 1,120	McCovey 1,974	McCovey 308	L. Doyle 117
Jackson 1,656	Jackson 6,086	McCovey 1,113	Tiernan 1,875	Jackson 291	Terry 112
L. Doyle 1,615	L. Doyle 5,995	Van Haltren 982	Jackson 1,768	L. Doyle 275	Ewing 108
Davenport 1,501	Tiernan 5,910	Connor 939	L. Doyle 1,751	G.J. Burns 267	G.S. Davis 97
Lockman 1,485	Lockman 5,584	L. Doyle 906	J. Moore 1,615	J. Moore 258	Youngs 93
Tiernan 1,474	J. Moore 5,427	G.J. Burns 877	Van Haltren 1,592	Tiernan 248	Van Haltren 90
G.J. Burns 1,362	G.J. Burns 5,311	G.S. Davis 844	Lockman 1,571	Connor 240	Jackson 86

CLUBS' ALL-TIME TOP TEN IN BATTING DEPARTMENTS

(Batting percentage column includes only players in 500 or more games.)

METS

HOME RUNS		TOTAL BASES		RUNS BATTED IN		EXTRA BASE HITS		BATTING AVG.		STOLEN BASES (Since 1898)	
Strawberry	252	Kranepool	2,047	Strawberry	733	Strawberry	469	Hernandez	.297	Wilson	281
H. Johnson	178	Strawberry	2,028	Kranepool	614	H. Johnson	381	Magadan	.294	Strawberry	191
Kingman	154	C. Jones	1,715	H. Johnson	560	Kranepool	368	Backman	.283	H. Johnson	174
Kranepool	118	H. Johnson	1,616	C. Jones	521	C. Jones	308	C. Jones	.281	Mazzilli	152
McReynolds	118	Wilson	1,586	Hernandez	468	Wilson	292	Dykstra	.278	Dykstra	116
Foster	99	Hernandez	1,358	McReynolds	435	McReynolds	272	Millan	.278	Harrelson	115
Milner	94	Grote	1,278	Staub	399	Hernandez	249	Wilson	.276	Backman	106
C. Jones	93	McReynolds	1,265	Kingman	389	Mazzilli	238	Staub	.276	Agee	92
Carter	89	Harrelson	1,260	Foster	361	Kingman	230	Youngblood	.274	C. Jones	91
Agee	82	Mazzilli	1,192	Grote	357	Staub	212	McReynolds	.273	Stearns	91

PHILLIES

HOME RUNS		TOTAL BASES		RUNS BATTED IN		EXTRA BASE HITS		BATTING AVG.		STOLEN BASES (Since 1898)	
Schmidt	548	Schmidt	4,404	Schmidt	1,595	Schmidt	1,015	Hamilton	.362	Magee	387
Ennis	259	Delahanty	3,197	Delahanty	1,286	Delahanty	667	Delahanty	.348	Bowa	288
Klein	243	Ennis	3,029	Ennis	1,124	Klein	643	Flick	.345	Samuel	249
Luzinski	223	Klein	2,898	Klein	983	Ennis	634	S. Thompson	.335	V. Hayes	202
F. Williams	217	Ashburn	2,764	S. Thompson	958	Magee	539	Klein	.326	Ashburn	199
R. Allen	204	F. Williams	2,539	Magee	889	Callison	534	V. Davis	.321	Maddox	189
Callison	185	Magee	2,463	Luzinski	811	F. Williams	503	Leach	.312	Schmidt	174
W. Jones	180	Callison	2,426	F. Williams	796	Luzinski	497	Ashburn	.311	Taylor	169
V. Hayes	124	Luzinski	2,263	W. Jones	753	R. Allen	472	Whitney	.307	R. Thomas	164
Seminick	123	W. Jones	2,236	Whitney	734	S. Thompson	456	F. Williams	.306	Paskert	149

PIRATES

HOME RUNS		TOTAL BASES		RUNS BATTED IN		EXTRA BASE HITS		BATTING AVG.		STOLEN BASES (Since 1898)	
Stargell	475	Clemente	4,492	Stargell	1,540	Stargell	953	P. Waner	.340	Carey	678
Kiner	301	Wagner	4,234	Wagner	1,475	Wagner	869	Cuyler	.336	Wagner	639
Clemente	240	Stargell	4,190	Clemente	1,305	P. Waner	850	E.E. Smith	.328	Moreno	412
Parker	166	P. Waner	4,120	Traynor	1,273	Clemente	846	Wagner	.328	Clarke	261
F. Thomas	163	Traynor	3,289	P. Waner	1,177	Traynor	593	M. Alou	.327	Leach	249
Bonds	142	Carey	3,285	Mazeroski	853	Carey	589	Vaughan	.324	Bonds	212
Mazeroski	138	L. Waner	2,898	Kiner	801	Parker	524	Beaumont	.321	Taveras	206
Oliver	135	Mazeroski	2,848	Suhr	789	Mazeroski	494	Traynor	.320	Beaumont	200
Hebner	128	Vaughan	2,484	Vaughan	764	Vaughan	491	L. Waner	.319	Bigbee	182
Stuart	117	Parker	2,397	Parker	758	Kiner	486	Clemente	.317	Traynor	158

CARDINALS

HOME RUNS		TOTAL BASES		RUNS BATTED IN		EXTRA BASE HITS		BATTING AVG.		STOLEN BASES (Since 1898)	
Musial	475	Musial	6,134	Musial	1,951	Musial	1,377	Hornsby	.359	Brock	888
K. Boyer	255	Brock	3,776	Slaughter	1,148	Hornsby	703	Mize	.336	Coleman	549
Hornsby	193	Hornsby	3,342	Bottomley	1,105	Brock	684	Medwick	.335	O. Smith	352
Bottomley	181	Slaughter	3,138	Hornsby	1,067	Slaughter	647	Musial	.331	McGee	274
Simmons	172	K. Boyer	3,011	K. Boyer	1,001	Bottomley	644	Hafey	.326	Frisch	195
Mize	158	Bottomley	2,852	Simmons	929	Medwick	610	Bottomley	.325	J. Smith	192
Medwick	152	Schoendienst	2,657	Medwick	923	K. Boyer	585	Frisch	.312	Huggins	174
Slaughter	146	Simmons	2,626	Brock	814	Simmons	541	Watkins	.309	L. Smith	173
White	140	Medwick	2,585	Frisch	720	Schoendienst	482	Torre	.308	Herr	152
Brock	129	Flood	2,464	Mize	653	Mize	442	J. Collins	.307	Konetchy	151

PADRES

HOME RUNS		TOTAL BASES		RUNS BATTED IN		EXTRA BASE HITS		BATTING AVG.		STOLEN BASES (Since 1898)	
Colbert	163	Gwynn	2,250	Winfield	626	Gwynn	373	Gwynn	.328	Gwynn	246
Winfield	154	Winfield	1,853	Gwynn	550	Winfield	372	Richards	.291	Richards	242
Martinez	82	Templeton	1,531	Colbert	481	Colbert	315	Grubb	.286	Wiggins	171
Gaston	77	Colbert	1,443	Templeton	427	Templeton	274	Winfield	.284	O. Smith	147
Kennedy	76	Richards	1,321	Kennedy	424	Kennedy	241	Garvey	.275	Winfield	133
Santiago	75	Kennedy	1,217	Martinez	337	Richards	212	Kennedy	.274	Hernandez	129
Tenace	68	Gaston	1,054	Santiago	333	Martinez	200	Salazar	.267	B. Roberts	107
McReynolds	65	Santiago	1,019	Garvey	316	Gaston	199	Santiago	.266	Templeton	101
Garvey	61	Martinez	948	Gaston	316	Santiago	193	Turner	.259	Salazar	93
Gwynn	53	Garvey	937	McReynolds	260	Garvey	176	Gaston	.257	R. Alomar	90

GIANTS

HOME RUNS		TOTAL BASES		RUNS BATTED IN		EXTRA BASE HITS		BATTING AVG.		STOLEN BASES (Since 1898)	
Mays	646	Mays	5,907	Ott	1,860	Mays	1,289	Terry	.341	Mays	336
Ott	511	Ott	5,041	Mays	1,859	Ott	1,071	G.S. Davis	.335	G. Burns	334
McCovey	469	McCovey	3,779	McCovey	1,388	McCovey	822	Connor	.334	L. Doyle	271
Cepeda	226	Terry	3,253	Terry	1,078	Terry	640	Van Haltren	.323	Devlin	264
Thomson	189	Tiernan	2,765	Jackson	929	Tiernan	515	Youngs	.322	Bonds	263
Bonds	186	Jackson	2,636	Tiernan	852	Jackson	512	Frisch	.321	Murray	231
J. Clark	163	L. Doyle	2,461	G.S. Davis	805	Cepeda	474	Lindstrom	.318	Frisch	224
Hart	157	Cepeda	2,234	Cepeda	767	Doyle	459	Tiernan	.317	Merkle	192
Mize	157	Lockman	2,216	Kelly	761	Connor	445	Ewing	.315	Snodgrass	190
Terry	154	J. Moore	2,216	L. Doyle	728	Thomson	437	E. Meusel	.314	Van Haltren	156

ALL-TIME HOME RUN LEADERS, SEASON—AT EACH POSITION

CATCHER

Team	Player	HR	Year
BOSTON	Walker Cooper	18	1951
MILWAUKEE	Joe Torre	27	1965
ATLANTA	Joe Torre	36	1966
CHICAGO	Gabby Hartnett	37	1930
CINCINNATI	Johnny Bench	45	1970
HOUSTON	John Bateman	17	1966
BROOKLYN	Roy Campanella	41	1953
LOS ANGELES	Joe Ferguson	25	1973
MONTREAL	Gary Carter	31	1977
NEW YORK Mets	Gary Carter	32	1985
PHILADELPHIA	Stan Lopata	32	1956
PITTSBURGH	Jim Pagliaroni	17	1965
ST. LOUIS	Ted Simmons	26	1979
SAN DIEGO	Terry Kennedy	21	1982
NEW YORK Giants	Walker Cooper	35	1947
SAN FRANCISCO	Tom Haller	27	1966

FIRST BASEMAN

Team	Player	HR	Year
BOSTON	Earl Torgeson	24	1951
MILWAUKEE	Joe Adcock	38	1956
ATLANTA	Hank Aaron	47	1971
CHICAGO	Ernie Banks	37	1962
CINCINNATI	Ted Kluszewski	49	1954
HOUSTON	Glenn Davis	34	1989
BROOKLYN	Gil Hodges	42	1954
LOS ANGELES	Steve Garvey	33	1977
MONTREAL	Andres Galarraga	29	1988
NEW YORK Mets	Dave Kingman	37	1982
PHILADELPHIA	Deron Johnson	34	1971
PITTSBURGH	Dick Stuart	35	1961
ST. LOUIS	Johnny Mize	43	1940
SAN DIEGO	Nate Colbert	38	1970
SAN DIEGO	Nate Colbert	38	1972
NEW YORK Giants	Johnny Mize	51	1947
SAN FRANCISCO	Orlando Cepeda	46	1961

SECOND BASEMAN

Team	Player	HR	Year
BOSTON	Rogers Hornsby	21	1928
MILWAUKEE	Frank Bolling	15	1961
ATLANTA	Dave Johnson	43	1973
CHICAGO	Rogers Hornsby	40	1929
CHICAGO	Ryne Sandberg	40	1990
CINCINNATI	Joe Morgan	27	1976
HOUSTON	Bill Doran	16	1987
BROOKLYN	Jackie Robinson	19	1951
BROOKLYN	Jackie Robinson	19	1952
LOS ANGELES	Dave Lopes	28	1979
MONTREAL	Pete Mackanin	12	1975
MONTREAL	Vance Law	12	1987
NEW YORK Mets	Gregg Jefferies	15	1990
PHILADELPHIA	Juan Samuel	28	1987
PITTSBURGH	Bill Mazeroski	19	1958
ST. LOUIS	Rogers Hornsby	42	1922
SAN DIEGO	Dave Campbell	12	1970
NEW YORK Giants	Rogers Hornsby	26	1927
SAN FRANCISCO	Robby Thompson	19	1991

SHORTSTOP

Team	Player	HR	Year
BOSTON	Eddie Miller	14	1940
MILWAUKEE	Denis Menke	20	1964
ATLANTA	Denis Menke	15	1966
CHICAGO	Ernie Banks	47	1958
CINCINNATI	Leo Cardenas	20	1966
CINCINNATI	Barry Larkin	20	1991
HOUSTON	Dickie Thon	20	1983
BROOKLYN	Glenn Wright	22	1930
LOS ANGELES	Don Zimmer	17	1958
MONTREAL	Hubie Brooks	14	1986
MONTREAL	Hubie Brooks	14	1987
NEW YORK Mets	Ed Bressoud	10	1966
NEW YORK Mets	Kevin Elster	10	1989
PHILADELPHIA	Granny Hamner	17	1952
PITTSBURGH	Arky Vaughan	19	1935
ST. LOUIS	Solly Hemus	15	1952
SAN DIEGO	Steve Huntz	11	1970
NEW YORK Giants	Alvin Dark	23	1953
SAN FRANCISCO	Daryl Spencer	17	1958

ALL-TIME RUNS-BATTED-IN LEADERS, SEASON—AT EACH POSITION

CATCHER

Team	Player	RBI	Year
BOSTON	Phil Masi	62	1946
MILWAUKEE	Joe Torre	109	1964
ATLANTA	Joe Torre	101	1966
CHICAGO	Gabby Hartnett	122	1930
CINCINNATI	Johnny Bench	148	1970
HOUSTON	John Bateman	70	1966
BROOKLYN	Roy Campanella	142	1953
LOS ANGELES	Joe Ferguson	88	1973
MONTREAL	Gary Carter	106	1984
NEW YORK Mets	Gary Carter	105	1986
PHILADELPHIA	Stan Lopata	95	1956
PITTSBURGH	Al Todd	86	1937
ST. LOUIS	Ted Simmons	103	1974
SAN DIEGO	Terry Kennedy	98	1983
NEW YORK Giants	Walker Cooper	122	1947
SAN FRANCISCO	Dick Dietz	107	1970

FIRST BASEMAN

Team	Player	RBI	Year
BOSTON	Stuffy McInnis	95	1923
MILWAUKEE	Joe Adcock	108	1961
ATLANTA	Hank Aaron	118	1971
CHICAGO	Ernie Banks	106	1965
CHICAGO	Ernie Banks	106	1969
CINCINNATI	Ted Kluszewski	141	1954
HOUSTON	Bob Watson	110	1977
BROOKLYN	Jack Fournier	130	1925
BROOKLYN	Gil Hodges	130	1954
LOS ANGELES	Steve Garvey	115	1977
MONTREAL	Al Oliver	109	1982
NEW YORK Mets	Dave Kingman	99	1982
PHILADELPHIA	Don Hurst	143	1932
PITTSBURGH	Gus Suhr	118	1936
ST. LOUIS	Jim Bottomley	137	1929
ST. LOUIS	Johnny Mize	137	1940
SAN DIEGO	Nate Colbert	111	1972
NEW YORK Giants	Johnny Mize	138	1947
SAN FRANCISCO	Orlando Cepeda	142	1961

SECOND BASEMAN

Team	Player	RBI	Year
BOSTON	Rogers Hornsby	94	1928
MILWAUKEE	Jack Dittmer	63	1953
ATLANTA	Dave Johnson	99	1973
CHICAGO	Rogers Hornsby	149	1929
CINCINNATI	Joe Morgan	111	1976
HOUSTON	Phil Garner	83	1982
BROOKLYN	Jackie Robinson	124	1949
LOS ANGELES	Charlie Neal	83	1959
MONTREAL	Vance Law	56	1987
NEW YORK Mets	Gregg Jefferies	68	1990
PHILADELPHIA	Juan Samuel	100	1987
PITTSBURGH	George Grantham	99	1930
ST. LOUIS	Rogers Hornsby	152	1922
SAN DIEGO	Roberto Alomar	60	1990
NEW YORK Giants	Rogers Hornsby	125	1927
SAN FRANCISCO	Tito Fuentes	63	1973

SHORTSTOP

Team	Player	RBI	Year
BOSTON	Eddie Miller	79	1940
MILWAUKEE	Johnny Logan	83	1955
ATLANTA	Andres Thomas	68	1988
CHICAGO	Ernie Banks	143	1959
CINCINNATI	Eddie Miller	87	1947
HOUSTON	Denis Menke	92	1970
BROOKLYN	Glenn Wright	126	1930
LOS ANGELES	Bill Russell	65	1974
LOS ANGELES	Bill Russell	65	1976
MONTREAL	Hubie Brooks	100	1985
NEW YORK Mets	Kevin Elster	55	1989
PHILADELPHIA	Granny Hamner	87	1952
PITTSBURGH	Glenn Wright	121	1925
ST. LOUIS	Doc Lavan	82	1921
SAN DIEGO	Garry Templeton	64	1982
NEW YORK Giants	Travis Jackson	101	1934
SAN FRANCISCO	Daryl Spencer	74	1958

NOTE—For purposes of this table, players who performed at more than one position are considered for the position they played most often that particular year and are credited with their entire season's home run and RBI totals.

ALL-TIME HOME RUN LEADERS, SEASON—AT EACH POSITION

Team	Third Baseman	HR	Year	Left Fielder	HR	Year	Center Fielder	HR	Year	Right Fielder	HR	Year
BOSTON	Chuck Workman	25	1945	Wally Berger	38	1930	Wally Berger	34	1935	Tommy Holmes	28	1945
	Ed Mathews	25	1952					34	1936			
MILWAUKEE	Ed Mathews	47	1953	Frank Thomas	25	1961	Hank Aaron	45	1962	Hank Aaron	44	1957
											44	1963
ATLANTA	Darrell Evans	41	1973	Rico Carty	25	1970	Dale Murphy	37	1985	Hank Aaron	44	1966
											44	1969
										Dale Murphy	44	1987
CHICAGO	Ron Santo	33	1965	Dave Kingman	48	1979	Hack Wilson	56	1930	Andre Dawson	49	1987
CINCINNATI	Tony Perez	40	1970	George Foster	52	1977	Eric Davis	37	1987	Wally Post	40	1955
HOUSTON	Doug Rader	25	1970	Jim Wynn	26	1968	Jim Wynn	37	1967	Roman Mejias	24	1962
										Jim Wynn	24	1972
BROOKLYN	Harvey Hendrick	11	1928	Andy Pafko	19	1952	Duke Snider	43	1956	Babe Herman	35	1930
LOS ANGELES	Pedro Guerrero	32	1983	Pedro Guerrero	33	1985	Jim Wynn	32	1974	Reggie Smith	32	1977
										Pedro Guerrero	32	1982
MONTREAL	Larry Parrish	30	1979	Mack Jones	22	1969	Andre Dawson	32	1983	Rusty Staub	30	1970
NEW YORK Mets	Howard Johnson	38	1991	Dave Kingman	36	1975	Tommie Agee	26	1969	Darryl Strawberry	39	1987
											39	1988
PHILADELPHIA	Mike Schmidt	48	1980	Greg Luzinski	39	1977	Cy Williams	41	1923	Chuck Klein	43	1929
PITTSBURGH	Frank Thomas	35	1958	Ralph Kiner	54	1949	Frank Thomas	30	1953	Bobby Bonilla	32	1990
ST. LOUIS	Ken Boyer	32	1960	Stan Musial	32	1951	Stan Musial	21	1952	Stan Musial	39	1948
SAN DIEGO	Dave Roberts	21	1973	Kevin McReynolds	26	1986	Clarence Gaston	29	1970	Dave Winfield	34	1979
NEW YORK Giants	Mel Ott	36	1938	Monte Irvin	24	1951	Willie Mays	51	1955	Mel Ott	42	1929
SAN FRANCISCO	Matt Williams	34	1991	Kevin Mitchell	47	1989	Willie Mays	52	1965	Bobby Bonds	39	1973

ALL-TIME RUNS-BATTED-IN LEADERS, SEASON—AT EACH POSITION

Team	Third Baseman	RBI	Year	Left Fielder	RBI	Year	Center Fielder	RBI	Year	Right Fielder	RBI	Year
BOSTON	Bob Elliott	113	1947	Wally Berger	119	1930	Wally Berger	130	1935	Tommy Holmes	117	1945
MILWAUKEE	Ed Mathews	135	1953	Rico Carty	88	1964	Hank Aaron	128	1962	Hank Aaron	132	1957
ATLANTA	Darrell Evans	104	1973	Rico Carty	101	1970	Dale Murphy	121	1983	Hank Aaron	127	1966
CHICAGO	Ron Santo	123	1969	Billy Williams	129	1970	Hack Wilson	190	1930	Andre Dawson	137	1987
CINCINNATI	Deron Johnson	130	1965	George Foster	149	1977	Cy Seymour	119	1905	Frank Robinson	136	1962
HOUSTON	Doug Rader	90	1972	Jose Cruz	95	1984	Jim Wynn	107	1967	Jim Wynn	90	1972
BROOKLYN	Cookie Lavagetto	87	1939	Zack Wheat	112	1922	Duke Snider	136	1955	Babe Herman	130	1930
LOS ANGELES	Ron Cey	110	1977	Tommy Davis	153	1962	Jim Wynn	108	1974	Frank Howard	119	1962
MONTREAL	Tim Wallach	123	1987	Mack Jones	79	1969	Andre Dawson	113	1983	Ken Singleton	103	1973
NEW YORK Mets	Howard Johnson	117	1991	Kevin McReynolds	99	1988	Lee Mazzilli	79	1979	Darryl Strawberry	108	1990
PHILADELPHIA	Pinky Whitney	124	1932	Greg Luzinski	130	1977	Cy Williams	114	1923	Chuck Klein	170	1930
PITTSBURGH	Pie Traynor	124	1928	Ralph Kiner	127	1947	Frank Thomas	102	1953	Paul Waner	131	1927
					127	1949						
ST. LOUIS	Joe Torre	137	1971	Joe Medwick	154	1937	Willie McGee	105	1987	Stan Musial	131	1948
SAN DIEGO	Graig Nettles	65	1984	Kevin McReynolds	96	1986	Joe Carter	115	1990	Dave Winfield	118	1979
NEW YORK Giants	Mel Ott	116	1938	Irish Meusel	132	1922	Willie Mays	127	1955	Mel Ott	151	1929
SAN FRANCISCO	Matt Williams	122	1990	Kevin Mitchell	125	1989	Willie Mays	141	1962	Jack Clark	103	1982

NOTE—For purposes of this table, players who performed at more than one position are considered for the position they played most often that particular year and are credited with their entire season's home run and RBI totals.

CLUBS' YEARLY RUNS-BATTED-IN LEADERS SINCE 1920

Year	BRAVES	CUBS	REDS	ASTROS	DODGERS	EXPOS	Year
1920	Holke 64	Robertson 75	Roush 90		Myers 80		1920
1921	Boeckel 84	Grimes 79	Roush 71		Wheat 85		1921
1922	Ford 60	Grimes 99	Duncan 94		Wheat 112		1922
1923	McInnis 95	Friberg-Miller 88	Roush 88		Fournier 102		1923
1924	McInnis 59	Friberg 82	Roush 72		Fournier 116		1924
1925	Burrus 87	Grimm 76	Roush 83		Fournier 130		1925
1926	Brown 84	Wilson 109	Pipp 99		F. Herman 73		1926
1927	Brown* 75	Wilson 129	C. Walker 80		F. Herman 73		1927
1928	Hornsby 94	Wilson 120	C. Walker 73		Bissonette 106		1928
1929	Sisler 79	Wilson 159	Kelly 103		F. Herman 113		1929
1930	Berger 119	**Wilson 190**	Heilmann 91		F. Herman 130		1930
1931	Berger 84	Hornsby 90	Cuccinello 93		F. Herman 97		1931
1932	Berger 73	Stephenson 85	F. Herman 87		Wilson 123		1932
1933	Berger 106	F. Herman 93	Bottomley 83		Cuccinello* 65		1933
1934	Berger 121	Hartnett 90	Bottomley 78		Leslie 102		1934
1935	Berger 130	Hartnett 91	Goodman 72		Leslie 93		1935
1936	Berger 91	Demaree 96	Cuyler 74		Hassett 82		1936
1937	Cuccinello 80	Demaree 115	Kampouris 71		Manush 73		1937
1938	Cuccinello 76	Galan 69	F. McCormick 106		Camilli 100		1938
1939	West 82	Leiber 88	F. McCormick 128		Camilli 104		1939
1940	Ross 89	Nicholson 98	F. McCormick 127		Camilli 96		1940
1941	West-Miller 68	Nicholson 98	F. McCormick 97		Camilli 120		1941
1942	West 56	Nicholson 78	F. McCormick 89		Camilli 109		1942
1943	Workman 67	Nicholson 128	Miller 71		W. Herman 100		1943
1944	Holmes 73	Nicholson 122	F. McCormick 102		Galan 93		1944
1945	Holmes 117	Pafko 110	F. McCormick 81		Walker 124		1945
1946	Holmes 79	Cavarretta 78	Hatton 69		Walker 116		1946
1947	R. Elliott 113	Nicholson 75	Miller 87		Walker 94		1947
1948	R. Elliott 100	Pafko 101	Sauer 97		Robinson 85		1948
1949	R. Elliott 76	Sauer* 83	Hatton 69		Robinson 124		1949
1950	R. Elliott 107	Sauer 103	Kluszewski 111		Hodges 113		1950
1951	Gordon 109	Sauer 89	Kluszewski 77		Campanella 108		1951
1952	Gordon 75	Sauer 121	Kluszewski 86		Hodges 102		1952
1953	**Mathews 135**	Kiner* 87	Kluszewski 108		Campanella 142		1953
1954	Mathews 103	Sauer 103	Kluszewski 141		Hodges-Snider 130		1954
1955	H. Aaron 106	Banks 117	Kluszewski 113		Snider 136		1955
1956	Adcock 103	Banks 85	Kluszewski 102		Snider 101		1956
1957	H. Aaron 132	Banks 102	Crowe 92		Hodges 98		1957
1958	H. Aaron 95	Banks 129	Robinson 83		Furillo 83		1958
1959	H. Aaron 123	Banks 143	Robinson 125		Snider 88		1959
1960	H. Aaron 126	Banks 117	Robinson 83		Larker 78		1960
1961	H. Aaron 120	Altman 96	Robinson 124		Moon 88		1961
1962	H. Aaron 128	Banks 104	Robinson 136	Mejias 75	**T. Davis 153**		1962
1963	H. Aaron 130	Santo 99	Pinson 106	Bateman 59	T. Davis 88		1963
1964	Torre 109	Santo 114	Robinson 96	Bond 85	T. Davis 86		1964
1965	Mathews 95	B. Williams 108	Johnson 130	Wynn 73	Fairly 70		1965
1966	H. Aaron 127	Santo 94	Cardenas-Johnson 81	Staub 81	Lefebvre 74		1966
1967	H. Aaron 109	Santo 98	Perez 102	Wynn 107	Fairly 55		1967
1968	H. Aaron 86	Santo-B. Williams 98	Perez 92	Staub 72	Haller 53		1968
1969	H. Aaron 97	Santo 123	Perez 122	Menke 90	Kosco 74	Laboy 83	1969
1970	H. Aaron 118	B. Williams 129	Bench 148	Menke 92	Parker 111	Staub 94	1970
1971	H. Aaron 118	B. Williams 93	May 98	Cedeno 81	Allen 90	Staub 97	1971
1972	E. Williams 87	B. Williams 122	Bench 125	May 98	W. Davis 79	Fairly 68	1972
1973	Evans 104	B. Williams 86	Bench 104	May 105	Ferguson 88	Singleton 103	1973
1974	Evans 79	Morales 82	Bench 129	Cedeno 102	Garvey 111	W. Davis 89	1974
1975	Evans 73	Morales 91	Bench 110	Watson 85	Cey 101	Carter 68	1975
1976	Wynn 66	Madlock 84	Foster 121	Watson 102	Cey-Garvey 80	Parrish 61	1976
1977	Burroughs 114	Murcer 89	**Foster 149**	**Watson 110**	Garvey 115	Perez 91	1977
1978	Murphy 79	Kingman 79	Foster 120	J. Cruz 83	Garvey 113	Perez 78	1978
1979	Horner 98	Kingman 115	Foster 98	J. Cruz 72	Garvey 110	Dawson 92	1979
1980	Horner-Murphy 89	Martin 73	Foster 93	J. Cruz 91	Garvey 106	Carter 101	1980
1981	Chambliss 51	Buckner 75	Foster 90	J. Cruz 55	Garvey 64	Carter 68	1981
1982	Murphy 109	Buckner 105	Cedeno-Driessen 57	Garner 83	Guerrero 100	Oliver 109	1982
1983	Murphy 121	Cey 90	Oester 58	J. Cruz 92	Guerrero 103	Dawson 113	1983
1984	Murphy 100	Cey 97	Parker 94	J. Cruz 95	Guerrero 72	Carter 106	1984
1985	Murphy 111	Moreland 106	Parker 125	J. Cruz 79	Marshall 95	Brooks 100	1985
1986	Horner 87	Moreland 79	Parker 116	G. Davis 101	Madlock 60	Dawson 78	1986
1987	Murphy 105	Dawson 137	E. Davis 100	G. Davis 93	Guerrero 89	**Wallach 123**	1987
1988	Murphy 77	Dawson 79	E. Davis 93	G. Davis 99	Marshall 82	Galarraga 92	1988
1989	Murphy 84	Grace 79	E. Davis 101	G. Davis 89	Murray 88	Galarraga 85	1989
1990	Gant 84	Dawson-Sandberg 100	E. Davis 86	Stubbs 71	Murray 95	Wallach 98	1990
1991	Gant 105	Dawson 104	O'Neill 91	Bagwell 82	Strawberry 99	Calderon 75	1991

In the ASTROS column, for years 1920–1961: "JOINED LEAGUE AS ACTIVE PARTICIPANT IN 1962".

In the EXPOS column, for years 1920–1968: "JOINED LEAGUE AS ACTIVE PARTICIPANT IN 1969".

(*)—1927, Brown topped by Eddie Farrell (92) who began season with New York; 1933, Cuccinello topped by Sam Leslie (73) who began season with New York; 1934, Moore's season total (98), balance made with Cincinnati; 1936, Camilli topped by Chuck Klein (104) who began season with Chicago; 1939, Fletcher's season total (77), balance made with Boston; 1940, Rizzo's season total (72), balance made with Pittsburgh and Cincinnati; 1943, Gordon topped by Medwick (70) who began season with Brooklyn; 1945, Kurowski topped by Adams (109) who began season with Philadelphia; 1949, Sauer's season total (99), balance made with Cincinnati; 1953, Kiner's season total (116), balance made with Pittsburgh; 1961, Demeter's season total (70), balance made with Los Angeles; 1990, V. Hayes topped by Dale Murphy (83), who began season with Atlanta.

Bold face type indicates team leader

CLUBS' YEARLY RUNS-BATTED-IN LEADERS SINCE 1920

The METS column is blank for 1920–1961 (arrow note: "JOINED LEAGUE AS ACTIVE PARTICIPANT IN 1962"). The PADRES column is blank for 1920–1968 (arrow note: "JOINED LEAGUE AS ACTIVE PARTICIPANT IN 1969").

Year	METS	PHILLIES	PIRATES	CARDINALS	PADRES	GIANTS	Year
1920		Williams 72	Whitted 74	Hornsby 94		Kelly 94	1920
1921		Williams 75	Grimm 71	Hornsby 126		Kelly 122	1921
1922		Williams 92	Bigbee 99	Hornsby 152		E. Meusel 132	1922
1923		Williams 114	Traynor 101	Stock 96		E. Meusel 125	1923
1924		Williams 93	Wright 111	Bottomley 111		Kelly 136	1924
1925		Harper 97	Wright 121	Hornsby 143		E. Meusel 111	1925
1926		Leach 71	Cuyler-Traynor 92	Bottomley 120		Kelly 80	1926
1927		Williams 98	**P. Waner 131**	Bottomley 124		Hornsby 125	1927
1928		Whitney 103	Traynor 124	Bottomley 136		Lindstrom 107	1928
1929		**Klein 145**	Traynor 108	Bottomley 137		**Ott 151**	1929
1930		**Klein 170**	Comorosky-Traynor 119	Frisch 114		Terry 129	1930
1931		Klein 121	Traynor 103	Hafey 95		Ott 115	1931
1932		Hurst 143	Piet 85	J. Collins 91		Ott 123	1932
1933		Klein 120	Vaughn 97	Medwick 98		Ott 103	1933
1934		J. Moore* 93	Suhr 103	J. Collins 128		Ott 135	1934
1935		J. Moore* 93	Vaughan 99	Medwick 126		Ott 114	1935
1936		Camilli* 102	Suhr 118	Medwick 138		Ott 135	1936
1937		Camilli 80	Suhr 97	**Medwick 154**		Ott 95	1937
1938		Arnovich 72	Rizzo 111	Medwick 122		Ott 116	1938
1939		Arnovich 67	Fletcher* 71	Medwick 117		Bonura 85	1939
1940		Rizzo* 53	Van Robays 116	Mize 137		Young 101	1940
1941		Etten 79	Di Maggio 100	Mize 100		Young 104	1941
1942		Litwhiler 56	Elliott 89	Slaughter 98		Mize 110	1942
1943		Northey 68	Elliott 101	Musial-Cooper 81		S. Gordon* 63	1943
1944		Northey 104	Elliott 108	Sanders 102		Medwick 85	1944
1945		DiMaggio 84	Elliott 108	Kurowski* 102		Ott 79	1945
1946		Ennis 73	Kiner 81	Slaughter 130		Mize 70	1946
1947		Ennis 81	Kiner 127	Kurowski 104		Mize 138	1947
1948		Ennis 95	Kiner 123	Musial 131		Mize 125	1948
1949		Ennis 110	Kiner 127	Musial 123		Thomson 109	1949
1950		Ennis 126	Kiner 118	Musial 109		Thompson 91	1950
1951		Jones 81	Kiner 109	Musial 108		Irvin 121	1951
1952		Ennis 107	Kiner 87	Slaughter 101		Thomson 108	1952
1953		Ennis 125	Thomas 102	Musial 113		Thomson 106	1953
1954		Ennis 119	Thomas 94	Musial 126		Mays 110	1954
1955		Ennis 120	Long 79	Musial 108		Mays 127	1955
1956		Ennis-Lopata 95	Long 91	Musial 109		Mays 84	1956
1957		Bouchee 76	Thomas 89	Ennis 105		Mays 97	1957
1958		Anderson 97	Thomas 109	Boyer 90		Cepeda-Mays 96	1958
1959		Post 94	Stuart 78	Boyer 94		Cepeda 105	1959
1960		Herrera 71	Clemente 94	Boyer 97		Mays 103	1960
1961		Demeter* 68	Stuart 117	Boyer 95		Cepeda 142	1961
1962	Thomas 94	Demeter 107	Mazeroski 81	White 102		Mays 141	1962
1963	Thomas 60	Demeter 83	Clemente 76	Boyer 111		Mays 103	1963
1964	Christopher 76	Callison 104	Clemente 87	Boyer 119		Mays 111	1964
1965	Smith 62	Callison 101	Stargell 107	Flood 83		Mays 112	1965
1966	Boyer 61	Allen 110	Clemente 119	Flood 78		Mays 103	1966
1967	Davis 73	Allen 77	Clemente 110	Cepeda 111		Hart 99	1967
1968	Swoboda 59	Allen 90	Clendenon 87	Shannon 79		McCovey 105	1968
1969	Agee 76	Allen 89	Stargell 92	Torre 101	Colbert 66	McCovey 126	1969
1970	Clendenon 97	Johnson 93	Stargell 85	Allen 101	Gaston 93	McCovey 126	1970
1971	Jones 69	Montanez 99	Stargell 125	Torre 107	Colbert 84	Bonds 102	1971
1972	Jones 52	Luzinski 68	Stargell 112	Simmons 90	Colbert 111	Kingman 83	1972
1973	Staub 76	Luzinski 97	Stargell 119	Simmons 91	Colbert 80	Bonds 96	1973
1974	Staub 78	Schmidt 116	Zisk 100	Simmons 103	Winfield 75	Matthews 82	1974
1975	Staub 105	Luzinski 120	Parker 101	Simmons 100	Winfield 76	Murcer 91	1975
1976	Kingman 86	Schmidt 107	Parker 90	Simmons 75	Ivie 70	Murcer 90	1976
1977	Henderson 65	Luzinski 130	Robinson 104	Simmons 95	Winfield 92	McCovey 86	1977
1978	Montanez 96	Luzinski 101	Parker 117	Simmons 80	Winfield 97	J. Clark 98	1978
1979	Hebner-Mazzilli 79	Schmidt 114	Parker 94	Hernandez 105	**Winfield 118**	Ivie 89	1979
1980	Mazzilli 76	Schmidt 121	Parker 79	Hendrick 109	Winfield 87	J. Clark 82	1980
1981	Kingman 59	Schmidt 91	Parker 48	Hendrick 61	Richards 42	J. Clark 53	1981
1982	Kingman 99	Schmidt 87	Thompson 101	Hendrick 104	Kennedy 97	J. Clark 103	1982
1983	Foster 90	Schmidt 109	Thompson 76	Hendrick 97	Kennedy 98	Leonard 87	1983
1984	Strawberry 97	Schmidt 106	Pena 78	Hendrick 69	Garvey 86	Leonard 86	1984
1985	Carter 100	Wilson 102	Ray 70	Herr 110	Garvey 81	Leonard 62	1985
1986	Carter 105	Schmidt 119	Morrison 88	Herr-Van Slyke 61	McReynolds 96	Maldonado 85	1986
1987	Strawberry 104	Schmidt 113	Van Slyke 82	J. Clark 106	Kruk 91	W. Clark 91	1987
1988	Strawberry 101	Samuel 67	Bonilla-Van Slyke 100	Brunansky 79	Gwynn 70	W. Clark 109	1988
1989	H. Johnson 101	V. Hayes 78	Bonilla 86	Guerrero 117	Ja. Clark 94	Mitchell 125	1989
1990	Strawberry 108	V. Hayes* 73	Bonilla 120	Guerrero 80	Carter 115	Williams 122	1990
1991	**Johnson 117**	Kruk 92	Bonds 116	Zeile 81	McGriff 106	W. Clark 116	1991

(*)—1927, Brown topped by Eddie Farrell (92) who began season with New York; 1933, Cuccinello topped by Sam Leslie (73) who began season with New York; 1934, Moore's season total (98), balance made with Cincinnati; 1936, Camilli topped by Chuck Klein (104) who began season with Chicago; 1939, Fletcher's season total (77), balance made with Boston; 1940, Rizzo's season total (72), balance made with Pittsburgh and Cincinnati; 1943, Gordon topped by Medwick (70) who began season with Brooklyn; 1945, Kurowski topped by Adams (109) who began season with Philadelphia; 1949, Sauer's season total (99), balance made with Cincinnati; 1953, Kiner's season total (116), balance made with Pittsburgh; 1961, Demeter's season total (70), balance made with Los Angeles; 1990, V. Hayes topped by Dale Murphy (83), who began season with Atlanta.

Bold face type indicates team leader

1991 PITCHING RECORDS AGAINST OPPOSING CLUBS

ATLANTA (94-68)

	Chi. W-L-S	Cin. W-L-S	Hou. W-L-S	L.A. W-L-S	Mon. W-L-S	N.Y. W-L-S	Phi. W-L-S	Pit. W-L-S	St.L. W-L-S	S.D. W-L-S	S.F. W-L-S	W	L	S	Pct.
Avery	1-0-0	2-1-0	2-1-0	3-0-0	0-1-0	1-1-0	1-1-0	2-0-0	3-0-0	2-1-0	1-2-0	18	8	0	.692
Berenguer	0-1-2	0-0-2	0-0-1	0-1-0	0-0-1	0-0-3	0-1-0	0-0-2	0-0-2	0-0-3	0-0-1	0	3	17	.000
Castillo	0-0-0	1-0-0	0-0-0	0-0-0	0-0-0	0-0-0	0-1-0	0-0-0	0-0-0	0-0-0	0-0-0	1	1	0	.500
Clancy	0-0-0	0-0-1	1-0-0	1-0-0	0-1-1	0-0-0	0-0-0	0-0-0	0-0-0	0-0-0	1-1-1	3	2	3	.600
Freeman	1-0-0	0-0-0	0-0-0	0-0-0	0-0-0	0-0-0	0-0-0	0-0-1	0-0-0	0-0-0	0-0-0	1	0	1	1.000
Glavine	2-0-0	2-1-0	0-2-0	2-2-0	1-2-0	2-0-0	3-0-0	2-1-0	2-0-0	2-2-0	2-1-0	20	11	0	.645
Leibrandt	0-2-0	2-2-0	2-1-0	0-2-0	1-0-0	2-1-0	1-0-0	1-1-0	2-1-0	2-1-0	2-2-0	15	13	0	.536
Mahler	0-0-0	0-0-0	0-0-0	0-1-0	0-0-0	0-0-0	0-0-0	1-0-0	0-0-0	0-0-0	0-0-0	1	1	0	.500
Mercker	0-1-1	0-0-1	0-1-0	1-0-0	0-0-1	1-0-0	0-0-0	0-0-3	1-0-0	2-0-0	0-1-0	5	3	6	.625
Parrett	0-0-0	0-0-0	0-0-1	0-0-0	0-0-0	0-0-0	0-1-0	1-0-0	0-0-0	0-1-0	0-0-0	1	2	1	.333
Pena	0-0-0	1-0-2	0-0-3	0-0-0	0-0-1	1-0-1	0-0-0	0-0-0	0-0-0	0-0-3	0-0-1	2	0	11	1.000
Reynoso	0-0-0	0-0-0	1-0-0	0-0-0	0-0-0	0-0-0	0-1-0	0-0-0	0-0-0	1-0-0	0-0-0	2	1	0	.667
Sisk	0-0-0	0-0-0	2-0-0	0-0-0	0-0-0	0-0-0	0-0-0	0-0-0	0-1-0	0-0-0	0-0-0	2	1	0	.667
P. Smith	0-1-0	0-1-0	0-0-0	0-0-0	0-0-0	1-0-0	0-1-0	0-0-0	0-0-0	0-0-0	0-0-0	1	3	0	.250
Smoltz	2-1-0	2-1-0	2-0-0	0-4-0	1-2-0	1-1-0	0-0-0	2-1-0	1-0-0	0-2-0	3-1-0	14	13	0	.519
Stanton	0-0-0	1-1-0	2-0-1	0-1-0	1-1-1	0-0-2	0-0-0	0-0-1	0-1-0	1-0-1	0-1-1	5	5	7	.500
Wohlers	0-0-0	0-0-0	1-0-0	0-0-0	1-0-0	0-0-0	0-1-1	0-0-0	0-0-0	1-0-1	0-0-0	3	1	2	.750
TOTALS	6-6-3	11-7-6	13-5-6	7-11-0	5-7-5	9-3-6	5-7-1	9-3-7	9-3-2	11-7-8	9-9-4	94	68	48	.580

NO DECISIONS OR SAVES: Bielecki, Petry, St. Claire.

CHICAGO (77-83)

	Atl. W-L-S	Cin. W-L-S	Hou. W-L-S	L.A. W-L-S	Mon. W-L-S	N.Y. W-L-S	Phi. W-L-S	Pit. W-L-S	St.L. W-L-S	S.D. W-L-S	S.F. W-L-S	W	L	S	Pct.
Assenmacher	2-0-2	0-0-2	0-0-2	0-2-0	3-1-0	1-1-1	1-3-0	0-1-1	0-0-4	0-0-0	0-0-3	7	8	15	.467
Bielecki	1-0-0	0-2-0	2-0-0	0-2-0	2-0-0	0-1-0	2-2-0	1-2-0	2-0-0	0-2-0	3-0-0	13	11	0	.542
Boskie	0-2-0	1-0-0	0-1-0	0-2-0	0-0-0	1-0-0	1-1-0	1-1-0	0-2-0	0-0-0	1-1-0	4	9	0	.308
Castillo	0-1-0	0-1-0	2-0-0	1-1-0	0-1-0	1-1-0	0-0-0	0-1-0	1-1-0	0-0-0	1-0-0	6	7	0	.462
Harkey	0-0-0	0-1-0	0-0-0	0-0-0	0-0-0	0-0-0	0-0-0	0-0-0	0-1-0	0-0-0	0-0-0	0	2	0	.000
Jackson	0-0-0	0-0-0	0-0-0	0-2-0	0-0-0	0-1-0	0-0-0	0-0-0	0-1-0	1-1-0	0-0-0	1	5	0	.167
Lancaster	1-1-0	1-0-0	1-0-0	0-0-0	1-1-2	2-0-1	0-3-0	1-1-0	1-0-0	1-0-0	0-1-0	9	7	3	.563
Maddux	1-0-0	0-1-0	3-0-0	0-0-0	0-1-0	4-1-0	3-0-0	0-2-0	2-1-0	1-3-0	1-2-0	15	11	0	.577
McElroy	1-0-1	0-1-0	0-0-0	1-1-0	1-0-2	0-0-0	0-0-0	1-0-0	1-0-0	0-0-0	0-0-0	6	2	3	.750
Perez	0-0-0	0-0-0	0-0-0	0-0-0	0-0-0	0-0-0	0-0-0	0-0-0	1-0-0	0-0-0	0-0-0	1	0	0	1.000
Renfroe	0-0-0	0-0-0	0-0-0	0-0-0	0-0-0	0-0-0	0-0-0	0-0-0	0-1-0	0-0-0	0-0-0	0	1	0	.000
Scanlan	0-1-0	0-0-0	1-1-0	0-0-0	2-2-0	2-1-0	0-0-0	1-0-1	1-1-0	0-2-0	0-0-0	7	8	1	.467
Slocumb	0-0-0	1-1-0	0-0-0	0-0-0	0-0-1	0-0-0	0-0-0	1-0-0	0-0-0	0-0-0	0-0-0	2	1	1	.667
Da. Smith	0-0-2	0-0-1	0-1-2	0-0-1	0-0-3	0-0-0	0-0-3	0-2-1	0-1-1	0-0-1	0-2-2	0	6	17	.000
Sutcliffe	0-1-0	1-1-0	0-0-0	0-0-0	1-1-0	0-1-0	0-1-0	1-0-0	2-0-0	1-1-0	0-0-0	6	5	0	.545
TOTALS	6-6-5	4-8-3	9-3-4	2-10-1	10-7-8	11-6-2	8-10-3	7-11-3	10-8-5	4-8-1	6-6-5	77	83	40	.481

NO DECISIONS OR SAVES: Dascenzo, S. May, Pavlas, Wilson.

CINCINNATI (74-88)

	Atl. W-L-S	Chi. W-L-S	Hou. W-L-S	L.A. W-L-S	Mon. W-L-S	N.Y. W-L-S	Phi. W-L-S	Pit. W-L-S	St.L. W-L-S	S.D. W-L-S	S.F. W-L-S	W	L	S	Pct.
Armstrong	2-2-0	1-0-0	1-1-0	0-1-0	0-2-0	0-0-0	0-1-0	0-1-0	1-1-0	1-1-0	1-3-0	7	13	0	.350
Browning	1-1-0	1-1-0	2-2-0	1-3-0	1-1-0	2-0-0	2-1-0	1-2-0	1-1-0	0-2-0	2-0-0	14	14	0	.500
Carman	0-0-0	0-0-0	0-1-0	0-0-0	0-1-0	0-0-0	0-0-1	0-0-0	0-0-0	0-0-0	0-0-0	0	2	1	.000
Charlton	0-0-0	0-1-0	0-1-0	0-1-0	1-0-0	0-0-0	0-0-0	0-1-0	1-0-0	1-1-0	0-0-1	3	5	1	.375
Dibble	0-1-1	1-0-3	0-1-6	1-1-2	0-0-2	0-1-2	0-0-6	0-0-1	0-1-3	0-0-2	1-0-3	3	5	31	.375
Gross	1-0-0	0-0-0	0-0-0	0-1-0	0-0-0	1-0-0	0-1-0	1-1-0	1-0-0	0-1-0	1-1-0	6	4	0	.600
Hammond	0-0-0	1-0-0	3-0-0	0-1-0	1-0-0	0-1-0	0-1-0	0-2-0	0-1-0	2-0-0	0-1-0	7	7	0	.500
Hill	1-0-0	0-0-0	0-0-0	0-1-0	0-0-0	0-0-0	0-0-0	0-0-0	0-0-0	0-0-0	0-0-0	1	1	0	.500
Layana	0-1-0	0-1-0	0-0-0	0-0-0	0-0-0	0-0-0	0-0-0	0-0-0	0-0-0	0-0-0	0-0-0	0	2	0	.000
Minutelli	0-0-0	0-0-0	0-0-0	0-0-0	0-0-0	0-0-0	0-0-0	0-1-0	0-1-0	0-0-0	0-0-0	0	2	0	.000
Myers	0-1-0	0-0-1	0-1-1	1-1-1	1-1-0	0-3-1	2-0-0	0-2-0	0-2-0	1-0-2	1-1-0	6	13	6	.316
Power	0-1-0	1-0-1	0-1-1	0-0-1	0-1-0	1-0-0	0-0-0	0-0-1	1-1-0	1-1-0	1-0-0	5	3	3	.625
Rijo	2-1-0	3-0-0	1-1-0	2-0-0	1-0-0	1-0-0	3-0-0	0-1-0	0-0-0	0-2-0	2-1-0	15	6	0	.714
Sanford	0-1-0	0-0-0	0-0-0	0-1-0	0-0-0	0-0-0	0-0-0	0-0-0	1-0-0	0-0-0	0-0-0	1	2	0	.333
Scudder	0-2-0	0-0-0	1-0-0	1-1-0	1-1-0	0-2-0	1-0-0	0-0-0	0-1-1	1-1-1	1-1-0	6	9	1	.400
TOTALS	7-11-1	8-4-5	9-9-7	6-12-4	6-6-2	5-7-3	9-3-7	2-10-2	4-8-3	8-10-5	10-8-4	74	88	43	.457

NO DECISIONS OR SAVES: Brown, Foster.

HOUSTON (65-97)

	Atl. W-L-S	Chi. W-L-S	Cin. W-L-S	L.A. W-L-S	Mon. W-L-S	N.Y. W-L-S	Phi. W-L-S	Pit. W-L-S	St.L. W-L-S	S.D. W-L-S	S.F. W-L-S	W	L	S	Pct.
Bowen	0-0-0	0-0-0	1-1-0	0-0-0	1-0-0	1-0-0	0-1-0	1-0-0	0-1-0	1-1-0	1-0-0	6	4	0	.600
Capel	0-0-0	0-1-1	0-0-0	0-0-0	0-0-0	1-1-1	0-0-1	0-0-0	0-0-0	0-1-0	0-0-0	1	3	3	.250
Clancy	0-1-0	0-1-0	0-0-1	0-0-0	0-0-0	0-0-1	0-0-1	0-1-2	0-0-0	0-0-0	0-0-0	0	3	5	.000
Corsi	0-1-0	0-0-0	0-1-0	0-2-0	0-1-0	0-0-0	0-0-0	0-0-0	0-0-0	0-0-0	0-0-0	0	5	0	.000
Deshaies	0-2-0	0-2-0	0-1-0	1-1-0	0-2-0	1-0-0	0-0-0	0-0-0	2-1-0	0-2-0	1-1-0	5	12	0	.294
Gardner	0-0-0	0-0-0	0-1-0	0-0-0	0-0-0	0-0-0	0-0-0	0-0-0	0-0-0	0-1-0	1-0-0	1	2	0	.333
Harnisch	2-1-0	2-0-0	1-2-0	2-1-0	0-2-0	1-0-0	1-0-0	0-2-0	0-1-0	1-0-0	2-0-0	12	9	0	.571
Henry	0-0-1	0-0-0	2-0-0	0-1-0	0-0-0	0-1-0	0-0-0	0-0-0	0-0-0	1-0-0	0-0-1	3	2	2	.600
Hernandez	0-2-0	0-1-0	2-0-1	0-2-0	0-0-0	0-0-0	0-0-0	0-0-0	0-1-0	0-1-1	0-0-1	2	7	3	.222
Jones	1-0-0	0-0-0	1-0-0	1-0-0	0-1-0	0-1-0	0-1-0	2-2-0	0-0-0	0-1-0	1-2-0	6	8	0	.429
Juden	0-1-0	0-0-0	0-1-0	0-0-0	0-0-0	0-0-0	0-0-0	0-0-0	0-0-0	0-0-0	0-0-0	0	2	0	.000
Kile	0-1-0	0-2-0	1-1-0	0-0-0	0-1-0	1-0-0	2-1-0	0-2-0	1-0-0	1-0-0	1-3-0	7	11	0	.389
Mallicoat	0-1-0	0-0-0	0-0-0	0-1-1	0-0-0	0-0-0	0-0-0	0-0-0	0-0-0	0-0-0	0-0-0	0	2	1	.000
Osuna	1-0-0	1-0-1	0-0-0	1-1-3	0-1-0	0-0-2	3-1-1	0-0-1	1-2-1	0-1-2	0-0-1	7	6	12	.538
Portugal	1-3-0	0-2-0	1-0-1	1-1-0	0-1-0	1-1-0	1-1-0	1-0-0	1-0-0	1-2-0	2-1-0	10	12	1	.455
Schilling	0-0-2	0-0-1	0-0-2	0-0-0	1-1-0	1-1-1	0-0-0	0-1-1	0-1-0	1-0-0	0-1-1	3	5	8	.375
Scott	0-0-0	0-0-0	0-1-0	0-0-0	0-0-0	0-0-0	0-0-0	0-0-0	0-0-0	0-0-0	0-1-0	0	2	0	.000
Wilkins	0-0-0	0-0-0	0-0-0	2-0-0	0-0-0	0-0-0	0-0-0	0-0-0	0-0-1	0-1-0	0-0-0	2	1	1	.667
Williams	0-0-0	0-0-0	0-0-0	0-0-0	0-0-0	0-0-0	0-0-0	0-0-0	0-0-0	0-1-0	0-0-0	0	1	0	.000
TOTALS	5-13-3	3-9-3	9-9-5	8-10-4	2-10-0	7-5-5	7-5-3	4-8-4	5-7-2	6-12-3	9-9-4	65	97	36	.401

LOS ANGELES (93-69)

	Atl. W-L-S	Chi. W-L-S	Cin. W-L-S	Hou. W-L-S	Mon. W-L-S	N.Y. W-L-S	Phi. W-L-S	Pit. W-L-S	St.L. W-L-S	S.D. W-L-S	S.F. W-L-S	W	L	S	Pct.
Belcher	1-2-0	1-0-0	2-0-0	2-0-0	2-0-0	0-2-0	0-1-0	1-0-0	0-1-0	0-1-0	3-0-0	10	9	0	.526
Candelaria	0-0-1	0-0-0	0-0-0	0-0-0	0-0-0	0-0-0	1-1-1	0-0-0	0-0-0	0-0-0	1-0-0	1	1	2	.500
Cook	0-0-0	0-0-0	0-0-0	0-0-0	0-0-0	0-0-0	0-0-0	0-0-0	0-0-0	0-0-0	1-0-0	1	0	1	1.000
Crews	0-0-0	0-0-1	0-0-1	0-0-0	1-0-0	1-0-1	0-1-0	0-0-1	0-1-1	0-0-1	0-1-0	2	3	6	.400
Gott	0-1-0	1-0-0	0-0-0	0-0-0	0-0-0	0-0-0	0-0-1	1-0-1	0-1-0	1-0-0	1-0-0	4	3	2	.571
Gross	0-1-3	0-1-0	2-0-0	2-2-0	1-1-0	0-0-0	1-1-0	0-0-0	1-3-0	1-2-0	1-0-0	10	11	3	.476
Hartley	1-0-0	1-0-1	1-0-0	1-1-0	0-0-0	0-0-0	0-0-0	0-0-0	0-0-0	2-0-0	0-1-0	6	2	1	.750
Hershiser	2-0-0	1-0-0	1-0-0	1-1-0	0-0-0	0-0-0	0-0-0	0-0-0	0-0-0	2-0-0	0-1-0	7	2	0	.778
Howell	0-0-0	1-0-3	0-1-1	1-2-2	1-0-2	0-0-2	1-1-2	0-0-1	2-1-0	0-0-1	0-0-2	6	5	16	.545
Martinez	3-1-0	2-1-0	1-3-0	0-1-0	1-1-0	3-1-0	2-0-0	0-0-0	1-1-0	3-0-0	1-4-0	17	13	0	.567
McDowell	1-1-2	1-0-0	1-1-2	1-0-1	0-0-0	0-0-0	0-0-0	1-0-0	1-0-0	0-0-2	0-0-0	6	3	7	.667
Morgan	3-0-1	2-0-0	1-0-0	2-2-0	0-2-0	0-1-0	2-0-0	2-2-0	0-1-0	2-1-0	0-1-0	14	10	1	.583
Ojeda	0-1-0	0-0-0	3-1-0	1-0-0	1-1-0	0-1-0	1-1-0	1-1-0	2-0-0	2-2-0	1-1-0	12	9	0	.571
Wetteland	0-0-0	0-0-0	0-0-0	0-0-0	0-0-0	0-0-0	0-0-0	0-0-0	0-0-0	0-0-0	0-0-0	1	0	1	1.000
Wilson	0-0-0	0-0-0	0-0-1	0-0-1	0-0-0	0-0-0	0-0-0	0-0-0	0-0-0	0-0-0	0-0-0	0	0	2	.000
TOTALS	11-7-7	10-2-5	12-6-5	10-8-4	5-7-3	7-5-5	7-5-3	7-5-3	6-6-1	10-8-4	8-10-2	93	69	40	.574

NO DECISIONS OR SAVES: Christopher.

MONTREAL (71-90)

	Atl. W-L-S	Chi. W-L-S	Cin. W-L-S	Hou. W-L-S	L.A. W-L-S	N.Y. W-L-S	Phi. W-L-S	Pit. W-L-S	St.L. W-L-S	S.D. W-L-S	S.F. W-L-S	W	L	S	Pct.
Barnes	0-1-0	1-0-0	0-2-0	0-0-0	1-0-0	1-0-0	0-2-0	0-1-0	1-1-0	1-1-0	0-0-0	5	8	0	.385
Boyd	1-0-0	0-0-0	1-0-0	0-0-0	1-1-0	0-2-0	0-2-0	0-2-0	0-1-0	1-0-0	2-0-0	6	8	0	.429
Burke	0-1-0	0-1-0	0-0-0	0-0-0	0-1-1	0-0-0	0-0-1	1-1-1	1-0-0	0-0-0	0-0-2	3	4	5	.429
Darling	0-0-0	0-0-0	0-0-0	0-0-0	0-0-0	0-0-0	0-0-0	0-0-0	0-0-0	0-0-0	0-2-0	0	2	0	.000
Fassero	0-0-0	0-1-2	0-0-1	2-0-2	0-0-0	0-0-1	0-0-0	1-0-0	0-0-0	0-1-2	0-0-0	2	5	8	.286
Frey	0-0-0	0-0-0	0-0-0	0-0-0	0-0-0	0-0-1	0-0-0	0-0-0	0-0-0	0-0-0	0-0-0	1	1	1	.500
Gardner	1-1-0	1-1-0	1-1-0	4-0-0	1-2-0	0-3-0	0-1-0	1-0-0	1-2-0	0-0-0	0-1-0	9	11	0	.450
Haney	0-0-0	1-0-0	1-1-0	0-0-0	0-1-0	0-2-0	0-0-0	0-1-0	1-0-0	0-0-0	0-0-0	3	7	0	.300
Jones	0-0-1	0-2-2	1-0-2	0-1-2	0-1-2	0-2-0	0-1-1	1-0-0	0-1-2	0-1-1	2-0-0	4	9	13	.308
Mahler	0-0-0	1-0-0	0-0-0	0-0-0	0-1-0	0-0-0	1-0-0	0-0-0	1-0-0	0-0-0	0-0-0	1	3	0	.250
De. Martinez	2-0-0	1-1-0	1-1-0	1-1-0	2-0-0	1-1-0	1-2-0	2-2-0	1-1-0	1-1-0	1-1-0	14	11	0	.560
Nabholz	0-1-0	0-1-0	1-1-0	1-0-0	1-0-0	1-2-0	2-0-0	1-1-0	1-1-0	0-1-0	0-0-0	8	7	0	.533
Rojas	1-0-0	1-0-2	0-0-1	1-0-0	0-0-0	0-0-1	0-1-0	0-0-2	0-1-0	0-1-0	0-1-0	3	3	6	.500
Ruskin	0-0-2	0-1-0	0-1-0	1-0-0	0-0-0	1-0-1	0-0-0	0-2-0	1-1-0	0-0-0	1-0-2	4	4	6	.500
Sampen	2-1-0	2-1-0	0-1-0	0-0-0	1-0-0	0-0-0	0-2-0	1-0-0	0-2-0	1-0-0	1-0-0	9	5	0	.643
Schmidt	0-0-0	0-0-0	0-0-0	0-0-0	0-0-0	0-0-0	0-0-0	0-0-0	0-1-0	0-0-0	0-0-0	0	1	0	.000
Wainhouse	0-0-0	0-0-0	0-0-0	0-0-0	0-0-0	0-0-0	0-1-0	0-0-0	0-0-0	0-0-0	0-0-0	0	1	0	.000
TOTALS	7-5-3	7-10-6	6-6-5	10-2-4	7-5-3	4-14-4	4-14-1	6-12-3	7-11-3	6-6-3	7-5-4	71	90	39	.441

NO DECISIONS OR SAVES: Long, Piatt.

1991 PITCHING RECORDS AGAINST OPPOSING CLUBS

NEW YORK (77-84)

	Atl. W-L-S	Chi. W-L-S	Cin. W-L-S	Hou. W-L-S	L.A. W-L-S	Mon. W-L-S	Phi. W-L-S	Pit. W-L-S	St.L. W-L-S	S.D. W-L-S	S.F. W-L-S	W	L	S	Pct.
Burke	0-0-0	0-2-0	0-0-0	0-0-0	1-1-0	0-0-0	0-0-0	1-0-0	1-0-1	0-0-0	0-0-0	3	3	1	.500
Castillo	0-0-0	1-0-0	0-0-0	0-0-0	0-0-0	0-0-0	0-0-0	0-0-0	0-0-0	0-0-0	0-0-0	1	0	0	1.000
Cone	0-0-0	1-2-0	3-1-0	0-2-0	1-2-0	2-1-0	2-0-0	1-2-0	2-2-0	1-1-0	1-1-0	14	14	0	.500
Darling	1-1-0	0-0-0	1-0-0	0-0-0	0-0-0	1-0-0	1-1-0	0-2-0	0-1-0	0-1-0	1-0-0	5	6	0	.455
Fernandez	0-0-0	0-0-0	0-0-0	0-0-0	0-0-0	0-0-0	0-0-0	0-2-0	1-0-0	0-1-0	0-0-0	1	3	0	.250
Franco	0-1-1	0-1-4	1-0-3	1-2-1	0-1-1	0-1-7	0-1-6	1-0-3	0-2-1	1-0-1	1-0-2	5	9	30	.357
Gooden	1-0-0	1-0-0	0-1-0	1-0-0	1-0-0	1-1-0	2-1-0	1-1-0	1-1-0	3-0-0	1-2-0	13	7	0	.650
Innis	0-0-0	0-0-0	0-0-0	0-0-0	0-0-0	0-0-0	0-1-0	0-1-0	0-0-0	0-0-0	0-0-0	0	2	0	.000
Pena	0-0-1	1-1-0	1-0-0	1-0-0	0-0-0	2-0-0	0-0-0	0-0-0	0-0-0	0-0-2	1-0-1	6	1	4	.857
Schourek	0-0-0	0-2-0	0-0-0	0-0-0	0-1-0	1-0-1	2-0-0	0-0-0	1-1-0	0-0-1	1-0-0	5	4	2	.556
Simons	0-0-0	0-0-0	0-0-1	1-0-0	0-1-0	0-0-0	1-1-0	0-1-0	0-0-0	0-0-0	0-0-0	2	3	1	.400
Viola	1-3-0	1-3-0	0-2-0	0-2-0	2-0-0	4-0-0	2-0-0	2-1-0	0-1-0	1-2-0	0-1-0	13	15	0	.464
Whitehurst	0-3-0	0-0-1	1-1-0	0-1-0	0-1-0	3-0-0	1-0-0	0-2-0	1-2-0	1-0-0	0-2-0	7	12	1	.368
Young	0-1-0	1-0-0	0-0-0	1-0-0	0-0-0	0-1-0	0-2-0	0-0-0	0-1-0	0-0-0	0-0-0	2	5	0	.286
TOTALS	3-9-2	6-11-5	7-5-4	5-7-1	5-7-1	14-4-8	11-7-6	6-12-3	7-11-2	7-5-4	6-6-3	77	84	39	.478

NO DECISIONS OR SAVES: Beatty, Bross, Sauveur, Valera.

PHILADELPHIA (78-84)

	Atl. W-L-S	Chi. W-L-S	Cin. W-L-S	Hou. W-L-S	L.A. W-L-S	Mon. W-L-S	N.Y. W-L-S	Pit. W-L-S	St.L. W-L-S	S.D. W-L-S	S.F. W-L-S	W	L	S	Pct.
Akerfelds	1-0-0	0-0-0	0-0-0	0-0-0	0-0-0	0-0-0	0-1-0	0-0-0	0-0-0	1-0-0	0-0-0	2	1	0	.667
Ashby	0-0-0	1-0-0	0-2-0	0-0-0	0-0-0	0-0-0	0-1-0	0-1-0	0-1-0	0-0-0	0-0-0	1	5	0	.167
Boever	0-0-0	1-0-0	0-0-0	0-1-0	0-2-0	0-0-0	0-1-0	0-1-0	0-0-0	0-0-0	2-0-0	3	5	0	.375
Brantley	0-0-0	0-0-0	0-1-0	0-0-0	0-0-0	0-0-0	1-0-0	0-1-0	1-0-0	0-0-0	0-0-0	2	2	0	.500
Combs	0-1-0	0-1-0	0-0-0	0-0-0	0-1-0	1-1-0	0-0-0	0-1-0	1-1-0	0-0-0	0-0-0	2	6	0	.250
Cox	0-0-0	1-0-0	0-0-0	1-1-0	0-1-0	0-0-0	1-1-0	0-1-0	0-0-0	1-0-0	0-2-0	4	6	0	.400
DeJesus	2-0-1	0-1-0	1-0-0	1-2-0	1-0-0	1-0-0	1-1-0	1-1-0	0-2-0	2-2-0	0-0-0	10	9	1	.526
Greene	1-1-0	2-0-0	1-1-0	0-0-0	1-0-0	3-0-0	0-1-0	2-1-0	1-2-0	0-0-0	2-1-0	13	7	0	.650
Grimsley	0-0-0	0-1-0	0-0-0	0-0-0	0-0-0	0-1-0	0-1-0	0-2-0	0-1-0	1-0-0	0-1-0	1	7	0	.125
Hartley	0-0-0	0-0-0	0-1-0	1-0-0	0-0-0	1-0-1	0-0-0	0-0-0	0-0-0	0-0-0	0-0-0	2	1	1	.667
LaPoint	0-0-0	0-0-0	0-0-0	0-0-0	0-0-0	0-0-0	0-0-0	0-0-0	0-1-0	0-0-0	0-0-0	0	1	0	.000
McDowell	0-0-0	0-1-0	0-1-1	0-2-0	0-1-0	0-0-0	2-0-0	0-0-0	1-1-0	0-0-1	0-0-1	3	6	3	.333
Mulholland	0-3-0	1-1-0	1-2-0	1-0-0	2-0-0	4-0-0	1-3-0	0-1-0	2-1-0	2-1-0	2-1-0	16	13	0	.552
Ritchie	0-0-0	1-0-0	0-0-0	0-0-0	0-0-0	0-1-0	0-1-0	0-0-0	0-0-0	0-0-0	0-1-0	1	2	0	.333
Ruffin	0-0-0	1-1-0	0-1-0	1-1-0	0-1-0	0-1-0	0-1-0	0-0-0	0-1-0	2-0-0	0-0-0	4	7	0	.364
Searcy	0-0-0	0-0-0	0-0-0	0-0-0	1-1-0	0-0-0	0-0-0	1-0-0	0-0-0	0-0-0	0-0-0	2	1	0	.667
Williams	3-0-1	2-2-4	0-0-2	0-0-2	0-0-3	4-0-3	1-0-3	2-2-2	0-1-4	0-0-3	0-0-3	12	5	30	.706
TOTALS	7-5-2	10-8-4	3-9-3	5-7-2	5-7-3	14-4-4	7-11-3	6-12-2	6-12-4	9-3-4	6-6-4	78	84	35	.481

NO DECISIONS OR SAVES: Carreno, Mauser.

PITTSBURGH (98-64)

	Atl. W-L-S	Chi. W-L-S	Cin. W-L-S	Hou. W-L-S	L.A. W-L-S	Mon. W-L-S	N.Y. W-L-S	Phi. W-L-S	St.L. W-L-S	S.D. W-L-S	S.F. W-L-S	W	L	S	Pct.
Belinda	0-0-2	2-2-0	1-0-1	0-0-2	0-1-1	0-0-4	0-0-3	1-1-2	2-1-0	0-0-0	1-0-1	7	5	16	.583
Drabek	1-2-0	2-2-0	1-1-0	1-2-0	1-2-0	2-2-0	1-1-0	2-0-0	1-2-0	2-0-0	1-0-0	15	14	0	.517
Heaton	0-0-0	0-0-0	0-0-0	1-0-0	0-0-0	1-0-0	0-0-0	0-1-0	1-0-0	0-1-0	0-1-0	3	3	0	.500
Kipper	0-0-0	0-0-0	0-0-1	1-0-0	0-0-1	1-0-1	0-1-0	0-1-0	0-0-0	0-0-1	0-0-0	2	2	4	.500
Landrum	0-1-0	0-1-1	0-0-2	0-0-1	0-0-2	0-0-3	2-0-0	0-1-2	0-0-3	2-1-2	0-0-1	4	4	17	.500
Mason	0-0-0	0-0-1	0-0-0	0-0-0	1-0-0	0-1-0	0-1-0	0-0-0	2-0-0	0-0-1	0-0-1	3	2	3	.600
Palacios	0-3-0	1-0-1	2-0-0	0-0-0	0-0-0	1-0-0	0-0-0	1-0-1	0-0-0	1-0-1	0-0-0	6	3	3	.667
Patterson	0-0-0	1-0-0	0-0-1	0-0-0	0-1-0	0-0-0	1-1-0	0-0-1	1-1-0	0-0-0	1-0-0	4	3	2	.571
Rodriguez	0-0-0	0-0-1	0-0-0	0-0-0	1-0-0	0-1-0	0-0-2	0-0-1	0-0-0	0-0-1	0-0-1	1	1	6	.500
Smiley	2-1-0	1-1-0	2-0-0	0-1-0	0-1-0	3-1-0	3-0-0	4-0-0	2-1-0	1-0-0	2-2-0	20	8	0	.714
Smith	0-2-0	3-0-0	1-0-0	3-1-0	1-1-0	2-0-0	1-2-0	2-0-0	2-0-0	1-2-0	0-2-0	16	10	0	.615
Tomlin	0-0-0	0-1-0	2-0-0	2-0-0	0-1-0	0-0-0	4-0-0	0-2-0	0-2-0	0-1-0	0-0-0	8	7	0	.533
Walk	0-0-0	1-0-0	1-1-0	0-0-0	1-0-0	2-1-0	0-0-0	2-0-0	0-0-0	0-0-0	2-0-0	9	2	0	.818
TOTALS	3-9-2	11-7-4	10-2-5	8-4-3	5-7-4	12-6-8	12-6-5	12-6-7	11-7-3	7-5-6	7-5-4	98	64	51	.605

NO DECISIONS OR SAVES: Fajardo, Huismann, Miller, Reed.

ST. LOUIS (84-78)

	Atl. W-L-S	Chi. W-L-S	Cin. W-L-S	Hou. W-L-S	L.A. W-L-S	Mon. W-L-S	N.Y. W-L-S	Phi. W-L-S	Pit. W-L-S	S.D. W-L-S	S.F. W-L-S	W	L	S	Pct.
Agosto	0-0-0	1-1-0	0-0-0	1-0-0	0-0-0	0-0-2	1-1-0	0-0-0	0-0-0	1-1-0	1-0-0	5	3	2	.625
Carpenter	1-0-0	0-0-0	1-0-0	1-1-0	1-0-0	1-0-0	2-0-0	0-1-0	1-0-0	0-2-0	2-0-0	10	4	0	.714
Clark	0-0-0	0-0-0	0-0-0	0-0-0	0-0-0	1-1-0	0-0-0	0-0-0	0-0-0	0-0-0	0-0-0	1	1	0	.500
Cormier	0-0-0	0-0-0	0-0-0	0-0-0	1-0-0	1-1-0	2-2-0	0-1-0	0-0-0	0-0-0	0-1-0	4	5	0	.444
DeLeon	0-1-0	0-4-0	1-0-0	1-1-0	0-0-0	0-1-0	0-0-0	1-0-0	1-1-0	0-0-0	1-1-0	5	9	0	.357
Fraser	0-0-0	1-1-0	1-0-0	0-0-0	1-0-0	0-0-0	0-1-0	0-0-0	0-1-0	0-0-0	0-0-0	3	3	0	.500
Hill	0-3-0	2-0-0	1-0-0	1-0-0	0-2-0	1-1-0	2-0-0	2-1-0	1-2-0	1-1-0	0-0-0	11	10	0	.524
McClure	0-0-0	0-0-0	0-0-0	0-0-0	0-1-0	0-0-0	0-0-0	0-0-0	1-0-0	0-0-0	0-0-0	1	1	0	.500
Moyer	0-0-0	0-0-0	0-2-0	0-0-0	0-0-0	0-1-0	0-0-0	0-1-0	0-1-0	0-0-0	0-0-0	0	5	0	.000
Olivares	0-1-0	1-1-0	1-1-0	0-0-0	1-0-0	3-1-0	2-0-0	2-0-1	1-1-0	0-1-0	0-1-0	11	7	1	.611
Perez	0-1-0	0-0-0	0-0-0	0-0-0	0-0-0	0-1-0	0-0-0	0-0-0	0-0-0	0-0-0	0-0-0	0	2	0	.000
B. Smith	0-2-0	1-2-0	1-0-0	2-1-0	1-1-0	2-0-0	1-1-0	3-0-0	1-1-0	0-0-0	0-1-0	12	9	0	.571
L. Smith	2-0-1	0-0-5	0-1-6	1-1-1	1-0-3	0-0-7	0-0-6	1-0-9	1-1-3	0-0-0	0-0-6	6	3	47	.667
Terry	0-0-0	0-0-0	0-0-0	0-0-0	0-2-0	1-0-0	0-0-0	1-0-0	0-0-1	0-2-0	2-0-0	4	4	1	.500
Tewksbury	0-1-0	2-1-0	2-0-0	0-1-0	0-0-0	1-0-0	1-2-0	2-2-0	0-3-0	1-2-0	2-0-0	11	12	0	.478
TOTALS	3-9-1	8-10-5	8-4-6	7-5-1	6-6-3	11-7-9	11-7-6	12-6-10	7-11-4	3-9-0	8-4-6	84	78	51	.519

NO DECISIONS OR SAVES: Grater, Oquendo, Sherrill.

SAN DIEGO (84-78)

	Atl. W-L-S	Chi. W-L-S	Cin. W-L-S	Hou. W-L-S	L.A. W-L-S	Mon. W-L-S	N.Y. W-L-S	Phi. W-L-S	Pit. W-L-S	St.L. W-L-S	S.F. W-L-S	W	L	S	Pct.
Andersen	0-0-2	0-0-1	0-0-2	0-1-3	1-1-0	1-0-2	0-1-0	0-0-0	1-0-0	0-1-0	0-0-3	3	4	13	.429
Benes	2-1-0	3-1-0	2-2-0	2-1-0	1-2-0	0-2-0	2-0-0	0-1-0	1-0-0	1-0-0	1-1-0	15	11	0	.577
Bones	0-2-0	0-0-0	1-1-0	0-0-0	0-2-0	0-0-0	0-0-0	0-0-0	1-1-0	1-0-0	1-0-0	4	6	0	.400
Clements	0-0-0	0-0-0	0-0-0	0-0-0	0-0-0	0-0-0	0-0-0	0-0-0	0-0-0	1-0-0	0-0-0	1	0	0	1.000
Costello	0-0-0	0-0-0	0-0-0	0-0-0	0-0-0	0-0-0	0-0-0	0-0-0	0-0-0	1-0-0	0-0-0	1	0	0	1.000
Gardner	0-0-0	0-0-0	0-0-0	0-0-0	0-0-1	0-1-0	0-0-0	0-0-0	0-0-0	0-0-0	0-0-0	0	1	1	.000
Hammaker	0-0-0	0-0-0	0-0-0	0-0-0	0-0-0	0-0-0	0-0-0	0-0-0	0-1-0	0-0-0	0-0-0	0	1	0	.000
Harris	1-1-0	0-0-0	2-1-0	1-0-0	2-1-0	0-0-0	1-0-0	0-0-0	0-0-0	1-0-0	0-0-0	9	5	0	.643
Hernandez	0-0-0	0-0-0	0-0-1	0-0-0	0-0-0	0-0-0	0-0-0	0-0-0	0-0-1	0-0-0	0-0-0	0	0	2	.000
Hurst	2-3-0	0-0-0	0-1-0	2-1-0	0-0-0	1-0-0	2-0-0	3-0-0	0-2-0	3-0-0	2-0-0	15	8	0	.652
Lefferts	0-2-0	0-1-0	0-0-2	0-0-7	0-0-2	0-0-0	0-0-4	0-0-1	1-1-1	0-0-2	0-2-4	1	6	23	.143
Lilliquist	0-0-0	0-0-0	0-0-0	0-0-0	0-0-0	0-0-0	0-1-0	0-1-0	0-0-0	0-0-0	0-0-0	0	2	0	.000
Maddux	0-0-0	1-0-0	2-0-1	0-1-0	0-0-1	1-0-0	0-0-0	0-1-0	1-0-1	1-0-0	1-0-2	7	2	5	.778
Melendez	0-0-0	1-2-2	2-1-0	2-0-0	1-0-0	1-0-0	0-0-0	0-1-0	0-0-0	1-1-1	0-0-0	8	5	3	.615
Nolte	0-0-0	0-0-0	0-0-0	0-0-0	2-0-0	0-0-0	0-1-0	0-1-0	0-0-0	1-0-0	0-0-0	3	2	0	.600
Peterson	0-0-0	0-0-0	0-0-0	1-0-0	1-1-0	0-0-0	0-1-0	0-2-0	0-0-0	1-0-0	0-0-0	3	4	0	.429
Rasmussen	0-1-0	3-0-0	0-2-0	3-0-0	0-0-0	0-1-0	0-1-0	0-2-0	0-2-0	0-0-0	0-2-0	6	13	0	.316
Rodriguez	0-0-0	0-0-0	0-0-0	1-0-0	0-0-0	1-1-0	0-0-0	0-0-0	0-0-0	1-0-0	0-0-0	3	1	0	.750
Rosenberg	1-1-0	0-0-0	0-0-0	0-0-0	0-0-0	0-0-0	0-0-0	0-0-0	0-0-0	0-0-0	0-0-0	1	1	0	.500
Whitson	0-0-0	0-0-0	0-0-0	0-0-0	1-0-0	1-2-0	1-1-0	0-0-0	0-0-0	0-1-0	1-2-0	4	6	0	.400
TOTALS	7-11-2	8-4-3	10-8-6	12-6-10	8-10-4	6-6-2	5-7-4	3-9-1	5-7-2	9-3-3	11-7-10	84	78	47	.519

NO DECISIONS OR SAVES: Jackson, Lewis, Scott.

SAN FRANCISCO (75-87)

	Atl. W-L-S	Chi. W-L-S	Cin. W-L-S	Hou. W-L-S	L.A. W-L-S	Mon. W-L-S	N.Y. W-L-S	Phi. W-L-S	Pit. W-L-S	St.L. W-L-S	S.D. W-L-S	W	L	S	Pct.
Beck	0-0-1	0-0-0	0-0-0	1-0-0	0-0-0	0-0-0	0-0-0	0-1-0	0-0-0	0-0-0	0-0-0	1	1	1	.500
Black	3-3-0	0-0-0	0-3-0	1-2-0	1-3-0	0-0-0	3-0-0	2-1-0	1-2-0	1-1-0	0-1-0	12	16	0	.429
Brantley	0-0-1	1-0-0	0-1-0	1-0-4	2-0-3	0-0-2	0-0-1	0-1-2	0-0-2	1-0-0	0-0-0	5	2	15	.714
Burkett	1-2-0	0-0-0	1-1-0	3-2-0	0-1-0	1-1-0	1-0-0	0-0-0	1-1-0	1-2-0	3-1-0	12	11	0	.522
Downs	1-1-0	2-0-0	0-0-0	1-0-0	3-0-0	1-0-0	0-1-0	2-1-0	0-1-0	0-0-0	0-1-0	10	4	0	.714
Garrelts	0-0-0	0-0-0	0-0-0	1-0-0	0-0-0	0-0-0	0-0-0	0-0-0	0-0-0	0-0-0	0-1-0	1	1	0	.500
Gunderson	0-0-0	0-0-0	0-0-0	0-0-0	0-0-1	0-0-0	0-0-0	0-0-0	0-0-0	0-0-0	0-0-0	0	0	1	.000
Heredia	0-0-0	0-1-0	1-0-0	0-1-0	0-1-0	0-0-0	0-0-0	0-0-0	1-0-0	0-1-0	0-0-0	2	2	0	.500
Hickerson	0-0-0	0-1-0	1-0-0	0-0-0	0-1-0	0-0-0	0-0-0	0-0-0	1-0-0	0-1-0	0-0-0	2	3	0	.400
LaCoss	0-0-0	0-0-0	0-0-0	0-0-0	1-1-0	0-2-0	0-1-0	0-0-0	0-0-0	0-1-0	0-0-0	1	5	0	.167
McClellan	0-1-0	0-2-0	2-1-0	0-0-0	0-0-0	0-0-0	1-0-0	0-0-0	0-1-0	0-1-0	0-0-0	3	6	0	.333
Oliveras	1-0-1	1-1-1	2-0-0	0-0-0	0-0-0	0-1-0	0-0-0	1-0-0	1-2-0	0-1-0	0-1-0	6	6	3	.500
Remlinger	0-0-0	0-0-0	0-0-0	0-0-0	1-0-0	0-0-0	0-0-0	0-0-0	0-0-0	0-0-0	0-0-0	1	2	0	.667
Reuschel	0-0-0	0-0-0	0-0-0	0-1-0	0-1-0	0-0-0	0-0-0	0-0-0	0-0-0	0-0-0	0-0-0	0	2	0	.000
Righetti	0-1-3	0-0-4	0-1-3	1-0-1	0-1-2	0-0-1	0-2-1	0-0-3	0-1-3	0-1-1	1-0-2	2	7	24	.222
Robinson	1-1-0	1-1-0	0-2-0	0-0-0	0-0-1	1-2-0	1-1-0	0-0-0	0-0-0	1-1-0	0-0-0	5	9	1	.357
Segura	0-0-0	0-0-0	0-0-0	0-0-0	0-0-0	0-0-0	0-0-0	0-0-0	0-1-0	0-0-0	0-0-0	0	1	0	.000
Wilson	2-0-0	2-1-0	2-1-0	0-2-0	2-0-0	2-1-0	1-1-0	0-1-0	1-0-0	1-3-0	0-1-0	13	11	0	.542
TOTALS	9-9-6	6-6-5	8-10-3	9-9-6	10-8-6	5-7-4	6-6-2	6-6-5	5-7-3	4-8-3	7-11-2	75	87	45	.463

NO DECISIONS OR SAVES: Litton.

PITCHERS' LIFETIME RECORDS AGAINST OPPOSING CLUBS

A.L. Records in Parentheses 10 OR MORE DECISIONS—PITCHERS ACTIVE IN 1991 SEASON OR ARE ON 1992 N.L. ROSTERS

	W	L	Pct.	Braves W	Braves L	Cubs W	Cubs L	Reds W	Reds L	Astros W	Astros L	Dodgers W	Dodgers L	Expos W	Expos L	Mets W	Mets L	Phillies W	Phillies L	Pirates W	Pirates L	Cardinals W	Cardinals L	Padres W	Padres L	Giants W	Giants L
Agosto, Juan (9-10)	29	19	.604	4	1	2	2	2	1	1	0	2	2	2	4	2	2	1	0	5	1	2	1	1	1	5	4
Akerfelds, Darrel (2-7)	7	3	.700	1	0	2	0	1	0	0	0	0	0	0	0	1	2	—	—	0	1	0	0	2	0	0	0
Andersen, Larry (3-4)	32	30	.516	3	4	2	1	4	4	0	2	6	2	6	1	0	4	2	3	3	3	3	4	1	0	2	2
Armstrong, Jack	25	32	.439	4	3	2	1	—	—	3	4	0	2	3	2	2	1	2	4	1	3	3	1	1	5	4	6
Assenmacher, Paul	33	25	.569	2	0	0	0	2	3	2	3	3	5	4	1	6	5	4	3	4	1	3	1	2	0	1	3
Avery, Steve	21	19	.525	—	—	2	0	2	3	2	3	5	0	0	2	1	3	1	1	2	2	3	0	2	2	1	3
Barnes, Brian	6	9	.400	0	1	1	0	0	2	0	0	1	0	—	—	0	1	1	3	0	1	1	1	1	1	0	0
Belcher, Tim	50	38	.568	5	3	5	3	5	7	7	3	—	—	3	3	1	4	5	3	7	1	1	3	5	5	6	3
Belinda, Stan	10	10	.500	0	0	3	3	1	1	0	0	0	1	0	3	0	0	2	1	—	—	3	1	0	0	1	0
Benes, Andy	31	25	.554	3	2	3	3	3	4	4	2	4	4	2	3	3	1	5	1	1	1	1	1	—	—	2	3
Berenguer, Juan (60-47)	3	10	.231	1	0	0	2	0	0	1	1	0	1	0	1	0	0	0	2	0	1	0	1	0	1	0	0
Bielecki, Mike	51	48	.515	5	3	0	1	4	8	4	2	3	2	8	4	2	4	7	5	4	6	4	3	4	8	6	2
Black, Bud (83-82)	12	16	.429	3	3	0	0	0	3	1	2	1	3	0	0	3	0	2	1	1	2	1	1	0	1	—	—
Boever, Joe	11	25	.306	0	0	1	0	0	4	1	3	1	6	0	1	1	1	0	2	0	3	2	2	2	3	3	0
Bones, Ricky	4	6	.400	0	2	0	0	1	1	0	0	0	2	0	0	0	0	0	1	1	1	1	0	—	—	1	0
Boskie, Shawn	9	15	.375	0	2	—	—	1	0	1	2	0	3	2	1	1	0	1	1	0	4	0	0	1	0	2	2
Bowen, Ryan	6	4	.600	0	0	0	0	1	1	—	—	0	0	1	0	1	0	0	1	1	0	0	1	1	1	1	1
Boyd, Dennis (62-63)	16	14	.533	3	0	0	1	1	1	0	0	2	1	—	—	1	3	1	3	1	2	2	2	3	1	2	0
Brantley, Jeff	17	7	.708	0	1	4	2	1	2	2	0	2	0	1	0	1	0	1	1	2	0	2	0	1	1	—	—
Browning, Tom	107	75	.588	13	4	9	8	—	—	13	10	12	9	6	5	8	6	8	7	8	7	8	6	12	7	10	6
Burke, Tim	46	29	.613	4	1	5	5	1	2	1	3	3	5	0	0	7	3	3	2	8	3	6	2	5	2	3	1
Burkett, John	26	18	.591	4	2	2	0	4	2	3	4	3	2	2	1	1	1	0	2	2	1	2	2	3	1	—	—
Candelaria, John (48-27)	127	87	.593	11	6	15	5	12	5	8	5	10	7	11	7	13	8	14	9	0	1	12	14	9	10	12	10
Carman, Don	53	54	.495	3	5	6	2	2	4	4	2	6	6	7	6	6	7	0	0	9	7	2	7	4	5	4	3
Carpenter, Cris	16	11	.593	1	0	3	1	1	1	1	3	2	0	1	2	2	1	2	1	1	0	—	—	0	2	2	0
Castillo, Tony (2-1)	7	3	.700	0	0	1	0	1	0	0	0	0	0	0	0	0	0	0	1	1	0	3	0	1	0	0	2
Castillo, Frank	6	7	.462	0	1	—	—	0	1	2	0	1	1	1	1	1	1	0	0	0	1	1	1	0	0	0	1
Charlton, Norm	27	22	.551	5	2	2	2	—	—	2	2	1	4	1	0	2	3	1	1	4	2	2	1	4	3	3	1
Clancy, Jim (128-140)	12	27	.308	2	3	0	2	1	3	1	0	2	1	0	3	0	3	0	1	1	3	0	0	4	3	1	5
Clements, Pat (8-3)	5	7	.417	0	0	0	0	1	0	0	1	1	0	0	0	1	2	0	0	0	0	4	0	0	0	0	1
Combs, Pat	16	16	.500	0	4	0	2	1	0	3	0	0	2	4	2	4	1	—	—	0	2	4	1	0	1	0	1
Cone, David (0-0)	67	41	.620	7	2	4	4	7	6	4	4	5	5	6	4	—	—	6	3	7	2	10	5	7	3	5	4
Cook, Dennis	19	13	.594	2	2	0	0	2	0	1	1	1	2	1	0	2	0	0	0	2	0	5	2	1	2	4	1
Costello, John	11	6	.647	1	0	0	2	2	0	0	1	2	0	0	0	1	1	3	2	0	0	—	—	1	0	1	0
Cox, Danny	60	62	.492	3	5	9	7	6	4	4	5	2	8	4	6	5	8	7	5	11	5	—	—	4	2	5	5
Crews, Tim	11	10	.524	1	0	0	0	0	2	1	0	—	—	2	1	1	1	0	0	2	0	1	2	2	2	1	2
Darling, Ron (3-7)	99	72	.579	13	3	8	9	10	5	6	5	8	4	12	10	0	0	11	9	11	6	8	7	6	7	6	7
DeJesus, Jose (0-1)	17	17	.500	2	0	1	2	2	1	2	2	1	1	1	1	4	1	—	—	1	2	0	4	3	3	0	0
DeLeon, Jose (15-17)	58	88	.397	6	4	10	11	5	9	6	5	2	8	9	7	4	12	4	6	3	6	0	6	4	7	5	7
Deshaies, Jim (0-1)	61	59	.508	10	7	2	5	6	7	—	—	10	4	2	6	5	1	3	5	5	4	8	4	3	11	7	5
Dibble, Rob	22	14	.611	1	3	3	0	—	—	3	1	3	2	2	1	0	2	2	0	1	0	3	2	2	1	2	2
Downs, Kelly	46	36	.561	7	5	4	1	2	4	2	4	9	6	6	2	1	3	4	4	2	5	2	1	7	1	—	—
Drabek, Doug (7-8)	77	51	.602	8	4	12	6	6	3	4	4	5	5	10	6	5	5	10	4	—	—	5	8	6	4	6	2
Fernandez, Sid	79	62	.560	4	4	8	5	5	7	9	3	5	6	6	6	0	0	13	8	11	6	10	5	4	8	4	4
Franco, John	52	42	.553	5	3	4	6	2	0	7	4	5	9	2	3	2	3	5	5	4	3	3	3	8	2	5	1
Freeman, Marvin	6	5	.545	0	0	2	0	0	0	0	1	0	1	1	0	1	1	0	0	1	0	0	1	0	0	1	1
Frey, Steve	11	5	.688	1	1	1	0	1	0	1	0	0	0	—	—	1	1	1	1	1	0	2	1	1	0	1	2
Gardner, Mark	16	23	.410	2	2	2	3	0	1	5	0	1	4	—	—	0	4	0	2	1	2	2	5	1	1	2	1
Garrelts, Scott	69	53	.566	12	4	7	4	6	8	6	6	6	8	4	5	7	1	5	3	4	5	7	3	5	6	—	—
Glavine, Tom	53	52	.505	—	—	2	3	10	3	0	8	6	9	2	8	2	2	8	1	6	5	3	2	9	6	5	5
Gooden, Dwight	132	53	.714	7	2	23	3	8	5	13	4	14	1	10	7	—	—	14	8	11	7	12	6	11	4	9	6
Gott, Jim (21-30)	21	26	.447	1	3	3	2	0	2	3	1	1	0	4	3	2	4	3	1	2	1	0	3	1	5	1	1
Greene, Tommy	17	12	.586	1	1	2	1	2	1	1	1	1	2	4	0	0	1	0	0	2	1	2	2	0	1	2	1
Grimsley, Jason	5	12	.294	0	0	0	2	0	0	0	0	0	0	2	1	0	3	—	—	0	4	1	1	1	1	0	1
Gross, Kevin	90	101	.471	6	7	6	14	7	8	8	9	11	8	12	4	13	11	2	3	10	8	4	14	4	9	7	6
Gross, Kip	6	4	.600	1	0	0	0	—	—	0	0	0	1	0	0	1	0	1	0	1	0	0	1	1	1	1	1
Hammaker, Atlee (1-3)	58	64	.475	6	5	5	7	8	6	9	10	1	5	5	5	4	5	9	5	3	2	4	4	4	9	0	1
Hammond, Chris	7	9	.438	0	0	1	0	—	—	3	0	0	1	1	0	0	1	0	1	0	4	0	1	2	0	0	1
Haney, Chris	3	7	.300	0	0	1	0	1	1	0	0	0	1	—	—	0	2	0	0	1	0	2	1	0	0	0	0
Harkey, Mike	12	11	.522	1	0	—	—	0	2	1	0	1	1	2	2	1	2	0	0	1	0	0	4	2	0	3	0
Harnisch, Pete (16-22)	12	9	.571	2	1	2	0	1	2	—	—	2	1	0	2	1	0	1	0	0	2	0	1	1	0	2	0
Harris, Greg W.	27	22	.551	1	2	0	1	6	4	7	0	4	1	0	1	3	2	1	3	0	2	1	4	—	—	4	2
Hartley, Mike	10	5	.667	3	0	2	0	0	1	1	0	0	0	1	1	2	0	0	0	0	0	0	0	0	2	1	1
Heaton, Neal (39-56)	37	39	.487	1	5	4	1	1	2	6	3	1	5	3	1	2	4	4	6	3	2	6	0	3	7	3	3
Henry, Dwayne (3-4)	5	6	.455	0	0	1	1	2	1	0	0	0	1	0	0	0	1	0	0	0	0	1	0	2	1	1	0
Hernandez, Xavier (1-0)	4	8	.333	0	2	0	1	3	1	—	—	0	2	0	0	0	0	0	0	0	0	0	0	0	1	1	0
Hershiser, Orel	106	67	.613	18	6	6	3	13	7	15	7	—	—	8	6	3	7	4	4	9	8	6	5	9	8	15	6
Hill, Ken	23	32	.418	1	4	3	3	1	3	2	2	2	3	3	4	4	1	3	3	2	6	—	—	2	1	0	2
Howell, Jay (27-30)	23	16	.590	2	0	1	0	2	3	3	3	0	0	3	2	0	0	4	2	2	1	2	1	2	2	2	2
Hurst, Bruce (88-73)	41	28	.594	6	4	0	2	2	2	5	3	3	3	2	2	5	1	5	0	3	4	6	3	—	—	4	4
Innis, Jeff	2	8	.200	0	2	1	1	0	0	0	0	0	0	0	0	—	—	1	1	0	2	0	1	0	0	0	1
Jackson, Danny (37-49)	36	30	.545	4	2	3	3	0	0	1	5	5	5	1	2	3	1	5	3	2	0	3	3	6	3	3	3
Jackson, Mike (22-25)	3	10	.231	0	0	0	1	1	1	0	2	0	0	1	3	0	0	—	—	1	0	1	0	1	0	0	0
Jones, Barry (16-8)	10	18	.357	0	0	3	2	2	1	0	1	0	0	0	2	0	2	2	1	0	4	1	1	1	2	1	2
Jones, Jimmy (3-3)	26	29	.473	4	2	1	1	3	2	3	0	5	1	2	4	2	3	1	4	3	5	0	1	0	1	2	5

PITCHERS' LIFETIME RECORDS AGAINST OPPOSING CLUBS

A.L. Records in Parentheses   10 OR MORE DECISIONS—PITCHERS ACTIVE IN 1991 SEASON OR ARE ON 1992 N.L. ROSTERS

Pitcher	W	L	Pct.	Braves W	Braves L	Cubs W	Cubs L	Reds W	Reds L	Astros W	Astros L	Dodgers W	Dodgers L	Expos W	Expos L	Mets W	Mets L	Phillies W	Phillies L	Pirates W	Pirates L	Cardinals W	Cardinals L	Padres W	Padres L	Giants W	Giants L
Kile, Darryl	7	11	.389	0	1	0	2	1	1	—	—	0	0	0	1	1	0	2	1	0	2	1	0	1	0	1	3
Kipper, Bob (0-1)	24	33	.421	3	1	2	1	1	4	1	3	5	3	3	1	4	9	1	6	—	—	2	2	0	2	2	1
LaCoss, Mike (1-1)	97	102	.487	10	7	6	5	8	7	7	10	12	10	8	13	5	8	6	6	10	8	9	8	12	10	4	10
Lancaster, Les	34	23	.596	3	1	—	—	4	1	3	1	1	4	4	3	5	2	3	4	2	3	4	2	3	0	2	2
Landrum, Bill	17	12	.586	3	1	0	2	0	1	0	0	1	0	2	2	4	1	2	3	0	0	1	0	4	2	0	0
Layana, Tim	5	5	.500	0	2	0	1	—	—	1	1	0	0	1	0	0	0	0	0	1	1	0	0	1	0	1	0
Leach, Terry (8-13)	24	9	.727	3	0	1	2	1	0	1	0	3	1	6	1	—	—	5	0	1	2	0	1	1	1	2	1
Lefferts, Craig	40	50	.444	4	4	2	6	3	2	8	7	9	1	1	2	0	7	1	4	4	8	1	4	3	2	4	3
Leibrandt, Charlie (76-61)	40	41	.494	2	1	2	3	3	2	6	6	0	5	3	2	3	3	3	1	2	2	5	4	7	5	4	7
Lilliquist, Derek	13	23	.361	0	2	2	1	3	2	1	2	1	0	1	2	1	2	1	1	1	1	0	3	1	2	1	5
Maddux, Greg	75	64	.540	6	2	—	—	4	7	9	4	4	2	9	7	9	8	10	5	5	10	5	9	8	4	6	6
Maddux, Mike	17	16	.515	0	1	4	4	3	0	0	3	1	2	2	1	0	0	0	1	3	1	2	2	0	0	2	1
Mallicoat, Rob	0	2	.000	0	1	0	0	0	0	—	—	0	1	0	0	0	0	0	0	0	0	0	0	0	0	0	0
Martinez, Dennis (108-93)	69	52	.570	5	3	8	5	7	5	5	5	4	5	—	—	7	9	7	4	9	4	7	4	5	4	5	4
Martinez, Ramon	44	26	.629	8	2	4	1	4	4	2	1	—	—	3	3	3	4	4	2	1	2	3	1	7	1	5	5
Mason, Roger (1-1)	8	10	.444	1	1	1	1	0	0	0	1	2	1	0	1	0	2	0	1	1	0	2	1	1	1	0	0
McClellan, Paul	3	7	.300	0	1	0	2	2	1	0	1	0	0	0	0	0	1	1	0	0	0	0	0	0	1	—	—
McClure, Bob (54-44)	11	10	.524	0	0	0	2	0	0	1	0	1	2	0	0	1	3	0	0	4	2	3	0	0	1	1	0
McDowell, Roger	51	49	.510	3	2	7	6	5	5	2	6	3	4	3	2	4	2	2	3	5	5	9	8	4	1	4	5
Melendez, Jose (0-0)	8	5	.615	0	0	1	2	2	1	2	0	1	0	1	0	0	0	0	0	0	0	1	1	1	1	—	—
Mercker, Kent	9	10	.474	—	—	0	2	0	0	1	3	1	0	1	0	3	0	0	0	0	1	1	0	2	0	0	2
Morgan, Mike (34-68)	33	36	.478	3	6	6	2	4	2	5	6	—	—	1	4	2	3	3	0	2	6	2	2	3	2	2	3
Moyer, Jamie (6-15)	28	39	.418	1	4	0	0	2	3	3	3	1	3	5	4	3	1	4	8	4	6	2	1	2	3	1	3
Mulholland, Terry	32	38	.457	2	5	4	4	1	5	1	3	3	3	5	1	1	6	0	0	1	2	5	3	4	3	5	3
Murphy, Rob (5-14)	14	11	.560	3	2	0	0	—	—	3	0	2	1	1	1	0	2	0	0	1	2	0	1	3	1	1	1
Myers, Randy	27	32	.458	1	2	1	3	3	0	3	4	2	3	2	2	0	3	4	1	2	7	3	2	2	3	4	2
Nabholz, Chris	14	9	.609	0	1	1	1	1	1	1	0	2	0	—	—	2	3	3	1	1	1	2	1	1	0	0	0
Nolte, Eric (0-0)	5	8	.385	0	2	0	0	0	1	0	0	2	1	0	0	0	2	1	1	0	0	0	0	—	—	1	1
Ojeda, Bob (44-39)	63	49	.563	4	5	2	4	7	4	3	3	5	0	6	6	0	1	7	4	13	6	7	4	5	3	4	9
Olivares, Omar	12	8	.600	0	1	1	1	1	1	1	0	1	0	4	2	2	0	2	0	1	1	—	—	0	1	0	1
Oliveras, Francisco (3-4)	8	8	.500	1	0	1	1	2	0	0	0	1	0	0	0	2	0	1	3	0	1	0	1	0	2	—	—
Osuna, Al	9	6	.600	2	0	1	0	0	0	0	2	0	0	1	0	0	1	3	1	1	0	0	1	2	0	1	0
Palacios, Vicente	9	6	.600	0	3	2	0	2	0	0	1	2	0	1	0	0	1	2	0	—	—	0	0	1	1	1	0
Parrett, Jeff	37	29	.561	6	1	4	4	1	2	4	3	4	1	1	3	1	1	3	2	7	2	5	3	1	7	0	0
Patterson, Bob	19	18	.514	5	0	5	0	0	2	0	2	1	3	0	0	1	6	3	2	0	0	5	1	2	1	2	1
Pena, Alejandro	49	42	.538	7	3	4	5	4	7	8	7	0	0	5	3	3	3	3	1	4	3	4	2	3	6	4	2
Portugal, Mark (11-19)	28	23	.549	4	3	3	3	3	2	—	—	2	2	1	1	2	3	2	1	1	1	1	0	1	5	8	2
Power, Ted (6-7)	57	55	.509	5	5	3	2	0	4	5	10	7	4	4	1	3	4	4	4	7	2	2	6	10	5	7	8
Rasmussen, Dennis (39-24)	47	49	.490	4	7	8	4	5	4	11	2	5	7	1	4	2	4	3	4	0	6	2	2	1	0	5	5
Reed, Rich	4	7	.364	1	0	0	1	0	1	0	0	1	0	0	1	1	0	1	2	—	—	0	1	0	0	0	1
Reuschel, Rick (4-4)	210	187	.529	23	7	11	3	19	16	16	15	12	19	26	21	14	25	20	20	13	24	19	13	20	12	17	12
Rijo, Jose (19-30)	49	28	.636	4	3	6	1	—	—	8	2	6	4	2	1	5	1	7	3	1	2	3	0	4	5	3	6
Robinson, Don	107	102	.512	11	7	11	11	8	12	10	10	6	9	11	9	10	9	10	12	2	3	13	8	10	6	5	6
Robinson, Jeff D. (3-9)	39	45	.464	3	2	4	1	6	4	1	7	2	2	5	4	1	5	4	6	2	2	5	3	3	3	1	1
Rojas, Mel	6	4	.600	1	0	1	0	0	0	1	0	0	1	—	—	1	0	0	1	1	0	0	0	0	1	1	1
Ruffin, Bruce	42	58	.420	7	5	5	6	4	5	6	4	2	4	1	5	4	6	—	—	4	7	3	6	4	3	2	7
Ruskin, Scott	7	6	.538	0	0	0	1	1	0	0	1	1	0	0	0	1	0	1	3	2	1	0	0	0	0	1	0
Sampen, Bill	21	12	.636	2	1	2	3	0	1	2	1	1	0	—	—	1	1	2	1	4	2	2	3	1	2	0	1
Scanlan, Bob	7	8	.467	0	1	—	—	0	0	1	1	0	0	2	2	2	1	0	1	1	0	1	0	0	2	0	0
Scott, Mike	124	108	.534	9	12	11	10	15	7	2	3	18	12	9	8	6	7	10	8	7	9	5	11	18	9	14	12
Scudder, Scott	15	23	.395	3	4	1	1	—	—	2	2	2	2	2	2	0	4	1	1	0	1	1	1	2	2	1	3
Sisk, Doug (3-3)	19	17	.528	1	2	2	4	0	0	3	1	1	1	3	2	0	0	2	4	2	0	1	2	2	1	2	0
Smiley, John	60	42	.588	4	4	5	5	5	0	5	5	4	4	6	9	10	3	5	2	—	—	6	4	3	1	7	5
Smith, Bryn	102	88	.537	13	5	12	12	8	5	7	5	7	10	3	1	8	12	15	8	4	9	12	9	9	3	9	4
Smith, Dave	53	53	.500	6	9	7	4	4	6	0	1	6	4	3	4	2	4	3	4	2	3	4	3	4	4	4	4
Smith, Lee (12-7)	49	58	.458	5	4	0	1	2	4	4	4	4	4	5	3	8	9	8	12	2	7	2	5	6	1	3	4
Smith, Pete	19	40	.322	—	—	3	4	1	4	0	2	3	4	1	4	0	2	3	5	2	5	0	3	3	3	2	5
Smith, Zane	67	78	.462	1	3	5	5	5	7	10	7	8	9	4	6	7	9	5	5	4	3	6	8	7	9	5	7
Smoltz, John	42	42	.500	—	—	6	2	4	6	4	4	3	7	2	3	3	1	5	1	4	2	3	4	2	5	6	7
Stanton, Mike	5	9	.357	—	—	0	0	1	1	2	0	0	1	1	1	0	2	0	1	0	0	0	1	1	1	0	2
St. Claire, Randy (1-0)	11	6	.647	1	0	2	1	0	3	1	0	0	0	2	1	0	3	1	0	0	0	1	0	2	0	1	1
Sutcliffe, Rick (35-24)	104	86	.547	1	8	1	3	13	4	8	7	6	4	14	6	10	9	12	6	12	11	11	11	10	8	6	9
Terry, Scott	24	28	.462	2	2	3	6	2	0	2	3	2	2	3	1	1	3	2	2	2	2	0	0	1	3	4	4
Tewksbury, Bob (10-9)	22	25	.468	0	2	4	1	3	0	1	1	0	2	3	2	1	4	3	4	2	5	0	0	3	3	2	1
Tomlin, Randy	12	11	.522	0	0	1	1	2	1	2	0	0	1	0	1	5	0	2	2	—	—	0	4	0	1	0	0
Viola, Frank (112-93)	38	32	.543	2	3	2	7	1	3	3	2	4	1	8	1	—	—	5	2	5	2	5	2	2	5	1	4
Walk, Bob	82	61	.573	5	8	11	3	8	4	7	6	8	4	5	8	4	7	6	2	10	8	11	5	7	4	4	4
Wetteland, John	8	12	.400	0	1	0	1	1	1	1	2	—	—	1	0	0	3	0	0	1	0	1	0	3	2	1	1
Whitehust, Wally	8	13	.381	1	3	0	1	1	1	1	1	0	1	3	0	0	0	1	0	0	2	1	2	0	0	0	2
Whitson, Ed (19-12)	107	111	.491	9	12	9	5	14	13	10	13	12	17	8	8	8	6	9	9	10	3	6	10	4	6	8	9
Williams, Mitch (18-19)	17	17	.500	5	3	2	2	1	1	0	0	0	1	4	1	3	2	0	0	2	3	0	3	0	0	0	1
Wilson, Steve	10	13	.435	0	1	0	0	0	1	0	0	2	0	0	0	1	2	2	4	3	1	1	2	1	0	0	0
Wilson, Trevor	23	23	.500	3	1	3	2	1	2	1	2	4	3	2	2	1	2	0	1	3	1	1	3	3	4	—	—

NATIONAL LEAGUE ACTIVE PITCHERS—LIFETIME MAJOR LEAGUE TOTALS—20 + DECISIONS

Pitcher	W	L	PCT.	ERA	G	SV	IP	H	R	ER	BB	SO
Agosto, Juan	38	29	.567	3.80	498	29	570.2	565	273	241	236	279
Andersen, Larry	35	34	.507	3.11	572	47	866.2	820	346	299	267	629
Assenmacher, Paul	33	25	.569	3.34	389	39	484.2	440	203	180	177	457
Avery, Steve	21	19	.525	4.10	56	0	309.1	310	168	141	110	212
Ballard, Jeff	36	51	.414	4.63	144	0	695.1	812	408	358	204	217
Bankhead, Scott	41	40	.506	4.24	126	0	689.1	682	350	325	203	469
Belcher, Tim	50	38	.568	2.99	138	5	806.0	680	309	268	261	633
Belinda, Stan	10	10	.500	3.67	123	24	147.0	111	61	60	66	136
Benes, Andy	31	25	.554	3.32	75	0	482.0	422	191	178	159	373
Berenguer, Juan	63	57	.525	3.79	443	31	1127.2	957	524	475	568	930
Bielecki, Mike	51	48	.515	4.19	184	1	846.2	842	434	394	349	489
Black, Bud	95	98	.492	3.74	333	11	1681.0	1598	777	698	499	850
Boever, Joe	11	25	.306	3.70	255	36	345.2	322	149	142	167	285
Boskie, Shawn	9	15	.375	4.57	43	0	226.2	249	120	115	83	111
Brantley, Jeff	17	7	.708	2.94	190	35	300.0	278	108	98	128	222
Browning, Tom	107	75	.588	3.80	256	0	1669.1	1617	774	704	445	889
Burke, Tim	46	29	.613	2.62	460	102	656.0	572	222	191	201	429
Burkett, John	26	18	.591	4.00	72	1	416.2	431	199	185	124	254
Candelaria, John	175	114	.606	3.30	526	23	2481.1	2354	1010	909	570	1633
Candiotti, Tom	84	78	.519	3.51	213	0	1404.2	1349	626	548	461	878
Carman, Don	53	54	.495	4.10	340	11	919.1	845	459	419	378	596
Carpenter, Cris	16	11	.593	3.99	107	0	189.2	184	92	84	57	112
Charlton, Norm	27	22	.551	3.00	174	3	419.1	350	155	140	164	331
Clancy, Jim	140	167	.456	4.22	472	10	2518.2	2513	1304	1182	947	1422
Clements, Pat	13	10	.565	3.89	238	12	312.0	314	144	135	137	138
Combs, Pat	16	16	.500	3.99	52	0	286.1	279	141	127	135	179
Cone, David	67	41	.620	3.18	166	1	1017.1	858	398	359	349	966
Cox, Danny	60	62	.492	3.51	175	0	1088.0	1089	491	424	336	539
Crews, Tim	11	10	.524	3.05	232	15	345.2	349	135	117	90	250
DeJesus, Jose	17	18	.486	3.77	58	1	322.1	257	151	135	214	209
DeLeon, Jose	73	105	.410	3.68	261	4	1579.2	1286	711	646	697	1343
Dibble, Rob	22	14	.611	2.21	246	44	338.2	234	89	83	119	460
DiPino, Frank	34	37	.479	3.80	494	56	673.0	643	318	284	260	502
Downs, Kelly	46	36	.561	3.65	158	1	699.2	640	311	284	243	461
Drabek, Doug	84	59	.587	3.19	192	0	1237.2	1135	486	438	333	719
Fernandez, Sid	79	62	.560	3.25	207	1	1256.1	930	496	453	500	1184
Fisher, Brian	32	31	.508	4.36	200	22	548.2	558	292	266	205	344
Franco, John	52	42	.553	2.53	500	211	651.0	587	223	183	249	468
Fraser, Willie	34	39	.466	4.39	208	5	619.0	595	328	302	223	309
Gardner, Mark	16	23	.410	3.76	61	0	347.1	294	156	145	147	263
Garrelts, Scott	69	53	.566	3.29	352	48	959.1	815	395	351	413	703
Gibson, Paul	18	21	.462	3.88	214	11	417.1	423	191	180	183	235
Glavine, Tom	53	52	.505	3.81	139	0	892.2	861	427	378	283	515
Gooden, Dwight	132	53	.714	2.91	238	1	1713.2	1467	609	554	505	1541
Gott, Jim	42	56	.429	3.98	362	55	886.2	854	446	392	376	647
Greene, Tommy	17	12	.586	3.75	55	0	285.1	249	128	119	98	192
Gross, Kevin	90	101	.471	3.99	311	4	1585.0	1570	767	702	633	1091
Hammaker, Atlee	59	67	.468	3.61	234	5	1071.0	1039	484	430	279	611
Harkey, Mike	12	11	.522	3.33	36	0	227.0	207	96	84	80	127
Harnisch, Pete	28	31	.475	3.74	84	0	521.2	468	230	217	242	374
Harris, Greg W.	27	22	.551	2.34	152	15	403.1	327	123	105	131	313
Heaton, Neal	76	95	.444	4.35	332	10	1438.0	1512	764	695	490	653
Hershiser, Orel	106	67	.613	2.77	256	5	1594.1	1378	563	490	470	1100
Hill, Ken	23	32	.418	4.03	84	0	470.2	428	226	211	205	297
Howell, Jay	50	46	.521	3.41	433	149	696.0	649	281	264	241	571
Howell, Ken	38	48	.442	3.95	245	31	613.1	534	296	269	275	549
Huismann, Mark	13	11	.542	4.40	152	11	296.1	305	163	145	83	219
Hurst, Bruce	129	101	.561	3.84	334	0	2149.1	2172	1005	918	667	1525
Jackson, Danny	73	79	.480	3.83	213	1	1277.0	1251	622	543	521	768
Jackson, Mike	25	35	.417	3.53	326	29	487.1	383	217	191	235	409

Pitcher	W	L	PCT.	ERA	G	SV	IP	H	R	ER	BB	SO
Jones, Barry	26	26	.500	3.16	281	22	356.0	316	145	125	156	213
Jones, Doug	26	32	.448	3.08	276	128	423.2	422	172	145	99	340
Jones, Jimmy	29	32	.475	4.42	116	0	576.0	627	333	283	191	286
Lancaster, Les	34	23	.596	3.82	232	22	555.2	558	255	236	189	337
Landrum, Bill	17	12	.586	3.13	232	58	319.2	315	126	111	109	197
Leach, Terry	32	22	.593	3.30	311	9	610.0	616	257	224	175	306
Lefferts, Craig	40	50	.444	3.03	582	100	831.1	742	318	280	241	530
Leibrandt, Charlie	116	102	.532	3.68	336	2	1964.2	2030	906	804	569	928
Maddux, Greg	75	64	.540	3.61	177	0	1174.0	1151	547	471	385	738
Maddux, Mike	17	16	.515	4.05	139	6	346.2	350	176	156	118	212
Magrane, Joe	42	42	.500	3.07	116	0	773.2	713	299	264	242	428
Martinez, Dennis	177	145	.550	3.71	491	5	2933.1	2878	1342	1209	866	1546
Martinez, Ramon	44	26	.629	3.15	90	0	589.0	487	234	206	199	485
Mathews, Greg	26	30	.464	3.96	79	0	461.2	437	216	203	178	224
McClure, Bob	65	54	.546	3.82	613	52	1098.1	1060	525	466	467	671
McDowell, Roger	51	49	.510	3.03	467	135	712.2	661	280	240	259	349
Morgan, Mike	67	104	.392	4.10	264	3	1385.1	1448	700	631	467	660
Moyer, Jamie	34	54	.386	4.56	141	0	700.0	766	394	355	282	435
Mulholland, Terry	32	38	.457	3.89	116	0	628.2	641	297	272	169	328
Murphy, Rob	19	25	.432	3.15	398	27	448.2	417	175	157	185	405
Myers, Randy	27	32	.458	2.85	309	93	458.2	354	164	145	215	470
Nabholz, Chris	14	9	.609	3.38	35	0	223.2	177	89	84	89	152
Ojeda, Bob	107	88	.549	3.60	311	1	1671.2	1605	746	668	568	1004
Olivares, Omar	12	8	.600	3.53	37	1	216.2	193	89	85	78	111
Oliveras, Francisco	11	12	.478	3.74	100	5	190.1	180	86	79	58	113
Parrett, Jeff	37	29	.561	3.80	275	21	409.2	378	196	173	199	337
Patterson, Bob	19	18	.514	4.53	150	8	270.1	289	143	136	74	195
Pena, Alejandro	49	42	.538	2.90	392	52	927.1	838	355	299	288	709
Portugal, Mark	39	42	.481	4.20	156	5	711.2	695	357	332	268	480
Power, Ted	63	62	.504	4.08	455	51	1015.0	1014	507	460	400	623
Rasmussen, Dennis	86	73	.541	4.09	234	0	1379.0	1339	699	627	492	805
Righetti, Dave	76	68	.528	3.13	583	248	1207.2	1063	477	420	501	991
Rijo, Jose	68	58	.540	3.39	223	3	1076.1	946	469	406	454	925
Robinson, Jeff D.	42	54	.438	3.87	405	38	823.1	804	404	354	309	583
Rosenberg, Steve	6	15	.286	4.94	87	1	209.2	222	129	115	87	115
Saberhagen, Bret	110	78	.585	3.21	252	1	1660.1	1551	650	593	331	1093
Sampen, Bill	21	12	.636	3.50	102	2	182.2	190	83	71	79	121
Sisk, Doug	22	20	.524	3.27	332	33	523.1	527	238	190	267	195
Smiley, John	60	42	.588	3.57	196	4	854.0	787	375	339	229	534
Smith, Bryn	102	88	.537	3.43	341	6	1740.1	1658	768	666	416	1010
Smith, Dave	53	53	.500	2.67	598	216	795.1	685	276	236	279	545
Smith, Lee	61	65	.484	2.84	717	312	992.1	857	347	313	376	990
Smith, Pete	19	40	.322	4.37	93	0	494.0	491	271	240	205	335
Smith, Zane	67	78	.462	3.58	258	3	1344.1	1335	636	535	464	772
Smoltz, John	42	42	.500	3.72	111	0	733.0	646	329	303	272	523
Swift, Bill	30	40	.429	4.04	253	24	759.0	827	395	341	253	292
Swindell, Greg	60	55	.522	3.79	153	0	1043.0	1059	487	439	226	756
Terry, Scott	24	28	.462	3.73	236	8	499.1	491	234	207	176	262
Tewksbury, Bob	32	34	.485	3.67	104	1	551.1	611	269	225	116	214
Tomlin, Randy	12	11	.522	2.85	43	0	252.2	232	99	80	66	146
Valdez, Sergio	8	12	.400	5.40	60	0	181.2	200	121	109	71	123
Walk, Bob	82	61	.573	3.88	282	3	1344.0	1325	654	580	493	708
Wetteland, John	8	12	.400	3.84	59	1	154.2	130	76	66	54	141
Whitehurst, Wally	8	13	.381	3.93	83	3	213.0	222	101	93	39	142
Whitson, Ed	126	123	.506	3.79	452	8	2240.2	2240	1045	944	698	1266
Williams, Mitch	35	36	.493	3.33	436	114	511.0	367	213	189	384	486
Wilson, Steve	10	13	.435	4.45	120	5	253.0	244	132	125	87	175
Wilson, Trevor	23	23	.500	3.81	89	0	373.2	313	173	158	158	242
Worrell, Todd	28	30	.483	2.64	281	126	361.2	300	118	106	142	301

CLUBS' ALL-TIME LEADERS IN PITCHING CATEGORIES

BRAVES

WINS	GAMES	SHUTOUTS	SAVES	INNINGS PITCHED	STRIKEOUTS
Warren Spahn 356	Phil Niekro 740	Warren Spahn 63	Gene Garber 141	Warren Spahn 5048.0	Phil Niekro 2912
Kid Nichols 328	Warren Spahn 714	Kid Nichols 44	Cecil Upshaw 78	Phil Niekro 4622.0	Warren Spahn 2493
Phil Niekro 268	Gene Garber 557	Phil Niekro 43	Rick Camp 57	Kid Nichols 4570.0	Kid Nichols 1684
Lew Burdette 179	Kid Nichols 543	Tommy Bond 30	Don McMahon 50	Lew Burdette 2638.0	Vic Willis 1161
Vic Willis 149	Lew Burdette 468	Lew Burdette 30	Steve Bedrosian 41	Vic Willis 2575.0	Jim Whitney 1157
Tommy Bond 149					

CUBS

WINS	GAMES	SHUTOUTS	SAVES	INNINGS PITCHED	STRIKEOUTS
Charles Root 201	Charles Root 605	Mordecai Brown 50	Lee Smith 180	Charles Root 3138.0	Ferguson Jenkins 2038
Mordecai Brown 188	Lee Smith 458	James Vaughn 35	Bruce Sutter 133	Bill Hutchinson 3026.0	Charles Root 1432
Bill Hutchinson 181	Don Elston 449	Ed Reulbach 31	Don Elston 63	Ferguson Jenkins 2672.2	Rick Reuschel 1367
Larry Corcoran 175	Guy Bush 428	Ferguson Jenkins 29	Phil Regan 60	Larry Corcoran 2337.2	Bill Hutchinson 1226
Ferguson Jenkins 167	Ferguson Jenkins 401	Orval Overall 28	Mitch Williams 52	Mordecai Brown 2329.0	James Vaughn 1138

REDS

WINS	GAMES	SHUTOUTS	SAVES	INNINGS PITCHED	STRIKEOUTS
Eppa Rixey 179	Pedro Borbon 531	Bucky Walters 32	John Franco 148	Eppa Rixey 2890.0	Jim Maloney 1592
Paul Derringer 161	Clay Carroll 486	Jim Maloney 30	Clay Carroll 119	Dolf Luque 2669.0	Mario Soto 1449
Bucky Walters 160	Joe Nuxhall 484	Johnny Vander Meer 30	Tom Hume 88	Paul Derringer 2616.0	Joe Nuxhall 1289
Dolf Luque 154	Tom Hume 457	Ken Raffensberger 25	Pedro Borbon 76	Bucky Walters 2355.0	Johnny Vander Meer 1251
Jim Maloney 134	Eppa Rixey 440	3 tied 24	Wayne Granger 73	Joe Nuxhall 2171.0	Paul Derringer 1062

ASTROS

WINS	GAMES	SHUTOUTS	SAVES	INNINGS PITCHED	STRIKEOUTS
Joe Niekro 144	Dave Smith 563	Larry Dierker 25	Dave Smith 199	Larry Dierker 2296.0	Nolan Ryan 1866
Larry Dierker 137	Ken Forsch 421	Joe Niekro 21	Fred Gladding 76	Joe Niekro 2271.0	J.R. Richard 1493
Mike Scott 110	Joe Niekro 397	Mike Scott 21	Joe Sambito 72	Nolan Ryan 1855.0	Larry Dierker 1487
J.R. Richard 107	Joe Sambito 353	Don Wilson 20	Ken Forsch 50	Don Wilson 1748.0	Mike Scott 1318
Nolan Ryan 106	Larry Dierker 345	J.R. Richard 19	Frank DiPino 43	Bob Knepper 1738.1	Don Wilson 1283

DODGERS

WINS	GAMES	SHUTOUTS	SAVES	INNINGS PITCHED	STRIKEOUTS
Don Sutton 233	Don Sutton 550	Don Sutton 52	Jim Brewer 125	Don Sutton 3815.1	Don Sutton 2696
Don Drysdale 209	Don Drysdale 518	Don Drysdale 49	Ron Perranoski 101	Don Drysdale 3432.0	Don Drysdale 2486
Dazzy Vance 190	Jim Brewer 474	Sandy Koufax 40	Clem Labine 83	Brickyard Kennedy 2857.0	Sandy Koufax 2396
Brickyard Kennedy 176	Ron Perranoski 457	Nap Rucker 38	Jay Howell 81	Dazzy Vance 2758.0	Dazzy Vance 1918
Sandy Koufax 165	Clem Labine 425	Claude Osteen 34	Tom Niedenfuer 64	Burleigh Grimes 2426.0	Fernando Valenzuela 1759

EXPOS

WINS	GAMES	SHUTOUTS	SAVES	INNINGS PITCHED	STRIKEOUTS
Steve Rogers 158	Tim Burke 425	Steve Rogers 37	Jeff Reardon 152	Steve Rogers 2839.1	Steve Rogers 1621
Bryn Smith 81	Steve Rogers 399	Bill Stoneman 15	Tim Burke 101	Bryn Smith 1400.1	Bryn Smith 838
Bill Gullickson 72	Jeff Reardon 359	Dennis Martinez 13	Mike Marshall 75	Steve Renko 1360.0	Bill Stoneman 831
Dennis Martinez 69	Woodie Fryman 297	Woodie Fryman 8	Woodie Fryman 52	Bill Gullickson 1186.0	Steve Renko 810
Steve Renko 68	Bryn Smith 284	Charlie Lea 8	Dale Murray 33	Dennis Martinez 1158.0	Dennis Martinez 688
		Scott Sanderson 8			
		Bryn Smith 8			

METS

WINS	GAMES	SHUTOUTS	SAVES	INNINGS PITCHED	STRIKEOUTS
Tom Seaver 198	Tom Seaver 401	Tom Seaver 44	Jesse Orosco 107	Tom Seaver 3045.0	Tom Seaver 2541
Jerry Koosman 140	Jerry Koosman 376	Jerry Koosman 26	Tug McGraw 86	Jerry Koosman 2545.0	Jerry Koosman 1799
Dwight Gooden 132	Jesse Orosco 372	Jon Matlack 26	Roger McDowell 84	Dwight Gooden 1713.2	Dwight Gooden 1541
Ron Darling 99	Tug McGraw 361	Dwight Gooden 21	Neil Allen 69	Ron Darling 1620.0	Sid Fernandez 1175
Jon Matlack 82	Roger McDowell 280	3 tied 10	Skip Lockwood 65	Jon Matlack 1448.0	Ron Darling 1148

PHILLIES

WINS	GAMES	SHUTOUTS	SAVES	INNINGS PITCHED	STRIKEOUTS
Steve Carlton 241	Robin Roberts 529	Grover Alexander 61	Steve Bedrosian 103	Robin Roberts 3740.0	Steve Carlton 3031
Robin Roberts 234	Steve Carlton 499	Steve Carlton 39	Tug McGraw 94	Steve Carlton 3696.1	Robin Roberts 1871
Grover Alexander 190	Tug McGraw 463	Robin Roberts 35	Ron Reed 90	Grover Alexander 2513.0	Chris Short 1585
Chris Short 132	Chris Short 459	Chris Short 24	Dick Farrell 65	Chris Short 2252.0	Grover Alexander 1409
Curt Simmons 115	Ron Reed 458	Jim Bunning 23	Jack Baldschun 59	Curt Simmons 1939.0	Jim Bunning 1197

PIRATES

WINS	GAMES	SHUTOUTS	SAVES	INNINGS PITCHED	STRIKEOUTS
Wilbur Cooper 202	ElRoy Face 802	Babe Adams 47	Roy Face 188	Bob Friend 3481.0	Bob Friend 1682
Sam Leever 194	Kent Tekulve 722	Sam Leever 39	Kent Tekulve 158	Wilbur Cooper 3201.0	Bob Veale 1652
Babe Adams 194	Bob Friend 568	Bob Friend 35	Dave Giusti 133	Babe Adams 2991.0	Wilbur Cooper 1191
Bob Friend 191	Vernon Law 483	Wilbur Cooper 34	Al McBean 59	Vernon Law 2673.0	John Candelaria 1142
Deacon Phillippe 165	Babe Adams 481	Lefty Leifield 29	Bill Landrum 56	Sam Leever 2645.0	Vernon Law 1092

CARDINALS

WINS	GAMES	SHUTOUTS	SAVES	INNINGS PITCHED	STRIKEOUTS
Bob Gibson 251	Jesse Haines 554	Bob Gibson 56	Bruce Sutter 127	Bob Gibson 3885.0	Bob Gibson 3117
Jesse Haines 210	Bob Gibson 528	Bill Doak 32	Todd Worrell 126	Jesse Haines 3203.0	Dizzy Dean 1087
Bob Forsch 163	Bill Sherdel 465	Mort Cooper 28	Lee Smith 74	Bob Forsch 2659.0	Bob Forsch 1079
Bill Sherdel 153	Bob Forsch 455	Harry Brecheen 25	Lindy McDaniel 64	Bill Sherdel 2450.0	Jesse Haines 979
Bill Doak 145	Al Brazle 441	Jesse Haines 24	Joe Hoerner 60	Bill Doak 2387.0	Steve Carlton 951
			Al Brazle 60		

PADRES

WINS	GAMES	SHUTOUTS	SAVES	INNINGS PITCHED	STRIKEOUTS
Eric Show 100	Craig Lefferts 348	Randy Jones 18	Rollie Fingers 108	Randy Jones 1765.0	Eric Show 951
Randy Jones 92	Eric Show 309	Steve Arlin 11	Rich Gossage 83	Eric Show 1603.1	Clay Kirby 802
Ed Whitson 77	Rollie Fingers 265	Eric Show 11	Mark Davis 74	Ed Whitson 1354.1	Ed Whitson 767
Andy Hawkins 60	Randy Jones 264	Andy Hawkins 7	Craig Lefferts 64	Clay Kirby 1129.0	Randy Jones 677
Dave Dravecky 53	Dave Tomlin 239	Clay Kirby 7	Gary Lucas 49	Andy Hawkins 1102.2	Andy Hawkins 489

GIANTS

WINS	GAMES	SHUTOUTS	SAVES	INNINGS PITCHED	STRIKEOUTS
Christy Mathewson 372	Gary Lavelle 647	Christy Mathewson 83	Gary Lavelle 127	Christy Mathewson 4772.0	Christy Mathewson 2502
Carl Hubbell 253	Christy Mathewson 634	Juan Marichal 52	Greg Minton 125	Carl Hubbell 3591.0	Juan Marichal 2281
Mickey Welch 243	Greg Minton 552	Carl Hubbell 36	Randy Moffitt 83	Mickey Welch 3579.0	Amos Rusie 1838
Juan Marichal 238	Carl Hubbell 535	Amos Rusie 29	Frank Linzy 78	Amos Rusie 3523.0	Carl Hubbell 1677
Amos Rusie 230	Randy Moffitt 459	Hal Schumacher 29	Marv Grissom 58	Juan Marichal 3443.0	Gaylord Perry 1606
		Hooks Wiltse 29			

YEARLY STRIKEOUT LEADERS

1900—George (Rube) Waddell, Pittsburgh .. 133
1901—Frank (Noodles) Hahn, Cincinnati 233
1902—Victor Willis, Boston 226
1903—Christopher Mathewson, New York 267
1904—Christopher Mathewson, New York 212
1905—Christopher Mathewson, New York 206
1906—Frederick Beebe, Chicago-St. Louis .. 171
1907—Christopher Mathewson, New York 178
1908—Christopher Mathewson, New York 259
1909—Orval Overall, Chicago...................... 205
1910—Christopher Mathewson, New York 190
1911—Richard (Rube) Marquard, New York 237
1912—Grover Alexander, Philadelphia 195
1913—Thomas Seaton, Philadelphia 168
1914—Grover Alexander, Philadelphia 214
1915—Grover Alexander, Philadelphia 241
1916—Grover Alexander, Philadelphia 167
1917—Grover Alexander, Philadelphia 200
1918—James (Hippo) Vaughn, Chicago....... 148
1919—James (Hippo) Vaughn, Chicago....... 141
1920—Grover Alexander, Chicago 173
1921—Burleigh Grimes, Brooklyn................. 136
1922—Arthur (Dazzy) Vance, Brooklyn 134
1923—Arthur (Dazzy) Vance, Brooklyn 197
1924—Arthur (Dazzy) Vance, Brooklyn 262
1925—Arthur (Dazzy) Vance, Brooklyn 221
1926—Arthur (Dazzy) Vance, Brooklyn 140
1927—Arthur (Dazzy) Vance, Brooklyn 184
1928—Arthur (Dazzy) Vance, Brooklyn 200
1929—Perce (Pat) Malone, Chicago 166
1930—William Hallahan, St. Louis 177
1931—William Hallahan, St. Louis 159
1932—Jerome (Dizzy) Dean, St. Louis 191
1933—Jerome (Dizzy) Dean, St. Louis 199
1934—Jerome (Dizzy) Dean, St. Louis 195
1935—Jerome (Dizzy) Dean, St. Louis 182
1936—Van Lingle Mungo, Brooklyn 238
1937—Carl Hubbell, New York 159
1938—Claiborne Bryant, Chicago 135
1939—Claude Passeau, Phila.-Chi. 137
      William (Bucky) Walters, Cincinnati .. 137
1940—W. Kirby Higbe, Philadelphia 137
1941—John Vander Meer, Cincinnati 202
1942—John Vander Meer, Cincinnati 186
1943—John Vander Meer, Cincinnati 174
1944—William Voiselle, New York 161
1945—Elwin (Preacher) Roe, Pittsburgh 148
1946—John Schmitz, Chicago 135
1947—Ewell Blackwell, Cincinnati 193
1948—Harry Brecheen, St. Louis.................. 149
1949—Warren Spahn, Boston 151
1950—Warren Spahn, Boston 191
1951—Warren Spahn, Boston 164
      Donald Newcombe, Brooklyn 164
1952—Warren Spahn, Boston 183
1953—Robin Roberts, Philadelphia 198

1954—Robin Roberts, Philadelphia 185
1955—Samuel Jones, Chicago 198
1956—Samuel Jones, Chicago 176
1957—John Sanford, Philadelphia................. 188
1958—Samuel Jones, St. Louis 225
1959—Donald Drysdale, Los Angeles...........242
1960—Donald Drysdale, Los Angeles...........246
1961—Sanford Koufax, Los Angeles 269
1962—Donald Drysdale, Los Angeles...........232
1963—Sanford Koufax, Los Angeles 306
1964—Robert Veale, Pittsburgh 250
1965—Sanford Koufax, Los Angeles 382
1966—Sanford Koufax, Los Angeles 317
1967—James Bunning, Philadelphia.............253
1968—Robert Gibson, St. Louis 268
1969—Ferguson Jenkins, Chicago 273
1970—G. Thomas Seaver, New York............283
1971—G. Thomas Seaver, New York............289
1972—Steven Carlton, Philadelphia 310
1973—G. Thomas Seaver, New York............251
1974—Steven Carlton, Philadelphia 240
1975—G. Thomas Seaver, New York............243
1976—G. Thomas Seaver, New York............235
1977—Philip Niekro, Atlanta.........................262
1978—James R. Richard, Houston 303
1979—James R. Richard, Houston 313
1980—Steven Carlton, Philadelphia 286
1981—Fernando Valenzuela, Los Angeles..... 180
1982—Steven Carlton, Philadelphia 286
1983—Steven Carlton, Philadelphia 275
1984—Dwight Gooden, New York 276
1985—Dwight Gooden, New York 268
1986—Michael Scott, Houston 306
1987—L. Nolan Ryan, Houston 270
1988—L. Nolan Ryan, Houston 228
1989—Jose DeLeon, St. Louis 201
1990—David Cone, New York 233
1991—David Cone, New York 241

NO-HIT AND ONE-HIT PITCHERS

The following pitchers (on N.L. rosters) have recorded
no-hit or one-hit games in N.L. competition:

NO-HIT GAMES

Tom Browning, Cin. vs. L.A., Sept. 16, 1988 (PERFECT GAME).
John Candelaria, Pitt. vs. L.A., Aug. 9, 1976.
Tommy Greene, Phil. at Mtl., May 23, 1991.
Dennis Martinez, Mtl. at L.A., July 28, 1991 (PERFECT GAME).
Terry Mulholland, Phil. vs. S.F., Aug. 15, 1990.

ONE-HIT GAMES

Reds: Tim Belcher, L.A. at Pitt., July 21, 1990.

Tom Browning (2), Cin. vs. Chi., June 4, 1986; Cin. at S.D., June 6, 1988.

Don Carman, Phil. vs. N.Y., Sept. 29, 1987.

Astros: Jimmy Jones, S.D. vs. Hou., Sept. 21, 1986.

Dodgers: Orel Hershiser (2), L.A. vs. S.D., April 26, 1985; L.A. vs. Pitt., July 23, 1985.

Expos: Chris Nabholz, Mtl. at N.Y., Sept. 20, 1990 (2nd game).

Terry Leach, N.Y. at Phil., Oct. 1, 1982 (10 innings).

Mets: Dwight Gooden, N.Y. vs. Chi., Sept. 7, 1984.

David Cone, N.Y. vs. S.D., Aug. 29, 1988; N.Y. vs. St.L., Sept. 20, 1991.

Pete Schourek, N.Y. vs. Mtl., Sept. 10, 1991.

Pirates: John Smiley (2), Pitt. vs. Mtl., June 3, 1988; Pitt. vs. N.Y., Apr. 17, 1991.

Doug Drabek (2), Pitt. at Phil., Aug. 3, 1990; Pitt. at St.L., May 27, 1991.

Zane Smith (2), Pitt. vs. N.Y., Sept. 5, 1990 (1st game); Pitt. at St.L., May 29, 1991.

Cardinals: Jose DeLeon (2), Pitt. vs. Cin., Aug. 24, 1984 (lost); St.L. vs. Pitt., Sept. 13, 1989 (6 innings).

Joe Magrane, St.L. at Chi., Aug. 12, 1988.

Bob Tewksbury, St.L. vs. Hou., Aug. 17, 1990.

Padres: Bruce Hurst, S.D. vs. Atl., April 10, 1989.

Giants: Trevor Wilson, S.F. at S.D., June 13, 1990.

Scott Garrelts, S.F. vs. Cin., July 29, 1990.

1991 AVERAGE TIME OF 9-INNING GAMES

	AT ATL	AT CHI	AT CIN	AT HOU	AT LA	AT MON	AT NY	AT PHI	AT PIT	AT STL	AT SD	AT SF	Avg. Games
ATLANTA	—	2:40	2:49	2:44	2:55	2:51	2:36	2:47	2:43	2:47	2:40	2:47	2:46
CHICAGO	2:54	—	2:30	2:34	2:57	2:54	2:47	2:43	2:36	2:41	2:51	2:52	2:45
CINCINNATI	2:38	2:46	—	2:35	2:51	2:47	3:05	2:35	2:27	2:32	2:37	2:33	2:40
HOUSTON	2:50	2:43	2:48	—	2:58	2:36	2:48	2:43	2:45	2:45	2:39	2:50	2:47
LOS ANGELES	2:44	2:47	2:53	2:54	—	2:46	3:09	2:54	2:54	2:45	2:48	2:45	2:51
MONTREAL	3:07	2:43	2:48	2:56	2:51	—	3:00	2:45	2:45	2:45	3:01	2:44	2:50
NEW YORK	2:34	2:45	3:07	2:53	3:01	2:43	—	2:41	2:33	2:42	2:41	2:37	2:44
PHILADELPHIA	3:03	2:37	2:33	2:37	2:53	2:27	2:42	—	2:36	2:33	2:31	2:43	2:39
PITTSBURGH	2:52	2:45	2:43	3:09	2:53	2:50	2:46	2:57	—	2:34	2:50	2:41	2:49
ST. LOUIS	2:40	2:35	2:52	2:55	2:58	2:34	2:51	2:42	2:44	—	2:30	2:46	2:44
SAN DIEGO	2:37	2:42	2:54	2:50	2:51	2:41	2:57	2:31	2:43	2:34	—	2:40	2:44
SAN FRANCISCO	2:56	2:41	2:36	2:55	2:58	2:54	2:55	2:50	2:40	2:44	2:37	—	2:48
Average Home Games	2:49	2:42	2:47	2:49	2:55	2:44	2:52	2:45	2:40	2:40	2:42	2:44	2:46
Average Home & Road	2:47	2:43	2:44	2:48	2:53	2:48	2:48	2:42	2:44	2:42	2:43	2:46	2:46

LEAGUE LEADER WON AND LOST PERCENTAGE
(15 or More Decisions)

Year	Pitcher, Club	W-L	Pct.
1901	Sam Leever, Pittsburgh	14- 5	.774
1902	Jack Chesbro, Pittsburgh	28- 6	.824
1903	Sam Leever, Pittsburgh	25- 7	.781
1904	Joe McGinnity, New York	35- 8	.814
1905	Sam Leever, Pittsburgh	20- 5	.800
1906	Ed Ruelbach, Chicago	19- 4	.826
1907	Ed Ruelbach, Chicago	17- 4	.810
1908	Ed Ruelbach, Chicago	24- 7	.774
1909	Howie Camnitz, Pittsburgh	25- 6	.806
	Christy Mathewson, New York	25- 6	.806
1910	Deacon Phillippe, Pittsburgh	14- 2	.875
1911	Rube Marquard, New York	24- 7	.774
1912	Claude Hendrix, Pittsburgh	24- 9	.727
1913	Bert Humphries, Chicago	16- 4	.800
1914	Bill James, Boston	26- 7	.788
1915	Grover Alexander, Philadelphia	31-10	.756
1916	Tom Hughes, Boston	16- 3	.842
1917	Ferdie Schupp, New York	21- 7	.750
1918	Claude Hendrix, Chicago	20- 7	.741
1919	Dutch Ruether, Cincinnati	19- 6	.760
1920	Burleigh Grimes, Brooklyn	23-11	.676
1921	Babe Adams, Pittsburgh	14- 5	.737
	Whitey Glazner, Pittsburgh	14- 5	.737
1922	Phil Douglas, New York	11- 4	.733
1923	Dolf Luque, Cincinnati	27- 8	.771
1924	Emil Yde, Pittsburgh	16- 3	.842
1925	Bill Sherdel, St. Louis	15- 6	.714
1926	Ray Kremer, Pittsburgh	20- 6	.769
1927	Larry Benton, New York	17- 7	.708
1928	Larry Benton, New York	25- 9	.735
1929	Charlie Root, Chicago	19- 6	.760
1930	Freddie Fitzsimmons, New York	19- 7	.731
1931	Jesse Haines, St. Louis	12- 3	.800
1932	Lon Warneke, Chicago	22- 6	.786
1933	Bud Tinning, Chicago	13- 6	.684
1934	Dizzy Dean, St. Louis	30- 7	.811
1935	Bill Lee, Chicago	20- 6	.769
1936	Carl Hubbell, New York	26- 6	.813
1937	Carl Hubbell, New York	22- 8	.733
1938	Bill Lee, Chicago	22- 9	.710
1939	Paul Derringer, Cincinnati	25- 7	.781
1940	Freddie Fitzsimmons, Brooklyn	16- 2	.889
1941	Elmer Riddle, Cincinnati	19- 4	.826
1942	Howie Krist, St. Louis	13- 3	.813
1943	Clyde Shoun, Cincinnati	14- 5	.737
	Whit Wyatt, Brooklyn	14- 5	.737
1944	Ted Wilks, St. Louis	17- 4	.810
1945	Harry Brecheen, St. Louis	15- 4	.789
1946	Schoolboy Rowe, Philadelphia	11- 4	.733
1947	Larry Jansen, New York	21- 5	.808
1948	Rip Sewell, Pittsburgh	13- 3	.813
1949	Ralph Branca, Brooklyn	13- 5	.722
1950	Sal Maglie, New York	18- 4	.818
1951	Preacher Roe, Brooklyn	22- 3	.880
1952	Hoyt Wilhelm, New York	15- 3	.833
1953	Carl Erskine, Brooklyn	20- 6	.769
1954	John Antonelli, New York	21- 7	.750
	Hoyt Wilhelm, New York	12- 4	.750
1955	Don Newcombe, Brooklyn	20- 5	.800
1956	Don Newcombe, Brooklyn	27- 7	.794
1957	Bob Buhl, Milwaukee	18- 7	.720
1958	Warren Spahn, Milwaukee	20-10	.667
	Lew Burdette, Milwaukee	20-10	.667
1959	ElRoy Face, Pittsburgh	18- 1	.947
1960	Lindy McDaniel, St. Louis	12- 4	.750
1961	John Podres, Los Angeles	18- 5	.783
1962	Bob Purkey, Cincinnati	23- 5	.821
1963	Ron Perranoski, Los Angeles	16- 3	.842
1964	Sandy Koufax, Los Angeles	19- 5	.792
1965	Sandy Koufax, Los Angeles	26- 8	.765
1966	Phil Regan, Los Angeles	14- 1	.933
1967	Nelson Briles, St. Louis	14- 5	.737
1968	Steve Blass, Pittsburgh	18- 6	.750
1969	Bob Moose, Pittsburgh	14- 3	.824
1970	Wayne Simpson, Cincinnati	14- 3	.824
1971	Tug McGraw, New York	11- 4	.733
1972	Gary Nolan, Cincinnati	15- 5	.750
1973	George Stone, New York	12- 3	.800
1974	Tommy John, Los Angeles	13- 3	.813
1975	Al Hrabosky, St. Louis	13- 3	.813
1976	Rick Rhoden, Los Angeles	12- 3	.800
1977	John Candelaria, Pittsburgh	20- 5	.800
1978	Gaylord Perry, San Diego	21- 6	.778
1979	Jim Bibby, Pittsburgh	12- 4	.750
1980	Jim Bibby, Pittsburgh	19- 6	.760
1981	Tom Seaver, Cincinnati	14- 2	.875
1982	Phil Niekro, Atlanta	17- 4	.810
1983	John Denny, Philadelphia	19- 6	.760
1984	Rick Sutcliffe, Chicago	16- 1	.941
1985	Orel Hershiser, Los Angeles	19- 3	.864
1986	Bob Ojeda, New York	18- 5	.783
1987	Dennis Martinez, Montreal	11- 4	.733
1988	David Cone, New York	20- 3	.870
1989	Sid Fernandez, New York	14- 5	.737
	Scott Garrelts, San Francisco	14- 5	.737
1990	Doug Drabek, Pittsburgh	22- 6	.786
1991	John Smiley, Pittsburgh	20- 8	.714
	Jose Rijo, Cincinnati	15- 6	.714

1991 LOW-RUN GAMES BY PITCHING STAFF

Club	Shutouts	1-Run	2-Run	Total
Atlanta	7	30	38	75
Los Angeles	14	23	27	64
St. Louis	5	30	26	61
Montreal	14	19	25	58
San Diego	11	19	26	56
Pittsburgh	11	25	19	55
New York	11	23	20	54
Philadelphia	11	15	25	51
San Francisco	10	17	22	49
Cincinnati	11	18	19	48
Houston	13	17	15	45
Chicago	4	14	21	39

1991 LOW-RUN COMPLETE GAMES

Pitcher and Club	Shutouts	1-Run	2-Run	Total
Martinez, D., Montreal	5	2	1	8
Mulholland, T., Philadelphia	3	4	0	7
Glavine, T., Atlanta	1	4	2	7
Martinez, R., Los Angeles	4	2	0	6
Smith, Z., Pittsburgh	3	2	0	5
Cone, D., New York	2	2	1	5
Morgan, M., Los Angeles	1	2	2	5
Smoltz, J., Atlanta	0	2	3	5
Harnisch, P., Houston	2	2	0	4
Maddux, G., Chicago	2	1	1	4
Castillo, F., Chicago	0	2	2	4
Hurst, B., San Diego	0	0	4	4
Black Jr., B., San Francisco	3	0	0	3
Tomlin, R., Pittsburgh	2	1	0	3
Harris, G., San Diego	2	1	0	3
Drabek, D., Pittsburgh	2	1	0	3
Benes, A., San Diego	1	2	0	3
Avery, S., Atlanta	1	2	0	3
Tewksbury, B., St. Louis	0	2	1	3
Smith, B., St. Louis	0	2	1	3
Greene, T., Philadelphia	2	0	0	2
Smiley, J., Pittsburgh	1	1	0	2
Gooden, D., New York	1	1	0	2
Burkett, J., San Francisco	1	1	0	2
Belcher, T., Los Angeles	1	1	0	2
Wilson, T., San Francisco	1	0	1	2
Ojeda, B., Los Angeles	1	0	1	2
Viola, F., New York	0	1	1	2
DeJesus, J., Philadelphia	0	1	1	2
Cormier, R., St. Louis	0	1	1	2
Schourek, P., New York	1	0	0	1
Ruffin, B., Philadelphia	1	0	0	1
Rijo, J., Cincinnati	1	0	0	1
Remlinger, M., San Francisco	1	0	0	1
Rasmussen, D., San Diego	1	0	0	1
Palacios, V., Pittsburgh	1	0	0	1
Leibrandt, C., Atlanta	1	0	0	1
Jones, J., Houston	1	0	0	1
Boyd, D., Montreal	1	0	0	1
Portugal, M., Houston	0	1	0	1
Nabholz, C., Montreal	0	1	0	1
McClellan, P., San Francisco	0	1	0	1
Gross, K., Cincinnati	0	1	0	1
DeLeon, J., St. Louis	0	1	0	1
Combs, P., Philadelphia	0	1	0	1
Deshaies, J., Houston	0	0	1	1
Barnes, B., Montreal	0	0	1	1
Armstrong, J., Cincinnati	0	0	1	1

FEWEST WALKS PER 9 INNINGS

1.1	Smith, Pit.
1.8	Tewksbury, St.L.
1.9	Mulholland, Phi.
1.9	Smiley, Pit.
2.0	B. Smith, St.L.
2.1	Viola, N.Y.
2.2	Browning, Cin.
2.2	Leibrandt, Atl.
2.3	Maddux, Chi.
2.3	Morgan, L.A.

STRIKEOUTS PER 9 INNINGS

9.3	Cone, N.Y.
7.6	Rijo, Cin.
7.1	Harnisch, Hou.
7.1	Gooden, N.Y.
7.0	Glavine, Atl.
6.8	Maddux, Chi.
6.7	Benes, S.D.
6.7	Belcher, L.A.
6.7	Greene, Phi.
6.5	DeLeon, St.L.

OPPONENTS BATTING AVERAGE AGAINST

.212	Harnisch, Hou.
.219	Rijo, Cin.
.222	Glavine, Atl.
.224	Hill, St.L.
.224	DeJesus, Phi.
.226	De. Martinez, Mon.
.226	Morgan, L.A.
.229	Martinez, L.A.
.230	Gardner, Mon.
.230	Greene, Phi.

LIFETIME SHUTOUTS

Active N.L. pitchers for 1992 and those
pitching N.L. shutouts in 1991
(A.L. shutouts in parentheses)

Player	Club	Total
Orel Hershiser	Dodgers	23
Dennis Martinez	Expos (10)	23
Dwight Gooden	Mets	21
Bruce Hurst	Padres (13)	19
Charlie Leibrandt	Braves (10)	16
Bob Ojeda	Dodgers (5)	15
Bret Saberhagen	Mets (14)	14
John Candelaria	Dodgers (4)	13
Tim Belcher	Reds	12
Doug Drabek	Pirates	12
Danny Jackson	Cubs (6)	12
Ed Whitson	Padres (3)	12
Bud Black	Giants (8)	11
Tom Browning	Reds	11
Jim Clancy	Cubs (11)	11
Kevin Gross	Dodgers	11
Zane Smith	Pirates	11
Oil Can Boyd	Expos (6)	10
David Cone	Mets	10
Joe Magrane	Cardinals	10
Greg Maddux	Cubs	9
Ramon Martinez	Dodgers	9
Tom Candiotti	Dodgers (8)	8
Mike Morgan	Cubs (3)	8
Bryn Smith	Cardinals	8
Jose DeLeon	Cardinals	7
Alejandro Pena	Braves	7
Greg Swindell	Reds (7)	7
Kelly Downs	Giants	6
Sid Fernandez	Mets	6
Atlee Hammaker	Padres	6
Neal Heaton	Pirates (5)	6
Terry Mulholland	Phillies	6
Bob Walk	Pirates	6
Danny Cox	Phillies	5
Tom Glavine	Braves	5
Scott Garrelts	Giants	4
Dennis Rasmussen	Padres (1)	4
Scott Bankhead	Reds (3)	3
Mike Bielecki	Braves	3
Pat Combs	Phillies	3
Mark Gardner	Expos	3
Jim Gott	Dodgers (3)	3
Tommy Greene	Phillies	3
Jimmy Jones	Astros	3
Terry Leach	Expos	3
Ted Power	Reds (2)	3
Jose Rijo	Reds	3
Bruce Ruffin	Phillies	3
John Smiley	Pirates	3
Pete Smith	Braves	3
Bob Tewksbury	Cardinals	3
Trevor Wilson	Giants	3
Steve Avery	Braves	2
Jeff Ballard	Cardinals (2)	2
Juan Berenguer	Braves (2)	2
Pete Harnisch	Astros	2
Greg W. Harris	Padres	2
Jamie Moyer	Cubs	2
Dave Righetti	Giants (2)	2
John Smoltz	Braves	2
Randy Tomlin	Pirates	2
Andy Benes	Padres	1
John Burkett	Giants	1
Norm Charlton	Reds	1
Jose DeJesus	Phillies	1
Mike Harkey	Cubs	1
Mike Hartley	Phillies	1
Ken Hill	Expos	1
Ken Howell	Phillies	1
Les Lancaster	Cubs	1
Mike Maddux	Padres	1
Greg Mathews	Cardinals	1
Bob McClure	Cardinals (1)	1
Chris Nabholz	Expos	1
Vicente Palacios	Pirates	1
Mark Portugal	Astros	1
Rick Reed	Pirates	1
Mike Remlinger	Giants	1
Pete Schourek	Mets	1
Bill Swift	Giants (1)	1

1991 SHUTOUTS BY PITCHING STAFF

Club	Shutouts
Los Angeles	14
Montreal	14
Houston	13
Cincinnati	11
New York	11
Philadelphia	11
Pittsburgh	11
San Diego	11
San Francisco	10
Atlanta	7
St. Louis	5
Chicago	4

NATIONAL LEAGUE SHUTOUT FACTS

Most Shutouts, Season—185-(1968)
Most Extra-Inning Shutouts, Season—12-(1976)
Fewest Shutouts, Season—48-(1925)
Most Shutouts, One Day—5-July 13, 1888 (6 games);
June 24, 1892 (8 games); July 21, 1896 (7 games); July
8, 1907 (5 games); Sept. 7, 1908 (8 games); Sept. 9,
1916 (7 games); May 31, 1943 (8 games); June 17, 1969
(9 games); Aug. 9, 1984 (6 games)
Most Shutouts, One Day, Both Leagues—8-June 4, 1972—
5 in A.L. (9 games), 3 in N.L. (7 games)

1991 NATIONAL LEAGUE SHUTOUTS

Individual

Dennis Martinez, Expos		5
Ramon Martinez, Dodgers		4
Bud Black, Giants		3
Terry Mulholland, Phillies		3
Zane Smith, Pirates		3
David Cone, Mets		2
Doug Drabek, Pirates		2
Tommy Greene, Phillies		2
Pete Harnisch, Astros		2
Greg Harris, Padres		2
Greg Maddux, Cubs		2
Randy Tomlin, Pirates		2
Steve Avery, Braves		1
Tim Belcher, Dodgers		1
Andy Benes, Padres		1
Dennis Boyd, Expos		1
John Burkett, Giants		1
Tom Glavine, Braves		1
Dwight Gooden, Mets		1
Jimmy Jones, Astros		1
Charlie Leibrandt, Braves		1
Mike Morgan, Dodgers		1
Bob Ojeda, Dodgers		1
Vicente Palacios, Pirates		1
Dennis Rasmussen, Padres		1
Mike Remlinger, Giants		1
Jose Rijo, Reds		1
Bruce Ruffin, Phillies		1
Pete Schourek, Mets		1
John Smiley, Pirates		1
Trevor Wilson, Giants		1

Combined

Pitchers	Club	SHO
Harnisch-Schilling	Astros	2
De. Martinez-Jones-Ruskin	Expos	2
Benes-Lefferts	Padres	2
Mercker-Wohlers-Pena	Braves	1
Smoltz-Bielecki	Braves	1
Smoltz-Stanton	Braves	1
Smoltz-Stanton-Berenguer	Braves	1
Bielecki-Assenmacher	Cubs	1
Maddux-D. Smith	Cubs	1
Armstrong-Power-Dibble	Reds	1
Browning-Dibble	Reds	1
Browning-Myers	Reds	1
Charlton-Myers	Reds	1
Gross-Dibble	Reds	1
Hammond-Myers-Dibble	Reds	1
Rijo-Charlton-Foster	Reds	1
Rijo-Hill	Reds	1
Rijo-Power	Reds	1
Scudder-Charlton-Power	Reds	1
Bowen-Mallicoat-Osuna	Astros	1
Deshaies-Clancy	Astros	1
Gardner-Mallicoat-Hernandez	Astros	1
Harnisch-Schilling-Mallicoat-Hernandez	Astros	1
Jones-Osuna-Henry	Astros	1
Kile-Mallicoat-Hernandez	Astros	1
Kile-Osuna-Schilling-Henry	Astros	1
Portugal-Osuna	Astros	1
Belcher-Candelaria-Howell	Dodgers	1
Belcher-Crews	Dodgers	1
Cook-Crews-Wilson-Christopher-Howell	Dodgers	1
Hershiser-Gross-Howell	Dodgers	1
Martinez-Wilson-McDowell	Dodgers	1
Ojeda-Candelaria-Crews	Dodgers	1
Ojeda-Gross-McDowell	Dodgers	1
Barnes-Jones	Expos	1
Gardner-Jones	Expos	1
Gardner-Rojas-Fassero	Expos	1
Haney-Fassero	Expos	1
Mahler-Jones-Ruskin	Expos	1
Sampen-Jones	Expos	1
Cone-Franco	Mets	1
Darling-Pena	Mets	1
Fernandez-Pena	Mets	1
Gooden-Franco	Mets	1
Gooden-Schourek-Burke	Mets	1
Viola-Franco	Mets	1
Whitehurst-Innis-Pena	Mets	1
Combs-McDowell-Boever-Greene	Phillies	1
DeJesus-Boever	Phillies	1
Greene-Ritchie-Williams	Phillies	1
Mulholland-Boever	Phillies	1
Ruffin-Williams	Phillies	1
Drabek-Patterson-Belinda-Landrum	Pirates	1
Smiley-Tomlin-Landrum	Pirates	1
Hill-McClure-Torry L. Smith	Cardinals	1
Hill-L. Smith	Cardinals	1
B. Smith-Agosto	Cardinals	1
B. Smith-Carpenter-L. Smith	Cardinals	1
Tewksbury-Fraser-L. Smith	Cardinals	1
Bones-Lewis-Rodriguez	Padres	1
Hurst-Andersen-Maddux	Padres	1
Hurst-Maddux	Padres	1
Maddux-Costello-Rodriguez	Padres	1
Rasmussen-Andersen-Rodriguez	Padres	1
Black-Righetti	Giants	1
LaCoss-Righetti	Giants	1
McClellan-Oliveras-Righetti	Giants	1
Wilson-Oliveras-Righetti-Brantley	Giants	1

1901

Bill Donovan, Dodgers	25 - 15
Deacon Phillippe, Pirates	22 - 12
Noodles Hahn, Reds	22 - 19
Jack Chesbro, Pirates	21 - 9
John Powell, Cardinals	21 - 20
Charles Harper, Cardinals	20 - 12
Al Orth, Phillies	20 - 12
Frank Donahue, Phillies	20 - 13
Charles Nichols, Braves	20 - 14
Christy Mathewson, Giants	20 - 17

1902

Jack Chesbro, Pirates	28 - 6
Charles Pittinger, Braves	27 - 14
Vic Willis, Braves	27 - 19
Noodles Hahn, Reds	22 - 12
Jack Taylor, Cubs	22 - 10
*Joe McGinnity, Balt.-Giants	21 - 18
Jess Tannehill, Pirates	20 - 6
Deacon Phillippe, Pirates	20 - 9

1903

Joe McGinnity, Giants	31 - 20
Christy Mathewson, Giants	30 - 13
Sam Leever, Pirates	25 - 7
Deacon Phillippe, Pirates	25 - 9
Noodles Hahn, Reds	22 - 12
Henry Schmidt, Dodgers	22 - 13
Jack Taylor, Cubs	21 - 14
Jake Weimer, Cubs	20 - 8
Bob Wicker, Cubs	20 - 9

1904

Joe McGinnity, Giants	35 - 8
Christy Mathewson, Giants	33 - 12
Charles Harper, Reds	23 - 9
Charles Nichols, Cardinals	21 - 13
Luther Taylor, Giants	21 - 15
Jake Weimer, Cubs	20 - 14
Jack Taylor, Cardinals	20 - 19

1905

Christy Mathewson, Giants	31 - 9
Charles Pittinger, Phillies	23 - 14
Leon Ames, Giants	22 - 8
Joe McGinnity, Giants	21 - 15
Sam Leever, Pirates	20 - 5
Bob Ewing, Reds	20 - 11
Deacon Phillippe, Pirates	20 - 13
Irving Young, Braves	20 - 21

1906

Joe McGinnity, Giants	27 - 12
Mordecai Brown, Cubs	26 - 6
Vic Willis, Pirates	23 - 13
Sam Leever, Pirates	22 - 7
Christy Mathewson, Giants	22 - 12
John Pfiester, Cubs	20 - 8
Jack Taylor, Cards-Cubs	20 - 12
Jake Weimer, Reds	20 - 14

1907

Christy Mathewson, Giants	24 - 12
Orval Overall, Cubs	23 - 8
Frank Sparks, Phillies	22 - 8
Vic Willis, Pirates	21 - 11
Mordecai Brown, Cubs	20 - 6
Al Leifield, Pirates	20 - 16

1908

Christy Mathewson, Giants	37 - 11
Mordecai Brown, Cubs	29 - 9
Ed Reulbach, Cubs	24 - 7
Nick Maddox, Pirates	23 - 8
Vic Willis, Pirates	23 - 11
George Wiltse, Giants	23 - 14
George McQuillan, Phillies	23 - 17

1909

Mordecai Brown, Cubs	27 - 9
Christy Mathewson, Giants	25 - 6
Howard Camnitz, Pirates	25 - 6
Vic Willis, Pirates	22 - 11
Orval Overall, Cubs	20 - 11
George Wiltse, Giants	20 - 11

1910

Christy Mathewson, Giants	27 - 9
Mordecai Brown, Cubs	25 - 14
Earl Moore, Phillies	22 - 15
Leonard Cole, Cubs	20 - 4
George Suggs, Reds	20 - 12

1911

Grover Alexander, Phillies	28 - 13
Christy Mathewson, Giants	26 - 13
Rube Marquard, Giants	24 - 7
Bob Harmon, Cardinals	23 - 16
Babe Adams, Pirates	22 - 12
Nap Rucker, Dodgers	22 - 18
Mordecai Brown, Cubs	21 - 11
Howard Camnitz, Pirates	20 - 15

1912

Larry Cheney, Cubs	26 - 10
Rube Marquard, Giants	26 - 11
Claude Hendrix, Pirates	24 - 9
Christy Mathewson, Giants	23 - 12
Howard Camnitz, Pirates	22 - 12

1913

Tom Seaton, Phillies	27 - 12
Christy Mathewson, Giants	25 - 11
Rube Marquard, Giants	23 - 10
Grover Alexander, Phillies	22 - 8
Jeff Tesreau, Giants	22 - 13
Babe Adams, Pirates	21 - 10
Larry Cheney, Cubs	21 - 14

1914

Dick Rudolph, Braves	27 - 10
Grover Alexander, Phillies	27 - 15
Bill James, Braves	26 - 7
Jeff Tesreau, Giants	26 - 10
Christy Mathewson, Giants	24 - 13
Ed Pfeffer, Dodgers	23 - 12
Jim Vaughn, Cubs	21 - 13
Erskine Mayer, Phillies	21 - 19
Larry Cheney, Cubs	20 - 18

1915

Grover Alexander, Phillies	31 - 10
Dick Rudolph, Braves	22 - 19
Al Mamaux, Pirates	21 - 8
Erskine Mayer, Phillies	21 - 15
Jim Vaughn, Cubs	20 - 12

1916

Grover Alexander, Phillies	33 - 12
Ed Pfeffer, Dodgers	25 - 11
Eppa Rixey, Phillies	22 - 10
Al Mamaux, Pirates	21 - 15

1917

Grover Alexander, Phillies	30 - 13
Fred Toney, Reds	24 - 16
Jim Vaughn, Cubs	23 - 13
Ferdie Schupp, Giants	21 - 7
Pete Schneider, Reds	20 - 19

1918

Jim Vaughn, Cubs	22 - 10
Claude Hendrix, Cubs	20 - 7

1919

Jess Barnes, Giants	25 - 9
Slim Sallee, Reds	21 - 7
Jim Vaughn, Cubs	21 - 14

1920

Grover Alexander, Cubs	27 - 14
Wilbur Cooper, Pirates	24 - 15
Burleigh Grimes, Dodgers	23 - 11
Fred Toney, Giants	21 - 11
Art Nehf, Giants	21 - 12
Jess Barnes, Giants	20 - 15
Bill Doak, Cardinals	20 - 12

1921

Burleigh Grimes, Dodgers	22 - 13
Wilbur Cooper, Pirates	22 - 14
Art Nehf, Giants	20 - 10
Joe Oeschger, Braves	20 - 14

1922

Eppa Rixey, Reds	25 - 13
Wilbur Cooper, Pirates	23 - 14
Dutch Ruether, Dodgers	21 - 12

1923

Adolfo Luque, Reds	27 - 8
John Morrison, Pirates	25 - 13
Grover Alexander, Cubs	22 - 12
Pete Donohue, Reds	21 - 15
Burleigh Grimes, Dodgers	21 - 18
Jesse Haines, Cardinals	20 - 13
Eppa Rixey, Reds	20 - 15

1924

Dazzy Vance, Dodgers	28 - 6
Burleigh Grimes, Dodgers	22 - 13
Carl Mays, Reds	20 - 9
Wilbur Cooper, Pirates	20 - 14

1925

Dazzy Vance, Dodgers	22 - 9
Eppa Rixey, Reds	21 - 11
Pete Donohue, Reds	21 - 14

1926

Remy Kremer, Pirates	20 - 6
Flint Rhem, Cardinals	20 - 7
Lee Meadows, Pirates	20 - 9
Pete Donohue, Reds	20 - 14

1927

Charles Root, Cubs	26 - 15
Jesse Haines, Cardinals	24 - 10
Carmen Hill, Pirates	22 - 11
Grover Alexander, Cardinals	21 - 10

1928

Larry Benton, Giants	25 - 9
Burleigh Grimes, Pirates	25 - 14
Dazzy Vance, Dodgers	22 - 10
Bill Sherdel, Cardinals	21 - 10
Jesse Haines, Cardinals	20 - 8
Fred Fitzsimmons, Giants	20 - 9

1929

Pat Malone, Cubs	22 - 10

1930

Pat Malone, Cubs	20 - 9
Remy Kremer, Pirates	20 - 12

1931

—None—

1932

Lon Warneke, Cubs	22 - 6
Watson Clark, Dodgers	20 - 12

1933

Carl Hubbell, Giants	23 - 12
Guy Bush, Cubs	20 - 12
Ben Cantwell, Braves	20 - 10
Dizzy Dean, Cardinals	20 - 18

1934

Dizzy Dean, Cardinals	30 - 7
Hal Schumacher, Giants	23 - 10
Lon Warneke, Cubs	22 - 10
Carl Hubbell, Giants	21 - 12

1935

Dizzy Dean, Cardinals	28 - 12
Carl Hubbell, Giants	23 - 12
Paul Derringer, Reds	22 - 13
Bill Lee, Cubs	20 - 6
Lon Warneke, Cubs	20 - 13

1936

Carl Hubbell, Giants	26 - 6
Dizzy Dean, Cardinals	24 - 13

1937

Carl Hubbell, Giants	22 - 8
Cliff Melton, Giants	20 - 9
Lou Fette, Braves	20 - 10
Jim Turner, Braves	20 - 11

1938

Bill Lee, Cubs	22 - 9
Paul Derringer, Reds	21 - 14

1939

Bucky Walters, Reds	27 - 11
Paul Derringer, Reds	25 - 7
Curt Davis, Cardinals	22 - 16
Luke Hamlin, Dodgers	20 - 13

1940

Bucky Walters, Reds	22 - 10
Paul Derringer, Reds	20 - 12
Claude Passeau, Cubs	20 - 13

1941

J. Whitlow Wyatt, Dodgers	22 - 10
Kirby Higbe, Dodgers	22 - 9

20 GAME WINNERS 1901—1991 (Continued)

1942

Mort Cooper, Cardinals	22 - 7
John Beazley, Cardinals	21 - 6

1943

Mort Cooper, Cardinals	21 - 8
Truett Sewell, Pirates	21 - 9
Elmer Riddle, Reds	21 - 11

1944

Bucky Walters, Reds	23 - 8
Mort Cooper, Cardinals	22 - 7
Truett Sewell, Pirates	21 - 12
Bill Voiselle, Giants	21 - 16

1945

Chas. Barrett, Braves-Cards	23 - 12
Hank Wyse, Cubs	22 - 10
†Hank Borowy, Yanks-Cubs	21 - 7

1946

**Howard Pollet, Cardinals	21 - 10
Johnny Sain, Braves	20 - 14

1947

Ewell Blackwell, Reds	22 - 8
Warren Spahn, Braves	21 - 10
Johnny Sain, Braves	21 - 12
Ralph Branca, Dodgers	21 - 12
Larry Jansen, Giants	21 - 5

1948

Johnny Sain, Braves	24 - 15
Harry Brecheen, Cardinals	20 - 7

1949

Warren Spahn, Braves	21 - 14
Howard Pollet, Cardinals	20 - 9

1950

Warren Spahn, Braves	21 - 17
Robin Roberts, Phillies	20 - 11
Johnny Sain, Braves	20 - 13

1951

**Larry Jansen, Giants	23 - 11
Sal Maglie, Giants	23 - 6
Preacher Roe, Dodgers	22 - 3
Warren Spahn, Braves	22 - 14
Robin Roberts, Phillies	21 - 15
Don Newcombe, Dodgers	20 - 9
Murry Dickson, Pirates	20 - 16

1952

Robin Roberts, Phillies	28 - 7

1953

Warren Spahn, Braves	23 - 7
Robin Roberts, Phillies	23 - 16
Carl Erskine, Dodgers	20 - 6
Harvey Haddix, Cardinals	20 - 9

1954

Robin Roberts, Phillies	23 - 15
John Antonelli, Giants	21 - 7
Warren Spahn, Braves	21 - 12

1955

Robin Roberts, Phillies	23 - 14
Don Newcombe, Dodgers	20 - 5

1956

Don Newcombe, Dodgers	27 - 7
Warren Spahn, Braves	20 - 11
John Antonelli, Giants	20 - 13

1957

Warren Spahn, Braves	21 - 11

1958

Warren Spahn, Braves	22 - 11
Bob Friend, Pirates	22 - 14
Lew Burdette, Braves	20 - 10

1959

Lew Burdette, Braves	21 - 15
Sam Jones, Giants	21 - 15
Warren Spahn, Braves	21 - 15

1960

Ernie Broglio, Cardinals	21 - 9
Warren Spahn, Braves	21 - 10
Vernon Law, Pirates	20 - 9

1961

Joey Jay, Reds	21 - 10
Warren Spahn, Braves	21 - 13

1962

Don Drysdale, Dodgers	25 - 9
Jack Sanford, Giants	24 - 7
Bob Purkey, Reds	23 - 5
Joey Jay, Reds	21 - 14

1963

Sandy Koufax, Dodgers	25 - 5
Juan Marichal, Giants	25 - 8
Warren Spahn, Braves	23 - 7
Jim Maloney, Reds	23 - 7
Dick Ellsworth, Cubs	22 - 10

1964

Larry Jackson, Cubs	24 - 11
Juan Marichal, Giants	21 - 8
Ray Sadecki, Cardinals	20 - 11

1965

Sandy Koufax, Dodgers	26 - 8
Tony Cloninger, Braves	24 - 11
Don Drysdale, Dodgers	23 - 12
Sammy Ellis, Reds	22 - 10
Juan Marichal, Giants	22 - 13
Jim Maloney, Reds	20 - 9
Bob Gibson, Cardinals	20 - 12

1966

Sandy Koufax, Dodgers	27 - 9
Juan Marichal, Giants	25 - 6
Gaylord Perry, Giants	21 - 8
Bob Gibson, Cardinals	21 - 12
Chris Short, Phillies	20 - 10

1967

Mike McCormick, Giants	22 - 10
Fergie Jenkins, Cubs	20 - 13

1968

Juan Marichal, Giants	26 - 9
Bob Gibson, Cardinals	22 - 9
Fergie Jenkins, Cubs	20 - 15

1969

Tom Seaver, Mets	25 - 7
Phil Niekro, Braves	23 - 13
Juan Marichal, Giants	21 - 11
Fergie Jenkins, Cubs	21 - 15
Bill Singer, Dodgers	20 - 12
Bob Gibson, Cardinals	20 - 13
Larry Dierker, Astros	20 - 13
Bill Hands, Cubs	20 - 14
Claude Osteen, Dodgers	20 - 15

1970

Bob Gibson, Cardinals	23 - 7
Gaylord Perry, Giants	23 - 13
Fergie Jenkins, Cubs	22 - 16
Jim Merritt, Reds	20 - 12

1971

Fergie Jenkins, Cubs	24 - 13
Steve Carlton, Cardinals	20 - 9
Al Downing, Dodgers	20 - 9
Tom Seaver, Mets	20 - 10

1972

Steve Carlton, Phillies	27 - 10
Tom Seaver, Mets	21 - 12
Claude Osteen, Dodgers	20 - 11
Fergie Jenkins, Cubs	20 - 12

1973

Ron Bryant, Giants	24 - 12

1974

Andy Messersmith, Dodgers	20 - 6
Phil Niekro, Braves	20 - 13

1975

Tom Seaver, Mets	22 - 9
Randy Jones, Padres	20 - 12

1976

Randy Jones, Padres	22 - 14
Jerry Koosman, Mets	21 - 10
Don Sutton, Dodgers	21 - 10
Steve Carlton, Phillies	20 - 7
J.R. Richard, Astros	20 - 15

1977

Steve Carlton, Phillies	23 - 10
Tom Seaver, Mets-Reds	21 - 6
John Candelaria, Pirates	20 - 5
Bob Forsch, Cardinals	20 - 7
Tommy John, Dodgers	20 - 7
Rick Reuschel, Cubs	20 - 10

1978

Gaylord Perry, Padres	21 - 6
Ross Grimsley, Expos	20 - 11

1979

Joe Niekro, Astros	21 - 11
Phil Niekro, Braves	21 - 20

1980

Steve Carlton, Phillies	24 - 9
**Joe Niekro, Astros	20 - 12

1981

—None—

1982

Steve Carlton, Phillies	23 - 11

1983

—None—

1984

Joaquin Andujar, Cardinals	20 - 14
#Rick Sutcliffe, Indians-Cubs	20 - 6

1985

Dwight Gooden, Mets	24 - 4
Joaquin Andujar, Cardinals	21 - 12
John Tudor, Cardinals	21 - 8
Tom Browning, Reds	20 - 9

1986

Fernando Valenzuela, Dodgers	21 - 11
Mike Krukow, Giants	20 - 9

1987

—None—

1988

Orel Hershiser, Dodgers	23 - 8
Danny Jackson, Reds	23 - 8
David Cone, Mets	20 - 3

1989

Mike Scott, Astros	20 - 10

1990

Doug Drabek, Pirates	22 - 6
Ramon Martinez, Dodgers	20 - 6
Frank Viola, Mets	20 - 12

1991

Tom Glavine, Braves	20 - 11
John Smiley, Pirates	20 - 8

*—Won 13 in A.L., 8 in N.L. (1902)
†—Won 10 in A.L., 11 in N.L. (1945)
#—Won 4 in A.L., 16 in N.L. (1984)
**—Includes playoff victory (1946, 1951, 1980)

30-GAME WINNERS
(since 1900)

41	Jack Chesbro, New York (AL)	1904
40	Ed Walsh, Chicago (AL)	1908
37	Christy Mathewson, New York (NL)	1908
36	Walter Johnson, Washington	1913
35	Joe McGinnity, New York (NL)	1904
34	Joe Wood, Boston (AL)	1912
33	Cy Young, Boston (AL)	1901
33	Grover Alexander, Philadelphia (NL)	1916
33	Christy Mathewson, New York (NL)	1904
32	Cy Young, Boston (AL)	1901
32	Cy Young, Boston (AL)	1902
31	Joe McGinnity, New York (NL)	1903
31	Christy Mathewson, New York (NL)	1905
31	Jack Coombs, Philadelphia (AL)	1910
31	Grover Alexander, Philadelphia (NL)	1915
31	Jim Bagby, Cleveland	1920
31	Lefty Grove, Philadelphia (AL)	1931
31	Denny McLain, Detroit	1968
30	Christy Mathewson, New York (NL)	1903
30	Grover Alexander, Philadelphia (NL)	1917
30	Dizzy Dean, St. Louis (NL)	1934

CLUBS' TOP MARKS SINCE 1900 (Individual Leaders)

BATTING

	BRAVES		CUBS		REDS		ASTROS	
Batting	Rogers Hornsby (1928)	.387	Rogers Hornsby (1929)	.380	Cy Seymour (1905)	.377	Rusty Staub (1967)	.333
Hitting Streak	Tommy Holmes (1945)	37	Jerome Walton (1989)	30	Pete Rose (1978)	44	Art Howe (1981)	23
Home Runs	Eddie Mathews (1953) / Hank Aaron (1971)	47 / 47	Hack Wilson (1930)	56	George Foster (1977)	52	Jim Wynn (1967)	37
Runs Batted In	Eddie Mathews (1953)	135	Hack Wilson (1930)	190	George Foster (1977)	149	Bob Watson (1977)	110
Hits	Tommy Holmes (1945)	224	Rogers Hornsby (1929)	229	Pete Rose (1973)	230	Enos Cabell (1978)	195
Runs	Dale Murphy (1983)	131	Rogers Hornsby (1929)	156	Frank Robinson (1962)	134	Jim Wynn (1972)	117
Extra Base Hits	Hank Aaron (1959)	92	Hack Wilson (1930)	97	Frank Robinson (1962)	92	Jim Wynn (1967) / Cesar Cedeno (1972)	69 / 69
One Base Hits	Ralph Garr (1971)	180	Earl Adams (1927)	165	Pete Rose (1973)	181	Sonny Jackson (1966)	160
Two Base Hits	Tommy Holmes (1945)	47	Billy Herman (1935, 1936)	57	Frank Robinson (1962) / Pete Rose (1978)	51 / 51	Rusty Staub (1967)	44
Three Base Hits	Ray Powell (1921)	18	Frank Schulte (1911) / Victor Saier (1913)	21 / 21	Sam Crawford (1902)	23	Roger Metzger (1973)	14
Total Bases	Hank Aaron (1959)	400	Hack Wilson (1930)	423	George Foster (1977)	388	Cesar Cedeno (1972)	300
Stolen Bases	Otis Nixon (1991)	72	Frank Chance (1903)	67	Bob Bescher (1911)	81	Gerald Young (1988)	65
At Bats	Ralph Garr (1973)	668	Billy Herman (1935)	666	Pete Rose (1973)	680	Enos Cabell (1978)	660
Bases on Balls	Bob Elliott (1948)	131	Jimmy Sheckard (1911)	147	Joe Morgan (1975)	132	Jim Wynn (1969)	148
Strikeouts (most)	Dale Murphy (1978)	145	Byron Browne (1966)	143	Lee May (1969)	142	Lee May (1972)	145
Strikeouts (fewest)*	Tommy Holmes (1945)	9	Charles Hollocher (1922)	5	Frank McCormick (1941)	13	Nellie Fox (1964)	13
Games	Felix Millan (1969) / Dale Murphy (1982, 1983, 1984, 1985)	162 / 162	Ron Santo (1965) / Billy Williams (1965)	164 / 164	Leo Cardenas (1964) / Pete Rose (1974)	163 / 163	Enos Cabell (1978) / Bill Doran (1987)	162 / 162
Grounded into Double Play (most)	Sid Gordon (1951)	28	Ron Santo (1973)	27	Ernie Lombardi (1938)	30	Doug Rader (1970)	23
Grounded into Double Play (fewest)*	Bill Bruton (1955) / Dave Justice (1990) / Lonnie Smith (1990)	2 / 2 / 2	Augie Galan (1935)	0	Lonnie Frey (1938)	1	Joe Morgan (1966, 1967) / Craig Reynolds (1979) / Omar Moreno (1983) / Craig Biggio (1991)	2 / 2 / 2 / 2

PITCHING

	BRAVES		CUBS		REDS		ASTROS	
Percentage**	Tom Hughes (1916) 16-3	.842	Rick Sutcliffe (1984) 16-1	.941	Tom Seaver (1981) 14-2	.875	Vern Ruhle (1980) 12-4	.750
Games (Appearances)	Rick Camp (1980)	77	Ted Abernathy (1965) / Dick Tidrow (1980)	84 / 84	Wayne Granger (1969)	90	Juan Agosto (1990)	82
Complete Games	Vic Willis (1902)	45	John Taylor (1903) / Grover Alexander (1920)	33 / 33	Noodles Hahn (1901)	41	Larry Dierker (1969)	20
Innings Pitched	Vic Willis (1902)	402	Grover Alexander (1920)	363	Noodles Hahn (1901)	375	Larry Dierker (1969)	305
Games Won	Vic Willis (1902); Chas. Pittinger (1902); Dick Rudolph (1914)	27	Mordecai Brown (1908)	29	Adolfo Luque (1923) / Bucky Walters (1939)	27 / 27	Joe Niekro (1979)	21
Games Lost	Vic Willis (1905)	29	Tom Hughes (1901) / Dick Ellsworth (1966) / Bill Bonham (1974)	22 / 22 / 22	Paul Derringer (1933)	25	Dick Farrell (1962)	20
Games Started	Vic Willis (1902)	45	Fergie Jenkins (1969)	42	Noodles Hahn (1901)	42	Jerry Reuss (1973)	40
Games Finished	Gene Garber (1982)	56	Ted Abernathy (1965)	62	Tom Hume (1980)	62	Joe Sambito (1979) / Dave Smith (1986)	51 / 51
Bases on Balls	Phil Niekro (1977)	164	Sam Jones (1955)	185	John VanderMeer (1943)	162	J.R. Richard (1976)	151
Strikeouts	Phil Niekro (1977)	262	Fergie Jenkins (1970)	274	Mario Soto (1982)	274	J.R. Richard (1979)	313
Shutouts	Charles Pittinger (1902), Irv Young (1905), Warren Spahn (1947, 1951, 1963)	7	Mordecai Brown (1906, 1908), Orval Overall (1907, 1909), Grover Alexander (1919), Bill Lee (1938)	9	Jake Weimer (1906), Fred Toney (1917), Hod Eller (1919), Jack Billingham (1973)	7	Dave Roberts (1973)	6

*Based on 400 or more at bats   **Based on 15 or more decisions

CLUBS' TOP MARKS SINCE 1900 (Individual Leaders)

BATTING

	DODGERS		EXPOS		METS		PHILLIES	
Batting	Babe Herman (1930)	.393	Tim Raines (1986)	.334	Cleon Jones (1969)	.340	Frank O'Doul (1929)	.398
Hitting Streak	Willie Davis (1969)	31	Warren Cromartie (1979) / Andre Dawson (1980)	19 / 19	Hubie Brooks (1984)	24	Chuck Klein (1930-twice)	26
Home Runs	Duke Snider (1956)	43	Andre Dawson (1983)	32	Darryl Strawberry (1987, 1988)	39	Mike Schmidt (1980)	48
Runs Batted In	Tommy Davis (1962)	153	Tim Wallach (1987)	123	Howard Johnson (1991)	117	Chuck Klein (1930)	170
Hits	Babe Herman (1930)	241	Al Oliver (1982)	204	Felix Millan (1975)	191	Frank O'Doul (1929)	254
Runs	Babe Herman (1930)	143	Tim Raines (1983)	133	Darryl Strawberry (1987) / Howard Johnson (1991)	108 / 108	Chuck Klein (1930)	158
Extra Base Hits	Babe Herman (1930)	94	Andres Galarraga (1988)	79	Howard Johnson (1989)	80	Chuck Klein (1930)	107
One Base Hits	Willie Keeler (1900) / Maury Wills (1964)	179 / 179	Tim Raines (1986)	140	Felix Millan (1973)	155	Frank O'Doul (1929) / Richie Ashburn (1951)	181 / 181
Two Base Hits	John Frederick (1929)	52	Warren Cromartie (1979)	46	Howard Johnson (1989)	41	Chuck Klein (1930)	59
Three Base Hits	Harry "Hi" Myers (1920)	22	Rodney Scott (1980) / Tim Raines (1985) / Mitch Webster (1986)	13 / 13 / 13	Mookie Wilson (1984)	10	Juan Samuel (1984)	19
Total Bases	Babe Herman (1930)	416	Andre Dawson (1983)	341	Howard Johnson (1989)	319	Chuck Klein (1930)	445
Stolen Bases	Maury Wills (1962)	104	Ron LeFlore (1980)	97	Mookie Wilson (1982)	58	Juan Samuel (1984)	72
At Bats	Maury Wills (1962)	695	Warren Cromartie (1979)	659	Felix Millan (1975)	676	Juan Samuel (1984)	701
Bases on Balls	Eddie Stanky (1945)	148	Ken Singleton (1973)	123	Keith Hernandez (1984) / Darryl Strawberry (1987)	97 / 97	Mike Schmidt (1983)	128
Strikeouts (most)	Billy Grabarkewitz (1970)	149	Andres Galarraga (1990)	169	Tommie Agee (1970) / Dave Kingman (1982)	156 / 156	Mike Schmidt (1975)	180
Strikeouts (fewest)*	James Johnston (1923)	15	Ron Hunt (1974)	17	Felix Millan (1974)	14	Emil Verban (1947)	8
Games	Maury Wills (1962)	165	Rusty Staub (1971) / Ken Singleton (1973) / Warren Cromartie (1980)	162 / 162 / 162	Felix Millan (1975)	162	Pete Rose (1979)	163
Grounded Into Double Play (most)	Carl Furillo (1956)	27	John Bateman (1971) / Ken Singleton (1973)	27 / 27	Cleon Jones (1970)	26	Del Ennis (1950) / Ted Sizemore (1977)	25 / 25
Grounded Into Double Play (fewest)*	John Roseboro (1961)	1	Ron Hunt (1971)	1	Len Dykstra (1987)	1	Richie Ashburn (1948)	1

PITCHING

	DODGERS		EXPOS		METS		PHILLIES	
Percentage**	Phil Regan (1966) 14-1	.933	Bryn Smith (1985) 18-5	.783	David Cone (1988) 20-3	.870	Robin Roberts (1952) 28-7	.800
Games (Appearances)	Mike Marshall (1974)	106	Mike Marshall (1973)	92	Roger McDowell (1986)	75	Kent Tekulve (1987)	90
Complete Games	Oscar Jones (1904)	38	Bill Stoneman (1971)	20	Tom Seaver (1971)	21	Grover Alexander (1916)	38
Innings Pitched	Oscar Jones (1904)	378	Steve Rogers (1977)	302	Tom Seaver (1970)	291	Grover Alexander (1916)	389
Games Won	Joe McGinnity (1900)	29	Ross Grimsley (1978)	20	Tom Seaver (1969)	25	Grover Alexander (1916)	33
Games Lost	George Bell (1910)	27	Steve Rogers (1974)	22	Roger Craig (1962) / Jack Fisher (1965)	24 / 24	Charles Fraser (1904)	24
Games Started	Don Drysdale (1963, 1965)	42	Steve Rogers (1977)	40	Jack Fisher (1965) / Tom Seaver (1970, 1973, 1975)	36 / 36	Grover Alexander (1916)	45
Games Finished	Mike Marshall (1974)	83	Mike Marshall (1973)	73	Jesse Orosco (1984) / Roger McDowell (1986)	52 / 52	Jim Konstanty (1950)	62
Bases on Balls	Bill Donovan (1901)	151	Bill Stoneman (1971)	146	Nolan Ryan (1971)	116	Earl Moore (1911)	164
Strikeouts	Sandy Koufax (1965)	382	Bill Stoneman (1971)	251	Tom Seaver (1971)	289	Steve Carlton (1972)	310
Shutouts	Sandy Koufax (1963)	11	Bill Stoneman (1969) / Steve Rogers (1979, 1983) / Dennis Martinez (1991)	5 / 5 / 5	Dwight Gooden (1985)	8	Grover Alexander (1916)	16

(Continued on next page)

*Based on 400 or more at bats **Based on 15 or more decisions

CLUBS' TOP MARKS SINCE 1900 (Individual Leaders)

BATTING

	PIRATES	CARDINALS	PADRES	GIANTS
Batting	Arky Vaughan (1935) .385	Rogers Hornsby (1924) .424	Tony Gwynn (1987) .370	Bill Terry (1930) .401
Hitting Streak	Danny O'Connell (1953) 26	Rogers Hornsby (1922) 33	Benito Santiago (1987) 34	Jack Clark (1978) 26
Home Runs	Ralph Kiner (1949) 54	Johnny Mize (1940) 43	Nate Colbert (1970, 1972) 38	Willie Mays (1965) 52
Runs Batted In	Paul Waner (1927) 131	Joe Medwick (1937) 154	Dave Winfield (1979) 118	Mel Ott (1929) 151
Hits	Paul Waner (1927) 237	Rogers Hornsby (1922) 250	Tony Gwynn (1987) 218	Bill Terry (1930) 254
Runs	Kiki Cuyler (1925) 144	Rogers Hornsby (1922) 141	Tony Gwynn (1987) 119	Bill Terry (1930) 139
Extra Base Hits	Willie Stargell (1973) 90	Stan Musial (1948) 103	Dave Winfield (1979) 71	Willie Mays (1962) 90
One Base Hits	Lloyd Waner (1927) 198	Jesse Burkett (1901) 180	Tony Gwynn (1984) 177	Bill Terry (1930) 177
Two Base Hits	Paul Waner (1932) 62	Joe Medwick (1936) 64	Terry Kennedy (1982) 42	Jack Clark (1978) 46
Three Base Hits	J. Owen Wilson (1912) 36	Tom Long (1915) 25	Tony Gwynn (1987) 13	Larry Doyle (1911) 25
Total Bases	Kiki Cuyler (1925) 366	Rogers Hornsby (1922) 450	Dave Winfield (1979) 333	Bill Terry (1930) 392
Stolen Bases	Omar Moreno (1979) 77	Lou Brock (1974) 118	Alan Wiggins (1984) 70	George Burns (1914) 62
At Bats	Matty Alou (1969) 698	Lou Brock (1967) 689	Steve Garvey (1985) 654	Joe Moore (1935) 681
Bases on Balls	Ralph Kiner (1951) 137	Jack Clark (1987) 136	Jack Clark (1989) 132	Eddie Stanky (1950) 144
Strikeouts (most)	Donn Clendenon (1968) 163	Jack Clark (1987) 139	Nate Colbert (1970) 150	Bobby Bonds (1970) 189
Strikeouts (fewest)*	Pie Traynor (1929) 7	Frank Frisch (1927) 10	Tony Gwynn (1991) 19	Don Mueller (1956) 7
Games	Bill Mazeroski (1967) 163 Bobby Bonilla (1989) 163	Jose Oquendo (1989) 163	Steve Garvey (1985) 162 Joe Carter (1990) 162	Jose Pagan (1962) 164
Grounded into Double Play (most)	Al Todd (1938) 25	Ted Simmons (1973) 29	Steve Garvey (1984, 1985) 25	Bill Jurges (1939) 26 Sid Gordon (1943) 26
Grounded into Double Play (fewest)*	Matty Alou (1966, 1967) 3 Barry Bonds (1988) 3	Lou Brock (1965, 1969) 2 Andy Van Slyke (1986) 2	Derrell Thomas (1973) 2 Alan Wiggins (1984) 2	Jose Uribe (1986) 2 Will Clark (1987) 2 Brett Butler (1988) 2

PITCHING

	PIRATES	CARDINALS	PADRES	GIANTS
Percentage**	ElRoy Face (1959) 18-1 .947	Howie Krist (1949) 13-3 .813 Al Hrabosky (1975) 13-3 .813	Gaylord Perry (1978) 21-6 .778 Dennis Rasmussen (1988) 14-4 .778	Hoyt Wilhelm (1952) 15-3 .833
Games (Appearances)	Kent Tekulve (1979) 94	Todd Worrell (1987) 75	Craig Lefferts (1986) 83	Greg Minton (1982) 78
Complete Games	Vic Willis (1906) 32	John Taylor (1904) 39	Randy Jones (1976) 25	Joe McGinnity (1903) 44
Innings Pitched	Burleigh Grimes (1928) 331	Grant McGlynn (1907) 352	Randy Jones (1976) 315	Joe McGinnity (1903) 434
Games Won	Jack Chesbro (1902) 28	Dizzy Dean (1934) 30	Randy Jones (1976) 22	Christy Mathewson (1908) 37
Games Lost	Murry Dickson (1952) 21	Grant McGlynn (1907) 25 Arthur Raymond (1908) 25	Randy Jones (1974) 22	Luther Taylor (1901) 27
Games Started	Bob Friend (1956) 42	John Taylor (1904) 39	Randy Jones (1976) 40	Joe McGinnity (1903) 48
Games Finished	Kent Tekulve (1979) 67	Bruce Sutter (1984) 63	Rollie Fingers (1977) 69	Greg Minton (1982) 66
Bases on Balls	Marty O'Toole (1912) 159	Bob Harmon (1911) 181	Steve Arlin (1972) 122	Jeff Tesreau (1914) 128
Strikeouts	Bob Veale (1965) 276	Bob Gibson (1970) 274	Clay Kirby (1971) 231	Christy Mathewson (1903) 267
Shutouts	Jack Chesbro (1902), Al Leifield (1906), Al Mamaux (1915) & Charles Adams (1920) 8	Bob Gibson (1968) 13	Fred Norman (1972) 6 Randy Jones (1975) 6	Christy Mathewson (1908) 12

*Based on 400 or more at bats **Based on 15 or more decisions

CLUB AND PLAYER STREAKS, ETC. DURING 1991 SEASON

EASTERN DIVISION

	CUBS	EXPOS	METS	PHILLIES	PIRATES	CARDINALS
Winning Streak	6 games	7 games	10 games	13 games	9 games	5 games
Losing Streak	9 games	11 games	11 games	7 games	8 games	5 games (2 times)
Runs, Game	12 (Apr. 21) (July 6)	12 (Sept. 27)	10 (3 times)	12 (May 28) (June 5)	13 (Apr. 21) (July 2)	14 (4 times)
Hits, Game	15 (3 times)	17 (Apr. 28)	16 (3 times)	17 (June 30)	22 (July 2)	23 (May 26)
Home Runs, Game	4 (3 times)	4 (May 6) (Aug. 2)	4 (June 20)	4 (Apr. 30) (Aug. 17)	4 (Aug. 25)	4 (Sept. 1)
Runs, Inning	7 (7th inn. May 26)	6 (8th inn. Sept. 27)	6 (5 times)	6 (3 times)	6 (5 times)	7 (6th inn. July 22)
Errors, Game	3 (3 times)	5 (Aug. 6)	5 (Aug. 16)	5 (Sept. 11)	4 (July 17)	4 (July 21)
Stolen Bases, Game	5 (Oct. 5, 2g)	5 (June 7) (June 16)	6 (Apr. 10)	4 (3 times)	3 (April 28) (June 1)	7 (May 10)
Double Plays, Game	3 (4 times)	3 (3 times)	3 (7 times)	3 (May 19; July 30)	4 (4 times)	5 (May 27)
Triple Plays, Game	None	1 (Sept. 8)	None	1 (April 28)	None	1 (Sept. 5)
Winning Streak, Pitcher	5 McElroy	6 Nabholz	6 Pena	6 Williams	7 Smiley	6 Carpenter
Losing Streak, Pitcher	6 Smith	5 Jones	7 Viola	6 McDowell	4 (3 times)	5 Moyer
Batting Streak	19 Grace	12 Grissom	12 Jefferies	15 Kruk	18 Bonilla	12 Guerrero, Lankford

WESTERN DIVISION

	BRAVES	REDS	ASTROS	DODGERS	PADRES	GIANTS
Winning Streak	8 games	5 games	9 games	5 games (3 times)	7 games	11 games
Losing Streak	5 games	10 games	7 games	7 games	5 games (2 times)	7 games
Runs, Game	17 (May 8)	13 (July 27, Sept. 13)	14 (July 4)	13 (June 10)	13 (3 times)	17 (July 14)
Hits, Game	17 (May 8; July 3)	20 (July 27)	18 (May 15)	16 (3 times)	20 (Aug. 2)	22 (July 14)
Home Runs, Game	4 (May 30; June 20)	5 (May 11)	3 (June 29; Sept. 4)	4 (May 21)	5 (Aug. 11)	4 (3 times)
Runs, Inning	8 (7th inn. May 8)	6 (4 times)	6 (3rd inn. Aug. 21)	6 (3 times)	7 (4th inn. Apr. 18) (2nd inn. June 4)	8 (7th inn. Apr. 13)
Errors, Game	6 (June 30)	4 (Sept. 7)	5 (May 1)	4 (Apr. 14)	5 (June 13)	4 (June 17; July 29)
Stolen Bases, Game	8 (June 16)	4 (3 times)	5 (Sept. 27)	4 (3 times)	4 (Sept. 21)	5 (May 26; June 25)
Double Plays, Game	4 (June 5; Oct. 2)	5 (July 20)	3 (6 times)	3 (9 times)	4 (Aug. 2)	4 (June 9; June 21)
Triple Plays, Game	None	None	1 (Apr. 16; Aug. 4)	None	None	None
Winning Streak, Pitcher	8 Glavine	7 Rijo	4 Osuna	7 Martinez	10 Benes	8 Downs
Losing Streak, Pitcher	5 Smoltz	5 Armstrong, Hammond	6 Portugal, Hernandez	3 (6 times)	9 Rasmussen	7 Righetti
Batting Streak	20 Nixon	19 Larkin	13 Bagwell	23 Butler	15 Gwynn	19 McGee

HOW THEY FINISHED 1900 - 1968 INCLUSIVE

Year	BRAVES ★ Fin.	Won—Lost	Pct.	CUBS Fin.	Won—Lost	Pct.	REDS Fin.	Won—Lost	Pct.	ASTROS Fin.	Won—Lost	Pct.	DODGERS # Fin.	Won—Lost	Pct.	EXPOS Fin.	Won—Lost	Pct.	Year
1900	4	66— 72	.478	5†	65— 75	.464	7	62— 77	.446				1	82— 54	.603				1900
1901	5	69— 69	.500	6	53— 86	.381	8	52— 87	.374				3	79— 57	.581				1901
1902	3	73— 64	.533	5	68— 69	.496	4	70— 70	.500				2	75— 63	.543				1902
1903	6	58— 80	.420	3	82— 56	.594	4	74— 65	.532				5	70— 66	.515				1903
1904	7	55— 98	.359	2	93— 60	.608	3	88— 65	.575				6	56— 97	.366				1904
1905	7	51—103	.331	3	92— 61	.601	5	79— 74	.516				8	48—104	.316				1905
1906	8	49—102	.325	1	116— 36	.763	6	64— 87	.424				5	66— 86	.434				1906
1907	7	58— 90	.392	1*	107— 45	.704	6	66— 87	.431				5	65— 83	.439				1907
1908	6	63— 91	.409	1*	99— 55	.643	5	73— 81	.474				7	53—101	.344				1908
1909	8	45—108	.294	2	104— 49	.680	4	77— 76	.503				6	55— 98	.359				1909
1910	8	53—100	.346	1	104— 50	.675	5	75— 79	.487				6	64— 90	.416				1910
1911	8	44—107	.291	2	92— 62	.597	6	70— 83	.458				7	64— 86	.427				1911
1912	8	52—101	.340	3	91— 59	.607	4	75— 78	.490				7	58— 95	.379				1912
1913	5	69— 82	.457	3	88— 65	.575	7	64— 89	.418				6	65— 84	.436				1913
1914	1*	94— 59	.614	4	78— 76	.506	8	60— 94	.390				5	75— 79	.487				1914
1915	2	83— 69	.546	4	73— 80	.477	7	71— 83	.461				3	80— 72	.526				1915
1916	3	89— 63	.586	5	67— 86	.438	7†	60— 93	.392				1	94— 60	.610				1916
1917	6	72— 81	.471	5	74— 80	.481	4	78— 76	.506				7	70— 81	.464				1917
1918	7	53— 71	.427	1	84— 45	.651	3	68— 60	.531				5	57— 69	.452				1918
1919	6	57— 82	.410	3	75— 65	.536	1*	96— 44	.686				5	69— 71	.493				1919
1920	7	62— 90	.408	5†	75— 79	.487	3	82— 71	.536				1	93— 61	.604				1920
1921	4	79— 74	.516	7	64— 89	.418	6	70— 83	.458				5	77— 75	.507				1921
1922	8	53—100	.346	5	80— 74	.519	2	86— 68	.558				6	76— 78	.494				1922
1923	7	54—100	.351	4	83— 71	.539	2	91— 63	.591				6	76— 78	.494				1923
1924	8	53—100	.346	5	81— 72	.529	4	83— 70	.542				2	92— 62	.597				1924
1925	5	70— 83	.458	8	68— 86	.442	3	80— 73	.523				6†	68— 85	.444				1925
1926	7	66— 86	.434	4	82— 72	.532	2	87— 67	.565				6	71— 82	.464				1926
1927	7	60— 94	.390	4	85— 68	.556	5	75— 78	.490				6	65— 88	.425				1927
1928	7	50—103	.327	3	91— 63	.591	5	78— 74	.513				6	77— 76	.503				1928
1929	8	56— 98	.364	1	98— 54	.645	7	66— 88	.429				6	70— 83	.458				1929
1930	6	70— 84	.455	2	90— 64	.584	7	59— 95	.383				4	86— 68	.558				1930
1931	7	64— 90	.416	3	84— 70	.545	8	58— 96	.377				4	79— 73	.520				1931
1932	5	77— 77	.500	1	90— 64	.584	8	60— 94	.390				3	81— 73	.526				1932
1933	4	83— 71	.539	3	86— 68	.558	8	58— 94	.382				6	65— 88	.425				1933
1934	4	78— 73	.517	3	86— 65	.570	8	52— 99	.344				6	71— 81	.467				1934
1935	8	38—115	.248	1	100— 54	.649	6	68— 85	.444				5	70— 83	.458				1935
1936	6	71— 83	.461	2†	87— 67	.565	5	74— 80	.481				7	67— 87	.435				1936
1937	5	79— 73	.520	2	93— 61	.604	8	56— 98	.364				6	62— 91	.405				1937
1938	5	77— 75	.507	1	89— 63	.586	4	82— 68	.547				7	69— 80	.463				1938
1939	7	63— 88	.417	4	84— 70	.545	1	97— 57	.630				3	84— 69	.549				1939
1940	7	65— 87	.428	5	75— 79	.487	1*	100— 53	.654				2	88— 65	.575				1940
1941	7	62— 92	.403	6	70— 84	.455	3	88— 66	.571				1	100— 54	.649				1941
1942	7	59— 89	.399	6	68— 86	.442	4	76— 76	.500				2	104— 50	.675				1942
1943	6	68— 85	.444	5	74— 79	.484	2	87— 67	.565				3	81— 72	.529				1943
1944	6	65— 89	.422	4	75— 79	.487	3	89— 65	.578				7	63— 91	.409				1944
1945	6	67— 85	.441	1	98— 56	.636	7	61— 93	.396				3	87— 67	.565				1945
1946	4	81— 72	.529	3	82— 71	.536	6	67— 87	.435				2**	96— 60	.615				1946
1947	3	86— 68	.558	6	69— 85	.448	5	73— 81	.474				1	94— 60	.610				1947
1948	1	91— 62	.595	8	64— 90	.416	7	64— 89	.418				3	84— 70	.545				1948
1949	4	75— 79	.487	8	61— 93	.396	7	62— 92	.403				1	97— 57	.630				1949
1950	4	83— 71	.539	7	64— 89	.418	6	66— 87	.431				2	89— 65	.578				1950
1951	4	76— 78	.494	8	62— 92	.403	6	68— 86	.442				2**	97— 60	.618				1951
1952	7	64— 89	.418	5	77— 77	.500	6	69— 85	.448				1	96— 57	.627				1952
1953	2	92— 62	.597	7	65— 89	.422	6	68— 86	.442				1	105— 49	.682				1953
1954	3	89— 65	.578	7	64— 90	.416	5	74— 80	.481				2	92— 62	.597				1954
1955	2	85— 69	.552	6	72— 81	.471	5	75— 79	.487				1*	98— 55	.641				1955
1956	2	92— 62	.597	8	60— 94	.390	3	91— 63	.591				1	93— 61	.604				1956
1957	1*	95— 59	.617	7†	62— 92	.403	4	80— 74	.519				3	84— 70	.545				1957
1958	1	92— 62	.597	5†	72— 82	.468	4	76— 78	.494				7	71— 83	.461				1958
1959	2**	86— 70	.551	5†	74— 80	.481	5†	74— 80	.481				1‡*	88— 68	.564				1959
1960	2	88— 66	.571	7	60— 94	.390	6	67— 87	.435				4	82— 72	.532				1960
1961	4	83— 71	.539	7	64— 90	.416	1	93— 61	.604				2	89— 65	.578				1961
1962	5	86— 76	.531	9	59—103	.364	3	98— 64	.605	8	64— 96	.400	2**	102— 63	.618				1962
1963	6	84— 78	.519	7	82— 80	.506	5	86— 76	.531	9	66— 96	.407	1*	99— 63	.611				1963
1964	5	88— 74	.543	8	76— 86	.469	2†	92— 70	.568	9	66— 96	.407	6†	80— 82	.494				1964
1965	5	86— 76	.531	8	72— 90	.444	4	89— 73	.549	9	65— 97	.401	1*	97— 65	.599				1965
1966	5	85— 77	.525	10	59—103	.364	7	76— 84	.475	8	72— 90	.444	1	95— 67	.586				1966
1967	7	77— 85	.475	3	87— 74	.540	4	87— 75	.537	9	69— 93	.426	8	73— 89	.451				1967
1968	5	81— 81	.500	3	84— 78	.519	4	83— 79	.512	10	72— 90	.444	7†	76— 86	.469				1968

The ASTROS column is marked **JOINED LEAGUE AS ACTIVE PARTICIPANT IN 1962**.
The EXPOS column is marked **JOINED LEAGUE AS ACTIVE PARTICIPANT IN 1969**.

HOW THEY FINISHED 1900 - 1968 INCLUSIVE

The Mets column carries the vertical note "JOINED LEAGUE AS ACTIVE PARTICIPANT IN 1962" (blank 1900–1961); the Padres column carries "JOINED LEAGUE AS ACTIVE PARTICIPANT IN 1969" (blank throughout).

Year	Fin. (METS)	Won—Lost (METS)	Pct. (METS)	Fin. (PHILLIES)	Won—Lost (PHILLIES)	Pct. (PHILLIES)	Fin. (PIRATES)	Won—Lost (PIRATES)	Pct. (PIRATES)	Fin. (CARDINALS)	Won—Lost (CARDINALS)	Pct. (CARDINALS)	Fin. (PADRES)	Won—Lost (PADRES)	Pct. (PADRES)	Fin. (GIANTS§)	Won—Lost (GIANTS§)	Pct. (GIANTS§)	Year
1900				3	75— 63	.543	2	79— 60	.568	5†	65— 75	.464				8	60— 78	.435	1900
1901				2	83— 57	.593	1	90— 49	.647	4	76— 64	.543				7	52— 85	.380	1901
1902				7	56— 81	.409	1	103— 36	.741	6	56— 78	.418				8	48— 88	.353	1902
1903				7	49— 86	.363	1	91— 49	.650	8	43— 94	.314				2	84— 55	.604	1903
1904				8	52—100	.342	4	87— 66	.569	5	75— 79	.487				1	106— 47	.693	1904
1905				4	83— 69	.546	2	96— 57	.627	6	58— 96	.377				1*	105— 48	.686	1905
1906				4	71— 82	.464	3	93— 60	.608	7	52— 98	.347				2	96— 56	.632	1906
1907				3	83— 64	.565	2	91— 63	.591	8	52—101	.340				4	82— 71	.536	1907
1908				4	83— 71	.539	2†	98— 56	.636	8	49—105	.318				2†	98— 56	.636	1908
1909				5	74— 79	.484	1*	110— 42	.724	7	54— 98	.355				3	92— 61	.601	1909
1910				4	78— 75	.510	3	86— 57	.562	7	63— 90	.412				2	91— 63	.591	1910
1911				4	79— 73	.520	3	85— 69	.552	5	75— 74	.503				1	99— 54	.647	1911
1912				5	73— 79	.480	2	93— 58	.616	6	63— 90	.412				1	103— 48	.682	1912
1913				2	88— 63	.583	4	78— 71	.523	8	51— 99	.340				1	101— 51	.664	1913
1914				6	74— 80	.481	7	69— 85	.448	3	81— 72	.529				2	84— 70	.545	1914
1915				1	90— 62	.592	5	73— 81	.474	6	72— 81	.471				8	69— 83	.454	1915
1916				2	91— 62	.595	6	65— 89	.422	7†	60— 93	.392				4	86— 66	.566	1916
1917				2	87— 65	.572	8	51—103	.331	3	82— 70	.539				1	98— 56	.636	1917
1918				6	55— 68	.447	4	65— 60	.520	8	51— 78	.395				2	71— 53	.573	1918
1919				8	47— 90	.343	4	71— 68	.511	7	54— 83	.394				2	87— 53	.621	1919
1920				8	62— 91	.405	4	79— 75	.513	5†	75— 79	.487				2	86— 68	.558	1920
1921				8	51—103	.331	2	90— 63	.588	3	87— 66	.569				1*	94— 59	.614	1921
1922				7	57— 96	.373	3†	85— 69	.552	3†	85— 69	.552				1*	93— 61	.604	1922
1923				8	50—104	.325	3	87— 67	.565	5	79— 74	.516				1	95— 58	.621	1923
1924				7	55— 96	.364	3	90— 63	.588	6	65— 89	.422				1	93— 60	.608	1924
1925				6†	68— 85	.444	1*	95— 58	.621	4	77— 76	.503				2	86— 66	.566	1925
1926				8	58— 93	.384	3	84— 69	.549	1*	89— 65	.578				5	74— 77	.490	1926
1927				8	51—103	.331	1	94— 60	.610	2	92— 61	.601				3	92— 62	.597	1927
1928				8	43—109	.283	4	85— 67	.559	1	95— 59	.617				2	93— 61	.604	1928
1929				5	71— 82	.464	2	88— 65	.575	4	78— 74	.513				3	84— 67	.556	1929
1930				8	52—102	.338	5	80— 74	.519	1	92— 62	.597				3	87— 67	.565	1930
1931				6	66— 88	.429	5	75— 79	.487	1*	101— 53	.656				2	87— 65	.572	1931
1932				4	78— 76	.506	2	86— 68	.558	6†	72— 82	.468				6†	72— 82	.468	1932
1933				7	60— 92	.395	2	87— 67	.565	5	82— 71	.536				1*	91— 61	.599	1933
1934				7	56— 93	.376	5	74— 76	.493	1*	95— 58	.621				2	93— 60	.608	1934
1935				7	64— 89	.418	4	86— 67	.562	2	96— 58	.623				3	91— 62	.595	1935
1936				8	54—100	.351	4	84— 70	.545	2†	87— 67	.565				1	92— 62	.597	1936
1937				7	61— 92	.399	3	86— 68	.558	4	81— 73	.526				1	95— 57	.625	1937
1938				8	45—105	.300	2	86— 64	.573	6	71— 80	.470				3	83— 67	.553	1938
1939				8	45—106	.298	6	68— 85	.444	2	92— 61	.601				5	77— 74	.510	1939
1940				8	50—103	.327	4	78— 76	.506	3	84— 69	.549				6	72— 80	.474	1940
1941				8	43—111	.270	4	81— 73	.526	2	97— 56	.634				5	74— 79	.484	1941
1942				8	42—109	.270	5	66— 81	.440	1*	106— 48	.688				3	85— 67	.559	1942
1943				7	64— 90	.416	4	80— 74	.510	1	105— 49	.682				8	55— 98	.359	1943
1944				8	61— 92	.399	2	90— 63	.588	1*	105— 49	.682				5	67— 87	.435	1944
1945				8	46—108	.299	4	82— 72	.532	2	95— 59	.617				5	78— 74	.513	1945
1946				5	69— 85	.448	7	63— 91	.409	1‡*	98— 58	.628				8	61— 93	.396	1946
1947				7†	62— 92	.403	7	62— 92	.403	2	89— 65	.578				4	81— 73	.526	1947
1948				6	66— 88	.429	2	83— 71	.539	2	85— 69	.552				5	78— 76	.506	1948
1949				3	81— 73	.526	6	71— 83	.461	2	96— 58	.623				5	73— 81	.474	1949
1950				1	91— 63	.591	8	57— 96	.373	5	78— 75	.510				3	86— 68	.558	1950
1951				5	73— 81	.474	7	64— 90	.416	3	81— 73	.526				1‡	98— 59	.624.	1951
1952				4	87— 67	.565	8	42—112	.273	3	88— 66	.571				2	92— 62	.597	1952
1953				3†	83— 71	.539	8	50—104	.325	3†	83— 71	.539				5	70— 84	.455	1953
1954				4	75— 79	.487	8	53—101	.344	6	72— 82	.468				1*	97— 57	.630	1954
1955				4	77— 77	.500	8	60— 94	.390	7	68— 86	.442				3	80— 74	.519	1955
1956				5	71— 83	.461	7	66— 88	.429	4	76— 78	.494				6	67— 87	.435	1956
1957				5	77— 77	.500	7†	62— 92	.403	2	87— 67	.565				6	69— 85	.448	1957
1958				8	69— 85	.448	2	84— 70	.545	5†	72— 82	.468				3	80— 74	.519	1958
1959				8	64— 90	.416	4	78— 76	.506	7	71— 83	.461				3	83— 71	.539	1959
1960				8	59— 95	.383	1*	95— 59	.617	3	86— 68	.558				5	79— 75	.513	1960
1961				8	47—107	.305	6	75— 79	.487	5	80— 74	.519				3	85— 69	.552	1961
1962	10	40—120	.250	7	81— 80	.503	4	93— 68	.578	6	84— 78	.519				1‡	103— 62	.624	1962
1963	10	51—111	.315	4	87— 75	.537	8	74— 88	.457	2	93— 69	.574				3	88— 74	.543	1963
1964	10	53—109	.327	2†	92— 70	.568	6†	80— 82	.494	1*	93— 69	.574				4	90— 72	.556	1964
1965	10	50—112	.309	6	85— 76	.528	3	90— 72	.556	7	80— 81	.497				2	95— 67	.586	1965
1966	9	66— 95	.410	4	87— 75	.537	3	92— 70	.568	6	83— 79	.512				2	93— 68	.578	1966
1967	10	61—101	.377	5	82— 80	.506	6	81— 81	.500	1*	101— 60	.627				2	91— 71	.562	1967
1968	9	73— 89	.451	7†	76— 86	.469	6	80— 82	.494	1	97— 65	.599				2	88— 74	.543	1968

HOW THEY FINISHED 1969-1991 INCLUSIVE

Year	BRAVES* Fin.	Won—Lost	Pct.	CUBS Fin.	Won—Lost	Pct.	REDS Fin.	Won—Lost	Pct.	ASTROS Fin.	Won—Lost	Pct.	DODGERS# Fin.	Won—Lost	Pct.	EXPOS Fin.	Won—Lost	Pct.	Year
1969	1W	93— 69	.574	2E	92— 70	.568	3W	89— 73	.549	5W	81— 81	.500	4W	85— 77	.525	6E	52— 110	.321	1969
1970	5W	76— 86	.469	2E	84— 78	.519	1W	102— 60	.630	4W	79— 83	.488	2W	87— 74	.540	6E	73— 89	.451	1970
1971	3W	82— 80	.506	3E†	83— 79	.512	4W†	79— 83	.488	4W†	79— 83	.488	2W	89— 73	.549	5E	71— 90	.441	1971
1972	4W	70— 84	.455	2E†	85— 70	.548	1W	95— 59	.617	2W	84— 69	.549	3W	85— 70	.548	5E	70— 86	.449	1972
1973	5W	76— 85	.472	5E	77— 84	.478	1W	99— 63	.611	4W	82— 80	.506	2W	95— 66	.590	4E	79— 83	.488	1973
1974	3W	88— 74	.543	6E	66— 96	.407	2W	98— 64	.605	4W	81— 81	.500	1W	102— 60	.630	4E	79— 82	.491	1974
1975	5W	67— 94	.416	5E†	75— 87	.463	1W*	108— 54	.667	6W	64— 97	.398	2W	88— 74	.543	5E†	75— 87	.463	1975
1976	6W	70— 92	.432	4E	75— 87	.463	1W*	102— 60	.630	3W	80— 82	.494	2W	92— 70	.568	6E	55— 107	.340	1976
1977	6W	61— 101	.377	4E	81— 81	.500	2W	88— 74	.543	3W	81— 81	.500	1W	98— 64	.605	5E	75— 87	.463	1977
1978	6W	69— 93	.426	3E	79— 83	.488	2W	92— 69	.571	5W	74— 88	.457	1W	95— 67	.586	4E	76— 86	.496	1978
1979	6W	66— 94	.413	5E	80— 82	.494	1W	90— 71	.559	2W	89— 73	.549	3W	79— 83	.488	2E	95— 65	.594	1979
1980	4W	81— 80	.503	6E	64— 98	.395	3W	89— 73	.549	1W‡	93— 70	.571	2W**	92— 71	.564	2E	90— 72	.556	1980
1981 (1H)	4W	25— 29	.463	6E	15— 37	.288	2W	35— 21	.625	3W	28— 29	.491	1W*	36— 21	.632	3E	30— 25	.545	(1H) 1981
1981 (2H)	5W	25— 27	.481	5E	23— 28	.451	2W	31— 21	.596	1W	33— 20	.623	4W	27— 26	.509	1E	30— 23	.566	(2H) 1981
1982	1W	89— 73	.549	5E	73— 89	.451	6W	61— 101	.377	5W	77— 85	.475	2W	88— 74	.543	3E	86— 76	.531	1982
1983	2W	88— 74	.543	5E	71— 91	.438	6W	74— 88	.457	3W	85— 77	.525	1W	91— 71	.562	3E	82— 80	.506	1983
1984	2W†	80— 82	.494	1E	96— 65	.596	5W	70— 92	.432	2W†	80— 82	.494	4W	79— 83	.488	5E	78— 83	.484	1984
1985	5W	66— 96	.407	4E	77— 84	.478	2W	89— 72	.553	3W†	83— 79	.512	1W	95— 67	.586	3E	84— 77	.522	1985
1986	6W	72— 89	.447	5E	70— 90	.438	2W	86— 76	.531	1W	96— 66	.593	5W	73— 89	.451	4E	78— 83	.484	1986
1987	5W	69— 92	.429	6E	76— 85	.472	2W	84— 78	.519	3W	76— 86	.469	4W	73— 89	.451	3E	91— 71	.562	1987
1988	6W	54— 106	.338	4E	77— 85	.475	2W	87— 74	.540	5W	82— 80	.506	1W*	94— 67	.584	3E	81— 81	.500	1988
1989	6W	63— 97	.394	1E	93— 69	.574	5W	75— 87	.463	3W	86— 76	.531	4W	77— 83	.481	4E	81— 81	.500	1989
1990	6W	65— 97	.401	4E†	77— 85	.475	1W*	91— 71	.562	4W†	75— 87	.463	2W	86— 76	.531	3E	85— 77	.525	1990
1991	1W	94— 68	.580	4E	77— 83	.481	5W	74— 88	.457	6W	65— 97	.401	2W	93— 69	.574	6E	71— 90	.441	1991
Total		6576—7590	.464		7218—6986	.508		7151—7057	.503		2307—2490	.481		7443—6749	.524		1767—1891	.483	

*Boston, 1900-1952, Incl.   Milwaukee, 1953-65, Incl.   *World Champions   †Tie for Place   **Lost Playoff   #Brooklyn, 1900-1957, Incl.   (E) East   (W) West

MOST CONSECUTIVE VICTORIES

	Club	H	R	Year
26	New York	26	0	1916
21	Chicago	11	10	1880
	Chicago	18	3	1935
20	Providence	16	4	1884
18	Chicago	14	4	1885
	Baltimore	13	5	1894
	New York	13	5	1904
17	Boston	16	1	1897
	New York	14	3	1907
	New York	0	17	1916
16	Philadelphia	5	11	1887
	Philadelphia	14	2	1890
	Philadelphia	11	5	1892
	Pittsburgh	12	4	1909
	New York	11	5	1912
	New York	13	3	1951
15	Detroit	12	3	1886
	Pittsburgh	11	4	1903
	Brooklyn	3	12	1924
	Chicago	11	4	1936
	New York	8	7	1936

MOST CONSECUTIVE LOSSES

	Club	H	R	Year
24	Cleveland	5	19	1899
23	Pittsburgh	1	22	1890
	Philadelphia	6	17	1961
20	Louisville	0	20	1894
	Montreal	12	8	1969
19	Boston	3	16	1906
	Cincinnati	6	13	1914
18	Cincinnati	9	9	1876
	Louisville	0	18	1894
17	Washington	7	10	1894
	New York	7	10	1962
	Atlanta	8	9	1977
16	Troy	5	11	1882
	Detroit	5	11	1884
	Cleveland	0	16	1899
	Boston	5	11	1907
	Boston	8	8	1911
	Brooklyn	0	16	1944
15	St. Louis	11	4	1909
	Boston	0	15	1909
	Boston	0	15	1927
	Boston	0	15	1935
	New York	8	7	1963
	New York	6	9	1982

LONGEST EXTRA-INNING GAMES

26 Brk. 1, Bos. 1, May 1, 1920
25 St.L. 4, N.Y. 3, Sept. 11, 1974 (n)
24 Hou. 1, N.Y. 0, Apr. 15, 1968 (n)
23 Brk. 2, Bos. 2, June 27, 1939
   S.F. 8, N.Y. 6, May 31, 1964 (2g)
22 Brk. 6, Pitt. 5, Aug. 22, 1917
   Chi. 4, Bos. 3, May 17, 1927
   Hou. 5, L.A. 4, June 3, 1989 (n)
   L.A. 1, Mtl. 0, Aug. 23, 1989
21 N.Y. 3, Pitt. 1, July 17, 1914
   Chi. 2, Phil. 1, July 17, 1918
   Pitt. 2, Bos. 0, Aug. 1, 1918
   S.F. 1, Cin. 0, Sept. 1, 1967 (n)
   Hou. 2, S.D. 1, Sept. 24, 1971 (1g, n)
   S.D. 11, Mtl. 8, May 21, 1977 (n)
   L.A. 2, Chi. 1, Aug. 17, 1982
20 Chi. 7, Cin. 7, June 30, 1892
   Chi. 2, Phil. 1, Aug. 24, 1905
   Brk. 9, Phil. 9, Apr. 30, 1919
   St.L. 8, Chi. 7, Aug. 28, 1930
   Brk. 6, Bos. 2, July 5, 1940
   Phil. 5, Atl. 4, May 4, 1973 (n)
   Pitt. 5, Chi. 4, July 6, 1980
   Hou. 3, S.D. 1, Aug. 15, 1980 (n)
19 Chi. 3, Pitt. 2, June 22, 1902
   Pitt. 7, Bos. 6, July 31, 1912
   Chi. 4, Brk. 3, June 17, 1915
   St.L. 8, Phil. 8, June 13, 1918
   Bos. 2, Brk. 1, May 3, 1920
   Chi. 3, Bos. 2, Aug. 17, 1932
   Brk. 9, Chi. 9, May 17, 1939
   Cin. 0, Brk. 0, Sept. 11, 1946
   Phil. 8, Cin. 7, Sept. 15, 1950 (2g, n)
   Pitt. 4, Mil. 3, July 19, 1955 (n)
   Cin. 2, L.A. 1, Aug. 8, 1972 (n)
   N.Y. 7, L.A. 3, May 24, 1973 (n)

19 Pitt. 4, S.D. 3, Aug. 25, 1979 (n)
   N.Y. 16, Atl. 13, July 4, 1985 (n)
   Mtl. 6, Hou. 3, July 7, 1985 (n)
   Atl. 7, St.L. 5, May 14, 1988 (n)
18 Prov. 1, Det. 0, Aug. 17, 1882
   Brk. 7, St.L. 7, Aug. 17, 1902
   Chi. 2, St.L. 1, June 24, 1905
   Brk. 4, St.L. 3, July 29, 1914
   Pitt. 3, Chi. 2, June 28, 1916 (2g)
   Phil. 10, Brk. 9, June 1, 1919
   N.Y. 9, Pitt. 8, July 7, 1922
   Chi. 7, Bos. 2, May 14, 1927
   N.Y. 1, St.L. 0, July 2, 1933 (1g)
   St.L. 8, Cin. 6, July 1, 1934 (1g)
   Chi. 10, Cin. 8, Aug. 9, 1942 (1g)
   Phil. 4, Pitt. 3, June 9, 1949
   Cin. 7, Chi. 6, Sept. 7, 1951 (2g)
   N.Y. 0, Phil 0, Oct. 2, 1965 (2g, n)
   Cin. 3, Chi. 2, July 19, 1966
   Phil. 2, Cin. 1, May 21, 1967
   Pitt. 1, S.D. 0, June 7, 1972 (2g, n)
   N.Y. 3, Phil. 2, Aug. 1, 1972 (1g, n)
   Mtl. 5, Chi. 4, June 27, 1973 (2g)
   Chi. 8, Mtl. 7, June 28, 1974 (1g, n)
   N.Y. 4, Mtl. 3, Sept. 16, 1975 (n)
   Pitt. 2, Chi. 1, Aug. 10, 1977 (n)
   Chi. 9, Cin. 8, May 10, 1979
   Hou. 3, N.Y. 2, June 18, 1979 (n)
   S.D. 8, N.Y. 6, Aug. 26, 1980
   St.L. 3, Hou. 1, May 27, 1983 (n)
   Pitt. 4, S.F. 3, July 13, 1984 (n)
   Atl. 3, L.A. 2, Sept. 6, 1984 (n)
   N.Y. 5, Pitt. 4, Apr. 28, 1985
   S.F. 5, Atl. 4, June 11, 1985
   Hou. 8, Chi. 7, Sept. 2, 1986
   Pitt. 5, Chi. 4, Aug. 6, 1989

HOW THEY FINISHED 1969-1991 INCLUSIVE

Year	METS Fin.	Won—Lost	Pct.	PHILLIES Fin.	Won—Lost	Pct.	PIRATES Fin.	Won—Lost	Pct.	CARDINALS Fin.	Won—Lost	Pct.	PADRES Fin.	Won—Lost	Pct.	GIANTS§ Fin.	Won—Lost	Pct.	Year
1969	1E*	100— 62	.617	5E	63— 99	.389	3E	88— 74	.543	4E	87— 75	.537	6W	52— 110	.321	2W	90— 72	.556	1969
1970	3E†	83— 79	.512	5E	73— 88	.453	1E	89— 73	.549	4E	76— 86	.469	6W	63— 99	.389	3W	86— 76	.531	1970
1971	3E†	83— 79	.512	6E	67— 95	.414	1E*	97— 65	.599	2E	90— 72	.556	6W	61— 100	.379	1W	90— 72	.556	1971
1972	3E	83— 73	.532	6E	59— 97	.378	1E	96— 59	.619	4E	75— 81	.481	6W	58— 95	.379	5W	69— 86	.445	1972
1973	1E	82— 79	.509	6E	71— 91	.438	3E	80— 82	.494	2E	81— 81	.500	6W	60— 102	.370	3W	88— 74	.543	1973
1974	5E	71— 91	.438	3E	80— 82	.494	1E	88— 74	.543	2E	86— 75	.534	6W	60— 102	.370	5W	72— 90	.444	1974
1975	3E†	82— 80	.506	2E	86— 76	.531	1E	92— 69	.571	3E†	82— 80	.506	4W	71— 91	.438	3W	80— 81	.497	1975
1976	3E	86— 76	.531	1E	101— 61	.623	2E	92— 70	.568	5E	72— 90	.444	5W	73— 89	.451	4W	74— 88	.457	1976
1977	6E	64— 98	.395	1E	101— 61	.623	2E	96— 66	.593	3E	83— 79	.512	5W	69— 93	.426	4W	75— 87	.463	1977
1978	6E	66— 96	.407	1E	90— 72	.556	2E	88— 73	.547	5E	69— 93	.426	4W	84— 78	.519	3W	89— 73	.549	1978
1979	6E	63— 99	.389	4E	84— 78	.519	1E*	98— 64	.605	3E	86— 76	.531	5W	68— 93	.422	4W	71— 91	.438	1979
1980	5E	67— 95	.414	1E*	91— 71	.562	3E	83— 79	.512	4E	74— 88	.457	6W	73— 89	.451	5W	75— 86	.466	1980
1981 (1H)	5E	17— 34	.333	1E	34— 21	.618	4E	25— 23	.521	2E	30— 20	.600	6W	23— 33	.411	5W	27— 32	.458	(1H) 1981
1981 (2H)	4E	24— 28	.462	3E	25— 27	.481	6E	21— 33	.389	2E	29— 23	.558	6W	18— 36	.333	3W	29— 23	.558	(2H) 1981
1982	6E	65— 97	.401	2E	89— 73	.549	4E	84— 78	.519	1E*	92— 70	.568	4W	81— 81	.500	3W	87— 75	.537	1982
1983	6E	68— 94	.420	1E	90— 72	.556	2E	84— 78	.519	4E	79— 83	.488	4W	81— 81	.500	5W	79— 83	.488	1983
1984	2E	90— 72	.556	4E	81— 81	.500	6E	75— 87	.463	3E	84— 78	.519	1W	92— 70	.568	6W	66— 96	.407	1984
1985	2E	98— 64	.605	5E	75— 87	.463	6E	57— 104	.354	1E	101— 61	.623	3W†	83— 79	.512	6W	62— 100	.383	1985
1986	1E*	108— 54	.667	2E	86— 75	.534	6E	64— 98	.395	3E	79— 82	.491	4W	74— 88	.457	3W	83— 79	.512	1986
1987	2E	92— 70	.568	4E†	80— 82	.494	4E†	80— 82	.494	1E	95— 67	.586	6W	65— 97	.401	1W	90— 72	.556	1987
1988	1E	100— 60	.625	6E	65— 96	.404	2E	85— 75	.531	5E	76— 86	.469	3W	83— 78	.516	4W	83— 79	.512	1988
1989	2E	87— 75	.537	6E	67— 95	.414	5E	74— 88	.457	3E	86— 76	.531	2W	89— 73	.549	4W	92— 70	.568	1989
1990	2E	91— 71	.562	4E†	77— 85	.475	1E	95— 67	.586	6E	70— 92	.432	4W†	75— 87	.463	3W	85— 77	.525	1990
1991	5E	77— 84	.478	3E	78— 84	.481	1E	98— 64	.605	2E	84— 78	.519	3W	84— 78	.519	4W	75— 87	.463	1991
Total		2241—2547	.468		6478—7691	.457		7424—6768	.523		7322—6873	.516		1640—2022	.448		7645—6548	.539	

*World Champions   †Tie for Place   ‡Won Playoff   §New York, 1900-1957, Incl.   (E) East   (W) West

INTER-CLUB TOTALS 1900 to 1991, INCLUSIVE

	Giants W-L	Dodgers W-L	Pirates W-L	Cards W-L	Cubs W-L	Reds W-L	Expos W-L	Astros W-L	Mets W-L	Braves W-L	Phils W-L	Padres W-L	Won	Lost	Pct.
N.Y.-San Francisco	-	953-928	937-810	902-833	914-835	1038-840	138-133	275-262	221-175	1038-827	1011-718	218-187	7645	6548	.539
Brk.-Los Angeles	928 953	-	898-842	870-871	868-874	952-929	161-110	303-232	224-171	1039-830	982-748	218-189	7443	6749	.524
Pittsburgh	810-937	842-898	-	986-890	995-886	900-839	223-185	234-161	280-247	955-778	1031-841	168-106	7424	6768	.523
St. Louis	833-902	871-870	890-986	-	915-957	928-818	204-205	214-182	286-245	951-788	1070-806	160-114	7322	6873	.516
Chicago	835-914	874-868	886-995	957-915	-	887-854	196-206	107-210	268-265	972-769	998-878	158-112	7218	6986	.508
Cincinnati	840-1038	929-952	839-900	818-928	854-887	-	150-123	291-242	229-169	1006-800	966-772	229-178	7151	7057	.503
Montreal	113-138	110-161	185-223	205-204	206-196	123-150	-	122-149	196-212	147-124	200-205	140-129	1767	1891	.483
Houston	262-275	232-303	161-234	182-214	210-187	242-291	149-122	-	221-176	254-276	179-221	215-191	2307	2490	.481
New York	175-221	171-224	247-280	245-286	265-268	169-229	212-196	176-221	-	189-207	247-289	145-126	2241	2547	.468
Bos.-Mil.-Atlanta	827-1038	830-1039	778-955	788-951	769-972	868-1006	124-147	276-254	207-189	-	892-846	217-193	6576	7590	.464
Philadelphia	718-1011	748-982	841-1031	806-1070	878-998	772-966	205-200	221-179	289-247	846-892	-	154-115	6478	7691	.457
San Diego	187-218	189-218	106-168	114-160	112-158	178-229	129-140	191-215	126-145	193-217	115-154	-	1640	2022	.448

CLUB ATTENDANCE HIGHS SINCE 1969

ATLANTA

53,575 (n)	4/ 8/74	vs. LA
50,597 (tn)	7/ 4/72	vs. Chi.
50,595 (n)	7/ 4/77	vs. Cin.
50,419 (tn)	7/24/76	vs. Cin.
48,905 (n)	7/ 7/82	vs. Cin.

CINCINNATI

55,438	4/ 4/88	vs. St.L.
55,385	4/ 3/89	vs. LA
55,205	4/ 8/91	vs. Hou.
55,166	4/ 6/87	vs. Mon.
54,960	4/ 7/86	vs. Phi.

LOS ANGELES

55,185 (n)	7/28/73	vs. SF
55,110 (n)	6/26/70	vs. SD
53,927 (n)	5/17/74	vs. Atl.
53,906 (n)	5/14/81	vs. Mon.
53,870 (n)	7/14/73	vs. Chi.

NEW YORK

59,083 (n)	7/ 9/69	vs. Chi.
58,874	9/20/69	vs. Pit.
55,901 (dh)	9/21/69	vs. Pit.
55,862 (dh)	6/22/69	vs. St.L.
55,391	7/27/69	vs. Cin.

PITTSBURGH

54,274 (n)	4/ 8/91	vs. Mon.
54,098 (n)	4/11/88	vs. Phi.
52,119 (n)	4/10/87	vs. St.L.
51,726	6/ 6/76	vs. SD
51,695	4/ 6/73	vs. St.L.

SAN DIEGO

54,841 (n)	5/10/91	vs. Mon.
54,732	6/ 7/86	vs. Atl.
54,517 (n)	6/ 1/91	vs. Hou.
54,490 (n)	4/15/85	vs. S.F.
54,395 (n)	5/11/85	vs. Chi.

CHICAGO

45,777	4/14/78	vs. Pit.
44,818	4/13/76	vs. NY
43,066 (dh)	8/ 8/71	vs. SF
42,497 (dh)	7/ 1/73	vs. NY
41,052 (dh)	7/22/79	vs. Cin.

HOUSTON

48,176 (n)	4/21/79	vs. Pit.
46,754 (n)	7/29/79	vs. LA
46,313 (n)	6/25/79	vs. Cin.
46,215 (n)	4/29/78	vs. Mon.
46,213 (n)	6/22/80	vs. Pit.

MONTREAL

59,282 (dh)	9/16/79	vs. St.L.
59,260 (tn)	7/27/79	vs. Pit.
57,694	8/15/82	vs. Phi.
57,592	4/15/77	vs. Phi.
57,121 (n)	10/ 3/80	vs. Phi.

PHILADELPHIA

63,816 (n)	7/ 3/84	vs. Cin.
63,501 (n)	7/ 5/82	vs. SF
63,346 (tn)	8/10/79	vs. Pit.
63,283 (n)	7/ 4/77	vs. NY
61,177 (tn)	7/15/77	vs. Chi.

ST. LOUIS

51,647 (n)	4/ 8/88	vs. Pit.
51,257 (n)	4/14/89	vs. NY
50,548	9/14/75	vs. NY
50,340 (n)	7/ 2/77	vs. Chi.
50,023 (n)	5/12/89	vs. Cin.

SAN FRANCISCO

56,196	4/10/79	vs. SD
56,103	5/28/78	vs. LA
55,920 (n)	6/20/78	vs. Cin.
55,883 (n)	4/15/91	vs LA
55,792	7/29/90	vs. Cin.

MOST VALUABLE PLAYER AWARD WINNERS

1931 - Frank Frisch, Cardinals	1962 - Maury Wills, Dodgers
1932 - Chuck Klein, Phillies	1963 - Sandy Koufax, Dodgers
1933 - Carl Hubbell, Giants	1964 - Ken Boyer, Cardinals
1934 - Dizzy Dean, Cardinals	1965 - Willie Mays, Giants
1935 - Gabby Hartnett, Cubs	1966 - Roberto Clemente, Pirates
1936 - Carl Hubbell, Giants	1967 - Orlando Cepeda, Cardinals
1937 - Joe Medwick, Cardinals	1968 - Bob Gibson, Cardinals
1938 - Ernie Lombardi, Reds	1969 - Willie McCovey, Giants
1939 - Bucky Walters, Reds	1970 - Johnny Bench, Reds
1940 - Frank McCormick, Reds	1971 - Joe Torre, Cardinals
1941 - Dolph Camilli, Dodgers	1972 - Johnny Bench, Reds
1942 - Mort Cooper, Cardinals	1973 - Pete Rose, Reds
1943 - Stan Musial, Cardinals	1974 - Steve Garvey, Dodgers
1944 - Marty Marion, Cardinals	1975 - Joe Morgan, Reds
1945 - Phil Cavarretta, Cubs	1976 - Joe Morgan, Reds
1946 - Stan Musial, Cardinals	1977 - George Foster, Reds
1947 - Bob Elliott, Braves	1978 - Dave Parker, Pirates
1948 - Stan Musial, Cardinals	1979 - Keith Hernandez, Cardinals
1949 - Jackie Robinson, Dodgers	Willie Stargell, Pirates
1950 - Jim Konstanty, Phillies	1980 - Mike Schmidt, Phillies
1951 - Roy Campanella, Dodgers	1981 - Mike Schmidt, Phillies
1952 - Hank Sauer, Cubs	1982 - Dale Murphy, Braves
1953 - Roy Campanella, Dodgers	1983 - Dale Murphy, Braves
1954 - Willie Mays, Giants	1984 - Ryne Sandberg, Cubs
1955 - Roy Campanella, Dodgers	1985 - Willie McGee, Cardinals
1956 - Don Newcombe, Dodgers	1986 - Mike Schmidt, Phillies
1957 - Hank Aaron, Braves	1987 - Andre Dawson, Cubs
1958 - Ernie Banks, Cubs	1988 - Kirk Gibson, Dodgers
1959 - Ernie Banks, Cubs	1989 - Kevin Mitchell, Giants
1960 - Dick Groat, Pirates	1990 - Barry Bonds, Pirates
1961 - Frank Robinson, Reds	1991 - Terry Pendleton, Braves

Prior to 1931, the League had awards that reflected what the MVP is today. Those early winners included:

1924 Vance, Arthur C., Brk. (P)
1925 Hornsby, Rogers, St.L. (2B)
1926 O'Farrell, Robert A., St.L. (C)
1927 Waner, Paul G., Pit. (OF)
1928 Bottomley, James L., St.L. (1B)
1929 Hornsby, Rogers, Chi. (2B)

Even earlier than 1924, the Chalmers Award carried the prestige of the MVP. Those winners included:

1911 Schulte, Frank, Chi. (OF)
1912 Doyle, Lawrence J., N.Y. (2B)
1913 Daubert, Jacob E., Brk. (1B)
1914 Evers, John J., Bos. (2B)

MVP

TERRY PENDLETON
ATLANTA BRAVES

Terry Pendleton, 1991 National League batting champion with a .319 average, led the Atlanta Braves to the Western Division title and was voted N.L. MVP with a total of 274 points in the balloting, defeating last season's MVP, Barry Bonds, by a 15-point margin. Pendleton also led the League in hits, 187, and multi-hit games, 52. He was tied for first in total bases, 303, third in slugging percentage, .517, tied for seventh in doubles, 34, tied for sixth in triples, 8, ninth in runs, 94, and tied for fifth in extra-base hits, 64. This is Pendleton's first MVP Award. The last Braves' player to win the N.L. MVP was Dale Murphy, who won back-to-back honors in 1982-83. It is also Pendleton's first batting title. The last Braves' player to win the batting championship was Ralph Garr in 1974.

1991 MVP VOTING

Player—Club	1	2	3	4	5	6	7	8	9	10	Pts.
Pendleton, Atlanta	12	10	2	—	—	—	—	—	—	—	274
Bonds, Pittsburgh	10	10	1	3	—	—	—	—	—	—	259
Bonilla, Pittsburgh	1	3	14	3	2	1	—	—	—	—	191
Clark, San Francisco	—	—	3	1	7	3	4	4	—	2	118
Johnson, New York	—	—	1	3	1	8	7	3	—	—	112
Gant, Atlanta	—	—	1	5	3	3	5	3	1	3	110
Butler, Los Angeles	1	1	1	4	1	3	3	2	2	1	103
L. Smith, St. Louis	—	—	1	2	4	4	2	2	2	5	89
Strawberry, Los Angeles	—	—	—	3	3	2	—	6	4	1	76
McGriff, San Diego	—	—	—	—	1	—	1	1	4	2	23
Glavine, Atlanta	—	—	—	—	2	—	—	—	2	—	16
Justice, Atlanta	—	—	—	—	—	—	1	1	2	—	11
Bell, Pittsburgh	—	—	—	—	—	—	1	1	1	2	11
Dawson, Chicago	—	—	—	—	—	—	—	1	1	—	5
Smiley, Pittsburgh	—	—	—	—	—	—	—	—	2	1	5
Gwynn, San Diego	—	—	—	—	—	—	—	—	2	—	4
Kruk, Philadelphia	—	—	—	—	—	—	—	—	1	—	2
Sandberg, Chicago	—	—	—	—	—	—	—	—	—	2	2
Larkin, Cincinnati	—	—	—	—	—	—	—	—	—	2	2
Martinez, Montreal	—	—	—	—	—	—	—	—	—	1	1
Sabo, Cincinnati	—	—	—	—	—	—	—	—	—	1	1
O. Smith, St. Louis	—	—	—	—	—	—	—	—	—	1	1

MVP AWARDS BY TEAM

Braves	5 Winners
Cubs	7 Winners
Reds	10 Winners
Astros	0 Winners
Dodgers	10 Winners
Expos	0 Winners
Mets	0 Winners
Phillies	5 Winners
Pirates	5 Winners
Cardinals	14 Winners
Padres	0 Winners
Giants	6 Winners

CY YOUNG AWARDS BY TEAM

Braves	2 Winners
Cubs	3 Winners
Reds	0 Winners
Astros	1 Winner
Dodgers	8 Winners
Expos	0 Winners
Mets	4 Winners
Phillies	6 Winners
Pirates	2 Winners
Cardinals	2 Winners
Padres	3 Winners
Giants	1 Winner

1991 PLAYERS OF THE MONTH

Month	Player & Club	Performance
April	FELIX JOSE, Cardinals	.354, 28/79, 9-2B, 2-3B, 2 HR, 16 R, 15 RBI, .595 SLG, 2 SB
May	DAVID JUSTICE, Braves	.381, 37/97, 9-2B, 5 HR, 19 R, 28 RBI, .629 SLG, 4 SB
June	BARRY LARKIN, Reds	.370, 34/92, 5-2B, 9 HR, 24 R, 23 RBI, .717 SLG, 13 SB
July	BARRY BONDS, Pirates	.362, 34/94, 4-2B, 2-3B, 6 HR, 20 R, 29 RBI, .638 SLG, 15 SB
August	WILL CLARK, Giants	.347, 41/118, 14-2B, 2-3B, 7 HR, 24 R, 28 RBI, .678 SLG
September	HOWARD JOHNSON, Mets	.296, 29/98, 7-2B, 1-3B, 10 HR, 27 R, 28 RBI, .694 SLG, 10 SB

1991 PITCHERS OF THE MONTH

Month	Pitcher & Club	Performance
April	LEE SMITH, Cardinals	2-0, 8 SV, 1.38 ERA, 10 G, 13 IP, 6 H, 14 SO, 2 BB
May	TOM GLAVINE, Braves	6-0, 1.76 ERA, 6 GS, 3 CG, 46 IP, 35 H, 33 SO, 6 BB
June	ROB DIBBLE, Reds	10 SV, 1.69 ERA, 15 G, 16 IP, 9 H, 22 SO, 7 BB
July	DENNIS MARTINEZ, Expos	2-1, 2.11 ERA, 5 GS, 38⅓ IP, 30 H, 17 SO, 9 BB, pitched perfect game 7/28
August	MITCH WILLIAMS, Phillies	8-1, 5 SV, 1.21 ERA, 15 G, 22⅓ IP, 10 H, 22 SO, 16 BB, M.L. record for wins in a month by a relief pitcher
September	CHRIS NABHOLZ, Expos	6-0, 2.23 ERA, 6 GS, 44⅓ IP, 34 H, 36 SO, 14 BB

NATIONAL LEAGUE BATTING CHAMPIONS

Year	Player, Team	Avg
1876	Roscoe Barnes, Chicago	.403
1877	James White, Boston	.385
1878	Abner Dalrymple, Milwaukee	.356
1879	Cap Anson, Chicago	.407
1880	George Gore, Chicago	.365
1881	Cap Anson, Chicago	.399
1882	Dan Brouthers, Buffalo	.367
1883	Dan Brouthers, Buffalo	.371
1884	Jim O'Rourke, Buffalo	.350
1885	Roger Connor, New York	.371
1886	Mike Kelly, Chicago	.388
1887	Cap Anson, Chicago	.421
1888	Cap Anson, Chicago	.343
1889	Dan Brouthers, Boston	.373
1890	Jack Glasscock, New York	.336
1891	Billy Hamilton, Philadelphia	.338
1892	"Cupid" Childs, Cleveland	.335
1892	Dan Brouthers, Brooklyn	.335
1893	Hugh Duffy, Boston	.378
1894	Hugh Duffy, Boston	.438
1895	Jesse Burkett, Cleveland	.423
1896	Jesse Burkett, Cleveland	.410
1897	Willie Keeler, Baltimore	.432
1898	Willie Keeler, Baltimore	.379
1899	Ed Delahanty, Philadelphia	.408
1900	Honus Wagner, Pittsburgh	.380
1901	Jesse Burkett, St. Louis	.382
1902	C.H. Beaumont, Pittsburgh	.357
1903	Honus Wagner, Pittsburgh	.355
1904	Honus Wagner, Pittsburgh	.349
1905	J. Bentley Seymour, Cincinnati	.377
1906	Honus Wagner, Pittsburgh	.339
1907	Honus Wagner, Pittsburgh	.350
1908	Honus Wagner, Pittsburgh	.354
1909	Honus Wagner, Pittsburgh	.339
1910	Sherwood Magee, Philadelphia	.331
1911	Honus Wagner, Pittsburgh	.334
1912	Heinie Zimmerman, Chicago	.372
1913	Jake Daubert, Brooklyn	.350
1914	Jake Daubert, Brooklyn	.329
1915	Larry Doyle, New York	.320
1916	Hal Chase, Cincinnati	.339
1917	Edd Roush, Cincinnati	.341
1918	Zack Wheat, Brooklyn	.335
1919	Edd Roush, Cincinnati	.321
1920	Rogers Hornsby, St. Louis	.370
1921	Rogers Hornsby, St. Louis	.397
1922	Rogers Hornsby, St. Louis	.401
1923	Rogers Hornsby, St. Louis	.384
1924	Rogers Hornsby, St. Louis	.424
1925	Rogers Hornsby, St. Louis	.403
1926	Bubbles Hargrave, Cincinnati	.353
1927	Paul Waner, Pittsburgh	.380
1928	Rogers Hornsby, Boston	.387
1929	Lefty O'Doul, Philadelphia	.398
1930	Bill Terry, New York	.401
1931	Chick Hafey, St. Louis*	.349
1932	Lefty O'Doul, Brooklyn	.368
1933	Chuck Klein, Philadelphia	.368
1934	Paul Waner, Pittsburgh	.362
1935	Arky Vaughan, Pittsburgh	.385
1936	Paul Waner, Pittsburgh	.373
1937	Joe Medwick, St. Louis	.374
1938	Ernie Lombardi, Cincinnati	.342
1939	Johnny Mize, St. Louis	.349
1940	Debs Garms, Pittsburgh	.355
1941	Pete Reiser, Brooklyn	.343
1942	Ernie Lombardi, Boston	.330
1943	Stan Musial, St. Louis	.357
1944	Dixie Walker, Brooklyn	.357
1945	Phil Cavarretta, Chicago	.355
1946	Stan Musial, St. Louis	.365
1947	Harry Walker, St. Louis-Philadelphia	.363
1948	Stan Musial, St. Louis	.376
1949	Jackie Robinson, Brooklyn	.342
1950	Stan Musial, St. Louis	.346
1951	Stan Musial, St. Louis	.355
1952	Stan Musial, St. Louis	.336
1953	Carl Furillo, Brooklyn	.344
1954	Willie Mays, New York	.345
1955	Richie Ashburn, Philadelphia	.338
1956	Hank Aaron, Milwaukee	.328
1957	Stan Musial, St. Louis	.351
1958	Richie Ashburn, Philadelphia	.350
1959	Hank Aaron, Milwaukee	.355
1960	Dick Groat, Pittsburgh	.325
1961	Roberto Clemente, Pittsburgh	.351
1962	Tommy Davis, Los Angeles	.346
1963	Tommy Davis, Los Angeles	.326
1964	Roberto Clemente, Pittsburgh	.339
1965	Roberto Clemente, Pittsburgh	.329
1966	Matty Alou, Pittsburgh	.342
1967	Roberto Clemente, Pittsburgh	.357
1968	Pete Rose, Cincinnati	.335
1969	Pete Rose, Cincinnati	.348
1970	Rico Carty, Atlanta	.366
1971	Joe Torre, St. Louis	.363
1972	Billy Williams, Chicago	.333
1973	Pete Rose, Cincinnati	.338
1974	Ralph Garr, Atlanta	.353
1975	Bill Madlock, Chicago	.354
1976	Bill Madlock, Chicago	.339
1977	Dave Parker, Pittsburgh	.338
1978	Dave Parker, Pittsburgh	.334
1979	Keith Hernandez, St. Louis	.344
1980	Bill Buckner, Chicago	.324
1981	Bill Madlock, Pittsburgh	.341
1982	Al Oliver, Montreal	.331
1983	Bill Madlock, Pittsburgh	.323
1984	Tony Gwynn, San Diego	.351
1985	Willie McGee, St. Louis	.353
1986	Tim Raines, Montreal	.334
1987	Tony Gwynn, San Diego	.370
1988	Tony Gwynn, San Diego	.313
1989	Tony Gwynn, San Diego	.336
1990	Willie McGee, St. Louis	.335
1991	Terry Pendleton, Atlanta	.319

*Hafey led with .3489, Bill Terry, New York, second with .3486, Jim Bottomley, St. Louis, third with .3482.

1991 PLAYERS OF THE WEEK

Week	Player, Team	Performance
4/8-14	Dwight Gooden, Mets	2-0, 21 SO, 4 BB, 13 H, 4 R, 17 IP
4/15-21	Andre Dawson, Cubs	.357, 2 grand slams, 1-2B, 1-3B, 10/28, 10 RBI, 6 R
4/22-28	Felix Jose, Cardinals	.500, 12/24, 2-2B, 2-3B, 1 HR, 6 RBI, 3 R
4/29-5/5	Fred McGriff, Padres	.423, 11/26, 1-2B, 1-3B, 3 HR, .885 slugging, 8 RBI, 5 R
5/6-12	Hal Morris, Reds	.533, 8/15, 5 R, 5 RBI, 2 SB, 1 HR, 6 BB, .652 on-base
5/13-20	Terry Pendleton, Braves	.611, 11/18, 2-2B, 1 HR, .889 slugging, .650 on-base, 4 RBI, 5 R, 1 SB
5/20-26	Tommy Greene, Phillies	pitched 1st career no-hitter vs. MTL 5/23, 10 SO, 7 BB
5/27-6/2	Mike Felder, Giants	.448, 13/29, 1-2B, 2-3B, 5 RBI, 8 R, 3 SB, .484 on-base
6/3-9	Tony Gwynn, Padres	.522, 12/23, 1-3B, 5 R, 4 RBI, 1 SB, .609 slugging, .542 on-base, current 15-game hitting streak
6/10-16	Dennis Martinez, Expos	0.56 ERA, 2-0, 1 ER, 16 IP, 1 CG, 14 H, 3 BB, 10 SO
6/17-23	Mike Morgan, Dodgers	2-0, 2 GS, 17.2 IP, 12 H, 5 R, 1 BB, 8 SO, 2.55 ERA
6/24-30	Barry Larkin, Reds	Tied ML record with 5 HR in 2 G (6/27, 28), .440, 11/25, 1-2B, 11 RBI, 7 R, 3 SB, 1.120 slugging
7/1-7	Pedro Guerrero, Cardinals	.367, 11/30, 1-2B, 3 HR, 9 RBI, 5 R, 2 SB, current 10-game hitting streak
7/11-14	Will Clark, Giants	.529, 9/17, 2-2B, 2 HR, 1 grand slam, 5 R, 10 RBI, 1 SB
	Barry Bonds, Pirates	.437, 7/16, 2-2B, 3 HR, 4 R, 11 RBI, 3 SB
7/15-21	Randy Tomlin, Pirates	2-0, 2 CG SHO, 8 H, 5 BB, 12 SO, 18 IP, no extra base hits, .142 opposing team BA
7/22-28	Dennis Martinez, Expos	Pitched perfect game on 7/28 vs. LA, 5 SO
7/29-8/4	Wes Chamberlain, Phillies	.478, 10 RBI, 3 3-run HR, 2-2B, 1-3B, 11/23, 6 R
8/5-11	Mitch Williams, Phillies	5 G, 3 W, 2 SV, 0.00 ERA, 2 H, 4 SO, 4 BB, 5.2 IP, 11.2 scoreless innings streak
8/12-18	Bobby Bonilla, Pirates	.577, 15/26, 5-2B, 1 HR, 10 R, 7 RBI, 7 multi-hit games, .633 on-base
8/19-25	Darryl Strawberry, Dodgers	.565, 13/23, 13 RBI, 4 HR, 5 R, 1-2B, 1 SB, 1.087 slugging
8/26-9/1	Ken Caminiti, Astros	.393, 11/28, 14 RBI, 2 HR, 2-2B, 3 R
9/2-8	Andujar Cedeno, Astros	.476, 10/21, 2-2B, 1-3B, 1 HR, 4 R, 4 RBI, 1 SB, hit safely in all 6 G
9/9-15	Mariano Duncan, Reds	.467, 14/30, 6 HR, 10 RBI, 11 R, 1 SB, 1.067 slugging
	Steve Avery, Braves	2-0, 2 R, 1 ER, 7 H, 2 BB, 10 SO, 17.2 IP, 1 CG, 0.51 ERA
9/16-22	John Kruk, Phillies	.480, 12/25, 3-2B, 1 HR, 3 RBI, 4 R
9/23-29	Lee Smith, Cardinals	3 SV, incl. 45th of season tying NL record, 3 G, 4 H, 0 R, 1 BB, 5 SO, 4 IP, 310 career SV, 3rd on ML all-time list
9/30-10/6	David Cone, Mets	Tied NL record of 19 SO vs. PHI 10/6
	Greg Maddux, Cubs	2 CG, 1 SHO, 9 H, 0 ER, 1 BB, 13 SO

NATIONAL LEAGUE HOME RUN CHAMPIONS 1900-1991

Year	Player	HR
1900	Herman Long, Boston	12
1901	Sam Crawford, Cincinnati	16
1902	Tom Leach, Pittsburgh	6
1903	Jim Sheckard, Brooklyn	9
1904	Harry Lumley, Brooklyn	9
1905	Fred Odwell, Cincinnati	9
1906	Tim Jordan, Brooklyn	12
1907	Dave Brain, Boston	10
1908	Tim Jordan, Brooklyn	12
1909	Red Murray, New York	7
1910	Fred Beck, Boston	10
	Frank Schulte, Chicago	10
1911	Frank Schulte, Chicago	21
1912	Heinie Zimmerman, Chicago	14
1913	Gavvy Cravath, Philadelphia	19
1914	Gavvy Cravath, Philadelphia	19
1915	Gavvy Cravath, Philadelphia	24
1916	Dave Robertson, New York	12
	Cy Williams, Chicago	12
1917	Gavvy Cravath, Philadelphia	12
	Dave Robertson, New York	12
1918	Gavvy Cravath, Philadelphia	8
1919	Gavvy Cravath, Philadelphia	12
1920	Cy Williams, Philadelphia	15
1921	George Kelly, New York	23
1922	Rogers Hornsby, St. Louis	42
1923	Cy Williams, Philadelphia	41
1924	Jack Fournier, Brooklyn	27
1925	Rogers Hornsby, St. Louis	39
1926	Hack Wilson, Chicago	21
1927	Cy Williams, Pittsburgh	30
	Hack Wilson, Chicago	30
1928	Jim Bottomley, St. Louis	31
	Hack Wilson, Chicago	31
1929	Chuck Klein, Philadelphia	43
1930	Hack Wilson, Chicago	56
1931	Chuck Klein, Philadelphia	31
1932	Chuck Klein, Philadelphia	38
	Mel Ott, New York	38
1933	Chuck Klein, Philadelphia	28
1934	Rip Collins, St. Louis	35
	Mel Ott, New York	35
1935	Wally Berger, Boston	34
1936	Mel Ott, New York	33
1937	Joe Medwick, St. Louis	31
	Mel Ott, New York	31
1938	Mel Ott, New York	36
1939	Johnny Mize, St. Louis	28
1940	Johnny Mize, St. Louis	43
1941	Dolf Camilli, Brooklyn	34
1942	Mel Ott, New York	30
1943	Bill Nicholson, Chicago	29
1944	Bill Nicholson, Chicago	33
1945	Tom Holmes, Boston	28
1946	Ralph Kiner, Pittsburgh	23
1947	Ralph Kiner, Pittsburgh	51
	Johnny Mize, New York	51
1948	Ralph Kiner, Pittsburgh	40
	Johnny Mize, New York	40
1949	Ralph Kiner, Pittsburgh	54
1950	Ralph Kiner, Pittsburgh	47
1951	Ralph Kiner, Pittsburgh	42
1952	Ralph Kiner, Pittsburgh	37
	Hank Sauer, Chicago	37
1953	Eddie Mathews, Milwaukee	47
1954	Ted Kluszewski, Cincinnati	49
1955	Willie Mays, New York	51
1956	Duke Snider, Brooklyn	43
1957	Hank Aaron, Milwaukee	44
1958	Ernie Banks, Chicago	47
1959	Eddie Mathews, Milwaukee	46
1960	Ernie Banks, Chicago	41
1961	Orlando Cepeda, San Francisco	46
1962	Willie Mays, San Francisco	49
1963	Hank Aaron, Milwaukee	44
	Willie McCovey, San Francisco	44
1964	Willie Mays, San Francisco	47
1965	Willie Mays, San Francisco	52
1966	Hank Aaron, Atlanta	44
1967	Hank Aaron, Atlanta	39
1968	Willie McCovey, San Francisco	36
1969	Willie McCovey, San Francisco	45
1970	Johnny Bench, Cincinnati	45
1971	Willie Stargell, Pittsburgh	48
1972	Johnny Bench, Cincinnati	40
1973	Willie Stargell, Pittsburgh	44
1974	Mike Schmidt, Philadelphia	36
1975	Mike Schmidt, Philadelphia	38
1976	Mike Schmidt, Philadelphia	38
1977	George Foster, Cincinnati	52
1978	George Foster, Cincinnati	40
1979	Dave Kingman, Chicago	48
1980	Mike Schmidt, Philadelphia	48
1981	Mike Schmidt, Philadelphia	31
1982	Dave Kingman, New York	37
1983	Mike Schmidt, Philadelphia	40
1984	Dale Murphy, Atlanta	36
	Mike Schmidt, Philadelphia	36
1985	Dale Murphy, Atlanta	37
1986	Mike Schmidt, Philadelphia	37
1987	Andre Dawson, Chicago	49
1988	Darryl Strawberry, New York	39
1989	Kevin Mitchell, San Francisco	47
1990	Ryne Sandberg, Chicago	40
1991	Howard Johnson, New York	38

MEL OTT AWARD
RBI LEADER

HOWARD JOHNSON
NEW YORK METS

Howard Johnson of the New York Mets won the 1991 Mel Ott Award for home runs with his League-leading 38 and the National League RBI Championship with 117. Johnson also led the League in extra-base hits with 76, was second in slugging percentage, .535, third in total bases, 302, tied for seventh in doubles, 34, and ninth in runs, 94. He was voted N.L. Player of the Month for September when he hit .296, 10 home runs and drove in 28 runs.

RBI RATIO
(At Bats Per RBI)

4.4	Bonds, Pit.
4.8	Johnson, N.Y.
4.9	Clark, S.F.
5.0	McGriff, S.D.
5.1	Strawberry, L.A.
5.3	Gant, Atl.
5.4	Dawson, Chi.
5.8	Bonilla, Pit.
5.8	O'Neill, Cin.
5.8	Kruk, Phi.

HOME RUN RATIO
(At Bats Per Home Run)

14.8	Johnson, N.Y.
17.0	McGriff, S.D.
17.3	Williams, S.F.
17.5	Gant, Atl.
18.0	Strawberry, L.A.
18.2	Dawson, Chi.
19.0	O'Neill, Cin.
19.5	Clark, S.F.
20.4	Bonds, Pit.
22.3	Bell, Chi.

NATIONAL LEAGUE 30-30 CLUB MEMBERS

Howard Johnson, Mets	1991	(38 HR, 30 SB)
	1989	(36 HR, 41 SB)
	1987	(36 HR, 32 SB)
Ron Gant, Braves	1991	(32 HR, 34 SB)
	1990	(32 HR, 33 SB)
Barry Bonds, Pirates	1990	(33 HR, 52 SB)
Darryl Strawberry, Mets	1987	(39 HR, 36 SB)
Eric Davis, Reds	1987	(37 HR, 50 SB)
Dale Murphy, Braves	1983	(36 HR, 30 SB)
Bobby Bonds, Giants	1973	(39 HR, 43 SB)
	1969	(32 HR, 45 SB)
Hank Aaron, Braves	1963	(44 HR, 31 SB)
Willie Mays, Giants	1957	(35 HR, 38 SB)
	1956	(36 HR, 40 SB)

RUNS BATTED IN LEADERS 1920-1991

Year	Player	RBI
1920	Rogers Hornsby, St. Louis	94
	George Kelly, New York	94
1921	Rogers Hornsby, St. Louis	126
1922	Rogers Hornsby, St. Louis	155
1923	Emil Meusel, New York	125
1924	George Kelly, New York	136
1925	Rogers Hornsby, St. Louis	143
1926	Jim Bottomley, St. Louis	120
1927	Paul Waner, Pittsburgh	131
1928	Jim Bottomley, St. Louis	136
1929	Hack Wilson, Chicago	159
1930	Hack Wilson, Chicago	190
1931	Chuck Klein, Philadelphia	121
1932	Frank Hurst, Philadelphia	143
1933	Chuck Klein, Philadelphia	120
1934	Mel Ott, New York	135
1935	Wally Berger, Boston	130
1936	Joe Medwick, St. Louis	138
1937	Joe Medwick, St. Louis	154
1938	Joe Medwick, St. Louis	122
1939	Frank McCormick, Cincinnati	128
1940	Johnny Mize, St. Louis	137
1941	Dolf Camilli, Brooklyn	120
1942	Johnny Mize, New York	110
1943	Bill Nicholson, Chicago	128
1944	Bill Nicholson, Chicago	122
1945	Dixie Walker, Brooklyn	124
1946	Enos Slaughter, St. Louis	130
1947	Johnny Mize, New York	138
1948	Stan Musial, St. Louis	131
1949	Ralph Kiner, Pittsburgh	127
1950	Del Ennis, Philadelphia	126
1951	Monte Irvin, New York	121
1952	Hank Sauer, Chicago	121
1953	Roy Campanella, Brooklyn	142
1954	Ted Kluszewski, Cincinnati	141
1955	Duke Snider, Brooklyn	136
1956	Stan Musial, St. Louis	109
1957	Hank Aaron, Milwaukee	132
1958	Ernie Banks, Chicago	129
1959	Ernie Banks, Chicago	143
1960	Hank Aaron, Milwaukee	126
1961	Orlando Cepeda, San Francisco	142
1962	Tommy Davis, Los Angeles	153
1963	Hank Aaron, Milwaukee	130
1964	Ken Boyer, St. Louis	119
1965	Deron Johnson, Cincinnati	130
1966	Hank Aaron, Atlanta	127
1967	Orlando Cepeda, St. Louis	111
1968	Willie McCovey, San Francisco	105
1969	Willie McCovey, San Francisco	126
1970	Johnny Bench, Cincinnati	148
1971	Joe Torre, St. Louis	137
1972	Johnny Bench, Cincinnati	125
1973	Willie Stargell, Pittsburgh	119
1974	Johnny Bench, Cincinnati	129
1975	Greg Luzinski, Philadelphia	120
1976	George Foster, Cincinnati	121
1977	George Foster, Cincinnati	149
1978	George Foster, Cincinnati	120
1979	Dave Winfield, San Diego	118
1980	Mike Schmidt, Philadelphia	121
1981	Mike Schmidt, Philadelphia	91
1982	Dale Murphy, Atlanta	109
	Al Oliver, Montreal	109
1983	Dale Murphy, Atlanta	121
1984	Gary Carter, Montreal	106
	Mike Schmidt, Philadelphia	106
1985	Dave Parker, Cincinnati	125
1986	Mike Schmidt, Philadelphia	119
1987	Andre Dawson, Chicago	137
1988	Will Clark, San Francisco	109
1989	Kevin Mitchell, San Francisco	125
1990	Matt Williams, San Francisco	122
1991	Howard Johnson, New York	117

JACKIE ROBINSON ROOKIE OF THE YEAR

JEFF BAGWELL
HOUSTON ASTROS

Jeff Bagwell of the Astros collected 23 of the 24 first place votes and a total of 118 points to win the 1991 Jackie Robinson Rookie of the Year Award, becoming the first Houston player to win the honor. Bagwell went to spring training as a non-roster player last season, won the first base job and played in all but six of the Astros' games. He led Houston with 82 RBI, hit 15 home runs and had a .294 batting average for the season.

1991 NATIONAL LEAGUE ROOKIE OF THE YEAR VOTING

	1	2	3	Pts.
Jeff Bagwell, Astros	23	1	0	118
Orlando Merced, Pirates	1	13	9	53
Ray Lankford, Cardinals	0	7	7	28
Brian Hunter, Braves	0	1	4	7
Bret Barberie, Expos	0	1	0	3
Wes Chamberlain, Philies	0	0	3	3
Chuck McElroy, Cubs	0	1	0	3
Mike Stanton, Braves	0	0	1	1

NATIONAL LEAGUE ROOKIE OF THE YEAR

*1947	Jackie Robinson, Dodgers
*1948	Alvin Dark, Braves
1949	Don Newcombe, Dodgers
1950	Sam Jethroe, Braves
1951	Willie Mays, Giants
1952	Joe Black, Dodgers
1953	Junior Gilliam, Dodgers
1954	Wally Moon, Cardinals
1955	Bill Virdon, Cardinals
1956	Frank Robinson, Reds
1957	Jack Sanford, Phillies
1958	Orlando Cepeda, Giants
1959	Willie McCovey, Giants
1960	Frank Howard, Dodgers
1961	Billy Williams, Cubs
1962	Ken Hubbs, Cubs
1963	Pete Rose, Reds
1964	Richie Allen, Phillies
1965	Jim Lefebvre, Dodgers
1966	Tommy Helms, Reds
1967	Tom Seaver, Mets
1968	Johnny Bench, Reds
1969	Ted Sizemore, Dodgers
1970	Carl Morton, Expos
1971	Earl Williams, Braves
1972	Jon Matlack, Mets
1973	Gary Matthews, Giants
1974	Bake McBride, Cardinals
1975	John Montefusco, Giants
1976	Pat Zachry, Reds
	Butch Metzger, Padres
1977	Andre Dawson, Expos
1978	Bob Horner, Braves
1979	Rick Sutcliffe, Dodgers
1980	Steve Howe, Dodgers
1981	Fernando Valenzuela, Dodgers
1982	Steve Sax, Dodgers
1983	Darryl Strawberry, Mets
1984	Dwight Gooden, Mets
1985	Vince Coleman, Cardinals
1986	Todd Worrell, Cardinals
1987	Benito Santiago, Padres
1988	Chris Sabo, Reds
1989	Jerome Walton, Cubs
1990	Dave Justice, Braves
1991	Jeff Bagwell, Astros

*One player selected as Major League Rookie of the Year in 1947 and 1948. Policy of naming a player from each league was inaugurated in 1949.

ROOKIE OF THE YEAR AWARDS BY TEAM

Team	
Braves	5 Winners
Cubs	3 Winners
Reds	6 Winners
Astros	1 Winner
Dodgers	11 Winners
Expos	2 Winners
Mets	4 Winners
Phillies	2 Winners
Pirates	0 Winners
Cardinals	5 Winners
Padres	2 Winners
Giants	5 Winners

CY YOUNG AWARD

Phil Davis

TOM GLAVINE
ATLANTA BRAVES

Tom Glavine led the Atlanta Braves to the Western Division title with his 20 wins and garnered 19 of 24 first place votes to be named the 1991 National League Cy Young Award winner. Glavine and John Smiley of the Eastern Division Champion Pittsburgh Pirates were the only N.L. 20-game winners for the 1991 season. Glavine also finished the season third in the League in ERA, 2.55, tied for first with 9 complete games, third in strikeouts, 192, second in innings pitched, 246.2, and eighth in winning percentage, .645. Opponents hit only .222 against Glavine, good for third in the League, and his strikeouts per 9 innings ratio was 7.0, fifth in the League. Glavine posted an 8-game winning streak, May 3-June 9. He was N.L. Pitcher of the Month for May with a 6-0 record, 1.76 ERA and 33 strikeouts.

1991 marks the first Cy Young Award for the left-handed Glavine and the first for an Atlanta pitcher. The last, and only other Braves' pitcher to win the award was Warren Spahn in 1957.

CY YOUNG AWARD
WINNERS

1956—Don Newcombe, Dodgers	1974—Mike Marshall, Dodgers
1957—Warren Spahn, Braves	1975—Tom Seaver, Mets
1958—Bob Turley, Yankees	1976—Randy Jones, Padres
1959—Early Wynn, White Sox	1977—Steve Carlton, Phillies
1960—Vernon Law, Pirates	1978—Gaylord Perry, Padres
1961—Whitey Ford, Yankees	1979—Bruce Sutter, Cubs
1962—Don Drysdale, Dodgers	1980—Steve Carlton, Phillies
1963—Sandy Koufax, Dodgers	1981—Fernando Valenzuela, Dodgers
1964—Dean Chance, Angels	1982—Steve Carlton, Phillies
1965—Sandy Koufax, Dodgers	1983—John Denny, Phillies
1966—Sandy Koufax, Dodgers	1984—Rick Sutcliffe, Cubs
1967—Mike McCormick, Giants	1985—Dwight Gooden, Mets
1968—Bob Gibson, Cardinals	1986—Mike Scott, Astros
1969—Tom Seaver, Mets	1987—Steve Bedrosian, Phillies
1970—Bob Gibson, Cardinals	1988—Orel Hershiser, Dodgers
1971—Ferguson Jenkins, Cubs	1989—Mark Davis, Padres
1972—Steve Carlton, Phillies	1990—Doug Drabek, Pirates
1973—Tom Seaver, Mets	1991—Tom Glavine, Braves

Note: From 1956-1966 there was only one Cy Young Award Winner for the Major Leagues. Beginning in 1967 a winner was selected for each league.

EARNED RUN AVERAGE LEADERS 1912-1991

Year	Leader	ERA
1912	Jeff Tesreau, New York	1.96
1913	Christy Mathewson, New York	2.06
1914	Bill Doak, St. Louis	1.72
1915	Grover Alexander, Philadelphia	1.22
1916	Grover Alexander, Philadelphia	1.55
1917	Grover Alexander, Philadelphia	1.85
1918	Hippo Vaughn, Chicago	1.74
1919	Grover Alexander, Chicago	1.72
1920	Grover Alexander, Chicago	1.91
1921	Bill Doak, St. Louis	2.58
1922	Rosy Ryan, New York	3.00
1923	Dolf Luque, Cincinnati	1.93
1924	Dazzy Vance, Brooklyn	2.16
1925	Dolf Luque, Cincinnati	2.63
1926	Ray Kremer, Pittsburgh	2.61
1927	Ray Kremer, Pittsburgh	2.47
1928	Dazzy Vance, Brooklyn	2.09
1929	Bill Walker, New York	3.08
1930	Dazzy Vance, Brooklyn	2.61
1931	Bill Walker, New York	2.26
1932	Lon Warneke, Chicago	2.37
1933	Carl Hubbell, New York	1.66
1934	Carl Hubbell, New York	2.30
1935	Cy Blanton, Pittsburgh	2.59
1936	Carl Hubbell, New York	2.31
1937	Jim Turner, Boston	2.38
1938	Bill Lee, Chicago	2.66
1939	Bucky Walters, Cincinnati	2.29
1940	Bucky Walters, Cincinnati	2.48
1941	Elmer Riddle, Cincinnati	2.24
1942	Mort Cooper, St. Louis	1.77
1943	Howie Pollet, St. Louis	1.75
1944	Ed Heusser, Cincinnati	2.38
1945	Hank Borowy, Chicago	2.14
1946	Howie Pollet, St. Louis	2.10
1947	Warren Spahn, Boston	2.33
1948	Harry Brecheen, St. Louis	2.24
1949	Dave Koslo, New York	2.50
1950	Jim Hearn, St. Louis-New York	2.49
1951	Chet Nichols, Boston	2.88
1952	Hoyt Wilhelm, New York	2.43
1953	Warren Spahn, Milwaukee	2.10
1954	John Antonelli, New York	2.29
1955	Bob Friend, Pittsburgh	2.84
1956	Lew Burdette, Milwaukee	2.71
1957	John Podres, Brooklyn	2.66
1958	Stu Miller, San Francisco	2.47
1959	Sam Jones, San Francisco	2.82
1960	Mike McCormick, San Francisco	2.70
1961	Warren Spahn, Milwaukee	3.01
1962	Sandy Koufax, Los Angeles	2.54
1963	Sandy Koufax, Los Angeles	1.88
1964	Sandy Koufax, Los Angeles	1.74
1965	Sandy Koufax, Los Angeles	2.04
1966	Sandy Koufax, Los Angeles	1.73
1967	Philip Niekro, Atlanta	1.87
1968	Bob Gibson, St. Louis	1.12
1969	Juan Marichal, San Francisco	2.10
1970	Tom Seaver, New York	2.81
1971	Tom Seaver, New York	1.76
1972	Steve Carlton, Philadelphia	1.98
1973	Tom Seaver, New York	2.08
1974	Buzz Capra, Atlanta	2.28
1975	Randy Jones, San Diego	2.24
1976	John Denny, St. Louis	2.52
1977	John Candelaria, Pittsburgh	2.34
1978	Craig Swan, New York	2.43
1979	J.R. Richard, Houston	2.71
1980	Don Sutton, Los Angeles	2.21
1981	Nolan Ryan, Houston	1.69
1982	Steve Rogers, Montreal	2.40
1983	Atlee Hammaker, San Francisco	2.25
1984	Alejandro Pena, Los Angeles	2.48
1985	Dwight Gooden, New York	1.53
1986	Mike Scott, Houston	2.22
1987	Nolan Ryan, Houston	2.76
1988	Joe Magrane, St. Louis	2.18
1989	Scott Garrelts, San Francisco	2.28
1990	Danny Darwin, Houston	2.21
1991	Dennis Martinez, Montreal	2.39

1991 NATIONAL LEAGUE CY YOUNG AWARD VOTING

	1	2	3	Pts.
Tom Glavine, Braves	19	5	0	110
Lee Smith, Cardinals	4	12	4	60
John Smiley, Pirates	0	4	14	26
Jose Rijo, Reds	1	2	2	13
Dennis Martinez, Expos	0	1	1	4
Steve Avery, Braves	0	0	1	1
Andy Benes, Padres	0	0	1	1
Mitch Williams, Phillies	0	0	1	1

ERA LEADER

DENNIS MARTINEZ
MONTREAL EXPOS

Dennis Martinez of the Montreal Expos was the National League ERA leader at 2.39. He also led the League in shutouts with 5 and was tied for first with 9 complete games. Opponents hit only .226 against him, sixth best in the League. He pitched a no-hitter on July 28, at Los Angeles. Martinez was voted National League Pitcher of the Month for July, when he was 2-1 with a 2.11 ERA.

SAVES LEADER

LEE SMITH
ST. LOUIS CARDINALS

Lee Smith of the St. Louis Cardinals set a new National League record for saves with 47 in 1991. His career total is not 312, third in the Major Leagues. Smith also led the League in games finished with 61. It is the second time Smith has led the League in saves. In 1983 while with the Chicago Cubs he led the N.L. with 29 saves.

NATIONAL LEAGUE RELIEF PITCHING RECORDS

Highest Percentage, Games Won—
.714, Hugh Casey, Chicago, Brooklyn, Pittsburgh

Most Games, Lifetime—
1,050, Kent Tekulve, Pittsburgh, Philadelphia, Cincinnati

Most Games, Season—
106, Mike Marshall, Los Angeles 1974

Most Games Won—
96, ElRoy Face, Pittsburgh, Montreal

Most Games Won, Season—
18, ElRoy Face, Pittsburgh 1959 (1 loss)

1991 RAWLINGS GOLD GLOVE AWARD WINNERS

POSITION	PLAYER, CLUB	YEARS WON
1B	Will Clark, Giants	1st
2B	Ryne Sandberg, Cubs	9th
3B	Matt Williams, Giants	1st
SS	Ozzie Smith, Cardinals	12th
OF	Tony Gwynn, Padres	5th
	Barry Bonds, Pirates	2nd
	Andy Van Slyke, Pirates	4th
C	Tom Pagnozzi, Cardinals	1st
P	Greg Maddux, Cubs	2nd

The Rawlings Gold Glove is presented annually to the best fielding players at their position as voted by the managers and coaches in their league.

1991 NATIONAL LEAGUE SILVER SLUGGER TEAM

(Top offensive player at each position)

1B—Will Clark, San Francisco Giants
2B—Ryne Sandberg, Chicago Cubs
3B—Howard Johnson, New York Mets
SS—Barry Larkin, Cincinnati Reds
OF—Barry Bonds, Pittsburgh Pirates
     Bobby Bonilla, Pittsburgh Pirates
     Ron Gant, Atlanta Braves
C —Benito Santiago, San Diego Padres
P —Tom Glavine, Atlanta Braves

TOP 1991 PINCH-HITTERS

(minimum: 20 AB)

Player, Club	AVG.	AB	H	2B	3B	HR	RBI
Walker, N.Y.	.406	32	13	1	0	1	6
Winningham, Cin.	.394	33	13	0	0	0	2
Lindeman, Phi.	.361	36	13	1	0	0	2
Thompson, St.L.	.357	28	10	0	1	1	6
Carreon, N.Y.	.343	35	12	1	0	3	7
Lemke, Atl.	.333	27	9	1	0	0	5
Jordan, Phi.	.321	28	9	3	0	0	6
Hansen, L.A.	.313	32	10	2	0	1	4
Jones, Cin.	.308	26	8	0	1	1	3
Noboa, Mon.	.304	46	14	2	0	1	2
Wilson, St.L.	.297	37	11	2	0	0	11
Redus, Pitt.	.290	31	9	1	0	1	3
Felder, S.F.	.278	36	10	1	0	0	3
McClendon, Pitt.	.273	33	9	1	0	2	8
Sharperson, L.A.	.273	22	6	1	0	0	3

MANAGER OF THE YEAR

BOBBY COX
ATLANTA BRAVES

Bobby Cox took the Atlanta Braves from last place in 1990 to the National League Championship in 1991 and for his efforts was voted National League Manager of the Year. He collected 96 points with 13 first place votes, 10 second place votes and one third place vote. He is the first manager to win Manager of the Year honors in both Leagues. He was the American League Manager of the Year in 1985 when he led the Toronto Blue Jays to a 99-62 record. The Braves posted a 94-68 record in 1991, Cox's first full season as Atlanta's manager this time around. He previously managed the Braves, 1978-81.

MANAGER OF THE YEAR VOTING

	1	2	3	Pts.
Bobby Cox, Braves	13	10	1	96
Jim Leyland, Pirates	9	7	8	74
Joe Torre, Cardinals	2	7	10	41
Tommy Lasorda, Dodgers ..	0	0	5	5

MANAGERS OF THE YEAR

1983	Tom Lasorda, Los Angeles Dodgers
1984	Jim Frey, Chicago Cubs
1985	Whitey Herzog, St. Louis Cardinals
1986	Hal Lanier, Houston Astros
1987	Buck Rodgers, Montreal Expos
1988	Tom Lasorda, Los Angeles Dodgers
1989	Don Zimmer, Chicago Cubs
1990	Jim Leyland, Pittsburgh Pirates
1991	Bobby Cox, Atlanta Braves

LOU BROCK AWARD

MARQUIS GRISSOM
MONTREAL EXPOS

Marquis Grissom of the Montreal Expos led the National League with 76 stolen bases, breaking the six-year reign of Vince Coleman as the League's base-stealing champion. It was Grissom's first Lou Brock Award. Prior to Coleman's tenure as the champion, the Expos had a hold on the title from 1980-84. Ron LeFlore won the award in 1980 and then Tim Raines was the N.L. base-stealing champion from 1981-84.

LOU BROCK AWARD

1977	Frank Taveras, Pittsburgh	70
1978	Omar Moreno, Pittsburgh	71
1979	Omar Moreno, Pittsburgh	77
1980	Ron LeFlore, Montreal	97
1981	Tim Raines, Montreal	71
1982	Tim Raines, Montreal	78
1983	Tim Raines, Montreal	90
1984	Tim Raines, Montreal	75
1985	Vince Coleman, St. Louis	110
1986	Vince Coleman, St. Louis	107
1987	Vince Coleman, St. Louis	109
1988	Vince Coleman, St. Louis	81
1989	Vince Coleman, St. Louis	65
1990	Vince Coleman, St. Louis	77
1991	Marquis Grissom, Montreal	76

STOLEN BASE LEADERS 1900-1991

1900	Jim Barrett, Cincinnati	46
1901	Honus Wagner, Pittsburgh	48
1902	Honus Wagner, Pittsburgh	43
1903	Frank Chance, Chicago	67
	Jim Sheckard, Brooklyn	67
1904	Honus Wagner, Pittsburgh	53
1905	Art Devlin, New York	59
	Bill Maloney, Chicago	59
1906	Frank Chance, Chicago	57
1907	Honus Wagner, Pittsburgh	61
1908	Honus Wagner, Pittsburgh	53
1909	Bob Bescher, Cincinnati	54
1910	Bob Bescher, Cincinnati	70
1911	Bob Bescher, Cincinnati	81
1912	Bob Bescher, Cincinnati	67
1913	Max Carey, Pittsburgh	61
1914	George Burns, New York	62
1915	Max Carey, Pittsburgh	36
1916	Max Carey, Pittsburgh	63
1917	Max Carey, Pittsburgh	46
1918	Max Carey, Pittsburgh	58
1919	George Burns, New York	40
1920	Max Carey, Pittsburgh	52
1921	Frank Frisch, New York	49
1922	Max Carey, Pittsburgh	51
1923	Max Carey, Pittsburgh	51
1924	Max Carey, Pittsburgh	49
1925	Max Carey, Pittsburgh	46
1926	Kiki Cuyler, Pittsburgh	35
1927	Frank Frisch, St. Louis	48
1928	Kiki Cuyler, Chicago	37
1929	Kiki Cuyler, Chicago	43
1930	Kiki Cuyler, Chicago	37
1931	Frank Frisch, St. Louis	28
1932	Chuck Klein, Philadelphia	20
1933	Pepper Martin, St. Louis	26
1934	Pepper Martin, St. Louis	23
1935	Augie Galan, Chicago	22
1936	Pepper Martin, St. Louis	23
1937	Augie Galan, Chicago	23
1938	Stan Hack, Chicago	16
1939	Stan Hack, Chicago	17
	Lee Handley, Pittsburgh	17
1940	Lonny Frey, Cincinnati	22
1941	Dan Murtaugh, Philadelphia	18
1942	Pete Reiser, Brooklyn	20
1943	Arky Vaughan, Brooklyn	20
1944	John Barrett, Pittsburgh	28
1945	Red Schoendienst, St. Louis	26
1946	Pete Reiser, Brooklyn	34
1947	Jackie Robinson, Brooklyn	29
1948	Richie Ashburn, Philadelphia	32
1949	Jackie Robinson, Brooklyn	37
1950	Sam Jethroe, Boston	35
1951	Sam Jethroe, Boston	35
1952	Pee Wee Reese, Brooklyn	30
1953	Bill Bruton, Milwaukee	26
1954	Bill Bruton, Milwaukee	34
1955	Bill Bruton, Milwaukee	25
1956	Willie Mays, New York	40
1957	Willie Mays, New York	38
1958	Willie Mays, San Francisco	31
1959	Willie Mays, San Francisco	27
1960	Maury Wills, Los Angeles	50
1961	Maury Wills, Los Angeles	35
1962	Maury Wills, Los Angeles	104
1963	Maury Wills, Los Angeles	40
1964	Maury Wills, Los Angeles	53
1965	Maury Wills, Los Angeles	94
1966	Lou Brock, St. Louis	74
1967	Lou Brock, St. Louis	52
1968	Lou Brock, St. Louis	62
1969	Lou Brock, St. Louis	53
1970	Bob Tolan, Cincinnati	57
1971	Lou Brock, St. Louis	64
1972	Lou Brock, St. Louis	63
1973	Lou Brock, St. Louis	70
1974	Lou Brock, St. Louis	118
1975	Dave Lopes, Los Angeles	77
1976	Dave Lopes, Los Angeles	63
1977	Frank Taveras, Pittsburgh	70
1978	Omar Moreno, Pittsburgh	71
1979	Omar Moreno, Pittsburgh	77
1980	Ron LeFlore, Montreal	97
1981	Tim Raines, Montreal	71
1982	Tim Raines, Montreal	78
1983	Tim Raines, Montreal	90
1984	Tim Raines, Montreal	75
1985	Vince Coleman, St. Louis	110
1986	Vince Coleman, St. Louis	107
1987	Vince Coleman, St. Louis	109
1988	Vince Coleman, St. Louis	81
1989	Vince Coleman, St. Louis	65
1990	Vince Coleman, St. Louis	77
1991	Marquis Grissom, Montreal	76

1991 LEADERS IN STOLEN BASES

Marquis Grissom, Montreal	76
Otis Nixon, Atlanta	72
Delino DeShields, Montreal	56
Ray Lankford, St. Louis	44
Barry Bonds, Pittsburgh	43
Brett Butler, Los Angeles	38
Vince Coleman, New York	37
Ozzie Smith, St. Louis	35
Steve Finley, Houston	34
Ron Gant, Atlanta	34

N.L. CAREER STOLEN BASE LEADERS
(1898-1991)

Lou Brock*	938
Max Carey*	738
Honus Wagner*	703
Joe Morgan*	681
Tim Raines	634
VINCE COLEMAN	586
Maury Wills	586
Cesar Cedeno	550
OZZIE SMITH	499
Davey Lopes	495

*IN HALL OF FAME
ALL CAPS—Active N.L. Player

TOM SEAVER

Tom Seaver was elected into the Hall of Fame in his first year of eligibility with the highest percentage of votes ever recorded, 98.8%. Seaver had a 311-205 record in his 20 years in the majors, playing for the Mets, Reds, White Sox and Red Sox. He recorded 3,640 strikeouts, third on the all-time Major League list, and 61 shutouts, 7th on the all-time list. His career ERA was 2.86. In three League Championship Series, 1969 and '73 with the Mets and 1979 with the Reds, he posted a 2-1 record, 2.84 ERA and 24 strikeouts. In two World Series he won 1, lost 2, struck out 27 and had a 2.70 ERA.

Rollie Fingers was also elected into the Hall of Fame. In 17 years with the A's, Padres and Brewers, Fingers recorded 341 saves, first on the Major League all-time list, in 944 games, fourth on the all-time list. He had a 107-102 record. His 107 wins rank third third on the all-time list for relievers.

The induction ceremonies will be held on Sunday, August 2, 1992, in Cooperstown, New York.

1992 HALL OF FAME GAME
New York Mets vs. Chicago White Sox
Monday, August 3
Doubleday Field
Cooperstown, New York

NATIONAL LEAGUE MEMBERS OF THE HALL OF FAME

Hank Aaron, Braves
Grover Cleveland Alexander, Phillies, Cubs, Cards
Adrian C. "Cap" Anson, Cubs
Earl Averill, Braves
Dave Bancroft, Phillies, Giants, Braves, Dodgers
Ernie Banks, Cubs
Al Barlick, Umpire
Jake Beckley, Pirates, Giants, Reds, Cardinals
Johnny Bench, Reds
Yogi Berra, Mets
James Bottomley, Cardinals, Reds
Roger Bresnahan, Giants, Cards, Cubs
Lou Brock, Cubs, Cardinals
Dennis "Dan" Brouthers, Braves, Dodgers, Phillies
Mordecai P. Brown, Cards, Cubs, Reds
Jesse C. Burkett, Cleveland (NL), Cards
Roy Campanella, Dodgers
Max Carey, Pirates, Dodgers
Frank Chance, Cubs
Jack Chesbro, Pirates
Fred Clarke, Pirates
John Clarkson, Cubs, Braves, Cleveland (NL)
Roberto Clemente, Pirates
James J. Collins, Braves
Charles Comiskey, Reds
John "Jocko" Conlan, Umpire
Roger Connor, Giants, Phillies, Cardinals
Samuel Crawford, Reds
Joe Cronin, Pirates
*W.A. "Candy" Cummings
Hazen "Kiki" Cuyler, Pirates, Cubs, Reds, Dodgers
Dizzy Dean, Cardinals, Cubs
Ed Delahanty, Phillies
Don Drysdale, Dodgers
Hugh Duffy, Cubs, Braves, Phillies
Johnny Evers, Cubs, Braves, Phillies

William "Buck" Ewing, Giants, Reds
Rollie Fingers, Padres
Elmer Flick, Phillies
*Ford Frick
Frankie Frisch, Giants, Cards
James "Pud" Galvin, Cardinals, Buffalo (NL), Pirates
Bob Gibson, Cards
Warren Giles, Reds, League President
Hank Greenberg, Pirates
Clark C. Griffith, Cubs, Reds
Burleigh Grimes, Pirates, Dodgers, Giants, Braves, Cards, Cubs
Charles "Chick" Hafey, Cardinals, Reds
Jesse "Pop" Haines, Reds, Cardinals
William "Billy" Hamilton, Phillies, Braves
Stanley "Bucky" Harris, Phillies (Mgr. only)
Charles "Gabby" Hartnett, Cubs, Giants
Billy Herman, Cubs, Dodgers, Braves, Pirates
Rogers Hornsby, Cards, Giants, Braves, Cubs
Waite Hoyt, Giants, Dodgers, Pirates
Carl Hubbell, Giants
Miller Huggins, Reds, Cards
Monte Irvin, Giants, Cubs
Travis Jackson, Giants
Ferguson Jenkins, Phillies, Cubs
Hugh Jennings, Dodgers, Phillies
Tim Keefe, Giants, Phillies
Willie Keeler, Giants, Dodgers
Joseph Kelley, Braves, Pirates, Baltimore (NL), Dodgers, Reds
George Kelly, Giants, Pirates, Reds, Cubs, Dodgers
Mike "King" Kelly, Reds, Cubs, Braves, Giants
Ralph Kiner, Pirates, Cubs
Chuck Klein, Phillies, Cubs
Bill Klem, Umpire
Sandy Koufax, Dodgers

Nap Lajoie, Phillies
Fred Lindstrom, Giants, Pirates, Cubs, Dodgers
Ernie Lombardi, Dodgers, Reds, Braves, Giants
Al Lopez, Dodgers, Braves, Pirates
Connie Mack, Pirates
*Larry MacPhail, Reds, Dodgers
Heinie Manush, Dodgers, Pirates
Rabbit Maranville, Braves, Pirates, Cubs, Dodgers, Cardinals
Juan Marichal, Giants, Dodgers
Richard "Rube" Marquard, Giants, Dodgers, Reds, Braves
Eddie Mathews, Braves, Astros
Christy Mathewson, Giants, Reds
Willie Mays, Giants, Mets
Joseph McCarthy, Cubs (Mgr. only)
Thomas F. McCarthy, Braves, Phillies, Dodgers
Willie McCovey, Giants, Padres
Joseph J. McGinnity, Dodgers, Giants
John J. McGraw, Cards, Giants
Bill McKechnie, Pirates, Cards, Giants, Braves, Reds
Joseph "Ducky" Medwick, Cardinals, Dodgers, Giants, Braves
Johnny Mize, Cardinals, Giants
Joe Morgan, Astros, Reds, Giants, Phillies
Stan Musial, Cardinals
Charles "Kid" Nichols, Braves, Cards, Phillies
James H. O'Rourke, Braves, Giants
Mel Ott, Giants
Gaylord Perry, Giants, Padres, Braves
Charles Radbourne, Braves, Reds
Harold "Pee Wee" Reese, Dodgers
*Branch Rickey, Cardinals, Dodgers, Pirates
Eppa Rixey, Phillies, Reds
Robin Roberts, Phillies, Astros, Cubs
Frank Robinson, Reds, Dodgers

Jackie Robinson, Dodgers
Wilbert Robinson, Baltimore (NL), Dodgers, Giants
Edd Roush, Giants, Reds
Amos Rusie, Giants, Reds
Red Schoendienst, Cardinals, Giants, Braves
Tom Seaver, Mets, Reds
George Sisler, Braves
Enos Slaughter, Cardinals, Braves
Duke Snider, Dodgers, Mets, Giants
Warren Spahn, Braves, Mets, Giants
*Albert Spalding
Willie Stargell, Pirates
Casey Stengel, Dodgers, Pirates, Phillies, Giants, Braves
Bill Terry, Giants
Sam Thompson, Detroit (NL), Phillies
Joe Tinker, Cubs, Reds
Harold "Pie" Traynor, Pirates
Arthur "Dazzy" Vance, Pirates, Giants, Dodgers, Cards, Reds
Arky Vaughn, Pirates, Dodgers
Honus Wagner, Pirates
Lloyd Waner, Pirates, Braves, Reds, Phillies, Dodgers
Paul Waner, Pirates, Dodgers, Braves
John Montgomery Ward, Giants, Dodgers
*George M. Weiss, Mets
Mickey Welch, Troy (NL), Giants
Zachary "Zack" Wheat, Dodgers
Hoyt Wilhelm, Giants, Cardinals, Braves, Cubs, Dodgers
Billy Williams, Cubs
Hack Wilson, Cubs, Dodgers, Phillies, Giants
George Wright, Red Stockings, Braves, Providence
Wm. Henry "Harry" Wright, Red Stockings, Braves, Providence, Phillies
Denton "Cy" Young, Cleveland (NL), Cards, Braves
Ross Youngs, Giants
*Selected for meritorious service to baseball

1991 NATIONAL LEAGUE HIGHS AND LOWS

CLUB

Most Runs, Game—
17, Atlanta vs. St. Louis, May 8
San Francisco at Philadelphia, July 14
Most Runs, Game, Both Clubs—
23, Montreal (9) at Atlanta (14), August 26
25, Chicago (12) at Pittsburgh (13), April 21 (11 inn.)
Most Runs, Inning—
8, San Francisco at Houston, April 13 (7th)
Atlanta vs. St. Louis, May 8 (7th)
Most Hits, Game—
23, St. Louis at New York, May 26
Most Hits, Game, Both Clubs—
34, St. Louis (21) at Chicago (13), June 28
36, San Francisco (19) at San Diego (17), April 11 (10 inn.)
Most Total Bases, Game—
40, Pittsburgh at Chicago, July 2
Most Doubles, Game—
6, Atlanta vs. St. Louis, May 8
Chicago at Los Angeles, June 19
San Francisco at Philadelphia, July 13
New York vs. Los Angeles, July 21
San Francisco at Houston, August 22
Philadelphia vs. Montreal, September 11
Most Triples, Game—
4, Pittsburgh at Chicago, July 2
Most Home Runs, Game—
5, Cincinnati at Chicago, May 11
San Diego vs. Cincinnati, August 11
Most Home Runs, Game, Both Clubs—
8, New York (4) at Atlanta (4), June 20
Most Home Runs, Doubleheader—
4, Atlanta vs. Pittsburgh, July 29
Most Extra Base Hits, Game—
8, Philadelphia vs. San Francisco, April 30
Atlanta vs. St. Louis, May 8
Pittsburgh at Chicago, July 2
San Diego vs. Cincinnati, August 11
Pittsburgh vs. New York, August 18
St. Louis vs. New York, September 15
Most Walks, Game—
11, Cincinnati at Philadelphia, June 16
Cincinnati vs. San Francisco, August 4
15, New York vs. Philadelphia, April 10 (10 inn.)
Most Walks, Game, Both Clubs—
16, St. Louis (7) at Chicago (9), October 5 (2g)
24, Philadelphia (9) at New York (15), April 10 (10 inn.)
Most Strikeouts, Game—
19, Philadelphia vs. New York, October 6
Most Strikeouts, Game, Both Clubs—
26, Philadelphia (13) at New York (13), September 27
New York (7) at Philadelphia (19), October 6
29, San Diego (16) at Houston (13), August 5 (12 inn.)
Most Stolen Bases, Game—
8, Atlanta at Montreal, June 16
Most Stolen Bases, Game, Both Clubs—
13, Atlanta (8) at Montreal (5), June 16

Most Double Plays, Game—
5, St. Louis vs. Pittsburgh, May 27
Cincinnati at Pittsburgh, July 20
Most Double Plays, Game, Both Clubs—
6, New York (3) at San Diego (3), July 27
Pittsburgh (4) at Houston (2), July 27
Atlanta (4) at Cincinnati (2), October 2
Most Errors, Game—
6, Atlanta vs. Los Angeles, June 30
Most Errors, Game, Both Clubs—
7, Philadelphia (3) at Houston (4), June 13
Los Angeles (1) at Atlanta (6), June 30
8, San Diego (3) at Atlanta (5), May 23 (12 inn.)
Most Left On Base, Game—
16, St. Louis vs. Houston, May 18
18, New York vs. Philadelphia, April 10 (10 inn.)
Most Left On Base, Game, Both Clubs—
23, Philadelphia (10) at Cincinnati (13), June 9
St. Louis (13) at San Francisco (10), June 17
Chicago (11) at St. Louis (12), September 29
31, Philadelphia (13) at New York (18), April 10 (10 inn.)
Chicago (17) at Philadelphia (14), May 17 (16 inn.)
Most Innings, Game—
16, Philadelphia vs. Chicago, May 17
Montreal vs. Houston, June 17
Longest Time, Game—
4:53, Los Angeles vs. Chicago, June 18 (13 inn.)
Shortest Time, Game—
1:45, Pittsburgh vs. Houston, May 3
Highest Attendance, Game—
55,882, San Francisco vs. Los Angeles, April 15
Longest Winning Streak—
13, Philadelphia, July 30-August 12
Longest Losing Streak—
11, Montreal, June 23-July 4
New York, August 9-21

INDIVIDUAL BATTING

Longest Hitting Streak—
23, Butler, Los Angeles, June 15-July 12
Most Runs, Game—
4, 16 players tied
Most Hits, Game—
5, Butler, Los Angeles vs. San Francisco, April 26
Grissom, Montreal at Atlanta, June 7
Felder, San Francisco at Los Angeles, June 25
Grissom, Montreal at New York, June 26
Bell, Pittsburgh vs. Chicago, June 26
Clark, San Francisco at Philadelphia, July 14
Wehner, Pittsburgh vs. Atlanta, July 23
Uribe, San Francisco at Houston, August 22
Santiago, San Diego at San Francisco, September 13
Most Total Bases, Game—
12, O'Neill, Cincinnati at Chicago, May 11
Larkin, Cincinnati vs. Houston, June 28

Most Doubles, Game—
3, Backman, Philadelphia vs. Atlanta, June 18
Santiago, San Diego at New York, July 11
Walker, Montreal at St. Louis, August 7
Mitchell, San Francisco at Houston, August 22
O'Neill, Cincinnati vs. Houston, September 13
Most Triples, Game—
2, Webster, Pittsburgh at St. Louis, May 27
Kruk, Philadelphia at Cincinnati, June 9
Clark, San Francisco vs. Atlanta, August 14
Dykstra, Philadelphia at Pittsburgh, August 14
Reed, Cincinnati vs. San Diego, September 29
Most Home Runs, Game—
3, Larkin, Cincinnati vs. Houston, June 28
Most Extra Bases, Game—
4, O'Neill, Cincinnati at Chicago, May 11
O'Neill, Cincinnati vs. Houston, September 13
Most Runs Batted In, Game—
7, Clark, San Francisco at Philadelphia, July 14
Strawberry, Los Angeles vs. San Diego, August 21
Most Stolen Bases, Game—
6, Nixon, Atlanta at Montreal, June 16

INDIVIDUAL PITCHING

Most Strikeouts, Game (Starter)—
19, Cone, New York at Philadelphia, October 6
Most Strikeouts, Game (Reliever)—
9, Gross, Los Angeles vs. New York, July 31
Most Innings, Game (Starter)—
10, Portugal, Houston vs. Philadelphia, June 11 (11 inn.)
Most Innings, Game (Reliever)—
7.2, Greene, Philadelphia at St. Louis, April 20 (1g)
Most Home Runs Allowed, Game—
4, Deshaies, Houston at Cincinnati, June 28
Darling, Montreal at San Francisco, July 30
Armstrong, Cincinnati vs. San Francisco, August 3
No-Hitters, Complete Game—
Greene, Philadelphia at Montreal, May 23
De. Martinez, Montreal at Los Angeles, July 28
One-Hitters, Complete Game—
Smiley, Pittsburgh vs. New York, April 17
Drabek, Pittsburgh at St. Louis, May 27
Smith, Pittsburgh at St. Louis, May 29
Schourek, New York vs. Montreal, September 10
Cone, New York vs. St. Louis, September 20
Longest Winning Streak—
10, Benes, San Diego, July 28-September 25
Longest Losing Streak—
9, Rasmussen, San Diego, June 26-August 9
Most Consecutive Scoreless Innings—
29, Greene, Philadelphia, May 7-June 2

1991 NATIONAL LEAGUE LEADERS

BATTING

BATTING AVERAGE

Terry Pendleton, Atlanta 319	Barry Larkin, Cincinnati 302
Hal Morris, Cincinnati................318	Bobby Bonilla, Pittsburgh 302
Tony Gwynn, San Diego 317	Will Clark, San Francisco 301
Willie McGee, San Francisco.....312	Chris Sabo, Cincinnati 301
Felix Jose, St. Louis.................305	Ivan Calderon, Montreal............300

ON-BASE PCT.

Barry Bonds, Pittsburgh 410
Brett Butler, Los Angeles.............401
Fred McGriff, San Diego 396
Bobby Bonilla, Pittsburgh............391
Jeff Bagwell, Houston..................387
Ozzie Smith, St. Louis.................380
Ryne Sandberg, Chicago.............379
Dave Magadan, New York 378
Barry Larkin, Cincinnati 378
Hal Morris, Cincinnati 374

SLUGGING PCT.

Will Clark, San Francisco..............536
Howard Johnson, New York 535
Terry Pendleton, Atlanta 517
Barry Bonds, Pittsburgh 514
Barry Larkin, Cincinnati 506
Chris Sabo, Cincinnati.................505
Matt Williams, San Francisco.......499
Ron Gant, Atlanta........................496
Fred McGriff, San Diego 494
Bobby Bonilla, Pittsburgh............492

RUNS SCORED

Brett Butler, Los Angeles.............. 112
Howard Johnson, New York 108
Ryne Sandberg, Chicago............. 104
Bobby Bonilla, Pittsburgh............ 102
Ron Gant, Atlanta....................... 101
Jay Bell, Pittsburgh 96
Ozzie Smith, St. Louis................. 96
Barry Bonds, Pittsburgh 95
Terry Pendleton, Atlanta 94
Chris Sabo, Cincinnati................. 91

HITS

Terry Pendleton, Atlanta 187
Brett Butler, Los Angeles.............. 182
Chris Sabo, Cincinnati.................. 175
Bobby Bonilla, Pittsburgh 174
Felix Jose, St. Louis..................... 173
Steve Finley, Houston................... 170
Will Clark, San Francisco.............. 170
Ryne Sandberg, Chicago............... 170
Mark Grace, Chicago.................... 169
Tony Gwynn, San Diego................ 168

RUNS BATTED IN

Howard Johnson, New York 117
Barry Bonds, Pittsburgh 116
Will Clark, San Francisco 116
Fred McGriff, San Diego 106
Ron Gant, Atlanta 105
Andre Dawson, Chicago 104
Bobby Bonilla, Pittsburgh............ 100
Ryne Sandberg, Chicago............. 100
Darryl Strawberry, Los Angeles 99
Matt Williams, San Francisco........ 98

DOUBLES

Bobby Bonilla, Pittsburgh................ 44
Felix Jose, St. Louis 40
Todd Zeile, St. Louis 36
Paul O'Neill, Cincinnati................... 36
Chris Sabo, Cincinnati.................... 35
Ron Gant, Atlanta 35
Terry Pendleton, Atlanta 34
Howard Johnson, New York 34
Hal Morris, Cincinnati..................... 33
Dale Murphy, Philadelphia.............. 33

TRIPLES

Ray Lankford, St. Louis................... 15
Tony Gwynn, San Diego 11
Steve Finley, Houston..................... 10
Luis Gonzalez, Houston.................... 9
Marquis Grissom, Montreal.............. 9
Jay Bell, Pittsburgh 8
Terry Pendleton, Atlanta 8
Spike Owen, Montreal 8
Casey Candaele, Houston 7
Will Clark, San Francisco................. 7
Shawon Dunston, Chicago 7
Andy Van Slyke, Pittsburgh............. 7

HOME RUNS

Howard Johnson, New York 38
Matt Williams, San Francisco......... 34
Ron Gant, Atlanta 32
Fred McGriff, San Diego 31
Andre Dawson, Chicago 31
Will Clark, San Francisco............... 29
Darryl Strawberry, Los Angeles 28
Paul O'Neill, Cincinnati.................. 28
Kevin Mitchell, San Francisco......... 27
Chris Sabo, Cincinnati................... 26
Ryne Sandberg, Chicago................ 26

PITCHING

WINS

Tom Glavine, Atlanta...................... 20
John Smiley, Pittsburgh.................. 20
Steve Avery, Atlanta....................... 18
Ramon Martinez, Los Angeles......... 17
Terry Mulholland, Philadelphia........ 16
Zane Smith, Pittsburgh.................. 16
Andy Benes, San Diego.................. 15
Doug Drabek, Pittsburgh................ 15
Bruce Hurst, San Diego.................. 15
Charlie Leibrandt, Atlanta 15
Greg Maddux, Chicago 15
Jose Rijo, Cincinnati....................... 15

EARNED RUN AVERAGE

Dennis Martinez, Montreal........2.39	Jose DeLeon, St. Louis.............2.71
Jose Rijo, Cincinnati 2.51	Mike Morgan, Los Angeles........2.78
Tom Glavine, Atlanta 2.55	Randy Tomlin, Pittsburgh.........2.98
Tim Belcher, Los Angeles 2.62	Andy Benes, San Diego 3.03
Pete Harnisch, Houston 2.70	Doug Drabek, Pittsburgh 3.07

INNINGS PITCHED

Greg Maddux, Chicago 263.0
Tom Glavine, Atlanta.................246.2
Mike Morgan, Los Angeles 236.1
Doug Drabek, Pittsburgh...........234.2
David Cone, New York 232.2
Terry Mulholland, Philadelphia....232.0
Frank Viola, New York 231.1
Tom Browning, Cincinnati...........230.1
Charlie Leibrandt, Atlanta..........229.2
John Smoltz, Atlanta 229.2

GAMES

Barry Jones, Montreal 77
Paul Assenmacher, Chicago 75
Mike Stanton, Atlanta...................... 74
Juan Agosto, St. Louis.................... 72
Tim Burke, Mon-N.Y....................... 72
Roger McDowell, Phi-L.A. 71
Chuck McElroy, Chicago 71
Al Osuna, Houston 71
Jeff Innis, New York 69
Mitch Williams, Philadelphia 69

COMPLETE GAMES

Tom Glavine, Atlanta......................... 9
Dennis Martinez, Montreal 9
Terry Mulholland, Philadelphia.......... 8
Greg Maddux, Chicago 7
Ramon Martinez, Los Angeles.......... 6
Zane Smith, Pittsburgh.................... 6
David Cone, New York 5
Doug Drabek, Pittsburgh.................. 5
Mike Morgan, Los Angeles 5
John Smoltz, Atlanta 5

SAVES

Lee Smith, St. Louis 47
Rob Dibble, Cincinnati.................... 31
Mitch Williams, Philadelphia 30
John Franco, New York 30
Dave Righetti, San Francisco.......... 24
Craig Lefferts, San Diego 23
Juan Berenguer, Atlanta................. 17
Bill Landrum, Pittsburgh................. 17
Dave Smith, Chicago...................... 17
Stan Belinda, Pittsburgh................ 16
Jay Howell, Los Angeles................. 16

STRIKEOUTS

David Cone, New York 241
Greg Maddux, Chicago 198
Tom Glavine, Atlanta...................... 192
Pete Harnisch, Houston................. 172
Jose Rijo, Cincinnati...................... 172
Andy Benes, San Diego.................. 167
Tim Belcher, Los Angeles............... 156
Tommy Greene, Philadelphia.......... 154
Dwight Gooden, New York 150
Ramon Martinez, Los Angeles 150

SHUTOUTS

Dennis Martinez, Montreal................ 5
Ramon Martinez, Los Angeles 4
Bud Black, San Francisco 3
Terry Mulholland, Philadelphia......... 3
Zane Smith, Pittsburgh.................... 3
David Cone, New York 2
Doug Drabek, Pittsburgh.................. 2
Tommy Greene, Philadelphia............ 2
Pete Harnisch, Houston................... 2
Greg Harris, San Diego.................... 2
Greg Maddux, Chicago 2
Randy Tomlin, Pittsburgh 2

INDIVIDUAL BATTING—1991

ALL PLAYERS LISTED ALPHABETICALLY

BATTER	TEAM	B	AVG	G	AB	R	H	TB	2B	3B	HR	RBI	SH	SF	HP	BB	IBB	SO	SB	CS	GIDP	SLG	OBP	E
Abner, S	SD	R	.165	53	115	15	19	28	4	1	1	5	1	1	1	7	4	25	0	0	3	.243	.218	10
Agosto, J	STL	L	.333	72	3	0	1	1	0	0	0	0	0	0	0	0	0	2	0	0	0	.333	.500	2
Akerfelds, D	PHI	R	.000	30	3	0	0	0	0	0	0	0	0	0	0	0	0	3	0	0	0	.000	.000	1
Aldrete, M	SD	L	.000	12	15	2	0	0	0	0	0	1	0	0	0	3	0	4	0	1	1	.000	.167	0
Alicea, L	STL	S	.191	56	68	5	13	16	3	0	0	0	0	0	0	8	0	19	0	1	0	.235	.276	0
Andersen, L	SD	R	.000	38	2	0	0	0	0	0	0	0	0	0	0	0	0	1	0	0	0	.000	.000	1
Anderson, D	SF	R	.248	100	226	24	56	71	5	2	2	13	2	0	0	12	2	35	2	4	8	.314	.286	11
Anthony, E	HOU	L	.153	39	118	11	18	27	6	0	1	7	0	2	0	12	1	41	1	0	2	.229	.227	1
Armstrong, J	CIN	R	.093	27	43	3	4	5	1	0	0	2	5	0	0	1	0	18	0	0	1	.116	.114	2
Ashby, A	PHI	R	.083	8	12	0	1	1	0	0	0	0	1	0	0	0	0	9	0	0	0	.083	.083	0
Assenmacher, P	CHI	L	.250	75	4	1	1	1	0	0	0	0	0	0	1	0	0	1	0	0	0	.250	.400	1
Avery, S	ATL	L	.215	37	79	4	17	20	1	1	0	2	5	0	0	4	0	31	1	0	1	.253	.253	1
Azocar, O	SD	L	.246	38	57	5	14	16	2	0	0	9	1	1	1	1	0	9	2	0	1	.281	.267	2
Backman, W	PHI	S	.243	94	185	20	45	57	12	0	0	15	2	3	0	30	0	30	3	2	2	.308	.344	4
Bagwell, J	HOU	R	.294	156	554	79	163	242	26	4	15	82	1	7	13	75	5	116	7	4	12	.437	.387	12
Banister, J	PIT	R	1.000	1	1	0	1	1	0	0	0	0	0	0	0	0	0	0	0	0	0	1.000	1.000	0
Barberie, B	MON	S	.353	57	136	16	48	70	12	2	2	18	1	3	2	20	2	22	0	0	4	.515	.435	5
Barnes, B	MON	L	.082	28	49	1	4	4	0	0	0	1	3	0	0	7	0	19	0	0	0	.082	.196	2
Barrett, M	SD	L	.188	12	16	1	3	7	1	0	1	3	0	0	1	0	0	3	0	0	0	.438	.235	0
Bass, K	SF	S	.233	124	361	43	84	132	10	4	10	40	2	3	4	36	8	56	7	4	12	.366	.307	4
Batiste, K	PHI	R	.222	10	27	2	6	6	0	0	0	1	0	0	1	1	0	8	0	0	0	.222	.250	1
Beck, R	SF	R	.500	31	2	0	1	1	0	0	0	0	0	0	0	0	0	0	0	0	0	.500	.500	0
Belcher, T	LA	R	.119	33	67	3	8	10	2	0	0	3	7	0	0	0	0	26	0	0	1	.149	.119	2
Belinda, S	PIT	R	.000	60	7	0	0	0	0	0	0	1	2	0	0	2	0	5	0	0	1	.000	.222	0
Bell, G	CHI	R	.285	149	558	63	159	261	27	0	25	86	0	9	4	32	6	62	2	6	10	.468	.323	10
Bell, J	PIT	R	.270	157	608	96	164	260	32	8	16	67	30	3	4	52	1	99	10	6	15	.428	.330	24
Bell, M	ATL	L	.133	17	30	4	4	7	0	0	1	1	0	0	0	2	0	7	1	0	2	.233	.188	2
Belliard, R	ATL	R	.249	149	353	36	88	101	9	2	0	27	7	1	2	22	2	63	3	1	4	.286	.296	18
Benavides, F	CIN	R	.286	24	63	11	18	19	3	1	1	1	1	1	1	15	1	15	1	0	1	.302	.303	2
Benes, A	SD	R	.032	33	62	4	2	5	0	0	1	1	7	0	2	6	0	29	0	0	2	.081	.143	0
Benjamin, M	SF	R	.123	54	106	12	13	22	3	0	2	8	3	2	2	7	2	26	3	0	1	.208	.188	3
Benzinger, T	CIN	S	.187	51	123	7	23	33	3	2	1	11	1	0	2	10	2	20	2	0	2	.268	.244	2
Berenguer, J	ATL	R	.000	49	5	0	0	0	0	0	0	0	0	0	0	0	0	3	0	0	0	.000	.000	0
Berryhill, D	CHI-ATL	S	.188	63	160	13	30	52	7	0	5	14	0	1	1	11	1	42	1	2	2	.325	.243	8
Bielecki, M	CHI-ATL	R	.065	41	46	1	3	3	0	0	0	0	0	0	0	1	0	21	0	0	1	.065	.122	0
Biggio, C	HOU	R	.295	149	546	79	161	204	23	4	4	46	5	3	2	53	3	71	19	6	2	.374	.358	11
Bilardello, D	SD	R	.269	15	26	4	7	11	2	1	0	5	0	0	0	3	0	4	0	0	0	.423	.345	0
Black, B	SF	L	.183	35	71	3	13	16	3	0	0	6	9	0	0	0	0	20	0	0	0	.225	.183	0
Blauser, J	ATL	R	.259	129	352	49	91	144	14	3	11	54	4	3	2	54	4	59	5	6	4	.409	.358	17
Boever, J	PHI	R	.333	68	3	0	1	1	0	0	0	0	0	0	0	0	0	0	0	0	0	.333	.333	0
Bonds, B	PIT	L	.292	153	510	95	149	262	28	5	25	116	0	13	4	107	25	73	43	13	8	.514	.410	3
Bones, R	SD	R	.077	11	13	1	1	1	0	0	0	1	4	0	0	2	0	5	0	0	0	.077	.200	0
Bonilla, B	PIT	S	.302	157	577	102	174	284	44	6	18	100	0	11	2	90	8	67	2	4	14	.492	.391	15
Booker, R	PHI	R	.226	28	53	3	12	13	1	0	0	7	1	1	0	1	1	7	0	0	1	.245	.236	0
Boskie, S	CHI	R	.171	30	41	3	7	12	0	1	1	2	3	0	0	3	0	15	0	0	0	.293	.227	2
Boston, D	NY	L	.275	137	255	40	70	106	16	4	4	21	0	1	0	30	0	42	15	8	2	.416	.350	3
Bowen, R	HOU	R	.182	17	22	2	4	5	1	0	0	0	1	0	0	3	0	11	0	0	0	.227	.280	2
Boyd, D	MON	R	.083	19	36	1	3	3	0	0	0	2	3	0	0	3	0	19	0	0	0	.083	.154	0
Braggs, G	CIN	R	.260	85	250	36	65	108	10	0	11	39	0	4	2	23	3	46	11	3	4	.432	.323	5
Brantley, C	PHI	R	.000	6	8	0	0	0	0	0	0	0	2	0	0	0	0	4	0	0	0	.000	.000	1
Brantley, J	SF	R	.000	67	3	0	0	0	0	0	0	0	1	0	0	0	0	1	0	0	0	.000	.000	0
Bream, S	ATL	L	.253	91	265	32	67	112	12	0	11	45	4	4	0	25	5	31	0	3	8	.423	.313	3
Brewer, R	STL	L	.077	19	13	0	1	1	0	0	0	1	0	0	0	0	0	5	0	0	0	.077	.077	1
Brooks, H	NY	R	.238	103	357	48	85	146	11	1	16	50	0	3	3	44	8	62	3	1	7	.409	.324	5
Browning, T	CIN	L	.171	36	70	3	12	18	3	0	1	5	10	0	0	3	0	19	0	1	0	.257	.205	5
Buechele, S	PIT	R	.246	31	114	16	28	47	5	1	4	19	1	1	2	10	0	28	0	1	3	.412	.315	4
Bullett, S	PIT	L	.000	11	4	2	0	0	0	0	0	0	0	0	1	0	0	3	1	1	0	.000	.200	0
Bullock, E	MON	L	.222	73	72	6	16	23	4	0	1	6	0	1	0	9	0	13	6	1	3	.319	.305	1
Burke, T	MON-NY	R	.000	72	6	0	0	0	0	0	0	0	0	0	0	0	0	4	0	0	0	.000	.000	2
Burkett, J	SF	R	.091	36	55	0	5	6	1	0	0	1	9	0	0	3	0	26	0	0	0	.109	.138	1
Butler, B	LA	L	.296	161	615	112	182	211	13	5	2	38	4	2	1	108	4	79	38	28	3	.343	.401	0
Cabrera, F	ATL	R	.242	44	95	7	23	41	6	0	4	23	0	1	0	6	0	20	1	1	5	.432	.284	3
Calderon, I	MON	R	.300	134	470	69	141	226	22	3	19	75	1	10	3	53	4	64	31	16	7	.481	.368	7
Caminiti, K	HOU	S	.253	152	574	65	145	220	30	3	13	80	3	4	5	46	7	85	4	5	18	.383	.312	23
Campusano, S	PHI	R	.114	15	35	2	4	7	0	0	1	2	1	0	0	1	0	10	0	0	0	.200	.139	0
Candaele, C	HOU	S	.262	151	461	44	121	167	20	7	4	50	1	3	0	40	7	49	9	3	5	.362	.319	10
Carman, D	CIN	L	.000	28	5	0	0	0	0	0	0	1	0	0	0	0	0	3	0	0	0	.000	.000	0
Carpenter, C	STL	R	.333	59	3	0	1	1	0	0	0	1	0	0	0	0	0	0	0	0	1	.333	.333	0
Carr, C	NY	S	.182	12	11	1	2	2	0	0	0	1	0	0	0	0	0	2	1	0	0	.182	.182	0
Carreno, A	PHI	R	.000	3	1	0	0	0	0	0	0	0	0	0	0	0	0	1	0	0	0	.000	.000	0
Carreon, M	NY	R	.260	106	254	18	66	84	6	0	4	21	1	1	2	12	2	26	2	1	13	.331	.297	3
Carter, G	LA	R	.246	101	248	22	61	93	14	0	6	26	1	2	7	22	1	26	2	2	11	.375	.323	5
Castilla, V	ATL	R	.200	12	5	1	1	1	0	0	0	0	1	0	0	0	0	2	0	0	0	.200	.200	0
Castillo, B	PHI	R	.173	28	52	3	9	12	3	0	0	2	0	0	0	1	0	15	1	1	1	.231	.189	1
Castillo, F	CHI	R	.143	18	35	0	5	5	0	0	0	1	6	0	0	2	0	13	0	1	0	.143	.189	0
Castillo, T	ATL-NY	L	.000	17	4	0	0	0	0	0	0	0	2	0	0	0	0	0	0	0	0	.000	.000	0
Cedeno, A	HOU	R	.243	67	251	27	61	105	13	2	9	36	1	2	1	9	1	74	4	3	3	.418	.270	18
Cerone, R	NY	R	.273	90	227	18	62	81	13	0	2	16	0	0	1	30	2	24	1	1	9	.357	.360	5
Chamberlain, W	PHI	R	.240	101	383	51	92	153	16	3	13	50	1	0	2	31	0	73	9	4	8	.399	.300	3
Charlton, N	CIN	S	.043	41	23	1	1	2	1	0	0	0	4	0	0	0	0	10	0	0	0	.087	.043	1
Clancy, J	HOU-ATL	R	.000	54	6	0	0	0	0	0	0	0	1	0	0	0	0	2	0	0	0	.000	.000	1
Clark, J	SD	R	.228	118	369	26	84	130	16	0	10	47	1	4	6	31	2	90	2	1	10	.352	.295	2
Clark, M	STL	R	.000	7	7	0	0	0	0	0	0	0	1	0	0	0	0	2	0	0	1	.000	.000	0
Clark, W	SF	L	.301	148	565	84	170	303	32	7	29	116	0	4	2	51	12	91	4	2	5	.536	.359	4
Clayton, R	SF	R	.115	9	26	0	3	4	1	0	0	2	0	0	0	1	0	6	0	0	1	.154	.148	3
Clements, P	SD	R	.000	12	1	0	0	0	0	0	0	0	0	0	0	0	0	1	0	0	0	.000	.000	0
Coleman, V	NY	S	.255	72	278	45	71	91	7	5	1	17	1	0	0	39	0	47	37	14	3	.327	.347	3
Coles, D	SF	R	.214	11	14	1	3	3	0	0	0	0	0	0	0	0	0	2	0	0	1	.214	.214	0
Combs, P	PHI	L	.133	14	15	5	2	2	0	0	0	0	2	0	1	2	0	7	0	0	0	.133	.278	0
Cone, D	NY	L	.125	34	72	3	9	9	0	0	0	5	6	1	2	3	0	14	0	0	3	.125	.179	4
Cook, D	LA	L	.000	20	1	0	0	0	0	0	0	0	1	0	0	0	0	1	0	0	0	.000	.000	0
Coolbaugh, S	SD	R	.217	60	180	12	39	55	8	1	2	15	4	1	1	19	2	45	0	3	8	.306	.294	7
Cooper, G	HOU	R	.250	9	16	1	4	5	1	0	0	2	0	0	0	3	0	6	0	0	0	.313	.368	1
Cormier, R	STL	L	.238	11	21	2	5	5	0	0	0	1	1	0	0	0	0	5	0	0	0	.238	.238	0
Corsi, J	HOU	R	.000	47	1	0	0	0	0	0	0	0	0	0	0	0	0	1	0	0	0	.000	.000	1
Costello, J	SD	R	.000	27	1	0	0	0	0	0	0	0	1	0	0	0	0	1	0	0	0	.000	.000	0
Cox, D	PHI	R	.103	23	29	4	3	3	0	0	0	1	4	0	0	2	0	16	0	0	0	.103	.161	0
Crews, T	LA	R	.000	60	1	0	0	0	0	0	0	0	0	0	0	1	0	1	0	0	0	.000	.500	1
Daniels, K	LA	L	.249	137	461	54	115	183	15	1	17	73	0	6	1	63	4	116	6	1	9	.397	.337	5
Darling, R	NY-MON	R	.125	20	40	0	5	9	4	0	0	3	6	0	0	0	0	16	0	0	0	.225	.125	6
Dascenzo, D	CHI	S	.255	118	239	40	61	75	11	0	1	18	6	1	2	24	2	26	14	7	3	.314	.327	2
Daulton, D	PHI	L	.196	89	285	36	56	104	12	0	12	42	2	5	2	41	4	66	5	0	4	.365	.297	8
Davidson, M	HOU	R	.190	85	142	10	27	39	6	0	2	15	0	0	2	12	0	28	0	0	2	.275	.263	0
Davis, B	LA	R	.000	1	1	0	0	0	0	0	0	0	0	0	0	0	0	0	0	0	0	.000	.000	0
Davis, E	CIN	R	.235	89	285	39	67	110	10	0	11	33	0	2	5	48	5	92	14	2	4	.386	.353	3
Dawson, A	CHI	R	.272	149	563	69	153	275	21	4	31	104	0	6	5	22	3	80	4	5	10	.488	.302	3
DeJesus, J	PHI	R	.129	31	62	3	8	8	0	0	0	4	4	0	0	2	0	39	0	0	0	.129	.156	1
DeLeon, J	STL	R	.043	28	46	0	2	2	0	0	0	0	5	0	0	0	0	17	0	0	0	.043	.043	0
Decker, S	SF	R	.206	79	233	11	48	72	7	1	5	24	2	4	3	16	1	44	0	1	7	.309	.262	7
Deshaies, J	HOU	L	.098	28	41	1	4	4	0	0	0	0	8	0	0	4	0	16	0	0	1	.098	.178	3
DeShields, D	MON	L	.238	151	563	83	134	187	15	4	10	51	8	5	2	95	2	151	56	23	6	.332	.347	27
Dibble, R	CIN	L	.000	67	2	0	0	0	0	0	0	0	1	0	0	0	0	0	0	0	0	.000	.000	1
Donnels, C	NY	L	.225	37	89	7	20	22	2	0	0	5	1	0	0	14	1	19	1	1	0	.247	.330	2
Doran, B	CIN	S	.280	111	361	51	101	135	12	2	6	35	0	3	0	46	1	39	5	4	4	.374	.359	7
Dorsett, B	SD	R	.083	11	12	0	1	1	0	0	0	1	0	0	0	0	0	3	0	0	0	.083	.083	0
Downs, K	SF	R	.087	45	23	3	2	2	0	0	0	1	2	0	0	1	0	5	0	0	0	.087	.125	1
Drabek, D	PIT	R	.179	36	84	6	15	16	1	0	0	2	4	0	0	1	0	28	0	0	0	.190	.188	5
Duncan, M	CIN	R	.258	100	333	46	86	137	7	4	12	40	5	3	3	12	0	57	5	4	0	.411	.288	9
Dunston, S	CHI	R	.260	142	492	59	128	200	22	7	12	50	4	11	4	23	5	64	21	6	9	.407	.292	21
Dykstra, L	PHI	L	.297	63	246	48	73	105	13	5	3	12	0	0	1	37	1	20	24	4	1	.427	.391	4
Elster, K	NY	R	.241	115	348	33	84	122	16	2	6	36	1	4	1	40	6	53	2	3	4	.351	.318	14
Espy, C	PIT	S	.244	43	82	7	20	27	4	0	1	11	3	2	0	5	0	17	4	0	0	.329	.281	2
Eusebio, T	HOU	R	.105	10	19	4	2	3	1	0	0	0	0	0	0	6	0	8	0	0	1	.158	.320	1
Fajardo, H	PIT	R	.000	2	3	0	0	0	0	0	0	0	0	0	0	0	0	1	0	0	1	.000	.000	0
Faries, P	SD	R	.177	57	130	13	23	28	3	1	0	7	4	0	1	14	0	21	3	1	5	.215	.262	2
Fassero, J	MON	L	.000	51	3	0	0	0	0	0	0	0	2	0	0	1	0	2	0	0	0	.000	.250	1
Felder, M	SF	S	.264	132	348	51	92	114	10	6	0	18	4	0	1	30	2	31	21	6	1	.328	.325	4
Fernandez, S	NY	L	.154	8	13	1	2	2	1	0	0	0	1	0	0	0	0	7	0	0	0	.231	.154	0
Fernandez, T	SD	S	.272	145	558	81	152	201	27	5	4	38	7	1	0	55	6	74	23	9	12	.360	.337	20
Finley, S	HOU	L	.285	159	596	84	170	242	28	10	8	54	10	6	2	42	5	65	34	18	8	.406	.331	5

INDIVIDUAL BATTING—1991

BATTER	TEAM	B	AVG	G	AB	R	H	TB	2B	3B	HR	RBI	SH	SF	HP	BB	IBB	SO	SB	CS	GI DP	SLG	OBP	E
Fitzgerald, M	MON	R	.202	71	198	17	40	61	5	2	4	28	1	3	0	22	4	35	4	2	5	.308	.278	2
Fletcher, D	PHI	L	.228	46	136	5	31	42	8	0	1	12	1	0	0	5	0	15	0	1	2	.309	.255	2
Foley, T	MON	L	.208	86	168	12	35	48	11	1	0	15	1	3	1	14	4	30	2	0	4	.286	.269	6
Franco, J	NY	L	.000	52	1	0	0	0	0	0	0	0	0	0	0	0	0	1	0	0	0	.000	.000	1
Fraser, W	STL	R	.000	35	2	0	0	0	0	0	0	0	0	0	0	0	0	2	0	0	0	.000	.000	0
Freeman, M	ATL	R	.000	34	7	0	0	0	0	0	0	0	0	0	0	0	0	5	0	0	0	.000	.000	0
Frey, S	MON	L	.000	31	2	0	0	0	0	0	0	0	0	0	0	1	0	2	0	0	0	.000	.333	0
Galarraga, A	MON	R	.219	107	375	34	82	126	13	2	9	33	0	0	2	23	5	86	5	6	6	.336	.268	9
Gant, R	ATL	R	.251	154	561	101	141	278	35	3	32	105	0	5	5	71	8	104	34	15	6	.496	.338	6
Garcia, C	PIT	R	.250	12	24	2	6	10	0	2	0	1	0	0	0	1	0	8	0	0	1	.417	.280	1
Gardner, C	HOU	R	.000	5	5	0	0	0	0	0	0	0	0	0	0	1	0	1	0	0	0	.000	.167	1
Gardner, J	NY	L	.162	13	37	3	6	6	0	0	0	1	0	1	0	4	0	6	0	0	0	.162	.238	6
Gardner, M	MON	R	.091	27	55	1	5	5	0	0	0	4	4	0	0	1	0	18	0	0	0	.091	.107	1
Gardner, W	SD	R	.000	14	2	0	0	0	0	0	0	0	0	0	0	0	0	2	0	0	0	.000	.000	0
Garrelts, S	SF	R	.000	11	4	1	0	0	0	0	0	0	1	0	0	0	0	1	0	0	0	.000	.000	0
Gedman, R	STL	L	.106	46	94	7	10	20	1	0	3	8	0	2	0	4	0	15	0	1	2	.213	.140	5
Gilkey, B	STL	R	.216	81	268	28	58	84	7	2	5	20	1	2	1	39	0	33	14	8	14	.313	.316	1
Girardi, J	CHI	R	.191	21	47	3	9	11	2	0	0	6	1	0	0	6	1	6	0	0	0	.234	.283	3
Glavine, T	ATL	L	.230	36	74	1	17	18	1	0	0	6	15	0	0	6	0	19	1	0	1	.243	.288	0
Gonzalez, J	LA-PIT	R	.042	58	48	5	2	5	0	0	1	3	2	1	0	2	0	15	0	0	0	.104	.078	0
Gonzalez, L	HOU	L	.254	137	473	51	120	205	28	9	13	69	1	4	8	40	4	101	10	7	9	.433	.320	5
Gooden, D	NY	R	.238	27	63	7	15	21	3	0	1	6	8	0	0	0	0	9	1	1	1	.333	.238	2
Goodwin, T	LA	L	.143	16	7	3	1	1	0	0	0	0	0	0	0	0	0	0	1	1	0	.143	.143	0
Gott, J	LA	R	.500	55	2	0	1	1	0	0	0	0	1	0	0	0	0	1	0	0	0	.500	.500	0
Grace, M	CHI	L	.273	160	619	87	169	231	28	5	8	58	4	7	3	70	7	53	3	4	6	.373	.346	8
Greene, T	PHI	R	.268	38	71	4	19	27	2	0	2	7	3	0	0	4	0	15	0	0	0	.380	.307	1
Gregg, T	ATL	L	.187	72	107	13	20	33	8	1	1	4	0	0	1	12	2	24	2	2	1	.308	.275	0
Griffin, A	LA	S	.243	109	350	27	85	95	6	2	0	27	7	5	1	22	5	49	5	4	5	.271	.286	22
Grimsley, J	PHI	R	.059	12	17	2	1	1	0	0	0	0	0	0	0	2	0	6	0	0	0	.059	.158	1
Grissom, M	MON	R	.267	148	558	73	149	208	23	9	6	39	4	0	1	34	0	89	76	17	8	.373	.310	6
Gross, K	LA	R	.280	48	25	4	7	8	1	0	0	3	2	0	0	2	0	14	0	0	0	.320	.333	1
Gross, K	CIN	R	.091	29	22	1	2	2	0	0	0	1	3	0	0	0	0	6	0	0	0	.091	.091	2
Guerrero, P	STL	R	.272	115	427	11	116	154	12	1	8	70	0	7	1	37	2	46	4	2	12	.361	.326	16
Gwynn, C	LA	L	.252	94	139	18	35	57	5	1	5	22	1	3	1	10	1	23	1	0	5	.410	.301	0
Gwynn, T	SD	L	.317	134	530	69	168	229	27	11	4	62	0	5	0	34	8	19	8	8	11	.432	.355	3
Hamilton, J	LA	R	.223	41	94	4	21	28	4	0	1	14	1	0	0	4	0	21	0	0	2	.298	.255	5
Hammaker, A	SD	S	.000	1	1	0	0	0	0	0	0	0	0	0	0	0	0	1	0	0	0	.000	.000	0
Hammond, C	CIN	L	.353	20	34	4	12	15	3	0	0	1	1	0	0	2	0	10	0	0	0	.441	.389	2
Haney, C	MON	L	.074	16	27	1	2	2	0	0	0	1	2	0	0	0	0	3	0	0	1	.074	.074	2
Hansen, D	LA	L	.268	53	56	3	15	22	4	0	1	5	0	0	0	2	0	12	1	0	2	.393	.293	0
Harkey, M	CHI	R	.400	4	5	2	2	2	0	0	0	0	0	0	0	1	0	0	0	0	0	.400	.500	0
Harnisch, P	HOU	R	.097	33	62	4	6	7	1	0	0	4	7	1	0	4	0	21	0	1	1	.113	.149	1
Harris, G	SD	R	.083	20	36	0	3	3	0	0	0	2	7	0	1	1	0	13	0	0	1	.083	.132	1
Harris, L	LA	L	.287	145	429	59	123	150	16	1	3	38	12	2	5	37	5	32	12	3	16	.350	.349	20
Hartley, M	LA-PHI	R	.000	58	5	0	0	0	0	0	0	0	0	0	0	0	0	1	0	0	1	.000	.000	1
Hassey, R	MON	L	.227	52	119	5	27	38	8	0	1	14	2	1	0	13	1	16	1	1	5	.319	.301	2
Hatcher, B	CIN	R	.262	138	442	45	116	159	25	3	4	41	4	3	7	26	4	55	11	9	9	.360	.312	5
Hayes, C	PHI	R	.230	142	460	34	106	167	23	1	12	53	2	1	1	16	3	75	3	3	13	.363	.257	15
Hayes, V	PHI	L	.225	77	284	43	64	81	15	1	0	21	0	5	3	31	1	42	9	2	6	.285	.303	2
Heath, M	ATL	R	.209	49	139	4	29	37	3	1	1	12	2	1	1	7	5	26	0	1	0	.266	.250	2
Heaton, N	PIT	L	.286	44	14	0	4	5	1	0	0	1	0	0	0	1	0	2	0	0	0	.357	.333	1
Heep, D	ATL	L	.417	14	12	4	5	6	1	0	0	3	0	0	1	0	0	1	0	1	0	.500	.462	0
Henry, D	HOU	L	.000	52	1	0	0	0	0	0	0	0	0	0	0	1	0	1	0	0	0	.000	.000	0
Heredia, G	SF	R	.429	7	7	0	3	3	0	0	0	0	0	0	0	0	0	0	0	0	0	.429	.500	0
Hernandez, C	LA	R	.214	15	14	1	3	4	1	0	0	1	0	1	1	0	0	5	1	0	2	.286	.250	1
Hernandez, J	SD	R	.000	9	2	0	0	0	0	0	0	0	0	0	0	0	0	0	0	0	0	.000	.000	0
Hernandez, X	HOU	R	.000	32	10	0	0	0	0	0	0	0	0	2	0	0	0	7	0	0	0	.000	.167	0
Herr, T	NY-SF	S	.209	102	215	23	45	58	8	1	1	21	2	2	0	45	2	28	9	2	4	.270	.344	0
Hershiser, O	LA	R	.258	21	31	6	8	10	2	0	0	2	4	0	0	3	0	11	0	0	1	.323	.324	1
Hickerson, B	SF	S	.000	17	12	0	0	0	0	0	0	0	0	0	0	0	0	5	0	0	0	.000	.000	0
Hill, K	STL	R	.100	30	50	2	5	5	0	0	0	3	7	0	0	4	0	12	0	0	0	.100	.167	2
Hill, M	CIN	R	.000	22	1	0	0	0	0	0	0	0	0	0	0	0	0	0	0	0	0	.000	.000	0
Hollins, D	PHI	S	.298	56	151	18	45	77	10	2	6	21	0	1	3	17	1	26	1	1	2	.510	.378	8
Howard, T	SD	S	.249	106	281	30	70	100	12	3	4	22	2	1	1	24	4	57	10	7	4	.356	.309	1
Howell, J	SD	L	.206	58	160	24	33	56	3	1	6	16	1	0	0	18	1	33	0	0	1	.350	.287	2
Hudler, R	STL	R	.227	101	207	21	47	64	10	2	1	15	2	2	0	10	1	29	12	8	1	.309	.260	2
Hundley, T	NY	S	.133	21	60	5	8	13	0	1	1	7	1	1	1	6	0	14	0	0	3	.217	.221	0
Hunter, B	ATL	R	.251	97	271	32	68	122	16	1	12	50	0	2	1	17	0	48	0	2	6	.450	.296	8
Hurst, B	SD	L	.134	31	67	3	9	10	1	0	0	6	12	0	0	4	0	23	0	0	0	.149	.183	2
Innis, J	NY	R	.000	69	2	0	0	0	0	0	0	0	0	0	0	0	0	1	0	0	0	.000	.000	1
Jackson, D	CHI	R	.087	17	23	1	2	2	0	0	0	1	2	0	0	0	0	13	0	0	0	.087	.087	1
Jackson, D	SD	R	.262	122	359	51	94	171	12	1	21	49	3	3	2	27	2	66	5	3	5	.476	.315	2
Javier, S	LA	S	.205	121	176	21	36	50	5	3	1	11	3	2	0	16	0	36	7	1	4	.284	.268	3
Jefferies, G	NY	S	.272	136	486	59	132	182	19	2	9	62	1	3	2	47	2	38	26	5	12	.374	.336	17
Jefferson, R	CIN	S	.143	5	7	1	1	4	0	0	1	1	0	0	1	1	0	2	0	0	0	.571	.250	0
Jefferson, S	CIN	R	.053	13	19	2	1	1	0	0	0	1	2	0	0	1	0	3	2	0	0	.053	.100	2
Johnson, H	NY	S	.259	156	564	108	146	302	34	4	38	117	0	15	1	78	12	120	30	16	4	.535	.342	31
Jones, B	MON	R	.000	77	1	0	0	0	0	0	0	0	0	0	1	0	0	0	0	0	0	.000	.000	3
Jones, C	CIN	R	.292	52	89	14	26	37	1	2	2	6	1	0	2	2	0	31	2	1	2	.416	.304	0
Jones, J	HOU	R	.184	26	38	4	7	8	1	0	0	2	0	0	3	0	0	11	0	0	0	.211	.244	2
Jones, R	PHI	L	.154	28	26	0	4	6	2	0	0	3	0	0	0	3	0	9	0	0	1	.231	.214	0
Jones, T	STL	L	.167	16	24	1	4	6	2	0	0	2	1	0	2	1	0	6	0	1	0	.250	.222	0
Jordan, R	PHI	R	.272	101	301	38	82	136	21	3	9	49	0	5	2	14	2	49	0	2	11	.452	.304	9
Jose, F	STL	S	.305	154	568	69	173	249	40	6	8	77	0	5	2	50	8	113	20	12	12	.438	.360	3
Juden, J	HOU	R	.000	4	5	0	0	0	0	0	0	0	0	0	0	0	0	3	0	0	0	.000	.000	0
Justice, D	ATL	L	.275	109	396	67	109	199	25	1	21	87	0	5	3	65	9	81	8	8	4	.503	.377	7
Karros, E	LA	R	.071	14	14	0	1	2	1	0	0	1	0	0	0	1	0	6	0	0	0	.143	.133	0
Kennedy, T	SF	L	.234	69	171	12	40	58	7	1	3	30	0	1	1	11	4	31	0	0	4	.339	.283	6
Kile, D	HOU	R	.000	37	38	2	0	0	0	0	0	0	4	0	0	0	0	23	0	0	0	.000	.073	3
King, J	PIT	R	.239	33	109	16	26	41	1	1	4	18	0	1	1	14	3	15	3	1	3	.376	.328	2
Kingery, M	SF	L	.182	91	110	13	20	26	2	2	0	8	0	0	0	15	1	21	1	0	3	.236	.280	1
Kipper, B	PIT	R	.000	52	1	0	0	0	0	0	0	0	0	0	0	1	0	0	0	0	0	.000	.000	2
Kruk, J	PHI	L	.294	152	538	84	158	260	27	6	21	92	0	9	1	67	16	100	7	4	11	.483	.367	3
LaCoss, M	SF	R	.222	18	9	2	2	2	0	0	0	0	0	0	0	0	1	6	0	0	0	.222	.300	1
LaPoint, D	PHI	L	.000	2	2	0	0	0	0	0	0	0	0	0	0	0	0	0	0	0	0	.000	.000	1
Lake, S	PHI	R	.228	58	158	12	36	45	4	1	1	11	4	0	0	2	1	26	0	0	5	.285	.238	2
Lampkin, T	SD	L	.190	38	58	4	11	16	3	1	0	3	0	0	0	8	0	9	0	0	0	.276	.230	0
Lancaster, L	CHI	R	.179	64	28	2	5	7	2	0	0	2	7	0	0	0	0	13	0	0	0	.250	.179	0
Landrum, B	PIT	R	.000	61	6	0	0	0	0	0	0	0	0	0	0	0	0	1	0	0	0	.000	.000	1
Landrum, C	CHI	L	.233	56	86	28	20	24	2	1	0	6	3	0	0	10	0	18	27	5	2	.279	.313	2
Lankford, R	STL	L	.251	151	566	83	142	222	23	15	9	69	4	3	1	41	1	114	44	20	4	.392	.301	6
Larkin, B	CIN	R	.302	123	464	88	140	235	27	4	20	69	3	2	3	55	1	64	24	6	7	.506	.378	15
LaValliere, M	PIT	L	.289	108	336	25	97	121	11	2	3	41	1	5	2	33	4	27	2	1	10	.360	.351	1
Layana, T	CIN	R	.000	23	1	0	0	0	0	0	0	0	0	0	0	0	0	2	0	0	0	.000	.000	0
Lee, T	CIN	R	.000	3	6	0	0	0	0	0	0	0	0	0	0	0	0	0	0	0	0	.000	.000	0
Lefferts, C	SD	L	.000	54	6	0	0	0	0	0	0	0	4	0	0	0	0	4	0	0	0	.000	.000	0
Leibrandt, C	ATL	R	.043	36	70	1	3	7	2	1	0	2	12	0	0	3	0	18	0	0	1	.100	.082	2
Lemke, M	ATL	S	.234	136	269	36	63	84	11	2	2	23	6	4	0	29	2	27	1	2	9	.312	.305	10
Leonard, M	SF	R	.240	64	129	14	31	46	7	1	2	14	1	2	1	12	1	25	0	1	3	.357	.306	0
Lewis, D	SF	R	.248	72	222	41	55	69	5	3	1	15	7	0	2	36	0	30	13	7	1	.311	.358	0
Lewis, J	SD	R	.000	12	2	0	0	0	0	0	0	0	0	0	0	0	0	1	0	0	0	.000	.000	1
Lilliquist, D	SD	L	.000	6	2	0	0	0	0	0	0	0	0	0	0	0	0	0	0	0	0	.000	.000	0
Lind, J	PIT	R	.265	150	502	53	133	170	16	6	3	54	5	6	2	30	10	56	7	4	20	.339	.306	9
Lindeman, J	PHI	R	.337	65	95	13	32	37	5	0	0	12	1	0	0	13	1	14	0	1	1	.389	.413	0
Lindsey, D	PHI	R	.000	1	3	0	0	0	0	0	0	0	0	0	0	0	0	3	0	0	0	.000	.000	0
Litton, G	SF	R	.181	59	127	13	23	35	7	1	1	15	3	1	1	11	0	25	1	0	2	.276	.250	2
Lofton, K	HOU	L	.203	20	74	9	15	16	1	0	0	0	2	1	0	5	0	19	2	1	0	.216	.253	1
Lyons, B	LA	R	.000	9	9	0	0	0	0	0	0	0	0	0	0	0	0	3	0	0	0	.000	.000	0
Maddux, G	CHI	R	.205	39	88	8	18	23	2	0	1	7	11	0	0	2	0	24	1	0	1	.261	.222	2
Maddux, M	SD	L	.077	64	13	1	1	1	0	0	0	0	0	0	0	3	0	4	0	0	0	.077	.200	1
Magadan, D	NY	L	.258	124	418	58	108	143	23	0	4	51	7	7	2	83	3	50	1	1	5	.342	.378	5
Mahler, R	MON-ATL	R	.143	23	14	0	2	3	1	0	0	1	2	0	0	0	0	4	0	0	0	.214	.143	1
Mallicoat, R	HOU	L	.000	24	1	0	0	0	0	0	0	0	0	0	0	0	0	0	0	0	0	.000	.000	0
Manwaring, K	SF	R	.225	67	178	16	40	49	9	0	0	19	7	2	3	9	0	22	1	1	2	.275	.271	4
Martinez, C	PIT-CIN	R	.234	64	154	13	36	59	5	0	6	19	0	3	0	16	1	39	0	0	3	.383	.301	0
Martinez, Da	MON	L	.295	124	396	47	117	166	18	5	7	42	5	3	3	20	3	54	16	7	3	.419	.332	4
Martinez, De	MON	R	.153	32	72	8	11	15	4	0	0	2	10	0	0	1	0	24	0	0	0	.208	.164	4
Martinez, R	LA	L	.117	33	77	6	9	13	1	0	1	4	8	0	0	1	0	25	0	0	1	.169	.128	2
Mason, R	PIT	R	.000	24	0	0	0	0	0	0	0	0	0	0	0	0	0	0	0	0	0	.000	1.000	0
Mauser, T	PHI	R	.000	3	3	0	0	0	0	0	0	0	0	0	0	0	0	2	0	0	0	.000	.000	0

INDIVIDUAL BATTING—1991

BATTER	TEAM	B	AVG	G	AB	R	H	TB	2B	3B	HR	RBI	SH	SF	HP	BB	IBB	SO	SB	CS	GIDP	SLG	OBP	E
May, D	CHI	L	.227	15	22	4	5	10	2	0	1	3	0	1	0	2	0	1	0	0	1	.455	.280	0
McClellan, P	SF	R	.143	13	21	0	3	3	0	0	0	1	2	0	0	1	0	3	0	0	0	.143	.182	0
McClendon, L	PIT	R	.288	85	163	24	47	75	7	0	7	24	0	0	2	18	0	23	2	1	2	.460	.366	3
McClure, B	STL	R	1.000	32	1	1	1	1	0	0	0	0	0	0	0	0	0	0	0	0	0	1.000	1.000	0
McDaniel, T	NY	S	.207	23	29	3	6	7	1	0	0	2	0	0	0	1	0	11	2	0	0	.241	.233	0
McDowell, R	PHI-LA	R	.000	72	2	0	0	0	0	0	0	0	0	0	0	0	0	0	0	0	0	.000	.000	3
McElroy, C	CHI	L	.300	71	10	1	3	4	1	0	0	2	0	0	0	0	0	3	0	1	0	.400	.300	0
McGee, W	SF	S	.312	131	497	67	155	203	30	3	4	43	8	2	2	34	3	74	17	9	11	.408	.357	6
McGriff, F	SD	R	.278	153	528	84	147	261	19	1	31	106	0	7	2	105	26	135	4	1	14	.494	.396	14
McLemore, M	HOU	S	.148	21	61	6	9	10	1	0	0	2	0	1	0	6	0	13	0	1	1	.164	.221	2
McReynolds, K	NY	R	.259	143	522	65	135	217	32	1	16	74	1	4	2	49	7	46	6	6	8	.416	.322	2
Melendez, J	SD	R	.100	31	20	1	2	3	1	0	0	0	0	0	0	0	0	14	0	0	0	.150	.143	2
Merced, O	PIT	S	.275	120	411	83	113	164	17	2	10	50	1	1	1	64	4	81	8	4	6	.399	.373	12
Mercker, K	ATL	L	.100	50	10	0	1	1	0	0	0	2	0	0	1	0	0	7	0	0	0	.100	.182	1
Miller, K	NY	R	.280	98	275	41	77	113	22	1	4	23	0	1	5	23	0	44	14	4	2	.411	.345	10
Miller, P	PIT	R	.000	1	3	0	0	0	0	0	0	0	0	0	0	0	0	1	0	0	0	.000	.000	0
Minutelli, G	CIN	L	.000	16	3	0	0	0	0	0	0	0	0	0	0	0	0	1	0	0	0	.000	.000	0
Mitchell, K	SF	R	.256	113	371	52	95	191	13	1	27	69	0	4	5	43	8	57	2	3	6	.515	.338	6
Mitchell, K	ATL	R	.318	48	66	11	21	27	0	0	2	5	0	0	0	3	1	12	3	1	1	.409	.392	1
Morandini, M	PHI	L	.249	98	325	38	81	103	11	4	1	20	6	2	2	29	0	45	13	2	7	.317	.313	6
Morgan, M	LA	R	.092	34	76	2	7	7	0	0	0	3	8	2	0	1	0	11	0	0	1	.092	.101	2
Morris, H	CIN	L	.318	136	478	72	152	229	33	1	14	59	5	7	1	46	7	61	10	4	4	.479	.374	9
Morris, J	PHI	L	.220	85	127	15	28	35	2	1	1	6	0	0	1	12	4	25	2	0	1	.276	.293	2
Mota, A	HOU	R	.189	27	90	4	17	22	2	0	1	6	0	0	0	1	0	17	2	0	0	.244	.198	3
Mota, J	SD	S	.222	17	36	4	8	8	0	0	0	2	2	0	1	2	0	7	0	0	0	.222	.282	3
Moyer, J	STL	L	.000	8	8	0	0	0	0	0	0	0	0	0	0	1	0	4	0	0	0	.000	.111	0
Mulholland, T	PHI	R	.088	35	80	3	7	7	0	0	0	0	5	0	1	1	0	32	1	0	2	.088	.110	5
Murphy, D	PHI	R	.252	153	544	66	137	226	33	1	18	81	0	7	0	48	3	93	1	0	20	.415	.309	5
Murray, E	LA	S	.260	153	576	69	150	232	23	1	19	96	0	8	0	55	17	74	10	3	17	.403	.321	7
Myers, R	CIN	L	.172	58	29	3	5	6	1	0	0	2	3	0	0	1	0	16	0	0	0	.207	.200	2
Nabholz, C	MON	L	.115	24	52	5	6	6	0	0	0	1	3	0	0	3	0	14	0	0	2	.115	.164	1
Nichols, C	HOU	R	.196	20	51	3	10	13	3	0	0	1	0	0	0	5	1	17	0	0	0	.255	.268	3
Nixon, O	ATL	S	.297	124	401	81	119	131	10	1	0	26	7	3	2	47	3	40	72	21	5	.327	.371	3
Noboa, J	MON	R	.242	67	95	5	23	29	3	0	1	2	0	0	0	1	1	8	2	3	1	.305	.250	1
Nolte, E	SD	L	.111	6	9	2	1	1	0	0	0	0	2	0	0	0	0	6	0	0	0	.111	.111	0
O'Brien, C	NY	R	.185	69	168	16	31	43	6	0	2	14	0	2	4	17	1	25	0	2	5	.256	.272	4
O'Neill, P	CIN	L	.256	152	532	71	136	256	36	0	28	91	0	1	1	73	14	107	12	7	8	.481	.346	2
Oberkfell, K	HOU	L	.229	53	70	7	16	20	4	0	0	14	0	0	0	14	4	8	0	0	0	.286	.357	2
Offerman, J	LA	S	.195	52	113	10	22	24	2	0	0	3	1	0	1	25	2	32	3	2	5	.212	.345	10
Ojeda, B	LA	L	.161	31	56	2	9	12	0	0	1	3	6	1	0	3	0	10	0	0	1	.214	.200	0
Olivares, O	STL	R	.226	28	53	4	12	15	3	0	0	6	4	0	0	2	0	16	0	0	0	.283	.255	2
Oliver, J	CIN	R	.216	94	269	21	58	102	11	0	11	41	4	0	0	18	5	53	0	0	14	.379	.265	11
Oliveras, F	SF	R	.200	55	10	0	2	2	0	0	0	0	0	0	0	0	0	4	0	0	0	.200	.200	1
Olson, G	ATL	R	.241	133	411	46	99	142	25	0	6	44	2	4	3	44	3	48	1	1	13	.345	.316	4
Oquendo, J	STL	S	.240	127	366	37	88	110	11	4	1	26	4	3	1	67	13	48	1	2	5	.301	.357	9
Ortiz, J	HOU	R	.277	47	83	7	23	32	4	1	1	5	0	0	0	14	0	14	0	0	3	.386	.381	0
Osuna, A	HOU	R	.000	71	2	1	0	0	0	0	0	1	1	0	0	0	0	1	0	0	0	.000	.000	1
Owen, S	MON	S	.255	139	424	39	108	155	22	8	3	26	4	4	1	42	11	61	2	6	11	.366	.321	8
Pagnozzi, T	STL	R	.264	140	459	38	121	161	24	5	2	57	6	5	4	36	6	63	9	13	10	.351	.319	7
Palacios, V	PIT	R	.071	36	14	0	1	1	0	0	0	0	5	0	0	0	0	7	0	0	0	.071	.071	0
Pappas, E	CHI	R	.176	7	17	1	3	3	0	0	0	2	0	0	0	1	0	5	0	0	0	.176	.222	0
Parker, R	SF	R	.071	13	14	0	1	1	0	0	0	1	0	0	0	1	0	5	0	0	0	.071	.133	0
Parrett, J	ATL	R	.000	18	0	0	0	0	0	0	0	0	0	0	0	1	0	0	0	0	0	.000	1.000	1
Patterson, B	PIT	R	.250	54	4	1	1	1	0	0	0	0	0	0	0	0	0	2	0	0	0	.250	.250	0
Pena, A	NY-ATL	R	.000	59	1	0	0	0	0	0	0	0	0	0	0	0	0	1	0	0	0	.000	.000	1
Pena, G	STL	S	.243	104	185	38	45	74	8	3	5	17	1	3	5	18	1	45	15	5	0	.400	.322	6
Pendleton, T	ATL	S	.319	153	586	94	187	303	34	8	22	86	7	7	1	43	8	70	10	2	16	.517	.363	24
Perezchica, T	SF	R	.229	23	48	2	11	17	4	1	0	3	0	0	0	2	0	12	0	1	0	.354	.260	2
Perry, G	STL	L	.240	109	242	29	58	92	8	4	6	36	0	3	0	22	1	34	15	8	2	.380	.300	5
Peterson, A	SD	R	.000	13	13	0	0	0	0	0	0	0	1	0	0	2	0	9	0	0	0	.000	.133	0
Petry, D	ATL	R	.200	10	5	1	1	1	0	0	0	0	0	0	0	0	0	0	0	0	0	.200	.200	0
Piatt, D	MON	L	.000	21	1	0	0	0	0	0	0	0	0	0	0	0	0	0	0	0	0	.000	.000	0
Portugal, M	HOU	R	.196	33	46	4	9	10	1	0	0	3	6	1	1	4	0	4	0	0	0	.217	.269	3
Power, T	CIN	R	.000	68	3	0	0	0	0	0	0	1	0	0	0	1	0	3	0	0	0	.000	.250	0
Presley, J	SD	R	.136	20	59	3	8	11	0	0	1	5	1	1	1	4	1	16	0	1	2	.186	.200	3
Prince, T	PIT	R	.265	26	34	4	9	15	3	0	1	2	0	0	1	7	0	3	0	0	3	.441	.405	1
Quinones, L	CIN	S	.222	97	212	15	47	69	4	3	4	20	1	1	2	21	3	31	1	2	2	.325	.297	7
Ramirez, R	HOU	R	.236	101	233	17	55	68	10	0	1	20	1	2	0	13	1	40	3	4	5	.292	.274	8
Rasmussen, D	SD	L	.136	25	44	3	6	7	1	0	0	3	0	0	0	5	0	12	0	0	0	.159	.224	1
Ready, R	PHI	R	.249	76	205	32	51	66	10	1	1	20	1	4	1	47	3	25	2	1	5	.322	.385	3
Redfield, J	PIT	R	.111	11	18	1	2	2	0	0	0	0	1	0	0	4	0	1	0	1	0	.111	.273	1
Redus, G	PIT	R	.246	98	252	45	62	99	12	2	7	24	1	4	3	28	2	39	17	3	0	.393	.324	6
Reed, J	CIN	L	.267	91	270	20	72	100	15	2	3	31	1	5	1	23	3	38	0	1	6	.370	.321	5
Reed, R	PIT	R	.500	1	2	0	1	2	1	0	0	2	0	0	0	0	0	0	0	0	0	1.000	.500	0
Remlinger, M	SF	L	.000	8	7	1	0	0	0	0	0	0	0	0	0	4	0	1	0	0	0	.000	.125	1
Renfroe, L	CHI	S	.000	4	1	0	0	0	0	0	0	0	0	0	0	0	0	0	0	0	0	.000	.000	0
Reuschel, R	SF	R	.000	4	2	0	0	0	0	0	0	0	0	0	0	0	0	0	0	0	0	.000	.000	0
Reyes, G	MON	R	.217	83	207	11	45	54	9	0	0	13	1	1	1	19	2	51	2	4	3	.261	.285	11
Reynoso, A	ATL	R	.000	6	7	0	0	0	0	0	0	0	0	0	0	1	0	5	0	0	0	.000	.125	0
Rhodes, K	HOU	R	.213	44	136	7	29	37	3	1	1	12	0	1	1	14	3	26	2	2	3	.272	.289	4
Richardson, J	PIT	R	.250	26	4	0	1	1	0	0	0	0	0	0	0	0	0	3	0	0	0	.250	.250	0
Riesgo, D	MON	R	.143	4	7	1	1	1	0	0	0	0	0	0	0	3	1	0	1	0	0	.143	.400	1
Righetti, D	SF	L	.000	61	3	0	0	0	0	0	0	0	0	0	0	0	0	2	0	0	0	.000	.000	0
Rijo, J	CIN	R	.209	31	67	7	14	14	0	0	0	5	9	0	2	13	1	0	1	0	0	.209	.232	3
Ritchie, W	PHI	L	.000	39	3	0	0	0	0	0	0	0	0	0	0	0	0	2	0	0	0	.000	.000	0
Roberts, L	SD	S	.281	117	424	66	119	147	13	3	3	32	4	3	4	37	0	71	26	11	6	.347	.342	10
Robinson, D	SF	R	.150	35	40	1	6	7	1	0	0	4	0	0	0	1	0	13	0	0	0	.175	.171	0
Rodriguez, R	PIT	L	.000	18	1	0	0	0	0	0	0	0	0	0	0	0	0	0	0	0	0	.000	.000	0
Rodriguez, R	SD	L	.000	65	5	0	0	0	0	0	0	0	0	0	0	0	0	5	0	0	0	.000	.000	0
Rohde, D	HOU	S	.122	29	41	3	5	5	0	0	0	0	0	0	0	5	0	8	0	0	1	.122	.217	0
Rojas, M	MON	R	.000	37	4	0	0	0	0	0	0	0	0	0	0	3	0	0	0	0	0	.000	.000	0
Rosenberg, S	SD	L	.000	10	1	0	0	0	0	0	0	0	0	0	0	1	0	1	0	0	0	.000	.000	0
Rossy, R	ATL	R	.000	5	1	0	0	0	0	0	0	0	0	0	0	0	0	0	0	0	0	.000	.000	0
Royer, S	STL	R	.286	9	21	1	6	7	1	0	0	1	0	0	0	1	0	2	0	0	0	.333	.318	0
Ruffin, B	PHI	S	.000	31	24	0	0	0	0	0	0	0	6	0	0	4	0	18	0	0	0	.000	.143	2
Ruskin, S	MON	R	.000	64	2	1	0	0	0	0	0	0	0	0	0	1	0	1	0	0	0	.000	.333	1
Sabo, C	CIN	R	.301	153	582	91	175	294	35	3	26	88	5	3	6	44	3	79	19	6	13	.505	.354	12
Salazar, L	CHI	R	.258	103	333	34	86	144	14	1	14	38	2	0	1	15	1	45	0	3	8	.432	.292	10
Sampen, B	MON	R	.231	43	13	2	3	3	0	0	0	0	0	0	0	1	0	10	0	0	0	.231	.231	1
Samuel, J	LA	R	.271	153	594	74	161	231	22	6	12	58	10	3	3	49	4	133	23	8	8	.389	.328	17
Sanchez, R	CHI	R	.261	13	23	1	6	6	0	0	0	2	0	0	0	3	0	3	0	0	0	.261	.370	1
Sandberg, R	CHI	R	.291	158	585	104	170	284	32	2	26	100	1	9	2	87	4	89	22	8	9	.485	.379	4
Sanders, D	ATL	L	.191	54	110	16	21	38	1	2	4	13	0	0	0	12	0	23	11	3	1	.345	.270	3
Sanders, R	CIN	R	.200	9	40	6	8	11	0	0	1	3	0	0	0	3	0	5	1	1	1	.275	.200	0
Sanford, M	CIN	R	.000	5	8	0	0	0	0	0	0	0	0	0	0	0	0	5	0	0	0	.000	.000	0
Santiago, B	SD	R	.267	152	580	60	155	234	22	3	17	87	0	7	4	23	5	114	8	10	21	.403	.296	14
Santovenia, N	MON	R	.250	41	96	7	24	35	5	0	2	14	0	4	0	2	0	18	0	1	4	.365	.255	3
Sasser, M	NY	L	.272	96	228	18	62	95	14	2	5	35	1	4	1	9	2	19	0	0	6	.417	.298	3
Scanlan, B	CHI	R	.042	40	24	0	1	1	0	0	0	0	1	0	0	1	0	10	0	0	3	.042	.080	2
Schilling, C	HOU	R	.333	56	3	0	1	1	0	0	0	0	0	0	0	1	0	0	0	0	0	.333	.333	1
Schourek, P	NY	L	.136	35	22	0	3	4	1	0	0	3	0	0	0	0	0	9	0	0	0	.182	.208	2
Schu, R	PHI	R	.091	17	22	1	2	2	0	0	0	0	0	0	0	1	0	1	0	0	0	.091	.125	1
Schulz, J	PIT	L	.000	3	1	0	0	0	0	0	0	0	0	0	0	0	0	0	0	0	0	.000	.000	0
Scioscia, M	LA	L	.264	119	345	39	91	135	16	2	8	40	5	4	3	47	3	32	4	3	5	.391	.353	7
Scott, D	CIN	S	.158	10	19	0	3	3	0	0	0	0	0	0	0	0	0	2	0	0	0	.158	.158	0
Scott, G	CHI	R	.165	31	79	8	13	19	3	0	1	5	0	0	3	13	4	14	0	1	2	.241	.305	2
Scott, M	HOU	R	.000	2	1	0	0	0	0	0	0	0	0	0	0	0	0	0	0	0	0	.000	.000	0
Scudder, S	CIN	R	.103	27	29	2	3	3	0	0	0	0	0	0	0	0	0	11	0	0	2	.103	.103	0
Searcy, S	PHI	L	.000	18	4	0	0	0	0	0	0	0	1	0	0	0	0	1	0	0	0	.000	.000	0
Servais, S	HOU	R	.162	16	37	0	6	9	3	0	0	6	1	0	0	5	0	5	0	0	1	.243	.244	1
Sharperson, M	LA	R	.278	105	216	24	60	81	11	2	2	20	10	0	1	25	0	24	1	3	2	.375	.355	4
Shipley, C	SD	R	.275	37	91	6	25	31	5	0	0	6	3	0	0	3	1	16	2	0	0	.341	.298	7
Simms, M	HOU	R	.203	49	123	18	25	39	5	0	3	16	0	2	0	18	0	38	1	0	2	.317	.301	6
Simons, D	NY	L	.000	42	3	0	0	0	0	0	0	0	0	0	0	0	0	5	0	0	0	.000	.000	0
Slaught, D	PIT	R	.295	77	220	19	65	87	17	1	1	29	5	3	1	21	1	32	1	0	6	.395	.363	5
Slocumb, H	CHI	R	.000	52	1	0	0	0	0	0	0	0	0	0	0	0	0	1	0	0	0	.000	.000	1
Smiley, J	PIT	L	.100	33	70	3	7	7	0	0	0	0	9	0	0	3	0	24	0	1	0	.100	.137	1
Smith, B	STL	R	.246	31	65	6	16	17	1	0	0	8	7	0	0	6	0	11	0	0	6	.262	.254	0
Smith, Da	CHI	R	.000	35	1	0	0	0	0	0	0	0	0	0	0	0	0	2	0	0	0	.000	.000	0
Smith, Dw	CHI	L	.228	90	167	16	38	58	7	2	3	21	1	0	1	11	2	32	2	3	2	.347	.279	3

INDIVIDUAL BATTING—1991

BATTER	TEAM	B	AVG	G	AB	R	H	TB	2B	3B	HR	RBI	SH	SF	HP	BB	IBB	SO	SB	CS	GI DP	SLG	OBP	E
Smith, G	LA	S	.000	5	3	1	0	0	0	0	0	0	1	0	0	0	0	2	0	0	0	.000	.000	0
Smith, L	ATL	R	.275	122	353	58	97	139	19	1	7	44	2	2	9	50	3	64	9	5	4	.394	.377	5
Smith, O	STL	S	.285	150	550	96	157	202	30	3	3	50	6	1	1	83	2	36	35	9	8	.367	.380	8
Smith, P	ATL	R	.167	14	12	1	2	2	0	0	0	1	0	0	1	0	1	5	0	0	0	.167	.231	0
Smith, Z	PIT	L	.183	36	71	3	13	16	3	0	0	10	13	1	1	3	0	8	0	0	0	.225	.224	3
Smoltz, J	ATL	R	.108	38	65	7	7	10	3	0	0	3	8	0	0	5	0	28	0	0	0	.154	.171	1
St. Claire, R	ATL	R	.500	19	2	0	1	1	0	0	0	0	0	0	0	0	0	0	0	0	0	.500	.500	0
Stanton, M	ATL	L	.500	74	6	0	3	4	1	0	0	1	0	0	0	1	0	1	0	0	0	.667	.571	0
Stephens, R	STL	R	.286	6	7	0	2	2	0	0	0	0	0	0	0	1	0	3	0	0	0	.286	.375	0
Stephenson, P	SD		.286	11	7	0	2	2	0	0	0	0	0	0	2	0	0	3	0	0	0	.286	.444	0
Strange, D	CHI	S	.444	3	9	0	4	5	1	0	0	1	0	1	1	0	0	1	1	0	0	.556	.455	1
Strawberry, D	LA	L	.265	139	505	86	134	248	22	4	28	99	0	5	3	75	4	125	10	8	8	.491	.361	5
Sutcliffe, R	CHI	L	.094	20	32	2	3	4	1	0	0	2	5	0	0	1	0	9	0	0	1	.125	.121	0
Sutko, G	CIN	R	.100	10	10	0	1	1	0	0	0	1	0	0	0	2	0	6	0	0	0	.100	.250	3
Templeton, G	SD-NY	S	.221	112	276	25	61	84	10	2	3	26	4	3	0	10	3	38	3	2	10	.304	.246	8
Terry, S	STL	R	.143	65	7	1	1	1	0	0	0	1	0	0	0	0	0	2	0	0	0	.143	.143	0
Teufel, T	NY-SD	R	.217	117	341	41	74	126	16	0	12	44	4	2	1	51	4	77	9	3	8	.370	.319	9
Tewksbury, B	STL	R	.155	30	58	5	9	10	1	0	0	2	7	0	0	4	0	16	0	0	1	.172	.210	2
Thompson, M	STL	L	.307	115	326	55	100	144	16	5	6	34	2	1	0	32	7	53	16	9	4	.442	.368	2
Thompson, R	SF	R	.262	144	492	74	129	220	24	5	19	48	11	1	6	63	2	95	14	7	5	.447	.352	11
Thon, D	PHI	R	.252	146	539	44	136	189	18	4	9	44	2	4	0	25	6	84	11	5	9	.351	.283	21
Tolentino, J	HOU	L	.259	44	54	6	14	21	4	0	1	6	0	1	0	4	0	9	0	0	2	.389	.305	1
Tomlin, R	PIT	L	.192	32	52	5	10	11	1	0	0	2	13	0	0	2	0	18	0	0	2	.212	.222	2
Torve, K	NY	L	.000	10	8	0	0	0	0	0	0	0	0	0	0	0	0	1	0	0	1	.000	.000	0
Treadway, J	ATL	L	.320	106	306	41	98	128	17	2	3	32	2	3	2	23	1	19	2	2	8	.418	.368	15
Uribe, J	SF	S	.221	90	231	23	51	70	8	4	1	12	1	0	0	20	6	33	3	4	2	.303	.283	11
Van Slyke, A	PIT	L	.265	138	491	87	130	219	24	7	17	83	0	11	4	71	1	85	10	3	5	.446	.355	1
VanderWal, J	MON	L	.213	21	61	4	13	22	4	1	1	8	0	1	0	1	0	18	0	0	2	.361	.222	0
Varsho, G	PIT	L	.273	99	187	23	51	78	11	2	4	23	1	1	2	19	2	34	9	2	2	.417	.344	1
Vatcher, J	SD	R	.200	17	20	3	4	4	0	0	0	2	0	0	0	4	0	6	1	0	0	.200	.333	1
Villanueva, H	CHI	R	.276	71	192	23	53	104	10	1	13	32	0	1	0	21	1	30	0	0	3	.542	.346	6
Viola, F	NY	L	.127	35	71	2	9	11	2	0	0	1	10	0	0	2	0	13	0	0	1	.155	.151	4
Vizcaino, J	CHI	S	.262	93	145	7	38	43	5	0	0	10	2	2	0	5	0	18	2	1	1	.297	.283	7
Walk, B	PIT	R	.205	25	39	2	8	12	1	0	1	5	2	0	0	1	0	11	0	0	1	.308	.225	2
Walker, C	CHI	S	.257	124	374	51	96	126	10	1	6	34	1	3	0	33	2	57	13	5	3	.337	.315	8
Walker, L	MON	L	.290	137	487	59	141	223	30	2	16	64	1	4	5	42	2	102	14	9	7	.458	.349	6
Wallach, T	MON	R	.225	151	577	60	130	193	22	1	13	73	0	4	6	50	8	100	2	4	12	.334	.292	14
Walton, J	CHI	R	.219	123	270	42	59	89	13	1	5	17	3	3	3	19	0	55	7	3	7	.330	.275	3
Ward, K	SD	R	.243	44	107	13	26	43	7	2	2	8	1	0	1	9	0	27	1	4	3	.402	.308	1
Webster, M	PIT-LA	S	.222	94	171	21	38	62	8	5	2	19	1	0	0	18	1	52	0	1	3	.363	.296	2
Wehner, J	PIT	R	.340	37	106	15	36	43	7	0	0	7	0	0	0	7	0	17	3	0	0	.406	.381	6
Whitehurst, W	NY	R	.182	36	33	2	6	7	1	0	0	5	0	0	2	0	0	6	0	0	0	.212	.229	2
Whitson, E	SD	R	.125	13	24	1	3	3	0	0	0	1	2	0	0	1	0	6	0	0	0	.125	.160	0
Wilkerson, C	PIT	S	.188	85	191	20	36	53	9	1	2	18	0	4	0	15	0	40	2	1	2	.277	.243	2
Wilkins, D	HOU	R	.000	7	1	0	0	0	0	0	0	0	0	0	0	0	0	1	0	0	0	.000	.000	0
Wilkins, R	CHI	L	.222	86	203	21	45	72	9	0	6	22	7	0	6	19	2	56	3	3	3	.355	.307	3
Willard, J	ATL	L	.214	17	14	1	3	6	0	0	1	4	0	0	0	2	0	5	0	0	0	.429	.313	0
Williams, B	HOU	R	.000	2	3	0	0	0	0	0	0	0	2	0	0	0	0	0	0	0	0	.000	.000	0
Williams, K	MON	R	.271	34	70	11	19	28	5	2	0	1	0	0	1	3	0	22	2	1	1	.400	.311	2
Williams, M	PHI	L	.000	69	1	0	0	0	0	0	0	0	0	0	0	1	0	1	0	0	0	.000	.500	3
Williams, M	SF	R	.268	157	589	72	158	294	24	5	34	98	0	7	6	33	6	128	5	5	11	.499	.310	16
Wilson, C	STL	R	.171	60	82	5	14	16	2	0	0	13	0	2	0	6	2	10	0	0	2	.195	.222	2
Wilson, S	CHI-LA	L	.000	20	2	0	0	0	0	0	0	0	0	0	0	0	0	1	0	0	0	.000	.000	0
Wilson, T	SF	L	.235	48	51	7	12	16	1	0	1	5	8	0	1	4	0	16	0	0	2	.314	.304	1
Winningham, H	CIN	L	.225	98	169	17	38	49	6	1	1	4	2	0	0	11	1	40	4	4	2	.290	.272	5
Wohlers, M	ATL	R	.000	17	1	0	0	0	0	0	0	0	0	0	0	0	0	0	1	0	0	.000	.000	0
Wood, T	SF	L	.120	10	25	0	3	3	0	0	0	1	1	0	0	2	0	11	0	0	0	.120	.185	1
Yelding, E	HOU	R	.243	78	276	19	67	83	11	1	1	20	3	1	0	13	3	46	11	9	4	.301	.276	20
Young, A	NY	R	.143	10	14	0	2	3	1	0	0	0	1	0	0	0	0	4	0	0	0	.214	.143	1
Young, G	HOU	S	.218	108	142	26	31	39	3	1	1	11	1	2	0	24	0	17	16	5	3	.275	.327	0
Zeile, T	STL	R	.280	155	565	76	158	233	36	3	11	81	0	6	5	62	3	94	17	11	15	.412	.353	25

BATSMEN AWARDED FIRST BASE ON INTERFERENCE OR OBSTRUCTION:
N.Y. (1): Herr (Wilkins, Chi.); S.F. (1): Kingery (Santiago, S.D.).

1991 CLUB BATTING

CLUB	AVG	G	AB	R	OR	H	TB	2B	3B	HR	GS	RBI	SH	SF	HP	BB	IBB	SO	SB	CS	GI DP	LOB	SHO	SLG	OB
PITTSBURGH	.263	162	5449	768	632	1433	2170	259	50	126	5	725	99	66	35	620	62	901	124	46	111	1188	6	.398	.338
CINCINNATI	.258	162	5501	689	691	1419	2215	250	27	164	2	654	72	41	32	488	54	1006	124	56	85	1110	9	.403	.320
ATLANTA	.258	162	5456	749	644	1407	2145	255	30	141	3	704	86	45	32	563	55	906	165	76	104	1111	9	.393	.328
ST. LOUIS	.255	162	5362	651	648	1366	1915	239	53	68	0	599	58	47	21	532	48	857	202	110	94	1072	14	.357	.322
CHICAGO	.253	160	5522	695	734	1395	2156	232	26	159	4	654	75	55	36	442	41	879	123	64	87	1074	4	.390	.309
LOS ANGELES	.253	162	5408	665	565	1366	1939	191	29	108	3	605	94	46	28	583	50	957	126	68	109	1151	8	.359	.326
SAN FRANCISCO	.246	162	5463	649	697	1345	2079	215	48	141	2	605	90	33	40	471	59	973	95	57	91	1110	13	.381	.309
MONTREAL	.246	161	5412	579	655	1329	1934	236	42	95	1	536	64	47	28	484	51	1056	221	100	97	1074	10	.357	.308
HOUSTON	.244	162	5504	605	717	1345	1908	240	43	79	1	502	63	43	35	502	45	1027	125	68	87	1131	16	.347	.309
SAN DIEGO	.244	162	5408	636	646	1321	1960	204	36	121	4	591	78	38	32	501	60	1069	101	64	122	1080	12	.362	.310
NEW YORK	.244	161	5359	640	646	1305	1954	250	24	117	4	605	60	52	27	578	53	789	153	70	97	1114	9	.365	.317
PHILADELPHIA	.241	162	5521	629	680	1332	1979	248	33	111	6	590	52	49	21	490	48	1026	92	30	114	1108	12	.358	.303
TOTALS	.250	970	65365	7955	7955	16363	24354	2819	441	1430	35	7438	891	562	367	6254	626	11446	1651	809	1198	13323	122	.373	.317

INDIVIDUAL FIELDING—1991

FIRST BASEMEN

PLAYER	TEAM	T	PCT	G	PO	A	E	TC	DP
Anderson, D	SF	R	1.000	16	85	9	0	94	3
Azocar, O	SD	L	1.000	1	5	0	0	5	0
Bagwell, J	HOU	R	.991	155	1270	106	12	1388	97
Barberie, B	MON	R	1.000	1	1	0	0	1	0
Bell, M	ATL	L	.975	14	72	5	2	79	7
Benzinger, T	CIN	R	.986	21	123	13	2	138	7
Bonilla, B	PIT	R	1.000	4	28	2	0	30	6
Bream, S	ATL	L	.996	85	668	50	3	721	53
Brewer, R	STL	L	1.000	15	27	3	0	30	2
Bullock, E	MON	L	.933	3	11	3	1	15	0
Cabrera, F	ATL	R	.973	14	65	7	2	74	3
Calderon, I	MON	R	1.000	4	28	2	0	30	4
Carter, G	LA	R	1.000	10	47	7	0	54	3
Clark, J	SD	R	.989	16	85	5	1	91	4
Clark, W	SF	L	.997	144	1273	110	4	1387	115
Coles, D	SF	R	1.000	1	4	0	0	4	0
Donnels, C	NY	R	1.000	15	123	12	0	135	10
Doran, B	CIN	R	1.000	4	19	0	0	19	3
Dorsett, B	SD	R	1.000	2	4	1	0	5	0
Fitzgerald, M	MON	R	1.000	3	15	3	0	18	1
Foley, T	MON	R	.994	31	148	9	1	158	8
Galarraga, A	MON	R	.991	105	887	80	9	976	68
Grace, M	CHI	L	.995	160	1520	167	8	1695	106
Gregg, T	ATL	L	1.000	13	105	9	0	114	6
Guerrero, P	STL	R	.985	112	953	66	16	1035	73
Heep, D	ATL	L	1.000	1	1	0	0	1	0
Hollins, D	PHI	R	.979	6	42	4	1	47	4
Hudler, R	STL	R	1.000	12	30	0	0	30	5
Hunter, B	ATL	L	.988	85	622	46	8	676	42
Javier, S	LA	R	.920	2	20	3	2	25	1
Jefferson, R	CIN	L	1.000	2	14	1	0	15	3
Jordan, R	PHI	R	.987	72	626	37	9	672	37
Karros, E	LA	R	1.000	10	33	2	0	35	5
Kennedy, T	SF	R	1.000	2	3	0	0	3	0
Kingery, M	SF	L	1.000	6	21	2	0	23	2
Kruk, J	PHI	L	.997	102	735	49	2	786	54
Lee, T	CIN	R	1.000	2	8	4	0	12	0
Lindeman, J	PHI	R	1.000	1	4	0	0	4	1
Litton, G	SF	R	.989	15	75	11	1	87	10
Magadan, D	NY	R	.996	122	1035	90	5	1130	73
Martinez, C	PIT-CIN	R	.977	33	239	12	6	257	15
McClendon, L	PIT	R	.986	22	132	10	2	144	12
McGriff, F	SD	R	.990	153	1370	87	14	1471	111
Merced, O	PIT	R	.988	105	911	60	12	983	64
Mitchell, K	SF	R	.000	1	0	0	0	0	0
Morris, H	CIN	L	.992	128	979	100	9	1088	87
Murray, E	LA	R	.995	149	1327	128	7	1462	96
Noboa, J	MON	R	1.000	1	1	0	0	1	0
Oberkfell, K	HOU	R	1.000	13	66	8	0	74	6
Oquendo, J	STL	R	.000	3	0	0	0	0	0
Pagnozzi, T	STL	R	1.000	3	9	0	0	9	1
Perry, G	STL	R	.989	61	407	28	5	440	30
Prince, T	PIT	R	1.000	1	1	0	0	1	0
Redus, G	PIT	R	.990	47	377	25	4	406	35
Rohde, D	HOU	R	1.000	1	3	0	0	3	0
Salazar, L	CHI	R	.969	7	30	1	1	32	2
Santovenia, N	MON	R	1.000	7	31	4	0	35	4
Sasser, M	NY	R	.988	10	80	5	1	86	5
Schu, R	PHI	R	1.000	1	13	1	0	14	0
Sharperson, M	LA	R	.983	10	46	12	1	59	5
Templeton, G	NY	R	.994	25	152	12	1	165	9
Teufel, T	SD	R	1.000	6	47	2	0	49	1
Tolentino, J	HOU	L	.982	10	49	5	1	55	3
Torve, K	NY	R	1.000	1	0	2	0	2	0
Varsho, G	PIT	R	1.000	3	11	0	0	11	0
Villanueva, H	CHI	R	1.000	6	17	1	0	18	2
Walker, L	MON	R	.988	39	313	30	4	347	28
Webster, M	LA	L	1.000	1	2	0	0	2	1
Wilson, C	STL	R	1.000	4	14	1	0	15	2

SECOND BASEMEN

PLAYER	TEAM	T	PCT	G	PO	A	E	TC	DP
Alicea, L	STL	R	1.000	11	17	22	0	39	3
Anderson, D	SF	R	1.000	6	6	3	0	9	1
Backman, W	PHI	R	.981	36	50	52	2	104	12
Barberie, B	MON	R	1.000	10	22	25	0	47	7
Barrett, M	SD	R	1.000	2	7	4	0	11	2
Benavides, F	CIN	R	1.000	3	7	4	0	11	1
Biggio, C	HOU	R	.929	3	5	8	1	14	1
Blauser, J	ATL	R	.983	32	48	66	2	116	15
Candaele, C	HOU	R	.982	109	197	301	9	507	52
DeShields, D	MON	R	.962	148	285	405	27	717	72
Doran, B	CIN	R	.981	88	153	208	7	368	47
Duncan, M	CIN	R	.974	62	116	144	7	267	29
Faries, P	SD	R	.988	36	67	92	2	161	18
Felder, M	SF	R	1.000	1	0	2	0	2	0
Foley, T	MON	R	1.000	2	6	8	0	14	3
Garcia, C	PIT	R	1.000	1	2	0	0	2	0
Gardner, J	NY	R	1.000	3	4	9	0	13	0
Harris, L	LA	R	.988	27	33	49	1	83	12
Herr, T	NY-SF	R	1.000	72	114	148	0	262	33
Hudler, R	STL	R	1.000	5	3	2	0	5	1
Jefferies, G	NY	R	.982	77	144	177	6	327	15
Jones, T	STL	R	1.000	4	0	3	0	3	0
Lemke, M	ATL	R	.978	110	159	205	8	372	39
Lind, J	PIT	R	.989	149	349	438	9	796	79
Litton, G	SF	R	1.000	15	29	24	0	53	7
McLemore, M	HOU	R	.975	19	25	54	2	81	8
Miller, K	NY	R	.972	60	129	148	8	285	28
Morandini, M	PHI	R	.986	97	183	254	6	443	45
Mota, A	HOU	R	.970	27	30	66	3	99	11
Mota, J	SD	R	.962	13	24	27	2	53	5
Noboa, J	MON	R	.962	6	11	14	1	26	3
Oquendo, J	STL	R	.988	118	244	346	7	597	60
Pena, G	STL	R	.976	83	95	146	6	247	28
Perezchica, T	SF	R	1.000	6	6	7	0	13	3
Quinones, L	CIN	R	.975	33	45	74	3	122	16
Ramirez, R	HOU	R	.978	27	35	52	2	89	9
Ready, R	PHI	R	.989	66	127	145	3	275	22
Roberts, L	SD	R	.978	68	128	185	7	320	35
Rohde, D	HOU	R	1.000	4	7	12	0	19	1
Samuel, J	LA	R	.978	152	300	442	17	759	73
Sanchez, R	CHI	R	1.000	2	1	8	0	9	0
Sandberg, R	CHI	R	.995	157	267	515	4	786	66
Sharperson, M	LA	R	1.000	5	5	8	0	13	3
Shipley, C	SD	R	.982	14	18	36	1	55	8
Smith, G	LA	R	.000	1	0	0	0	0	0
Teufel, T	NY-SD	R	.987	66	102	124	3	229	22
Thompson, R	SF	R	.985	144	320	402	11	733	98
Treadway, J	ATL	R	.960	93	155	206	15	376	33
Vizcaino, J	CHI	R	.929	9	8	18	2	28	4
Walker, C	CHI	R	1.000	6	11	16	0	27	1
Wilkerson, C	PIT	R	.992	30	50	80	1	131	15
Wilson, C	STL	R	1.000	3	0	2	0	2	1

THIRD BASEMEN

PLAYER	TEAM	T	PCT	G	PO	A	E	TC	DP
Alicea, L	STL	R	1.000	2	1	0	0	1	0
Anderson, D	SF	R	.842	11	8	8	3	19	0
Backman, W	PHI	R	.939	20	4	27	2	33	1
Barberie, B	MON	R	1.000	10	11	17	0	28	1
Barrett, M	SD	R	1.000	2	0	2	0	2	0
Benjamin, M	SF	R	.000	1	0	0	0	0	0
Blauser, J	ATL	R	.911	18	13	28	4	45	1
Bonilla, B	PIT	R	.932	67	43	134	13	190	13
Booker, R	PHI	R	1.000	3	1	4	0	5	0
Buechele, S	PIT	R	.956	31	22	64	4	90	5
Caminiti, K	HOU	R	.948	152	129	293	23	445	29
Candaele, C	HOU	R	.958	11	7	16	1	24	1
Coolbaugh, S	SD	R	.952	54	32	108	7	147	8
Cooper, G	HOU	R	.833	4	3	2	1	6	0
Donnels, C	NY	R	.938	11	8	22	2	32	3
Faries, P	SD	R	1.000	12	5	13	0	18	0
Felder, M	SF	R	.857	3	1	5	1	7	1
Foley, T	MON	R	.857	6	1	5	1	7	0
Garcia, C	PIT	R	1.000	2	4	5	0	9	0
Hamilton, J	LA	R	.928	33	21	43	5	69	2
Hansen, D	LA	R	1.000	21	4	18	0	22	1
Harris, L	LA	R	.943	113	77	155	14	246	16
Hayes, C	PHI	R	.958	138	85	237	14	336	25
Hernandez, C	LA	R	.000	1	0	0	0	0	0
Herr, T	SF	R	1.000	3	2	3	0	5	0
Hollins, D	PHI	R	.922	36	25	58	7	90	2
Howell, J	SD	R	.985	54	33	98	2	133	7
Jefferies, G	NY	R	.916	51	26	94	11	131	6
Johnson, H	NY	R	.927	104	55	173	18	246	11
King, J	PIT	R	.975	33	15	62	2	79	0
Lemke, M	ATL	R	.867	15	3	10	2	15	1
Litton, G	SF	R	.958	11	5	18	1	24	1
Miller, K	NY	R	1.000	2	2	1	0	3	0
Murray, E	LA	R	.000	1	0	0	0	0	0
Noboa, J	MON	R	1.000	2	1	3	0	4	1
Oberkfell, K	HOU	R	.818	4	4	5	2	11	0
Pendleton, T	ATL	R	.950	148	108	349	24	481	31
Presley, J	SD	R	.923	16	13	23	3	39	0
Quinones, L	CIN	R	.914	19	12	20	3	35	2
Ramirez, R	HOU	R	1.000	2	0	1	0	1	0
Redfield, J	PIT	R	.917	9	4	7	1	12	3
Richardson, J	PIT	R	.000	3	0	0	0	0	0
Rohde, D	HOU	R	1.000	3	0	3	0	3	0
Royer, S	STL	R	1.000	5	5	4	0	9	0
Sabo, C	CIN	R	.966	151	86	255	12	353	24
Salazar, L	CHI	R	.956	86	46	151	9	206	5
Schu, R	PHI	R	.667	3	2	0	1	3	0
Scott, G	CHI	R	.969	31	13	50	2	65	6
Sharperson, M	LA	R	.981	68	30	71	2	103	5
Slaught, D	PIT	R	.000	1	0	0	0	0	0
Strange, D	CHI	R	.800	3	1	3	1	5	0
Templeton, G	SD-NY	R	.967	17	4	25	1	30	3
Teufel, T	NY-SD	R	.947	53	29	79	6	114	4
Vizcaino, J	CHI	R	.947	57	10	26	2	38	1
Walker, C	CHI	R	.929	57	22	69	7	98	7
Wallach, T	MON	R	.968	149	107	310	14	431	27
Wehner, J	PIT	R	.936	36	23	65	6	94	9
Wilkerson, C	PIT	R	.974	14	14	24	1	39	4
Williams, M	SF	R	.964	155	131	293	16	440	30
Wilson, C	STL	R	.905	12	8	11	2	21	3
Zeile, T	STL	R	.943	154	124	290	25	439	18

SHORTSTOPS

PLAYER	TEAM	T	PCT	G	PO	A	E	TC	DP
Alicea, L	STL	R	1.000	1	1	1	0	2	1
Anderson, D	SF	R	.956	63	68	107	8	183	25
Barberie, B	MON	R	.931	19	19	48	5	72	7
Batiste, K	PHI	R	.970	7	10	22	1	33	4
Bell, J	PIT	R	.968	156	239	491	24	754	78
Belliard, R	ATL	R	.967	145	168	361	18	547	53
Benavides, F	CIN	R	.974	20	26	49	2	77	5
Benjamin, M	SF	R	.984	51	64	123	3	190	23
Blauser, J	ATL	R	.948	85	75	125	11	211	21
Booker, R	PHI	R	1.000	20	16	29	0	45	2
Castilla, V	ATL	R	1.000	12	6	6	0	12	0
Cedeno, A	HOU	R	.930	66	88	151	18	257	36
Clayton, R	SF	R	.880	8	16	6	3	25	1
Duncan, M	CIN	R	.983	32	46	68	2	116	12
Dunston, S	CHI	R	.968	142	261	383	21	665	69
Elster, K	NY	R	.970	107	149	299	14	462	39
Faries, P	SD	R	1.000	8	8	12	0	20	2
Fernandez, T	SD	R	.972	145	247	440	20	707	78
Foley, T	MON	R	.967	43	45	71	4	120	12
Garcia, C	PIT	R	.947	9	5	13	1	19	3
Gardner, J	NY	R	.818	8	7	20	6	33	2
Griffin, A	LA	R	.961	109	186	349	22	557	45
Hamilton, J	LA	R	.000	1	0	0	0	0	0
Hansen, D	LA	R	1.000	1	1	1	0	2	1
Harris, L	LA	R	.924	20	15	46	5	66	7
Hayes, C	PHI	R	.857	2	3	3	1	7	0
Johnson, H	NY	R	.924	28	45	88	11	144	15
Jones, T	STL	R	1.000	14	5	13	0	18	3
Larkin, B	CIN	R	.976	119	226	372	15	613	65
Litton, G	SF	R	1.000	9	7	12	0	19	3
Miller, K	NY	R	.667	2	1	3	2	6	1
Mota, J	SD	R	.750	3	1	2	1	4	0
Noboa, J	MON	R	1.000	2	0	2	0	2	0
Offerman, J	LA	R	.945	50	50	121	10	181	17
Oquendo, J	STL	R	.961	22	27	22	2	51	5
Owen, S	MON	R	.986	133	189	376	8	573	64
Perezchica, T	SF	R	.947	13	14	22	2	38	3
Quinones, L	CIN	R	.958	5	11	12	1	24	5
Ramirez, R	HOU	R	.953	45	51	71	6	128	13
Richardson, J	PIT	R	1.000	2	0	1	0	1	0
Rohde, D	HOU	R	1.000	3	3	8	0	11	1
Rossy, R	ATL	R	.000	1	0	0	0	0	0

INDIVIDUAL FIELDING—1991

SHORTSTOPS (Continued)

PLAYER	TEAM	T	PCT	G	PO	A	E	TC	DP
Sanchez, R	CHI	R	1.000	10	10	17	0	27	1
Sharperson, M	LA	R	.960	16	8	16	1	25	2
Shipley, C	SD	R	.902	19	21	34	6	61	6
Smith, O	STL	R	.987	150	244	387	8	639	79
Templeton, G	SD-NY	R	.963	41	54	104	6	164	18
Thon, D	PHI	R	.969	146	234	412	21	667	65
Uribe, J	SF	R	.966	87	98	218	11	327	35
Vizcaino, J	CHI	R	.972	33	31	74	3	108	14
Wilkerson, C	PIT	R	1.000	15	9	20	0	29	5
Williams, M	SF	R	1.000	4	3	2	0	5	2
Yelding, E	HOU	R	.939	72	113	166	18	297	31

OUTFIELDERS

PLAYER	TEAM	T	PCT	G	PO	A	E	TC	DP
Abner, S	SD	R	1.000	39	86	1	0	87	0
Aldrete, M	SD	L	1.000	5	7	1	0	8	0
Anthony, E	HOU	L	.986	37	64	5	1	70	1
Azocar, O	SD	L	.875	13	14	0	2	16	0
Bass, K	SF	R	.977	101	159	9	4	172	2
Bell, G	CHI	R	.962	146	249	6	10	265	0
Benzinger, T	CIN	R	1.000	15	23	0	0	23	0
Biggio, C	HOU	R	1.000	2	0	1	0	1	0
Bonds, B	PIT	L	.991	150	321	13	3	337	1
Bonilla, B	PIT	R	.989	104	176	8	2	186	0
Boston, D	NY	L	.981	115	156	2	3	161	1
Braggs, G	CIN	R	.966	74	139	2	5	146	1
Brewer, R	STL	L	.750	3	3	0	1	4	0
Brooks, H	NY	R	.972	100	166	6	5	177	0
Bullett, S	PIT	L	1.000	3	2	0	0	2	0
Bullock, E	MON	L	1.000	9	11	0	0	11	0
Butler, B	LA	L	1.000	161	372	8	0	380	3
Calderon, I	MON	R	.974	122	256	3	7	266	1
Campusano, S	PHI	R	1.000	15	27	1	0	28	0
Candaele, C	HOU	R	1.000	26	40	1	0	41	0
Carr, C	NY	R	1.000	9	9	0	0	9	0
Carreon, M	NY	L	.971	77	96	4	3	103	1
Castillo, B	PHI	R	.977	26	40	2	1	43	1
Chamberlain, W	PHI	R	.985	98	199	4	3	206	0
Clark, J	SD	R	.994	96	160	5	1	166	2
Coleman, V	NY	R	.979	70	132	5	3	140	0
Coles, D	SF	R	.000	3	0	0	0	0	0
Daniels, K	LA	R	.979	132	220	9	5	234	0
Dascenzo, D	CHI	L	.985	86	134	0	2	136	0
Davidson, M	HOU	R	1.000	63	71	1	0	72	0
Davis, E	CIN	R	.985	81	190	5	3	198	2
Dawson, A	CHI	R	.988	137	243	7	3	253	2
Doran, B	CIN	R	1.000	6	11	0	0	11	0
Duncan, M	CIN	R	1.000	7	7	0	0	7	0
Dykstra, L	PHI	L	.977	63	167	3	4	174	2
Espy, C	PIT	R	.966	35	54	3	2	59	2
Felder, M	SF	R	.985	107	192	3	3	198	2
Finley, S	HOU	L	.985	153	323	13	5	341	2
Fitzgerald, M	MON	R	1.000	3	10	0	0	10	0
Gant, R	ATL	R	.983	148	338	7	6	351	1
Gilkey, B	STL	R	.994	74	164	6	1	171	1
Gonzalez, J	LA-PIT	R	1.000	41	38	1	0	39	0
Gonzalez, L	HOU	R	.984	133	294	6	5	305	1
Goodwin, T	LA	R	1.000	5	8	0	0	8	0
Gregg, T	ATL	L	1.000	14	16	0	0	16	0
Grissom, M	MON	R	.984	138	350	15	6	371	2
Gwynn, C	LA	L	1.000	41	37	2	0	39	0
Gwynn, T	SD	L	.990	134	291	8	3	302	2
Harris, L	LA	R	.000	1	0	0	0	0	0
Hatcher, B	CIN	R	.981	121	248	4	5	257	0
Hayes, V	PHI	R	.990	72	202	3	2	207	2
Heep, D	ATL	L	.000	1	0	0	0	0	0
Herr, T	SF	R	.000	1	0	0	0	0	0
Howard, T	SD	R	.995	86	182	4	1	187	1
Hudler, R	STL	R	.981	58	97	4	2	103	0
Hunter, B	ATL	L	1.000	6	2	0	0	2	0
Jackson, D	SD	R	.992	98	243	2	2	247	2
Javier, S	LA	R	.986	69	70	1	1	72	0
Jefferson, S	CIN	R	1.000	5	4	0	0	4	0
Johnson, H	NY	R	.970	30	61	3	2	66	0
Jones, C	CIN	R	1.000	26	27	1	0	28	0
Jose, F	STL	R	.990	153	268	15	3	286	2
Justice, D	ATL	L	.968	106	204	9	7	220	0
Kingery, M	SF	L	.975	38	39	0	1	40	0

OUTFIELDERS (Continued)

PLAYER	TEAM	T	PCT	G	PO	A	E	TC	DP
Kruk, J	PHI	L	.992	52	113	4	1	118	1
Landrum, C	CHI	R	.968	44	61	0	2	63	0
Lankford, R	STL	L	.984	149	367	7	6	380	2
Leonard, M	SF	R	1.000	34	41	0	0	41	0
Lewis, D	SF	R	1.000	68	159	2	0	161	0
Lindeman, J	PHI	R	1.000	30	31	1	0	32	0
Litton, G	SF	R	1.000	6	2	0	0	2	0
Lofton, K	HOU	L	.977	20	41	1	1	43	0
Martinez, C	CIN	R	1.000	16	35	1	0	36	0
Martinez, D	MON	L	.982	112	213	10	4	227	0
May, D	CHI	R	1.000	7	11	1	0	12	0
McClendon, L	PIT	R	.966	32	26	2	1	29	1
McDaniel, T	NY	R	1.000	14	18	0	0	18	0
McDowell, R	LA	R	.000	2	0	0	0	0	0
McGee, W	SF	R	.978	128	259	6	6	271	3
McReynolds, K	NY	R	.993	141	281	9	2	292	1
Merced, O	PIT	R	1.000	7	5	0	0	5	0
Miller, K	NY	R	1.000	28	33	2	0	35	1
Mitchell, K	SF	R	.970	100	188	6	6	200	1
Mitchell, K	ATL	R	.970	34	31	1	1	33	0
Morris, H	CIN	R	.000	1	0	0	0	0	0
Morris, J	PHI	R	.974	57	73	1	2	76	0
Murphy, D	PHI	R	.983	147	287	6	5	298	0
Nixon, O	ATL	R	.987	115	218	6	3	227	1
Noboa, J	MON	R	1.000	7	7	0	0	7	0
O'Neill, P	CIN	L	.994	150	301	13	2	316	2
Ortiz, J	HOU	R	1.000	24	27	2	0	29	1
Parker, R	SF	R	1.000	4	5	0	0	5	0
Pena, G	STL	R	1.000	4	6	0	0	6	0
Perry, G	STL	R	1.000	5	6	1	0	7	0
Redus, G	PIT	R	.931	33	26	1	2	29	0
Rhodes, K	HOU	L	.958	44	87	4	4	95	1
Riesgo, D	MON	R	.500	2	0	1	1	2	0
Roberts, L	SD	R	.974	44	111	0	3	114	0
Salazar, L	CHI	R	.000	1	0	0	0	0	0
Sanders, D	ATL	L	.952	44	57	3	3	63	0
Sanders, R	CIN	R	1.000	9	22	0	0	22	0
Santiago, B	SD	R	.000	1	0	0	0	0	0
Sasser, M	NY	R	.967	21	26	3	1	30	1
Simms, M	HOU	R	.889	41	44	4	6	54	0
Smith, D	CHI	R	.962	42	73	3	3	79	1
Smith, L	ATL	R	.965	99	134	5	5	144	2
Strawberry, D	LA	L	.978	136	209	11	5	225	2
Templeton, G	NY	R	.000	2	0	0	0	0	0
Thompson, M	STL	R	.991	91	207	8	2	217	1
Tolentino, J	HOU	L	1.000	1	4	0	0	4	0
VanderWal, J	MON	L	1.000	17	29	0	0	29	0
Van Slyke, A	PIT	R	.996	135	273	8	1	282	1
Varsho, G	PIT	R	.989	54	84	2	1	87	1
Vatcher, J	SD	R	.900	11	8	1	1	10	0
Walker, C	CHI	R	.987	53	73	4	1	78	1
Walker, L	MON	R	.991	102	223	6	2	231	2
Walton, J	CHI	R	.983	101	170	2	3	175	1
Ward, K	SD	R	.982	33	54	0	1	55	0
Webster, M	PIT-LA	L	.978	65	85	2	2	89	0
Williams, K	MON	R	.957	24	42	3	2	47	0

OUTFIELDERS (Continued)

PLAYER	TEAM	T	PCT	G	PO	A	E	TC	DP
Wilson, C	STL	R	1.000	5	8	0	0	8	0
Winningham, H	CIN	R	.953	66	99	2	5	106	0
Wood, T	SF	L	.909	8	10	0	1	11	0
Yelding, E	HOU	R	.333	4	1	0	2	3	0
Young, G	HOU	R	1.000	84	96	4	0	100	1

CATCHERS

PLAYER	TEAM	T	PCT	G	PO	A	E	TC	DP	PB
Berryhill, D	CHI-ATL	R	.967	49	214	24	8	246	2	8
Biggio, C	HOU	R	.990	139	889	64	10	963	10	13
Bilardello, D	SD	R	1.000	13	59	6	0	65	1	0
Cabrera, F	ATL	R	.987	17	72	6	1	79	0	3
Carter, G	LA	R	.988	68	355	45	5	405	2	4
Cerone, R	NY	R	.987	81	424	36	6	466	0	6
Daulton, D	PHI	R	.985	88	493	33	8	534	5	2
Decker, S	SF	R	.984	78	385	41	7	433	5	7
Eusebio, T	HOU	R	.981	9	49	4	1	54	0	1
Fitzgerald, M	MON	R	.994	54	306	24	2	332	3	2
Fletcher, D	PHI	R	.992	45	242	22	2	266	1	1
Gedman, R	STL	R	.976	43	192	13	5	210	4	3
Girardi, J	CHI	R	.972	21	95	11	3	109	1	1
Hassey, R	MON	R	.989	34	172	13	2	187	1	4
Heath, M	ATL	R	.991	45	192	33	2	227	1	6
Hernandez, C	LA	R	.966	13	24	4	1	29	0	1
Hundley, T	NY	R	1.000	20	85	11	0	96	1	1
Kennedy, T	SF	R	.978	58	237	36	6	279	2	2
Lake, S	PHI	R	.993	58	277	25	2	304	1	5
Lampkin, T	SD	R	1.000	11	49	5	0	54	0	1
LaValliere, M	PIT	R	.998	105	565	46	1	612	4	5
Lindsey, D	PHI	R	1.000	1	8	0	0	8	0	1
Litton, G	SF	R	1.000	1	3	0	0	3	0	0
Lyons, B	LA	R	1.000	6	12	1	0	13	1	0
Manwaring, K	SF	R	.988	67	315	28	4	347	7	0
McClendon, L	PIT	R	1.000	2	5	0	0	5	0	0
Nichols, C	HOU	R	.971	17	86	14	3	103	2	2
O'Brien, C	NY	R	.991	67	396	37	4	437	7	2
Oliver, J	CIN	R	.980	90	496	40	11	547	6	10
Olson, G	ATL	R	.995	127	721	48	4	773	7	5
Pagnozzi, T	STL	R	.991	139	673	81	7	761	8	5
Pappas, E	CHI	R	1.000	6	35	1	0	36	0	0
Prince, T	PIT	R	.984	19	52	9	1	62	0	1
Reed, J	CIN	R	.991	89	527	29	5	561	7	7
Reyes, G	MON	R	.975	80	375	61	11	447	4	10
Santiago, B	SD	R	.985	151	830	100	14	944	14	8
Santovenia, N	MON	R	.976	30	109	12	3	124	3	6
Sasser, M	NY	R	.904	43	165	13	1	179	0	3
Scioscia, M	LA	R	.990	115	677	51	7	735	8	3
Scott, D	CIN	R	1.000	8	19	0	0	10	0	2
Servais, S	HOU	R	.988	14	77	4	1	82	0	0
Slaught, D	PIT	R	.987	69	338	31	5	374	4	3
Stephens, R	STL	R	1.000	6	16	2	0	18	0	0
Sutko, G	CIN	R	.875	9	16	5	3	24	0	1
Villanueva, H	CHI	R	.979	55	259	26	6	291	2	4
Wilkins, R	CHI	R	.993	82	373	42	3	418	6	6
Willard, J	ATL	R	1.000	1	3	0	0	3	0	0

1991 N.L. CLUB PINCH-HITTING

Club	AVG.	AB	H	2B	3B	HR	RBI
St. Louis	.254	209	53	9	2	2	38
Philadelphia	.241	245	59	13	0	2	33
Montreal	.239	213	51	8	1	5	25
Atlanta	.233	253	59	11	0	3	26
Chicago	.233	223	52	8	3	7	35
Pittsburgh	.226	217	49	8	2	6	29
Cincinnati	.222	234	52	4	2	6	22
San Francisco	.216	259	56	7	3	0	26
New York	.212	231	49	3	0	8	28
Houston	.182	274	50	12	0	3	35
Los Angeles	.180	305	55	10	2	4	42
San Diego	.176	238	42	8	2	4	28
TOTALS	.216	2901	627	101	17	50	367

1991 INDIVIDUAL PINCH-HITTING

Hits
14 Noboa, Mon.
13 Gwynn, L.A.
13 Lindeman, Phi.
13 Walker, Chi.
13 Winningham, Cin.
12 Carreon, N.Y.
11 D. Smith, Chi.
11 Kingery, S.F.
11 Perry, St.L.
11 Wilson, St.L.

Home Runs
3 Carreon, N.Y.
2 Bell, Chi.
2 Braggs, Cin.
2 Bream, Atl.
2 Dawson, Chi.
2 Gwynn, L.A.
2 McClendon, Pitt.
2 Sasser, N.Y.
1 33 players tied.

Runs Batted In
13 Gwynn, L.A.
13 Perry, St.L.
11 Wilson, St.L.
8 Backman, Phi.
8 McClendon, Pitt.
8 Oberkfell, Hou.
7 5 players tied.

INDIVIDUAL PITCHING RECORDS—1991

ALL PITCHERS LISTED ALPHABETICALLY

PITCHER	TEAM	T	W	L	ERA	G	GS	CG	SHO	GF	SV	IP	H	TBF	R	ER	HR	SH	SF	HB	BB	IBB	SO	WP	BK	OPP AVG
Agosto, J	STL	L	5	3	4.81	72	0	0	0	22	2	86.0	92	377	52	46	4	11	3	8	39	4	34	6	0	.291
Akerfelds, D	PHI	R	2	1	5.26	30	0	0	0	11	0	49.2	49	229	30	29	5	6	2	3	27	4	31	4	0	.257
Andersen, L	SD	R	3	4	2.30	38	0	0	0	24	13	47.0	39	188	13	12	0	4	2	0	13	3	40	1	0	.232
Armstrong, J	CIN	R	7	13	5.48	27	24	1	0	1	0	139.2	158	611	90	85	25	6	9	2	54	2	93	2	1	.293
Ashby, A	PHI	R	1	5	6.00	8	8	0	0	0	0	42.0	41	186	28	28	5	1	3	3	19	0	26	6	0	.256
Assenmacher, P	CHI	L	7	8	3.24	75	0	0	0	31	15	102.2	85	427	41	37	10	8	4	3	31	6	117	4	0	.223
Avery, S	ATL	L	18	8	3.38	35	35	3	1	0	0	210.1	189	868	89	79	21	8	4	3	65	0	137	4	1	.240
Barnes, B	MON	L	5	8	4.22	28	27	1	0	0	0	160.0	135	684	82	75	16	9	5	6	84	2	117	5	1	.233
Beatty, B	NY	L	0	0	2.79	5	0	0	0	1	0	9.2	9	42	3	3	0	1	1	0	4	1	7	1	0	.250
Beck, R	SF	R	1	1	3.78	31	0	0	0	10	1	52.1	53	214	22	22	4	4	2	1	13	2	38	0	0	.273
Belcher, T	LA	R	10	9	2.62	33	33	2	1	0	0	209.1	189	880	76	61	10	11	3	2	75	3	156	7	0	.240
Belinda, S	PIT	R	7	5	3.45	60	0	0	0	37	16	78.1	50	318	30	30	10	4	3	4	35	4	71	2	0	.184
Benes, A	SD	R	15	11	3.03	33	33	4	1	0	0	223.0	194	908	76	75	23	5	4	4	59	7	167	3	4	.232
Berenguer, J	ATL	R	0	3	2.24	49	0	0	0	35	17	64.1	43	255	18	16	5	2	2	3	20	2	53	0	0	.189
Bielecki, M	CHI-ATL	R	13	11	4.46	41	25	0	0	9	0	173.2	171	727	91	86	18	10	6	2	56	6	75	6	0	.262
Black, B	SF	L	12	16	3.99	34	34	3	3	0	0	214.1	201	893	104	95	25	11	7	4	71	8	104	6	6	.251
Boever, J	PHI	R	3	5	3.84	68	0	0	0	27	0	98.1	90	431	45	42	10	3	6	0	54	11	89	6	1	.245
Bones, R	SD	R	4	6	4.83	11	11	0	0	0	0	54.0	57	234	33	29	3	0	4	0	18	0	31	4	0	.269
Boskie, S	CHI	R	4	9	5.23	28	20	0	0	2	0	129.0	150	582	78	75	14	8	6	5	52	4	62	1	1	.294
Bowen, R	HOU	R	6	4	5.15	14	13	0	0	0	0	71.2	73	319	43	41	4	2	6	3	36	1	49	8	1	.268
Boyd, D	MON	R	6	8	3.52	19	19	1	1	0	0	120.1	115	496	49	47	9	2	4	0	40	2	82	2	3	.256
Brantley, C	PHI	R	2	2	3.41	6	5	0	0	0	0	31.2	26	140	12	12	0	2	3	2	19	0	25	2	0	.228
Brantley, J	SF	R	5	2	2.45	67	0	0	0	39	15	95.1	78	411	27	26	8	4	4	5	52	10	81	6	0	.225
Bross, T	NY	R	0	0	1.80	8	0	0	0	4	0	10.0	7	39	2	2	1	1	0	0	3	0	5	0	0	.200
Brown, K	CIN	R	0	0	2.25	11	0	0	0	3	0	12.0	15	56	4	3	0	1	0	0	6	1	4	1	0	.306
Browning, T	CIN	L	14	14	4.18	36	36	1	0	0	0	230.1	241	983	124	107	32	8	9	4	56	4	115	3	1	.266
Burke, T	MON-NY	R	6	7	3.36	72	0	0	0	31	6	101.2	96	421	46	38	8	3	3	4	26	8	59	3	0	.249
Burkett, J	SF	R	12	11	4.18	36	34	3	1	0	0	206.2	223	890	103	96	19	8	8	10	60	2	131	5	0	.277
Candelaria, J	LA	L	1	1	3.74	59	0	0	0	10	2	33.2	31	138	16	14	3	1	3	0	11	2	38	1	1	.252
Capel, M	HOU	R	1	3	3.03	25	0	0	0	13	3	32.2	33	143	14	11	3	3	1	0	15	1	23	0	0	.266
Carman, D	CIN	L	0	2	5.25	28	0	0	0	10	1	36.0	40	164	23	21	8	3	1	1	19	1	15	2	0	.286
Carpenter, C	STL	R	10	4	4.23	59	0	0	0	19	0	66.0	53	266	31	31	6	3	2	0	20	9	47	1	0	.220
Carreno, A	PHI	R	0	0	16.20	3	0	0	0	1	0	3.1	5	20	6	6	1	0	0	2	3	0	2	0	0	.333
Castillo, F	CHI	R	6	7	4.35	18	18	4	0	0	0	111.2	107	467	56	54	5	6	3	0	33	2	73	5	1	.252
Castillo, T	ATL-NY	L	2	1	3.34	17	3	0	0	6	0	32.1	40	148	16	12	4	2	1	0	11	1	18	0	0	.299
Charlton, N	CIN	L	3	5	2.91	39	11	0	0	10	1	108.1	92	438	37	35	6	7	1	6	34	4	77	11	0	.236
Christopher, M	LA	R	0	0	0.00	3	0	0	0	2	0	4.0	2	15	0	0	0	0	0	0	3	0	2	0	0	.167
Clancy, J	HOU-ATL	R	3	5	3.91	54	0	0	0	22	8	89.2	73	368	42	39	8	2	4	1	34	4	50	10	0	.223
Clark, M	STL	R	1	1	4.03	7	2	0	0	1	0	22.1	17	93	10	10	3	0	3	0	11	0	13	2	0	.215
Clements, P	SD	L	1	0	3.77	12	0	0	0	4	0	14.1	13	63	8	6	0	0	3	0	9	4	8	0	0	.255
Combs, P	PHI	L	2	6	4.90	14	13	1	0	0	0	64.1	64	300	41	35	7	1	2	2	43	1	41	7	0	.254
Cone, D	NY	R	14	14	3.29	34	34	5	2	0	0	232.2	204	966	95	85	13	13	7	5	73	2	241	17	1	.235
Cook, D	LA	L	1	0	0.51	20	1	0	0	5	0	17.2	12	69	3	1	0	1	2	0	7	1	8	0	0	.203
Cormier, R	STL	L	4	5	4.12	11	10	2	0	1	0	67.2	74	281	35	31	5	1	3	2	8	1	38	2	1	.277
Corsi, J	HOU	R	0	5	3.71	47	0	0	0	15	0	77.2	76	322	37	32	6	3	2	0	23	5	53	1	1	.259
Costello, J	SD	R	1	0	3.09	27	0	0	0	6	0	35.0	37	157	15	12	2	4	2	0	17	3	24	2	0	.276
Cox, D	PHI	R	4	6	4.57	23	17	0	0	2	0	102.1	98	433	57	52	14	6	7	1	39	2	46	7	1	.258
Crews, T	LA	R	2	3	3.43	60	0	0	0	17	6	76.0	75	318	30	29	7	4	2	0	19	11	53	3	1	.256
Darling, R	NY-MON	R	5	8	4.37	20	20	0	0	0	0	119.1	121	508	66	58	15	7	4	7	33	1	69	13	4	.265
Dascenzo, D	CHI	L	0	0	0.00	3	0	0	0	3	0	4.0	2	15	0	0	0	0	0	0	2	0	2	0	0	.154
DeJesus, J	PHI	R	10	9	3.42	31	29	3	0	1	1	181.2	147	801	74	69	7	11	3	4	128	4	118	10	0	.224
DeLeon, J	STL	R	5	9	2.71	28	28	1	0	0	0	162.2	144	679	57	49	15	5	4	6	61	1	118	1	1	.239
Deshaies, J	HOU	L	5	12	4.98	28	28	1	0	0	0	161.0	156	686	90	89	19	4	7	1	72	5	98	0	5	.259
Dibble, R	CIN	R	3	5	3.17	67	0	0	0	57	31	82.1	67	334	32	29	5	5	3	0	25	2	124	5	0	.223
Downs, K	SF	R	10	4	4.19	45	11	0	0	4	0	111.2	99	479	59	52	12	4	4	3	53	9	62	4	1	.239
Drabek, D	PIT	R	15	14	3.07	35	35	5	2	0	0	234.2	245	977	92	80	16	12	6	3	62	6	142	5	0	.274
Fajardo, H	PIT	R	0	0	9.95	2	2	0	0	0	0	6.1	10	35	7	7	0	0	0	0	7	0	8	3	0	.357
Fassero, J	MON	L	2	5	2.44	51	0	0	0	30	8	55.1	39	223	17	15	1	6	0	1	17	1	42	4	0	.196
Fernandez, S	NY	L	1	3	2.86	8	8	0	0	0	0	44.0	36	177	18	14	4	5	1	0	9	0	31	0	0	.222
Foster, S	CIN	R	0	0	1.93	11	0	0	0	5	0	14.0	7	53	5	3	1	0	0	0	4	0	11	0	0	.143
Franco, J	NY	L	5	9	2.93	52	0	0	0	48	30	55.1	61	247	27	18	2	3	0	1	18	4	45	6	0	.271
Fraser, W	STL	R	3	3	4.93	35	0	0	0	16	0	49.1	44	210	28	27	9	1	3	3	21	3	25	4	0	.242
Freeman, M	ATL	R	1	0	3.00	34	0	0	0	6	1	48.0	37	190	19	16	2	1	1	2	13	1	34	4	0	.214
Frey, S	MON	L	0	1	4.99	31	0	0	0	5	1	39.2	43	182	31	22	3	3	1	2	23	4	21	3	1	.281
Gardner, C	HOU	R	1	2	4.01	5	4	0	0	0	0	24.2	19	103	12	11	5	2	0	0	14	1	12	0	0	.218

MAJOR LEAGUE RECORDS SET

Most putouts, catcher, lifetime—11,304, Gary Carter, Los Angeles

Most chances accepted, catcher, lifetime—12,455, Gary Carter, Los Angeles

Most years, club—116, Chicago*

Most games, club, lifetime—17,072, Chicago*

Most games won, club, lifetime—8,774, Chicago*

Most games lost, club, lifetime—8,745, Philadelphia*

MAJOR LEAGUE RECORDS TIED

Most home runs, two consecutive games—5, Barry Larkin, Cincinnati, June 27 (2), 28 (3)

Most home runs by pinch-hitters, club, inning—2, New York (Sasser, Carreon), May 4, 9th inning

Most grand slams, two consecutive games—2, Fred McGriff, San Diego, August 13, 14

Most stolen bases, game, since 1900—6, Otis Nixon, Atlanta, June 16

Three strikeouts on nine pitched balls, inning—Andy Ashby, Philadelphia, June 15, 4th inning; Pete Harnisch, Houston, September 6, 7th inning

Highest fielding average, outfielder, season (minimum: 150 games)—1.000, Brett Butler, Los Angeles

Fewest errors, outfielder, season (minimum: 150 games)—0, Brett Butler, Los Angeles

Most consecutive errorless games, club, season—15, St. Louis, May 24 through June 9

Fewest doubleheaders, club, season—0, Houston, San Diego, San Francisco

Fewest tie games, league, season—0

* Extended own record

NATIONAL LEAGUE RECORDS SET

Most saves, season—47, Lee Smith, St. Louis

Most years leading league in fielding average, shortstop—7, Ozzie Smith, St. Louis

Fewest errors, shortstop, season (minimum: 150 games)—8, Ozzie Smith, St. Louis

Most consecutive errorless games, outfielder, lifetime—242, Doug Dascenzo, Chicago, September 2, 1988 through August 21, 1991

Most games, catcher, lifetime—1,971, Gary Carter, Los Angeles*

NATIONAL LEAGUE RECORDS TIED

Most home runs, switch-hitter, two consecutive seasons—61, Howard Johnson, New York

Most consecutive doubles, club, inning—4, New York, July 21, 3rd inning

Most sacrifice flies, lefthanded batter, season—13, Barry Bonds, Pittsburgh

Most sacrifice flies, switch-hitter, season—15, Howard Johnson, New York

Most strikeouts, game—19, David Cone, New York, October 6

Most consecutive strikeouts, relief pitcher, game—6, Rob Dibble, Cincinnati, April 23

Highest fielding average, league, season—.980

* Extended own record

PITCHER	TEAM	T	W	L	ERA	G	GS	CG	SHO	GF	SV	IP	H	TBF	R	ER	HR	SH	SF	HB	BB	IBB	SO	WP	BK	OPP AVG
Gardner, M	MON	R	9	11	3.85	27	27	0	0	0	0	168.1	139	692	78	72	17	7	2	4	75	1	107	2	1	.230
Gardner, W	SD	R	0	1	7.08	14	0	0	0	2	1	20.1	27	99	16	16	1	0	0	0	12	1	9	1	0	.310
Garrelts, S	SF	R	1	1	6.41	8	3	0	0	2	0	19.2	25	90	14	14	5	0	1	0	9	0	8	0	0	.313
Glavine, T	ATL	L	20	11	2.55	34	34	9	1	0	0	246.2	201	989	83	70	17	7	6	2	69	6	192	10	2	.222
Gooden, D	NY	R	13	7	3.60	27	27	3	1	0	0	190.0	185	789	80	76	12	5	4	3	56	2	150	5	2	.257
Gott, J	LA	R	4	3	2.96	55	0	0	0	26	2	76.0	63	322	28	25	5	6	1	1	32	7	73	6	3	.223
Grater, M	STL	R	0	0	0.00	3	0	0	0	2	0	3.0	5	15	0	0	0	0	0	0	2	0	0	0	0	.385
Greene, T	PHI	R	13	7	3.38	36	27	3	2	3	0	207.2	177	857	85	78	19	9	11	3	66	4	154	9	1	.230
Grimsley, J	PHI	R	1	7	4.87	12	12	0	0	0	0	61.0	54	272	34	33	4	3	2	3	41	3	42	14	0	.242
Gross, K	LA	R	10	11	3.58	46	10	0	0	16	3	115.2	123	509	55	46	10	6	4	2	50	6	95	3	0	.275
Gross, K	CIN	R	6	4	3.47	29	9	1	0	6	0	85.2	93	381	43	33	8	6	2	0	40	2	40	5	1	.279
Gunderson, E	SF	L	0	0	5.40	2	0	0	0	1	1	3.1	6	18	4	2	0	0	0	0	1	0	2	0	0	.353
Hammaker, A	SD	L	0	1	5.79	1	1	0	0	0	0	4.2	8	27	7	3	0	2	0	0	3	0	1	1	0	.364
Hammond, C	CIN	L	7	7	4.06	20	18	0	0	0	0	99.2	92	425	51	45	4	6	1	2	48	3	50	3	0	.250
Haney, C	MON	L	3	7	4.04	16	16	0	0	0	0	84.2	94	387	49	38	6	6	1	1	43	1	51	9	0	.280
Harkey, M	CHI	R	0	2	5.30	4	4	0	0	0	0	18.2	21	84	11	11	3	0	1	0	6	1	15	1	0	.273
Harnisch, P	HOU	R	12	9	2.70	33	33	4	2	0	0	216.2	169	900	71	65	14	9	7	5	83	3	172	5	2	.212
Harris, G	SD	R	9	5	2.23	20	20	3	2	0	0	133.0	116	537	42	33	16	9	2	1	27	6	95	2	0	.233
Hartley, M	LA-PHI	R	4	1	4.21	58	0	0	0	16	2	83.1	74	368	40	39	11	2	1	6	47	8	63	10	2	.237
Heaton, N	PIT	L	3	3	4.33	42	1	0	0	5	0	68.2	72	293	37	33	6	3	3	4	21	2	34	0	1	.275
Henry, D	HOU	R	3	2	3.19	52	0	0	0	25	2	67.2	51	282	25	24	7	6	2	2	39	7	51	5	0	.219
Heredia, G	SF	R	0	2	3.82	7	4	0	0	1	0	33.0	27	126	14	14	4	2	1	0	7	2	13	1	0	.233
Hernandez, J	SD	R	0	0	0.00	9	0	0	0	7	2	14.1	8	56	1	0	0	0	0	0	5	0	9	2	0	.157
Hernandez, X	HOU	R	2	7	4.71	32	6	0	0	8	3	63.0	66	285	34	33	6	1	1	0	32	7	55	0	0	.263
Hershiser, O	LA	R	7	2	3.46	21	21	0	0	0	0	112.0	112	473	43	43	3	2	1	5	32	6	73	2	4	.259
Hickerson, B	SF	L	2	2	3.60	17	6	0	0	4	0	50.0	53	212	20	20	3	2	0	0	17	3	43	2	0	.275
Hill, K	STL	R	11	10	3.57	30	30	0	0	0	0	181.1	147	743	76	72	15	7	7	6	67	4	121	7	1	.224
Hill, M	CIN	R	1	1	3.78	22	0	0	0	8	0	33.1	36	137	14	14	1	4	3	0	8	2	20	1	0	.295
Howell, J	LA	R	6	5	3.18	44	0	0	0	35	16	51.0	39	202	19	18	3	5	2	1	11	3	40	0	0	.213
Huismann, M	PIT	R	0	0	7.20	5	0	0	0	0	0	5.0	7	25	6	4	0	0	0	0	2	1	5	0	0	.304
Hurst, B	SD	L	15	8	3.29	31	31	4	0	0	0	221.2	201	909	89	81	17	8	4	3	59	3	141	5	1	.241
Innis, J	NY	R	0	2	2.66	69	0	0	0	29	0	84.2	66	336	30	25	2	6	5	0	23	6	47	4	0	.219
Jackson, D	CHI	L	1	5	6.75	17	14	0	0	0	0	70.2	89	347	59	53	8	8	2	1	48	4	31	1	1	.309
Jackson, D	SD	R	0	0	9.00	1	0	0	0	1	0	2.0	3	10	2	2	0	0	0	0	2	0	0	0	0	.375
Jones, B	MON	R	4	9	3.35	77	0	0	0	46	13	88.2	76	353	35	33	8	7	3	1	33	8	46	1	1	.246
Jones, J	HOU	R	6	8	4.39	26	22	1	1	0	0	135.1	143	593	73	66	9	7	2	3	51	3	88	4	0	.270
Juden, J	HOU	R	0	2	6.00	4	3	0	0	0	0	18.0	19	81	14	12	3	2	3	0	7	1	11	0	1	.275
Kile, D	HOU	R	7	11	3.69	37	22	0	0	5	0	153.2	144	689	81	63	16	9	5	6	84	4	100	5	4	.246
Kipper, B	PIT	L	2	2	4.65	52	0	0	0	18	4	60.0	66	264	34	31	7	1	2	0	22	3	38	0	1	.276
LaCoss, M	SF	R	1	5	7.23	18	5	0	0	6	0	47.1	61	225	39	30	4	3	2	2	24	0	30	2	0	.314
Lancaster, L	CHI	R	9	7	3.52	64	11	1	0	21	3	156.0	150	653	68	61	13	9	4	4	49	7	102	2	2	.256
Landrum, B	PIT	R	4	4	3.18	61	0	0	0	43	17	76.1	76	322	32	27	4	1	1	0	19	5	45	3	2	.252
LaPoint, D	PHI	L	0	1	16.20	2	2	0	0	0	0	5.0	10	32	10	9	0	1	1	1	6	0	3	0	0	.435
Layana, T	CIN	R	0	2	6.97	22	0	0	0	9	0	20.2	23	95	18	16	1	1	0	0	11	0	14	3	0	.277
Lefferts, C	SD	L	1	6	3.91	54	0	0	0	40	23	69.0	74	290	35	30	5	10	5	1	14	3	48	3	1	.285
Leibrandt, C	ATL	L	15	13	3.49	36	36	1	1	0	0	229.2	212	949	105	89	18	19	6	4	56	3	128	5	3	.245
Lewis, J	SD	R	0	0	4.15	12	0	0	0	2	0	13.0	14	64	7	6	2	2	0	0	11	2	10	1	0	.275
Lilliquist, D	SD	L	0	2	8.79	6	2	0	0	1	0	14.1	25	70	14	14	3	0	0	0	4	1	7	0	0	.379
Litton, G	SF	R	0	0	9.00	1	0	0	0	1	0	1.0	1	7	1	1	0	0	0	0	3	0	0	0	0	.250
Long, B	MON	R	0	0	10.80	3	0	0	0	1	0	1.2	4	12	2	2	0	0	0	0	4	0	0	0	0	.500
Maddux, G	CHI	R	15	11	3.35	37	37	7	2	0	0	263.0	232	1070	113	98	18	16	3	6	66	9	198	6	3	.237
Maddux, M	SD	R	7	2	2.46	64	1	0	0	27	5	98.2	78	388	30	27	4	5	2	1	27	3	57	5	0	.221
Mahler, R	MON-ATL	R	2	4	4.50	23	8	0	0	2	0	66.0	70	291	37	33	4	5	1	2	28	1	27	1	0	.275
Mallicoat, R	HOU	L	0	2	3.86	24	0	0	0	4	1	23.1	22	103	10	10	2	1	2	2	13	1	18	1	0	.259
Martinez, De	MON	R	14	11	2.39	31	31	9	5	0	0	222.0	187	905	70	59	9	7	3	4	62	3	123	3	0	.226
Martinez, R	LA	R	17	13	3.27	33	33	6	4	0	0	220.1	190	916	89	80	18	8	4	7	69	4	150	6	0	.229
Mason, R	PIT	R	3	2	3.03	24	0	0	0	6	3	29.2	21	114	11	10	2	1	1	1	6	1	21	2	0	.200
Mauser, T	PHI	R	0	0	7.59	3	0	0	0	1	0	10.2	18	53	10	9	3	1	0	0	3	0	6	0	0	.367
May, S	CHI	R	0	0	18.00	2	0	0	0	1	0	2.0	6	12	4	4	0	0	0	0	1	0	1	1	0	.545
McClellan, P	SF	R	3	6	4.56	13	12	1	0	1	0	71.0	68	300	41	36	12	3	1	1	25	1	44	5	0	.252
McClure, B	STL	L	1	1	3.13	32	0	0	0	9	0	23.0	24	98	8	8	1	1	3	1	8	2	15	0	0	.282
McDowell, R	PHI-LA	R	9	9	2.93	71	0	0	0	34	10	101.1	100	445	40	33	4	11	3	2	48	20	50	2	0	.262
McElroy, C	CHI	L	6	2	1.95	71	0	0	0	12	3	101.1	73	419	33	22	7	9	6	0	57	7	92	1	0	.210
Melendez, J	SD	R	8	5	3.27	31	9	0	0	10	3	93.2	77	381	35	34	11	2	6	1	24	3	60	3	2	.221
Mercker, K	ATL	L	5	3	2.58	50	4	0	0	28	6	73.1	56	306	23	21	5	2	2	1	35	3	62	4	1	.211

THE FOLLOWING PITCHERS APPEARED AS PINCH-HITTERS/PINCH-RUNNERS:

PITCHER	TEAM	TOTAL GAMES	
Avery, S	ATL	37	1 GAME AS PINCH-RUNNER
			1 GAME AS PINCH-HITTER
Black, B	SF	35	1 GAME AS PINCH-HITTER
Boskie, S	CHI	30	1 GAME AS PINCH-RUNNER
Bowen, R	HOU	17	3 GAMES AS PINCH-RUNNER
Charlton, N	CIN	41	2 GAMES AS PINCH-RUNNER
Drabek, D	PIT	36	1 GAME AS PINCH-HITTER
Garrelts, S	SF	11	3 GAMES AS PINCH-RUNNER
Glavine, T	ATL	36	1 GAME AS PINCH-HITTER
			1 GAME AS PINCH-RUNNER
Greene, T	PHI	38	2 GAMES AS PINCH-HITTER
Gross, K	LA	48	2 GAMES AS PINCH-HITTER
Heaton, N	PIT	44	1 GAME AS PINCH-RUNNER
			1 GAME AS PINCH-HITTER
Layana, T	CIN	23	1 GAME AS PINCH-HITTER
Maddux, G	CHI	39	2 GAMES AS PINCH-HITTER
Martinez, D	MON	32	1 GAME AS PINCH-HITTER
McElroy, C	CHI	71	1 GAME AS PINCH-HITTER
Minutelli, G	CIN	16	1 GAME AS PINCH-HITTER
Mulholland, T	PHI	35	1 GAME AS PINCH-RUNNER
Portugal, M	HOU	33	1 GAME AS PINCH-HITTER
Rasmussen, D	SD	25	1 GAME AS PINCH-HITTER
Rijo, J	CIN	31	1 GAME AS PINCH-HITTER
Robinson, D	SF	35	2 GAMES AS PINCH-HITTER
Rodriguez, R	SD	65	1 GAME AS PINCH-RUNNER
Smith, Z	PIT	36	1 GAME AS PINCH-HITTER
Smoltz, J	ATL	38	2 GAMES AS PINCH-HITTER
Sutcliffe, R	CHI	20	1 GAME AS PINCH-HITTER
Tomlin, R	PIT	32	1 GAME AS PINCH-RUNNER
Wilson, S	CHI	9	1 GAME AS PINCH-RUNNER
Wilson, T	SF	48	4 GAMES AS PINCH-RUNNER

THE FOLLOWING PLAYERS HAD PITCHING APPEARANCES AS INDICATED:

PITCHER	TEAM	TOTAL GAMES	
Dascenzo, D	CHI	118	3 GAMES PITCHED
Jackson, D	SD	122	1 GAME PITCHED
Litton, G	SF	59	1 GAME PITCHED
Oquendo, J	STL	127	1 GAME PITCHED

1991 statistics compiled by Major League Baseball-IBM Baseball Information System. Other statistics were compiled by the Elias Sports Bureau, the official statistician for the National League.

INDIVIDUAL PITCHING RECORDS—1991

PITCHER	TEAM	T	W	L	ERA	G	GS	CG	SHO	GF	SV	IP	H	TBF	R	ER	HR	SH	SF	HB	BB	IBB	SO	WP	BK	OPP AVG
Miller, P	PIT	R	0	0	5.40	1	1	0	0	0	0	5.0	4	21	3	3	0	0	0	0	3	0	2	0	0	.222
Minutelli, G	CIN	L	0	2	6.04	16	3	0	0	2	0	25.1	30	124	17	17	5	0	2	0	18	1	21	3	0	.288
Morgan, M	LA	R	14	10	2.78	34	33	5	1	1	1	236.1	197	949	85	73	12	10	4	3	61	10	140	6	0	.226
Moyer, J	STL	L	0	5	5.74	8	7	0	0	1	0	31.1	38	142	21	20	5	4	2	1	16	0	20	2	1	.319
Mulholland, T	PHI	L	16	13	3.61	34	34	8	3	0	0	232.0	231	956	100	93	15	11	6	3	49	2	142	3	0	.260
Myers, R	CIN	L	6	13	3.55	58	12	1	0	18	6	132.0	116	575	61	52	8	8	6	1	80	5	108	2	1	.242
Nabholz, C	MON	L	8	7	3.63	24	24	1	0	0	0	153.2	134	631	66	62	5	2	4	2	57	4	99	3	1	.237
Nolte, E	SD	L	3	2	11.05	6	6	0	0	0	0	22.0	37	111	27	27	6	0	3	0	10	0	15	1	1	.378
Ojeda, B	LA	L	12	9	3.18	31	31	2	1	0	0	189.1	181	802	78	67	15	15	9	3	70	9	120	4	2	.257
Olivares, O	STL	R	11	7	3.71	28	24	0	0	2	1	167.1	148	688	72	69	13	11	2	5	61	1	91	3	1	.243
Oliveras, F	SF	R	6	6	3.86	55	1	0	0	17	3	79.1	69	316	36	34	12	5	3	1	22	4	48	2	2	.242
Oquendo, J	STL	R	0	0	27.00	1	0	0	0	1	0	1.0	2	7	3	3	0	0	0	0	2	0	1	0	0	.400
Osuna, A	HOU	L	7	6	3.42	71	0	0	0	32	12	81.2	59	353	39	31	5	6	5	3	46	5	68	3	1	.201
Palacios, V	PIT	R	6	3	3.75	36	7	1	1	8	3	81.2	69	347	34	34	12	4	1	1	38	2	64	6	2	.228
Parrett, J	ATL	R	1	2	6.33	18	0	0	0	9	1	21.1	31	109	18	15	2	2	0	0	12	2	14	4	0	.326
Patterson, B	PIT	L	4	3	4.11	54	1	0	0	19	2	65.2	67	270	32	30	7	2	2	0	15	1	57	0	0	.267
Pavlas, D	CHI	R	0	0	18.00	1	0	0	0	1	0	1.0	3	5	2	2	1	1	0	0	0	0	0	0	0	.750
Pena, A	NY-ATL	R	8	1	2.40	59	0	0	0	36	15	82.1	74	331	23	22	6	3	4	0	22	4	62	1	2	.245
Perez, M	STL	R	0	2	5.82	14	0	0	0	2	0	17.0	19	75	11	11	1	1	0	1	7	2	7	0	1	.288
Perez, Y	CHI	L	1	0	2.08	3	0	0	0	0	0	4.1	2	16	1	1	0	0	2	0	2	0	3	2	0	.167
Peterson, A	SD	R	3	4	4.45	13	11	0	0	0	0	54.2	50	241	33	27	10	4	2	0	28	2	37	7	1	.242
Petry, D	ATL	R	0	0	5.55	10	0	0	0	4	0	24.1	29	116	17	15	2	3	0	1	14	1	9	2	0	.296
Piatt, D	MON	R	0	0	2.60	21	0	0	0	3	0	34.2	29	145	11	10	3	2	0	0	17	0	29	1	0	.230
Portugal, M	HOU	R	10	12	4.49	32	27	1	0	3	1	168.1	163	710	91	84	19	6	6	2	59	5	120	4	1	.256
Power, T	CIN	R	5	3	3.62	68	0	0	0	22	3	87.0	87	371	37	35	6	6	4	2	31	5	51	6	1	.265
Rasmussen, D	SD	L	6	13	3.74	24	24	1	1	0	0	146.2	155	633	74	61	12	4	6	2	49	3	75	1	1	.271
Reed, R	PIT	R	0	0	10.38	1	1	0	0	0	0	4.1	8	21	6	5	1	0	0	0	1	0	2	0	0	.400
Remlinger, M	SF	L	2	1	4.37	8	6	1	1	1	0	35.0	36	155	17	17	5	1	1	0	20	1	19	2	1	.271
Renfroe, L	CHI	R	0	1	13.50	4	0	0	0	2	0	4.2	11	27	7	7	1	0	0	0	2	1	4	1	0	.440
Reuschel, R	SF	R	0	2	4.22	4	1	0	0	1	0	10.2	17	54	5	5	0	1	0	0	7	1	4	0	0	.370
Reynoso, A	ATL	R	2	1	6.17	6	5	0	0	1	0	23.1	26	103	18	16	4	3	0	3	10	1	10	2	0	.299
Righetti, D	SF	L	2	7	3.39	61	0	0	0	49	24	71.2	64	304	29	27	4	4	2	3	28	6	51	1	1	.240
Rijo, J	CIN	R	15	6	2.51	30	30	3	1	0	0	204.1	165	825	69	57	8	4	8	3	55	4	172	2	4	.219
Ritchie, W	PHI	L	1	2	2.50	39	0	0	0	13	0	50.1	44	213	17	14	4	2	4	2	17	5	26	1	0	.234
Robinson, D	SF	R	5	9	4.38	34	16	0	0	7	1	121.1	123	525	64	59	12	4	5	1	50	7	78	1	0	.265
Rodriguez, R	PIT	L	1	1	4.11	18	0	0	0	8	6	15.1	14	67	7	7	1	1	0	1	8	0	10	2	0	.246
Rodriguez, R	SD	L	3	1	3.26	64	1	0	0	19	0	80.0	66	335	31	29	8	7	2	0	44	8	40	4	1	.234
Rojas, M	MON	R	3	3	3.75	37	0	0	0	13	6	48.0	42	200	21	20	4	0	2	1	13	1	37	3	0	.228
Rosenberg, S	SD	L	1	1	6.94	10	0	0	0	5	0	11.2	11	49	9	9	3	0	0	0	5	1	6	2	0	.250
Ruffin, B	PHI	L	4	7	3.78	31	15	1	1	2	0	119.0	125	508	52	50	6	6	4	1	38	3	85	4	0	.272
Ruskin, S	MON	L	4	4	4.24	64	0	0	0	24	6	63.2	57	275	31	30	4	5	0	3	30	2	46	5	0	.241
Sampen, B	MON	R	9	5	4.00	43	8	0	0	8	0	92.1	96	409	49	41	13	4	4	3	46	7	52	3	1	.273
Sanford, M	CIN	R	1	2	3.86	5	5	0	0	0	0	28.0	19	118	14	12	3	0	0	1	15	1	31	4	0	.186
Sauveur, R	NY	L	0	0	10.80	6	0	0	0	0	0	3.1	7	19	4	4	1	2	0	0	2	0	4	0	0	.467
Scanlan, B	CHI	R	7	8	3.89	40	13	0	0	16	1	111.0	114	482	60	48	5	8	6	3	40	3	44	5	1	.269
Schilling, C	HOU	R	3	5	3.81	56	0	0	0	34	8	75.2	79	336	35	32	2	5	1	0	39	7	71	4	1	.271
Schmidt, D	MON	R	0	1	10.38	4	0	0	0	1	0	4.1	9	24	5	5	2	1	0	0	2	0	3	0	0	.429
Schourek, P	NY	L	5	4	4.27	35	8	1	1	7	2	86.1	82	385	49	41	7	5	4	2	43	4	67	1	0	.248
Scott, M	HOU	R	0	2	12.86	2	2	0	0	0	0	7.0	11	35	10	10	2	0	0	1	4	1	3	0	0	.367
Scott, T	SD	R	0	0	9.00	2	0	0	0	0	0	1.0	2	5	2	1	0	0	0	0	0	0	1	0	0	.400
Scudder, S	CIN	R	6	9	4.35	27	14	0	0	4	1	101.1	91	443	52	49	6	8	3	6	56	4	51	7	0	.246
Searcy, S	PHI	L	2	1	4.15	18	0	0	0	4	0	30.1	29	134	16	14	2	3	2	0	14	1	21	1	1	.252
Segura, J	SF	R	0	1	4.41	11	0	0	0	2	0	16.1	20	72	11	8	1	1	0	0	5	0	10	2	0	.303
Sherrill, T	STL	L	0	0	8.16	10	0	0	0	3	0	14.1	20	67	13	13	2	1	2	2	3	1	4	1	0	.339
Simons, D	NY	L	2	3	5.19	42	1	0	0	11	1	60.2	55	258	40	35	5	9	4	2	19	5	38	3	0	.246
Sisk, D	ATL	R	2	1	5.02	14	0	0	0	2	0	14.1	21	73	14	8	1	1	1	0	8	2	5	0	0	.333
Slocumb, H	CHI	R	2	1	3.45	52	0	0	0	21	1	62.2	53	274	29	24	3	6	6	3	30	6	34	9	0	.231
Smiley, J	PIT	L	20	8	3.08	33	32	2	1	0	0	207.2	194	836	78	71	17	11	4	3	44	0	129	3	1	.251
Smith, B	STL	R	12	9	3.85	31	31	3	0	0	0	198.2	188	818	95	85	16	10	7	7	45	3	94	3	1	.251
Smith, Da	CHI	R	0	6	6.00	35	0	0	0	28	17	33.0	39	151	22	22	6	2	0	1	19	5	16	1	1	.302
Smith, L	STL	R	6	3	2.34	67	0	0	0	61	47	73.0	70	300	19	19	5	5	1	0	13	5	67	1	0	.249
Smith, P	ATL	R	1	3	5.06	14	10	0	0	2	0	48.0	48	211	33	27	5	2	4	0	22	3	29	1	4	.262
Smith, Z	PIT	L	16	10	3.20	35	35	6	3	0	0	228.0	234	916	95	81	15	7	5	2	29	3	120	1	0	.268
Smoltz, J	ATL	R	14	13	3.80	36	36	5	0	0	0	229.2	206	947	101	97	16	9	9	3	77	1	148	20	2	.243
St. Claire, R	ATL	R	0	0	4.08	19	0	0	0	5	0	28.2	31	123	17	13	4	3	1	0	9	3	30	4	0	.282

1992 IMPORTANT DATES TO REMEMBER

Feb. 21 First date injured players, pitchers and catchers may be invited to attend spring training workouts.

Feb. 26 First date all other players may be invited to attend spring training workouts.

Mar. 2 First date to renew contracts. Ten day renewal period ends on March 11th.

Mar. 4 Mandatory date players are required to report for first spring training workout.

Mar. 17 First date draft excluded/selected players may be assigned to a National Association club.

Mar. 21 Last day to assign an injured player to a National Association club until the close of the championship season (OUTRIGHT or OPTIONALLY) provided that:
 a) The player has less than 3 years of Major League service.
 b) The assignment would not be the player's second (or subsequent) career outright since 3/19/90.
 c) The player had NO MAJOR LEAGUE SERVICE the prior championship season.
 d) The player was not selected by the assignor Major League club in the immediately preceding Rule 5 Draft.

Apr. 6 Official opening of the 1992 championship season. All clubs are required to have their active (25 man) rosters transmitted to their league office by 12:00 noon EDT.

May 1 Earliest date former clubs may re-sign free agent players who refused arbitration and were unsigned after Jan. 8th.

May 5 Waivers secured on/after Nov. 11th expire 5:00 p.m. EDT.

May 6 This is the 31st day of the 1992 championship season. New waiver period begins. Waivers secured on/after this date are good through 5:00 p.m. EDT July 31st.

May 15 Earliest date clubs may re-sign players whom they unconditionally released after midnight Aug. 31st, 1991.

June 1-3 Summer Free Agent Draft.

July 14 All Star Game in San Diego (N.L.).

July 31 Waivers secured on/after May 6, 1992 expire at 5:00 p.m. EDT. Players may be traded between major league clubs until MIDNIGHT tonight without any waivers in effect.

Players recalled not to report after midnight tonight for the purpose of securing outright waivers for assignment to the National Association can ONLY be outrighted to the N.A. club they were recalled from.

Aug. 1 Beginning this date and ending on the day following the close of the championship season, players may be assigned between major league clubs ONLY after major league waivers have been secured during the current waiver period.

Aug. 3 Hall of Fame Game at Cooperstown (Chicago White Sox vs. New York Mets).

Aug. 15 Last date to bring player up for "full trial" to exclude draft excluded status.

Aug. 31 Any player released after midnight tonight may not be re-signed to a major league contract by the club that released him until May 15th of the following season.

Postseason rosters are established at midnight tonight. To be eligible, a player must be a bona fide member of a qualifying team on Aug. 31st and must remain a bona fide member until the end of the season. (See MLR 40 and League Constitutions regarding eligible players that become injured.)

Sept. 1 Active player limit increased from 25 to 40. Beginning today outright assignments to the National Association may be made ONLY with special waivers in effect.

Oct. 1 All players on optional assignment must be recalled.

Oct. 4 Official closing of the 1992 championship season.

Oct. 5 Beginning today, players may be traded between major league clubs without any type of waivers in effect.

Oct. 9 Last date to request waivers on draft excluded players until 25 days prior to the opening of the following season. This is also the beginning of the closed period for major league waiver requests. Special waivers may still be requested on players that are not draft excluded for the next preceding Rule 5 draft.

Oct. 15 Last day (5 p.m.) to assign a potential National Association 6-year free agent outright to the N.A.

Oct. Day following the last game of the World Series is the commencement of 15-day period during which eligible players may elect free agency.

Nov. 10 Waivers secured on/after Aug. 1, 1992, Expire 5:00 p.m. EST.

Nov. 11 New waiver period begins. Major League waiver requests may be withdrawn by a club on a player only once in each waiver period; subsequent Major League waiver requests in that period are irrevocable.

Waivers (exclusive of special waivers) secured today and after shall be in effect until the 30th days of the following championship season.

Nov. (TBA) Dates for filing Rookie, A, AA, AAA and Major League Reserve lists will be announced as soon as the dates are determined.

Dec. 20 Last date to tender contracts.

INDIVIDUAL PITCHING RECORDS—1991

PITCHER	TEAM	T	W	L	ERA	G	GS	CG	SHO	GF	SV	IP	H	TBF	R	ER	HR	SH	SF	HB	BB	IBB	SO	WP	BK	OPP AVG
Stanton, M	ATL	L	5	5	2.88	74	0	0	0	20	7	78.0	62	314	27	25	6	6	0	1	21	6	54	0	0	.217
Sutcliffe, R	CHI	R	6	5	4.10	19	18	0	0	0	0	96.2	96	422	52	44	4	5	8	0	45	2	52	2	2	.264
Terry, S	STL	R	4	4	2.80	65	0	0	0	13	1	80.1	76	339	31	25	1	2	0	0	32	14	52	0	0	.249
Tewksbury, B	STL	R	11	12	3.25	30	30	3	0	0	0	191.0	206	798	86	69	13	12	10	5	38	2	75	0	0	.281
Tomlin, R	PIT	L	8	7	2.98	31	27	4	2	0	0	175.0	170	736	75	58	9	5	2	6	54	4	104	2	3	.254
Valera, J	NY	R	0	0	0.00	2	0	0	0	1	0	2.0	1	11	0	0	0	0	0	0	4	1	3	0	0	.143
Viola, F	NY	L	13	15	3.97	35	35	3	0	0	0	231.1	259	980	112	102	25	15	5	1	54	4	132	6	1	.286
Wainhouse, D	MON	R	0	1	6.75	2	0	0	0	1	0	2.2	2	14	2	2	0	0	1	0	4	0	1	2	0	.222
Walk, B	PIT	R	9	2	3.60	25	20	0	0	0	0	115.0	104	484	53	46	10	7	4	5	35	2	67	11	2	.240
Wetteland, J	LA	R	1	0	0.00	6	0	0	0	3	0	9.0	5	36	2	0	0	0	1	1	3	0	9	1	0	.161
Whitehurst, W	NY	R	7	12	4.19	36	20	0	0	6	1	133.1	142	556	67	62	12	6	3	4	25	3	87	3	4	.274
Whitson, E	SD	R	4	6	5.03	13	12	2	0	0	0	78.2	93	337	47	44	13	6	3	0	17	3	40	1	1	.299
Wilkins, D	HOU	R	2	1	11.25	7	0	0	0	3	1	8.0	16	51	14	10	0	2	0	0	10	2	4	1	0	.410
Williams, B	HOU	R	0	1	3.75	2	2	0	0	0	0	12.0	11	49	5	5	2	0	0	1	4	0	4	0	0	.250
Williams, M	PHI	L	12	5	2.34	69	0	0	0	60	30	88.1	56	386	24	23	4	4	4	8	62	5	84	4	1	.182
Wilson, S	CHI-LA	L	0	0	2.61	19	0	0	0	5	2	20.2	14	81	7	6	1	0	1	0	9	1	14	0	0	.197
Wilson, T	SF	L	13	11	3.56	44	29	2	1	6	0	202.0	173	841	87	80	13	14	5	5	77	4	139	5	3	.234
Wohlers, M	ATL	R	3	1	3.20	17	0	0	0	4	2	19.2	17	89	7	7	1	2	1	2	13	3	13	0	0	.239
Young, A	NY	R	2	5	3.10	10	8	0	0	2	0	49.1	48	202	20	17	4	1	1	1	12	1	20	1	0	.257

1991 CLUB PITCHING

CLUB	W	L	ERA	G	CG	SHO	REL	SV	IP	H	R	ER	HR	HB	BB	IBB	SO	WP	BK	OPP AVG
LOS ANGELES	93	69	3.06	162	15	14	367	40	1458.0	1312	565	496	96	28	500	77	1028	48	12	.241
PITTSBURGH	98	64	3.44	162	18	11	353	51	1456.2	1411	632	557	117	30	401	34	919	40	12	.256
ATLANTA	94	68	3.49	162	18	7	345	48	1452.2	1304	644	563	118	28	481	39	969	66	13	.240
NEW YORK	77	84	3.56	161	12	11	314	39	1437.1	1403	646	568	108	25	410	41	1028	59	14	.257
SAN DIEGO	84	78	3.57	162	14	11	334	47	1452.2	1385	646	577	139	13	457	56	921	49	13	.252
MONTREAL	71	90	3.64	161	12	14	367	39	1440.1	1304	655	583	111	32	584	42	909	51	9	.244
ST. LOUIS	84	78	3.69	162	9	5	369	51	1435.1	1367	648	588	114	47	454	52	822	33	7	.255
CINCINNATI	74	88	3.83	162	7	11	354	43	1440.0	1372	691	613	127	28	560	41	997	60	9	.253
PHILADELPHIA	78	84	3.86	162	16	11	321	35	1463.0	1346	680	628	111	43	670	58	988	81	6	.246
HOUSTON	65	97	4.00	162	7	13	365	36	1453.0	1347	717	646	129	29	651	62	1033	46	17	.247
SAN FRANCISCO	75	87	4.03	162	10	10	334	45	1442.0	1397	697	646	143	36	544	60	905	44	14	.257
CHICAGO	77	83	4.03	160	12	4	360	40	1456.2	1415	734	653	117	28	542	64	927	48	12	.257
TOTALS	970	970	3.68	970	150	122	4183	514	17387.2	16363	7955	7118	1430	367	6254	626	11446	625	138	.250

1991 CLUB FIELDING

CLUB	PCT	G	PO	A	E	TC	DP	TP	PB
ST. LOUIS	.982	162	4306	1689	107	6102	133	1	8
SAN FRANCISCO	.982	162	4326	1753	109	6188	151	0	9
CHICAGO	.982	160	4370	1830	113	6313	120	0	19
SAN DIEGO	.982	162	4358	1731	113	6202	130	0	9
PITTSBURGH	.981	162	4370	1846	120	6336	134	0	9
PHILADELPHIA	.981	162	4389	1623	119	6131	111	1	9
LOS ANGELES	.980	162	4374	1795	123	6292	126	0	8
CINCINNATI	.979	162	4320	1615	125	6060	131	0	20
MONTREAL	.979	161	4321	1796	133	6250	128	1	22
ATLANTA	.978	162	4358	1834	138	6330	122	0	14
NEW YORK	.977	161	4312	1766	143	6221	112	0	12
HOUSTON	.974	162	4359	1617	161	6137	129	2	16
TOTALS	.980	970	52163	20895	1504	74562	1527	5	155

TEN TOUGHEST TO FAN

(minimum: 502 PA)

Player and Club	Games	PA	SO	SO Rate*
Gwynn, S.D.	134	569	19	29.9
O. Smith, St.L.	150	641	36	17.8
Jefferies, N.Y.	136	539	38	14.2
Grace, Chi.	160	703	53	13.3
McReynolds, N.Y.	143	578	46	12.6
Magadan, N.Y.	124	517	50	10.3
Candaele, Hou.	151	505	49	10.3
Bonilla, Pitt.	157	680	67	10.1
Finley, Hou.	159	656	65	10.1
Lind, Pitt.	150	545	56	9.7

*Average plate appearances per strikeout.

TEN TOUGHEST TO DOUBLE

(minimum: 502 PA)

Player and Club	Games	PA	GIDP	DP Rate*
Biggio, Hou.	149	609	2	273.0
Butler, L.A.	161	730	3	205.0
Lankford, St.L.	151	615	4	141.5
Johnson, N.Y.	156	658	4	141.0
Morris, Cin.	136	537	4	119.5
Clark, S.F.	148	622	5	113.0
Grace, Chi.	160	703	6	103.2
Thompson, S.F.	144	573	5	98.4
Van Slyke, Pitt.	138	577	5	98.2
DeShields, Mon.	151	673	6	93.8

*Average at bats per grounded into double play.

TOP TEN CONTROL ARTISTS

(minimum: 162 innings)

Pitcher and Club	Games	IP	BB	BB/ 9 INN
Smith, Pitt.	35	228.0	29	1.14
Tewksbury, St.L.	30	191.0	38	1.79
Mulholland, Phil.	34	232.0	49	1.90
Smiley, Pitt.	33	207.2	44	1.91
B. Smith, St.L.	31	198.2	45	2.04
Viola, N.Y.	35	231.1	54	2.10
Browning, Cin.	36	230.1	56	2.19
Leibrandt, Atl.	36	229.2	56	2.19
Maddux. Chi.	37	263.0	66	2.26
Morgan, L.A.	34	236.1	61	2.32

NATIONAL LEAGUE ANNUAL ATTENDANCE FIGURES—1901-1991

1901—1,920,031	1920—4,036,575	1938— 4,560,837	1956— 8,994,525	1974—16,978,314
1902—1,683,012	1921—3,986,984	1939— 4,707,177	1957— 8,819,601	1975—16,600,490
1903—2,390,362	1922—3,941,820	1940— 4,389,693	1958—10,164,596	1976—16,660,529
1904—2,664,271	1923—4,069,817	1941— 4,777,647	1959— 9,994,525	1977—19,070,228
1905—2,734,310	1924—4,340,644	1942— 4,353,353	1960—10,684,963	1978—20,106,921
1906—2,781,213	1925—4,353,704	1943— 3,769,342	1961— 8,731,502	1979—21,178,419
1907—2,640,220	1926—4,920,399	1944— 3,974,588	1962—11,360,159	1980—21,124,084
1908—3,512,108	1927—5,309,917	1945— 5,260,703	1963—11,382,227	1981—12,478,390
1909—3,496,420	1928—4,881,097	1946— 8,902,107	1964—12,045,190	1982—21,507,425
1910—3,494,544	1929—4,925,713	1947—10,388,470	1965—13,581,136	1983—21,549,285
1911—3,231,768	1930—5,446,532	1948— 9,770,743	1966—15,015,471	1984—20,781,436
1912—2,735,759	1931—4,583,815	1949— 9,484,718	1967—12,971,430	1985—22,292,154
1913—2,831,531	1932—3,841,334	1950— 8,320,616	1968—11,758,358	1986—22,333,471
1914—1,707,397	1933—3,162,821	1951— 7,244,002	1969—15,094,946	1987—24,734,155
1915—2,430,142	1934—3,200,105	1952— 6,339,148	1970—16,662,198	1988—24,499,268
1916—3,051,634	1935—3,657,309	1953— 7,419,721	1971—17,324,857	1989—25,323,834*
1917—2,361,136	1936—3,903,691	1954— 8,013,519	1972—15,529,730	1990—24,491,508
1918—1,372,127	1937—4,204,228	1955— 7,674,412	1973—16,675,322	1991—24,696,172
1919—2,878,203				Total—848,912,350

*National League Record.

ATTENDANCE—1991-1990

CLUB	1991 Openings	HOME 1991	HOME 1990	ROAD 1991	ROAD 1990
Atlanta	78	2,140,217	980,129	1,927,285	1,851,517
Chicago	81	2,314,250	2,243,791	2,039,465	2,160,568
Cincinnati	80	2,372,377	2,400,892	2,060,205	2,174,093
Houston	81	1,196,152	1,310,927	2,039,738	1,831,131
Los Angeles	81	3,348,170	3,002,396	2,483,818	2,113,630
Montreal	67	934,742	1,373,087	2,021,866	1,941,918
New York	79	2,284,484	2,732,745	2,139,475	2,349,021
Philadelphia	83	2,050,012	1,992,484	1,907,597	1,985,844
Pittsburgh	83	2,065,302	2,049,908	2,060,949	2,033,535
St. Louis	82	2,448,699	2,573,225	1,796,933	1,908,633
San Diego	81	1,804,289	1,856,396	2,025,196	1,911,315
San Francisco	81	1,737,478	1,975,528	2,193,645	2,230,303
TOTALS	957	24,696,172	24,491,508	24,696,172	24,491,508

1992 NATIONAL LEAGUE TICKET PRICES

ATLANTA
Club & Dugout Level $12.00
Field Level $10.00
Upper Level $8.00
Lower Pavilion $8.00
General Admission $4.00
   Children $1.00

CHICAGO#
Club Box $16.00
Field Box $16.00
Terrace Box $11.00
Upper Deck Box $11.00
Terrace Reserved $8.00
Upper Deck Reserved (Adult) $6.00
Upper Deck Reserved (Children) ... $4.00
Bleachers $6.00

CINCINNATI
Blue Level Box Seats $10.00
Green Level Box Seats $9.00
Yellow Level Box Seats $9.00
Red Level Box Seats $8.00
Green Level Reserved $7.00
Red Level Reserved $6.00
"Top Six" Reserved $3.50

HOUSTON
Field Level $12.00
Mezzanine Level $10.00
Loge Level $8.00
Upper Box Terrace $7.00
Upper Box $6.00
Upper Reserved $5.00
Pavilion (Adult) $4.00
Pavilion (Children) $1.00

LOS ANGELES
Box Seats $11.00
Reserved Seats $8.00
General Admission $6.00
Children General Admission $3.00
  (at game time)

MONTREAL*
VIP Box $22.00
Box Seats $15.25
Terrace $9.00
General Admission $5.50
Bleachers $4.00
*Figures are Canadian dollars.

NEW YORK
Box Seats $15.00
Upper Deck Box $12.00
Loge & Mezzanine Reserved $12.00
Upper Deck Reserved $6.50
Picnic Area
  (Groups of 100 or more) $12.00
Senior Citizen (Day of Game Only) $1.00

PHILADELPHIA
Field Boxes $10.00
Terrace Boxes $9.00
Loge Boxes $9.00
Reserved .... $4.00 & $6.50

PITTSBURGH
Club Boxes $14.00
Terrace Boxes $10.00
Reserved Seats $8.00
General Admission $5.00
Youth General Admission $2.50
  (12 and under)

ST. LOUIS
Box Seats $12.00
Loge & Terrace Reserved $9.50
Bleachers $4.00
General Admission $5.50

SAN DIEGO
Reserved (Field, Plaza, Press) $11.00
Reserved (Loge, View) $9.50
Reserved (Grandstand) $7.00
General Admission $5.00

SAN FRANCISCO
MVP Box $14.25
Lower Stand Box $12.25
Lower Stand Reserved $11.25
Upper Stand Box $10.25
Upper Stand Reserved $8.25
Pavilion $5.25
General Admission $2.75

#Prices listed are for weekday afternoon games. For weekends, nights, holidays, Opening Day and exhibition games, prices are $1.00 higher in each category.

CLUB	SEASON AT HOME	SEASON ON ROAD	SINGLE DAY GAMES	NIGHT GAMES	DOUBLEHEADERS (DAY)
Atlanta	2,140,217 in 1991	1,985,595 in 1982	51,275 vs. Los Angeles—6/26/66	53,775 vs. Los Angeles—4/8/74	46,489 vs. San Francisco—7/18/71
Chicago	2,491,942 in 1989	2,271,855 in 1989	46,572 vs. Brooklyn—5/18/47	39,002 vs. Montreal—8/7/89	46,965 vs. Pittsburgh—5/31/48
Cincinnati	2,629,708 in 1976	2,320,616 in 1978	55,438 vs. St. Louis—4/4/88	53,790 vs. Houston—9/17/83	52,147 vs. Atlanta—6/23/74
Houston	2,278,217 in 1980	1,996,660 in 1989	49,442 vs. Los Angeles—9/5/65	50,908 vs. Los Angeles—6/22/66	45,115 vs. Atlanta—8/4/79
Los Angeles	*3,608,881 in 1982	2,250,191 in 1982	78,672 vs. San Francisco—4/18/58	72,140 vs. Cincinnati—8/16/61 (tn)	53,856 vs. Cincinnati—7/7/63
Montreal	2,320,651 in 1983	2,083,277 in 1989	57,592 vs. Philadelphia—4/15/77	57,121 vs. Philadelphia—10/3/80	59,282 vs. St. Louis—9/16/79
New York	3,055,445 in 1988	*2,553,582 in 1988	56,738 vs. Los Angeles—6/23/68	56,658 vs. San Francisco—5/13/66	57,175 vs. Los Angeles—6/13/65
Philadelphia	2,775,011 in 1979	2,061,384 in 1987	60,120 vs. Atlanta—5/6/73	63,816 vs. Cincinnati—7/3/84	40,720 vs. Brooklyn—5/11/47
Pittsburgh	2,065,302 in 1991	2,197,247 in 1980	51,726 vs. San Diego—6/6/76	54,274 vs. Montreal—4/8/91	49,341 vs. Houston—7/16/72
St. Louis	3,080,980 in 1989	2,321,960 in 1987	50,548 vs. New York—9/14/75	51,647 vs. Pittsburgh—4/8/88	49,743 vs. Atlanta—6/23/68
San Diego	2,210,352 in 1985	1,994,464 in 1985	53,375 vs. San Francisco—6/22/85	54,841 vs. Montreal—5/10/91	43,473 vs. Philadelphia—6/13/76
San Francisco	2,059,701 in 1989	2,230,659 in 1989	56,196 vs. San Diego—4/10/79	55,920 vs. Cincinnati—6/20/78	53,179 vs. Los Angeles—7/31/83

*National League Record.